ISBN 978-1-332-13151-8
PIBN 10288945

JOHN KEMPE, CARDINAL, ARCHBISHOP OF CANTERBURY.
LORD CHANCELLOR OF ENGLAND.

A GENERAL HISTORY OF THE KEMP AND KEMPE FAMILIES

Of Great Britain and Her Colonies

WITH

Arms, Pedigrees, Portraits, Illustrations of Seats, Foundations, Chantries, Monuments, Documents, Old Jewels, Curios, &c.

BY

FRED. HITCHIN-KEMP

ASSISTED BY

DANIEL WM. KEMP, J.P., Edinburgh (Author of works on Sutherland, &c.),

AND

JOHN TABOR KEMP, M.A.,

AND WITH THE SUPPORT OF

SIR KENNETH HAGAR KEMP, Twelfth Baronet of Gissing; GEORGE KEMP, Esq., M.P., Rochdale;
J. A. KEMPE, Esq., C.B., Deputy Chairman of H.M. Customs;
REV. PREBENDARY KEMPE, M.A., Chaplain in Ordinary to the late Queen Victoria;
CHARLES N. KEMPE, late of the Admiralty;
ALFRED BRAY KEMPE, Esq., F.R.S., Chancellor of the Dioceses of St. Albans, Newcastle and Southwell

AND WITH ILLUSTRATIONS BY

MISS LUCY E. KEMP-WELCH

AND OTHERS.

LONDON: PUBLISHED BY
THE LEADENHALL PRESS, LTD: 50, LEADENHALL STREET, E.C.
NEW YORK: CHARLES SCRIBNER'S SONS, 153-157, FIFTH AVENUE.

The Leadenhall Press, Ltd:
50, LEADENHALL STREET, LONDON, E.C.
T 4,753.

PREFACE.

THE question has so constantly been asked, with whom did the idea of compiling a history of the Kemps originate? that it seems fitting to preface the work with a brief account of its inception and achievement. In order to simplify matters the chief writer will, with the reader's leave, speak in the first person singular.

I was on a visit to an elderly cousin, living near Ashford, in 1896, when, finding that the topics of modern conversation failed to interest him, I sought something to read in an old library adjacent, of which my relative was trustee. My first inspection of the shelves inclined me to think that the ancient volumes with which they were loaded would afford me no entertainment, for I was neither an antiquarian nor interested in history or genealogy. I came, however, to a copy of Hasted's "History of Kent," which I took down with some curiosity as to what it might say about the places of interest around my cousin's home, and finding that I had thus dropped upon an account of a great man of my own name—Archbishop Kemp—I read page after page concerning him and his relations. This exhausted I turned to the index for the name of Kemp in order to discover more information concerning my namesakes.

During the next few days I frequently returned to the library and found that the name of Kemp appeared prominently in numerous volumes, while the crest and arms closely resembled those granted to my father on accession to certain Kemp estates. What connexion, I naturally asked, was there between this Kentish family and those of Hendon, Middlesex, from whom we were descended?

On my return to town, after visiting Wye College, Chilham Castle, and other places connected with the Kemps, my desire to determine this question took definite shape, and I made enquiries at the Heralds' College. The officials could not give a ready reply, as the pedigree of my people was not recorded when the present arms were granted. I then sought admission to the British Museum Library intent upon a search which might solve the problem. I did not anticipate that this would be a very difficult matter, for "The History of Hendon" (by E. T. Evans, 1890) mentioned our Kempes as being at Hendon in 1610, the very year in which Ollantigh and other Kentish property was distributed among the four daughters of the last Sir Thomas Kempe of Wye. This Kentish Knight had no sons, but as he had brothers and uncles, I reasoned might not one of these have founded the family at Hendon?

Genealogists will smile at this, for the longer one studies pedigrees the more one realises how difficult it is to adduce conclusive evidence in proof of descent from a family, or individual, living at a remote period. They will not wonder that I soon collected a mass of information pertaining to various Kemps and Kempes which in no way threw light on my family's connexion with Wye. This collection must, however, relate to various living representatives of the name, I thought! Why not offer it to them? So I took the liberty of addressing Sir Kenneth Kemp, Baronet, and one or two others, saying that I had a collection of notes relating to the Kemp and Kempe families which I thought might be printed privately for those whom it might interest.

Lady Kemp favoured me with an interview in London the following year (1897), and shortly after this I was delighted with an invitation to Mergate Hall, near Norwich, to have a look at the deeds and records relating to the long pedigree and large estates of the Kemp Baronets. Sir Kenneth most kindly gave me access to his great chests full of Manorial Rolls and documents ranging from the reign of King John to the present time. It need hardly be said that these records contain the most valuable genealogical evidence, but to examine them fully would require close attention for quite a year, and I was unable to do much more than note each series and the dates, except where a definite query suggested a closer investigation. With the assistance of Sir Kenneth I have reproduced in this history a few of the documents which are of the chief general interest to Kemps.

After this first visit to Mergate and Gissing Halls, George Kemp, Esq., M.P. for the Heywood Division of Lancashire, helped the project of publishing the result of my researches by handing me a cheque which covered the cost of addressing circulars to Kemps and Kempes throughout England. In response to the first issue of about one hundred some twenty-five replies were received warmly supporting the scheme. The chief result, however, of this circular was the very unexpected news to me that Mr. Daniel W. Kemp, of Edinburgh, had issued a somewhat similar circular a year or two previously, saying that having collected Kemp items for some twenty-five years he proposed to issue in periodical form "Notes on Kemps of Great Britain." To this circular he had had many replies, but having other literary work in hand, as well as numerous municipal and business engagements, he had postponed the publication indefinitely. He therefore offered to hand over to me the whole of his collection for me to deal with. This very generous offer was gladly accepted, and a visit to Scotland in the interests of the Scottish Kemps followed. By this time the work assumed large proportions, and I felt it necessary to obtain the services of some gentleman who had both the time and the means to render me assistance in the great work of arranging, selecting and editing the matter. I deem myself fortunate in having found Mr. John Tabor Kemp, M.A. (Camb.), willing to devote a great deal of his time to this honorary work.

The second circular was addressed in 1899 to Kemps in India, Australia, United States and elsewhere, and advertisements calling for information concerning Kemp(e)s abroad were inserted in the *Times* and several American and Colonial papers. The letters received were so numerous, and requests for special researches so many, that the whole of my time for more than two years was devoted to the necessary correspondence and to researches at Somerset House, the Record Office, British Museum, Provincial District Probate Courts, ancient libraries and other store-houses of historical and genealogical facts. The notes personally collected from these sources fill forty-eight octavo manuscript books, each of over one hundred pages; while the annotations and indexes relating to these fill another twenty-five books, half of which are quarto, and amount to an aggregate of 1,500 pages of manuscript. In addition to this bulk of matter requiring sorting and arrangement, the collection of manuscript and books, by and concerning Kemps, sent by Daniel William Kemp, J.P., weighs about one hundredweight. Mr. John Tabor Kemp has also gathered a valuable amount of useful information, but the work for which Kemps and Kempes in general must be indebted to him is his editorial share of the work, for while it has fallen upon myself to write the matter, space at our disposal has made it necessary for him to cut down to the lowest consistent form the histories of the numerous distinct families of the names of Kemp and Kempe.

Subscribers will, I trust, find, that where possible, some details of their family are included, and I hope will realise that we have treated their family traditions with respect, even where evidence was against them. History, however, is valueless if not true, and we have in a few cases to show that errors have been found in some ancient as well as modern pedigrees, while others lack documentary evidence.

To all subscribers and others (Kemps, Kempes, Kempts, and even Camps and Campes) I may here say that the mass of information in our hands is far greater than space permits us to print in full. Those interested in making further research concerning their family history should communicate with me, and I will place other details at their disposal. I may add, also, that where any statement in this work is found to be in error, I shall welcome correction or addition in view of a possible reprint of the work.

In conclusion I may be permitted to say the cost of research has fallen almost entirely upon the joint compilers. Mr. Daniel W. Kemp, two years ago, found that he had expended £100 in research, collecting and circulars. Mr. John Tabor Kemp has travelled extensively in quest of records, the cost of all fares and hotel, as well as other incidental fees, being borne by himself. My own time devoted to the work represents five years of close study and journeys all over England, and a visit to the Record House, Edinburgh. In most cases the illustrations in this work are from photographs taken personally, but I am also greatly indebted to Miss Lucy Kemp-Welch for giving her valuable time to reproduce (in black and white) some portraits and the tomb of Archbishop Kempe.

To many gentlemen who have considerable collection of Kemp(e) notes I also owe my thanks, but their names being many I omit the list here, as in most cases their loans are mentioned in the text.

Fred. Hitchin-Kemp.

6, Beechfield Road, Catford,
London, S.E.
June, 1902.

William Kempe, Shakespeare's Comedian, the celebrated Morris Dancer who danced from London to Norwich in nine days.

History of the Kemp and Kempe Families.

CHAPTER I.

INTRODUCTORY BY JOHN TABOR KEMP, M.A.

THE name Kemp or Kempe is widely distributed among the population of the British Islands. Nevertheless, except in certain regions, it cannot be considered a very common surname. It abounds chiefly in the eastern and southern counties of England, notably in Norfolk, Suffolk, Essex, Kent, Middlesex and Sussex, to which may be added Surrey and Hampshire. It is also tolerably frequent in the adjacent counties. In these parts families bearing the name, or recognised variants thereof, have dwelt since the period of the earliest existing records. For a thousand years, it is safe to assert, the stock of the modern Kemps * has occupied an important place among the people of East Anglia. Although no contemporary documents as old as this are extant, the earliest references to the name (dating from a period soon after the Norman Conquest) testify its representatives as being above the class of villeins. The popular etymology of Kemp, countenanced by the high authority of Prof. Skeat, regards it as the Anglo-Saxon word CEMPA, a champion, in modern spelling. Reasons for doubting whether this is the true explanation are set forth in the chapter on the origin of the name (Chapter II.) One point, however, in favour of the accepted derivation, is the early period at which Kemps came to the fore in the social life of the nation. If champions they were, the qualities, to wit, strength of limb united with force of character, which gave them that position naturally fitted them to be leaders in other affairs than war.

But the name is not by any means confined to East Anglia, either in early or modern times. In the south it extends to Wales and Cornwall. It is sparsely disseminated throughout the midland and northern counties, and even reaches the Highlands of Scotland. The Scottish Kemps, though few in numbers, have been far from undistinguished. Some of these scattered families, no doubt, migrated from the south-east of England at various periods. In very many cases, however, there is no evidence, apart from their name, to connect them with the Kemps of the south. We may not designate them, after Jewish analogy, as "the Kemps of the Dispersion" on the assumption that they are descendants of one original stock. In all probability the name has arisen independently in different localities. It may also have had more than one derivation.

Among the vast English-speaking populations beyond the seas, in the United States of America, in South Africa and Australia, the name of Kemp is well known. References to the career of the more distinguished bearers of the name outside the British Islands will be found in

* In order to avoid needless repetition of the phrase "Kemps and Kempes," and the like, it will be convenient to state once for all that, except where the contrary is indicated by the context, the term Kemps includes the Kempes.

other parts of the present work. Some of the Colonial and American Kemps are, however, not of English origin at all, but are the descendants of emigrants from the Low Countries. This meeting and commingling of English and Dutch Kemps is no new event, for the ancestors of many of the Kemp families of the old country are known to have come over from Flanders at various periods. A noteworthy man was John Kemp, the weaver, who settled at Carlisle about 1335. The name is frequent among weavers in many parts of Great Britain till quite recent times. The entries in the Scottish Registers relating to the Kemps often specify the occupation as that of a weaver. It is a somewhat curious coincidence that "kemp" is a technical term in connexion with weaving, denoting a bristly hair often found among wool. "Kemb" is an old spelling of comb. Referring to the English and Dutch Kemps, it may here be noted that they have fought against one another in the present war.

Families vary enormously in the proportion of distinguished individuals which they have produced to the total number of bearers of the name. It is customary to speak of those families whose members were persons of importance centuries ago as "old" families. "Historic" would be the more correct term, since it is equally certain that the obscurest of the poor at the present day are descended from individuals who lived a thousand years ago, as that the representatives of the noblest houses are so descended. Their "simple annals" have not been recorded except in very fragmentary form in the parish registers of the land or the tenant rolls of estates, and now and again in the records of crime. More rarely have the memories of their simple goodness been handed down in such stories as "The Shepherd of Salisbury Plain" and the "Dairyman's Daughter." Some families are distinguished by many illustrious names. Others, like the Shakespeares and the Bunyans, have flashed forth in glory once and for all; the posterity, if any, of their one famous name is hardly more noted than was his ancestry. The Kemps do not fall exactly under any of these categories. Their families are unquestionably "historic," for their records reach back unbroken for at least five hundred years. They are by no means lacking in famous names as the following pages amply testify. Yet they have produced no celebrity of the first rank—no name which stands for an epoch in the annals of his own vocation, like Milton, Newton, Darwin, Wellington or Nelson. Not a few of them have received marks of honour from their Sovereign for their services to the State. Though they do not stand foremost among the truly great families of the land—families that are great on account of the noble deeds of their members, and not because the creatures of some early king—they do claim rightly that they have enriched the nation's life. And herein lies the justification for the publication of the present history. Every man or woman who takes any delight in the records of worthy actions, or who cares to know anything of the personality of the authors of inspiring utterances, must feel a special pleasure in becoming acquainted with such memorials when connected with their own ancestors or namesakes. "I hope for light," expresses the feeling with which many readers will open the present work, light which will reveal to them fragments of history in which they may justly feel a peculiar pride. "Lucem spero," again, may voice the hope that something herein recorded may in some way be helpful in their own lives, if only by directing their attention to forgotten worthies.

The rest of this chapter will be devoted to brief references to some of the more notable Kemps in various walks in life. The connexion of Kemps with the Courts of the English Kings and Queens is noticed *in limine*, because earliest in date, while the names of some deservedly famous individuals can be introduced here who do not come under any of the subsequent categories.

Kemps appear in close association with royalty almost from the first known appearance of the name to the present day. One, Stephen Kempe, was fined for leaving the Court in 1127.

Archbishop Kempe, of Canterbury, in virtue of his office, was necessarily much in touch with the king, as was also Thomas Kempe, his nephew, the Bishop of London. The Archbishop was frequently sent abroad by the king on important missions. For many years he held the office of Lord Chancellor. Elizabeth, daughter of Robert Kempe of Gissing, was Lady of the Bedchamber to Elizabeth of York, the Consort of Henry VII. Sir Thomas, Sir William and Lady Kempe of Wye, attended the Court of Henry VIII. in various capacities, and were present at the Field of the Cloth of Gold. A Lady Kempe was prominent at the Court of Queen Mary. During the long reign of Elizabeth, at least a dozen Kempes, both of Norfolk and Kent were active. A Robert Kempe of Gissing was gentleman of the Bedchamber to Charles I., who first knighted him and afterwards raised him to the dignity of a baronet. He raised arms for the King at the outbreak of the Cromwellian troubles, sacrificing much of his property in so doing. John Kemp, of Boldre, a representative of the Kentish stock was a prominent Roundhead. Various Kemps of minor note from time to time appear at Court under the Georges. At the present time two Kempes are Chaplains to the King. Some of the living branches of the Kemps possess royal blood. Pedigrees of their descent will be found in other chapters.

The Kemp families have given some very high dignitaries to the church, including the Archbishop of Canterbury and the Bishop of London above mentioned. The second Bishop of Maryland was James Kemp, a native of Scotland. Various Kemps have held canonries and prebends. But while Kemps have risen to fame in the church none of them can be claimed as great divines in the restricted sense of the word as applied to Hooker or Pearson. They make up, however, for any lack of distinction in scientific theology by the fervent piety and practical philanthropy which many of them have exhibited. One of the earliest productions of the printing press, issued by Wynkyn de Worde, was "A Short Treatyse of Contemplacyon taught by the Lorde Jhesu Cryste, taken out of the Boke of Margerie Kempe of Lyn." Her writings resemble those of the Quietists and Quakers. Grover Kemp was a leading member of the Society of Friends. Among the victims of the Boxer massacres in China was Mrs. T. W. Pigott, *née* Kemp, murdered with her husband and son at Tai-Yuen-Fu.

Kempt is a well ascertained variant of the name Kemp as will appear in the pages of this history. It is specially frequent in Scotland, but is known elsewhere. This being the case it is legitimate to name here Sir James Kempt, G.C.B., Governor-General of Canada from 1828 to 1830. He served under the Duke of Wellington in the war against Napoleon, when he distinguished himself on many occasions, including the Battle of Waterloo, and was frequently mentioned in despatches. He was of Scottish parentage.

The most eminent Kempe who ever served in the Navy was Admiral Arthur Kempe of the Cornish stock. A Kempe sailed with Captain Cook in his celebrated voyages of discovery. Another individual of the same family was granted by royal patent the privilege of catching whales. The late Mr. Dixon Kemp, the celebrated yachtsman and writer on ship building, may be mentioned here. He was yachting editor to the ***Field*** newspaper.

Art, science, and literature claim a considerable number of Kemps. A lady of the name still living is the only woman artist, any of whose paintings have been purchased by the Chantrey Trustees for the National Gallery. As a connoisseur in the fine arts John Kemp, who died in 1717, was renowned. The contents of his collection of antiquities was described in a volume written in Latin and published after his death entitled, "Monumenta Vetustatis Kempiana." Alfred John Kempe, who died in 1846, was the author of many articles in the ***Gentleman's Magazine*** on antiquarian subjects. As an architect John Meikle Kemp, designer of the Scott Monument at Edinburgh, occupies a distinguished place. The most noted musician bearing the name is Joseph Kemp, some time organist of Bristol Cathedral. His brother, James, was a minor poet. One, Andrew Kemp, who has left a setting of the Te Deum, was master of the Song School at St. Andrew's in 1575. A William Kemp, contemporary with Shakespeare, achieved fame as a comic actor and dancer.

John Kemp, F.R.S., Edin., a native of Aberdeenshire, was a noted mathematician. Other Kemps have also distinguished themselves in the same study. Medical science has been advanced by several Kemps who have written upon different subjects in connexion therewith. Two brothers named Kemp taught chemistry at Edinburgh University during the first half of the nineteenth century. Both were cut off under forty years of age after careers of great promise.

To conclude this review it may be added that a valuable dictionary of the Maori language was compiled by a Kemp, who abandoned civilised society and took up his residence among the natives of New Zealand, who recognised him as a chief, using his portrait on their tribal banner.

Kemps have taken their full share in mercantile pursuits. Many noted business houses bear their name. For several generations they have likewise been connected with banking. Of late the name has become famous in connexion with sport. References to living Kemps who have in any way distinguished themselves, and to existing firms founded by Kemps, will be found elsewhere in the present work.

The compilers of this history would here express the hope that their readers who possess the ability and leisure to continue the researches which they have begun will do so. Much work remains to be done in the patient examination of ancient records of many kinds. The systematic search of parish registers would probably repay the time and labour spent on it in clearing up many doubtful points in descent. Of the relationship of some of the famous Kemps little or nothing is known. To discover their family connexion would be to earn the gratitude of future biographers and historians. Again, to trace out the migrations of the families of any one name would be a distinct addition to the history of the social life of the nation, still more, if the causes which determined the movement could also be ascertained. The history of a family if truly written is no mere monument of that selfish pride known as snobbery, but a valuable contribution to human knowledge.

The Kemp and Kempe Families of Kent.

CHAPTER II.

(By John Tabor Kemp, M.A.)

ORIGIN OF THE NAME.

THE prevalence of the surname Kemp in the eastern counties of England indicates it as of probably Saxon origin. Students of old English ballads are familiar with the word "kemp," signifying a fighting man or champion, derived from the Anglo-Saxon *Cempa*, a soldier. Since warfare occupied an important place in ordinary life during the period when surnames were coming into vogue, there is an antecedent likelihood that such a word as "kemp" would be found among them. Arguing from these premises many writers have concluded somewhat hastily that the question of the origin of the name was settled beyond dispute, Kemp the surname and "kemp" the soldier being certainly regarded as one and the same word. Plausible as what we may term the accepted derivation appears at first sight, some weighty evidence against its validity will be adduced in the sequel. It is almost certain, however, that the name has arisen in more than one way. The divergent physical types presented by its bearers afford clear evidence of descent from more than one racial stock. The Kemps of the east of England belong generally to the Saxon and Danish types, with light hair and skin and blue or grey eyes. In the west Kemps are met with distinguished by the dark features which characterize the modern Kelts.

The English language presents numberless instances of identical collocations of letters having divers meanings and derivations. For example, "host" in its different senses represents the three Latin words *hostis* (enemy, hence multitude), *hostia* (victim) and *hospes* (entertainer). Another and even better instance is furnished by the word "lime" in "quicklime," "birdlime," "lime-tree," and "lime-fruit." Similar instances are not unknown among English surnames, while it is very probable that they would be found more common than they appear in the light of present knowledge had as much attention been bestowed on personal names as on the language generally. The surname Samson may represent either a contraction of Samuelson, *i.e.* son of Samuel or Sam, or it may point to the exceptional strength of some remote ancestor recalling the prowess of the hero and judge of that name. Craven, again may be and probably is in many cases equivalent to coward; its frequency in the north of England, however, points to the Craven district of Yorkshire whence the Earls of that ilk derive their title. With regard to the name Kemp, it is well within the compass of possibility in the case of different families bearing it, that it may be taken in some instances from the calling of some remote ancestor, in others from his place of abode, in others from some physical or moral characteristic, and in others again from some object adopted as a tribal or family badge or used as a sign for some purpose. Etymologically the modern name may represent Saxon, Danish, Keltic or other appellatives. Apart, however, from any prepossessions or suspicions which the philologist may entertain his first duty is to collect and examine the various forms through which the name has passed wherever it is found.

Before dealing more particularly with the question of derivation it will be convenient to mention the fact that in Anglo-Saxon, as in modern Welsh, likewise in Gaelic and Irish, the symbol *c* universally possessed the sound of *k*. Hence, as would naturally be expected, many of the early forms of the name KEMP are written with a C even before the vowels *e*, *i*, and *y*, in which positions modern usage gives *c* the sound of *s*. The spelling Cemp met with in early documents survived as late as the latter half of the eighteenth century. Among the wills proved in the Norwich Consistory Court is that of Mary Cemp, of Great Yarmouth, who died in 1759.

The earliest examples of the forms KEMP or KEMPE date from about the middle of the twelfth century, but the spelling with a *k* did not become frequent till considerably later. One Gotfred Kemp is recorded as living at Norwich in 1154. No Kemp is found in Domesday, the nearest approach being *de Campo*.

Much uncertainty prevails as to the connexion between the forms KEMP and KEMPE and the earlier forms from which they certainly arose, which the researches of the present writers have only partially enabled them to clear up. Many names which may have passed into Kemp are met with in early registers and other documents, but the proof that they actually did so is often wanting. Only in very few cases can we discover the individual who changed the spelling of his name, or whose name was changed for him by the officials of the time. In Domesday and other ancient records, prior to the period when surnames had come into general use, we find various descriptive terms relating to place of abode or occupation, appended to baptismal names for the purpose of distinguishing the bearers from others of the same name. Among instances may be mentioned *de Campo*, *de Campis*, *de Combes or Compes*, *and Campio*. In the sixteenth century we find their place taken by the regular surnames Camp, Kemp, Campion and so forth. The inference is that the latter are the historical successors of the former, but it is only rarely that the transition can be traced in any given family line.

According to the Roll of Battle Abbey, ***Radulphus de Campis*** held land at Wye from the Abbey. He is also known as ***Ralph Kemp***, of Wye. The same Roll contains the names of several tenants called ***de Cumbe***, ***de Combe*** and ***Kempe***.

Edmund Campian, the Jesuit, executed in 1581 for treasonable correspondence, was arrested and tried as ***Edmund*** KEMP.

The family of ***John Kemp*** the Archbishop, are known to have changed the spelling of their name from ***de Campis***.

As late as 1624 the author of a will signed his name ***Thos. Champe***, while his son witnessing the same document wrote ***Thomas Kempe***.

The author of the "Worthies of Devon" (1701) says the members of the Champernown family formerly wrote their name "*De Campo Arnulphi* from a certain Champion Country where one Arnulphus lived or had his seat." The Inquisitio 30, Edward I., records that Lady John Champernown granted land for the celebration of masses for her father *William de Campo Arnulphi*, and her husband Ralph de Willington. If the following entries in the Probate Registry of Canterbury represent mere coincidencies they are sufficiently curious. Under Archdeaconry of Canterbury, 1493 (fol. b.) is mentioned the will of one ***Arnolphus Kempe***, of Boughton Aluph. In 1517 (lib. 12) we find ***Arnoldus Kempe*** of Newenden. Another ***Arnold Kempe*** is mentioned in the Norwich Charter Rolls ***temp.*** Edward I.

Among the Essex wills is one dated 1539 of Henry Camp *al.* Kamp of Nasing, and another dated 1551 of John Camp *al.* Kempe of the same place.

Many Kemps and Kempes in various parts of England are met with in early documents claiming descent from the Earls of Warwick, who had the title of de Bello Campo. The number of Kemps known to have been tenants or recipients of patronage from the House of Warwick is certainly remarkable.

In the Canterbury Probate Registers (1396-1496) the earliest spelling is Combe. No spelling with an *a* occurs.

In Essex, *Combes* seems to be the chief early spelling, giving place to Kemp about 1370. *Compes* is known as an alternative form in connexion with the Kemps of Finchingfield.

In Norfolk, *Campe* or *de Campo* is said to give place to Kemp about 1270. Comp occurs frequently in the fifteenth century in the records of the Norwich Consistory Court.

In Wiltshire, *de Campo* appears to be the forerunner of the name Kemp.

The will of John *Compos* is preserved in the Archdeaconry of St. Albans.

Among the Archers of the Vale of Revill the name of *Thomas atte Campe* is recorded.

Arnaldus de Campis was Master of the Knights Hospitallers in 1160. Bertrand de Campis succeeded to the office in 1231.

No Kemps are known in Cornwall till about 1400, but *Kemys*, *Camois*, *Cames* and similar forms occur from the time of the Norman Conquest. The pedigree of the Cornish Kempes commences in 1544. They claim descent from the Kemps of Kent. The Manors of Blisland and Liskeard belonged to the Earls of Warwick. In the Manorial Rolls the form *Kympe* (rare in other parts of England) occurs repeatedly from 1500 to 1618. The name Kemys and its variants occur in the Battle Abbey Roll.

In the Exchequer Receipts for 1185 the name of Umfrid de la Cumb occurs in the Buckinghamshire section.

"Kemp" was, as has been already mentioned, an old English word signifying a soldier, also a contender in single combat, being the philological successor of the Anglo-Saxon *Cempa.* Examples of its use may be found in the Ballad of King Estmere, printed in Bishop Percy's "Reliques of Ancient Poetry."

"They had not ridden scant a myle
A myle forthe of the towne,
But in did come the kyng of Spayne,
With kempès many one."

And again—

"'And how nowe, kempe,' said the kyng of Spain
'And how what aileth thee?'"

In the same ballad the derivative kempery occurs more than once :—

"Downe then came the kemperye man,
And looked him in the eare."

Again—

"And aye their swords soe sore can fyte,
Through help of gramaryè
That soone they had slayne the kempery men,
Or forst them forth to flee."

"Kemp" being an actual English word, and moreover, one designating an occupation or profession of universal importance, it would seem *à priori* probable that it would be met with among modern surnames. As the case of Edmund Campian, *alias* Kemp, above quoted shews, the accepted derivation possesses some historical support. In early Latin documents such entries as *Galfredus Campio*, *Ricardus Campio* are frequent, where Campio signifies a champion or fighting man, being the nearest equivalent of "Kemp." The frequent occurrence of such phrases as de Campo, de Campis, atte-Campe and, we may add, Champe to designate members of the Kemp family, indicates that the name was regarded as having reference to abode rather than occupation. In other words the name Kemp represents the Anglo-Saxon *Cempa* only exceptionally, not universally as many have supposed.

The "Historical English Dictionary" has not yet reached the word Kemp. We are, therefore, unable to obtain any direct assistance from it on the present subject. There are, however, six distinct words, "Camp," viz., four substantives and two verbs, under more than one of which information is given which may guide us to the origin and meaning of the name KEMP. The four substantives are designated Camp, sb.[1], sb.[2], sb.[3] and sb.[4]. We shall consider them in the reverse order.

"Camp, sb.[4]" is a rare obsolete word defined as meaning "whiskers of a cat, stout bristly hairs" The only known example of its use dates from the fifteenth century. It would seem to have no bearing on the present subject but for the significant note "Cf KEMP sb."

"Camp, sb.[3]" is a modern dialect word of uncertain origin and history, signifying "a conical or ridge-shaped heap of potatoes or turnips in the open air, covered with straw and earth for winter storage."

The earliest known example of the word in use is dated 1713. Could the word be traced back to the twelfth or thirteenth century with some such sense as a hill or ridge, it were plausible to conjecture that it and the surname KEMP might be one and the same word, the Latin scribe being guided by sound rather than sense when he rendered, say, "John-atte-Camp" by Johannes-de-Campo."

"Camp sb.[2]" is the military camp. The following quotation from the "Historical Dictionary" disposes of the hypothesis that Camp in this sense can have given rise to the surname KEMP. "Although *camp* was the Norman form of *champ*, no trace of it appears in ME., which had only CHAMP from central OF., in the senses of field of duel or tournament and heraldic 'field.' *Camp* was introduced early in the 16th c., from contemporary Fr. and with the sense *castra*, but was also at first used to render L. *campus* in other senses, as well as occasionally in the sense of the earlier *champ* 'field of combat.'" Camp in this sense, not having been introduced into the English language until centuries after Kemp had become a well established name, cannot be the original of it.

One other substantive *Camp* distinguished in the Historical English Dictionary remains to be noticed. This word was sometimes spelled *comp* during the period 1000-1300; *komp* is found in the thirteenth and *kamp* in the fourteenth century. The sense is given as "Martial contest, combat, fight, battle, war." The latest illustrative quotation is taken from the *Morte Arthur* which was composed *ante* 1400, and runs thus:—"Alle the kene mene of kampe, knyghtes and other." The same word enters into the compound *camp-ball*, "an ancient form of football in which large numbers engaged on both sides." The earliest quoted instance of the word is dated *circa* 1600, but under the verb "camp" much earlier references to the game are found.

Of the two verbs "camp," one corresponds to the military camp and therefore possesses no further interest in the present connexion.

The etymology of the Old English verb "camp" is thus stated, "OE. campian, compian, from *camp*, fight." The primary signification of the word is "To fight; to contend in battle."

The *Morte Arthur* has the following :—" There es no kynge undire Criste may kempe with hym one ! " It is also applied to contending in athletic sports. Enclosures where such contests were wont to be held were known as " camping closes." The sense was further extended to include any kind of competition, *e.g.* in drinking. Sir James Melvill (1587) mentions a " banquet of wat and dry confectiones, with all sortes of wyne wharat his Majestie camped verie mirrelie a guid whyll ! " The game camp-ball gave rise to another use of the word. Thus, Tusser in his *Five Hundred Good Points of Husbandry* :—

" Get campers a ball to campe therewithal ; "

and again—

" In meadow or pasture (to grow the more fine)
Let campers be camping in any of thine."

Tusser, it may be noted, spent his life chiefly in the eastern counties. Sir Thomas Browne, author of *Religio Medici*, who practised as a physician at Norwich, and who had travelled extensively in England, speaks of camp as a Norfolk word.

None of the words passed in review appears at first sight to furnish a completely satisfactory explanation of the surname Kemp. Further consideration may possibly modify this conclusion. It should, however, be borne in mind that the name has almost certainly more than one origin.

The grand objection to the popular derivation from the Anglo-Saxon *Cempa* is that early forms, whether Latin, English, or French point to the name as possessing a local signification. Two of the substantives " camp," as we have seen above, designate places or features of the ground. Unfortunately, however, as far as is known, they only came into use as English words centuries after the surname of Kemp was well established.

" Camp," with the meaning contest, requires further notice. In this sense which appears to be the only one known to literature, it scarcely meets the necessities of the case as the original of the name Kemp. It seems, however, extremely probable that the word may have been transferred from the contest itself to the place where contests were accustomed to take place. Whether this be so or not, plots of ground on which athletic contests were held used to be known as " camping closes." A deed of 1466 relating to Hawsted in Suffolk speaks of the " camping pightel joined to the east side of the churchyard." These terms correspond accurately with one of the uses of the Latin word *campus*, meaning originally a level place, but which came specially to be applied to such places as adapted for battles or athletic contests. A John or Richard distinguished by having his dwelling by a " camping close " or " pightel " would naturally be described in Latin as Johannes or Richardus de Campo, even if the old English substantive camp were not applied to such a locality. The descriptive phrase noted above, viz., " atte camp " (*i.e.* at the camp) favours the presumption that the substantive was used in the sense indicated. In schoolboys' slang, about 1612, the " campo " was a term for the playground. Examples of this usage are given in the " Historical English Dictionary " under that word.

" Camp " is an element in many English place names. In Cambridgeshire are the parishes of Castle Camps and Shudy Camps. Camps End and Camps Green are localities in the said parishes. Camp is a hamlet of Miserden in Gloucestershire. In the same county are Chipping Campden with Broad Campden. Campsall is a parish in Yorkshire, Campton one in Bedfordshire. Near Hatfield is a place named Camfield. There is a Camping Hill in the parish of Stiffkey in Norfolk. Many other instances might be adduced. In some cases the syllable camp has evident reference to the existence of an ancient entrenchment near the spot so named. Most Scottish examples must be thus explained.

We have seen that *comp* is a variant of camp with the sense of contest. The question at once suggests itself whether the syllable "comp" in place-names such as Compton be the same word. Most of the places so designated are situated in narrow valleys, "combes" they are called in the West of England, where also the majority of Comptons are found. It is evident, therefore, that Compton means the town in the combe. There is, however, a hamlet named Comp in the parish of Leybourne, Kent, and another called Great Comp in the parish of Wrotham, in the same county. In these instances it is very possible that comp may be a variation of camp. Comp appears as an early surname in the county.

In favour of the accepted derivation it may be submitted (1) that the Anglo-Saxon *Cempa* actually gave rise to the English word "Kemp"; (2) that Cemp survived as a variant of Kemp till a very late period; (3) that Campian is found as an alias of Kemp. On the other hand, the forms *de Campo* and *de Campis* with "*atte Campe*" shew that the name was certainly regarded as taken from a place of some sort. With this also agrees the alias *Champ*. In early documents as already mentioned, we find *Campio* used to distinguish certain individuals. This word is undoubtedly a Latin translation of *Cempa*. From it comes the modern surnames Campion and Champion, which are, therefore, the true representatives of the Anglo-Saxon *Cempa*, rather than Kemp, though it may be freely conceded without detriment to the validity of other proposed derivations, that the latter name in some cases probably comes ultimately from the same source.

Among the early representatives of the name Kemp the phrases "de Combes" or "de Compes" occur frequently in the eastern counties. In Suffolk is a parish named Combs, while Sussex has a parish of Coombs. There is evidence that in a few instances "de Combes" or "de Compes" passed into Kemp, but it is more probable that these forms are represented by the modern surname Coombs.

The early spelling of the name of the Cornish Kempes appears to have been Camois, Kemys or Cames, variants of the Welsh place-name Cemmaes or Cemmes. Kemes is the name of one of the hundreds of Pembrokeshire. There are two parishes named Kemeys on the River Usk in Monmouthshire, viz., Kemeys Commander and Kemeys Inferior. Kemmaes or Cemmaes Head is a promontory on the north of Pembrokeshire. Cemmaes is a hamlet of Llanbadrig, Anglesey. In Montgomeryshire is a parish and village of Cemmes. In Pughe's Welsh Dictionary *Cemmaes* is defined as an amphitheatre for games, while *Maes* is stated to signify "that which is spacious, clear or open; an open region; a plain, an open field." *Kemeys* appears, therefore, to have nearly the same meaning as *Kemp*, in the sense of camping close. Possibly it may be a translation. Cornwall is a county with a peculiar history. The Keltic language there survived till the latter half of the eighteenth century. Yet the landholders in the time of Edward the Confessor as recorded in Domesday without exception possess Saxon names. Nowhere else did such a large Keltic population pass under Saxon rule. Under such circumstances it is reasonable to think that names may have been translated from one language to the other. Where a similarity in sound between the forms occurred such translations would be almost certain to "catch on" and become better known than the original. It will be noted that the Kempes of Cornwall being known as Kemys favours the theory set forth in this chapter as to the origin of the name Kemp.*

As it has been shewn highly probable that Kemys is a translation of the name Kemp, it is possible that the name Kemys may have in turn given rise to Kemp through hasty pronunciation: Kemys, Kemmis, Kemms and Kemps are all existing surnames. When it is remembered that Pepys and Sandys are pronounced as Peps and Sands, the transition from Kemys to Kems appears natural. Kemps again illustrates the tendency to insert an unnecessary *p* after the letter *m* as in

* An actual instance of Kemp giving place to Kemys occurs on p. 22.

Thompson. Finally, what can be more probable than the dropping of the final s by bearers of the name Kemps, thus making it identical with a well-known English surname?

But an *s* may have been cut off at the beginning of a name making it into Kemp. Skemp, like Kemps, represents an existing English name. Kemp, it will at once be admitted, is more euphonious than Skemp. It is also more easily understood when spoken. "My name is Skemp"; "Kemp did you say?" "No, Skemp" is a dialogue with which bearers of the name Skemp must be painfully familiar. The name is moreover suggestive of Scamp, to which, indeed, it may be equivalent. Thus on many grounds Skemps would be disposed to transform themselves into Kemps. It should perhaps be added that the writers have not met with any actual instance of the transition from Skemp or Kemps to Kemp.

The Danish word *Kimpe*, a giant has been suggested as a possible original of the name Kemp, but no evidence of much weight has been adduced. The spelling with an *i* or a *y* in place of *e* is very rare in old documents except in Cornwall as above noticed. Among the Gloucester wills is that of William Kympe, *alias* Kempe, of Maismore, dated 1566. The absence of such variant spellings in the eastern counties where the Danes principally settled is an objection to this derivation.

Among the Flemish weavers of whom many have settled in England, Kemp was a common surname. It is at least a curious circumstance that more than one technical term connected with their industry suggests a plausible origin of the name. "Kemb" was an old spelling of comb. From it was derived the word "kembster" or "kempster," signifying a woolcomber. *Kemb* is found as a surname at Bristol in the sixteenth century. It may very probably bave been exchanged for the better known Kemp. If Kemb the surname be the same word as kemb, a comb, its adoption as a family appellation, most probably arose through the ancestors of its bearers being engaged in wool or perhaps flax combing and using the chief implement of their trade as a sign of their abode.

Kempt is a variant of Kemp occasionally met with. Among the Lincoln wills is that of *Thomas Kempt* of Dunston, who died in 1558. The form also occurs frequently in Scotland. "Kempt" is the past participle of the old English verb kemb, signifying to comb. "Unkempt" is still in use in the sense of rough or shaggy-haired. Kempt would thus be the sobriquet of a man who paid more than usual attention to his personal appearance, "well groomed" as we say. As a surname the final *t* would almost certainly tend to be dropped in course of time.

The stiff coarse hairs which grow among the finer wool and prevent it becoming matted are known as "kemps." They are very brittle and will not take any dye. Hence they have to be carefully removed before the wool is manufactured. It will be noted that this word is evidently identical with "Camp sb[4]" previously mentioned. "Kemp" or "kempe" appears also to have been used as an adjective in the sense of shaggy or rough. Thus in Chaucer's Knights' Tale l. 1276, it is said of the King of Thrace:—

"Lik a grifphon looked he aboute
With kempe heeris on hise browes stoute."

It should be added, however, that there is a variant reading "kemped" found in some copies of the "Canterbury Tales."

According to the "Century Dictionary" the word kemp, besides being used in the above-mentioned senses, is applied to (1) an eel; (2) a boar; (3) various species of plantain. It is possible that each one of these senses may have caused the adoption of the word as a surname in some cases, though we have no proof that it did so. Many surnames are taken from fishes. Herring, Roach, Salmon, Sturgeon are examples. Eel as a surname is not known to the present writers, though they have met with Eeles. Quadrupeds furnish another important category, including Bull and Bullock, Fox, Hare, Lyon, Pigg.. A small class of names are taken from plants. Examples are Fennel, Moss, Parsley, Rose and Primrose. It would be out of place to enter into the reasons for which such names were originally bestowed. The fact of their being so numerous is a proof of the possibility of the word "Kemp" in the senses here enumerated having been so applied.

"Kempie" is a term of reproach applied in Scotland to a contemptible rascally fellow. Among the Edinburgh wills is preserved that of John Kempie, Maltman, Burgess of Perth, who died in 1598. In the same collection is the will of William Kempyew proved in 1569. Kempie is another name which would naturally tend to be changed into Kemp. (See Scottish section.)

Kemp (with its variants) is used throughout northern Europe as a surname, and from at least as early as the time of Edward III. Kemps from the Continent have frequently settled in this country. Holland and Germany have given many Kemps to Britain whose descendants little imagine that their ancestors were of foreign stock. From the lowlands of Scotland the name has almost disappeared, through migration to other parts of the kingdom or the colonies. At the present time numerous Dutch Kemps are living side by side with Scottish and English Kemps in the Transvaal, and it will be well nigh impossible in the future to trace their origin, unless the present generation take the trouble to record their facts. The compilers of the present History will gladly welcome information.

Appendix to Chapter II.

I.

Since this chapter was written a note has appeared in *Notes and Queries* (9th S. VIII. August 3rd, 1901, p. 113) by Dr. G. Krueger, of Berlin, in reply to an inquiry by the writer in a previous issue.

Dr. Krueger states that the Latin word *campus*, with the primary meaning field, passed into the Old English, Frisian and Low German languages as well as French. It formerly denoted an enclosed piece of land belonging to a single owner as distinguished from one belonging to the community. In Westphalia it now-a-days simply signifies a field. It is found in various place names. Many surnames contain it as one of their elements, especially in Westphalia, of which the Doctor cites numerous instances. His conclusion is that the name has reference to the place of abode only, being the original usage of the word.

II.

An important event has occurred in the publication of the fifth volume of the "Historical English Dictionary," which includes the letters H, I, J, K.

The Dictionary gives no less than five substantives "kemp"—

Kemp sb[1]=champion. It also signifies a reaper. From a game with the seed-stalks of the ribwort plantain, in which each competitor tried with his own, of which he held a certain number, to strike off as many heads as possible from the stalks held by his opponent, the word was transferred to this plant.

Kemp sb[2]=a coarse hair.

Kemp sb[3] is given as doubtfully signifying a barrel or cask. Illustrative quotations mention "kemps" of ale (1391) and also of herrings (c 1440).

Kemp sb[4]=a kind of eel. Its use belongs to the fifteenth and sixteenth centuries.

Kemp sb[5]=a contest of reapers.

Kemb appears in the sense of comb as a substantive and as a verb. From the latter comes the participle adjective kempt found in use soon after the year 1000. The surname Kempt is doubtless the same word.

CHAPTER III.

THE EARLY KEMPES OF WYE.

ALFRED JOHN KEMP, the antiquary, who, perhaps, took more trouble in comparing the Kempe pedigrees with original and authoritative sources of information than any previous compiler, had not the facilities for verifying and correcting them which we enjoy to-day. Had the Record Office been as advanced towards order as it is now, there is little doubt that he would have made good use of its wealth of documents before writing the interesting articles on the family which appeared in the *Gentleman's Magazine* in 1823, 1829, and 1845.

With regard to the Kentish Kempes he seems to have relied on the statement contained in a chart pedigree of the family privately printed in 1808 for the use of the Cornish Kempes, the information in which is apparently drawn from the printed pedigree of the family given in "Stemmata Chicheleana" (1765), which is repeated in Berry's "Kent Genealogies" (1830).

"Stemmata Chicheleana" is a work which is generally accepted as an authority, but is not without important errors. Its full title is "Stemmata Chicheleana: A Genealogical Account of some of the Families derived from Thomas Chichele, of Higham Ferrers, Co. Northampt., all whose descendants are held entitled to Fellowships in All Souls' College." The author was Dr. Buckler.

Hasted in his "History of the County of Kent," published in 1798, gives as his authorities for the ancestors of the Kempe family a book in the Heralds' Office marked "H. 2. Kent," a manuscript in the possession of Thomas Knight of Godmersham Park and the "Stemmata Chicheleana."

Robert Kempe, of Gissing, about 1680 collected the various pedigrees of Kempe families. These in his own hand-writing are now in the British Museum (Harl. MSS. 901).

Other MSS. might be mentioned, but as they appear to have been derived from the same sources, and vary little in their main features, it is not necessary here to specify their differences.

The general statement made by A. J. Kempe that the first known ancestor of the Kempes of Wye came "from the North," and that he was "connected with the Nevils of Raby" appears never to have been satisfactorily proved or disproved. It will be well, therefore, first of all to inquire what is meant by the very indefinite "North," and how the Nevils and the Kempes were connected.

Northumberland would seem to be the region probably indicated as the "North," for we know of a Kempe there to whom King John in 1205 gave land at Newcastle of the annual value of 50*s.* "till he could provide for him in marriage." This Kempe, whose Christian name is not given, was *balistarius*, or bowmaker to the King. Evidently he had powerful family connexions since the King considered it necessary thus to provide for him. How long he enjoyed the above-named provision, or what other lands he eventually obtained, we have not traced; but we find from the Pipe Rolls for Northumberland that in 1277 the lands at Newcastle which had belonged to "Kempe the bowmaker," were then held by the burgessess of the town, who paid £5 10*s.* 6*d.* per annum. As the Nevills were Earls of Northumberland, the bowmaker, an important follower of the King, would certainly be familiar with them. It may be possible some day to prove that the families were linked by marriage. Meanwhile we can show many *later* instances of Kempes being associated with the Neville family. The tradition as to the origin of the Kempes of Wye recorded by A. J. Kempe, though not proven, is easily credible. As Kempe is by no means a common name in the North of England the probability that Kempe *balistarius* was of the same family, if not a progenitor, of the Kempes of Wye (admitting the truth of the tradition), is distinctly strengthened. Long before this day, however, Kempes had settled in Norfolk, and it is probable that the north country Kempes came originally from the East Anglian stock.

The Kempes and Nevilles may have been linked in another way. A. T. Kempe, as above noted, specifies the "Nevilles of Raby." Now Isabel de Neville, daughter and heiress of Geoffrey de Neville, Governor of Berwick-on-Tweed, married Robert Fitz Maldred, Lord of Raby, in the County of Durham, of the stock of the Earls of Northumberland. Her son, who assumed the name of Neville, was an ancestor of the Earls of Westmoreland and of the Marquises of Abergavenny. From the Kalendar of Inquisitions, post mortem, of 16 Edward IV. (1477), we learn that Edward Nevill, Knight, Lord Abergavenny owned, among other real estate, land at Morley and Birlingham in Norfolk, of which one, Roger (or Robert) Kempe was tenant. These lands had descended to the Nevills from William de Bello Campo, Knight and Lord Bergaveney, of the family of the Earl of Warwick, who died possessed of them in 1436 when the above Roger or Robert was already tenant.

When, therefore, we find Thomas de Bello Campo, the powerful Earl of Warwick, interceding on behalf of a Thomas Kempe of Rochester, who had lost his estates for misdemeanour, we can hardly doubt that this was a case of an influential man assisting an unfortunate relative. It was in February, 1381, that Thomas Kempe, having failed to render an account to William de Gadesby for his stewardship was outlawed, and his goods forfeited. In the following April a petition was presented to the King on his behalf by the Earl with the result that a pardon was obtained and the estate restored. This interesting episode is recorded in the Patent Rolls, while the existence of Thomas Kempe is further attested by the Inquisition made at the time which is given in the Escheat Rolls, where he is called "Thomas Kempe atte Raven," "de Ravene" * or "de Rochester." He was found to possess a tenement, "Bogham de Boldye," and ten acres of arable land in "Bowte-walle," both in Kent, though these places have not been certainly identified.

The identity of this Thomas Kempe is involved in obscurity. He may be the father of Archbishop Kempe, who was born in 1380. If he was a kinsman of the Kempes of Wye at all (for even this is uncertain) the above event shows that this family are probably connected with those Norfolk Kemps who held land from the Earls of Warwick, the Bello Campo and Neville families.

There is another point from which our inquiries into the origin of the Kempes of Wye might start.

The pedigrees above mentioned generally agree in stating that the head of the family held Bilting (or Bileting) with Ollantigh, as early as the time of Edward III., both of which manors are in Wye. Although Wye is but a village to-day it was a place of considerable importance at that period. The Conqueror bestowed it on his newly-founded Battle Abbey by the name of the Royal Manor of Wye, which, it is said, contained twenty-two towns. Fortunately the Custumals of Battle Abbey from Edward I. to Edward III. are in existence, the substance of the earlier portion (1283-1313) having been printed by the Camden Society. These show the various properties held by the Abbey with the names of the chief tenants. On pp. 101-136 are given the tenants of the Royal Manor of Wye. Among them is RADULPHUS DE CAMPIS, who is, of course, identical with Ralph Kempe, the accredited ancestor of the Wye Kempes. In Sussex they had a tenant

* The Bishop of Rochester still signs himself "Roffen," *i.e.*, Roffensis.

named Galfridus (*i.e.*, Geoffrey) Kempe holding "messuagium et dimidiam acram." One, Johannes de Campo, is their tenant in Wilts. Willielmus de Combe, or Coumbe, is also at Wye with Hamo de Cambe. All these names occur before 1312 when the spelling *Kempe* was rare.

Another origin is suggested by the author of the "Scotts of Scott's Hall," who tells us that the Kempes of Wye were probably descendants of John Kempe, the Flemish weaver, who settled in this country under Royal protection in 1331. In support of this view he tells us that a John Kempe, who witnessed a Scott deed, described himself as a "scissor," which the author of that work says means a cutter and hence a tailor. The fact of the Kempes having been established at Wye before the time of the arrival of the Flemish weaver and his relatives of the same name sufficiently refutes this theory, which but for the distinguished support it has received, would be unworthy of notice.

CHAPTER IV.

THE KEMPES OF WYE.

THE earliest ancestor of the Wye Kempes, of whose existence and relationship to the house we possess any certain knowledge, is RADULPHUS DE CAMPIS, otherwise Ralph Kempe, whose name occurs among the tenants of the manor from 1283 to 1313. He is the first-known holder of Ollantigh.

He left a son, Sir John Kempe, of Wye, who held Boxley, Birling, Stentor, and other estates. The Christian name of his wife is unknown. But among the deeds at the Public Record Office is one dated 5 May, 3 Edward III. (1330), granting pieces of land called "Kingscroft," in the parish of Maidstone, and "Bromfield *alias* Freynhill," in the parish of "Boxle," to "Agnes Kempe, widow," John Payne and William Harding, the grantors being John Scot and Stephen Wolf. This is the earliest known deed relating to the Kentish Kempes. Although historians have not told us the name of Sir John Kempe's wife, we know that he married a daughter of Sir Thomas Aldon, by whom he had two sons, Roger and Peter, and possibly others.

SIR ROGER KEMPE inherited Ollantigh. He died without issue leaving his property to his next of kin, viz., his brother, Peter, who appears as already possessed of a portion of Brabourne. Now Brabourne was at this time, and for many generations, a seat of the Scots with whom the Kempes intermarried several times. The John Scot above mentioned was undoubtedly of this family. PETER KEMPE was certainly living at Brabourne in 1352, for at Michaelmas in that year he made a perpetual grant of a plot with a messuage at "Colmannes," in the parish and in the tenure of Brabourne (? Manor); also an acre near the Rectory of which he was presumably proprietor. This deed is quoted in brief in the history of the Scotts of Scott's Hall. It was witnessed by one, Rado Kempe. As Ralph Kempe of Wye must have been dead by this time, this must have been a relative of whom we have no other record. He may have been the ancestor of one of the lines which are found existing soon after.

David, King of Scotland=Maud of Northumberland.

Adama de Warrene=Henry, Prince of Scotland, Earl of Huntingdon.

Maud de Meschines=David, Earl of Huntingdon, went with King Richard I to the Crusades, died 1219.

Hugh Balliol, Lord of Teesdale and Marwood Forests, temp. Henry III.

Allan, Lord of Galloway, Steward of Scotland=Margaret, of Huntingdon. Isabelle, of Scotland, mar. Robert de Ros. Ada, of Huntingdon=Henry Hastings, Lord Hastings, died 1250.

John Balliol, Lord of Bywell, Founder of Balliol College, Oxford; died 1269.=Dornagieen, of Galloway.

Sir William Balliol, called le Scott=

John Scott, of Brabourne, Kent.

Sir William Scott, of Brabourne.

Michael Scott=Emma.

William Scott=Matilda.

. . . . the heiress of Cumbe, Brabourne=John Scott.

William Scott, of Scott's Hall, Smeeth, East Kent, =Isabel Herbert or Fynche.

Sir Robert Scott.

Alice Scott=WILLIAM KEMPE.

Sir John Scott, of Scott's Hall=Agnes Beaufitz.

Sybilla Lewknor=Sir William Scott, of Scott's Hall.

Anne Pympe=Sir John Scott, of Scott's Hall and of Iden, Sussex.

Sir Reginald Scott, of Scott's Hall=EMMELINE KEMPE.

The connexion of the Kempes with the Scots is of great interest, both because it is through this line that some of the Kempes inherit royal blood, and because, apart from all such considerations, some members of the Scot family were persons of great personal distinction. The pedigree of the Scots from David, King of Scotland, who married Maud of Northumberland, to Sir Reginald Scott, who took as his wife Emmeline Kempe, is here given, having been kindly supplied with other royal descent by Herbert Robertson, Esq., author of "Stemmata Robertson et Durden." Further reference to this subject will be made when we come to speak more particularly of the marriages between the families.

PETER KEMPE probably moved to Ollantigh on the death of his brother. His wife's name is unknown. He left two sons, viz., Sir Roger Kempe, who like his uncle died without issue in 1425, and Sir Thomas Kempe, who consequently succeeded to the family property.

This THOMAS KEMPE appears to have been escheater to the King, for we find that one of this name living at "Wy" was frequently called upon in and about 1388 to admit clergy and others to lands which had escheated to the Crown. It was usual for sheriffs and others of standing in a county to undertake this office. "Thomas Kempe of Wy" must therefore have been known as a fit person for this responsibility. According to the Close Rolls recently printed his jurisdiction was not confined to Kent, for we have his name mentioned in connexion with Middlesex. He died in 1428. He probably held some minor office, in the discharge of which he distinguished himself before he became escheater to the Crown, and was consequently regarded as likely to rise to some much higher position, for long before he could have entertained any prospect of being heir to the chief estates of the family he made a very good match, securing as his wife Beatrice, the daughter of Sir Thomas Lewknor, whose family exceeded his own in importance and extent of possessions. Roger Lewknor had been Sheriff of Sussex in 1284, while his son, Roger, was Sheriff for the same county in the 14th and 20th years of Edward III. The latter married Barbara Bardolph, whose arms he quartered with his own, and whose coat is quartered by the Kempes of Gissing. By her he had a son, Thomas, who was, we believe, father of the Thomas Lewknor, whose daughter, Beatrice, wedded Sir Thomas Kempe. The date of this marriage is not precisely known. John Kempe, who became Archbishop of Canterbury, was their second son. The date of his nativity is given as 1380.

Some authorities state that Beatrice Lewknor was also married to a Ralph Roper, but as to whether before or after her union with Sir Thomas Kempe they differ. In "Segar's Baronage" it is said that *her daughter* married this individual, which seems far more likely. In any case, the pedigree makers are right in stating that both Kempes and Ropers, who were subsequeutly jointly interested in certain estates, were equally descended from her.

Sir Thomas Kempe's eldest son, Roger, succeeded to the Wye estates. Besides the somewhat hypothetical Beatrice, or Joan, who married Ralph Roper, he undoubtedly had a daughter, Isabelle, who married Sir Robert Strelley. A separate chapter is devoted to the life of Archbishop John Kempe.

Camden and others describe the parentage of the Archbishop as "mean," by which they did not, of course, intend to convey the idea of contemptible or really low rank. But when after a succession of archbishops drawn from the noblest families of immense wealth John Kempe was appointed, a host of disappointed expectants must have relieved their feelings by gibing at the comparative obscurity and poverty of his family. The Cardinal was certainly not of this opinion, judging both from the fact that all the time he could snatch from the onerous and multifarious duties of state he delighted to spend under the parental roof. The monument which he erected in Wye Church confirms the esteem in which he held his home. The tomb disappeared when the church was destroyed by fire, but the inscription which follows is given in Parson's "Monuments of Kent":—

HIC SISTUNT OSSA THOMÆ KEMPE MARMORE FOSSA
CUJUS OPUS PRONUM SE PROBAT ESSE BONUM.
DUM VIXIT LÆTUS FUIT ET BONITATE REPLETUS
MUNIFICUS VIGUIT, PAUPERIBUS TRIBUIT.
JUNGITUR HUIC SATRIX VIRTUTUM, SPONSA BEATRIX
QUÆ PARTITUR OPES, SPONTE JUVANS INOPES.
EX HIS PROCESSIT, UT RAMUS AB ARBORE CRESCIT
CLERI PRÆSIDIUM, DUX SAPIENS OVIUM.
CHRISTI(ANUS) LECTOR CUNCTIS SUPPLICET HORIS
UT PATRIS DEITAS LUMINET HAS ANIMAS.

CHAPTER V.

THE KEMPES OF WYE—*continued.*

THE biography of John Kempe we shall give in subsequent chapters. We now pass to the elder brother Robert.

The name of this brother has been omitted in several pedigrees, as also the name of his wife, while some entirely ignore him and make his son William brother to the Cardinal. Certainly there seems no satisfactory evidence of his holding Ollantigh. If he did so it was probably for but a short period, for we find no Robert as a payer of subsidy in the Lathes of Scray or Saint Augustine in the year 1440, by which time the nephew of the Archbishop had come into the estates.

The Subsidy Roll for that year is still in existence at the Record Office, and the Kempes on it include the following:—

In St. Augustine's Lathe.

Hundred of Ringslow.	Simon	Kempe	paid,	12	pence.	
Do.	"	"	"	12	"	
Do.	"	"	"	2	"	
Do.	"	"	"	2	"	
Do.	Stephen	"	"	12	"	
Do.	"	"	"	12	"	
Do.	"	"	"	3	"	
Do.	"	"	"	2	"	
Do.	Thomas	"	"	4	"	
Do.	Nicholas	"	"	20	"	
Do. (Luke or ?)	"	"	"	20	"	
Hundred of Blengate	"	"	"	12	"	
Do.	John	"	"	14	"	
Do.	"	"	"	11	"	

Lathe of Shipway.					
	(Hundred doubtful)				
	John	Kempe	paid	8	pence.
	"	"	"	11	"
	"	"	,	9	"
	William	"	"	16	"
	"	"	"	8	"
	"	"	"	8	"
Hundred of Bircholt.	John	"	"	6	"

In some cases the individuals of the same name may be identical, being rated in each of the parishes where they held lands. The William and John in the Lathe of Shipway may represent William Kempe of Wye and Archbishop Kempe, but if so it is singular that they do not appear under the Lathe of Scray.

It will be noticed from the above that the names in each case occur more than once, and this may indicate that since 1418, when only three Kempes occur on the Kentish Subsidy Roll, the property had descended to the sons, nephews and grandsons of the then holders, according to the custom of gavelkind. The amounts are all small compared with others paid at this time, but it does not necessarily follow that these were *all* poor people. In the Subsidy Roll of 1418 Hamo Kempe of Ringslow hundred paid two shillings. It was a common practice to name two sons alike; hence it is probable that the Simons, Stephens, Thomases and Nicholases of Ringslow in 1440 were his descendants. Hugh Kempe appears in the hundred of Heane in 1418. This hundred lies around Hythe, which ancient port was in constant communication with Romney. Hence the Kempes of the latter may thus have originated here as they crop up soon after this date. Of them we shall give some account in due course.

Neither in 1418 nor in 1440 does a Roger or Robert appear, and no inquisition post mortem, or a will is forthcoming; but it is yet early for these documentary evidences to be obtainable. We must merely credit the existence of this elder brother of Cardinal Kempe, who was father of William Kempe the next heir, and Thomas Kempe, who became in time Bishop of London.

This William Kempe married Alice, daughter and heiress of Sir Robert Scott. By her the Manor of Hinxhill (between Brabourne and Ashford), passed to the Kempes, but it was alienated by her grandson, Sir William Kempe, about the end of the reign of Henry VIII. Her father was Lieutenant of the Tower of London in 1424, and hence a man of considerable importance.

William and Alice had at least two sons, Thomas and William. The latter was educated for the church, and is mentioned in the will of Bishop Thomas Kempe in 1488. It was doubtless due to the influence of this uncle that he obtained his preferments in the church. Newcourt in his "Repertorium," in giving a list of his livings, calls him "doubtless a relation of Thomas Kempe, at this time Bishop of London." He may in early life have had one of the Kentish churches of which his relations were patrons. He first appears, however, in the Diocese of London in 1473, when he was elected to the Prebend of Hoxton in St. Paul's Cathedral. This stall derives its stipend from Shoreditch, in which parish a family of Kempes were settled for a very long period, as will be seen under that head. (Middlesex, Shoreditch.) In February, 1476, he was made Rector of Stepney. On March 2, 1478, he was transferred to the Prebendal Stall of Kentish Town, that stall being worth about three times as much as his former one. Before his death Kempes had established themselves at Kentish Town and St. Pancras, in which the corpus of this prebend lies. Noticing how frequently this settlement of Kempes follows the course of the favoured ecclesiastics of the family, one cannot fail to infer that they thus obtained leasehold property on very easy terms. On the 28th March, 1489, being then B.D., William was presented to the Rectory of Orset in Essex, which he retained with Stepney until the end of December,

1522. He, perhaps, died at this time, as we find no further trace of him. His will has not been discovered; it would in the ordinary way have been proved in the Court of the Dean and Chapter of St. Paul's. The first extant register of Probates belonging to this court commences in 1535.

His brother, THOMAS KEMPE, was Sheriff of Kent in 1493 and again in 1506. At the marriage of Prince Arthur, the eldest son of Henry VII., in 1510, he was made a Knight of the Bath, and in 1508 he rebuilt his mansion at Ollanty. He married Emelyn, daughter of Sir Valantyne Chiche, by Phillippa, daughter and heir of Robert Chichley, who was son of Sir Robert Chichley, Knight, Lord Mayor of London, and nephew of Henry Chichele, Archbishop of Canterbury and Founder of All Souls' College, Oxford.

This marriage was one of very great importance to the succeeding generations; as being descendants of the "Founder's Kin" they were entitled to election as Fellows of All Souls, a privilege which was eagerly claimed for hundreds of years, not only by the Kempes but by the innumerable other descendants of this marriage. The College at last sought to limit the claim, but litigation failed to relieve them of this wide-spreading bequest of the founder, and, providing claimants were in a position to show their lawful relationship, their claim could not be set aside.

The arms of the family of Chicheley, who were descended from Thomas of High Ferrars, Northamptonshire, were:—Azure, three lions rampant and a bordure argent. The tomb of Archbishop Chichley is the most resplendent in Canterbury Cathedral. It stands exactly opposite that of Archbishop Kempe, and has recently been most gorgeously regilt and highly coloured by Charles Eamer Kemp, M.A. (the noted stained window manufacturer), at the expense of All Souls' College. On the tomb is the very fleshy form of the Archbishop in full episcopal vestments, and beneath in striking contrast is a ghastly representation of his skeleton, devoid of all earthly pomp.

Emelyn Chiche presented Sir Thomas Kempe with a numerous family, at least seven sons and half a dozen daughters. There is, however, a curious error in the pedigrees widely printed. It has been standing now so many years, and having received even the apparent approval of Sir Edmund Burke in his "History of the Commoners of England," it is difficult to set this right without hurting the susceptibilities of some who feel themselves bound to stand up for their family traditions. The editors would infinitely have preferred to confirm such traditions rather than to upset them, but the sacred duty of the historian is to administer the truth, so far as possible. The error to which we refer is the insertion of the name of Edmund Kempe, "Citizen and Mercer of London" among the children of Sir Thomas Kempe. This Edmund Kempe was, in fact, a native of Suffolk, bore the arms of that family, with the quarterings of his father, who resided at Gissing, and is shown in the visitation of London made in 1563 to be son of Robert Kempe, of Weston, in Suffolk, by Anne, daughter of John Clifford, of Holmdale, Kent. This association with Kent, coupled with the fact that he married Bridget, daughter of John Style, sister to Sir Humphrey Style, of Beckenham, in Kent, was quite sufficient to lead to the mistake. Consequently persons mentioned in his will (1542) were added to the pedigree of Kentish Kempes as well as himself, notwithstanding the fact that in the Harleian MSS. (1154) he is said to be "Heire elect to Robert Kempe of Gissing and Weston." This Edmund had two sons, both mentioned in his will. James, the eldest, was of Acton, Middlesex, and was married in 1544 to Anne Powle. Humphry Kempe, the second son, was evidently not married till some years later, hence it is quite impossible for this Edmund to have been ancestor to the Kempes of Cornwall, as stated by Burke, for Richard Kempe was at Levethan with a family in 1544. Added to which is the statement of Sir John Maclean in his "History of Trigg Minor," that the seat of the Kempes of Cornwall was at Trevelver in 1475, in which year they removed to Levethan.

Edmund Kempe, Citizen and Mercer of London, will be therefore more fully dealt with under the Kempes of Norfolk, and the Cornish family by themselves.

We now give the names of those who are duly authenticated as children of the above Sir Thomas Kempe and Emelyn Chiche, which are as follows:—Christopher, William, Richard,

26

19

Brass to the memory of John Toke, in the Church of Great Chart, near Ashford.

John, Andrew, Edward, George, and Cecilia, the last of whom married John Toke of Godinton. To their memory there is still a fine brass, with figures and inscription, in the Church of Great

Chart, near Ashford, of which an illustration is given in "Belcher's Kentish Brasses." It must not be taken for granted that these figures are actual likenesses of the persons they commemorate, for a number of brasses were often made from the same drawing. In this case the effigies of seven children of this couple are also represented. Cecilia died in 1559, her husband on 7th November, 1568, aged eighty. In this church there are other monuments to the Tokes, extending faom 1513 to 1680.

The arms and pedigree of this family are given in the "Visitation of Kent." Their initial coat is :—Per chevron sable and argent, three griffins' heads erased counterchanged. To this eight quarterings are attached.

Christopher Kempe, the eldest son of Sir Thomas Kempe, by Emelyn Chiche, married Mary, daughter of Sir Richard Guildford,* Knight.

By her he had a daughter, Mary, born in 1508, who married Lawrence Finch of the Mote (brother to Sir Thomas Finch, of Eastwell). She became heir to her father (who died without leaving a son) before 1518, as appears from the will of Sir Thomas. Mary, his widow, afterwards married Sir William Haut, or Hawte. There are in the British Museum (Add. Char., F49 & 54-5) two deeds executed when Christopher's daughter was eighteen, at which Kentish maidens come of age. These deeds are chiefly interesting for their seals, one of which has the initials "I. C.," which it is quite possible was the signet of John Kempe. The signatures and seals of William and Mary Haute are appended. By the will of Sir Thomas Kempe, proved in 1520, "Mary, wife of William Haute, Esq., formerly wife of Christopher Kempe," was bequeathed certain tenements in Warehorne, Newchurch, Roking, and Snave, in accordance with some indenture made 27th June in the second year of Henry VIII. (1511). We are unable to say who were the parties to this deed, perhaps it was executed by way of provision for his child in accordance with the will of Christopher Kempe, but there is no such will registered at Canterbury or in the Perogative Court of that See.

William Kempe, the second son of Sir Thomas and Emelyn, became heir to the Ollantigh estates, and of him we shall speak later ; Richard Kempe, the third son, under his father's will, was to receive the reversion of the family mansion and chief lands in the case of this William dying without male heir ; this, however, did not occur, and Richard seems to have left the neighbourhood. Possibly it was he who obtained a licence to marry Katherine Catesby, of the Diocese of Worcester in 1547. She was one of seven daughters of Will. Willington, a wealthy merchant of Oxford, Barcheston, in Warwickshire, and other places. Her first husband was William Catesby, of Lapworth ; after the death of Richard Kempe she married Anthony Throckmorton, a younger son of Sir George Throckmorton. Richard Kempe, who describes himself as of Longdon, in the Parish of Treddington, and Diocese of Worcester, made his will in the fifth year of Edward VII. (P. C. C. 17 Buck). In it he mentions his wife, Katherine, Anthony, his son, his daughter Ann, John Bradley, son of William Bradley, sisters named Anne and Jane, and Phillip Rawlins. The will of his wife as Katherine Throckmorton, proved 1594 (P. C. C. 69 Dixy), mentions her cousin "Rawlins," her "brother's sons, Richard and Anthony Kemys," and many other relatives. She desired to be buried in the Church of St. Martin Orgar, London, with the body of her late husband, Anthony Throckmorton. (*See* Throckmorton under Norfolk Kempes.)

It is open to doubt, however, if Richard of Longdon, Treddington, was of the Wye family. Possibly the following will may represent the third son of Thomas and Emelyn Kempe—

* Arms of Guildford, with quarterly of four, as given in the Visitation of Kent are: Or, a saltire between four martletts, sable. Crest: a tree couped or, from the three branches fire issuant proper.

Richard :—Richard Kempe, of London, dated 9th March, 1547, proved the last day of that month (P. C. C. 5 Popuwell), leaves "to myne hoste John Barton the goodman of the 'George' besides Fleet Bridge 40/-, to Harry Bennet 20/- and the residue to Nicholas Udall of London gentleman. Nicholas Udall, M.A., was a celebrated schoolmaster and playwright in the employ of Stephen Gardiner, Bishop of Winchester. The latter, in his will of 1557, bequeathes £4 to Francis Kempe, who witnessed the will.

A third Richard, who might prove to be the son of William of Ollantigh, was a husbandman of Whatlington, Sussex, whose will was proved in 1558. (*Vide* Sussex Section.)

John, the fourth son of Sir Thomas Kempe and Emelyn Chiche, was an "F.S.A." in 1541; this does not mean that he was a Fellow of the Society of Antiquaries, as some writer in the *Gentleman's Magazine* supposes "Berry's Pedigrees" to have inferred, but that he became a Fellow of All Souls' College in virtue of his descent from Chichley before explained. It may have been this individual who, after being a preacher throughout Kent and Essex, was parson of Freshwater, and a friend of John Foxe, with whom we shall deal under the Isle of Wight Kempes.

Andrew, the fifth son of Sir Thomas Kempe, is probably the same as one of that name who constantly appears as a Notary Public engaged in making probate valuations in London, as given in Inquisitones Post Mortem, 1485-1561, but the identity is not clear. There is a will proved in 1575 (Arch. of London, No. I., 139) of an Andrew Kempe, whose profession and parish are not given; he mentions his sister, Margaret Lynicke, his sister, Julian Viggas, Joan Hill, his wife's sister, and Sara, the wife of John Spylsbury, his kinswoman; also a Robert Kempe, who is to divide the chief part of his estate with one, John Hankes, a barber surgeon; and some other names occur.

No definite account is given of Edward and George Kempe, the two youngest sons of Sir Thomas Kempe, except that Edward was not to inherit any estates (even if his elder brothers died without issue) if he became a priest. There is an Edward Kempe in the "Alumni Oxonienses" who became B.A. 26th January, 1519-20, and was a Fellow of Merton (where Archbishop and Bishop Kempe were educated) in 1521. This looks like the son who desired to enter the church.

The name of George was not very common—at least among the Kempes—so early as this; we do not find another in Kent till the next generation. There was a George Kempe at Hampstead, in Middlesex, in 1523; there is nothing, however, to connect the one name with the other.

Sir Thomas Kempe, by deed dated 4th March, 1503, gave all the trees on the west side of the Church of Crundal, as a succour of defence to that church. He served as Sheriff of the County of Kent for the fourth time in 1513-4. In 1520, the year of the "Field of the Cloth of Gold," the Kempes were well to the front. Mistresses Margaret and Margery Kempe attended the Queen of England at the interview with the French King, while John Kempe was master of the *Lesse Barke*, one of the chief ships fitted out for this great State function. The identity of these individuals is uncertain, but they were most probably connected in some way with the distinguished Kentish family. Sir Thomas made his will in 1518, and it was proved in 1521, he having died in 1520. His chief mansion house of "Ollanty" and estates were strictly entailed to his heirs male. His wife, Emelyn, was to have the lease of the messuage in the town of Wye known as the "Bell," held from the Master and brethren of the College of Wye. She is also to enjoy the use of all the furniture and other goods at "Olantye." Cecile, his daughter, is to receive 300 marks on her marriage, 100 in cash on her wedding day, and the remainder from the income derived from the testator's Manor of Boughton Aluph. William, the eldest surviving son, is to pay out of this manor to each of *his five brothers* five marks every half year ; if he fail to do so the brothers have right of entry, or to a grant of sufficient demise to satisfy this bequest. The tenements and lands in Warehorn, Newchurch, Roking and Snave, after the decease of the widow of Christopher Kempe are to revert to William Kempe and his heirs. The testator desires to be buried in the Parish Church of Wye, in the chancel of Our Lady, "beside the sepulchres of my grandfadres and grand-dams." He leaves the usual bequests, for the good health of his soul and "all Christian souls," and donations to the poor. Sir Lawrence Broke, parson of Boughton Aluph, with the eldest son, is to be executor. Elinor, the wife of William Kempe, is mentioned, and the will is witnessed by John Roos, Esq., John Hales, Christopher Hales and Humphrey Gage.

Sir Thomas gives his widow the option of using that part of "Olantye" within the Mote, containing the "chamber wherein I usually lye," for her own habitation, on the south side of the mansion. She is also to have an acre in Boughton Wood cleared for her fowls.

CHAPTER VI.

THE KEMPES OF WYE—*continued.*

AS we have said WILLIAM, the second, but eldest surviving son, succeeded to Ollantigh and the chief Kempe estates in 1520. He had married some time before this Elenor, daughter and coheir of Sir Robert Browne, Knight, and widow of Thomas Fogg, Esq., Sergeant Porter of Calais.

This marriage was, like that of his grandfather with Alice Scot, of Scotshall, the means of bringing more royal ancestors to the family, and the subsequent generations were always anxious to claim the connection with the Earls of Arundel, as shown in the accompanying sketch of this Elenor's descent. It is interesting to notice that the Kemp baronets of Gissing, by a later intermarriage with these Brownes, enjoy the same line of royal descent as the issue of this Kentish Kempe-Browne alliance. *(See Chart.)*

We cannot dwell upon the honours and distinctions of the Brownes of Betchworth Castle ; their history will be found in Surrey county works. Many illustrations have appeared of their fine seat. Their arms were :—Sable, three lions passant in bend between two double cotises argent. And their crest :—A griffin's head erased or. Their pedigree was duly registered at the Visitation of Surrey, and is printed by the Harleian Society, and appears also in Berry's Surrey pedigrees. William Kempe is said to have been born in 1487. In 1523 he paid a subsidy as one of the persons in the Royal Household (his kinsman, John Roper, being also in that favoured list). This John Roper was steward of the Liberty of "Battle Abbey in the town of Wye" (*sic*), and in this capacity—as well as because of his relationship—he was much concerned with the late Sir Thomas Kempe and the present William Kempe in the control of their estates, and was party with them and other influential landed gentry of Kent in petitioning for amendments in the laws

RFOLK.

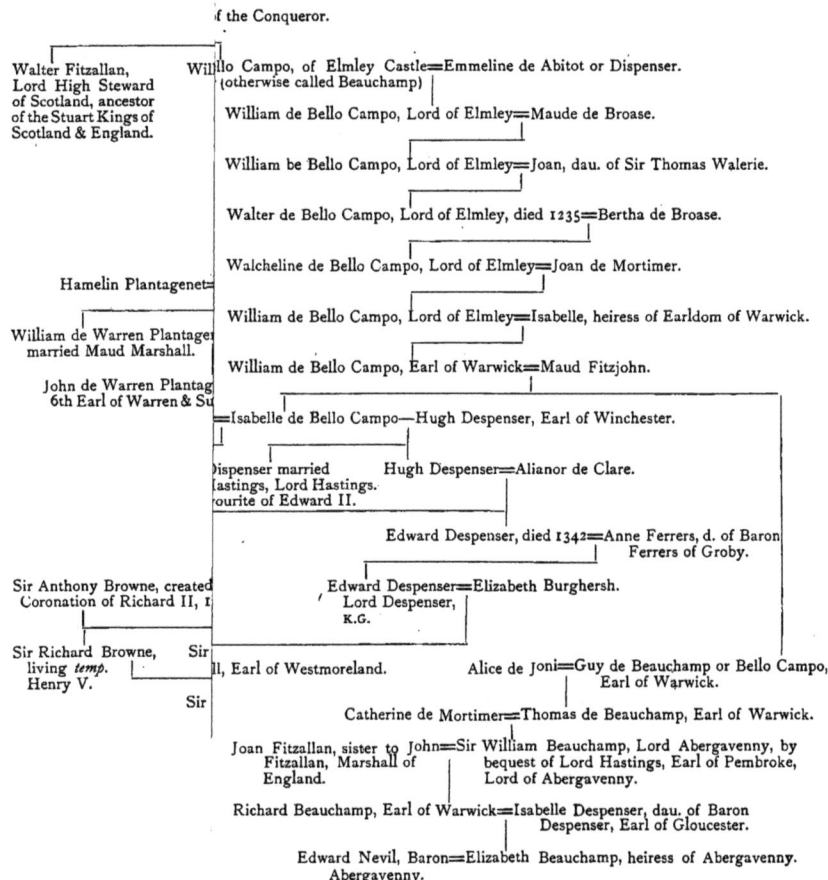

f the Conqueror.

Walter Fitzallan, Lord High Steward of Scotland, ancestor of the Stuart Kings of Scotland & England.

Wil[llo] Campo, of Elmley Castle=Emmeline de Abitot or Dispenser.
(otherwise called Beauchamp)

William de Bello Campo, Lord of Elmley=Maude de Broase.

William be Bello Campo, Lord of Elmley=Joan, dau. of Sir Thomas Walerie.

Walter de Bello Campo, Lord of Elmley, died 1235=Bertha de Broase.

Walcheline de Bello Campo, Lord of Elmley=Joan de Mortimer.

Hamelin Plantagenet=

William de Bello Campo, Lord of Elmley=Isabelle, heiress of Earldom of Warwick.

William de Warren Plantage[net] married Maud Marshall.

William de Bello Campo, Earl of Warwick=Maud Fitzjohn.

John de Warren Plantag[enet] 6th Earl of Warren & Su[rrey]

=Isabelle de Bello Campo—Hugh Despenser, Earl of Winchester.

[D]ispenser married [H]astings, Lord Hastings. [fav]ourite of Edward II.

Hugh Despenser=Alianor de Clare.

Edward Despenser, died 1342=Anne Ferrers, d. of Baron Ferrers of Groby.

Sir Anthony Browne, created Coronation of Richard II, 1

Edward Despenser=Elizabeth Burghersh.
Lord Despenser, K.G.

Sir Richard Browne, living *temp.* Henry V.

Sir

[Nevi]ll, Earl of Westmoreland.

Alice de Joni=Guy de Beauchamp or Bello Campo, Earl of Warwick.

Sir

Catherine de Mortimer=Thomas de Beauchamp, Earl of Warwick.

Joan Fitzallan, sister to John Fitzallan, Marshall of England.=Sir William Beauchamp, Lord Abergavenny, by bequest of Lord Hastings, Earl of Pembroke, Lord of Abergavenny.

Richard Beauchamp, Earl of Warwick=Isabelle Despenser, dau. of Baron Despenser, Earl of Gloucester.

Edward Nevil, Baron Abergavenny.=Elizabeth Beauchamp, heiress of Abergavenny.

[V]ernon, Surrey, Knight.

pay out of this manor to each of *his five brothers* five marks every half year ; if he fail to do so the brothers have right of entry, or to a grant of sufficient demise to satisfy this bequest. The tenements and lands in Warehorn, Newchurch, Roking and Snave, after the decease of the widow of Christopher Kempe are to revert to William Kempe and his heirs. The testator desires to be buried in the Parish Church of Wye, in the chancel of Our Lady, "beside the sepulchres of my grandfadres and grand-dams." He leaves the usual bequests, for the good health of his soul and "all Christian souls," and donations to the poor. Sir Lawrence Broke, parson of Boughton Aluph, with the eldest son, is to be executor. Elinor, the wife of William Kempe, is mentioned, and the will is witnessed by John Roos, Esq., John Hales, Christopher Hales and Humphrey Gage.

Sir Thomas gives his widow the option of using that part of "Olantye" within the Mote, containing the "chamber wherein I usually lye," for her own habitation, on the south side of the mansion. She is also to have an acre in Boughton Wood cleared for her fowls.

CHAPTER VI.

THE KEMPES OF WYE—*continued.*

As we have said WILLIAM, the second, but eldest surviving son, succeeded to Ollantigh and the chief Kempe estates in 1520. He had married some time before this Elenor, daughter and coheir of Sir Robert Browne, Knight, and widow of Thomas Fogg, Esq., Sergeant Porter of Calais.

This marriage was, like that of his grandfather with Alice Scot, of Scotshall, the means of bringing more royal ancestors to the family, and the subsequent generations were always anxious to claim the connection with the Earls of Arundel, as shown in the accompanying sketch of this Elenor's descent. It is interesting to notice that the Kemp baronets of Gissing, by a later intermarriage with these Brownes, enjoy the same line of royal descent as the issue of this Kentish Kempe-Browne alliance. *(See Chart.)*

We cannot dwell upon the honours and distinctions of the Brownes of Betchworth Castle ; their history will be found in Surrey county works. Many illustrations have appeared of their fine seat. Their arms were :—Sable, three lions passant in bend between two double cotises argent. And their crest :—A griffin's head erased or. Their pedigree was duly registered at the Visitation of Surrey, and is printed by the Harleian Society, and appears also in Berry's Surrey pedigrees. William Kempe is said to have been born in 1487. In 1523 he paid a subsidy as one of the persons in the Royal Household (his kinsman, John Roper, being also in that favoured list). This John Roper was steward of the Liberty of "Battle Abbey in the town of Wye" (*sic*), and in this capacity—as well as because of his relationship—he was much concerned with the late Sir Thomas Kempe and the present William Kempe in the control of their estates, and was party with them and other influential landed gentry of Kent in petitioning for amendments in the laws

ROYAL DESCENT OF THE KEMPES OF KENT AND NORFOLK.

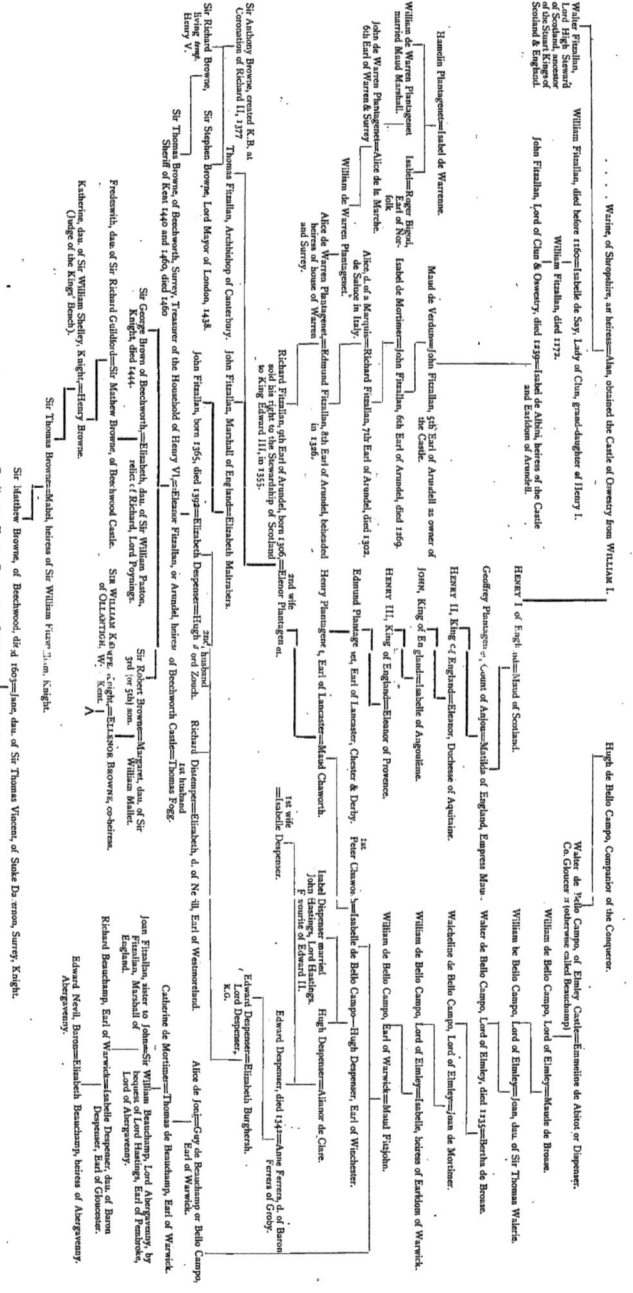

. . . . Warine, of Shropshire, an heiress=Alan, obtained the Castle of Oswestry from William I.

Walter Fitzallan, Lord High Steward of Scotland, ancestor of the Stuart Kings of Scotland & England.

William Fitzallan, died before 1160=Isabelle de Say, Lady of Clun, grand-daughter of Henry I.

William Fitzallan, died 1172.

John Fitzallan, Lord of Clun & Oswestry, died 1239=Isabel de Albini, heiress of the Castle and Earldom of Arundell.

Hamelin Plantagenet=Isabel de Warrenne.

William de Warren Plantagenet married Maud Marshall.

Isabel=Roger Bigod, Earl of Norfolk

John de Warren Plantagenet=Alice de la Marche. 6th Earl of Warren & Surrey

William de Warren Plantagenet.

Maud de Verdun=John Fitzallan, 5th Earl of Arundell as owner of the Castle.

Isabel de Mortimer=John Fitzallan, 6th Earl of Arundel, died 1269.

Alice, d. of a Marquis=Richard Fitzallan, 7th Earl of Arundel, died 1302. de Saluce in Italy.

Alice de Warren Plantagenet,=Edmund Fitzallan, 8th Earl of Arundel, beheaded in 1326. heiress of house of Warren and Surrey.

Richard Fitzallan, 9th Earl of Arundel, born 1306,=Elenor Plantagenet. (2nd wife) sold his right to the Stewardship of Scotland to King Edward III, in 1355.

Henry I of England=Maud of Scotland.

Geoffrey Plantagenet, Count of Anjou=Matilda of England, Empress Maud.

Henry II, King of England=Eleanor, Duchesse of Aquitaine.

John, King of England=Isabelle of Angoulême.

Henry III, King of England=Eleanor of Provence.

Edmund Plantagenet, Earl of Lancaster, Chester & Derby.

Henry Plantagenet, Earl of Lancaster=Maud Chaworth.

Hugh de Bello Campo, Companion of the Conqueror.

Walter de Bello Campo, of Elmley Castle=Emmeline de Abitot or Dispenser. Co. Gloucester (otherwise called Beauchamp)

William de Bello Campo, Lord of Elmley=Maude de Brosse.

William be Bello Campo, Lord of Elmley=Joan, dau. of Sir Thomas Walerie.

Walter de Bello Campo, Lord of Elmley, died 1235=Bertha de Brosse.

Walcheline de Bello Campo, Lord of Elmley=Joan de Mortimer.

William de Bello Campo, Lord of Elmley=Isabelle, heiress of Earldom of Warwick.

William de Bello Campo, Earl of Warwick=Maud Fitzjohn.

Peter Chaworth (1st)=Isabelle de Bello Campo—Hugh Despenser, Earl of Winchester.

Isabel Dispenser married John Hastings, Lord Hastings. Favourite of Edward II.

Hugh Despenser=Alianor de Clare.

1st wife =Isabelle Despenser.

Edward Despenser, died 1342=Anne Ferrers, d. of Baron Ferrers of Groby.

Edward Despenser=Elizabeth Burghersh. Lord Despenser, K.G.

Sir Anthony Browne, created K.B. at Coronation of Richard II, 1377

Thomas Fitzallan, Archbishop of Canterbury.

John Fitzallan, Marshall of England=Elizabeth Maltrabers.

Sir Richard Browne, living *temp.* Henry V.

Sir Stephen Browne, Lord Mayor of London, 1438.

John Fitzallan, born 1365, died 1392=Elizabeth Despenser=Hugh Lord Zouch. (2nd husband)

Richard Distemper=Elizabeth, d. of Nevill, Earl of Westmoreland. (1st husband)

Alice de Joni=Guy de Beauchamp or Bello Campo, Earl of Warwick.

Sir Thomas Browne, of Beechworth, Surrey, Treasurer of the Household of Henry VI,=Eleanor Fitzallan, or Arundel, heiress of Beechworth Castle=Thomas Fogg. Sheriff of Kent 1440 and 1460, died 1460

Catherine de Mortimer=Thomas de Beauchamp, Earl of Warwick.

Sir George Brown of Beechworth,=Elizabeth, dau. of Sir William Paston, Knight, died 1444. relict of Richard, Lord Poynings.

Sir Robert Browne=Margaret, dau. of Sir 3rd (or 5th) son. William Mallet.

Joan Fitzallan, sister to John Fitzallan, Marshall of England.=Sir William Beauchamp, Lord Abergavenny, by bequest of Lord Hastings, Earl of Pembroke, Lord of Abergavenny.

Fredeswith, dau. of Sir Richard Guildford=Sir Mathew Browne, of Beechwood Castle.

Sir William Kempe, Knight,=Ellenor Browne, co-heiress. of Ollantigh, W. Kent.

Richard Beauchamp, Earl of Warwick=Isabelle Despenser, dau. of Baron Despenser, Earl of Gloucester.

Katherine, dau. of Sir William Shelley, Knight,=Henry Browne. (Judge of the Kings' Bench).

Edward Nevil, Baron=Elizabeth Beauchamp, heiress of Abergavenny. Abergavenny.

Sir Thomas Browne=Mabel, heiress of Sir William Fitzwilliam, Knight.

Sir Matthew Browne, of Beechwood, died 1603=Jane, dau. of Sir Thomas Vincent, of Stoke Dabernon, Surrey, Knight.

Sir Robert Kempe, Baronet of Gissing=Jane Browne. and Flordon, Norfolk, died 1647.

of gavelkind, by which much of their land was held. This petition resulted eventually in certain land belonging to the Kempes being disgavelled in the 31st year of Henry VIII. under an Act of Parliament. (*See* Patent 12 Henry VIII., p. 2, m. 14d.; Ped. Fin., 11 Henry VII. Hil.). There is, in the Beaney Institute at Canterbury, a printed volume on the law of gavelkind, and to this we would refer those of our Kentish readers who are interested in the subject. To others it may be well to explain that this ancient law was peculiar to a few parts of the United Kingdom. It has been abolished by Statute in Ireland and Wales, but it still exists in Kent where the custom is recognised by 4 & 5 Vic. c. 35. It appears to be a survival of the ancient Saxon law of landed property. The continuance of the custom is due to the demand of the men of Kent backed by the supreme resistance which they offered to the Conqueror. The chief features of this are that all lands (held under that law) were divided equally among the male issue, and in absence of male issue among the daughters. The heirs entered their estates at fifteen years of age, and they had a right to part with their share by sale, gift or otherwise. This practice must in the case of landowners, whose property was extensive, have tended to keep the younger members of the family from seeking their fortunes at a distance from the paternal home.

By his wife Elenor Browne, Sir William Kempe had a large family. Five daughters lived to be married as follows:—

Mary, to Sir Nicholas Boughton, son of Sir Edward Boughton, of Plumstead;
Faith, to Francis Neale (or Mayall, or Naylor), of Lancashire;
Emelyn, to Sir Reginald Scott, of Scott's Hall and Netsted, Kent;
Margaret, to Sir George Fogg—related to her mother's first husband, and
Cecilia or Cicily, to William Latham, whose wife she was in 1558, and afterwards to William Strangeman, of Hadley Castle, Essex.

He had also six sons living at his death, as follows:—

Thomas, his heir, of whom later;
John (the second son), of Wye, who died wealthy in 1598;
Edward (the third), who went to live in the New Forest, and died in 1605, leaving issue;
Anthony, an important man at Court, and founder of the Slindon Kempes; (*See* Sussex.)
Francis Kempe, a lawyer, who had no male issue, and
George, the youngest, who appears to have lived in London, and died in 1588.

Of each we have some account, but first we must say that after serving as Sheriff of his County in 1529 and 1538, Sir William Kempe died on Tuesday, 28th January, and was buried at Wye, 30th January 1538-9.

His will was dated 28th November, 30 Henry VIII., and describes him as Knight of "Olenty." The usual items of money "for tythes negligently forgotten," and the Church come first. He then bequeaths to his daughter "Ciceley" 300 marks on her marriage, and the same sum each to Faith and Mary. A like amount is given to Margaret, provided she be "putt owte of the house where she is now Nunn, and then she be disposed to marry." The testator doubtless felt convinced that the monasteries must all go, as he had witnessed the dissolution of that of Wye and many others. The daughter we have seen did leave her nunnery and become a mother of a family, one of whom Ezecias Fogg was presented by his uncle, Sir Thomas Kempe, to the church of Chilham. The will proceeds to provide for the maintenance of Elenor, the testator's widow, for which purpose the messuage of "Olenty" has been demised for twenty years to Reginald Scott, Esq. and John "Took" Gent, to raise the 1,200 marks above given to the daughters, and 40*s.* per annum to each of the five younger sons, Elenor, the widow, to have the use of the mansion for the term of her life after providing for the above payments from this Estate.

She is further to have the profits arising from the estates of Henry Idon during his nonage, she, meanwhile, providing his keep. The reversion of Ollantigh and the residue of the estate passes, of course, to the eldest son, he paying to his five brothers £10 each per annum. (This is doubtless, by way of giving them a share equivalent to what they should receive under the law of gavelkind. The inquisition showing his estates is number 34 in "31st Henry VIII. Kent."

ELENOR, the relict of Sir William, may have continued to live at Wye for a time, but it doubtless was her pleasure to be amidst the Court, and her will is dated from the Savoy, where at the time the ladies of Queen Mary had apartments. It is dated 21st August, 1560, and bears witness to the Roman faith to which she and her son Anthony Kempe were staunchly attached. She desires to be buried in the Savoy according to the rites of the "Catholic Church of Christ." She left a rather liberal sum to be expended on her funeral, and for distribution among the poor and the prisoners at Ludgate, Newgate, and Fleet Prison, and the poor of the "Galdhouse" of Westminster. To Sir Thomas Kempe she left her "ring with diamonds," and a pair of gilt saltcellars weighing twenty ounces. To Anthony, a gilt bowl weighing twenty-two ounces, a great flat standard (family banner) and furniture. Francis Kempe was also to have a standard, a ring set with a ruby, a gilt goblet of twenty-one ounces and tapestry. To Edward, her son, she bequeathed six spoons with gilt ends; to John, a little gilt saltcellar, and to George, her youngest son, the bed which she "lay in at Court" and more gilt-ended spoons. To her daughters, Cecily Latham and Mary Boughton (as well as her daughters by her first husband whose names appear in the will as Pollard and Ann Cross), she left a large quantity of dresses and finery, the list of which is too long to insert here; furs, velvet, damask, silk, satin, and fine linen, with chests of household linen and blankets are included. The daughters, like their brothers, each are to have a piece of plate weighing about twenty-two ounces.

She does not forget to reward her faithful servants; those mentioned being William Bowth, Francis Hitchcock, and William Kitt or Kyttes. The latter is to enjoy his "lease of the manor of Marie Court," and the others are provided with pensions. Her other manors are Morris Court, Kent (which had belonged to the Brownes from the time of Henry IV.), Tonge, Redmersham, Murston and Lynsted, all of which she settled on her son John and his heirs, failing issue to revert to his brothers in succession and their issue.

Others mentioned are the Vicar of Colman Street, Mrs. Brent, Mrs. Cisley Barnard, Master Robert Alce, William Roper of Eltham (her overseer), and Sir Thomas Oxenbridges, who was one of her Executors, and the husband to one of her daughters, Fogge.

JOHN KEMPE, the second son, and chief legatee of his mother, who thus received the manors of Morris Court, Tonge, Redmersham, Murston and Lynsted, married a woman named Jane . . . who died in 1597. He was buried at Wye 30th July, 1598, and his will dated 27th November, 1597, was proved on 8th September, 1599 (Arch. Cant., 51. fo. 360), the executors being his nephew, Thomas Kempe, of "Olentigh," and Ezechias Fogge, of Chilham. The will is remarkable for the number of pieces of silver bearing "the Kempe sheaves" which he distributed among his brothers and other relatives. He left the house in which he was living called "Fancocke," in "Wie," to his nephew, Thomas Kempe. To his brother, Francis Kempe, he bequeathed £100; to the wife of his nephew Thomas, a "jewell of gold with two diamonds therein; to their daughters, Ann (the eldest), Dorothy, and Mary, silver pieces and "fine Holland sheets"; to his nephew, "Raynold" (Reginald), £50 instead of "my household stuff which I purposed to have given him," also a "deaths-head ring of gold" and a cloak. To his godson, John Kempe, a great silver saltcellar and a dozen silver spoons "with the Kempe Sheaves graven on them."* It is not stated whose son this John was; Reginald had a son of that name by Mary Argyll, who was married to him in 1590. Possibly this is the relative intended.

Unfortunately the testator does not mention any of his estates by name except the above house at Wye. We do not, therefore, know whether these were disposed of by him or passed to his nephew under the "residue" clause.

Space will not permit us to give details of the numerous legacies, but a list of the other names occurring in the will may prove of interest. They are briefly as follows:—Mr. Jackson, Minister of Wye; Mr. Nicholls, Parson of Eastwell; his nephew, Anthonie Broughton, and his daughter, Marie Broughton; his niece, Richard Fogge's daughter, and William, the son of nephew Ezichias Fogge; nephew Duddlie Lullgrave; Mr. Thomas Moile, of Molash; Francis Hill and wife; Goodwife Evans (?) of Wye; Mrs. Morehouse, Roger Moste, Richard Cooke, John Tittenden, Edward Earnet and Thomas Cottum. To his servant, Miss Drewe, he left a tenement near "Knockseale," which he bought from Henrie Bronde, of Canterbury. His other servants mentioned are Alice Marsh and William Carter; witnesses to the document are John Kempe, Thomas Hall or (Haull) and Terras, and Thomas Cock or Cocke. The will is duly registered in the Archdeaconry Court of Canterbury. (Liber 51, folio 360).

The further details of EDWARD KEMP, the next brother to this testator will be given under Hampshire Kempes.

For the account of ANTHONY KEMPE, the next brother, see under Sussex.

FRANCIS KEMPE was Clerk of the Hanaper, and Attorney of Court of Chancery. Amongst the Stowe Manuscripts in the British Museum (415 f. 86) is a complaint of the Clerk of the Hanaper concerning his grievances against Sir Nicholas Bacon.† The date is 1564; the matter is as to the profits, which had provided a very handsome income to these officers, whose clerks practically did all the work. Sir Nicholas Bacon's reply is worded with much caution and with evident justice, to the effect that it is quite time that the office should be reformed and regulated. Francis Kempe, therefore, does not appear to have gained by his petition.

Francis Kempe appears to have held some 10½ acres of pasture and "appertenances" in Mitcham ‡ about 1592, and he certainly had a share of some 200 acres of land at Plumstead in Kent, which he held with his brother Edward. Of the latter we shall have to give further notice, as in and around it the Kempes held lands from a much earlier date, while as we have said a sister of this lawyer had married a Boughton who held the manor.

The land at Mitcham he doubtless held in right of his wife who was Elianor, daughter and coheir of Henry Carew, brother to Wymond Carew, whose family long had property here. Sir Francis Carew in 1592 was directed by Her Majesty to hold an inquisition of the property here belonging to John Gage (related to the Gage who married Anthony Kempe), whose estates were forfeited owing to his having concealed a Roman Catholic missionary named Beesley. By this wife Francis had two or more daughters who were his coheirs, he having no surviving son. One of them, named Ann, married Gamaliel Jerins of Letheringset, in Norfolk, who was living in 1634: they also had a son, Richard Jerins, who was then 18, the "only son and heir apparent."

* John had a definite right to both the arms of his father, *viz:* three sheaves on a red ground surrounded by a border engrailed and the crest, the pelican "vulning," *i.e.*, pecking her breast, providing merely that the cadence marks were added; but, like the archbishop, he deemed it sufficient to use the sheaves merely,—in allusion to his arms. Families who believe themselves entitled to arms will do well to follow this ancient custom of using a badge in allusion thereto instead of the crest which they consider theirs by descent. Then, should they find that the arms of their ancestors were not the same as those they had believed to be theirs, they will not have the ignominy of haviug to retract when their veritable arms have been discovered or a new coat granted to them by the Heralds. A badge, it may be mentioned, is distinguished from a crest by the omission of the wreath on which a crest always stands. Kemps of to-day may use any badge they please without infringing on the rights of the Heralds, but the use of a crest or arms without the sanction of the College of Arms and Royal consent is as wrong and foolish as one styling himself "Lord" or "Baronet" without such authority. It may also be noted here that it is quite wrong for ladies to use a crest.

† It is singular that Bacons and *Kempes of Norfolk* were related and much connected with the law at this time. (*See* Norfolk section.)

‡ "Collectanea Top. et Genealogica," vol iii. An account of the Manor of Hayling, in the parish of Croydon, Surrey.

Sir Wymond Carew was of Anthony in Cornwall, and was connected by marriage also with the Kempes of Gissing. Indeed, it is singular to notice how closely the four chief Kempe families of Kent, Norfolk, Essex and Cornwall were drawn together at about this period by inter-marriages with the same families, and by their various properties.

In later times certain Kempes have purposely sought to purchase lands and houses formerly connected with others of their name, but at this time the distinct families actually exchanged and bought one from another, and have made the matter of distinguishing one from the other very puzzling.

Among the manuscripts of Lieut.-Colonel Carew at Crowcomb Court, Somerset, a notice of which is given by the Historical MSS. Commission (Report 4th, p. 371), mention is made of letters concerning Francis Kempe, but the actual date is unfortunately not stated.

George, the youngest brother to this Francis Kempe, inherited jointly with his brothers the Manor of Chelworth, out of which his mother ordered that (40*s*.) forty shillings yearly should be paid to her servant, William Bowth, during his life. Edward seems to have released his share of this manor to George, and perhaps the other brothers did the same. His will is dated 28th February, 1567, but was not proved till 1588, and we fairly conclude that he did not die much before then, although we have no direct evidence to establish this as a fact. He does not mention any wife or children, but gives back to his brother Edward the fifth part of the manor which he had acquired by "bargain, sale, or gift" from him. This brother, Edward and Anthony were the executors, and employed Thomas Wheeler, a notary, to prove the will on their behalf. (P.C.C. 37 Rutland).

CHAPTER VII.

KEMPES OF WYE, 1539-1591.

Sir Thomas Kempe, who succeeded to Olantigh in 1539, was perhaps the most active and illustrious of the Kentish Kempe knights, much of his power being but the outcome of position he had gained by a line of knightly ancestors and the prestige obtained from his mother, Lady Ellenor Browne. He was, doubtless, a capable governor and good man of business, otherwise he would not have kept himself so much in the foreground of the Royal Court and field of politics. His marriages were all apparently the outcome of negotiation, rather than prompted by passion. He first married Katherine, daughter, and eventually co-heir, of Sir Thomas Chaney, K.G., who was Treasurer of the Royal Household; a favourite and privy councillor to four successive Kings and Queens; twice Sheriff of Kent; proxy to Queen Elizabeth, as godparent to the Dolphin of France; Governor of Rochester Castle, and one of the challengers of all men at the "Field of the Cloth of Gold"; besides numerous other offices of distinction and profit.

Katherine's mother, too, was the heiress to a famous name and considerable estates, which must be mentioned as having, in time, some effect on the issue of her daughters. She was Frideswide, daughter of Sir Thomas Frowick, her father being the last of his name and family. His will, dated 14th October, 1505, leaves his Manor Place and messuage at Finchley, Middlesex, to his wife, and large estates at South Mimms and other places devolved upon his daughters. Thus, from Frowick to Chaney, and Chaney to Kempe, certain property passed. A sister to this Catherine (or Katherine) Chaney, named Margaret, married to George Nevill, Lord Bergaveney, a descendant of the Bello Campo or Beau-Champ family, Earls of Warwick, whose consanguinity with these Kempes we have before remarked upon and shown in the descent of Browne.

Thomas Chaney had the honour of entertaining King Henry VIII at his house at Eastchurch, and was buried at Minster, in the Isle of Sheppey, in 1558, where a brass to his memory still remains.

By Katherine Chaney, Sir Thomas Kempe had several children, of whom short notices are appended :

Fryswyde was baptized at Wye 26th December, 1544 (doubtless named after her grandmother.)

Margaret, married Sir Thomas Shirley, at Wye, 20th February, 1560, to whom Sir Thomas Kempe conveyed the Manor of Wadling, in Ripple, Walmer, Deal and Monham (which had formed the marriage portion of Amy Moyle, his second wife.) This Sir Thomas Shirley was treasurer of the war in the Low Countries. He rebuilt his family seat of Wiston Manor House, in Sussex, in which the Countess of Phillip, Earl of Arundell, was committed to his wardship, and where subsequently was born Elizabeth, the Earl's only daughter. Sir Thomas Shirley died in 1597, aged sixty-seven. Portions of his mansion are still in existence, and many of his families' tombs, from an early period, will be found in Wiston Church.

Alice (the third surviving daughter of Katherine and Sir Thomas Kempe) married Sir James Hales, of the "Dungeon," Canterbury. His family had a grant of the Nunnery of St. Sepulchres, in the same city, at the suppression of the monasteries, and this property he sold to Sir Thomas Kempe about 1572. He seems to have died at sea, for on the fine mural monument to his memory, still in the nave of the Cathedral, he is represented as being lowered into the deep, over the side of a ship, wearing his full armour. On this monument his wife Alice Kempe is mentioned, and the various arms of his family are shown.

Katherine had died before 1550' for, on the 19th January of that year, Sir Thomas Kempe married, at Eastwell Church, Amy daughter of Sir Thomas Moyle, of Eastwell Place, ancestor of the Earls of Winchelsea, who died in 1560, leaving considerable landed estates in Kent and Somerset. By his will he devises the property as follows : to his son-in-law, Sir Thomas Kempe, Knight, the lease of Rokyng Court ; to Thomas, the son of the latter, his Manors of Preston, Grandisons, Waldyslands in Kent, and lands at Dartford, Sutton-at-Hone and Chatham, also in Kent, and the Manors of King's Weston, Wythys and Lottsham, in Somerset. His house at Newgate, in London, he left between his grandsons, Reginald, Moyle and William Kempe ; and Moyle, Thomas and Henry Finch. Sir Thomas Kempe and Sir Thomas Finch, Knight, were the executors, Anthony Kempe being a witness. This Sir Thomas Finch had married the other daughter and co-heir of Sir Thomas Moyle (and was brother to Thomas Finch who married Mary, daughter of Christopher Kempe) and they were ancestors of the Earls of Winchelsea.

By Amy his second wife Sir Thomas Kempe had :

Thomas Kempe, his eldest son, baptized at Wye, 7th November, 1551, who became his heir, and of whom we shall give further details later.

Reginald Kempe, baptized at Eastwell on 18th May, 1553, and who also eventually owned Olantigh, and died in 1612.

Moyle Kempe, baptized at Wye, 24th August, 1554, buried there in December.

* Moyle Kempe, baptized also at Wye, 30th September, 1555, who was entered at Exeter College in 1573, aged eighteen (? and was "recusant" in Cornwall in 1590), buried at Wye, 17th March, 1585.

William Kempe, baptized 17th February, 1556, (?) buried at Wye, 22nd March, 1597; probably the founder of the Dartford Kempes.

George Kempe, baptized 24th January, 1557; possibly identical with George Kempe, of Northaw, in Middlesex, in 1593, assessed at thirty pounds for the defence of the Kingdom, and who was prosecuted as a Jesuit concerned in Clerkenwell and Edmonton plots.

Lady Anne Kempe appears as buried at Wye on August 17th, 1557; this is doubtless *Amy* Kempe, for she had died before the Will of Sir Thomas Moyle was made.

Sir Thomas Kempe was created a Knight of the Carpet on Tuesday, 22nd February, 1546, and was Sheriff of his County in 1548, 1549 and again in 1563. In 1565 the "History of Juan de Mendoca," was dedicated to him, so we may presume that he was a patron of literature.

In 1567 he, with the other chief gentlemen of Kent (many of whom were his relatives), met at Ashford as Commissioners for the defence of the sea coast. They developed a definite arrangement of signalling by means of fire beacons, and provided for the raising of an organised force of "Hobelers" or light horse. The long and careful report of this Commission to the Privy Council is considered one of the most praiseworthy schemes for defence ever suggested, and even two hundred years later the precedents then made were followed, when a descent on the English coast was expected under the first Emperor Napoleon. (*Vide* "Scott of Scott's Hall.")

In 1588 Sir Thomas Kempe, Sir Thomas Scott (his nephew) and others, were officers commanding these bands of Kentish men-at-arms on the approach of the Spanish Invincible Armada. We know that their fighting qualities were not actually put to the test, but half the difficulties of war consists of organizing and arming, in suitable manner, a well-trained army. This we know they had duly and most successfully accomplished, largely at their own costs; and the fact that they were ready and able to back up the work of their fellow defenders on the high seas, doubtless had much to do with the tremendous victory which our first line of defence then, and ever since have, looked upon as one of the most glorious to the credit of our nation.

It will be seen that this Sir Thomas Scott was the son of Sir Reginald Scott by Emelyn Kempe. A fine portrait of him in armour was in the possession of Thomas Fairfax Best, Esq., of Chilston Park, Kent. His helmet still hangs in Brabourne Church, where he was first buried; and an epitaph, with sixteen verses telling of his fame, was erected in Scott's Chapel where his body was removed. One verse must suffice as a specimen, as follows:

"Here lyes Sir Thomas Scott, by name;
O happy KEMPE that bore him
Sir Raynold, with four knights of fame,
Lyved lyneally before him."

He was called by his contemporaries, "Father of Romney Marsh and Founder of Dover Haven"; having, as said, protected the district of the former and been chief commissioner in the construction of the latter. He died in 1594.

We may here say that this marriage between Reginald and a daughter of the Kempes was the outcome of an interesting family agreement, duly attested by deed, dated 9th December, 1522, between Sir William Scott and William Kempe and Elenor, the latter's wife. It was agreed that

* Perhaps there was a third son baptized Moyle, who was thus living in 1590.

in the event of either Edward Scott, son of Sir William Scott, or of the eldest son of Sir John Scott (who was eldest son of Sir William) marrying either of the daughters of William Kempe and Elenor, these Kempes would settle land of the annual value of £20 upon the Scott during his life, on his wife after his decease, and eventually on the children of the marriage. Edward Scott married Alice Fogge, who was the daughter of this Elenor by her first husband, Thomas Fogge; at the making of this agreement she seems to have been but twelve years of age, she was therefore placed under the wardship of Sir William Scott, who paid £200 for the grant of her custody till she reached the age of fourteen, when her consent to the marriage was considered valid. Thomas Fogge at his death held the Manor of Walmer (as the Manor of Folkestone), and during the minority of his children this and other estates were administered by William and Elinor Kempe.

Anne Fogge married William Scott, a brother of Sir Reginald Scott, so the families were related in very many ways.

Sir Thomas Kempe married for his third wife Dame Joan, the daughter of . . . . Farmer, of . . . . . . and widow of Lord Mordant. She was recusant with her stepson, Moyle Kempe, residing in Cornwall in 1592.

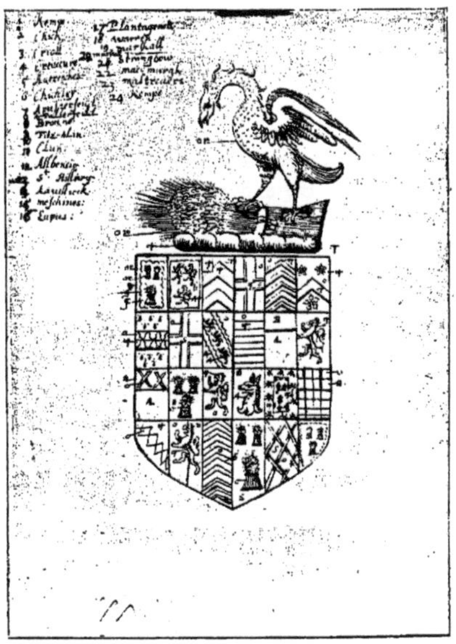

Arms claimed by the Kempes of Wye but not fully authorized by the Heralds' College.

The Mordant arms were argent, a chevron between three estoiles sable, which closely resembles, in all but the tinctures, the arms used by the Kempes of Spain's Hall, Finchingfield, Essex. So far as can be ascertained, however, there was no reason for the two coats to be in any way associated; there are over a dozen such coats, varied by tinctures and minor changes, all or most dating from *before* the visitations of the sixteenth century. Indeed it would hardly be worth mentioning the fact but for the chance of the coats, when appearing without the tinctures being indicated, giving a wrong impression.

The descent of the Mordants is given on a very curious and handsome tomb in Fulham Church, an illustration of which, with much concerning the family, is given in Fèret's "Fulham Old and New."

By this wife Sir Thomas Kempe seems to have left no issue. He was buried at Wye on 22nd March, 1590. His Post Mortem Inquisition is dated 1591 (No. 49 Kent, Anno 33 Elizabeth.) Where his will was proved does not appear.

(There is a grant of administration in 1587 (P.C.C. 10th June) to John Kempe, husband of Elizabeth Mordant alias Kempe, late of the parish of St. Dunston's-in-the-West, London.)

Before recording the details known concerning the issue of this Sir Thomas Kempe, we must revert to an earlier period, as, although his sister and he were both interested in fresh acquisitions of land at Plumstead, Kempes had long before this held property around that place which lies between the great ancient Manor of Lewisham and Greenwich.

CHAPTER VIII.

BLACKHEATH HUNDRED.

THE name of Kempe is said by Hasted, in his "History of Kent," to be frequently met with in the Court Rolls of Lewisham. It is rather singular, therefore, in so large a parish that from 1558 to 1750 no Kempe or Kemp appears in the church register, neither does the name occur on any of the innumerable monuments, the inscriptions of which have been printed.

Greenwich was anciently the harbour of the Danes, and the early occurrence of the name of Kempe here and along the shores of the Thames, where they settled, or wintered, has given rise to the claim of some Kempes of Teddington that they owe their origin to these early invaders. The word *kimpe* in the Danish language means a giant. It is just *possible* that the word in that sense survived down to the period that surnames became customary in England, but extremely *improbable* that these humble fisherfolk and watermen passed down the surname continuously from such an early time. "Kempe's Tenement" was the name of a house at Fulham before the time of Edward III. In this ancient town the Danes were for long resident; but when we consider the other occupants of the place subsequently, and recall the fact that some 400 years intervened before the first known mention of this messuage as "Kempes," it seems the more absurd to ascribe such an origin to the name.

At Greenwich, however, so early as the 16th year of Edward I. (1288) William Kemp held "Uplands" in East Greenwich. At a later date Ranulph, Vicar of Greenwich, paid to the Abbot and Convent of *Gand* the sum of fourpence, being quit for a field called "Uplands" or "Upfield," in the Ville of Lewisham, receivable from the heirs of William Kempe. Blackheath is certainly *high land* and adjoins the manor, if it was not actually in it. And in the hundred of Blackheath, which included Lewisham, Greenwich and other manors, we find a John Kempe paid one shilling and a halfpenny as his assessment in the subsidy collected in the first year of Edward III. (1327). Compared with other items, which vary from 6*d.* to 25*s.* 4*d.*, this amount is but small. The fact of this holding being from the Convent of Gand or Ghent is interesting as suggesting a connection between the Kempes of Ghent from whom descended the great Flemish weaver, John Kempe of Flanders (of whom see under Kendal) and the Kempes of Wye. (Chapter III.)

Communication between Kent and the opposite coast was very frequent at this period. Under the auspices of the various abbots even humble individuals found frequent opportunity of transit, and as even now practised, those connected with a monastery or convent would travel provided with a recognised introduction to a fraternity of the same order in a foreign land, or those who held lands or office under them.

Humphrey, Duke of Gloucester, built a noble palace here, which eventually became a much frequented royal residence in the time of Henry VI. and Henry VII., and both Queens Mary and Elizabeth were born there. During this time the Bishops Kempe must have often been here, and it was on the adjoining "Blackheath" that the two rebels, Wat Tyler and Jack Cade—whose insurrections marked the beginning and the end of the life of Archbishop Kempe—gathered their bands of malcontents. In the following of Cade in 1450 there was a John Kempe, a *labourer*, from Mundefeld in Sussex, and from the same county a *husbandman* named Richard Roper;

perhaps these *claimed* the other Kempes and Ropers as kin, and personal ill-will actuated their taking part in a feud which was largely aimed at the aged prelate.

Except for these passing Kempes we know of none at Greenwich from about 1299 till 1499. In the latter year Henry Hurst, a citizen and tailor of London, having property in Greenwich, made Thomas Kempe, Esq., and John Roper, respectively, executor and overseer to his will.

About this time (1 Henry VII. or ? VIII.) THOMAS KEMPE, Gent., William Kempe, Clerk, John Fineaux (Justice of the King's Bench), John Woode, John Roper, and Richard Stevens, conveyed lands at Greenwich, Charlton, Plumstead, Woolwich and Westerham to John Pole and Margery, his wife (Ped. Fin.)

* (In the 12 of Henry VIII. Sir Thomas Kempe, John Roper, Steward of the Liberty, John Fineaux, Sir William Scott, and others, are mentioned as having obtained a grant under Royal Patent concerning property in the town of Wye.)

The Manor of Plumstead belonged to Sir Nicholas Boveton or Boughton, who died possessed of it in 1517, leaving it to his son, Sir Edward Boughton. The latter married Joan, daughter of Sir William Scott, by Sibbela, a daughter of Sir Thomas Lewknor. His will was proved in 1550, and left the bulk of his local property to his son, Sir Nicholas Boughton, who as we have said, married Mary, daughter of Sir William Kempe of Ollantigh. This Sir Nicholas left by his will, proved 9th February, 1559 (14 Maellershe) lands called Shooter's Hill in Plumstead, and his residence called "Plumstead Park," providing for the maintenance of his wife, Mary, his four sons and a daughter. He made SIR THOMAS KEMPE and Sir Robert Oxenbridge his overseers.

It may be that part of this estate passed by subsequent will, by sale or gift to Anthony, Francis and Edward Kempe, sons of Sir William Kempe of Ollantigh, who held over 200 acres of land there in the reign of Elizabeth, the details of which will appear under their respective names.

There are in the registers of the Rochester Probate Court two Wills, both proved in 1548, relating to the little estates of a couple named Jasper and Jertrude Kempe of Greenwich. These individuals do not appear on any pedigree we have seen, and may not be connected with the Wye family; there is, however, some chance of their being traced to that origin. The husband's will is dated 6th July, 1548, he makes his wife, "Jertrude," executrix, and mentions his two kinswomen, Jermyn and Powell (*sic*). Henry Hall, Vicar of Greenwich, and Erasmas Kyrknor (? Lewknor) are witnesses.

The widow's will is dated 6th May the same year. She mentions many relatives and friends, among whom she distributes silver spoons, rings, clothes and "angels"—which, of course, are pieces of money. The list is a long one and cannot be given fully here, but the following names may lead to identification. Some names certainly are *Dutch*, the name of Conelius Jansen occurs and is given as the painter of the portrait of Sir Nicholas Kempe who married a daughter of Roger James of Holland (in Essex).

She mentions, "my brother Barnard, wholemaker, if he be alive." Many Johnsons are named,—Corneles or Cornilis and his wife, Christopher, Alis, Peter, Garrett, Egbart, Jasper, his son, his mother, and Perter's children, Leonard Vanwanary, Hans Mitris, Lucas Goldsmyth, Leonard Gibbes' wife, Agnes Powell. The will is witnessed by the same Vicar of Greenwich, Roger Rogerson of London, Hans Myter, John Mylles and others.

Cornelius Johnson and Henry Blewe were the executors. No real estate is mentioned, and the testator's rank or trade is not mentioned. The mention of Roger Rogerson of London would

* This note might seem rather out of place here, but the names being almost the same as in the preceding it is inserted.

lead us to suppose relatives might be found there. Powell or Powle was the surname of the wife of James Kempe of London and Acton, belonging to the Suffolk Kempes, while the names of Hall, Johnson, and Gybbes were all connected with the Kempes of Willesden and that part of Middlesex.

Perhaps Garret Kempe, of Slinden, derived his name from the Garrets mentioned in the will, as his father, Anthony Kempe, in addition to having the property at Plumstead close by, was much at Greenwich Palace.

We find that an Agnes Kempe, of Poplar, married Thomas Loone, of Woolwich, at St. Dunstan's, Stepney, in 1588. But of them we have no further knowledge. These riverside places had a large proportion of migratory people, and there is frequently an intermarriage of mariners' families extending from Stepney right down the river and round the coast to Rye.

The Rochester Calendars of Wills commence in 1440. The surname of KENT is from the first found at Malling, Cowling, Charlton, West'ram and Hadlow, and many similar names occur, such as Kemby, Combe, Kempsay, Kene, Kember, and Kempall. The present work cannot enter into these, although some might prove to be actual corruptions or variants of Kempe. Particularly should we suspect this to be the case at Lewisham, Charlton and Westerham.

Francis Bacon, who was closely related and most intimate with the Gissing Kempes, had much property in Woolwich, and had the Queen's licence to alienate 130 acres there, and at East and West Ham, in Essex, to Francis Kempe and his heir, in 1583. At this time there was a Francis Kempe belonging to each of the principal families, and all three were more or less frequently concerned with London ; it is not certain which of these was the purchaser of this.

The manor and advowson of Charlton were conveyed to Sir Henry Puckering, als. Newton, in 1658, by Henry Kempe, Gent., and others.

Close by Lewisham is Deptford, at which place Kempes have been a numerous, if not a long staying family. This part must be given some consideration later, as we must now return to the remaining generation of the Kempes of Wye, who we have shown to be definitely associated with this neighbourhood in the fifteenth and sixteenth centuries.

CHAPTER IX.

THE KEMPES OF WYE—*continued.*

SIR THOMAS KEMPE (the son of the previous one of his name, by Amy Moyle) inherited Olantigh in or about 1591. He was knignted at Charterhouse in 1603. He took some part in county affairs and also provided suitable husbands for his daughters. He has, however, left no record of any great service to the community, and seems to have lived a rather uneventful life. He married, as his second wife, Dorothy, daughter of John Thompson or Tomson, Esq., of London. The surname of his first wife is unknown ; she was the mother of his daughters Mary and Anne.

It was, doubtless, a great sorrow that there was no son to continue the knightly line of these Kempes. By the second marriage there were only two daughters, whose names were Dorothy and

Amy Kempe. Of these we will give a few particulars, but before doing so we append the inscription which was placed on the tomb of this last Sir Thomas Kempe, of Ollantigh, in Wye Church. The original has now been lost, and the following is taken from "Archæologia Cantiana," vol. 5, p. 117.

"Sir Thomas Kempe of Olantigh Knt. Heir male of the Kempes of Olantigh, by Dame Emelyn Daughter and Coheyr of Sr. Valentine Chich, by the Heir of Sr. Robt. Chichley, left his Heyre Sir William Kempe, that by dame Eleanor widdow of Sir Thomas Fogge, being ye Heir of Browne, by an heir of Sr. Thomas Arundel left his heyre Sr. Thomas Kempe Knt., that by Dame Amie Daur. and coheyr of Sir Thomas Moyle, left his Heyr this last Sir Thomas Kempe."

He died in 1607 and was buried in the family chapel with his ancestors. His Inquisition Post Mortem is registered in the 7th year of James I.

The Subsidy Roll of 1593-4 for the Hundred of Wye gives an idea of the then comparative values of his own and other local Kempes' estates.

The Hundred of Wye, with Hundreds of Folkestone, Oxney and Stowting. At the head of the lists of landholders at Wye is—

Thomas Kempe, Esquire, in land, £40, for which he pays £8.

The second name under Wye is—

Reginald Kempe, Esquire, in goods, £4, for which he pays 18*s*. 8*d*.

Their uncle John Kempe, Esquire, in Wye, has £18 in lands, for which he pays £3 13*s*.

There is on this Roll, but under which hundred is not quite clear, a Roger Kempe whose goods are rated at £8, and he pays 21*s*. 4*d*.

In the Hundred of Aloes Bridge there is a William Kempe rated for goods at £3, paying 8*s*.

The above Reginald either inherited Olantigh as heir male under the entailing clause in the will of Sir Thomas Kempe proved in 1520, or, having lost it under the law of gavelkind, acquired it by purchase, as appears by his will hereafter given.

The above John, as we have said, died in 1599, and we can identify Roger as one who was living at Boughton Aluph, and his will, proved in 1602 will be given under Boughton Aluph Kempes.

In the Hundred of Aloes Bridge is New Romney, where there was a William Kempe whose will was proved in 1600, and whose family will be mentioned under Lydd.

Mary, the eldest daughter of Sir Thomas Kempe, was baptized at Wye, 14th March, 1590, and married Sir Dudley Digges, who was the son of Thomas Digges, of Digges Court, Barham, Kent, by Ann, daughter of Sir Warren St. Ledger. Both his father and grandfather, Leonard Digges, had been great mathematicians and he had a decided bent in that direction. He was born in 1583 and matriculated at Oxford in 1601. In his early life he travelled a good deal.

In 1618 he was sent by James I. as Ambassador to Russia, and in 1620, with Sir Maurice Abbott, was commissioned to go to Holland to obtain restitution of certain goods seized by the Dutch from some Englishmen in the East Indies; he was at this time a director of the Virginia Company, of London, and was associated in the East India Company with Sir Nicholas Kempe, who had £2,500 invested in East India Stock. Sir Dudley was a member of the third Parliament of Charles I, and was made Master of the Rolls in April, 1636.

On the distribution of the Kempe property in 1610, his wife secured, by arrangement with her sisters, the castle and lands at Chilham, which her grandfather, Sir Thomas Kempe, had bought from his first wife's relative—Henry, Lord Chaney—and to the church of which the Kempes had presented clergy.

Mary Kempe found the Castle in decay and set about, at considerable expense, to rebuild it. This she took some years to accomplish, and she thought it desirable to record the fact by inserting a prominent memorial stone on which her name appears, and the text, "The Lord is my house of defence and my castle."

The castle is still standing in very much the same state as then built, and the above inscription may be seen. The entrance to the castle forms one side of the picturesque village square, the church standing to the rear of the old houses which face the castle grounds. On either side the square are little primitive shops and a typical Kentish inn. The church, which is very full of

Chilham Castle, Kent, rebuilt by Mary Kempe—Lady Digges—about 1610.

interest, contains a lofty and handsome tomb to the memory of "Mary Kempe—Lady Digges." A well-known antiquary remarks that this entirely spoils the appearance of the south aisle, others may be of his opinion, but the inscription, with its quaint pomposity, will be none the less interesting:

"Mary Kempe, Lady Digges Daughyer and Coheire of Sr Thomas Kempe of Olentigh Knight by Sir Thomas Moyle's Daughter and Coheire, Son of Sir Thomas Kempe Knight, by an heir of Brown and Arundel, Son of Sir William Kempe Knight, who by Emelyn daughter and coheir of Sir Valentine Chichley and Phillipa daughter and heire of Sir Robert Chiche, Mayor of London, and brother to Henry the Archbishop, was son of Sir Thomas Kempe Knight, nephew to Thomas Kempe, Bishop of London, the nephew of John Kempe Archbishop of York, then of Canterbury, Cardinal, Lord Chancellor, Lyes here buried to-gether with Francis her 4th and Richard her eighth son."

Several coats of arms with various impalements and quarters are displayed on the tomb. The three sheaves within a bordure engrailed, duly occur in the usual manner, and for Digges, Gules, on a cross argent, five eagles displayed, sable.

Sir Dudley became one of the administrators of the estates of the last Sir Thomas Kempe and his widow Dorothy, on the death of the latter in 1629. He died 8th March, 1639, and on his monument the following eulogy is given :

"He was a pious son, a careful father, a loving husband, a fatherly (*sic*) brother, a courteous neighbour, a merciful landlord, a liberal master, a noble friend."

By his will (said to have been proved in 1638) he left a sum for the winners of a competition to be contested for on the 19th of May yearly. Two young men and two maidens between the ages of sixteen and twenty-four ran a tye on "Old Wives Lees," the winners receiving £10 each. This sum has been appropriated to the National Schools. The will, which has been recently required in connexion with the charity, appears to be missing, and we understand that a search in the P.C C. and Canterbury Courts has failed to trace the probate of this important will.

Dorothy (the first daughter by the second wife) married Sir Thomas Chichley, of Wimpole, Cambridgeshire. He died before 1626, as appears from the will of Lady Dorothy Kempe. The latter mentions her *grand*-daughter, Dorothy Chichley, and other children of her daughter Lady Dorothy Chichley. The eldest son, Sir Thomas Chichley, died old at Bloomsbury Square, London, in 1698.

This family were descended from the same stock and bore the same arms as the Chichleys, of Higham Ferrers.* Thus a second time they were connected by marriage with the Kempes of Ollantigh.

Amy Kempe, the fourth co-heiress of Sir Thomas Kempe, had for her husband Sir Henry Skipworth, Baronet. Their children, William and Elizabeth Skipworth, as well as Lady and Sir Henry, were mentioned by Lady Kempe in her will as living in 1626.

Sir Thomas Kempe had also a son by his second wife, whose baptism is entered in Wye Register as Isaac, son of Thomas Kempe and Anne, 1st October, 1586. We know that this son did not live to succeed his father, but the date of his burial or death is unknown. The surname of this wife is not given in the usually recognized pedigrees, although it generally appears that Dorothy Thompson was his second wife.

Anne Kempe was baptized at Wye, 19th June, 1589, and, as we have said, married Sir John Cutts, an Alderman of London, who served the office of Lord Mayor. There is an amusing story told concerning some Spanish Grandees who were invited to meet him ; it is said that they were deeply aggrieved at being asked to a banquet by a man with *so short a name*, for they reasoned that a man with so brief a title could not be a man of importance, when however they saw the sumptuous provision made for them, they changed their opinion.

The following is a copy of an inscription to Anne Cutts, which is to be seen in Swavesey Church, Cambridge, for which we are indebted to Captain William Kemp, of Arundel :

"ANNE KEMP. — LADY CUTT,

"eldest daughter and co-heir of Thomas Kempe of Ollantigh Knt. by Sir Thomas Moyles daughter and co-heir, sonne of Sir Thos. Kempe Knt. by Ann heire or Browne and Arundell sonne of Sir William Kempe Knt. who by Emline daughter and coheire of Sir Valentine Chich and Philip(a) daughter and heire of Sir Robert Chichley, Mayor of London and brother to Henry the Archbishop, was sonne of Sir Thomas Kempe Knt. Nephew to Thomas Kempe Bishop of London, the nephew of John Kempe, Archbishop of York, then of Canterbury, Cardinal, Lord Chancellor, lies buried here, she lived 48 years and dyed the 13th March 1631."

Dorothy Kempe, the mother of this Anne Cutts, mentions several treasures which she had at Swavesey, perhaps these had been left there when visiting this daughter.

Lady Dorothy Kempe (*née* Tomson or Thompson) had a grant of administration of Sir Thomas Kempe's estates on 10th December, 1607, and this was re-granted 23rd June, 1609.

She lived till 1629, and by her will, dated 14th November, 1626 (P.C.C. 49 Ridley, 1629),

* For the line see "Burke's Commoners" and the "Northamptonshire County Histories."

she desired to be buried "decently but not sumptuously," in the parish church of Wye, "by the ashes of my dear husband Sir Thomas Kempe." Being in London at the time the will was made, she provided £100 for the conveyance of her body to Wye, an amount which seems extremely large for mere conveyance. Doubtless this would include something of a state funeral by easy stages. Dr. Jackson, who we take to be the then Vicar of Wye, is bequeathed £10 for a gown, and a considerable sum is distributed among her relations and others for "blacks" (*i.e.* mourning.) Sums of money are left to her four daughters, the three living sons-in-law, and several grand-children, as well as to the poor at Shelford, Childerley, Lolworth and Swavesey in Cambridgeshire.

The list of chests, jewels and clothes would afford interesting reading, but space is limited, and we will only mention that "the Great Standard," doubtless the family banner borne by the successive Kempes when Sheriffs of Kent and at other functions, was left to Sir Dudley Digges, who was the most distinguished of the four sons-in-law.

Her personal effects were evidently scattered at the various residences she frequented. "Olenty," of course, contained the bulk of her personal treasures, but some were at Shelford House and others at Childerly. There is a mention of "russet curtains at Shelford with Sir Thomas Kempe his colours," and his armour, these also going to the Digges.

Others whose names appear in the will are briefly as follows: Marie Charnworth, Lady Bowles, Mr. Jacob Bridgeman and Mr. Thomas Adye, Mr. John Marchinoff, Thomas Osbourne and John Collier.

Nothing is said of real estate, only "residue to be divided" between the four daughters.

Reginald Kempe, the next younger brother of the last Sir Thomas Kempe, of Ollantigh, was, as we have said, born in 1553, and baptized at Eastwell, his mother's native place a few miles from Wye. We have also shown that when only some seven years of age he had a legacy from his grandfather, Sir Thomas Moyle, in the form of a share in his town house in Newgate Street, London. Under this will his elder brother inherited lands at Dartford, Sutton-at-Hone and Chetham, which property seems to have also come to him. He married Mary, the daughter of Richard Argyl or Argall, of East Sutton (by licence from the Archbishop of Canterbury) in 1590.

The licence is dated 11th December; he is described as a "gent. of Wye," and she as "of Sutton, virgin." The one Sutton is quite distinct from the other, the former being by Dartford, in the north-west of the county, and the latter—with Sutton Valance and Chart Sutton—near Maidstone and within some twelve miles of Wye.

The pedigree of Argal is given in the "Visitation of *Essex*," of 1612.

By his wife he had the following children:

Thomas, who was to inherit Olantigh.

John, baptized at Wye, 26th March, 1594, to have the reversion of Ollantigh under certain limitations.

Ann, baptized at Wye, 20th January, 1595, married Josias Clarke, to whom she conveyed the Manor of Stowting, Kent, in 1622. She died at Wethersfield, *Essex*, her husband having letters of administration for her estate 12th May, 1623.

Amy, baptized at Wye, 1st October, 1598, married Maurice Tuke, Esq., of Layer Marney, *Essex*, whose family had held that manor. She left a daughter (who inherited her portion of the Kempe property) named Dorothy. The latter married Sir Robert Filmer, Baronet,* of East Sutton. He died 22nd March, 1675-6, and Dorothy died 10th June, 1671.

* Arms of Filmer: Sable, three bars and in chief as many cinquefoils or crest. On a ruined tower or a falcon argent, wings expanded proper beaked and belled or. *See* "Visitation of Kent."

Dorothy, baptized at Wye, 17th February, 1599, married Sir William Denny, of Gray's Inn, Knight, by licence from the Archbishop of Canterbury, dated 18th February, 1632-3. This gentleman wrote the "Shepherd's Holiday," which he dedicated to "Lady Kemp."

We have seen that in 1593-4 Reginald Kempe was assessed at £18, and that in 1599 he received a legacy that did not greatly increase his property, the bulk of his estate therefore must have come to him on decease of his father and brother, but there is little to prove the exact means. Hasted says he died at Tremworth and was buried at Crundell, close to Wye. His will was proved in the Archdeaconry Court of Canterbury, by his widow Mary, on 12th September, 1612. It is dated 2nd January, 1610, and he therein describes himself as "Renold Kempe, of Tremworth, in Co. Kent, Esq." He desires to be buried at Wye, amongst the "reste of my ancestors." The will recites that he had, by a deed dated 26th November, 3-4 James, passed all his lands to his son Thomas Kempe, "for the continuance of our SHEEFE (chief) House of Olantye," the testator accordingly leaves the lands and "Ollanty" to Thomas, his son, for his life only, giving him power to make a jointure for his (Thomas's) wife; after her decease the whole estate undivided is to pass to the lawful heir male of this eldest son, and for want of an heir male the whole undivided estate is to pass to John Kempe—the testator's second son. The following abstract from the will shows the intent, which is briefly summed up in the words "strictly entailed to the heirs male":

"If such son attempt or goe about to do any act or acts to alien or discontinue the said howse, lands, tenements, &c." . . . . "so that it cannot, or any part of it be alienated, then their interest to cease and be thereby determined and extinguished, that then ymediately and from thenceforth the same shall remain and be to such person by this my will is limited, &c." . . . . "the estate of apportionment to the wife of John Kempe excepted."

A second important item in the will is that under date of 1st November, 1606, he passed the Park of Stowting, limited for certain uses to his "cousin" Thomas Scott, of Eggerton, and to Mr. George Finch, that when his son comes of age, or his, the testator's, "sister Kempe" dies, which shall first happen, the park is to be sold and £1,400 out of the produce to be paid to Sir Dudley Digges according to the purchase made by the testator: meanwhile the profits from the manor to go to the advancement of his daughters in marriage. The daughters were also to have the overplus (after the payment of the £1,400) from Stowting, and of 100 marks issuing out of Chilham by the year, until the said "sister Kempe" die or marry. Mr. Balford to have the next advowson of the church of Crondell. The will contrasts with the previous ones in the absence of the religious bequests and petty legacies. The children being minors, their mother, doubtless, had the use of all the household effects, and her income was presumably provided by a settlement at the time of her marriage, as the will does not give her anything more than the reversion of the daughters' portions in case of their dying unmarried.

The inquisition of Reginald Kempe appears in the Calendar in the 10th year of James I. The parchment on which the original report of his possessions was made has, however, been so saturated with wet, at some period, that little or nothing could be deciphered by an expert.

In 1617 (22nd November) Commission was granted to administer the effects of Mary Kempe, widow, deceased, late of the parish of St. Mary the Virgin, in the town of Colchester, Anne Kempe, the daughter, being the grantee.

Ann having married and died before the 29th March, 1622, a fresh grant was made, on that date, of Mary Kempe's estate to John Argall, Gent., brother of the deceased.

It may here be noted that *Mr.* Kempe was Head Master of Colchester School at this time, his term of office extending from 1598 till 1637. During the last years of his life the school dwindled down to ten boys, whereas in the following eighteen months eighty were admitted. The Christian name of this master does not appear in the history of the school (by J. H. Round). His identity is at present unknown.

It is evident that before 1617 the sons of Reginald Kempe were dead, otherwise the administration of his widow's estate would have been granted to the eldest son instead of a daughter. The date of their death, however, is not known, and we cannot taace the Kempes whc ppear at Wye later than this to the same stock; in the adjoining parish of Boughton Aluph, however, a line of Kempes continued to the eighteenth century, and there can be little doubt as to these being a collateral line of the Kempes of Ollantigh, although the date at which this branch started is left uncertain.

It must not, however, be thought that, with the co-heiresses of the last Sir Thomas Kempe of Wye and Reginald Kempe, the family became extinct. Those branches best known, which continued much later, are those of Slindon, Sussex; the issue of Edward Kempe, of Hampshire, who spread into Herefordshire, Buckinghamshire and other counties; and it seems that the Kempes of Dorset, from whom the Kemp-Welches descended, were also of the Ollantigh stock, as they were landholders in Hampshire and the Isle of Wight, where their properties appear to be close to, if not identical with, the lands belonging to the known individuals of the Archbishop's family. The exact connexion, however, has not been traced.

CHAPTER X.

THE ARCHBISHOP OF CANTERBURY, LORD CHANCELLOR OF ENGLAND.

JOHN KEMPE, who eventually became practically head of both Church and State, could hardly, even in the moments of boyish enthusiasm, have hoped that such positions were in store for him. For although his father was of knightly family and his mother's relatives held large estates, both were comparatively poor people until some years after John had made his first great impression as a man of keen intelligence.

It was, therefore, the necessity of carving out a position for himself that stimulated him to make the utmost use of his opportunities, and to apply himself to study. Further than this we have ample evidence of his good physique, and, perhaps, chief of all, of his strong self-control, and moderation in times of extravagance and passion.

His rapid rise shows that he possessed great abilities, and that his character was one on which men could rely. The latter quality is specially attested by his maintaining his high positions for so many years, during a period when public opinion and court influence underwent such great and sudden changes. Doubtless he was always ready to seize any opportunity of adding to his estate, and it may have been galling to others when he instituted his own kin to lucrative posts. In his times, and for very long afterwards, positions were obtained far more by favour than they are in these days of acute competition, with railways and newspapers providing communication with the whole kingdom. An official would naturally have to draw his subordinates from his

I, KENT.

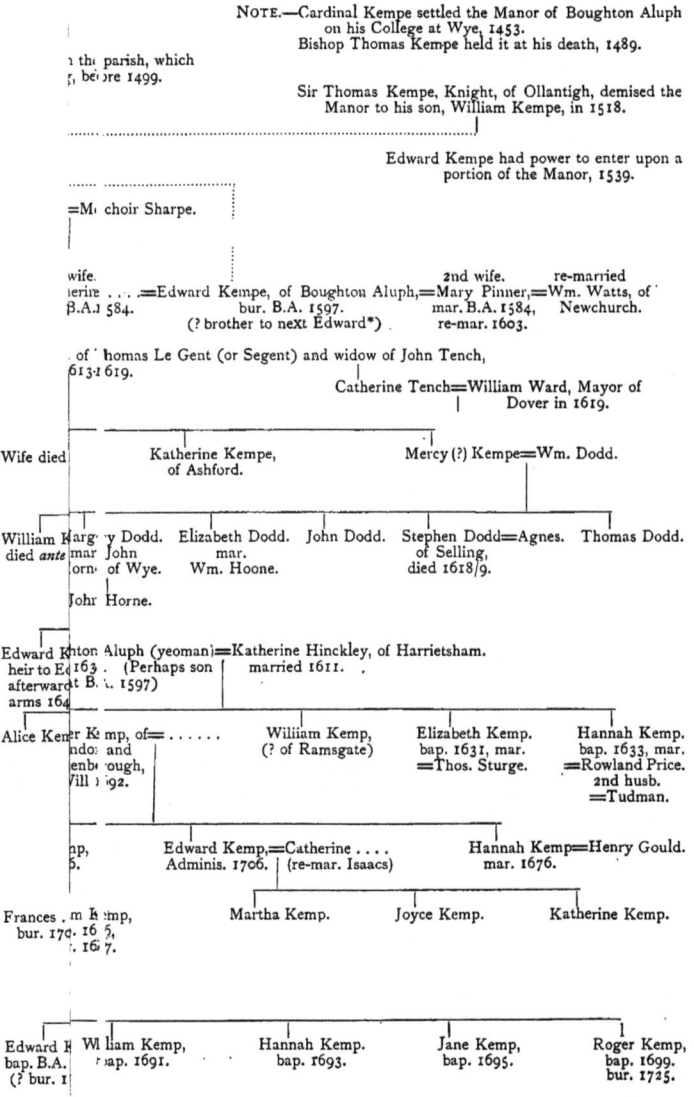

NOTE.—Cardinal Kempe settled the Manor of Boughton Aluph on his College at Wye, 1453.
Bishop Thomas Kempe held it at his death, 1489.

ı thı parish, which
;, beı ɔre 1499.

Sir Thomas Kempe, Knight, of Ollantigh, demised the Manor to his son, William Kempe, in 1518.

Edward Kempe had power to enter upon a portion of the Manor, 1539.

=Mı choir Sharpe.

wife.
ıeriı . . . . =Edward Kempe, of Boughton Aluph, bur. B.A. 1597. (? brother to next Edward*)
β.A.ı 584.

2nd wife. =Mary Pinner, mar. B.A. 1584, re-mar. 1603.

re-married =Wm. Watts, of Newchurch.

. of ' homas Le Gent (or Segent) and widow of John Tench,
613-1619.

Catherine Tench=William Ward, Mayor of Dover in 1619.

Wife died

Katherine Kempe, of Ashford.

Mercy (?) Kempe=Wm. Dodd.

William K died *ante*

Marg· ·y Dodd. mar John Horn· of Wye.
John Horne.

Elizabeth Dodd. mar. Wm. Hoone.

John Dodd.

Stephen Dodd=Agnes. of Selling, died 1618/9.

Thomas Dodd.

Edward K heir to E afterward arms 164

·hton Aluph (yeoman)=Katherine Hinckley, of Harrietsham. married 1611.
163 . (Perhaps son
t B. ·. 1597)

Alice Ken

·r Kemp, of=. . . . . .
ndo: and
enbı ·ough,
Vill ı ·92.

William Kemp, (? of Ramsgate)

Elizabeth Kemp. bap. 1631, mar. =Thos. Sturge.

Hannah Kemp. bap. 1633, mar. =Rowland Price. 2nd husb. =Tudman.

np,
5.

Edward Kemp,=Catherine . . . . Adminis. 1706. (re-mar. Isaacs)

Hannah Kemp=Henry Gould. mar. 1676.

Frances . bur. 170

m Kemp,
16 5,
. 16 7.

Martha Kemp.

Joyce Kemp.

Katherine Kemp.

Edward K bap. B.A. (? bur. 1

William Kemp, bap. 1691.

Hannah Kemp. bap. 1693.

Jane Kemp, bap. 1695.

Roger Kemp, bap. 1699. bur. 1725.

down to ten boys, whereas in the following eighteen months eighty were admitted. The Christian name of this master does not appear in the history of the school (by J. H. Round). His identity is at present unknown.

It is evident that before 1617 the sons of Reginald Kempe were dead, otherwise the administration of his widow's estate would have been granted to the eldest son instead of a daughter. The date of their death, however, is not known, and we cannot taace the Kempes whc ppear at Wye later than this to the same stock; in the adjoining parish of Boughton Aluph, however, a line of Kempes continued to the eighteenth century, and there can be little doubt as to these being a collateral line of the Kempes of Ollantigh, although the date at which this branch started is left uncertain.

It must not, however, be thought that, with the co-heiresses of the last Sir Thomas Kempe of Wye and Reginald Kempe, the family became extinct. Those branches best known, which continued much later, are those of Slindon, Sussex; the issue of Edward Kempe, of Hampshire, who spread into Herefordshire, Buckinghamshire and other counties; and it seems that the Kempes of Dorset, from whom the Kemp-Welches descended, were also of the Ollantigh stock, as they were landholders in Hampshire and the Isle of Wight, where their properties appear to be close to, if not identical with, the lands belonging to the known individuals of the Archbishop's family. The exact connexion, however, has not been traced.

CHAPTER X.

THE ARCHBISHOP OF CANTERBURY, LORD CHANCELLOR OF ENGLAND.

JOHN KEMPE, who eventually became practically head of both Church and State, could hardly, even in the moments of boyish enthusiasm, have hoped that such positions were in store for him. For although his father was of knightly family and his mother's relatives held large estates, both were comparatively poor people until some years after John had made his first great impression as a man of keen intelligence.

It was, therefore, the necessity of carving out a position for himself that stimulated him to make the utmost use of his opportunities, and to apply himself to study. Further than this we have ample evidence of his good physique, and, perhaps, chief of all, of his strong self-control, and moderation in times of extravagance and passion.

His rapid rise shows that he possessed great abilities, and that his character was one on which men could rely. The latter quality is specially attested by his maintaining his high positions for so many years, during a period when public opinion and court influence underwent such great and sudden changes. Doubtless he was always ready to seize any opportunity of adding to his estate, and it may have been galling to others when he instituted his own kin to lucrative posts. In his times, and for very long afterwards, positions were obtained far more by favour than they are in these days of acute competition, with railways and newspapers providing communication with the whole kingdom. An official would naturally have to draw his subordinates from his

PEDIGREE OF THE KEMPES OF BOUGHTON ALUPH, KENT.

NOTE.—Cardinal Kempe settled the Manor of Boughton Aluph on his College at Wye, 1453.
Bishop Thomas Kempe held it at his death, 1489.

Arnold Kempe possessed land and a tenement in the parish, which he had purchased of Wm. Brent, of Charing, before 1499.

Sir Thomas Kempe, Knight, of Ollantigh, demised the Manor to his son, William Kempe, in 1518.

Richard Kempe married Monnsyn Pett, at Boughton Aluph, 1558.

Edward Kempe had power to enter upon a portion of the Manor, 1539.

Aleringe Sharpe=Anne Kempe. | Dennis Kempe=Melchoir Sharpe. mar. B.A. 1565, living 1602.

William Kempe, buried at Wye 1560.

Mary Kempe, bap. Wye 1555. | Jane Kempe, bap. Wye 1558. | Joane Kempe, bap. Wye 1549. | William Kempe, living 1580,=Mary Derne. ? m. 1569. ? bap. at Wye 1556.

1st wife. Katherine . . . bur. B.A. 1584.=Edward Kempe, of Boughton Aluph,=2nd wife. Mary Pinner,=re-married Wm. Watts, of Newchurch. bur. B.A. 1597. (? brother to next Edward*) mar. B.A. 1584, re-mar. 1603.

Richard Kempe, bap. B.A. 1580, living 1604. . . . . . Kemp.

* Edward Kempe, of Dover,=Alice, dau. of Thomas Le Gent (or Segent) and widow of John Tench, died before 1613. Will 1613-1619.

Catherine Tench=William Ward, Mayor of Dover in 1619.

Wife died *ante* 1582=John Kempe, of Kennington. Will 1582. | Roger Kempe, of Boughton Aluph, Eastwell, Wye and Kennington (Yeoman). Will 1662, bur. B.A. S.P. | Mary Kempe, living 1582. | Elizabeth Kempe, living 1582. | Edward Kempe, of Maidstone, Gent.=Katherine, daughter of Christopher Bachelor. and of Dover, Boughton Aluph and Kennington. Will 1620. (? Will 1670/1) | Katherine Kempe, of Ashford. | Mercy (?) Kempe=Wm. Dodd.

William Kempe,=(?) Judith Gibson, died *ante* 1618. mar. at Maidstone 1629. | 1st husb. Trindall=Mercy Kempe,=2nd husb. Boghurst. of Longham.

John Chapman=Mary Trindall.

Alice Kempe,=Rand. Partridge, mar. 1610. of Lenham. | Ann Kempe. | Mary Kempe.

Edward Dodd. (eldest son) | Mary Dodd. mar. John Horne of Wye. | Elizabeth Dodd. mar. Wm. Hoone. | John Dodd. | Stephen Dodd=Agnes. of Selling, died 1618/9. | Thomas Dodd.

John Horne.

Edward Kempe, of Biddenden, a minor in 1618,=(? Alice Basedon, mar. at Maidstone 1662, heir to Edward Kempe, of Maidstone. (Perhaps afterwards of Dover and obtained grant of arms 1645) she re-married, 1668, Thomas Savage) | Two daughters. | William Kempe, living 1618.

Edward Kempe, of Boughton Aluph (yeoman)=Katherine Hinckley, of Harrietsham. Buried B.A. 1638. Will 163[illegible]. (Perhaps son of Edward Kemp bur. at B.A. 1597) married 1611.

Alice Kempe. | Anne Kempe,=Robert Curtis, mar. 1638. of Tenterden. | Mary Kempe.

(These children were minors in 1638)

Edward Kempe, of=Sarah . . . . Boughton Aluph, (eldest son) bap. B.A. 1618, bur. B.A. 1693. | Katherine Kempe, bap. 1612, mar. 1638, =Thomas Fogg. | Frances Kempe, bap. 1615, mar. 1st=Robt. Green. 2nd=Thos. Mascall. | Mary Kempe, S.P. Will 1674. | Roger Kemp, of=. . . . . . London and Queenborough, Will 1692. | William Kemp, (? of Ramsgate) | Elizabeth Kemp. bap. 1631, mar. =Thos. Sturge. | Hannah Kemp. bap. 1633, mar. =Rowland Price. 2nd husb. =Tudman.

Roger Kemp, Will 1696. | Edward Kemp,=Catherine . . . . Adminis. 1706. (re-mar. Isaacs) | Hannah Kemp=Henry Gould. mar. 1676.

Frances . . . =Edward Kemp bur. 1700. (yeoman) bap. B.A. 1649, bur. B.A. 1708. | Mary Booth=Thomas Kemp, bap. 1651, mar. 1681, living 1696, "Fellmonger," of Wye. | Roger Kemp, bap. 1652, Will 1696, Bootmaker, of Hornsey. | 1st husb. John Hope,=Mary Kempe=2nd husb. Norton mar. 1667. mar. | Sarah Kemp=Philip Smith, of Eastwell, mar. 1667. | William Kemp, bap. 16[illegible], bur. 16[illegible].

Martha Kemp. | Joyce Kemp. | Katherine Kemp.

Edward Kemp, bap. B.A. 1676, (? bur. 1700) | Frances Kemp, bap. B.A. 1678. | Thomas Kemp, bap. 1681, bur. 1681. | Thomas Kemp, bap. 1682. | Mary Kemp,=John Wood. bap. 1683. | Sarah Kemp, bap. 1687. | John Kemp, bap. 1689. | William Kemp, bap. 1691. | Hannah Kemp. bap. 1693. | Jane Kemp, bap. 1695. | Roger Kemp, bap. 1699. bur. 1725.

own acquaintances, and he would, of course, select those on whom he could rely for suitable service. Positions were sold frequently to the highest bidder, or arrangements made for the reversion of an office by payment of a considerable sum down (with an indefinite period of waiting for the vacancy), or by the undertaking to pay to the retiring person the income for a term of years during which the new officer must be dependent on other income, perhaps that raised by a similar sale of minor posts, or by the illegal enforcement of payments. It was this injustice which prepared the way for Jack Cade's rebellion of which we shall have to speak later. But looking down the long list of those appointed to various valuable posts during the long period of his governing of the church, we do not find a large percentage of relatives presented to the "fat livings," nor do we find an undue portion of the vacancies filled up by men who were in a position to pay premiums to the Archbishop. It is only fair to point this out, as he been has repeatedly

The Norman Stairs, Ganterbury.

charged with nepotism and greed. The rules which he so carefully compiled for the regulation of his College at Wye, bear the strongest testimony in his favour. He held his ecclesiastical appointments with great dignity—we are inclined to-day to look upon his grave hauteur, such as demanding it as his right to sit before the king wearing his cardinal's hat, as popish arrogance. Yet here it must be borne in mind that the Roman Church was still regarded as the chief authority in matters concerning Christian Religion, while in the Bishop of Rome was recognised the faithful and inspired representative of Christ. Archbishop Kempe believed in the reality and sacredness of his authority, and felt that in maintaining his own position with prescribed insignia of his various powers he was upholding the dignity (*i.e.* greatness) and reality of Christ through the church.

John Kempe was sent at an early age to Canterbury (some nine miles from his home). Here we are unable to find that he distinguished himself, but he must have shown an aptitude for study, otherwise being but the second son of a small property holder, he would not have been sent to college. At what age exactly he went to Oxford no record shows—probably at about sixteen.

There he quickly made his presence felt as a brilliant debater. Doubtless the puzzles with which he embarrassed his learned masters made him popular among his fellow students. Eventually, having more than mastered the legal conundrums of the day, and the usual subjects taught, he became both Doctor of Divinity and Doctor of Laws. He entered the legal profession which, be it remembered was then recognised as a clerical calling. At this time he was probably about twenty. We do not know the date of his ordination, but we find him as Rector of both Saint Michael's,* Crooked Lane, London, and of of Slapton in Bucks, before 1407, for in that year he resigned both livings. It seems that about the same time he was also Rector of Southwich, Sussex, which, perhaps, was due to his relatives' influence with the patron of that living. It is, however, quite possible that at Slapton, at least, he did not personally officiate, as one of the evils of the time arose from the fact that many livings were held by one man who put a badly paid clerk in charge. At his city church he probably exercised his powers of preaching, and thus doubtless spread his fame. In any case, he was so well known as a learned man and clever barrister in 1413 that Thomas Arundel, Archbishop of Canterbury, engaged his services in the most memorable trial of Lord Cobham, otherwise called Sir John Oldcastle, who was looked upon as a dangerous enemy of the church.

This gentleman, whose family held considerable property in Kent, had imbibed the doctrines of John Wyckliffe (who died four years after the death of John Kempe). His chief offence was that he denied that the clergy had any priestly power; for this he was brought before an assembly of the greatest ecclesiastics, who were soon deeply involved in discussing the matters which then, and ever since, have been such serious matters of difference between Christian communities. The account of the trial is extremely interesting; we must, however, confine ourselves to the questions put by the young barrister, John Kempe, and the answers given.

At the trial of Lord Cobham, † 25th September, 1413, it is thus recorded:

". . . . When a Doctour of Lawe, called Master Johan Kempe, plucked out of his bosome a copye of that Byll which they had afore sent into the Tower, by the Archbishop's Council, thinking thereby to make shorter work of him. For they were so amased with his answers . . . . that they knew not well howe to occupye the tyme. . . . .

"'My lord Cobham' (saythe this doctor) 'we must brefely know your mynde concernyng these 4 poynts here following. The first of them is thys, And then he redde vpon the Byll. The Fayth and Determinacion of holy Church touching the Blessed Sacrement of the Alter is this, that after the sacramentall words be once spoken by a pryst in hys masse, the materyall bread that was before bread, is turned into Christes very blode. And so there remaineth in the sacrement of the Aulter from thens forth no materyall bread nor materyall wyne, which were there before the sacrementall words spoken; Sir, beluve ye not this?'

"Then Lord Cobham sayed, 'This is not my Beleue; but my Faith is (as I sayed to you afore) that in the worshipfull sacrament of the aulter, is very Christes body in fourme of bread.' Than said the Archbishop, 'Sir Johan, ye must saye otherwise.' Then Lord Cobham saide, 'Nay, that I shall not, if God be vpon my syde (as I trust he is) but that there is Christes bodye in fourm of bread, as the comon beleue is.'

"Then redde the doctor again. 'The second Point is this: Holy Churche hath determined that euery Christen man lyuing here bodely vpon earth, ought to be shryen to a priest ordained by th' church, if he may come to him. Sir, What say ye to this?'

"The Lord Cobham answered and said, 'a diseased or sore wounded man had nede to have a sure wyse chyrurgion, and a true; knowing both the ground and the danger of the same. Moost necessary were it therefore, to be fyrst shryuen vnto God, which only knoweth our diseases and can help us. I deny not in this the going to a priest, if he be a man of good lyfe and learning: for the lawes of God are to be required of the Priest which is godly learned, But if he be an Ydiote, or a man of viciouse lyuing that is my curate, I ought rather to flee him than to seke vnto him. For souner might I catch yll of him that is nought, than any goodnesse towards my soule helth.'

"Then redde the doctour againe, 'The third Point is this, Christe ordained Saint Peter ye Apostle to be his Vicar here in earth, whose see is the church of Rome. And he granted that the same power which he gave vnto Peter, should succeed

* *See* Dr. Thomas Kempe was also Rector of this church, 1747-1763, in our Middlesex section. The church was pulled down in 1832 to make space for London Bridge. The Rector of that time, Dr. Dakins, has published a Parish History of it and Alfred J. Kempe wrote an account of Roman Antiquities found on the site.

† "Cobbett's State Trials," 1163-1600, vol. i.

to all Peter's successors, which we call now Popes of Rome. By whose special power in churches partycular he ordained prelates, archbishops, parsons, curates, and other degrees more; vnto whom christen men ought to obeye after the lawes of the church of Rome. This is the determination of Holy church; Sir, belieue ye not this?'

"To this he answered, and said, 'He that followeth Peter moost nighest in pure lyuing, is next vnto him in succession; but your Lordly ordre estemeth not greatly the lowly behauer of pore Peter; what soeuer ye prate of him: neither care you greatly for the humble maners of them that succeeded him tyll the time of Sylvester, which for the most part were martirs, as I told ye afore. You can lett all their good condicions go by you, and not hurt your selues with them at all; all the world knows thys well enough by you, and ye can meke boast of Peter.'

"Then redde the Doctor again: 'The fourth Pointe is this, holy Church hath determined, that it is meretorious to a chrysten manne to go on pilgrimage to holy places, and there specially to worship holy relicks and images of saintes, apostles, martirs, confessors, and all other saintes besides, approued by the Church of Rome; Sir, what say ye to this?'

"Whereunto he answered: 'I owe them no seruice by any commandent of God, and therefore I minde [? you] not to seke them for your coueteovsness; It were best ye swept them fayre from cobwebs and duste, ...'"

John Oldcastle was condemned to be burnt as a heretic, in accordance with a law made in 1401 for the suppression of the Lollard doctrines. He, however, escaped into Wales, and it was not until 1417 that he was executed. A most ghastly picture of his execution is given in "Foxe's Book of Martyrs," it depicts the Lollard hung in chains nude, over a great pile of burning faggots, an aged bishop on horseback, and many clergy and officers are represented as looking on.

The able way in which John Kempe had conducted the prosecution led to the next step in his now rapid promotion. Archbishop Chichele introduced him to King Henry V., who soon made use of his services. In July, 1415, he was sent, attended by a large retinue, and provided with what seems an enormous amount of plate and money to negotiate with the King of Arragon for peace, and for the hand of his daughter, Princess Catherine. It was not unusual for clerics to be sent on State negotiations, but the very delicate and difficult task entrusted to him in his thirty-fifth year—when older and more experienced men were available—shows how greatly the king and great officers of State esteemed his talents. Although these desired objects were not attained, he was soon dispatched on a second mission to France, and afterwards to Burgundy in 1417 and 1418. In April, 1419, Henry V. made him keeper of his Privy Seal, and in less than two years he was appointed Chancellor of the Duchy of Normandy, during which office he on one occasion at least held a review of the troops, he being the inspecting general! He had, meanwhile, been successively appointed Archdeacon of Durham, Dean of Arches, Vicar-General to Archbishop Chichele, and Chief Justiciary of the Province of Canterbury. In the same year he was appointed Bishop of Rochester, the Papal provision being dated 26th June, 1419, and the temporalities of the see being delivered to him by the Archbishop of Canterbury on the 9th December following. It is probable that his consecration as bishop took place at Rouen at the same time as that of Bishop Morton, who about this time was appointed Bishop of Winchester, and who it is known was consecrated at Rouen Cathedral on 3rd December that year. In this see he remained till 1421, when he was appointed to that of Chichester; he was, however, never enthroned there, nor did he perform any episcopal act in that diocese, as the more important bishopric of London becoming vacant, he claimed that see under a Papal provision dated 17th November, 1420. This provision, however, was felt by the London clergy to be an encroachment on the right exercised by the Dean and Chapter of St. Paul's, of selecting a candidate and submitting his name to the Pope. They had in this case elected Thomas Polton, Bishop of Hereford, and thus to compromise matters the Pope translated the latter to the See of Chichester, while John Kempe received the spirituals of London from the Archbishop on 20th May, 1422, and the temporals from the King on the 20th of the following month. It is interesting to notice as one of the results of this struggle between the Dean and Chapter of St. Paul's on the one hand, and the Pope on the other, for the right of nominating a new Bishop to the See, that at the Court General of the Manor of Fulham held on 2nd October, 1421, it was decreed as follow :—

"Presented that the Dean and Chapter claim one shilling during the vacancy of the See as recognizance from the Customary Tenants, and the same to be levied forthwith."

When at length John Kempe was presented to the temporalities pertaining to his Bishopric of London, all the tenants of his manors had to attend to do fealty. We may here digress to note the very considerable lands which the Bishop of London then held, in addition to his chief seat, Fulham Palace. The Manor of Fulham alone included Hammersmith and *Finchley* covering about 4,000 acres. The Bishop held the manors of the following places in Middlesex, Herts, and Essex with the advowson of several of them :—*Acton*, Ealing, Ashwell, Drayton, Feering, Greenford, *Hanwell*, *Rickmansworth*, Hornsey, *Hadham*, Kelvedon, Layndon, Steavenage, Stortford, Wickham, and *Paddington*. Granting that both the Kempe bishops were guilty of remembering their relatives and introducing them to positions of advantage, it will be interesting for us to bear in mind these places, with those which they held personally, and others like the lands held by the Dean and Chapter of St. Paul's to which the bishops' influence doubtless extended. In many cases the ancient Manor Rolls go back to their times or nearly so, and we may thus obtain a trace of Kempes who settled down on these episcopal lands during the period over which the Kempes were Lords of these Manors. This subject will be followed in our Middlesex section more particularly, and it will seem evident that the Kempes of Norfolk were recognized as kinsmen by both John and Thomas Kempe, although even then the connexion between the two families of Norfolk and Kent must have been remote and merely supported by tradition. In any case, both Kentish and Norfolk Kempes became holders of land in some of the above manors (indicated by italics) within a short time.

In his London bishopric, John Kempe could have found but little time to devote to the improvement of his manorial residence at Fulham, his numerous offices must have necessitated his being much in London, and frequently he was away on missions, so that his stay at Fulham could not have been prolonged, yet it seems that at least he had meditated the alterations and improvements which his nephew eventually carried out. This rebuilding of the episcopal seat will therefore be mentioned at a greater length under our notice of Bishop Thomas Kempe.

On the accession of Henry VI. Bishop John Kempe resigned the post of Chancellor of Normandy in order to become a member of the Council appointed to act for the boy-king during his minority. In this he took no small part, for the Duke of Bedford, who had been appointed Protector, tried to ignore the Council, and it was necessary to check his arrogance. This duty fell upon Kempe, and Bedford was summoned to the Star Chamber at Westminster. At first he refused, then he made excuses for non-attendance, but eventually he appeared, and before a great gathering of noblemen, prelates, and the King's Council Bishop Kempe addressed him with a long and powerful reprimand. The whole is too long to be given here, but the opening sentences as recorded in the Parliament Rolls, will afford an idea of its tone :—

> "Furste, after protestation made, that it is in no wyse th'entent of my said Lordes of the Counsaille, to with drawe from the saide Lorde of Bedford, Worship, Reverence, or enything that thei owe unto him, considering his birth, the state that God hath sette hymne ynne ; but to do him all Worship, Reverence, and Pleasure ; it was rememboud howe that after the time of his last coming unto this land, he had made unto the saide Lordes of the Counsaille many notable good and great exhortations." . . .

With many such polished speeches Kempe made it distinctly understood that the noble lord must not trifle with the Council, and great and powerful as was the Duke of Bedford he had to at least nominally assent to the rulings of this "Kempe of mean origin."

The King's education was one of the chief concerns of this Council. In the British Museum is an interesting document relating to this subject, in which directions "for the better rule and government of the King" are laid down. It is signed by all the members of the Council.

Kempe, who had by the date when the document was drawn up become Archbishop of York, signs himself "J. Ebor."

At the assembling of Parliament in the Painted Chamber, Westminster, in 1428, John Kempe, then being Archbishop of York and Chancellor of England, opened the Cause of the Summons with a sermon based on the words, "Sine Providentia Regali impossibile est Pacem Rebus dare," from the Book of Maccabees, deducing therefrom two heads of discourse which are given in the Parliamentary History, vol. ii., para. 201, as follows:—

"The first was the duty of the Prince towards his Subjects, and the other the duty of the Subjects to their Prince. The first of these he again subdivided into three other points that the Subjects should be defended from any foreign invasion; that Justice should be indifferently administered, and that Peace should be kept within the Realm. Three things he said also belonged to the subjects; first, that they should grant large supplies for their better defence in time of war; in Peace, that they should readily obey their Majesties and meekly to submit themselves to the known Laws of the Land. All which the better to accomplish, the King had called this Parliament and confirmed all their Liberties; and, that business might be sooner begun and ended, he desired the Commons to make choice of a Speaker and present him the next day before the King." (John Tyrrel, Esquire, was the Speaker, who was then accordingly presented.)

At the opening of Parliament at Westminster, in 1429, Archbishop Kempe addressed the assembly, taking for his text the words "Quomodo stabit Regnum" (Lk. xi., 18), from which he argued "That in the Realm of England three Causes were to be noted which hindered its advancement:

1. "Want of Faith, which is the root of all good works: quod sine Fide impossibile est placere Deo;

2. "Want of Fear, which was the chief in every good mind: Nam qui timet nihil, negliget;

"And lastly. The want of upright Justice, the pillar of every Kingdom, for, Ex Justitia sequitur Pax et Pace Rerum Abundantia maxime procreatur.

"Instead of these three virtues three abominable Vices," he said, "were sprung up, namely, Infidelity, through Errors and Heresies; Obstinacy, instead of fear; and Oppression in place of Justice. Through infidelity he told them that the troubles in Germany had happened. Fear he again divided into two parts, the one Spiritual and virtuous, as fearing God and man for God, the other, Carnal and Vicious, from whence sprung murmurs and rebellion which would procure such destruction as happened to Dathan and Abiram.

"From oppression ensued the transferring of the King's arms, according to the Wise Man, 'Regnum a gente in gentem transferetur propter Injustitias aut Injurias! But that if true Faith, due Fear and strict Justice were restored, there was then no doubt but this would be a flourishing Kingdom.' He concluded, That as the Prince was bound to defend the Subjects and to keep Peace, so ought the Subjects to grant largely to the Prince out of their goods that he might be enabled to perform the same, to which end the said Parliament was called." (Parl. Hist., vol. ii., pp. 205-6.)

The substance of the addresses at the Assembling of Parliament here recorded are given in the Parl. Hist. II., 258 and II., 262 in the years 1428-9. During the years of his office Kempe seems to have opened Parliament each year with only one exception, when illness prevented him from doing so.

John Kempe, soon after the address to the Duke above recorded, was sent to the Duke, then acting as Regent of France, and was employed to treat for the release of the King of Scots (Acts of Privy Council, III., 83, 137.) On 16th March, 1426, he was raised to the Chancellorship of England, and on the 8th of April following was elected Archbishop of York. As Lord Chancellor he remained for nearly six years, resigning the Great Seal on 25th February, 1432. This resignation is believed to have been due to the friction between the two factions of the governing powers—Bedford and Gloucester. The Archbishop was one of those who signed the "Answers" of the latter Duke resisting the other's claim to govern at his own will and pleasure and explaining the limitation of his authority as Protector (Rot. Parl. IV., 327). He, however, continued to take an active part in, and assiduously attended the Council, notwithstanding his relinquishment of the Purse.

We have mentioned that Kempe held for a time the post of Chancellor of Normandy, and it will be of interest to further note that when his other duties prevented his personally executing the acts of that position his seal was affixed by Jehan Brinkley, his Esquire, Lieutenant at Caen.

The impression of this seal is preserved among the additional charters in the British Museum (No. 114), though slightly damaged it will be found to bear the inscription "myn. J.K." in old English characters and "an eagle displayed," which being similar to his badge, "a bird in her piety," may be also a cognizance worn by the personal following of the Chancellor in Normandy. We may here venture to say that just as our regiments wear the present Royal badges in various forms, so the servants of a lord possessing numerous seats and offices would frequently be distinguished by a badge which would serve readily to identify the individual both with his lord and also with the seat or office to which he was attached. Such badge was not subject to the decrees of the Heralds as Arms were and still are, thus many badges have passed out of mind and are entirely unrecorded. Archbishop Kempe used as his badge when Archbishop of York and Canterbury a pelican or similar bird plucking her breast, commonly termed a "bird in her piety," and so frequently used in churches to allude to the self-sacrifice of Christ. It was probably due to his using this as a badge that a crest of such a bird, standing on a wheatsheaf, was adopted by his family and the Kempes of Norfolk, who had previously used "a hooded hawk" as their crest.

CHAPTER XI.

ARCHBISHOP KEMPE—*continued.*

As at his appointment to the See of London, there was opposition to John Kempes' translation to the Archbishopric of York. In this case the Pope had preferred Richard Fleming of Lincoln to this province, but the King, with the Dean and Chapter, taking advantage of the law against the usurpations of Rome, stoutly opposed him, and the Pope had practically to withdraw his nominee. Again, however, the Roman Pontiff did not acknowledge that the King had either the right or power to instal any to the See without his direct sanction; thus obliged to give way to the King he yet claimed the prerogative, and issued a letter to the clergy of the province directing in rather odd terms that Kempe should be acknowledged as the Archbishop of York.

During the long period of twenty-six years which he occupied this position he was so occupied with the more secular offices connected with the State politics that suffragan bishops discharged most of his episcopal functions. He, however, seems to have been very mindful of his parishes, and there can be no doubt that out of his revenues he spent yearly large sums in restoring the churches in his province which specially required such outside help. He made good use of his nephew, Thomas Kempe, as we shall presently see, and, doubtless, this relative was the factotum who was entrusted with the administration of the Archbishop's charitable funds. Perhaps it was to acknowledge the generosity of this Archbishop, or, perhaps, out of esteem for his personal qualities, that many churches displayed some allusion to his name or arms. For instance, in the Church of St. George, at Doncaster, over the principal eastern arch of the interior, there is a demi-figure archangel in ecclesiastical vestments, pall, &c., the right hand raised in the act of benediction, in the left an episcopal mitre, and on a shield supported by two smaller figures the coat of arms of the See of York impaling the coat of Cardinal Kempe (three sheaves within a bordure engrailed). Over the angels' heads the sacred monogram I.H.S. And there also was a carving in the masonry, representing a woolsack with the letter K, in allusion to Archbishop Kempe being Lord Chancellor of England.*

Archbishop Kempe left various material memorials of his occupation of the See of York. He beautified Southwell Minster, and to a great extent rebuilt it. He built the Gatehouse to the Palace of Cawood, which he adorned inside and out with his arms and insignia as Cardinal and Archbishop. His arms, badges, and motto are also to be seen in the now decayed woodwork of the palace itself. An illustration of the gateway is given in Drake's "Eboracum," page 443, showing the shield, three sheaves within an engrailed border, being supported by birds—possibly meant for hawks, presumably in allusion to the early crest of his family. In the engraving the birds appeared to be strangled by a cord, but this line may be the lower edge of a hood such as the hawk crest often had. The Cardinal's hat was used here and in other places as Kempe's crest. His personal motto was "Loue soit Dieu," *i.e.*, God be praised. We have not, however, actually seen these relics at Southwell Palace, and are relying upon Drake for these details. He also speaks in the above-mentioned work of the existence of "vestry furniture cloth" at York Minster bearing Kempe's arms. These may, however, have disappeared before now.

The beautiful window of Bolton Percy Church, near York, contains in the centre section a portrait figure of Archbishop Kempe, which was doubtless placed there at the cost of Thomas Kempe when rector of that church in recognition of his uncle's generosity and patronage. Unfortunately the glass with the head of the figure is modern. Hence it cannot be relied on as an actual likeness. We give a small illustration of the whole window which will give an idea of the figure, and below may be seen a shield bearing his arms.

The Archbishop was prepared to attend the Council at Basle, and his credentials and passport were made out and permission given him to take £2,000 sterling, with plate valued at 1,000 marks, in 1433, when a change in the policy of the Kingdom occasioned a delay. He addressed letters to the Council in consequence. These are said to be very verbose in character. They may be seen in the British Museum Library (Harl. MS., 826). The year is not mentioned, but the month is July, probably 1433.

In 1435 he represented England at the great European Congress held at Arras, when he declared with immense vigour and dignity the King's desires, which were for peace. As representing the King, rather than in his Ecclesiastical capacity, he went on this important mission in greater state than before. The gold, silver plate and jewels which he took with him on this occasion were valued at three million marks. Other officials he took with him must, according to the permission granted to them, have taken altogether more than twenty million marks in similar valuables. His principal commission was to arrange a marriage between one of the daughters of Charles of Valois and Henry VI., but this he failed to accomplish. On his return he resumed his many State duties within this realm.†

In 1439 he was again engaged in a fruitless mission to France with the object of arranging peace.

The embassy consisted of the Duke of Norfolk with a long retinue of nobles, prelates, lawyers and their respective suites, with a following of armed soldiery. Dr. Thomas Beckington was secretary to Archbishop Kempe, and Sir Thomas Wotton, Knight (formerly esquire to King

* "History of St. George's, Doncaster," by Rev. Jackson, 1855.

† "Foedera," v, 1, 18. "Acts of Privy Councils," iv, 302.

Henry VI.), was now one of his esquires. The secretary kept a voluminous diary, and the minutes, of which three contemporary copies are extant.* From these a book might be written; we must, however, give here but few of the graphic details to enable us to enter a little into the reality of this long-forgotten but memorable mission.

It was on Friday, the 26th June, that the Ambassadors landed at Calais, where on the following Sunday they received news of the approach of the French Embassy, headed by Count de Vendome and Archbishop of Rheims, and accordingly rode out in great state to meet them. Next day both parties dined with the Archbishop of York at ten o'clock, excepting the Count de Vendome, who made the excuse that on that day he kept a fast. The arrangements for the conference were made on a magnificent scale, the preparations requiring over a week to complete. On Monday, 6th July, at six o'clock in the morning, the English Legation left Calais, a sufficient guard being stationed there to prevent the town being taken unawares in order to rescue the Duke of Orleans, who was then a prisoner in the hands of the English. At eight o'clock they arrived at the place of Convention, the Gravelines being seven miles distant, when refreshments were in readiness for the whole cavalcade, the chief of the party being entertained in the tent of the Archbishop of Rheims. The Duchess of Burgundy on the one side and Cardinal Beaufort on the other were the appointed mediators, and before them the Ambassadors of England and Charles laid their proposals. Great friction, however, again prevailed, and each party was so little assured of the other's honour that their camps were surrounded by trenches in which the armed soldiers kept continual watch, ready for an outbreak of hostilities at any moment. The object of the Council was not accomplished, but the Archbishop of York was not held to have erred in judgment or ability, for not only did he continue to hold his many high offices, but further dignities were conferred on him.

In the December of the same year (1439) Pope Eugenius IV., at his third creation of Cardinals, made John Kempe Cardinal Priest of Santa Balbina. This led to a controversy between the Archbishop of Canterbury (Stafford) and himself as to which provincial had the precedence. On this matter being referred to the Pope it was decreed in favour of Archbishop Kempe, on the ground that an Archbishop, even in his own province, must go after a Cardinal, the latter office being second in the church only to the papacy.

Some two years later Cardinal Kempe, with Archbishop Chichley and Cardinal Beaufort, had to judge Alenor or Elenor Cobham, who was charged with conspiracy, with her acquaintance, Roger Onley, otherwise called Bolingbroke, for planning to cause the King's death. This lady was the daughter of Reginald, Lord Cobham, and wife of Humphry, Duke of Gloucester. She is said to have been a weak-minded person and the dupe of Bolinbroke, who is called a necromancer. The ignorance of the time is shown by these three learned men judging her for the offence of procuring a wax effigy of the King, by burning which she would cause the King's actual body to waste away in death. Both she and Bolingbroke protested that they had never intended more than to foretell when the King should die by means of the wax figure. This trial was held in St. Stephen's Chapel, Westminster, where she had taken sanctuary, according to the custom of the times. The verdict was that she should be imprisoned at Leeds Castle, in Kent, but the villainy of her enemies (her husband), who sought by this charge to get rid of her, having been foiled by this comparatively mild sentence, they soon brought her to the Guildhall, London, where, on a false charge of having by means of witchcraft induced her betrayer, the Duke, to marry her, she was condemned to do public penance (1441).

* "Harl. M.S.," 861 and 4,763. "Cotton M.S. Tiberius," B. xii.

In 1443 Cardinal Kempe granted an indulgence to those who gave to the building of a bridge at Oxhead, Norfolk, the charter concerning which is among the Stowe MSS. (Charter 608.)* Oxhead is a parish on the River Bure, about nine miles north of Norwich, and close to Brampton. It will be noticed in our Norfolk section of this work that Alice, the daughter of Robert, Duke of Brampton, married John Kempe of Weston. It is just possible that Archbishop Kempe recognised these persons, or rather their ancestors, as kinsmen and the senior line of his own family, and that consequently he was easily induced to render this favour. Archbishop Kempe was one of those who signed the great Charter granted to the City of Norwich in 1452, and this act may also indicate that he used his influence to obtain the advancement of a place so intimately connected with Kempes.

On 31st January, 1450, Kempe was again called upon to fill the offices of Chancellor and received the Great Seal on the resignation of John Stafford, Archbishop of Canterbury.

In 1450, when the Cardinal was seventy years of age, he had to go forth to meet the formidable rising headed by Jack Cade. This rebellion was supposed to have been instigated by the Yorkists, and had it been successful the king would probably have been deposed. But timely warning was carried to the City of London, which immediately turned out its pikemen and sent for the venerable Chancellor and Archbishop to come to direct their operations. The insurgents were met at the south side of London Bridge, where the two forces met, and a furious but indecisive fight occurred. It was then arranged that Cade and Kempe should hold a parley in St. Margaret's Church, Southwark (now Southwark Cathedral), and the Archbishop Kempe agreed that Jack Cade should be pardoned, provided the rising was quelled. The pardon was dated Monday, 12th July, 1450, but it took the Council a full month before all concerned in the rising had been brought to justice. During that time a Commission was issued in Kent to enquire by whom the disturbances had been instigated; the Cardinal was naturally one of this Commission, and opened the proceedings at Canterbury. Eight men were executed at that City as the outcome of the enquiry, and many minor offenders punished.

Archbishop Stafford having died on 6th July, 1452, John Kempe was elected Primate in his stead on the 21st of the same month. The Pope again demurred, for he held that this appointment rested with the Pontiff, as, however, he had every reason to approve of the elected bishop, he issued his usual mandate, and Cardinal Kempe was duly enthroned at Canterbury on December 11th that year.

At this time the Pope, doubtless in recognition of his powerful influence in England, created an extraordinary cardinal bishopric by separating the See of Porto from that of Salva Candida, or Santa Rufina, and constituted Kempe Cardinal Bishop with the latter title. He received the Pall at the hands of his nephew, Thomas Kempe, Bishop of London, at Fulham Palace, on 24th September, 1452.

Still retaining the Great Seal, he remained till his death, both head of the Church and Lord Chancellor of the Kingdom. His age led his enemies to hope for more power, and getting impatient for his death, it appears that the rival political parties were preparing for hostilities which they felt must follow. Thus we find that only two months before he died the aged Archbishop was actively trying to stave off nobles and others who desired the King's dethronement. In a letter privately sent to John Mowbray, Duke of Norfolk, and one of the most powerful of the Yorkist Lords, written by some paid spy, within the Court at Windsor, we find trace of the plotting of these enemies. The letter is quoted in "Annals of Windsor," and contains the following "item":—

* This Charter may now be seen in the Castle Museum, Norwich, bearing the signature of Archbishop Kempe.

"The Cardinalle (Kempe) bathe charged and commanded alle his servaunts to be redy with bowe and arwes, swerd and bokeler, crosse-bowes and alle other habillements of Werre, suche as as thei kun meidle wt., to awaite upone the safe guard of his persone." (*See* "Archaeologia," vol. XXIX., p. 310).

Another war-like duty which fell upon Cardinal Kempe in his declining years will be worthy of mention. A warrant was issued in the name of the King in 1453, addressed to "the moost revend ffadre in god Joh'n Cardinal Archbishop of Canterbury," commanding him to erect barriers for a battle upon an appeal of High Treason. The appellant in this case was John Hatton, and the defendant Robert Norreys. Doubtless the Archbishop had to be present at this "Battle" or tournament, which took place in London.

Canopy over Tomb of Archbishop Kempe in Canterbury Cathedral.
Specially drawn by Miss Lucy Kemp-Welsh.

This may have been his last public function, for on 22nd March, 1453, the aged Archbishop died. The King was at the time lying ill at Windsor, suffering from that strange disorder of mind, bordering on insanity, which caused him to evince no interest in events. In the letter above mentioned, for instance, it is recounted how, when his infant son, the Prince of Wales, was brought to him for the first time, the King looked upon the babe without the smallest change of countenance or word. When, however, the Bishops of Winchester, Ely and Chester, with other Lords deputed by Parliament, told the King of the Lord Chancellor Kempe's death, the King for a moment awoke from his protracted silence and indifference and remarked with emphasis: "One of the wisest Lords in this Land is dead." The detailed account, written as a report to the House of Lords by this deputation, will be found in the "Annals of Windsor" and in the "Parliamentary History."

During the closing years of his life, Archbishop Kempe took steps to found and endow liberally a College for Secular Priests—a Collegiate Church and School in his native town of Wye, and we can feel sure that, from the time of his becoming Archbishop of Canterbury, he was as frequently resident in Kent as his duties of state would allow. He, doubtless, was frequently the guest of his nephew at Ollantigh, and thence watched the rebuilding of the church and the erection of his college and schools; to the subject of his foundations we shall, however, give a separate chapter.

One other important item should be mentioned here. Some accounts tell us that Archbishop Kempe performed the ceremony of marriage between the King and Margaret of Anjou, on the

Cardinal Kempe's Tomb, Canterbury Cathedral.

continent. It seems well within reason that he should be the officiating bishop at this marriage, but there is some doubt about it. The King was represented by the Earl of Suffolk, and the wedding was solemnized in the Cathedral of Tours, 18th April, 1445, the King and Queen of France being present. There is a celebrated picture of the marriage, by Jan Mabuse, which was in the Walpole collection at Strawberry Hill. This picture, and the portrait of Archbishop Kempe, passed to the present Duke of Sutherland, and both have been reproduced, the wedding having appeared in "England's History," by A. G. Temple, F.S.A., in 1897-8.

In the picture of the marriage Archbishop Kempe is represented in full Ecclesiastical Vestments—Albe, Tunicle, Chasuble, Pall, Cope, Amice, and a jewelled Mitre. The Archbishop is said to have worn yellow gauntlets, but from the reproduction one would judge that the painting merely represented his old wrinkled hands. The Morse worn on the Cope is apparently a very large example, like a cruciform broach of gold with pictures in enamel. If it is somewhat doubtful if this marriage was actually performed by Cardinal Kempe, we have at least a reliable record of his having stood as god-father for the Prince of Wales, who was born in 1453.

With the death of Archbishop Kempe the political troubles, which are known as the Wars of the Roses, commenced, and within a few years the House of Lancaster was succeeded by the House of York.

John Kempe, Archbishop of Canterbury, Cardinal of the Church of Rome and Lord Chancellor of England, was buried in the Chancel of Canterbury Cathedral, on the south side and just opposite the tomb of his friend and patron, Archbishop Chichele. The tomb erected over him is a fine example of fifteenth century work, and it is greatly to be regretted that it has been allowed to fall into decay. In 1899 the editor of *The Kentish Gazette and Canterbury Press* called attention to the urgent need of repair in which the handsome canopy of this tomb stood. Dean Farrar was approached on the subject and expressed his desire to see the restoration accomplished; there had, however, arisen much discussion among antiquaries as to the manner in which this work should be carried out, the exceedingly gorgeous colours and amount of gold recently used to re-decorate Archbishop Chichele's tomb having given rise to much dissatisfaction, the general opinion being that the high colours were entirely out of harmony with the surroundings. Doubtless Mr. Charles Eamer Kempe, who had been entrusted with this restoration by the authorities of All Souls' College, carried out their wishes, but as this gentleman is a well-known designer of church furniture and stained glass he would be conscious of this and would treat Archbishop Kempe's tomb in a suitable manner if funds for the restoration were placed at his disposal.

With the sanction of the Dean it was proposed to start such a fund, and the compiler of this work volunteered to send out an appeal for donations for this object to every Kemp and Kempe in the Directories of Great Britain and her Colonies and the English-speaking world. The outbreak of the war in South Africa at this moment, and the many calls upon the charitable, was deemed a reason for delaying this appeal; now, however, those who feel disposed to aid in the restoration of this ancient memorial of the greatest man of the name of Kempe, should intimate the amount which they are prepared to subscribe to the editors of this history, and should more than sufficient be received to accomplish this restoration, the surplus would be devoted to similar restoration of other Kemp or Kempe relics.

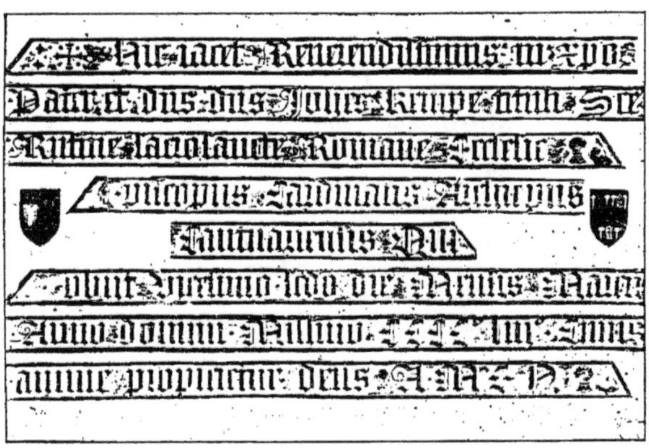

Rubbing of Inscription on Tomb of Archbishop Kempe, 1452.

The inscription round the bevelled edge of the tomb is deeply cut in abbreviated Latin, the annexed illustration being from a rubbing specially made for this work, with the Dean's kind permission. It will be noticed that sheaves occur at the end of the principal lines in *allusion* to the arms of his family. The cross at the commencement probably has reference to his office as bishop.

The inscription on the tomb, if given in full, would read as follows:

Hic jacet Reverendissimus in Christo Pater et dominus Johannes Kempe tituli * Sanctae Rufinae sacrosanctae Romanae Ecclesiae Episcopus Cardinalis Archiepiscopus Cantuariensis Qui obiit vicesimo secundo die Mensis Marcii Anno Domini Millesimo CCCC liij. Cuius animae propicietur Deus. AMEN.

Neither the actual will of the Archbishop nor even a copy has been found, but it appears that it was duly proved in 1454. The executors, however, having declined to act as such, the Prior of Christ Church, "auctoritate prerogativa Ecclesiae Xpi, que hac vice ad nos plenarie spectat" appointed as administrators, the Bishop of London (Thomas Kempe, the Archbishop's nephew), Judge Fortescue, two Kentish Knights, Dr. Packenham and Robert Ballad, a priest, in their place.

In the ordinary course an "inquisition" was held to ascertain what lands and property the Archbishop held at the time of his decease. This document, recording his possessions and personal effects, is extant, and the following details are given in the appendix to the ninth volume of the "Historical MSS. Report," pages 104-5. We do not know if any books are in existence which can be identified as having been in his collection when this inventory was prepared, but possibly a few may be found in the Bodleian and other libraries of Oxford, to which university he is likely to have bequeathed them.

"INVENTARIUM DNI. JOHIS KEMPE CARDINALIS."

The ready money amounted to - - -	£899	10	11
The Vestments in the Chapel - - -	827	1	6
The Silver, Jewels and Ornaments of the Chapel -	398	1	4½
The Gold Plate of the Chapel and Pantry - -	501	15	10
The Silver Vessels in the Cellarer's Office - -	485	0	11
The Silver Vessels used for Spices - - -	60	5	2½
The (Silver) in the Pantry - - - -	74	2	5
The Linen in the Pantry - - - -	33	4	4
The Silver Vessels for Water - - -	158	4	3
The Silver in the Kitchen - - - -	234	13	11
The Books for the Chapel - - - -	98	16	8
The Books of Divinity and Law - - -	255	18	10
Brass and other ware - - - -	19	9	2
Horses and other property in the Stables - -	23	13	4
Total -	£4,069	18	8

This is certainly a large sum, but it must not be taken to be, as has been said, a reflection on his greed or love of display; he had to keep up an official and palatial retinue, not only as Archbishop but as Lord Chancellor, and yet Archbishop Arundel's Inventory for similar effects was half as much again!—£6,008 12*s*. 7¼*d*. in 1413.

In a Metrical History of the Archbishops of York the following lines, commemorating Archbishop Kempe, occur, and are thence quoted by Weever in his "Funeral Monuments," from wh we take them:

Tunc Johannes nobilis Kemp vociferatus
  Prius in Londoniis presul instalatus.
Et erectus pontifex metropolitanus,
  Presul Archipresulem confirmat Romanus,
Mandans sibi pallium Martini; erectus
  Sagax Cancellarius regis est effectus.
Cardinalis presbyter digne sublimatur

Sub Balbinae titulo; sic laus cumulatur.
In Suthwell manerium fecit preciosum,
Multis artificibus valde sumptuosum.
Annis multis prospere curam sui gregis,
Rexit per insticiam, et per normam legis.
Tandem Archiepiscopus est inthronizatus
Apud Lambeth. Abiit, labor iam finitur,
Et in Cantuaria corpus sepelitur.
Licet prohibuerit abbas rigorose.
Iacet ibi condita gleba, gloriose.

CHAPTER XII.

WYE COLLEGE.

OF Ollantigh we have no illustration. The present structure is modern and possesses no feature of special interest. There is nothing, we believe, in evidence at the mansion connecting it with the Kempes, but there is, or lately was, a bell, marked Thomas a Kempis, which had evidently been purchased as a suitable relic. We need hardly say here that Thomas, the reputed author of "The Imitation of Christ," was in no way connected with Archbishop Kempe, but was living a monk on the continent when Kempe was flourishing in this country, both having been born about 1380.

The Church of Wye is also disappointing. Through fire and lightning the church as built by Archbishop Kempe has disappeared, and the present erection on its site would not be recognised by those who knew it in the days of the founder. No tomb marks the long connexion of his family with the parish, all having been destroyed.

The graveyard is rather a large one. Adjoining it at the east end of the church is what remains of the college and school founded by Archbishop Kempe, with numerous additions in red brick, easily distinguished from the original buildings.

A fine view of the church, college, and the mansion and grounds of Ollantigh may be obtained from the train when travelling from London to Margate on the South Eastern Railway.

The college, as an institution, was doomed to but a short career, for founded with much care by a man with good foresight in 1447, it fell into the grasping hands of Henry VIII. in 1545, thus existing less than a century. The Thornhill family, who afterwards lived at Ollantigh, established a school in the building, but this, too, fell into disuse, and the old buildings are utilised for an agricultural college. We are indebted to the secretary of this institution (Mr. Hall) for the illustrations and for much of our information. Those who have an opportunity to visit the vicinity should not fail to call at the college, where, under ordinary circumstances, they will be permitted to see the library, in the window of which are the genuine arms of the founder. This fragment of glass was found by Mr. Parsons in one of the windows of a farmhouse at Wye, whither it had doubtless heen carried for safety; perhaps at the time when a battle between Royalists and Roundheads occurred in the parish. Mr. Parsons effected its return to the college. The fragments include a shield, on which the arms of the See of Canterbury impale three sheaves within a border (all yellow) the field being red. (The border is not engrailed, possibly this was effected by painting out in black by hand, which painting would be likely to wear off in time.) In addition to the chasuble and cross of Canterbury there is a cross of yellow, which we take to represent that the founder was Primate of all England as well as Bishop of that See, while a red circle below the chasuble was intended, we believe, to represent the Cardinal's hat, as that appears above his arms in the chief boss over the Martyrdom in Canterbury Cathedral.

NORTH-EAST FRONT.

SOUTH FRONT.

VIEWS OF WYE COLLEGE. S.E.

SOUTH-EAST FRONT.

QUADRANGLE.

We have not space to describe the building, the illustrations giving a good idea of the original structure before the alterations of the last century. The chief interior features are the staircase, library and kitchen. For further details we must refer our readers to "The History of Wye," by Dr. W. Leliven Morris, F.R.C.S., a copy of which is at the Canterbury Public Library.

In the Library of the British Museum there is a bound manuscript entitled, "Wye College: Being an Abstract of Statutes made for the Good Government of the said College." In addition to the statutes this manuscript gives details of the college history and possession, collected by Dr. Brett, of Wye, and written down to about 1735.

Space at our disposal prevents us printing the statutes, which are most interesting, and show that Archbishop Kempe took the greatest care to establish his college on scriptural lines. He frequently refers to Apostolic teaching, and strongly enforces sobriety upon the clergy and choristers forming the staff. He directs that their dress shall not be of a dark, dull colour nor yet glaring. The outer garment is to reach to their heels and to have proper sleeves, but not unduly long ones. Their shoes are not to have "beaks." In the other parts they are to be like other grave clergymen. The cost of their clothes, which are to be renewed annually, is as follows: the Master, thirteen shillings and fourpence per year; Fellows, ten shillings, and Clerks, seven shillings. The choristers' clothing and keep is not to exceed forty shillings a year. The members of the college are not even to look upon others playing with dice or other games of chance, are never to go into taverns, nor even the town unless accompanied by another member of the college. "Honest women are not to be admitted to the college unless for some necessary, useful, or lawful cause, those of suspicious character never."

Every person admitted to the college as a member must have been born in lawful wedlock. The entertainment of guests and visitors of other orders is allowed, and a scale fixed for the cost of feasting such. The member intoducing the guest is required to defray half the cost out of his stipend. When guests are present at meals conversation is permitted in English, but at other times only necessary speaking is allowed at such times, and then only in Latin. When desired, one of the staff may read or lecture to the others while at dinner. All food must be taken in the common hall to avoid private gluttony or tippling. The time for meals and daily services may be given generally as follows: Fellows were to rise at five and begin mattins at six, to have mass at eight o'clock, and finish all canonical hours by eleven to have a convenient hour for dinner. Vespers were to be said at three or four and to finish at five. In the interval of these services study or manual labour were to form part of the day's occupation. Fines had to be paid for absence from services, the amounts of which helped to swell the property of the college and also to benefit those who most regularly attended to their duties.

CHAPTER XIII.

BISHOP THOMAS KEMP.

THOMAS KEMP, who eventually became Bishop of London, had certainly better prospects at his birth than had his uncle, who at that time had already become famed as a lawyer. The son of Sir Roger Kempe of Ollantigh, he was probably born at the chief mansion of the family, Ollantigh, in 1405. His education was similar to that of his uncle. At first he daily attended at the old school of Christ Church, or the "King's School."

He was in due time entered at Merton, Oxford, and there his benefactions to the University, both during his lifetime and after his death, caused him, like his uncle, to be designated the

Macænas of the University, while special prayers were ordered to be recited for them at the Commemoration of Benefactors.

He was elected proctor of his college in 1437, to which, as well as to the Divinity Schools he was a liberal benefactor. Weaver states that it was this Bishop, and not Humphry, Duke of Gloucester, as it is commonly supposed, who was the chief builder of the "Divine School" as it stood before Bodley's foundation. Weaver enlarges on its beautiful "walls, arches, vaults, doors, towers and pinicales, all of square, smooth polisht stone and artificially depainted." He also speaks of "the Doctor's chair" and the "lively representation of the glorious frame of the celestial globe." It was, indeed, as old drawings show, a handsome building, but looking on such as this and the College at Wye and the schools there, we cannot but feel that these were after all but small institutions compared with the great buildings which the modern supporters of education put up. Yet in their day the money expended was a fair proportion of the donors' fortunes, and must be appreciated as works of very useful charity.

Speaking of his munificent gifts to the University, we are bound to say that the latter was not always content with freewill offerings, and seems to have pressed for funds for this purpose, even threatening to throw aside the prayers for the Kempes unless a large sum was given.

It appears that a Thomas Kemp was Rector Warden of the hospital called Eastbridge or Kingsbridge, in Canterbury, sometime between 1429-45. We do not know whether such an office could be held without the holder residing in the house, but it seems likely that this was one of the many positions which he filled. In any case we may remark here that this hospital had as part of its endowment two salt pits near Whitstable, and the windmills at Reculver and West-Halimot, in Thanet, as well as the tithes of Westgate Mill (Canterbury). This may have something to do with the later Kempes of those places settling, as they could under his influence obtain their leases on very favourable terms.

By this time his uncle had become Archbishop of York, and thus it was that Thomas Kempe was made a Canon of that Cathedral in 1431. In April, 1435, he received the Prebend of Stillington, which he vacated on the 7th July following on being presented to the Prebendal Stall of Driffield; he was subsequently made Prebendary of Langtoft. From 1439 till 1442 he held the Stall of Southcore, resigning this in the latter year, but was again admitted to it in 1447. On his first resignation he had been made Archdeacon of Richmond, and afterwards Chancellor of the See of York. During this time he was also Rector of Bolton Percy—a very fine church some six miles out of York—the patron of which was the Archbishop. It is likely that Thomas Kempe made this rectory his residence for a time, as he took considerable trouble to improve the church, erecting a large east window of well executed stained glass, in the centre of which he placed the portrait of his revered uncle, John Kempe, with his arms. This window was taken out to save it from destruction by fanatics, but has been recently replaced, and the Bishop of Beverley, who is now rector, took much trouble to point out to the writer the various ages of restoration indicated. Unfortunately the portion representing the Archbishop's face is among the modern pieces. The accompanying illustration shows the window in its present state.*

To the rear of the present rectory is a great tythe barn of ponderous carved timber, which must date back to the time when Prebendary Kempe stored his own grain there. Doubtless the humbler followers in the train of distinguished visitors were frequently provided with a night's shelter in this barn's upper story, which is now often used for parochial meetings and as a school.

About 1442 Thomas Kempe was Archdeacon of Middlesex, but the date of his appointment

* The arms contained in the window were noted by Sir William Dugdale in 1641, the book in the Herald's Office records no less than thirty-three coats in this window. Those that were original are noted in Drake's "Eboracum," page 386, Kempe being one.

and resignation is not recorded, the probability is that he resigned when he was re-admitted to the Prebendal Stall of Southcore, and became Archdeacon of Richmond in 1447. This, however, he did not hold long, for by virtue of a Bull, published by Pope Nicholas, he was proclaimed Bishop of London 21st August, 1448.

As in other instances of presentation by the Pope, the English Church objected to his appointment without first being elected by the Chapter of St. Paul's, and afterwards obtaining the approval of the King. Thus it was not until a year and a half after that he was consecrated Bishop by the hands of his uncle, the Archbishop of York, assisted by five Suffragans of the province of Canterbury, the ceremony taking place at York Place, now known as Whitehall. It is interesting to note that while the uncle thus consecrated his nephew, that nephew two years later (1452) had the pleasure of investing his uncle with the insignia of the Archbishopric of Canterbury and Cardinal Bishopric of Santa Rufina, this function being performed in the Bishop's Palace at Fulham.

During his long episcopate he must have lived the greater part of his time at that Palace, and arranged for the restoration and alteration of this official residence and manor house. The work, however, was not complete, even at his death, although the arms of the Kempes were the most prominent in the Bishop's Hall and the chief apartments as denoting that mnch of the palace was constructed by him. Bishop Fitz-James, who succeeded to the See in 1506, has the credit for what is now said to be the oldest existing portions of the palace. On this subject we would refer our readers to Fèret's "Fulham Old and New," in which full details of the palace are given, and in which many records of the various Kempes of that ancient parish are included. Those visiting Fulham will not fail to see the arms, mottoes, badges and other allusions to the Kempes, who together held the manor longer than those of any other name or family.

In 1456 we have an interesting specimen of the Bishop's mode of settling a dispute, and his independence and originality in administering the work of his diocese. The chapel of St. Stephen, in Coleman Street, had anciently belonged to the Canons of St. Paul's, who annexed it to St. Olave's, Jewry; with the latter it became appropriated to the Priory of Butley in Suffolk, and eventually a parish church. Between these various bodies a contention had long existed as to the right of presentation to the living; on the matter being placed before Bishop Kemp he ordered that in future *the parishoners should elect their own pastor*, which they have done ever since.

Bishop Thomas Kempe set a higher value on the use of sermons than many of his immediate predecessors, for he rebuilt the pulpit of St. Paul's Cross, which remained standing until the Puritans ruthlessly pulled it down, although it "was guilty of no superstition." There are numerous illustrations of St. Paul's Cross, differing much, but the original materials have entirely disappeared, and we can obtain no trace of any relics.

About the year 1478 the Bishop founded and endowed a chantry for one priest, at the Altar of the Holy Trinity, and instituted the Office of Penitentiary. To this he united the Church of Chigwell, Essex, and the Prebend of St. Pancras, from which the prebend has since been called the "Office or Dignity of the Penitentiary."

This chantry priest was to celebrate Divine Service daily at the High Altar of the Holy Trinity "for the good estate of the King, Queen Elizabeth, his wife, and the Bishop during their abode in this world, and also after their departure." We are told that the chantry was one of the most beautiful in Old St. Paul's At the destruction of the Cathedral in the great Fire of London this, of course, perished, but among the fragments of the old masonry, now treasured in the present edifice, there are pieces of stonework, the carving of which correspond with the illustration which we give of the fine tomb to this bishop, who, according to his desire, was buried within the chapel. Doubtless, the chapel and the tomb were of uniform style. The inscription on Bishop Kempe's tomb as given in "Tombs, Monuments, &c., in London Churches," was as follows:

"Infra Capellam istam requiescit corpus Domini Thomae Kempe quondam Episcopi Londinensis, Fundatoris eiusdem, et unius Cantariae perpetuae in eadem; qui multa bona tempore vitae suae Ecclesiae S. Pauli dedit et stetit XXXIX Annis LXXXIV diebus Episcopus Lond. ac obiit XXVIII die mensis Martli, anno Domini MCCCCLXXXIX. Cujus animae propitietur Deus. Amen.

This being rendered into the following English:

Beneath this chapel resteth the body of Thomas Kempe, sometime Bishop of London and founder of this chapel and of a chantry therein, forever. In his lifetime he was a bountiful benefactor to St. Paul's Church. He sat as Bishop of London thirty-nine years four-score and four days, and died 28th March, in the year of Grace 1489. On whose soul God have mercy."

Seal of Thomas Kempe,
Bishop of London, about 1475.

The various Episcopal Act books in use during Thomas Kempe's Episcopate are still to be seen, but we know of no other impression of his official seal than that here illustrated. This original, which is very imperfect, is exhibited with other seals of the diocese in a large case in the centre of the library over the Consistory Court in St. Paul's Cathedral, where it is accessible to the public. Among other important documents existing which was witnessed and signed by him, is the Charter to the City of Norwich, which was signed also by his uncle, Archbishop Kempe. We have not heard of any portrait or effigy of this Bishop, unless that on the seal represents himself.

His will was proved in the Prerogative Court of Canterbury. The original is lost, though the probate is extant. It is written in Latin and dated 4th February, 1488. He describes the chapel in St. Paul's, where he desires to be buried, as St. Erkinwold's. To his nephew, William Kempe, he left his missal; he also mentions his relatives, Thomas Kempe, John Kempe; the latter's son, John Kempe; Sir Robert Strelley, Knight, and his children; his kinsman, William Upton; John Read or Reede, boy of his chapel; the Archdeacon of Essex, Richard Lichfield, Archdeacon of Middlesex, and others.

A writ was issued for an inquisition of the late Bishop's estate on the 5th April, and the result of the inquiry was dated 8th May in the fourth year of Henry VII. The document, which is given in English in the "Calendar of Inquisition Post Mortem," printed by the British Record Office, is too long to be given here in full. It is, however, important as giving how his various properties were held.

A messuage or tenement called "Clente," with 200 acres of land, 24 acres of meadow, 120 acres of pasture, and 140 acres of wood in Wye, Crundel, Godmersham and Walham, held by the tenure of gavelkind, whereof 16 acres in Crundel were held from John Lee, the Master of the College of All Saints' at Maidstone; 26 acres of land at Wye, held of Thomas Combes, Esq., as of the Manor of Combe; 24 acres of pasture in Godmersham, held from the Prior of Christ Church, Canterbury; 7 acres of wood in Walham, held from the *Prior of St. John of Jerusalem*,* and the messuage called "Clente," and the residue of land worth 100*s*. of the Abbot of St. Martins, at Battle, Co. Sussex.

Besides these estates, which were all in one district, he held the Manor of Boughton Aluph, direct from the King, as of the Manor of Boulogne, by service of one Knight's fee; and the Manor of Stowting, from the Archbishop of Canterbury: the Manor of Ashemersfield, from the "Abbott of St. Augustines without the walls of Canterbury"; the Manor of Hadlow, from Jasper, Duke of Bedford, as of the Manor of Tunbridge, Kent; an acre of land at Staplehurst and the advowson of the church there, held from the Lordship of Merden; 60 acres in Staplehurst, called Henhurst, held from Alexander Clifford, Esq., as of the Manor of Sutton Valance, and other lands called Sandling, Saltwood, Postling. These lands the Bishop had entrusted to John Roper, Gent., Nicholas Wright, Clerk, and John Chauncey to the use of his will. The estate to be entailed on the male heirs of his nephew, Thomas Kempe, with remainder to daughters.

The escheators found that the Bishop had died on "Saturday after the Feast of Annunciation, and that Thomas Kempe, Esq., aged forty-four and more, is his cousin and heir, being son of William Kempe, the Bishop's brother.

* See other Kempe tenants under this Priory in Norfolk and Middlesex sections.

Tomb of Bishop Thomas Kempe in old St. Paul's.

Numerous other Kentish Kempes have been traced, and *all* their wills have been searched at Canterbury and London, but space at our disposal prevents us including details of them here.

Sir Robert Kempe—First Baronet.

Section II.

The Kemp and Kempe families of Norfolk and Suffolk.

The Kemp and Kempe Families of Norfolk and Suffolk.

CHAPTER I.

EARLY NORFOLK AND SUFFOLK KEMPES.

APART from tradition it is antecedently probable that the Kempes of Norfolk and Suffolk are of Saxon origin. Many facts support the belief which is current in the family. The significance of the name has already been discussed in another chapter, but it will be convenient to refer to it again. According to popular etymology, Kemp and Kempe are modern English forms of the Anglo-Saxon *Cempa*, a soldier. Whether the name means soldier or field of contest (for which view there is strong evidence) its Saxon derivation is undisputed.

A fact which was not mentioned in the chapter on the derivation of the name is the designation "Kemping" applied to competitions among reapers in the harvest field. This usage is found both in the south of Scotland and East Anglia, and probably in other parts of the country. Its history has not been traced, but were it proved to have existed, as in all probability it did, earlier than the custom of distinguishing families by heraldic arms it would account for the adoption of the three sheaves in the Kempe coat. The country folk in the eastern counties speak of the best sheaves in a field as "Battle" sheaves, from the belief that where human blood has been shed the corn grows more luxuriantly. Whatever sense the invention of the arms ascribed to the name the appropriateness of the sheaves is obvious.

There were in Norfolk before 1300, one or more members of the family known as Belle Kempe, signifying beautiful field. They survive to the present as Belkemps and Beauchamps. In Latin the name appears as Bello Campo, borne by the noble house of Warwick. By a play in words, though in total defiance of grammar, it might be rendered battlefield.

Such playful twistings of a name were dear to our mediæval forefathers. The very motto used by the Kempes of Norfolk supplies a rather far-fetched pun on the name. LuCEM sPero (Lucem Spero) has but a vague significance except in allusion to the name. Perhaps it is worth noting here that it reminds one of the dying words of Goethe, "Light, more light," the meaning of which has been variously interpreted as a request that the window of his chamber might be opened, or as a prayer for higher knowledge of spiritual truth. Even in the latter sense the words *Lucem Spero* are hardly likely to have suggested themselves to a warrior five hundred years ago as a family motto. Such an aspiration would be more likely to have emanated from a monastic cell. The present baronet suggests that "I hope for light" was the cry of the hooded hawk which is one of the crests of the family. When the identification of Kempe with CEMPA is borne in mind the word play appears much more natural than it does to modern ears.

There is a story current in the family concerning the origin of the shield. A king (whose name is not recorded) with his followers, being tired of falconry, were attracted by the shoutings of a band of reapers engaged in gathering in their equally allotted portions of their lord's harvest, this being one of the customary services in lieu of rent. "What game is this?" inquired the king. "Kemping" was the reply, followed by further explanation. The young men goaded to fresh efforts by their anxiety to display their skill before so noble a company presented a lively scene. His Majesty, in order to spur them to yet keener contest, promised three hundred acres and some kine to the man who first laid three sheaves at his feet. Hardly had the reaper laid his last sheaf down when one of the royal birds returning from his flight alighted upon it, whereupon the king granted him as arms and crest three sheaves and a hawk, an appropriate memorial of the incident whereby he obtained his estate. In the hall at Gissing there was formerly an old picture of unknown date representing the "Kempers" or reapers competing, but without the royal party. Also in the church reapers were introduced as supporters of the Kemp arms with evident allusion to the family tradition.

There is in Suffolk, near Blythburg, on the river Blyth, a locality known as Bulchamp, with a hamlet of the same name. In the immediate neighbourhood is the traditional site of a fierce battle in which the Christian Saxons of East Anglia were defeated by Penda, the ruler of the still heathen kingdom of Mercia. From this event the name is supposed by some to be derived. Camp, as stated in a former chapter, has among other meanings that of battle or contest, while the syllable bul is believed to represent the Anglo-Saxon bald, *i.e.*, bold. Hence, the name would signify "bold fight." It is quite possible that the name Kemp, meaning field of contest, may have reference to the traditional site of this battle being in the midst of the ancient settlements of the Kemps. It may be added that Kemps are known as tenants of Blythburg Abbey as early as 1187.

In 1154, a Gotfred Kempe was living at Norwich, his daughter having married that year Jevan Bladwell. From this time numerous individuals of the name occur in records of Norfolk and Suffolk. At Gasthorpe, on the border of these counties we know that there was a manor called "Kempes" before 1288, where at that date was living as its Lord, one, ADAM KEMPE, who paid two shillings and sixpence annually to the Abbey at Bury St. Edmunds. In the following year it was held by Gilbert Kempe, and in 1294 William Kempe gave part of it as a marriage portion to his daughter Lettice, on her marriage with William, of Norwich. This husband having died three years later, she married again, and her portion thus passed to Simon de la Majorwaring of Herling, and was afterwards considered part of East Hall Manor. The other portion in 1330 is recorded to have passed from Emma Kempe, a widow, to her son, JOHN KEMPE What remained of the manor after numerous charitable gifts and other assignments, decended to WILLIAM KEMP before 1341.

This manor was within ten miles of Gissing, and we suggest that Adam de Gissing, a Knight, who with Sir Nicholas Hastings founded and endowed the chapel to "All the Saints," at Gissing, in 1280, was one and the same with Adam Kempe of Kempe's Manor. We have ample proof that the Kempe and Hastings families were much together during the fourteenth century, and must have had interests in common, despite the fact that their properties were adjacent might tend to differences over boundaries and privileges. Of the marriage between Kempe and Hastings families we shall speak later, when we come to consider the recorded pedigree. Long before the above Kempes are known to have had Kempe's Manor, we find some of the name as land holders in in Norfolk and Suffolk.

To begin with, we may ask whether there is any known reason for the Kempes being associated with the Abbey of Bury St. Edmunds. In the study of small holdings in early times, it is noticeable that the tenants were closely attached to their greater owners. Even when they removed from one place to another they generally remained on the rolls of the same landlords. (We do not refer here to the vassels who were actually the property of the landlord, and could not quit the manor without his permission.) If, therefore, we find other early Kempes associated with the Abbey of Bury, we may infer a possible connexion with the families. Anyway, this Kempe Manor connected them with Suffolk.

A William Kempe was a tenant under St. Augustine's Priory, Blythburg, in that county 100 years earlier than the first date mentioned at Gasthorpe. This William and Ermesent, his wife, were living in 1187, and had a son named Bartholomew, who joined in the sale of their property at Darsham, to "Ralph de Bulitot, son of Geoffrey."

Among other property belonging to the Priory of Blythburg were lands at *Stubbing*, Heveningham, *Redisham*, Rushmere, and also at *Canterbury*. At Little *Redisham*, Robert Kempe was a witness to a deed (now among the Stow MSS.) dated 1411. William Kempe was possessed

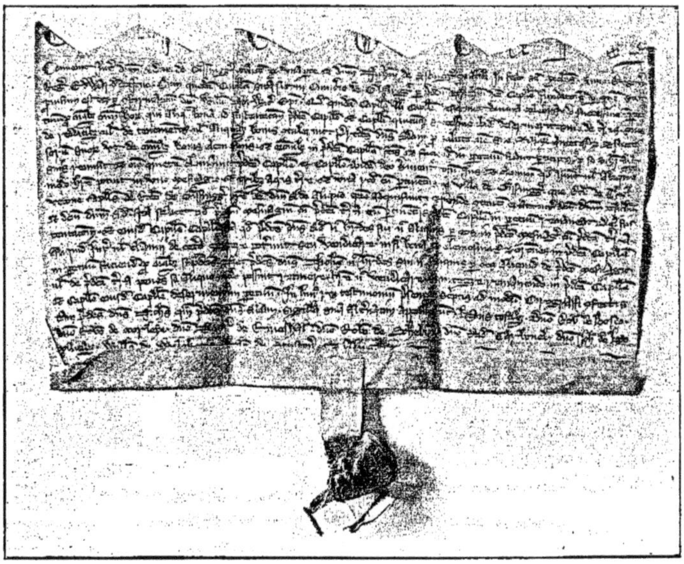

Royal Grant to Adam de Gissing and Sir Nicholas Hastings for founding a Chapel at Gissing in 1280.

of tenements at Heveringland, Norfolk, in 1343-4, and Isabelle Kempe had land called *Stubbing*, at Wenham Parva, as well as other lands in Chatsham and Belstede Magna, in Suffolk in 1347, which had been settled upon her by her son in 1327. Deeds relating to these are in the Record Office, and with them several which are dated in 1287, and witnessed by Geoffrey Kempe, Warden of Ipswich.

This name brings us to the first occurrence of the name of Kempe on the Norwich Charter Rolls, and although Kempes were even then numerous in East Anglia, we consider it probable that this Geoffrey was connected with, if not the same as Geoffrey Kempe, a citizen of Norwich, who, in 1294, had a grant of land in the parish of St. Lawrence. He had a son then living named Thomas. The next year Geoffrey Kempe le Clerke and Cecilia, his wife, are mentioned in

St. John, "Woddermarket" (? Maddermarket), Norwich, and twice more in 1305-6. This couple are also named in connexion with land and other property in St. Lawrence and the Market, which had formerly belonged to Arnold Kempe. (*See* Arnold Kempe under Boughton Aluph, Kent).

Geoffrey, we need hardly say, is rendered in Latin as Galfridus, and as such is recorded in "Rotuli Hundredorum." He is termed "Clerk of Norwich," but does not seem to have been either a city clerk or a clergyman. In the same record, and at the same period, "GALFRID KEMPE balli de Castello" is entered, which may represent him to be a Bailiff of the Castle, an office likely to be held by the same individual as he who was Warden of Ipswich.

In **1298** and 1305 Richard, son of GEOFFREY KEMPE and *Matilda*, is mentioned also in connexion with St. Lawrence, Norwich, and St. Margaret, Westwick.

In 1306, John Kempe appears with his wife Pleysinica, who was previously wife of Mathew de Swathing, a goldsmith of St. John, Maddermarket.

From the Close Rolls we find that one, Galfrid Kempe, was imprisoned at Norwich, with other persons, on a malicious charge of having been the cause of the death of "Thomas, the son of John de Ladnes," but the King sent authority to the Sheriff of the County to bail him out.

In **1321** RICHARD KEMPE was presented to the fifth Prebend or Provostship in Norwich Cathedral; perhaps it was the same Richard who was Rector of St. George's in Tombland, in Norwich in 1326, and the "Sir Richard Kempe," who as Chaplain of Hingham, was buried in that Church as mentioned by Blomfield. No monument now remains to his memory.

In 1349 a Walter Kempe was presented to the Vicarage of East Walton, from which he was transferred to the Rectory of St. Matthew the Apostle, Norwich, in 1364. A Walter Kempe was also a Rector of Narborough in 1370. From the fact that the Kempes of Essex were constantly represented in the West of Norfolk from early times until the last century, it is probable that this cleric was one of that family.

In 1346 Nicholas Kempe of Westwych, or West Winch, held a portion of the manor called Dovedales, in Newton, of which Peter de Ovedale was then, or previously, Lord. It was doubtless a kinsman of this Nicholas, who was in 1612 Rector of West Winch, both being, we believe, of the Essex stock, by whom at an early date the name of Nicholas was used. This is, perhaps, the first Nicholas Kempe of whom we find record, unless one Nicholas Kempyn, of North Erpingham, can be claimed as a Kemp. This latter was living old, blind and infirm in 1256, for which reason he could not attend a court, to which he owed homage. (Crown Plea Rolls). He may also be the first Kempe known in the Hundred. But it is doubtful if any Kempes were his offspring, for nearly a century later when the subsidies were collected we find only two Kempes in the Hundred. These are both found on the coast, and pay but small sums; it is, therefore, not improbable that they were foreigners, who had but recently settled, perhaps relatives of the Flemish Kempe weavers who had license to establish their craft in England in the reign of Edward III. (the King to whom these subsidies were paid). Their names were Thomas Kempe of Beeston, who paid two pence, the lowest amount collected in 1334-5. Roger Kempe of Sherringham, who paid the same amount in 1327, when other people paid from twelve to eighteen pence each.

In **1374** a William Ke*nt*pe witnessed the will of Sir John de Reppes, one of whose daughters was Alice de Redisham. This testator mentions the Church of Antingham, and from the names of other witnesses, it seems likely that William was related to him, thus for the first time on record, ***Kempe and Antingham*** are brought together. It was not, however, until two hundred years later that the Kempes made Antingham one of their favourite seats.

In 1379 we find that Richard Kempe, a tanner of Fletcham, was made a Freeman of Norwich. The same honour was conferred upon Thomas Kimmppe in 1405, and Gregory Kempe soon afterwards. John Kempe, a carpenter in the reign of Henry VI., was also a Freeman of this City; also Thomas Kempe, a tailor, in 1456. When we recall the fact of the woollen industry, having an early home at Worsted, and that much of their manufacture was shipped from Norwich to the Continent, it seems probable that these tailors, mercers, and tanners were also of *foreign* origin.

In 1451-2 Norwich obtained the great Charter which may still be seen at the Castle Museum. This was signed by John Kempe, Cardinal and Archbishop of York, and Lord Chancellor of England, and his nephew, Thomas Kempe, then Bishop of London. Among other names thereon are the Duke of Norfolk as Marshal of England, and Duke of Somerset as Constable of England.

CHAPTER II.

ROOTS OF THE TREE.

JUST south of Gasthorpe and Garboldisham, but in Suffolk, lie two Westons, Coney Weston and Market Weston. Owing to their proximity to "Kempe's Manor," and being on the route which must have been taken by these Kempes when they repaired to Bury St. Edmunds to pay their dues, it would be easy to believe that one of these was the Weston, which according to the pedigree was the earlier seat of the Kemps of Gissing.

We have, however, evidence that it was another Weston in the north-east corner of Suffolk. In the "Rotuli Hundredorum" for the county, we find that in the time of Edward I. Alan Kempe was rated at five shillings for land which he held at *Weston in the Hundred of Waynesford*, and William Kempe and his sons, John and Alan are mentioned. This Weston is further identified by the deeds now at the Records Office, which as we have said relate to Redisham, the adjoining parish to this.

For further proof of the Kempes being here we turn to the Suffolk fines (for which details we are indebted to Mr. Walter Rye). The most important item touching the present question is an entry made in the 11th year of Edward II. (1318), which runs as follows:—"Henry, son of Robert le Clerk, of Carlton, and Aullina, his wife, V. Geoffrey, son of Alan Kempe, of Weston, in Carlton, Rushmere, Mutford, Barnaby and Honberg."

The Carlton here referred to is, doubtless, Carlton Colville, which is close to Mutford and Barneby, and Rushmere is just south of these. A few miles southward again we come to Blythburg, the priory at which received dues or charities from the Kempes as early as 1187, and as we have said owned land at some of those places, at which the Kempes also had possessions.

It would then be reasonable to suppose that at some earlier period, for which no records now exist, an ancestor of the family settled or bequeathed a portion of his lands on this Priory of St. Augustine, and that others of the family caused a charge to be made on their estates to the end that in return for these benefactions the monastery would "pray for the health of their souls."

We have before spoken of the custom of one religious house entertaining the friends and tenants of another of the same order; and we suggest that in this way these Suffolk Kempes were likely to communicate with those in Kent, some of whom we have seen were tenants of the St. Augustine at Canterbury, in which city this Blythburgh Priory also had property. The frequent interchange of Combe and Kempe in early documents has been notified. We here call attention to the coincidence, that while Alan Kempe held his property at Weston the same authority tells us that Alan Combe held a messuage and lands in Kent from Alic de Schalar, by service of three capons, and that at this time also "Barthus * de Combis" paid fourteen pence as rent for his lands at "Blackburn," in Suffolk, and another three pence for other neighbouring property.

The Calendars of Wills for Norfolk do not commence until 1416, they show that *Comp* was the favourite spelling between that date and 1450; Thomas Comp of Ashfield, there can be little doubt, belonged to the same family as William Kempe of Griston, who in 1304 had some interest in that place. In course of another half century *Campe* had become a common rendering.

In the Calendar of Ipswich Wills, which commences in 1400, no *Comp* or *Cemp* occurs at this period, the Kempes there having settled upon the spelling, which they continued uninterruptedly until about the end of the seventeenth century, when they dropped the final E.

William Kempe, of Griston, was also concerned with lands in Walsham and Stanton, as well as Ashfield Parva in 1304, and in 1313 William and John Kempe paid a fine relative to properties in "Elgh and Wylyngham," which were also the subject of a fine in 1327, the parties then being William Kempe and Agnes Kempe, with Walter de Blyford. (Blyford is close to Blythburgh.) The identity of these places is not quite clear, but we presume that Ellough and Wellingham, near Weston, are meant.

It is interesting to find that Ubbeston, which was centuries later a seat of the family, was so early as 1311 partly held by one Roger Kempe. He, with his wife, Alice, was concerned that year with Adam Love, of Westhale, in settlements of land situated in *Ubbeston*, *Laxfield*, and Huntingfield. Laxfield is the place of residence of the first Kempe, whose will is preserved in the Ipswich Probate Court. His Christian name was GODFRID, the date of proving being 1444 or 1445. The will of Alice Kempe, of Laxfield, also appears in the Calendar, between 1458 and 1477.

Summing up the groups of Kempes, so far briefly reviewed in Norfolk and Suffolk, we find them as follows:—

At Darsham, as tenants of St. Augustine's, Blythburg, in 1187.

At Kempe's Manor, Garboldisham, from 1288 till 1330, as tenants of the Abbey of Bury St. Edmunds.

At Weston, *circa* 1300 to 1555.

At Norwich, from 1150.

At Ipswich and around, from 1294.

And in and around Monks Eleigh, from 1372.

It is noticeable that Darsham is just equi-distant from Norwich and Ipswich, although not in a direct line between them. The dates, so far ascertained, would lead us to suppose that the Ipswich family came to Norwich, and as the land around the former was acquired soon after the Geoffrey Kempe was Warden of that borough, it would appear probable that his office led to his settling in or near the latter place. This supposition is in accord with the suggestion made by Blomfield, in the "History of Norfolk," who, however, had it seems even slighter evidence to guide him. The other ancestors which he gives, as additional to those authorised by the

* Contraction for Bartholomaeus.

"Heraldic Visitations," he appears to have obtained from the collections made by Robert Kempe about the end of the sixteenth century.

This collection of matter relating to the county families of Norfolk and Suffolk, as well as the Kempes of Kent, is now at the British Museum (Harl. MSS., 901.) It has his arms inside the cover—three sheaves within a bordure engrailed, and a crescent for difference. On page 10 he starts the "Descent of Kempe of Weston, in Suffolk," with Norman de Campo, Rogerus de Campo, and a remark to the effect that these were "vulgarly called Kempe." These are followed by Roger Kempe, Ralph Kempe, William Kempe, and then the Allan Kempe, the latter being the first on the pedigree of "Herald's Visitation."

It is certainly rather curious if the family at so early a date attributed their name to their Saxon origin, as Blomfield states, that they should have started their pedigree with a Norman Kempe.

Accepting for the moment these ancestors, we find Ralph Kempe to be the grandfather of Allan Kempe of Weston. The latter we have shown was living in 1318, and he is said to have married before 1324. At that time his grandfather might reasonably be living; but he does not so far as we have traced appear as a land-holder in Norfolk or Suffolk. Now we find from the custumals of Battle Abbey that Radulphus de Campis, otherwise RALPH KEMPE, was between 1283 and 1312 a tenant of that monastery as stated under our records of the Kempes of Wye, and that at this time Galfrid Kempe was also a tenant of the same house, having his holding situated in the Manor of "Lymenesfield," in Sussex. Thus, so far as dates are concerned, Ralph Kempe, of Kent, and Galfrid Kemp, of Sussex, might be the same individuals as those connected with this Norfolk pedigree.

It has, apparently, *always* been claimed that those of Wye and those of Gissing were of the same original stock, and the early authorised use of the same coat would seem to acknowledge this. Yet the relationship has, it seems, never been traced.

Taking another aspect of the matter, and adhering to our theory of migration as influenced by monastic tenures, we revert to Bury St. Edmunds.

The only portrait claimed as that of Archbishop Kempe was formerly in the "Abbey of St. Edmundsbury"—so Lyson in his work on London tells us. The question as to whether it really represents him has been threshed out in the pages of *Notes and Queries*, with the result that we may rest assured that the portrait is his, and that beyond doubt it was at Bury with that of Humphrey, Duke of Gloucester, both of whom were benefactors of this place and of Oxford. The original Register of Expenses at Bury St. Edmunds is in the Harleian Library (645), it is entitled on the vellum cover as follows:—

"Registrum KEMPE olim ad Abbattiam Sci. Edmundi, in agro Suffolciensi pertinens."

Either the paintings themselves, or replicas, were placed in the Abbey of Barking, in Essex, about the time of Bishop Thomas Kempe's death. This convent was founded by Saint Erkenwold, by whose shrine in St. Paul's this bishop desired to be buried. St. Erkenwald was a Saxon, great grandson of Uffa, the first King, and second son of Anna, the seventh King of the East Angles, which may account for the especial veneration in which the Kempes held him. (He was made bishop of London in 675.)

Alice Kempe, of the Weston family, became a nun at this abbey at Barking. Why she should enter so distant a convent when there were many nearer is a mystery, unless due to the same esteem for the founder, or for its being patronised by her renowned kinsmen, Archbishop and Bishop Kempe. She must have been there some forty years after the death of the latter, possibly until the suppression under Henry VIII.

Between this house and the Convent of Chertsey there were great disputes as to the interment of the body of this St. Erkenwald, each claiming exclusive right to the bones of the venerable prelate The connection between these houses may have occasioned the settlement of Kempes at Chertsey. John Kempe had a grant of a toft of land in that place in 1379-80, the deed making this grant is preserved at the Record Office. The grantor was John de Thorpe. This was not the first Kempe in Chertsey, for back in 1235 one, Gilbert Kempe, of Chertsey (Certesey), conveyed a portion of his estate to Phillip de Henley.

Gilbert being one of the names associated with Kempe's Manor in Norfolk, there may be a connexion between the two; while Ailwin Kempe, who was a landowner in the Hundred of Blackheath, Surrey, in 1205, suggests by his name a distinctly Saxon origin. Perhaps Ailwin became corrupted in time to Allan, for so far the Kempes had not come into touch with Scotland, whence it would be expected the name of Allan might be derived.

If, however, Allan Kempe of Weston was neither connected with Ailwin Kempe, of Surrey, nor drew his name from the name of Allan so prevalent in Scotland, he may yet have been connected through the Scotts of Brabourne, in Kent, with North Britain as recorded in our Kentish section of this work. We must also bear in mind the tradition of the Kentish Kempe family, that their ancestors came from "the North," from which we may further argue, that if this tradition holds good for Kent it may do so also for those of Weston and Gissing. We fear that all evidence in favour of this is, however, prehistoric. One more word, however, may be said in support of the connexion between Scottish and English Kempes. This Allan Kempe of Weston, we are told, had at least two sons, John, who succeeded him at Weston, and Alexander Kempe, of whose further existence we have no trace in Norfolk, Suffolk, Essex or Kent. He appears to have left the country. One of the earliest Kempes whom we find in Scotland, though at a much later date, is an Alexander Kempe, who was a favourite of King James V. It is very possible that the Christian name was handed down from the one to the other. Alexander is one of the names oftenest used by the Kempes of Edinburgh and the Lowlands since 1500.

With regard to the early ancestors named by Blomfield in his account of the Kempes of Gissing, in his great "History of Norfolk," beyond the facts that such individuals did live about the time he ascribes to them, there is no conclusive evidence that they were the progenitors of the Weston or Gissing Kempes. When, however, he tells us that Ralph Kempe married a daughter of De la Haute, and that their son, William, married a daughter of Barstaple or Bainspath,* we must think that he had some reasonable ground for making such a statement. We have sought to trace these ladies in records of their respective families, and among the ancient documents of the present Baronet, but have found nothing more than the bare repetition of the statements dating apparently no further back than the eighteenth century. When the family histories connected with these names come to be written these points may be cleared up. Meanwhile we cannot feel quite certain that these early ancestors of the Kempes are correctly recorded. While there is no reason why we should set them entirely aside we yet suggest that like the de Campos they were but individuals of whose existence Blomfield had but a bare knowledge. Had it been possible to establish a claim to them as direct ancestors, the Elizabethan Kempes of Gissing would have effected their being recorded as such in the official "Heraldic Visitations."

We have shown that the Ralph Kempe and Geoffrey Kempe claimed by Blomfield as progenitors of the Weston and Gissing Kempes synchronize with individuals of the same name in Kent and Sussex, and that Blythburgh Abbey had communication with Canterbury. It is feasible therefore to believe that at about this time (1180) the Norfolk Kempes held lands in each county;

* Bainspath sounds like a northern name. Cf. Brancepeth, Copeth, Morpeth. Bain is a Scottish name.

Norman de Camp *d for leaving the King's Court, 1127.*

Gotfred Kempe, lived at Norwich in 1154=

Rogerus de Campe *Master of the Knight's Hospitallers, 1160.* *Anne Kempe=Jwan Bladwell.*

Ralf Kempe (said *do. do. 1231.*

t Chertsey, Surrey. Living 1235.

William Kempe (s *horpe, Norfolk, in 1288. Gilbert Kemp held* "KEMPE'S MANOR" *in 1289.*

held "Kempe's Manor," Gasthorpe in 1294=Emma Kempe of same, living 1330.

Arnold Kempe, of *1st husband.* *2nd husband.*

William de Norwich=Lettice Kempe=Simon de la Mainwaring.

Geofrey Kempe, W *the same as William K. of "Ely," living in 1327 with his wife Agnes.*

of the City of N *d Kempe, of Monk's Eleigh, living in 1372.*

?

John Kempe, of W d Kempe (perhaps Rector of Heigham) | Anne or Margaret Kempe, mar. . . Loveday, of Norwich. | Alice Kempe.

bur. there 1459 (?

er to Robert Beuteveleyn=a co-heir of Thomas Gardiner.

William Beuteveleyn, an idiot, died S.P.

? 1st wife

=Elizabeth, sister to Robert Beuteveleyn.

eth Kempe,=Thomas Herteshorne, of Gissing, Esq.

f Beuteveleyn.

Elizabeth, dau. and | Richard Kempe. | Cicely Kempe=John Moulton. | Alice Kempe, a Nun at Barking.

of Mergate Hall,

Ann=Sir Richd. B | Kempe=Robert Blaverhausett, of Princethorpe, Warwickshire. | Florence Kempe=Sir Philip Woodall, of Frampton, Suffolk.

of Harlston,

Elizabeth, d. of Ed e, | William Kempe. | Francis Kempe, of Little Hadham. | Elizabeth Kempe=Lionel Throgmorton, of Flixton, Suffolk.

of Bucking

Alice, d. of Phillip | obert Kempe, of ry St. Edmunds, =Agnes, dau. of illiam Staunton. | William Kempe, of Cambridge. | Edward Kempe. | Elizabeth Kempe, =John Buxton.

Hampstead, Mdse

Robert Kempe, of

at Hampstead 15

Jane, d. of Sir Ma | Kempe, ham. on 1642. | Col. Matthew Kempe, of Virginia. | Dorothy Kempe, =William Jackman. | Elizabeth Kempe, =Sir Robert Kempe, Knight, of Finehingfield.

of Betchworth C

Bart.

1st wife.

Mary, d. of Thoma | e Kempe=Thomas Waldegrave. | Maurice Shelton=Elizabeth Kempe.

Shelley, Suffolk,

Jane Waldegrave.

1st wife.

Letitia, d. of Robe | pe, ois, | Elizabeth Kempe, died unmarried. | Elizabeth, d. of Henry Shardelow (or ? Shallcross)=William Kempe, Esq., of Antingham, died 1744. Tomb in Antingham Church.=Jane Coleman, mar. 1704, died 1705.

of Thurlow, Suf

the widow of Sir

Kempe, Knight.

Letitia Kempe, M

born 1694. Ed | cilla, d. and co-heir of Thos. Holden. arried A. Merry. | Sir Benjamin Kemp, 7th Bart., Physician of Coln St. Dennis, Glo. born 1708, died 1777.

1st husb. 2nd husb.

Sir John Kemp, | John Cook,=Elizabeth Kemp,=James Gay, of | of Horsted. died 1803 North Walsham.

born 1754, died un

Sir William Rober

died Octo

The Rev. Sir Will | Francis Woodrow. | Melissa=Capt. Thos. Withers, R.N. | Elinora=Shephard Holmes. | Sarah=Richd. Fish.

10th Bart., Rect

Flordon, born 17

Mary, d. of Admir | Sarah, infant. | Elinora Sarah Caroline, S.P. | Lucretia Melissa, S.P. died 1901. | Jane Louise, died an infant.

Hagar.

Ca . . . ar Ke aroline Russell Kemp=Rev. John Sharp, D.D., late Rector of Elmle Lovets.

of the body of this St. Erkenwald, each claiming exclusive right to the bones of the venerable prelate The connection between these houses may have occasioned the settlement of Kempes at Chertsey. John Kempe had a grant of a toft of land in that place in 1379-80, the deed making this grant is preserved at the Record Office. The grantor was John de Thorpe. This was not the first Kempe in Chertsey, for back in 1235 one, Gilbert Kempe, of Chertsey (Certesey), conveyed a portion of his estate to Phillip de Henley.

Gilbert being one of the names associated with Kempe's Manor in Norfolk, there may be a connexion between the two; while Ailwin Kempe, who was a landowner in the Hundred of Blackheath, Surrey, in 1205, suggests by his name a distinctly Saxon origin. Perhaps Ailwin became corrupted in time to Allan, for so far the Kempes had not come into touch with Scotland, whence it would be expected the name of Allan might be derived.

If, however, Allan Kempe of Weston was neither connected with Ailwin Kempe, of Surrey, nor drew his name from the name of Allan so prevalent in Scotland, he may yet have been connected through the Scotts of Brabourne, in Kent, with North Britain as recorded in our Kentish section of this work. We must also bear in mind the tradition of the Kentish Kempe family, that their ancestors came from "the North," from which we may further argue, that if this tradition holds good for Kent it may do so also for those of Weston and Gissing. We fear that all evidence in favour of this is, however, prehistoric. One more word, however, may be said in support of the connexion between Scottish and English Kempes. This Allan Kempe of Weston, we are told, had at least two sons, John, who succeeded him at Weston, and Alexander Kempe, of whose further existence we have no trace in Norfolk, Suffolk, Essex or Kent. He appears to have left the country. One of the earliest Kempes whom we find in Scotland, though at a much later date, is an Alexander Kempe, who was a favourite of King James V. It is very possible that the Christian name was handed down from the one to the other. Alexander is one of the names oftenest used by the Kempes of Edinburgh and the Lowlands since 1500.

With regard to the early ancestors named by Blomfield in his account of the Kempes of Gissing, in his great "History of Norfolk," beyond the facts that such individuals did live about the time he ascribes to them, there is no conclusive evidence that they were the progenitors of the Weston or Gissing Kempes. When, however, he tells us that Ralph Kempe married a daughter of De la Haute, and that their son, William, married a daughter of Barstaple or Bainspath,* we must think that he had some reasonable ground for making such a statement. We have sought to trace these ladies in records of their respective families, and among the ancient documents of the present Baronet, but have found nothing more than the bare repetition of the statements dating apparently no further back than the eighteenth century. When the family histories connected with these names come to be written these points may be cleared up. Meanwhile we cannot feel quite certain that these early ancestors of the Kempes are correctly recorded. While there is no reason why we should set them entirely aside we yet suggest that like the de Campos they were but individuals of whose existence Blomfield had but a bare knowledge. Had it been possible to establish a claim to them as direct ancestors, the Elizabethan Kempes of Gissing would have effected their being recorded as such in the official "Heraldic Visitations."

We have shown that the Ralph Kempe and Geoffrey Kempe claimed by Blomfield as progenitors of the Weston and Gissing Kempes synchronize with individuals of the same name in Kent and Sussex, and that Blythburgh Abbey had communication with Canterbury. It is feasible therefore to believe that at about this time (1180) the Norfolk Kempes held lands in each county;

* Bainspath sounds like a northern name. Cf. Brancepeth, Copeth, Morpeth. Bain is a Scottish name.

DESCENT OF THE KEMP BARONETS OF NORFOLK AND SUFFOLK.

Norman de Campo, otherwise called Norman Kempe.
Rogerus de Campo or Roger Kempe.
Ralf Kempe (said to have) married a dau. of De la Haute.
William Kempe (said to have) married a dau. of Barstaple or Bainspath.

1170—1187. William Kempe, a tenant of lands under=Ermesent, living 1187. the Abbey of Blythburg, Suffolk.
Bartholomew Kempe, living 1187.
Robert de Gissing.
Sir Nicholas Hastings and Sir Adam de Gissing, Knt., founded Gissing Church, 1280.

Sweetman Kempe fin'd for leaving the King's Court, 1127.
Golfred Kempe, lived at Norwich in 1154=
Amaldus de Campis, Master of the Knight's Hospitallers, 1160. *Anne Kempe=Juan Bladwell.*
Bertrand de Campis do. do. 1231.
Gilbert Kempe, lived at Chertsey, Surrey. Living 1235.
Adam Kempe held "Kempe's Manor," Gasthorpe, Norfolk, in 1288. Gilbert Kemp held "KEMPE'S MANOR" in 1289.
William Kempe held "Kempe's Manor," Gasthorpe in 1294=Emma Kempe of same, living 1330.

Arnold Kempe, of Norwich, living in 1305.
Isabelle, daughter of Edmund and Philippa Hastings=Allan Kempe, Lord of Weston, Suffolk, (Isabelle Kempe, widow at Little Wenham, Suff. 1347) living in 1318 (had mar. before 1324)
John Kempe,= living 1330. | ob. ante 1341.
1st husband. William de Norwich=Lettice Kempe=Simon de la Maimwaring. 2nd husband.
William Kempe, perhaps the same as William K. of "Ely," living in 1327 with his wife Agnes.
Edmund Kempe, of Monk's Eleigh, living in 1372.

Geofrey Kempe, Warden of Ipswich and=Matilda, living 1305. of the City of Norwich, 1287-1318.
Richard Kempe, living 1305.
Alice or Agnes, living in 1350=John Kempe, of Weston, (said to be heiress of Duke and Beutevelyn) living in 1347 and perhaps 1376.

? John Kempe, of Woodbridge,=Margaret. bur. there 1459 (? 2nd son) 1st
2nd Joan. 3rd Margaret.
1st wife. Mary, dau. of Bartholomew White,=Robert Kempe,=Agnes. 2nd wife. of Shotisham, Norfolk. of Weston. 3rd wife. =Katherine, dau. of Roger Hawker, of Redenhall, living 1473.
Ralph Kempe (3rd son) perhaps Rector of Harlow, 1429.
Richard Kempe (perhaps Rector of Heigham)
Anne or Margaret Kempe, mar. . . Loveday, of Norwich.
Alice Kempe.

Margaret, dau. of . . . . Sherrington,=Jeffrey Kempe, of Weston, of Cranworth, Norfolk, Esq. living 1440. (Perhaps also of Woodbridge, a will proved 1444.
John Kempe=Alice, dau. of Robert Duke, of Brampton, Suffolk, by Julian, sister to Robert Beuteveleyn=a co-heir of Thomas Gardiner.
William Beuteveleyn, an idiot, died S.P.

(Margaret or) Elizabeth, dau. of William Curzon, of Stutton=Robert Kempe, of Weston, co-heir of Duke, Beuteveleyn and Gardiner. Deed of Settlement, 1473=Elizabeth, sister to Robert Beuteveleyn. ? 1st wife or Sturton, Suffolk (? at Fundenhall in 1521) buried at Gissing about 1518.
Elizabeth Kempe,=Thomas Herteshorne, of Gissing, Esq. co-heir of Beuteveleyn.

Elizabeth, dau. and heir of John Appleyard,=Robert Kempe, of Weston, Flordon and=Anne, dau. of John Clifford, of Mergate Hall, Braconash. Gissing, died 1526. P.M.I, 1527 of Holmedale, Kent.
2nd Edmund Kempe, Merchant, of London.
John Kempe, (? of Fundenhall)
William Kempe, Rector of Sproughton.
Ralf Kempe
Richard Kempe.
Cicely Kempe=John Moulton.
Alice Kempe, a Nun at Barking.

Anne=Sir Richd. Bacon, of Harlston, Norf.
Mary=Thomas Jernygan, of Cove, Suffolk.
Elizabeth, Lady of Bed-chamber to Qn. Catherine.
Bartholomew Kempe, of Weston, Gissing, Flordon, &c.=Anne, dau. of John Alleyn, aged 35 in 1527, died 1554, I.P.M. 1554. of Bury St. Edmunds.
Lewis Kempe, living in 1529.
Margaret Kempe=Robert Blaverhassett, of Princethorpe, Warwickshire.
Florence Kempe=Sir Philip Woodall, of Frampton, Suffolk.

Elizabeth, d. of Edmund Smythwin,=Robert Kempe, of Gissing & Flordon,=Elizabeth, d. of Edmund de Grey, of Buckinghamshire died 1594, aged 80. of Merton, Norfolk.
Bartholomew Kempe, of London, M.P. for Eye 1586-8 & Shaftesbury.
Anthony Kempe, of Flordon, S.P.
Edward Kempe, Merchant, of Lon.
John Kempe, S.P.
William Kempe.
Francis Kempe, of Little Hadham.
Elizabeth Kempe=Lionel Throgmorton, of Flixton, Suffolk.

Alice, d. of Phillip Cockeram, of=Richard Kempe, Councillor of Ipswich, of Hampstead, Mdsex. mar. 1566. Washbrook, Gissing & Flordon, died 1600.
John Kempe, of Antingham, died 1610. Left a son Robert Kempe, who gave his estates to his cousin Sir Robert Kempe, of Gissing, 1626.
Margaret Kempe, =Thos. Rouse.
Anne Kempe, =Anthony Drury.
Other children died infants.
Thomas Kempe, of Little Bricit & Beccles. (see Thwaite Pedigree)
Robert Kempe, of Bury St. Edmunds, =Agnes, dau. of William Staunton.
William Kempe, of Cambridge.
Edward Kempe.
Elizabeth Kempe, =John Buxton.

Robert Kempe, of Gissing & Flordon, bap.=Dorothy, d. of Arthur Harris, of at Hampstead 1567, bur. at Gissing 1612. Cricksea, Essex. Will 1626.

Jane, d. of Sir Matthew Browne,=Sir Robert Kempe, Knight & Baronet, of Betchworth Castle, Surrey, Gent. of the Privy Chamber to Bart. Charles I., of Gissing, Flordon and Antingham. Will 1647.
John Kempe, =Amphillis Bigot.
Rev. Arthur Kempe, of Cricksea. Will 1645. S.P.
Richard Kempe, Secretary of Virginia,=Dame Eliz. Lunsford.
Edmund Kempe, of Virginia.
Edward Kempe, of Virginia.
Thomas Kempe, of Antingham. Administration 1642.
Col. Matthew Kempe, of Virginia.
Dorothy Kempe, =William Jackman.
Elizabeth Kempe, =Sir Robert Kempe, Knight, of Finchingfield.

1st wife. Mary, d. of Thomas Kerridge, of=Sir Robert Kempe, 2nd Bart.,=Mary, d. and sole heir of John Sone, 2nd wife. Shelley, Suffolk, died 1655. born at Walshingham Abbey 1627, died 1710. of Ubbeston, Suffolk. died 1705.
Thomas Kempe.
Matthew Kempe, of Virginia.
Richard Kempe. Will 1714, S.P.
Jane Kempe=Thomas Waldegrave.
Jane Waldegrave.
Maurice Shelton=Elizabeth Kempe.

1st wife. Letitia, d. of Robert King,=Sir Robert Kempe, 3rd Bart.,=Mary Elizabeth, d. of=Martha, d. of William=Amy, d. of RichardP of Thurlow, Suffolk, by of Ubbeston, born 1667, John Brand Colt, of Blackwell, of Mortlock, Phillips, of the widow of Sir Robert died 1734. Edwardeston, d. 1709 Surrey, died 1727. Edwardeston, widow Kempe, Knight. of John Burroughs, died 1745. (2nd wife. 3rd wife. 4th wife.)
John Kempe, died young.
Robert Kempe, died young.
Jane Kempe. =John Dade, M.D., of Tannington, Suffolk.
Mary Kempe, =Sir Charles Blois, mar. 1680.
Elizabeth Kempe, died unmarried.
Elizabeth, d. of=William Kempe, Esq.=Jane Coleman, Henry Shardelow (or ? Shallcross) of Antingham, died 1744. Tomb in Antingham Church. mar. 1704, died 1705.
Martha K.=Darell Short.
William, died young.

Letitia Kempe, born 1694.
Mary Kempe=Sir Edmund Bacon, Bart., of Garboldisham
Sir Robert Kemp, 4th Bart., born 1699, died unmar. 1752.
Sir John Kemp, 5th Bart.=Elizabeth, d. of Thos. Mann born 1700, died S.P. 1761. and widow of John Colt.
Isaac. d. young.
Edward. d. young.
Anne, d. of . . . Mallum, Esq.=Rev. Thomas Kemp,=Priscilla, d. and co-heir Rector of Gissing, of Thos. Holden. born 1706, d. 1761. re-married A. Merry.
Sir Benjamin Kemp, 7th Bart., Physician of Coln St. Dennis, Glo. born 1708, died 1777.

Sir John Kemp, 6th Bart. born 1754, died unmarried 1771.
Robert Kemp. unmarried.
Mary Kemp, S.P. died 1784.
Sir William Kemp, 8th Bart.=Mary, d. of . . . Ives, of died at Worstead 1799 Coltshall, died 1762.
Robert Kemp, died S.P.
1st husb. John Cook,=Elizabeth Kemp,=James Gay, of 2nd husb. of Horsted. died 1803 North Walsham.

Sir William Robert Kemp, 9th Bart.=Sarah, d. of Thomas Adcock, died October, 1804. of Carlton.
Sarah, d. of . . . Cooke=Thomas Benjamin Kemp, of Swaffield, died 1837.
1st wife. Mary, d. of . . . Groat,=John Kemp,= & widow of . . . Chandler. S.P. 2nd wife.

The Rev. Sir William Robert Kemp,=Mary, d. of Charles Saunders, 10th Bart., Rector of Gissing and Esq., of Camberwell. Flordon, born 1791, died 1874.
Sir Thomas Kemp, 11th Bart. S.P. died 1874.
Rev. Thomas Cooke Kemp,=Jane, d. of Robt. Pretyman, Rector of East Meon, b. 1787. Esq., of Eye, Suffolk.
Clarissa=Ebenezar Randall.
Lucretia=Francis Woodrow.
Melissa=Capt. Thos. Withers, R.N.
Elinora=Shephard Holmes.
Sarah=Richd. Fish.

Mary, d. of Admiral=The Rev. Nunn Robert Hagar. Pretyman Kemp.
Mary Louisa, d. of A. Canham,=Thomas Cooke Kemp. of Fordam, Cambs. S.P.
(Two sons of same names died as infants)
Martha Maria,=James Barnard, mar. 1830. of Bordean.
Jane Sarah, died infant.
Elinora Sarah Caroline, S.P.
Lucretia Melissa, S.P. died 1901.
Jane Louise, died an infant.

Captain Edgar Kemp, of=Ellen, d. of Alfred Giles, Esq., M.P. the 4th King's Own. S.P. died 1873.
Sir Kenneth Hagar Kemp, 12th Bart.,=Henrietta Mary Eva, d. of Henry Hamilton, Esq., of born at Erpingham, 1853. Chilham, Kent, and late of Blackrock, Ireland.
Caroline Russell Kemp=Rev. John Sharp, D.D., late Rector of Elmley Lovets.
Edgar Sharp, born 1887.

Robert Hamilton Kemp (only son and heir) Lieut. 3rd Batt. Norfolk Regiment.
Eva Constance Kemp.
Margaret Hagar Kemp.
Violet Mary Kemp.
Ida Dorothy Kemp, mar. at Flordon, 1901=Robert Gwilt, Esq., Hartest, Suffolk.

and that their property being thus divided the senior branch would naturally retain the ancestral holdings in Norfolk, the Kempes of Wye being the junior branch. This hypothesis best meets the tradition that the Kempes of Ollantigh came "from the North," and that they were of the same stock (indicated by a common heraldic coat) as those of Norfolk.

There is one other little point which we may mention here, Adam Kempe, of Kempe's Manor, Adam de Gissing, and Allan Kempe of Weston, were living about the same time, and knowing how often at this period a man was given a variety of appellations it seems quite within probability that these three names represented one and the same individual.

CHAPTER III.

THE SUFFOLK ANCESTORS.

WE now come to the consideration of the accepted and official pedigree of the Kempes of Norfolk. This certainly dates from before the time of Elizabeth, for in the "Visitation of London" the arms are given of EDMUND KEMPE, citizen of London, who died in 1542, being one of the Weston (Suffolk) family. The earliest official record of which we have actual knowledge is Harvey's "Visitation of Norfolk," in 1563 (printed by the Harleian Society), but it is likely that an earlier but undated Visitation, now preserved in the College of Arms, which has not been printed or published, may include the Kempe pedigree. On the occasion of this Visitation the Kempes of Weston and Gissing took the opportunity of obtaining several official copies with the arms differenced for each son. There were then living six brothers, for whom (if not for their sons) the pedigree and arms, with their respective marks of cadency, were prepared. The copy belonging to the eldest was very likely destroyed by the Cromwellian party when they visited Gissing to apprehend the faithful Royalist Sir Robert Kempe, Bart., for the original copy now in possession of the present Baronet belonged, it will be seen, to the sixth son as indicated by the fleur-de-lis. The accompanying illustration shows only the commencement and end of the roll, which was brought down to 1592 by Robert Cooke, Clarenceux King of Arms; Robert Kempe, who was head of the family in 1563, being still alive.

It will be noticed from this that the pedigree starts with Sir Philip Hastings, son of Sir Edward Hastings, whose daughter Isabel married ALLAN KEMPE, ESQUIRE. This Allan Kempe, there can be no doubt, is the same Allan of Weston mentioned in the foregoing chapters, but this copy omits to state his residence or seat.

The second point, which is one of considerable interest and importance, is that Isabel is not claimed to be the *heiress* of Hastings, and that even as late as 1592 the Hastings coat was not quartered by the family. If then the quartering was not theirs by right at that date, the family cannot have any right to it through *this* marriage at the present time. Some historians tell us that the quartering came through the next marriage on the pedigree, viz., John Kempe with Alice Duke, heiress to both Duke and Butvilleyn. If this was the case the same objection would arise, as the Hastings quartering would have been quartered then with Butvilleyn and Duke and thus handed down, but this was not done. What then can we say in support of this use of the Hastings quarter by the Norfolk family? It is stated in the "Visitation of Norfolk" that the coat as now used, comprising eight quarterings, was set out by Raven, Richmond Herald; the actual date is not given, but as his "Visitation of Norfolk" was made in 1613, that date is doubtless about the time of the enlarged coat. He gives the fourth quartering as Or, a maunch gules, which is the well known Hastings arms. Thus placed, the right to quarter it would occur between that of Duke and that of Blackwell, the latest quartering being the arms of Lomnor of Maningham. Both Blackwell and Lomner arms were shown in the east window of Gissing Church as being impaled by Kempe quartering Buttveleyn, and Kempe quartered with Buttveleyn also as impaling Hastings. These of course each point to a direct marriage between Kempe and the families they represent; thus Kempe, *after* marriage with the heiress of Butteveleyn, must have married a Hastings. It is, therefore, singular that we find neither of these marriages in the pedigree which accompanies the enlarged Kempe shield.

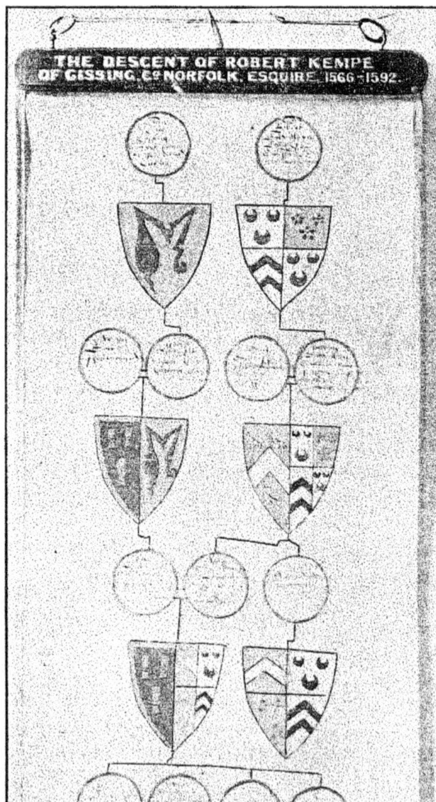

Another clue is given by an ancient gold signet ring still in the possession of the Baronet's family. This ring has engraved upon it the coat of six quarters as given in our illustration of the pedigree roll, with the addition of a maunch on a shield of pretence. The tinctures are not indicated, which gives rise to the question as to whether the coat is in reality that of Hastings or another of the same charge, but distinctive of another family. Mistakes have frequently occurred from this cause, while often an ignorant painter, by "restoring" coats in colours to suit his own fancy, has caused far-reaching errors. Even families interested in heraldry are liable to trip in blazoning their arms, as will be seen by comparing the following coat given as that of the above-mentioned Edmund Kempe, citizen of London, with the correct description.

Edmund Kempe's coat was said to be (in 1542) as follows:

1.—Gules, three garbs or. 2.—Argent, three crescents gules. 3.—Azure, two chevrons sable. 4.—*Sable*, a lion rampant argent. 5.—Sable, three bars argent, on a canton gules, a saltire of the second. 6.—Ermine, a bend chequy sable and argent. The tinctures of the generally recognized arms are: 1.—Gules, three garbs or. 2.—Argent, three crescents gules. 3.—Azure, two chevrons sable. 4.—*Azure*, a lion rampant argent. 5.—Sable, three bars argent, on a canton gules, a saltire gules. 6.—Ermine, a bend chequy sable and argent. To mistake azure for sable, when the coats become black with age, is a most frequent occurrence, but how they came to drop out of the above shield, the Duke quartering, which brought the quarterings 2 and 3, is inconceivable—except as an ignorant blunder. Then, too, the quartering for Bardolph is omitted, while we find that this Edmund claims three coats which were not granted to his brother's descendants until 1587 or 1613.

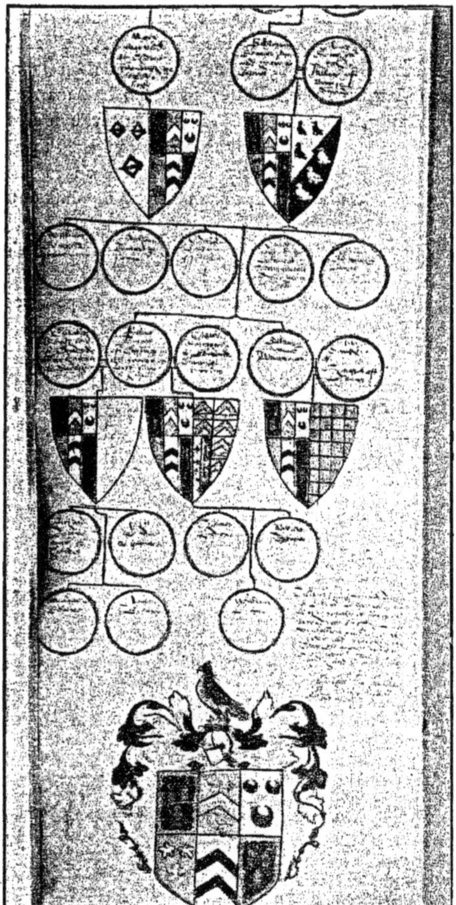

This late blunder would not be cited here but for the additional object of further showing that, although these latest coats *were* claimed by him, the Hastings arms, most to be coveted, were *not* claimed. The same negligence which caused him to omit the other quarters might be considered sufficient to account for this, or it might be possible to show that the elder branch did obtain a subsequent right to the Hastings quarter through a later marriage with that family, as indicated by the signet ring. No Kempe and *Hastings* direct intermarriage is traced occurring at a suitable date, but the explanation appears to be given by the pedigree of Calthorp of Antingham. It is to the effect that Ann, daughter of Sir Edmund Hastings (and relict of Robert Raynes of Oxstrand) married Richard Calthorp, of Antingham; their daughter Ann married John Kempe, second son of Robert Kempe, of Gissing. This John Kempe died in 1610, leaving his estate to his son Robert, who gave it to his cousin Robert Kempe, of Gissing. Thus we presume the ring represented *Calthorp*, of Orthonby, Norfolk, whose arms were *Ermine*, a maunch gules, in allusion, we may believe, to Hastings. Their arms, however, as shown in Antingham Church, impaled by Kempe, are: Or and azure chequy a fesse ermine. This latter coat also impales "Or a maunche gules quartering gules a bend argent" for Hastings.

While it may yet be possible to find another union between Kempe and Hastings, it is clear from the pedigree that there was no second marriage in the direct senior male line of the Kempes of Gissing, and that the Baronets attributed their right to the quartering to the alliance by which the Hastings property in and around Gissing passed to them. At what date then, we may ask, did this actually pass to them? According to the pedigrees in 1324! Allan Kempe was then living as the husband of Isabella Hastings, so that it has been frequently stated that the Gissing Manors have belonged to the Kempes from that time; but Mr. Walter Rye, who has made a considerable study of this matter (as well as Norfolk pedigrees in general) points out, in an article on the subject in *Notes and Queries*, that Gissing Manor was held by the Hastings until 1353, Ralph Hastings being Lord of it in 1347, as is authoritively recorded in the "Book of Aids," 20th year of Edward III. It was sold about 1353 to Thomas Gardiner, of Gissing, whose daughter Joan, dying without issue in 1400, left it to her brother-in-law Sir Robert Buttevileyn who had married her half-sister. It remained with the Buttevileyn family till 1465, when William Buttevileyn died and the Manors of Gissing and Florden came to his *sister* Julian, who by marriage conveyed these to Robert Duke, of Brampton, in Suffolk. This gentleman's daughter Alice, as shown in the pedigree, married John Kempe. The date, however, attributed to this match, Mr. Rye points out, is much earlier than was actually the case.

Among the Norris MSS., a collection of pedigrees and family evidences now in Mr. Rye's possession, there is the following remark against this Duke-Kempe alliance:

"Here is a notorious mistake in Mr. Blomfield's from whom the former part of the pedigree is taken, but how to correct it I know not yet. and also Alice daughter and only child of Robert Duke of Brampton in Suff., by Julian his 2nd wife who was sister and coheir of Wm. Butteveleyn who died s.p. 1465, therefore she could not be wife to this John who was born before 1324."

Both Mr. Rye and Norris seem to be corrected by the author of the "History of Northampton," vol. i, p. 354. He states, under an account of the Cotesbrook property held by the Butteveleyn family, that the Manor of Cotesbrook belonged, in the reign of Henry V., to Robert Butteveleyn, Esquire, who, in the fifth year of that reign, going to "foreign parts," conveyed this property to the Duke of Clarence and other feoffees for the time of his absence out of the kingdom, with remainder after his decease to William, his son and heir, and for want of such heir then to the right heirs of himself, Robert. He, however, died seized of it in the 9th year of Henry V. (1422) and was succeeded by William Butteveleyn, Esquire, his son, who leaving no issue it devolved to his *cousins* and heirs, Elizabeth, the wife of Thomas Herteshorne, of Gissing, Esquire, the daughter of Elizabeth, one of the sisters of his father Robert Butteveleyn, and (upon) Robert Kempe, of Weston, in Suffolk, Gent., son and heir of Alice Kempe, daughter of Julian, another of the sisters of Robert Butteveleyn, *between whom partition was made 6 Edward IV.* (1467) of the Manor and advowson of Cotesbrook *and lands in other counties*. The Inquisition Post Mortem of William Butteveleyn, made 30th Henry VI. (1451-2) in which he is described as "fatuus," is given in the "History of Northampton," (vol. iv, p. 150.)

There can be no doubt that at this time part of the Gissing Manors became the property of the Kempes, but even at this date (1467) it is doubtful if the whole became theirs, for we are told by Blomfield that, in 1548, Sir Anthony Hevenyngham, Knight, Lord of Gissing cum Dagworth, settled three acres of land upon the churchwardens for the poor, and *ordered* Bartholomew Kempe and his heirs to pay three shillings a year to the same use out of his estate. This is recorded in the Manorial Rolls now in the present Baronet's yossession.

It is evident from these facts that generations elapsed between Allan Kempe, whom we positively know as being at Weston in 1318, and the marriage of the heiress who brought the chief part of the Gissing property to the family in 1456-7. To set this right we must therefore remove the Duke marriage from the second generation of the Heraldic pedigree and place it about one hundred years later. We have further to attempt to set straight the intervening generations.

Allan Kempe, we know (from the "Suffolk Feet of Fines"), had a son Geoffrey, otherwise called Jeffry or Galfrid Kempe. This son was interested in land at Carlton, Rushmere, Mutford, Barneby and Honbergh.

It is not recorded in the "Suffolk Fines," or in other records searched, that Allan had also a son named John, but we find that a John Kempe and a William Kempe paid fines for land in Elough and Wellingham in 1313, which places, like those of Galfrid's, are close around the patronal seat of Weston. William was of Griston, in Norfolk, and was interested in lands at Walsham, Stanton, Ashfield Parva, Elough and "Wyrlyngham" (? Worlingham) between 1304 and 1372, his wife's name occurring as Agnes. Of John Kempe we find no further trace in the fines, but the deeds relating to holdings at Chattisham, Belstead Magna and Reddenhall, before mentioned, seem to be his, as he granted parts of these lands to his mother Isabel in 1327. This same John then was the father of Robert, John, Richard and other children. Robert, the son and heir, is said by Norris to have married Mary, daughter of Bartholomew White, by 1350, but the only reason for giving this date appears to have been a conjecture based on the 1324 given as a date at which Allan Kempe was living. Bartholomew White was "of Shotisham, in Norfolk." There are two Shotteshams close to Florden and Braconash, where the Kempes were afterwards seated; if it is a fact that the Whites belonged to either of these they would have been near neighbours, and the match might be thought to have been the natural outcome of local social life. It is, however, necessary to point out that Braconashe did not pass to the Kempes until some generations later, and that Florden was one of the possessions of the Butteveleyns, the last of whom in the male line was, as we have said, William Buttevelyn, who being an idiot in 1447 his estates were controlled by his guardians. These guardians were Sir Thomas Tudenham, Knight, Willm. de la Pole, Marquess of Suffolk, and Thomas Brewer, who together committed the care of this idiot to *William White*, Esq., of Shotesham, 1450.

This fact throws some light on the matter, and the connexion between Kempe and White does not seem quite so likely to have been "purely for love" as for the possible annexation of "a desirable freehold property." The Whites may certainly have lived at Shottesham, in Norfolk, but it is very singular that in 1440 John Kempe, John Dod of Woodbridge, Thomas Ward, Reginald Rous and William "Jenny" (? Jermy) should have been concerned with property at Shotesham and other places near Woodbridge, in Suffolk, while we have no mention of Shotisham in Norfolk among our collection of Notes from the ancient Kempe records.

In 1381 Robert Kempe and Mary (or Margaret) his wife, with others, were jointly interested in the Manor of Blounts, in Suffolk. This couple, it seems, would correspond with the more probable date at which Robert married the Mary White, who after her death married successively two other wives. Of his second wife we do not know the surname, her Christian appellation being Agnes; by her no issue is recorded. His third wife was Katherine, daughter of Robert Hawker, of Redenhall. At the latter place, in 1376, John Kempe, of Weston, had property which seems to have remained with the Kempes until 1536 and perhaps later. This place may be seid to be the "half-way house" between Weston and Florden or Braconash, and it is very likely to have been used as such. This John was probably the father of Robert and grandfather of another John, who was half-brother to "Jeffrey Kempe" of the fourth generation shown on the official Heraldic pedigree. Geoffrey Kempe, as stated, was by the first wife, Mary White, and if the property around Woodbridge, noted above, belonged to her this would be sufficient to account for his settling there during his father's lifetime; while John Kempe, who is stated in the Norris MSS. to be the son of Robert Kempe's third wife, is more likely to have been provided temporally with a residence at Redenhall or on any other of his father's estates. It was then this Geoffrey and his half-brother John who, in 1440, paid a fine, with their respective wives and John Somerset, for the property at Woodbridge, as recorded in the "Suffolk Feet of Fines." Both Geoffrey and John's wives are there stated to be named Margaret, of them we shall have more to say, but first we venture upon rather a hazardous suggestion.

Those familiar with the earliest parochial registers and wills of the fifteenth and sixteenth centuries will readily admit that Agnes and Alice were, during that period, often taken to represent the same name. Now if the second wife of the above Robert Kempe was Agnes Duke, the properties would of course devolve upon her husband or his children. Under this hypothesis, Geoffrey, John and *all* other children might have interests in the estates, or, as is frequently the case, only the children of the heiress would participate. If John Kempe was half-brother to Geoffrey, by his father's second wife, he might have become sole heir to the Manors of Gissing, while the elder son perhaps used the heiress' arms with his own, although not strictly entitled to them. If however John, as it seems, had these Duke estates, he and not Geoffrey, the eldest son, was the ancestor of the subsequent Gissing line. To explain how Weston also passed to the younger branch we must further presume that the male issue of Geoffry became extinct.

The entire absence of wills purporting to belong to Kempes of Weston forces us to base our further investigations on the Woodbridge line, of which we have some records; as however this is entirely outside the scope of the official pedigree we will deal with it in a separate chapter, which the sceptical can "skip" to follow the later and more certain generations.

CHAPTER IV.

WOODBRIDGE AND EARLY SUFFOLK KEMPES.

WOODBRIDGE is situated about seven miles east-north-east of Ipswich on the river Deben, and like the latter place stands at the head of a creek some ten miles from the sea. Its proximity to both Ipswich and the sea would make it a suitable residence for that Geoffrey Kempe, who, at the end of the thirteenth and commencement of the fourteenth centuries, was Warden of the Port and perhaps also an official of the City of Norwich, which he could thus reach by water as conveniently as by land. We know that at Chattisham, Wenham Parva and Belstead, near Ipswich, the Kempes had property in 1327 and 1347, and at Bucklesham and Rushmere juxta Ipswich about 1385, Edmund Kempe, of Saxthorp, in Norfolk, paying a fine for his possessions at the last two places in that year. The first mention of Kempes actually connected with Woodbridge occurs in 1440, when, as stated, Geoffrey and John Kempe, with John Somerset, paid a fine for property there. In 1455, all the following names were jointly parties to some settlement of local property lying in Sutton, Shottisham, Ramsholt, Alderton, Bawdsey, Henley, and Newbourne, together with lands at Thornham and Gislingham in the north of the country; Philip Wentworth, Knight; Robert Wylieghby, Robert Wyngefield, Thomas *Drewes*, Gilbert *Debenham*, John Heydon, Reginald *Rous*, William *Jenney*, Walter Fulburne, Richard

Chiche, William Boundis, Thomas Kene, John Prylle, Thomas *Ward*, John Kempe and John *Dod* of Woodbridge, with John Tymperley and Margaret, his wife. The manors concerned in this agreement were Pettistrees, Osmondis and Talvos or Salvos.

Many of the above names are familiar in connexion with Kempes of Kent as well as of Norfolk; Chiche is associated with the Kentish stock of this date. Debenham occurs in the will of John Kempe of Woodbridge, proved in 1459, while Ward is variously stated to have married either Alice Duke herself, or Alice, the daughter of Robert Kempe by that heiress. "Collin's Peerage" states that Robert Ward of Kirby Bedon, married Alice Kempe of Gissing; the date is not given, but from the context the middle of the fifteenth century is inferred. Drewes in various spellings is a prominent name in the Kempe wills of this and subsequent periods, as also is Rous or Rowse.

We have nothing to show that the Geoffrey of Ipswich ever took up his residence at the Weston seat. Although we have every reason to believe that the family retained their property there, they *appear* to have resided chiefly around Ipswich from about 1440. The will of Geoffrey Kempe of Woodbridge, was proved in the Suffolk Archdeaconry between 1444 and 1455; we have not, however, been able to obtain a copy of this. The pedigree tells us that he married Margaret, daughter of Sherrington, a gentleman, having a seat at Cranworth in Norfolk. By her, so the pedigree says, he had a son Robert, who became heir to the numerous scattered estates and ancestor to all the Kempes of Gissing. There is no reason to doubt the fact of his marriage, but if he had a son, we think he must have been *John* Kempe, the husband of Alice Duke, for Robert, the son of *John*, not Geoffrey, had grant of the manors of Butteveleyns and Dallings in 1473, as given in Dalry's MSS. (19, 138 add. MSS.) in the British Museum. Although we are unable to give the whereabouts of the original deed, we must credit Dalry's statement that such a document existed signed by "Robert Kempe, *son of John*."

A will dated and proved in 1465 commences "Ego Dns Robertus Kempe." Perhaps this Robert was a son of Geoffrey, hence he would be lord of several manors. He mentions the Curates of Whitton and Thurlston, his Lord and patron, Peter of Claydon, and William ffyshlie, Rector of Blakenham. He leaves bequests to amend the bridge at Claydon, to provide candelabra and lamps for the church and for other charitable objects. He mentions, however, neither wife nor children, but leaves legacies to his nephew and niece, William and Katherine. These are the only relatives mentioned, and their surname does not appear. We know of no Kempe named William as *connected* with this family at this time.

The earliest monument on record to a Kempe in Suffolk or Norfolk is that of John Kempe at Woodbridge. It is described in Weaver's "Funeral Monuments," under the Diocese of Norwich, and the inscription is given as follows:—

> "ORATE . . . JOHANNIS KEMPE, QUI OBIIT 3 JULII 1459, ET PRO ANIMABUS MARGARET, JOHANNE ET MARGARET UXORUM."

The church at Woodbridge was founded by Sir Hugh Rufus and Alice, his wife. It is very probable that these were closely related to the Kempes, and it may be that their settlement at Woodbridge was influenced by this as well as the site being a convenient one for communication with Ipswich. For many generations the Rouse (*alias* Rufus) and Kempe families were intimate, and later we know of intermarriages.

The will of this John Kempe, of Woodbridge was proved in the Suffolk Archdeaconry Court, and also in the Prerogative Court of Canterbury. The fact of it having been proved in the second court probably indicates that the testator had properties in more than one diocese or county. The various estates are not, however, enumerated in the will, and we are not aware of the existence of any Post Mortem Inquisition. The descent of property was so definitely settled by the customs of manors and other written and unwritten laws that even if the ancestors had not entailed their freeholds, it was hardly necessary to mention either the lands or the heirs, and thus numerous wills of considerable landowners only deal with petty bequests and charitable deeds, and give us no clue as to what estates they owned at their death. A late example of this is the will of Sir Benjamin Kemp, the seventh Baronet, who in his will of 1777 leaves "all real and personal estate whatsoever to his sister, Martha Short, of Sevenoaks," and does not mention Gissing, Florden, Braconash, or other family estates which, of course, duly passed to the next male heir without any difficulty. Thus John Kempe, of Woodbridge, ordains that Thomas Kempe, his son, Margaret Kempe, his wife, and Thomas Alnard, his son (in law) should be executors, but gives no directions for the disposal of his real estate. He mentions the poor of Orford, Rosamond Dalie, of Clopton, Thomas Panwed, Thomas Stub, John *Debenham*, and his son, "Thomas Kempe, of Woodbridge." The mention of Margaret Kempe as his widow, and the three wives named on the brass shews that it was not this John who married Alice Duke. The will, however, of Margaret, *alias* Alice Kempe, of Ipswich, was proved in the Consistory Court of Norwich, in February 1480.

The chief point of interest is the fact of the Curzons being mentioned as relatives. The will commences "Domina Margaret Kempe, vidua de Ipswich." The original will is, we understand, not in existence, but in the margin and index of the Probate Register the name of the testatrix is given as *Alice* Kempe. She desired to be buried in the Monastery of SS. Peter and Paul, at Ipswich, to which and to the Priories of Butley and Letheringham she leaves legacies, as also for repairs to the churches of the Carmelites, Friars Preachers, Friars Minor, and others at Ipswich, and also to St. Margaret's Chapel, Cretingham. Out of the goods of her "husband, John Kempe," she gives £20 for the repair of the highways. She speaks of her *sister*, Edith Curzon, also of William and Thomas Curzon. Margaret *Alverd*, Robert Chapman, Richard Wengfield, Richard Osberne, who also appear, may be relatives. Thomas Goodwyn she calls her son, and John *Drewry*, her nephew. Among others who are mentioned, the following are all styled "Dominus :—Thomas *Drewry*, John Fert, John Reigner, John Bridgewater, Thomas Baker, John Lacye, William Smith, John *Debenham*, John Clar, Robert Stowe, Robert Beenlie, and Thomas Goodwyn. To the last of these, evidently her son, she leaves the residue of her estate after numerous small bequests. We may further note that the churches of St. Clement's Norwich, "Mowlesford" and "Waloughby" are to receive small doles, which may show that she was formerly resident or connected with those places. Persons of the name of KENE and KEME are also mentioned in this will. We cannot say with certainty that these were Kempes, but it is known that Kene and Keme were sometimes used as variants of the name.

There cannot be much doubt as to this will being that of the widow of John Kempe, of Woodbridge, for she mentions her late husband of that name, while Margaret *Alverd* must be his daughter "Aluard" or Alnard. William Curzon died in 1485, for in that year Robert Kempe, and his wife Margaret, daughter of the said William Curzon, were made feoffees of his estate, as appears from Dalry's MSS. before cited.

From this point it would seem the chief branch became again more intimately associated with Norfolk. With the subsequent representatives of the Gissing line we shall deal in our next chapter. Here we must follow the issue of the Woodbridge couple.

The first couple whose wills are given above had, besides the daughter who married Alvard, a son, THOMAS KEMPE, who in 1459 was of Woodbridge. He evidently remained there till his death, his will being proved in the Norwich Consistory Court in 1474 (Herbert fo. 54). He therein desires to be buried in the church of Woodbridge, doubtless beside his father. He leaves his house at Woodbridge, which was late the tenement of "Wm. Cane" (another likely variant of Kempe), to his wife for life, and afterward to his son, Galferd or Geoffrey Kempe, to whom also all the testator's other lands at Woodbridge were bequeathed. All residue was to be equally divided between his sons John and Galfred, but a "*dividend*" of his houses was reserved for his daughters Anne and Agnes. Thomas Kempe is also mentioned, but his relationship is not indicated. Other places are spoken of in the will; these have not all been identified, as the spelling is eratic. "Dallings" evidently stands for Dallinghoe, as Debach, the next parish occurs in the same clause, otherwise this might have been taken to refer to the manor of Dallings, at Gissing. "Chenlye" might stand for Shenley, in Buckinghamshire, where Kempes flourished, or for Shenley, in Hertfordshire, but it is as likely to mean Shelly, in Suffolk, which long after this was a possession of the Kempes. "Pytyste," doubtless stands for Pettistree by Dallinghoe; "Sabyley" is a name with which we are unfamiliar.

Of Galfred we find no further trace, but it is probable that he was the father of a THOMAS KEMPE, of Woodbridge, whose will was proved with that of Katherine Kempe of the same place, in the Suffolk Archdeaconry Court (1518-24). In the same Court about 1477 was proved the will of John Kempe, of Ipswich. That of Henry Kempe, also of Ipswich, is recorded in the same register as the last, the date being before 1524. The will of Joan Kempe, of Ipswich, is registered between 1564 and 1566, and one of Nicholas Kempe, of the same place, occurs between 1647 and 1649, and in 1734 in the same Court was a will of William Kemp, of Ipswich. During the period covered by these Ipswich wills, relatives naturally were settled around, while those who had settled at Gissing were frequently reconnected by marriage with the town as will be seen in the following chapters. It cannot, however, be said that Ipswich was ever a centre from which Kempes multiplied or where any subsequent branch remained for generations. The Registers of St. Nicholas, Ipswich, have been printed, covering the period from 1539 to 1710; during that long period only three marriages of Kempes are there recorded which are as follows:—

1570 (no day or month given) George Kempe to Helen. . . . (blank).

29th November. 1599. Elias Kempe to Susan Silverside.

8th November, 1677. Robert Jacob and Grace Kempe.

We have said that the early Kempes of Ipswich had property at Dallinghoe. The following items are taken from the registers of that parish. ("Visitation of Suffolk," J. J. Howard, 1866):

1568. 8th April. Anthonie Kempe, son of John and Maria, baptized.
1571. 1st May. Marie Kempe, daughter of John, baptized.
1574. 13th December. John Kempe, buried.
1579. 16th September. Susan Kempe, son (*sic*) of Robert Kempe, baptized.
1583. 9th June. Robert Kempe, son of Robert, dwelling in Bynghall, baptized.
1583. 12th February. Robert Kempe, buried.
1589. 14th July. William Kempe, Son of Robert, baptized.
1592. 11th March. Anne Kempe, daughter of John, baptized.
1603. 16th August. Henry Kempe, son of Robert Kempe, buried.
1618. 14th September. William Thompson and Susan Kempe, daughter of John Kempe the elder, married.
1631. 18th April. Anne Kempe, wife of John Kempe, buried.

The following wills will add to the information thus given:

1574-5. John Kempe, of Dallinghoe, proved in the Suffolk Archdeaconry, Ipswich.
1606. Jane Kempe, Dallinghoe, proved in the Norwich Consistory Court.
1638-40. John Kempe, of Dallinghoe, proved in the Suffolk Archdeaeonry, Ipswich.
1638-40. Bridget Kempe, of Dallinghoe, proved in the Suffolk Archdeaconry, Ipswich.

Of these wills the only one examined is that of Jane Kempe. She mentions Mary May, a widow, of Dallinghoe, and Robert, Margaret and James May, sons and daughter of this widow;

also Thomas *Gardener* and a friend named Elmes and widow London. The only relative is her brother Robert Kempe, of "F," which may stand for Fakenham, where Anne and William Kempe lived at this time. Around Dallinghoe, at Parham, Wickham Market and between these places and Ipswich, some of this line certainly remained down to recent times, and there seems little room for doubting that the celebrated preacher and author, the Rev. Edward Curtis Kempe, Chaplain to the late Duke of Cambridge (who came from this part), was a representative of this line; with him and his distinguished descendants we, however, shall deal later. The three following Wills very probably refer to his near relatives. They will be found in the Probate Office at Ipswich under the dates given: Henry Kempe, of Parham, 1769; John Kempe, of Woodbridge, 1771-2, and Amy Kempe (widow), of Felixstow, 1783. The Index to the Administrations at the same office mentions James Kemp, of Parham, 1716-19, and Mary Kemp, of Wickham Market, 1795.

As early as 1518-24 there is a will of Cicely Kempe, of Parham, which is close to Marlesford, which appears to be the "Mowlesford" in the testament of Margaret Kempe in 1480; thus one may consider Dallinghoe, with Parham, a nest of a branch of the Kempes, of Woodbridge, from about 1480 down to late in the nineteenth century. Tuddenham, Westerfield, Sproughton, Clopton, Claydon and perhaps Henley were early homes of the Kempes around Ipswich; most, if not all, of these were of the old Norfolk stock dating from the fourteenth century.

CHAPTER V.

KEMPES OF WESTON AND GISSING.

AT the end of Chapter III. we suggested that a Geoffrey Kempe, of Woodbridge, whose will appears in the Ipswich Calendar between 1444 and 1445, was identical with Geoffrey or JEFFREY KEMPE OF WESTON. In the last chapter we have shown that Kempes remained at Woodbridge and around Ipswich for some generations, during which, however, Weston was continuously held by the family. It is, however, still an open question as to whether JOHN KEMPE, the next on the pedigree (as of Weston), was son or half brother to Geoffrey. It is remarkable that we can find no will which can be positively identified as this John's, and the more so since it was in his time that the Gissing lands were settled on his son Robert. Dalry in his MSS. collections (Brit. Mus., Add. MSS., 19, 138) mentions a deed dated 1473 of ROBERT KEMPE, CO-HEIR OF BUTTEVELYN, OF GISSING, concerning the manors there, and another dated 1485, being a grant by John and Robert Norman to RICHARD AND EDMUND KEMPE, Gents, sons of Robert Kempe and "Margaret, daughter of William Curzon." William Curzon was of "Sturton," otherwise "Stutton," a parish on the Stour just south of Ipswich. It would appear from this last-mentioned deed that he died in or before 1485; he was, we know, living in 1480, as he is mentioned in the will of Margaret, the widow of John Kempe, of Woodbridge.

Dalry gives us another note concerning this "Robert, son of *John* Kempe and Alice Duke," stating that in his grant of the Manors of Buttevelyns and Dallings in 1473 he used a seal bearing the impression or device of a squirrel sitting and cracking a nut upon his head. Where these deeds now are we have not discovered ; possibly they may be among the large collection of ancient documents belonging to the present Sir Kenneth H. Kempe. Dalry also states that a Ralph Kempe was co-feoffee of the Manor of Gissing. He does not give the date, but it was probably about 1467 or 1473. No RALPH KEMPE is entered in the various Probate Calendars of Norfolk and Suffolk. This Ralph evidently settled in Middlesex and was a merchant of London, his will being proved in the Prerogative Court of Canterbury in 1477. As he founded a line of his family in Middlesex the records of his estates and issue will be treated with under that county. Norris in his MSS., now in possession of Walter Rye, Esq., of the Priory, Norwich, shows a Ralph Kempe on the Norfolk pedigree as a brother of Robert, and uncle of Geoffrey and John Kempe. This seems quite compatible with the other facts we have given, but we know of no better authority for this Ralph being so placed on the pedigree. Norris also informs us that Margaret, widow of one Drewry, married John Kempe, Gent., and died as widow of the latter in 1483 at Ipswich. This date would seem to be a mistake for 1480, as the will of Domina MARGARET KEMPE, Vidua de Ipswich, given in our last chapter accords with that statement except as to date. This will, mentioning as it does Will. Curzon, would at least appear to be a close relation to Robert Kempe, the co-heir to the Duke estates. We suggest that her husband, John Kempe, was brother to Ralph Kempe.

Dalry states that a Richard was a mercer of London ; he does not say which this Richard was. But there is little doubt that he was the brother of Edmund, another mercer of London, both being recipients of the grant mentioned above, dated 1485, as sons of Robert Kempe and Mary or Margaret Curzon. The Harleian Manuscripts (1154) contain a sixteenth century pedigree showing the issue of the last-named couple, placing Robert Kempe as the eldest son, but curiously stating that Edmund, the second son, was then "heere electe." His issue is also shown and is continued to 1585 ; but we suppose for the sake of excluding the junior line from participation in arms and property the line is made to die out with "Pawle" Kempe, son of James Kempe, of Acton, Middlesex, the eldest son of Edmund Kempe, the Citizen and Mercer of London, who died in 1542. His line will also be reserved for the Middlesex section of our work, he being chiefly connected with that county. We will here only say that his daughter Margaret, as widow of William Dane, an Alderman of London, was a great benefactor to the City Guilds, and that her portrait still hangs in the Ironmongers' Hall. She left a sum of money to purchase a necklace for Queen Elizabeth with whom she was on intimate terms.

JOHN, the third son of Robert by Margaret Curzon, is said in the Norris MSS. to have been living in 1539, married and left issue. There is a will in 1557 of John Kempe of Fundenhall, Norfolk, which might be his ; if so he appears to be the founder of a family who continued around Bunwell and Carlton Rode down to last century, and is now represented by a Quaker family of Kempes at Norwich, Manchester and London (*Vide post*).

WILLIAM KEMPE, the third son of Robert, and next younger brother to this John, was a clergyman, of "Sprockton," probably Sproughton, near Ipswich. Perhaps it is his will as of Cratfield which appears in the Norwich Consistory Court Calendar between 1546 and 1548, John Kempe of that place appears in the same calendar in 1606, so presumbly he too had issue which continued in the north-east of Suffolk.

RALPH or "Rarfe" Kempe is shown as the fifth son of Robert, this may be a mistake for Richard, who does not appear on the pedigree quoted (Harl. 1154). No Kempe appears in the various Probate Courts of Norfolk, Suffolk, or Essex to correspond with this name, nor do we trace any Ralph Kempe as living nearer than Middlesex, and the one of the name there was grandson to that Ralph of London mentioned above. "Raffe" Kempe, however, witnessed the will of Robert Kempe of Winchcomb, with whom Sir Nicholas Kempe and his heir, Ralph Kempe, were connected. Thus a west country branch may have been established by this "Rarfe" Kempe from Weston and Gissing. Such a distant settlement might seem unlikely to many who have studied the Norfolk families, but as the grandchildren of Edmund Kempe of London are recorded as intermarrying with families resident in Somerset and Surrey, the distance of Winchcomb from Gissing cannot be looked upon as too great for these Kempes to cover at one migration.

Alice Kempe (sister to the above Edmund, John, William, and Rarfe) became a nun at the beautiful Saxon Abbey of Barking, the reason for her choosing a convent so distant from her native home may reasonably be atttributed to her venerating the Saxon founder of that abbey to whose race she claimed to belong.

Her sister, Ciseley Kempe, married John Moulton, or Melton, of "Sturston," which is undoubtedly the modern Stuston in the north of Suffolk near to Diss.

A John Moulton at this period had extensive possessions in Gloucestershire, his will, which describes him as of Toddenham, in that county, was proved in 1563 (P.C.C., 9 Stevenson). If this is a relation to Cicely Kempe's husband it may perhaps account for her younger brother Ralph being in that county. "Cicely Melton" is mentioned as living in 1542 in her brother Edmund's will.

Before we take leave of this generation we may here note, as we have stated in the Kentish section, that this last mentioned Edmund Kempe, and some of those enumerated as his relatives by his will, have by an error been repeatedly attached to the pedigree of the Kentish Kempes. All the Kempes of Cornwall have also claimed this Edmund Kempe to be their ancestor in order to link themselves with the family of Archbishop Kempe, a distinction greatly coveted. They state that his son, Humphrey Kempe, was father of Richard Kempe, who was living a married man at Levethan, Cornwall, in 1544, whereas Sir John MacLean, in his careful history of that family in "Trigg Minor," states that even in 1475, when Edmund Kempe was but a boy, ancestors of the Cornish Kempes were already *seated* in Cornwall. Then, too, James Kempe, the eldest son of Edmund Kempe, did not marry until 1544, and Humphrey Kempe, the younger brother, must have married even later. Perhaps it is but fair to add that this unfortunate error does not necessarily deprive them from sharing either kinship with both Norfolk and Kentish stocks, but their pedigree goes back to such remote times that we fear that proofs of the common origin of the three great families of the same arms will never be forthcoming.

Robert Kempe, on whom the Gissing Manors were settled, thus left behind him by his wife, Mary or Margaret Curzon, a numerous issue, who, even at his death must have spread out into half a dozen counties. His newly-augmented estates had permitted him to send his family forth well portioned, and as time proceeded it is natural to imagine that he found the ancient home at Weston too confined for his status. Hence he had doubtless arranged before his decease for the transfer of the chief family seat to Gissing. We do not know for certain the date of his death; there is an Inquisition of a Robert Kempe of Norfolk and Suffolk indexed as taken in the eleventh year of Henry VIII. (1518), but this seems to be a mistake for the nineteenth year of that reign, when his son Robert Kempe's estate was the subject of an Inquisition.

Robert Kempe must have married Elizabeth Appleyard, heiress of Mergate Hall, Braconash, before 1470, for as we shall see he had married a second wife before 1474, the first one having left no son but three daughters. Mary, the eldest child, married Thomas Jernygan, of Cove, Suffolk, and had by him at least four children living in 1527. Elizabeth Kempe, the second daughter of the heiress of Braconash, became Lady of the Bedchamber to Queen Catherine, and died in 1536.

She states in her will * that she was born at Gissing, being daughter of Robert Kempe late of that place.

The third daughter of Robert Kempe and Elizabeth Appleyard was Anne, who married Sir Richard Bacon, of Harleston, Norfolk, of whose family were Lord Keeper Sir Nicholas Bacon and Sir Francis Bacon. It was, doubtless, due to these being in the Royal Court, with other relatives of the Kempes, that Queen Elizabeth stayed at Mergate Hall on one of her state progresses to Norwich. This occurred on Saturday, 16th August, 1578, and it is duly recorded in the official records of the Queen's "Progresses" that the Queen and Court were there entertained at dinner, after which the company proceeded to the city. At this time Lady Style was residing at Mergate Hall, her sister-in-law, Bridget Style, having married Edmund Kempe of London, son of Robert Kempe, of Weston. Margaret Kempe, the daughter of this Edmund, had married Sir William Dane, Lord Mayor of London, and was at the time of this progress a lady of the Royal Court. She died the following year bequeathing £200 to the Queen for a necklace.

Robert Kempe's second wife was Anne, daughter of John Clifford, of Holmdale, Kent (probably related to Richard Clifford, Archdeacon of Canterbury, and afterwards Bishop of Worcester and London), who died in 1421. By this wife he had several children, Bartholomew, the eldest son, being declared to be aged fifty-five at his father's death in 1527; thus this second marriage must have taken place before 1474. He inherited the chief estates as we shall presently notice. Margaret Kempe, a daughter of Robert, married Robert Blaverhauset, of Princethorpe, Warwickshire; Florence, another daughter, married Sir Phillip Woodhall, of "Frampton," † Suffolk, and was living in 1542; Lewis Kempe, a younger son, was to have the remainder of his father's estate, but we find but little local trace of him except that he joined his elder brother in a deed relating to some land in which his name is rendered as Ludovicus Kempe, the deed concerning which is noted by Dalry in the MSS. before quoted. No will of any Kempe of his name occurs in the calendars of the various Probate Courts of Norfolk, Suffolk, Essex, Kent, or Lincoln, but "Sir" John Kempe, Vicar of Hungerton, Leicestershire, in a will dated, 1539 speaks of his brother, "Ludwyke Kempe," and the latter's son, Ludwick. We have not traced the exact abode of this elder Ludwick Kempe, but his sons and their issue lived at Croxton, and established a family who have continued in Leicestershire and Lincolnshire to the present day. Other Kempes of Leicestershire came from Staffordshire and Warwickshire, perhaps these also, although apparently an earlier branch, may be akin to those of Norfolk stock, and thus account for Margaret's marriage with Blaverhauset of Warwickshire.

The Blenerhauset marriage is one of much interest, as it opens up many complex relationships between Kempes of Norfolk and other families of Kempes about the Kingdom. The family had been long seated at Frenze, Norfolk, in the church of which many brasses and monuments to their family exist. John Bleverhausett, who died 1510, married first Jane, daughter of Thomas Higham, of Higham Green, Suffolk (whose family afterwards intermarried with Kempes of Essex), and secondly Jane, daughter of Thomas Tyndale, of Norfolk. By these wives he had a numerous issue, of whom not all are shown in the Heraldic Pedigree as given in the "Norfolk Visitation." Sir Thomas Bleverhauset, his eldest son, was of Frenze, and had seats in Suffolk and Essex. His will was proved in 1532 (P.C.C., 17 Thower); Robert, the second son, married Margaret Kempe as we have said; Margaret Bleverhauset was the Prioress of Kempsey, Gloucestershire, and John Bleverhauset was of Hampstead, Middlesex, where a line of Kempes were established as early as 1520. The will of this John Bleverhauset has been examined, it was proved the same year as

* *See* mention of this will under the Middlesex section of this work.

† Perhaps this may be Framsden, near Letheringham, where the Kempes, of Woodbridge, held property.

that of his brother, and is registered in the same court (16 Thower). Among those he mentions are "his cozen, Christopher Jermyn," his brothers, Sir Thomas and Robert Bleverhauset, Sir Henry Grey, Knight, Sir John Corwallis, Knight, and Sir Phillip Calthorp. His properties mentioned are the leases of his house at Hampstead, held from St. Bartholomew's Hospital, leases of the parsonages of "Brome, Southell, and Camfield, in Essex," and an interest in the Manor of Frenze, also a lease of Lyston Farm. To the High Altars of Marylebone and Ridge he bequeaths sums of money. To his wife, Margaret, and after her death to their son, Edmund Bleverhauset, he leaves the reversion of his leases and estates. The mention of Marylebone was doubtless occasioned by the association therewith of this testator's mother, Jane Bleverhauset, who obtained a portion of the Tyburn Manors from the Knights of St. John of Jerusalem. Her will, in which she is called "Jane Blenerhasseth, formerly Hobson," describes her as of St. John of Jerusalem, London. We are inclined to believe that it was due jointly to this Blenerhauset lease of Marylebone that Kempes were established at Marylebone, these being associated as will be seen with the Hampstead Kempes. Of this interesting point we shall have more to say in the Middlesex section, the facts, however, require mentioning here, as shortly after this Richard Kempe of Gissing, then studying the law in London, selected his bride from Hampstead, whither presumably, he went to visit his kinsmen. Before leaving the Bleverhausetts we may add another mention of them in a relatives will. Richard Hungerford, Esq., in his will dated and proved in 1510, mentions "My cousin, Margaret Kempe, and my cousin, Robert Blaynerhauset." This testator was buried at Blackfriars, and was possessed in right of his wife, Jane, widow of Sir Edmund Lucy, of the Manor of Charlecote, Warwick. The Bleverhausett arms were Gules, a chevron ermine between three dolphins naiant embowed argent, and five quarterings.

ROBERT KEMPE (father of Bartholomew and Lewis Kempe) made his will 8th September, 1526, and it was proved at Hoxne on the 22nd January following. Dalry in giving an abstract from it describes the testator as of Weston, but in the Norwich Register (224 Briggs) he is stated to be "of Gissing, Esquire." Dalry says that his will recites that whereas his son, Bartholomew Kempe, stands indebted to him for two hundred marks, this sum shall be expended in employing some "honest" priest to sing for the soul of the testator, his wife's, the souls of his father and mother and ancestors, for ten years to come. He desired to be buried by his wife in the Lady Chapel of Gissing Church, and left bequests to the altar of that church and to the high altars of Florden, Burston and Tivetshall. The most important item in the will is the statement that the Manors of Dallings and Hastings in Gissing belonged to his father, while other lands "in the said town" had been purchased from "various persons." These Gissing lands he settled on his eldest son, Bartholomew, and his heirs male, with remainder entailed on Lewis, his second son, and his issue. The testator says that Bartholomew had then (1526) five sons and one daughter, the names of these are not given, but bequests of money are left to each. The testator also leaves £10 to his "godson," Robert Bacon,* son of (Sir) Richard Bacon by his third daughter, Ann Kempe. The executors are Bartholomew Kempe, William Chowte or Haute, and Sir Philip Tylney (related to the Bleverhausets and Kempes of Thweyt), the supervisor was Sir John Shelton, Knight, and Richard Bacon ; John Chapman and Robert Kene were witnesses.

* It is interesting to note that the first of his family, of whom we have actual praof as living at that place, viz., "Dominus Allan Kempe," in the time of Edward I., had for his neighbour "Dominus Ad(am) Bacon"; thus for over two hundred years the Kempes and Bacons had already been closely connected. We shall see that this connection became even closer for the next century at least, while it is probable that the families were connected by common descent from William de Roos, of Bulchamp and Woodbridge, for Bulchamp by Blythburg, as we have intimated, seems to have been the actual place whence the Kempes of Weston first derived their name. (*See* Chapter I. Norfolk Section.)

CHAPTER VI.

KEMPES OF GISSING.

ACCORDING to the Inquisition Post Mortem made in 1527 of the property lately held by Robert Kempe, of Weston, Gissing and Flordon, BARTHOLOMEW KEMPE was fifty-five years of age at his father's death, and was found to be duly entitled to the estates at each of these places. With his brother Lewis, he was, as we have said, concerned in the settlement of some part of the lands in 1529; perhaps this was a partition in settlement of Lewis's interest in the reversion, for as previously stated, Lewis Kempe does not appear to have remained in the county. It is likely that he had settled long before his father's death at some place at Leicestershire, or perhaps Northampton, for in the latter county his ancestors, the Dukes, held property, which may have been his portion during the father's lifetime.

Bartholomew, like his father, had an invincible desire to get the whole of the Gissing Estates into his hands. It was this doubtless that led to his parting with Weston, so long the seat of his ancestors. Did Bartholomew believe that Gissing had formerly belonged to his ancestors in the person of Adam de Gissing or Adam Kempe, of Kempe's Manor? It is possible that such a tradition had been handed down, and that in all good faith the wife of Allan Kempe (whose name at least was Isabel), was put down as the daughter of Sir Edward Hastings by his wife Phillipa, which in time became corrupted into the daughter of Sir Philip Hastings. Bartholomew, at least, knew that the house of Hastings had held the lordship of Gissing, and claiming descent from them, he would be the more anxious to have entire possession of the manors comprised in Gissing. Thus in 1532 he sold the seat at Weston, and as opportunity occurred he bought off the interests held by others in the Manors of Gissing. That Bartholomew Kempe was a good business man there can be little doubt, the sale of Weston, and the additional acquirements and building at Gissing, demonstrate that he had a definite purpose in view, which is further manifested by his seeking and obtaining from the king a confirmation of his free warren in the demesne lands at Gissing, which the grant recites, were originally granted by Henry III. to Nicholas Hastings on 23rd May in the 54th year of that King's reign (1270). The Patent to Bartholomew is dated at Westminster, 4th May, in the 21 Henry VIII. (1529), and is mentioned in vol. iv., part. 3, of "Letters and Papers of Henry VIII."

Nor did Bartholomew neglect his religious duties, for we find him in possession of the Church Funds in 1537. These funds probably were raised for the purpose of restoration, very likely at his instigation, for we may judge that he was anxious for the welfare of the church as well as all else at Gissing. The advowson of the rectory of this church was not yet in his family, for we are told by Blomfield that it was purchased by Robert Kempe, his son, on 17th February, 1574. In the Subsidy Roll of 1523, when Bartholomew was but eldest son of the Lord of these Manors, he is rated as the chief "gentleman" residing in the Hundred of Diss, his land being then valued at £8 yearly, for which he paid 8*s*. as his proportion of the rate levied. In the reign of Mary, as Lord of Gissing and Dallings, he paid £4 subsidy for his lands, they being then valued at £80 per annum.* Bartholomew Kempe, be it remembered, was the son of Robert Kempe's second wife, Anne Clifford, of Kent. It is possible that he was named after a Bartholomew Kempe, of that county, who died a few years after the birth of this namesake. Bartholomew may have had some property in Kent from his mother, which may account for his son, Edward Kempe, retiring

* On this Subsidy Roll appear John Kemp, at Shelfhanger; Thomas Kemp, at Starston; William Kemp, at Shelton, and Robert Kemp, at Forncett St. Mary, all within the Hundred of Diss.

to that county after an active life in London as a merchant ; of such maternal estate, however, we have no actual knowledge. He married Anne, daughter of John Alleyn, of Bury St Edmunds, by Constance, daughter and heiress of William Gedding. (This John Alleyn, with a Godfrey Kempe and others, petitioned the King to translate Thetford Monastery to a Dean and Chapter of Thetford Church, at the time of the suppression of the monasteries).

Bartholomew had a very large family, some of whom died in infancy. We know that at the decease of his father in '1526' he had five sons and a daughter, after which, at least, two more sons were born. The order of the sons is not uniformly given, the cadency marks to their arms being shifted evidently on the decease of a brother without issue to make their line appear as close as possible to the head of the family. The following order we think most probable :—(1) Robert, who in time succeeded to the Gissing and Flordon estates ; (2) Bartholomew, who settled in London and became founder of the Kempes of Croydon ; (3) Anthony, who died old and childless in 1612 ; (4) Edward Kempe, a mercer, of London, and afterwards of Shorn, Kent ; (5) John, who died a bachelor ; (6) William Kempe ; (7) Francis Kempe, who settled at Little Hadham, Herts ; (8) Thomas, whose effects and estates were administered by his brother Edward in 1562 ; and a daughter named Elizabeth, who married into the Throgmorton family, and of whom we shall have more presently to say.

Bartholomew (the elder) died in 1554, in which year there is recorded an Inquisition, which may now be seen by any interested at the Record Office, London. Besides Gissing and Dallings it mentions Shimpling as one of the places where he had property.* William and Thomas Poley, Robert, Elizabeth, Dorothy and Anne Kemp are mentioned therein.

Details of the issue of Bartholomew Kemp, junior, will be given under Surrey ; of Edward, further notice will be found under Shorne, Kent. Of the other sons John, William and Thomas, we know nothing more than is recorded above. Francis Kempe, of Little Hadham, married Armynell, daughter of John Brooke, of London, by whom he had a son named Francis Kempe, said to be the same as one of that name settled at Fulham.

FRANCIS, the elder, had also two sons, William and Thomas, and perhaps a daughter, Dorothy, who was baptized at St. Dunstan's in the West, London, 30th June, 1579. William entered the Merchant Taylors' School, 6th March, 1574, and is marked in the school books as having died young. Thomas, perhaps, was of Sandon, Herts, for in 1646 a grant of administration was made to Joanne Kempe, *alias* Allen (? Tillon), widow, of the goods, credits, and estate of Thomas Kempe, a minor, her son. The Fulham line will be given under Middlesex, but we may here note that thence it branched out to Lincolnshire, where the name is largely represented from many distinct sources. Francis, of Little Hadham, besides being credited by the Heralds as the ancestor of these lines, is said by the author of the "History of Hendon," to be probably the ancestor of Hendon Kempes, but this will be seen to be impossible, as the latter were established before Francis Kempe, of Little Hadham, could have married.

The will of ANTHONY KEMPE (third son of Bartholomew, of Gissing) was proved in 1614 (P.C.C. 37 Lawe), and is interesting chiefly as confirming relationships. He is, of course, styled "gent." He says rather pathetically "I am set as you know at board with my nephew, Edward Rous, of Flordon, in Co. Norfolk, Clerk," adding that whereas he is an "ould man," he cannot ride for his money to Cambridge and other places, he has, therefore, become indebted to this nephew for his keep, therefore, and considering the kindness of his nephew, he leaves all he possesses at the time of his death to him. It appears that this Rev. Edward Rous was Anthony's

* This is presumably Shimpling, in Norfolk, near to Diss. There is another place of the same name in Suffolk, not far from Lavenham.

grand-nephew, being the son of Thomas Rous, otherwise Rowse, who married Margaret Kempe, of whom we shall speak again.

Anthony Kempe's sister Elizabeth married Lyonell Throckmorton, of Flixton, Suffolk, and South Elmham, and Bungay in Norfolk. This Lionel was under twenty-one in 1540, and died in 1599. By this wife he is said to have had no issue and he married again, his second wife being Elizabeth, daughter of John Blenerhausett, of Barsham, related to the Bleverhausett's before mentioned, and thus a second time connected with the Kempes, while Catherine, daughter of Wm Willington, had married first William Catesby, of Lapworth, secondly in 1547, *Richard* Kempe, and as her third husband she had Anthony Throckmorton, whose widow she died in 1594. Her will is recorded in that year (P.C.C., 69 Dixy), and in it she speaks of her brother's sons, Richard and Anthony Kemys, which probably is the scribe's error for Kempe; she also mentions her beloved son, Richard Butler, her cousin, Richard Rawlins, Thomas Palmer, of Holbourne, and numerous relations and friends known or related to Kempes of both Norfolk and Kent, thus it is difficult to say with certainty how her husband, Richard Kempe, was connected. His will describes him as of Longton, in the Parish of Tredington, Worcester, and was proved 1552 (P.C.C. 17 Buck).

The arms of Throckmorton, as given with the pedigree in the "Visitation of Norfolk," are Gules, on a chevron argent, two bars gemelles sable, with five quarterings.

Robert Kempe, the eldest son of Bartholomew, succeeded to the Gissing estates in 1554 on his father's decease. He married first Elizabeth, daughter of John Smythwyn, some authorities say Edmund Smythwyn, and both differ as to the County to which he belonged, Berks or Bucks, the place of his abode having been omitted in the pedigrees. We find that at Gissing Church the epitaph to Robert Kempe states that the father-in-law's name was John, and that by this first wife Robert had two sons and three daughters; these represent only those who survived infancy, for she had besides Bartholomew, Genehide, Edward and John, who died as children. Those who attained majority were Richard, the eventual heir; John, of Antingham; Margaret, who married Thomas Rous; Ann, the wife of Anthony Drury, and another daughter (perhaps named Dorothy, the wife of Norton). Robert Kempe's second wife was Elizabeth, daughter of Edmund de Grey, of Merton, whose sister Margaret had already married Edward Kempe, this Robert's brother. Edmund de Grey died 12th May, 1562, and was buried at Merton Church, Norfolk, where tombs to him, Thomas de Grey, his son, and others of the family exist. This marriage again not only complicated the relationships between the brothers, but also made a connexion between the Norfolk Kempes and Francis Kempe, of the Kentish family through the Carews, Thomas de Grey having married a daughter of Sir Wymond Carew, of Anthony, Cornwall, and Elianor Carew, the latter's neice, having become wife of the said Francis Kempe, son of William Kemp, Knight of Wye.

By Elizabeth de Grey, his second wife, Robert Kempe had the following issue:—Thomas Kempe, of Bricett Parva and Beccles, founder of the Kempe family of Thwaite; Robert, who married and left issue; William Kempe, of Cambridge; Edward, who appears to have been a clergyman of Oakington, Cambridgeshire; and Elizabeth, who married John Buxton, whose family resided at Channonz Hall, at Tibenham, the adjoining parish to Gissing.

Before dealing with these children and their respective families, we must note a few facts concerning Robert, their father, who lived to be 80. Following the example of Bartholomew Kempe, he endeavoured to improve the ancestral estates and to raise the status of the family in various ways. It was he who purchased the adwowson of Gissing Church in 1574. With Charles Le Grey, John Hastings, Jennys Bygott, and others, he founded a free chapel at Moulton, Norfolk, the deed concerning which bearing his signature and seal is preserved at the British

Museum (Add. Charters 874). He also re-roofed Gissing Hall, the account of which, with the cost and his domestic expenses, from about 1584 to his decease, is entered in the Museum with other Kempe documents. We are chiefly indebted to him, however, for collecting the scattered pedigrees of the different Kempe families, and other families of Norfolk, to which we have repeatedly referred (Brit. Mus. Harl. 901). During the earlier days of his married life he was, it would seem, in London, for a family corresponding to his were baptized at St. James', Clerkenwell, Richard being baptized in 1545, John in 1547, and Margaret in 1548. It is antecedently probable that until after his father's decease he may have been engaged in London where his uncles and other relatives were established as merchants. It must be admitted that the Clerkenwell Register may refer to quite a different line, for as has been noticed both Kempes of Kent and Kempes of Cornwall certainly resided in that parish, and appear in the church books.

Robert Kempe, of Gissing died 27th April, 1594, and was buried with his wife or wives at Gissing, where, as we have said, is a monument to his and their memory, with his arms displayed impaling theirs and the motto "Spero Lucem" (now written generally in the reverse order), the earliest instance of its use actually found, although doubtless this motto had been used from remote times. The Inquisition Post Mortem of this Robert Kempe was made in 1595, and may be seen at the Record Office. His name figures in the Close Rolls of Elizabeth, with the following names, at the dates indicated, but the nature of the transaction has not been followed up: 1566 with William Grice and 1575 with Edward Dyer.

He was succeeded by his son Richard, before dealing with whom we will give some account of the younger sons of this Robert Kempe and their issue.

John Kempe, the second son of Robert Kempe, of Gissing, by Elizabeth Smythwin (or Smithwine) married first Anne, daughter of Robert Cuddon, of Weston, in Suffolk, Esquire, by whom he had a son Robert and a daughter who married Robert Palgrave, of Bradfield, in Norfolk, Gent., second son of Clement Palgrave, of Barningham, Norfolk, Esquire. During the life of this first wife John Kempe probably lived at Cromer, for we find that a John Kempe had a lease of the Manors of Uffords and Tomlyns in that town from 1561.

He married as his second wife, Ann, daughter of Robert Calthorpe, of Antingham (which is near Cromer), who had married as her first husband Robert Jermy (sometimes corruptly called Germy and even Gerry) by whom she had several children. We do not know the date of her first husband's death or of her second marriage, but as we find John Kemp obtained property in and around Antingham, in 1587, his second marriage was most probably prior to that date. The lands which he held included the Manor of Callyce, in Suffield, and lands at Colby, Felmingham, North Walsham, Gunton and Antingham. They were not all his freehold property, but we cannot say on what terms he held the several estates, though we know that these, with other lands at Antingham St. Mary, Antingham St. Margaret, Gunthorp, Thorp Market, Bradfield and other properties, descended to his son, who held them in 1610-11.

This first Robert, of Antingham, acquired additional land at Thorp Market by marriage with Mary, daughter of Edmund Gresham and sister to Sir Richard Gresham, of Thorp Market. Her father, Edmund Gresham, had also a seat at this place and made his will in 1586, it being witnessed by Robert and John Kempe, William Jermy, William Hall and others, it was proved in London that year (P. C. C. 64 Windsor) and a copy may be seen printed in "Miscellanea Genealogica," vol. ii, pp. 264-5. At the time of his decease Mary, his daughter, was a minor and unmarried; the marriage, however, must have taken place soon afterwards, probably the following year. We may here call attention to the long connexion and friendship which had existed between the Greshams and Kempes. Edmund Kempe, four generations earlier, had left legacies to Sir Richard Gresham, Sir John Gresham and William Gresham, with whom, as a Citizen and Merchant of London, he had become intimately acquainted; he had succeeded the first Richard Gresham in the honourable office as surveyor and accountant of St. Paul's School, which the latter vacated in 1533. He was the father of the celebrated Sir Thomas Gresham, founder of the Royal Exchange, near whom, in the parish of St. Michael, Basinghall, Edmund Kempe lived. Within that parish church Sir Richard Gresham, Sir John Gresham, Edmund Kempe and others of his family were buried side by side. Margaret Dane, Edmund Kempe's daughter, kept up the intimacy. The wife of a John Kempe, of Birchington, Kent, was godmother to Mildred, daughter of Edward Gresham, in 1579, but how this Gresham was connected with the others we do not know. Fèret, who gives a good account of the Greshams, shows that one Edmund is also repeatedly called Edward; his father was of Mayfield, Sussex, and was son of Sir John Gresham of the Norfolk family. Thomas Gresham, brother to this Edward or Edmund, lived at Fulham, where he also was intimate with the Kempes.—(*vide* Fèret's "Fulham Old and New.") After this long family connexion it is no wonder that an intermarriage should take place, nor that John Kempe, of Antingham, should direct that Sir Richard Gresham should nominate feoffees for his estate to assure the payment of certain annuities. The will of this first John Kempe, of Antingham, was dated and proved in 1610 (Norwich Cons. 164 Harman). The testator leaves sums to the poor and for the reparation of the churches at North Walsham, Worsted, Fritton and Antingham; to his wife £20 over and above what she "brought out of Suffolk," as well as the annuity of £50; to his nephew Rowse, "parson of Flordon," his stepson William Jermy, his sister Lawrence, his wife's son William Grudgfield and other relatives, he leaves rings and other small legacies. To the wife of John Neave, Gent., of Banningham, he leaves a yearly rent of £100, and to his godson, the son of his nephew Robert Kempe, of Gissing, £5. The same amount is bequeathed to Thomas Kempe, son of his brother Robert Kempe. His son Robert Kempe is to be executor and chief legatee, but to be supervised by the testator's nephew Robert Kempe, of Gissing. The will is witnessed by William Jermy, Gent., Thomas Cully, Samuel Mackett (clerk to the testator) and John Albon (? Allen).

He was buried in Antingham Church, where a monument was erected to him bearing the following inscription:

"Here Resteth in the Lord the Body of John Kempe, Esq., Second son to Robert Kempe of Gissing Esq., who had issue by Anne the daughter of Robert Cuddon Esq. Robert sonne and Heire who made this monument remembering immortality in the hope of Resurrection the XVIII of November. Anno D'ni. 1610 aetatis 76."

The arms of the Gissing Kempes, with seven quarterings and four smaller shields referring to to the deceased, were displayed on the tomb.

Robert Kempe, the only son, duly inherited the whole of the estates, and, having no children, settled the whole of his lands upon his nephew Sir Robert Kempe, of Gissing. This settlement was evidently made during his life, as we find that he left no will, an administration being granted in 1626 to John Cudden, Gent., who was doubtless his cousin.

Thomas Kempe, Gent., next occupied the seat at Antingham, for we find that on 21st January, 1642, William Cock was granted to administer his estate, which, as we shall see, then became the favourite residence of Sir Robert Kempe.

CHAPTER VII.

KEMPES OF THWAITE AND BRICETT.

THE founder of the Kempe family at Thwaite was THOMAS KEMPE, the third surviving son of Robert Kempe, of Gissing, and next younger brother to the John Kempe who first settled at Antingham. He probably became connected with the Thwaite district through visiting his brother. It was not, however, until the next generation that Thwaite was, as we shall see, acquired.

THOMAS KEMPE was a "councellor of law" practising, doubtless, chiefly at Ipswich, where Richard, his eldest brother, was the official lawyer to the borough. In the "Calendar of Pleadings" (Ducatus Lancastriae) we find, during the reign of Elizabeth, that a case of Thomas Kempe *versus* John Layton is entered. This concerns an Ingress Fine at "Brissett, otherwise Talmays Manor, in Little Brissett, Clare Honor, Suffolk," which actually concerned Tallmach Hall, at Bricett. The exact year is not given, but a second suit between the parties is dated 1590, and this doubtless marks the time when the young counsellor made his home at that place, which would be conveniently placed for business requiring frequent journeys into Ipswich. He further identified himself with that town by marrying Ann, daughter and co-heir of John Moore, "Portman of Ipswich"; by this lady he had two sons, Thomas and John, and three daughters, Anne, Martha and Elizabeth. The last-named child married Josias Faweather (? Fairweather), of Halesworth (at which place some Kempes had been living shortly before this time). Thomas, the elder son, seems to have died before his father, for John, the second son, became heir. Thomas Kempe, the father, removed from Little Brissett to Beccles some time after 1595, perhaps on his retiring from his profession; it is said that he died in 1623, but no will or other evidence of his death has been traced by the present writers.

John Kempe, the succeeding son, first lived at Beccles, where he married Jane, one of the co-heirs of Thomas Hobart, of Thwaite, by Anne, daughter of William Raynes, of Overstrand, of whom we have spoken as connected with the John Kempe who settled at Antingham. This wife was to inherit—jointly with her sisters, Mary, the wife of Dr. Colby, and Elizabeth Peters—the Thwaite property, including Somerton Hall Manor, which had been in the Hobart family some generations. These sisters released their interest in the estate to John and Jane Kempe, who in time settled it upon their son Thomas Kempe.

This Thomas was a clergyman, but what cures he held is not known. At his death he seems to have been on the Norwich Cathedral staff, for he dated his Will from the precincts of that church, though he desired to be buried in the south isle of Thwaite church. He seems to have been married about 1649 to Frances, daughter of Sir Thomas Corbet, for a deed dated 26th September that year was made between Thomas Kempe, Sir Thos. Corbett, Sir Robert Kempe, William Kempe and John Gosling, Gent., settling the Manor of Somerton Hall and divers other lands in Norfolk as provision for his wife and her issue. Subsequently—doubtless owing to Cromwellian troubles—the estate was made over to Clement Kempe, their son, who was therefore at his father's death enjoined, "as he hoped for God's blessing," to faithfully pay to his mother an annuity of £80 during her life, paying this to her regularly at the Feasts of the Annunciation, Nativity, St. John the Baptist and St. Michael, in the porch of the parish church of Thwaite. These instructions he seems to have faithfully carried out.

Besides this son, Thomas and Frances had a son Hobart Kempe (named after his grandmother) who visited Bombay and died at sea on his way home in 1689. There was a bookseller of his name, at the sign of the "Ship," in London, in 1672, but we cannot say whether this is the same individual. The estate of Hobart, who died at sea, was granted in 1689 to his mother Frances Kempe, and after her decease a fresh power of administration was granted in 1693 to his brother Robert Kempe. This son left no issue, being a bachelor at his death. Robert acted also as executor to his mother, but of his later movements we are not certain.

The Reverend Thomas Kempe left children named Thomas, Elizabeth and Frances, the last-named daughter married the Rev. Thomas Benyon, of Ely, in 1684, at St. George's-in-Tombland, Norwich, she being then a resident in the precincts of Christ Church, Norwich. (At the same church an Elizabeth Kempe was married, in 1699, to Thomas Chitting of that parish, it would seem likely that she was the sister of the Frances married there, but we have no proof of this.)

The Reverend Thomas Kempe dated his will 23rd March, 1667, it was not proved until 1670, we do not know exactly the date of his death. His will, besides directing Clement, his eldest son, to provide for his mother out of the Thwaite estates, required him to pay £300 to each of the testator's daughters (Frances and Elizabeth). In case the mother died before receiving her legacies Clement was to allow £6 per annum to each of his younger brothers until they came of age, and to the daughters each £12 until their legacies were paid. Thomas Kempe mentions also his "good sisters-in-law" Mrs. Elizabeth Gostling, the Lady Alford and Mrs. Katherine Corbet, and he constituted his "honorable and dear friend and kinsman" Sir Robert Kempe, of Gissing, Baronet, supervisor. Robert, the youngest son, was to be brought up in "the schools of good learning," to be afterwards sent to the university and to study Divinity. Charities were left to the poor of Thwaite and Alby. This will, with many pious paternal injunctions, is registered in the Prerogative Court of Canterbury (61 Penn) with a carefully made list of outstanding debts.

The will of Frances Kempe, the widow, was proved in the same court in 1690 (27 Vere). She was living at Ely, Cambridge, when it was drawn up, presumably as a guest of her daughter Frances Benyon, whose husband and children are mentioned, with her grandchild Frances Kemp and her sister Katherine, who is one of the witnesses. The chief property appearing is a lease from the Bishop of Norwich which, with £100, she left to the Rev. Thomas Benyon her son-in-law; this son however died before December, 1690, and the lease and money passed direct to Frances Benyon his wife. (Thomas, as well as her son Hobart, are mentioned as having died before February, 1689.)

She died on January 12th, 1691, aged sixty-nine, and was buried at St. Mary's, Ely, where there is a mural tablet to her memory. Her maiden name being Corbett has led to a correspondent in the ***Gentleman's Magazine*** connecting the Kempes of Thwaite with the Essex family, George Kempe, of Pentlow and Tottenham, having married, for his third wife, Mary, daughter of John Corbet, of Sproughton, Norfolk, whose first husband was Sir Roger Woodhouse. George Kempe will be seen by our Essex section of this work to have a distinct line of Kempe ancestors (back to 1296) from those of Norfolk, but a double intermarriage had occurred before the above Frances Kempe died, which closely linked two Sir Robert Kempes of the distinct families together. In this way, if not directly through the Corbets, there was a relationship between those of Thwaite and Pentlow.

The inscription referred to is as follows:

"Near this stone lyeth the body of Frances Kemp late widow of Thomas Kemp of Thwait Hall in Co. Norfolk Gent, who departed this life January 12th in the year 1691, aged 67."

Clement Kemp married a daughter of one Whitton, of Wilby, by whom he had only a daughter, who became sole heiress and conveyed the Thwaite estates by marriage to John Horne, of Witchingham, Gent. The name of this daughter and heiress was, we believe, Frances, as mentioned in the will of Frances her grandmother. The Hornes and Kempes were frequently after this united by marriages both in Norfolk and others of the same name having estates in Kent, the relationship between the various Hornes has not however been ascertained. These Kemps appear to be extinct in the male line unless Robert Kemp had issue. We have no trace of a clergyman of his name at this period, and can only suggest that one of the following wills might be his and that, if examined, it is possible that the pedigree may be brought down to recent times:

Robert Kemp, Hunstanton, 1719-20, Norfolk Arch. Court, fo. 23.

Roger Kemp, Wrentham 1719 and 1734, Suffolk Arch. Court.

In attempting to trace further descent it will be well to notice that, living within the same Norwich Cathedral precincts and attending the same church of St. George's-in-Tombland, there were Kempes of the Pentlow stock before mentioned who had much property throughout Norfolk, chiefly round Lyng, Heydon and Wood Dalling.

CHAPTER VIII.

KEMPES OF GISSING—*continued.*

ROBERT, the fourth son of Robert Kempe, of Gissing (by Elizabeth Grey), married Ann, co-heir of William Stanton or Staunton, Esq., and had two sons, Robert and Thomas Kempe, but of the place of their abode or of further issue we have no details. William Kempe, of Cambridge, who married Thomazine, daughter of William Waldegrave, of Hitcham, Suffolk, does not appear to have left any issue. His widow married Samuel Harsnet, Bishop of Chichester, afterwards of Norwich, who died in 1629. Her arms were Per pale, argent and gules, with eleven other quarterings. Edward we have not identified with any will or local record; it is, therefore, open to question whether he reached manhood.

We now return to RICHARD KEMPE, the eldest brother of these, and son and heir of "old" Robert Kempe of Gissing, by Elizabeth Smythwime. We find his name enrolled as a student at Gray's Inn, 1556, and also in the registers of that Inn in 1582 as being one of the "Readers of this House." We may remark that two earlier entries concerning Kempes entering Gray's Inn as students of the law occur, the first being a John Kempe in 1544, who may have been this Richard's bachelor uncle, and the second Edmund or Edward Kempe who was admitted in 1552. It is possible that the latter belonged to the same family, but of this we have no evidence other than the fact that Edward Kempe, of Gissing, who settled in London as a mercer, had a son named Edmund, who would be of a suitable age to be a student at this date.

Richard Kempe married Alice Cockerham, the daughter of Phillip Cockerham, of Hampstead, whose family were connected with the Cockerhams of Cornwall. They sometime spelled their name as Corkrom and Kockrom, as appears from their Signatures to the will of John Kempe of Hampstead, in 1574 (Com. Court, London, 35 Martyn) and the Parish Register, 1566 to 1584. The Arms of Cockerham, of Hampstead, Middlesex, are given in the Harleian MSS., 1551, as

Argent, on a bend sable three (? tigers') heads caboshed or. Their pedigree appears in the "Visitation of Devon."

Hampstead had been separated from the parish of Hendon by Bishop Thomas Kempe, and as he considerable episcopal property in this district it is not unlikely that some of his own kinsmen had were admitted to his lands as tenants in his time, but the Subsidy Rolls do not give names of residents in this part until 1520, when the chief inhabitants of Hampstead are William, George and (widow) Margaret Kempe. These, however, must have gone to Hendon Church, as did their descendants, for the first entry of a Kempe in the Hampstead Register is that recording that on January 22, 1566, Richard Kemp and Alice "Kockrom" were married. Perhaps the couple resided in the Parish of Hampstead for a while, for certainly their son and heir (from whom all the Baronets are descended), was baptized at the same church on 28th December, 1567, this being the second Kemp entry. It was so usual for the young wife to be with her mother for the first confinement that we must not necessarily conclude that Richard Kempe the lawyer, was a householder here. There can, however, be no doubt that three other Kempes holding the chief establishments were in this parish at the time, while in Hendon adjoining Humphrey Kempe was a "considerable" landowner, and Bartholomew Kempe had also an interest in land there. We learn the latter fact from the Feet of Fines for Middlesex, in 1567 (printed). Concerned with Bartholomew in the Hendon property are Thomas Andrews, Edward Wyseman, and Richard Nicholles. This Bartholomew has not certainly been identified with Bartholomew Kempe of Gissing, but it will be recollected that Bartholomew, the Lord of the Manor of Gissing, died in 1554, leaving a son of the same name, who was at this time married and living in London. As there is no record of any other Bartholomew Kempe in or near London at this time it is very likely that Bartholomew had a suburban retreat at Hendon, as did so many of his relatives. Of this we shall have more to say in our Middlesex section. Meanwhile we must follow Richard from Hampstead to Ipswich. That ancient and important borough, whose interest had been dear to other Kempes, called for the services of Richard Kempe and appointed him to the post of Councillor of the Law to the town. In the Archives of Ipswich, as given in the Ninth Report of the Royal Historical Commission, it is officially recorded as follows:

"23rd March, 14 Elizabeth (1571-2) Order for the appointment of Richard Kempe, Esquire, learned in the law, to be Councel for the town during pleasure; at a yearly fee of twenty shillings."

We need scarcely remark upon the handsome retaining fee; we feel sure that the barrister made a very substantial addition to his income by the appointment, and that as we have remarked he managed to put professional fees in the way of his eldest brother, who also practised as a lawyer in the Ipswich Courts.

This appointment necessitated residence in the neighbourhood. The place he selected was "Wasbrooke," *hodie* Washbrook, situated about three miles to the south-west of the town. Here, doubtless, other children were born who presumably died in youth, for we are informed that the son baptized at Hampstead was the only son, while no daughters are mentioned. Blomfield gives a few abstracts from the Gissing Church Registers, only one of which refers to this Richard, who is entered as having been buried there on 5th April, 1600. We can only infer from this that Richard probably removed from Washbrook to Gissing on the death of his father, about six years previous to this date, by which time he was fifty-four years of age (at which age also Bartholomew had succeeded to the estates). We do not know much concerning the Gissing property during his tenure, except that it was made subject to a marriage settlement for his wife. The deed was made between Richard Kempe, described as of Gissing, and Alice Cockerham, of Hampstead, and concerns the Manors of Hastings, in Gissing, Flordon, Dallings and Redisham in Suffolk. The last-named property is mentioned in a Kempe of Weston deed as having been in possession of those Kempes in 1411. The original is among the Stowe MSS. at the British Museum (Ch. 250). This alone is good evidence of the direct descent of the Norfolk family from the Weston Kempes.

After the decease of Richard, his widow, Alice, married again, her second husband being Edmund Poley, Gent., of Badley, near Stowmarket. The wedding is duly reeorded as having taken place at Gissing Church on 17th September, 1601. In the church of Badley there is a long inscription to the Poleys, including this Edmund Poley, who died the last day of October, 1613, aged sixty-nine. His marriage with "Alice, relict of Ricard Kemp," of Gissing, is likewise mentioned. The pedigree and notes concerning the Poleys of Badley is given in Jackson's edition of "The Visitation of Suffolk."

We do not know if the property at Washbrook was handed down by Richard to his son. Possibly it was settled on the widow outright in place of the charge on the Gissing and other properties. Richard added at least one other possession to the family estates, for in (or soon after) 1579 he purchased the manor afterwards known as that of "Gissing Hall," in Roydon. Thus his manors practically extended from Braconash to Diss, along the present route of the Great Eastern Railway from Ipswich to Norwich. Richard desired to be buried in the Chapel of Gissing "with the rest of my ancestors." His Will was proved in the Norwich Consistorial Court on 7th May, 1600, by his son and his wife.

The Will states that the Manors of Gissing, Flordon, and Burnells had been charged with a dowry for the wife of his son, which the testator had confirmed since the son's marriage. It settles £3 6*s*. 8*d*. per annum on the deceased's sister Margaret, the wife of Daniel Cotton, who was also to receive a mourning ring and gown. Rings and gowns are also given to Richard's brother-in-law, Drury ; his sister, Buxton ; his nephew and niece Harbourne ; his brother at Antingham, and Thomas Kempe, of Beccles ; his niece, Dorothy Norton ; his cousin, Robert Kempe, of Bury St. Edmunds ; his god-daughter, Ann Lany (or Lang) ; his nephews, Thomas Kemp, then a scholar in Cambridge, and Edward Rowse. Robert and John, sons of his son Robert, are to have a sum of money when they go to Gray's Inn to study the law, and a Mr. Sherwood, of Tivetshall, with servants and maids, are remembered. Roger Payne, John Buxton and Henry Horseman were the witnesses.

Anne Kempe's marriage with Mr. Anthony Drury, above named, took place at Gissing, 26th May, 1567. This gentleman was seated at Besthorp. Their daughter or grandchild married Henry Roswood the Lord of Weston.

At the call to arms in 1599 this Richard Kempe, of Norfolk, with William Kempe, of Spain's Hall, and George Kempe, of Middlesex, each provided one lance and two light horsemen at their own expense.

As already indicated, the estates next devolved upon the only son of Richard Kempe, of Gissing, in 1600. This Robert, who was born at Hampstead, Middlesex, in 1567, was entered as a student at Gray's Inn on 9th May, 1582. We do not know that he ever practised as a lawyer, he may however have assisted his father as a councillor at Ipswich and afterwards taken over the duties on his father's removal to Gissing. The supposition consists with the fact that his first two children are not recorded as having been baptized at Gissing, while on his accession to the manors he evidently settled there at once with his wife and infant sons, for Richard, his third son, was baptized there in 1600 and Arthur, his fourth son, was also baptized there in 1601. Of the subsequent baptisms we have no knowledge ; Blomfield, who gives some extracts, tells us that the registers were partially burnt, which fact prevents us making a search for these details ; however, in the present case it is unimportant, so fully are the relationships supported by other evidence. We may, however, say that Blomfield mentions the burial of a Robert Kempe at Gissing in 1600, as well as the burial of Richard; perhaps this relates to Robert, the brother of the last Lord of Gissing, though mentioned in the Will above recorded, or perhaps the son of Robert Kempe, of Bury.

Robert Kempe, of Gissing, had married (about 1596) Dorothy, daughter of Arthur Harris, of Cricksea and Woodham Mortimer, Essex, by Dorothy, daughter of Sir William Waldegrove, of Smallbridge, Suffolk, and sister of Sir William Harris, of Cricksea. Their pedigree is duly set out

This portrait, which is at Mergate Hall, is marked in pencil "Mrs. Sone," but the dress and features suggest that it more probably represents Dorothy Harris, the mother of the First Baronet.

in the "Essex Visitation" of 1612. Her father was buried with Heraldic formality, by Segar Norroy, in Mortimer Church. (While speaking of Woodham Mortimer we may note that connected with this parish and Althorne there were several generations of Kempes, ancestors of the present Charles Fitch Kemp, Esq. of Hildenborough, Kent, whose seat is celebrated for its fine pack of hounds.

The Waldegrave who was the mother of this Dorothy Harris makes the third relationship existing at this period between Kempes and that family.

Besides the four sons already mentioned, Robert had the following children by this wife (who outlived him): Edmund, who acted as the first Baronet's attorney in Virginia; Thomas, who appears to have been living in 1626; Edward, who went to Virginia, and Matthew Kempe, a colonel who played a prominent part in the settlement of Virginia, of which Colony Richard, the third son, was the first Secretary. Of John, the second son, we are told by Blomfield that he married Amphillis, daughter of Roger Bigot (ancestor of the Earls of Norfolk), who was possessed of the Manor of Antingham, which thus came to the Kempes. John and Amphillis are said, by the same authority, to have settled it upon Robert Kempe, Esquire, their nephew, who was Lord of it in 1700; this may be quite in order but the proofs have not been searched for by the present compilers. The fourth son, Arthur, took holy orders and preached at Gissing in 1639 with the Bishop's licence, having studied at Pembroke College, Cambridge, between 1620-23, and obtained a curacy at Cricksea, Essex, From 1631 to 1635 he was Rector of Mapiscombe, in Kent. He used frequently to write little moral essays to his relatives in the form of letters, some of which may be seen at the British Museum (Add. MSS., 10,435). An idea of the contents may be gathered from the following titles: 1.—"Upon the death of her younger son"; 2.—"Upon the death of her daughter"; 3.—"To one going to reside as Factor at Constantinople"; 4.—"To Mrs. . . . upon the death of his wife"; 5.—"Advices concerning marriage"; 7.—"To a gentleman tortured with gout." The last covers 207 pages of manuscript. These manuscripts were reviewed in the *Gentleman's Magazine* of 1814. The reviewer was not aware of their having been published, and one would hardly expect that their sale would be profitable. They were, however, printed in 1641 and dedicated to "The Noble and Virtuous Lady the Lady Waldegrave." The author soon afterwards became the Rector of St. Michael-at-Thorne, in Norwich, where he died in 1644, or the following year. His Will was proved in 1645 (P.C.C. Rivers, 68). It leaves bequests to the poor of the two parishes of Antingham, Flordon, St. Michael-at-Thorn and to the City of Norwich. He mentions the following: the four eldest children of his brother Edmund; his nieces Dorothy Jackman, Wal(de)grave and Elizabeth; "his cozen Freeman's wife"; Thomas Cain, of Best Street; his sister Lady Kempe, of Spain's Hall, in Essex; his cousin Thomas Rous, of Flordon, and his cousin Porter, of Dover; cousin "Tom Kempe the Minister"; his brother Sir Robert Kempe and Doctor Thomas Browne. The last named was the celebrated Sir Thomas Browne, author of "Religio Medici." The cousin Porter, at Dover, we do not know. The Reverend Arthur Kempe seems to have accumulated a good collection of books. He leaves a choice copy of "Tolosinus" to Browne, while all those at his London Chambers as well as those at Norwich were to go to the Gissing Hall Library. His niece Dorothy Jackman was the daughter of his sister Dorothy Kempe, she having married William Jackman, the sister having died before this. The other nieces were daughters of Sir Robert Kempe.

Judging from these Wills it would seem that little thought was bestowed upon those of the family who had emigrated, although one was attorney to Sir Robert and Colonel Matthew was over again in this country. News however travelled so slowly and uncertainly that it doubtless seemed useless to leave bequests to those who were out of reach and might have been dead months before tidings could reach home.

Robert Kempe died in 1612, when none of his children had reached manhood. He was buried at Gissing, where the inscription to his memory runs as follows:

"Robert Kemp only sonne of Richard Kempe of Gissing Esquire and Alice Cockerham of Hampstead . . . . married Dorothy Harris of Crixeth, Essex, by whom he had VIII sons and III daughters, seven sons and two daughters survived him. He died, 23 October MDCXII, aged 47 years and having been married 17 years."

Dorothy, his widow, lived after his death at the Manor House at Flordon, of which we give an illustration. It remains to-day much the same in external appearance as it did in her day, the arms will be seen over the porch, just the Kempe shield without quarters. Although much of the oak panelling has been removed to Mergate Hall by the present Baronet, one can well picture the interior as the widow Dorothy Kempe knew it. There, in the great drawing-room in the

Flordon Hall, built about 1500 on the site of a previous Manor House, which passed to the Kempes by intermarriage with the heiress of Duke and Butteveleyn.

south wing, its floor laid with unusually broad oaken boards, she sat day after day with her unmarried daughter spinning the thread and making, and carefully marking with their respective initials, the hoards of fine household linen which she prepared for each of her children "against their marriage." In her will she gives us a glimpse of this outcome of her domestic activity, even explaining that Edward and Edmund Kempe having the same initials she had distinguished the linen intended for Edmund by an E being "let in the corner." In the early days of her widowhood she had, of course, the usual trouble which seven boys in a house are bound to cause. Robert, the eldest, must have been a young incorrigible and a constant anxiety to his pious mother, for, with the daring and gaiety which manifested itself in his manhood, we are sure that he demanded obedience from the servant and the homage of his future tenants, while his amorous proclivities must have got him into numerous scrapes with the fair young ladies and beautiful rustic maidens of the district, but college days then commenced earlier and in a few years the widow was much left to the company of her daughters and divided her time between the devotions prescribed by strict Puritan views and the linen for her sons and daughters. She died at Flordon in 1626, and was buried, as she desired, beside her husband in the family chapel at Gissing. Her will was proved that year (P.C.C., 120 Hele.) and is expressive of her maternal affection and Puritan feelings. She mentions certain wills under which her family were to receive legacies, viz., those of her late husband; Alice Poley, the children's grandmother; Roger Payne and Grizzell Herbert. Of this last we shall be glad to gain some knowledge, for it would appear likely that this "Grissell Herbert, of Gissing," was the Lady Herbert who married a John Kempe in 1572. A mystery hangs round the marriage for no Grizzell or Grace Herbert appears in the pedigrees of that family. The Herberts were at this time successors to the Greys, both as Lords of Powis Castle and Lords of Hendon, where the Kempes were their neighbours. Between the Herberts and Greys a very long litigation was carried on as to right to the title and certain Welsh estates, the cause being an Edward (Kempe) who was claimed to be son of Edward Lord Powis, by one Jane Kempe *alias* Jane Orwell. Whether she was akin to the Norfolk Kempes we do not know. Any information concerning Lady Grace Herbert and Grissell Herbert, of Gissing, will be welcomed by the editors of this work. Dorothy Kempe mentions the following children: Robert, Arthur, Edmund, Edward, Thomas, Dorothy and Elizabeth; her daughter-in-law Dame Jane Kemp; her "cousin" Thomas Kempe, of Barrow Hampton, and Dorothy the daughter of her "cousin" Clere Tolbot, of Wymondham; Prudence the daughter of her cousin Edward Rouse, of Flordon, and Henry Bing, Sergeant at Law of Grantchester, Cambridgeshire. The testatrix mentions that she holds a lease of a house in Finsbury from Sir William Parkhurst, Knight. If this refers to Finsbury, Middlesex, it might represent a London residence, perhaps mentioned by Arthur Kempe as his Chambers in London. She also speaks of her personal property at "Hopen" and Eye, in Suffolk, and land in Old Buckenham, Norfolk. Her chief jewels she left to her daughter-in-law Lady Jane Kempe.

The Rev. Edward Rous was evidently not only a beloved relative of Dorothy and the Rev. Arthur Kempe, but also an acceptable teacher of the Puritan beliefs and practices, perhaps he was related to that Francis Rous who was created a peer by Cromwell and at an advanced age was one of his Privy Council; the portrait of this "speaker of the House of Commons" hangs in the Hall of Pembroke College, Oxford; he was buried at Acton, in Middlesex, where a branch of the Norfolk Kempes had a house. It must have created domestic difficulties when Sir Robert became a Royalist, while this his cousin Rous was a pronounced Roundhead.

CHAPTER IX.

THE FIRST BARONET.

ROBERT KEMPE, who was destined to become both a Knight and the first of the line of Baronets, was, as already shown, an infant at the death of his grandfather, Richard Kempe, the Councillor of Ipswich, who hoped that this grandchild would follow the law as his profession. At his father's death, though only about fifteen years of age, he was even then averse to following the studies which he had been desired to take up, reasoning, no doubt, that he had but to wait until his twenty-first birthday before he could enjoy the income of the family estates, and that hence there was no need of any occupation (other than pleasure) for him.

He was nevertheless entered as a student of Gray's Inn, his name being enrolled on 26th February, 1614, as "son and heir of Robert Kempe, Esquire, of Gissing." It is unlikely that he ever practised as a lawyer, but it seems probable that he obtained some office in the Court of Faculties, as for some years a Robert Kempe issued marriage licences. This office, if he actually held it, may well have opened the way to his becoming intimate with many influential people, but it must be remembered, that apart therefrom, he had a "friend at court" in the person of his kinsman Bacon, and must have been familiar with many of the ladies of the Royal circle. Young and wealthy as he was, he soon found favour, with the result that in 1618 he was Knighted by James I., at his Palace at Theobalds, Herts., on the 12th November. In the same year Robert Kempe retired from the Court of Faculties.

From that date Sir Robert Kempe became closely attached to the King's person, and doubtless with Sir Francis Bacon, enjoyed both pleasure and profit. From the bonds of matrimony, however, he kept himself free till he reached middle life, although it is impossible that he lacked admirers, for his portrait (frontispiece) which must have been painted about this time, shows that his face was almost as attractive as his fortune. Eventually, however, before 1626, he married the heiress of Sir Matthew Browne, of Betchworth Castle, a gentleman who could boast of long descent, and moreover, possessed connexions with exceptional influence at Court. Jane Browne, too, if she bore him children, would link them with the descendants of her kinswoman, Eleanor Browne, the wife of Sir William Kempe, of Wye, at the same time providing Royal ancestors for their children. From how many Royal personages and other worthies this Jane Browne was descended, we must leave our readers to ascertain from the tables of Kempe descent drawn up by the author of "Stemmata Robertson et Durdin," from which the Royal descent given in the Kentish section of this work is extracted. That table shows a few of the lines which can easily be multiplied by a little patient study of the above-mentioned tables and other works on regal lineage. This being merely a history of the Kemps and Kempes, we must not devote pages to this very interesting but remote ancestry.

Jane Brown, wife of the First Baronet. (*Circa* 1620)

Sir Robert Kempe naturally accompanied the Court in its peregrinations, while he had many friends of his own, at whose houses he was a frequent guest. We are not surprised, therefore, to find that his eldest son, Robert, was born at Walsingham Abbey, whose charming ruins are one of the glories of his native county. The date of his birth was 2nd February, 1627, and the heir was soon conveyed in safety to Gissing Hall. Lady Kempe, doubtless, found Gissing rather quiet after the life at Court to which she had been accustomed, and consequently preferred living in London; when a retreat to the country became imperative, she preferred Antingham as a home rather than Gissing Hall. The Antingham residence we find described as their "winter" house in 1643.

The year 1641 will ever be a memorable in the annals of the Kempes of Gissing. Generation after generation had for centuries led a prosperous but somewhat uneventful life, escaping the attainders and escheats which upset many landed families. Except once when a member was detained at Norwich Castle on a false charge of manslaughter, for which he received a so-called "pardon," the chief members of the family have never figured in the records of disgrace. This year, however, gaiety and pleasure gave place to trouble in the prospect of civil war. Sir Robert Kempe as became a Knight and personal attendant of the King, determined to stand by his colours and made no secret of his aversion to the policy of the Parliamentary party. Foremost among the Norfolk Royalists was Sir William D'Oyley, whom Sir Robert Kempe, of Gissing, calls in his will "his cousin." With this Knight Sir Robert shared the honour of raising among their tenantry and friends a band of soldiers as a King's body-guard, while from time to time they raised at their own expense further forces, providing the necessary supplies for their maintenance, and otherwise assisting the King with funds. Before the war actually broke out the King recognised the long personal devotion of Sir Robert by raising him from the rank of Knight to that of Baronet. As an especial mark of Royal favour he directed that the usual heavy fees for the Patent, the charges of the Heralds, scribes and other officials should be borne by the Royal purse instead of devolving, as is usual, upon the recipient of the honour.

Royal Patent granting the Baronetcy to Sir Robert Kempe, of Gissing, 1641.

The original Patent is extant and quite perfect, the great seal attached not even being cracked. The portrait of the King in the initial letter of the document is, as will be seen from the illustration here given, a very good portrait of His Majesty.

At this time there were two Sir Robert Kempes resident in Norfolk, the other being Sir Robert Kempe, of Heydon, and afterwards of Spains Hall, Essex. He had married Elizabeth

Kempe, sister to the first Kempe Baronet of Gissing. Thus they were brothers-in-law, but were otherwise of quite distinct descent and diverse arms. They are believed to have come from entirely different stocks, the earliest known ancestors of the one being styled "de Campo" and the other "de Combes." The two Sir Robert Kempes were most intimate friends, and seem to have been companions at Charles's Court, both in days of peace, and during the exciting times of the Great Rebellion. Nor was this all, for as in war so in love, they seem to have risked even their ancestral domains to gain their desires. Surely nothing but a sporting propensity could have called for a bond so great as the whole of one's Hall and Manors to be pledged to secure a wife. Yet such a bond is recorded as having been made between the two Sir Roberts. Later on, as we shall see, the widow of Sir Robert Kempe, of Spain's Hall, became the wife of the second Sir Robert Kempe, of Gissing, thus further confusing and complicating the relationships. Further than this, by mere chance, it seems Lady Jane Kempe, of Gissing, being an heiress of the Brownes, held the advowson of Finchingfield Church, which was afterwards held by the Kempes of Spain's Hall, in that parish, so that both Kempe families were in turn patrons of the living.

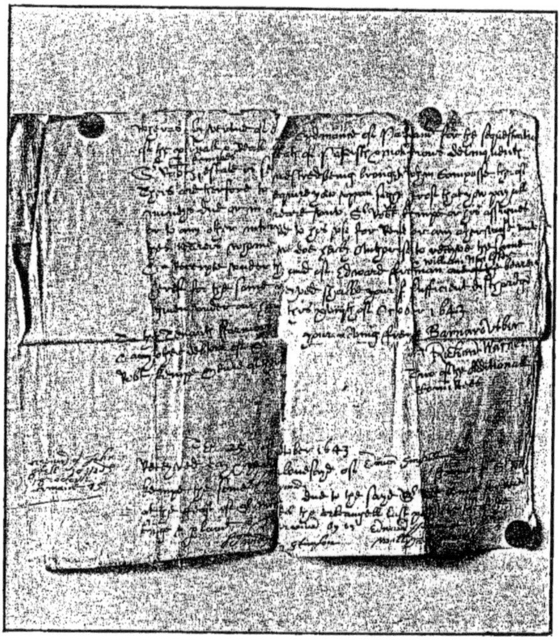

Warrant issued under Cromwell for the sequestration of Sir Robert Kempe, 1643.

One other point in common possibly helped to cement their friendship. Both their mothers held pronounced Puritan views, which they endeavoured to impress on their children with the result that they worked to the opposite extreme. We shall deal more particularly with the Sir Robert Kempe, of Heydon, when we come to the Essex section, though he remained in close association with the Gissing family.

When the war broke out, in 1642, the little force raised by Sir Robert Kempe, and others, was found to be helpless against Cromwell. Sir William D'Oyley and Sir Robert Kempe had, therefore, to fly for safety to Rotterdam, as is fully told in the history of the D'Oyley family.

How long Sir Robert actually remained at Rotterdam and "parts beyond the sea" we are unable to say, but in October, 1643, he was at least in hiding, for a warrant was issued for the sequestration of his personal and real estate on the sixteenth of that month. This interesting document, with others mentioned in this chapter, are still in the hands of the Kemps of Gissing. It is addressed to the "Tenant ffarmers and any other debtors of Sir Robert Kempe," and is signed by (Captain) Richard Warner and Bernard Uther (or Utberd), "Two of the Additional Committee." Edward Freeman and William Walter were the bearers of the warrant and collectors of the rents and moneys demanded. Edward Singleton paid on the 25th October, 1643, £60 due to Sir Robert Kempe, and John Stell paid £10 on the 18th of the month, leaving a balance due of £15.

Between these dates and November 27th of that year, Gissing was threatened with an attack from the "unruly people in Essex and Suffolk," in consequence of which the valuables there were hidden or removed with all speed to places less likely to be plundered. A letter signed by "J.D." addressed to a "Mr. Bradley," tells us of this, and in a friendly way pleads with the appraisers not to interfere unreasonably with the personal effects of Lady Kempe, or to do wanton mischief to the family pictures or the place. The letter was evidently a kind service of some friend of both parties, who calls himself a cousin of the Kempes, and had the desired effect of restraining the Cromwellian officer and his men from pillaging and damaging the property, otherwise many treasures still held by the family must have been lost. We gather from the various documents that Lady Kempe was at Gissing in the memorable October, and afterwards retreated to Antingham, which was deemed a safer residence. Even there, however, the collectors seem to have demanded payment for things which had been brought thither from Gissing after being appraised, which were deemed subject to further fine demanded from Sir Robert Kempe for his "delinquences."

In the absence of Sir Robert, the Parliamentary Committee had granted a lease to Edward Singleton, giving him a reduction of one-fourth the rent he had formerly paid to the Baronet. Notwithstanding a previous agreement, this tenant was declared as not liable for the full rent to Sir Robert, even after the latter had compounded for his estate. In this way alone Sir Robert suffered heavily for years. His fine paid on 3rd March, 1645 was £112 18*s*. 4*d*., as appears by the original receipt signed by Hugh Newhouse, Clerk to the Committee of Accounts for Norfolk and Norwich

In order to release himself from the consequences of his heavy expenditure in raising troops and the subsequent fine, he was forced to sell some of his estates. These lands have now returned to the family by the present Baronet purchasing them.

On 29th April, 1647, Sir Robert Kempe, styling himself Knight and Baronet of Gissing, made his will. The opening sentence indicates his religious views. He commends his soul "to God and Jesus Christ my sweet Saviour and redeemer," phraseology not favoured by the Puritans. He gave the usual bequests to the poor, but abstains from tributes to the clergy or churches. The will was not proved until 6th September, 1647, by which time his late Royal master was a prisoner in the hands of the Roundheads. (Norwich Cons. 1647, fo. 93b)

The will mentions Antingham, Diss, North Walsham, Cromer, Dicklesburgh and Burston, in all of which the first Sir Robert Kempe had property as well at Gissing, Flordon, Braconash and other parishes. To his wife, Dame Jane Kempe, he bequeathed his coach and horses, jewels, and the use of his ready money for "the bringing up of the children," five of whom it seems had been placed out to board during the war. A marriage settlement having been made, it was not necessary to mention other provision for his wife in the will.

To his eldest son, Robert Kempe, he particularly bequeathed his "yellow diamond ring"; this, it seems, has now been lost. It is thought that it passed out of the family with other trinkets; the widow Kempe married Anthony Merry, of whom we shall speak in due course. Sir Robert further left his books to his son Robert, and £80 per annum from his 17th year. To his other sons he left the following annuities:—To Thomas, his second son, £60; to Matthew, his third, £50 from 16, and £30 until he reached that age. To Maurice Shelton and his Wife,

£10, and to Dorothy, daughter of his late sister, Dorothy Jackman, £100, on her marriage with consent of his "sister, Lady Kempe, *in Essex*," with £10 per annum until her wedding. To his "brother, Sir Robert Kempe, of Finchingfield, Essex," and to his sister, his wife, also to each of his sisters and his son, Thomas Waldegrave, he left sums for mourning. To his grandchild, Jane Waldegrave, he gave £20, and to his executors £40 each; these being Dame Jane Kempe, the Baronet's wife, and Sir William D'Oyley, who had shared so many ot his escapades. The witnesses to the will were William Starkey, Junior, and Thomas Thurston.

We may here note that Maurice Shelton and the daughter of Sir Robert Kempe were ancestors of Lord Nelson, of whom we shall have occasion to speak again. Sir Robert died on 20th August, 1647.

CHAPTER X.

THE SECOND BARONET

SIR ROBERT KEMPE, the second Baronet, was born, as above stated, at Walsingham Abbey, where his parents were visiting with the Court. His baptism is entered in the register of Walsingham Church, the entry being as follows:

"Robertus Kempe filius Roberti. 14 Februarii 1627."

We are told that he was born on the second of that month, thus he was baptized when only twelve days old. At the death of his father he was but little over twenty years of age. Before he was twenty-four he married Mary, daughter of Thomas Kerridge, of Shelley, in Suffolk, the wedding taking place at that parish church 15th July, 1650. This lady gave birth to three children, all of whom died young, they were probably born and baptized at Antingham, as the following inscriptions to their memory were erected in Antingham Church. The first runs:

"Here lyeth interred the body of Elizabeth Kemp ye Daughter of Sir Robert Kemp of Antingham in the County of Norfolk, Baronet, and Mary his wife ye Daughter of Thomas Kerridge of Shelley in the County of Suffolk, Esq. She was born the 23 of April 1655 and Died on the 17th day of March 1657."

The second differs only in the child's name and date, which was Mary Kemp, who was born on the 20th and buried on the 29th January, 1654. The other child was a son, who also died in infancy. Lady Kempe's death occurred in 1655.

Sir Robert married for his second wife Mary, daughter of John Sone, of Ubbeston, Gent. The wedding took place at St. Andrew's Church, Holborn, London, in 1657. It is probable that the marriage was celebrated here owing to Sir Robert being a barrister belonging to Gray's Inn, the members of which were considered parishioners of St. Andrews. If, like most of his family, he ever qualified as a lawyer, it would seem that he rarely or never practised. On the death of his first wife he left Antingham for Gissing Hall, but Ubbeston Hall passing to him on his second

Mary Sone, second wife of Second Baronet.

Sir Robert Kemp, Second Baronet, M.P., North Norfolk, 1668.

marriage he removed thither. Thus his second family were baptized at Ubbeston Church, the entries being as follows:

Mary Kemp the first daughter of Sir Robert and Mary, born 20 March 1659.
Jane Kemp the second daughter of the same, baptized 23 November 1662.
Robert Kemp son of Sir Robert and Mary born 25 Jan. 1667.
William Kemp son of Sir Robert and Mary baptized 5 December 1675.

Besides these, two sons, named John and Robert, are recorded to have died in infancy. Mary, the eldest child, married at Ubbeston, Charles Blois, Esq., on 11th May, 1680; Jane, the younger daughter, was also married there on 15th March, 1694, to Dr. John Dade; William Kemp, the younger son, was of Antingham, and became the ancestor of the eighth and subsequent Baronets, we shall therefore return to him and his issue after following the senior branch.

Sir Robert, the second Baronet, was Lord of the Gissing, Flordon, and other family manors for the long period of sixty-two years; the estates on his entry were, as we have said, encumbered with charges, and Gissing Hall at least was much despoiled and in want of repair. This hall had been rebuilt about the beginning of the sixteenth century and re-roofed in or about 1595, but doubtless the fire which caused the necessity for the new roof had weakened the walls, and as the family treasures had been carried to Antingham at the outbreak of the Civil War, there was little to make it attractive as a residence. Sir Robert, therefore, decided to pull the whole place down, and the materials were soon made use of for local buildings. All that remains to mark the site of the old hall is the wide and deep moat. The actual island site is now the home of ducks, the only access to the island being by means of a tree trunk, which is thrown across the stream at a spot where the fragments of the ancient bridge are just traceable.

The Moat round the site of the old Gissing Hall.
(From a photograph by F. H. Kemp, taken in 1899.)

For some 150 years the family lived at Ubbeston, and when at length they decided to build a new Gissing Hall, they selected the crest of the hill instead of the ancient site on the lower ground, over which the new hall has a commanding view. The old hall had a large amount of heraldic glass, all the quarterings and arms of the Kempes and their kinsmen being displayed in a variety of forms, most of which had been duly recorded by the heralds at their visitations. Many of these arms were doubtless destroyed by the fire; some perhaps were maliciously damaged by the Cromwellian soldiers, who made many visits to the place. What remained must have been treasured by Sir Robert and were probably removed to Ubbeston and thence to Gissing, Flordon and Bracon Ash. From the time it left Ubbeston until recently, much of this old glass with glories of heraldic signification lay hidden in boxes, which had evidently escaped the observation of the successive baronets. When the present Lady Kemp attempted to fit the pieces together so many were missing or shattered that the hope of restoring them was regretfully abandoned.

It was also in this old Gissing Hall that the picture of "two labourers threshing wheat-sheaves" was preserved. The Rev. William Kemp, in his "History of Norfolk," says that the subject alluded to the family arms. A similar representation, either painted or carved, is said to have been in Gissing Church; possibly this was the same picture. Its disappearance is due to a fire which damaged the church, destroying the early parish registers at the same time.

In 1660, the year of the accession of Charles II., Sir Robert Kempe was elected the Tory Member of Parliament for the County of Norfolk. It is therefore evident that he had kept up the loyal traditions of his family, and as he must have been intimate with the King when they were boys together, there is little doubt that he shared in the renewed Court fêtes. Sir Robert was again elected for his county in 1668, and in 1679 and 1700 he was returned "Tory" member for Dunwich. In addition to his Parliamentary duties he was a Justice of the Peace for Norfolk. We find that on 10th of October, 1670, he was appointed, with his father's old friend, Sir William D'Oyly, to hear a case of William Clerk, a churchwarden, *versus* Richard Huntingdon, at the Angel, Norwich.

In 1693, Sir Robert Kemp introduced into Parliament "the Kerridge Estate Bill," which sought powers to purchase certain lands from Maurice Shelton which adjoined the property of Thomas Kerridge, a minor, who was a ward of Sir Robert Kemp and Sir Thomas Gerrard, of Green Street, East Ham, Essex, Bart. This ward was a son of Samuel Kerridge, of Shelley, nephew of Mary Kerridge, the first wife of this Sir Robert Kemp(e), while Maurice Shelton was the latter's brother-in-law. The properties which had descended to the minor were in Shelly, Laybourne, and Polsted, Suffolk, and in Codenham, Creeting St. Mary, Creeting All Saints, Bricet, Ringsale, Trimley St. Mary, Trimley St. Martin, Walton, and Bildeston in the same county, a messuage in Broad Street, St. Peter le Poor, London, and at Hampstead, Middlesex. The mother of the ward was said to have agreed to pay £9,000 for the Manors of Reydon Hall, Marks or Martins and Sullies or Selvies, for which purpose it was necessary to mortgage the Kerridge property. After considerable trouble for so simple a matter, the Bill was passed, subject to due provision being made for Thomas Kerridge's sisters. The digest of the Bill and the details of the case will be found in the "House of Lords MSS," vol. i. (new series) 1900.

With Thomas Kerridge, Sir Robert Kemp had a good deal more to do of which some record may be found in the Additional MSS. (19, 185) in the British Museum. The papers referred to were the original bonds for money lent, and such documents which passed from the Kempes to Dr. Dade, of Ipswich and Tammington, the son-in-law of this Baronet, and who had subsequently much to do with the property of Kemps and their kinsmen.

Jane Kempe (born 1662, died 1724) the wife of Dr. John Dade, of Ipswich.

Mary Kemp (born 1659) the wife of Sir Charles Blois.

Among the same collection of papers are numerous Dade documents, including the marriage settlement of Jane Kemp with this Doctor of Physic. (It is, of course, mere coincidence that the arms of Dade as shown on the seal to this document closely resemble that of some Kemps, namely, *three sheaves* with a chevron between them). There is also among these manuscripts a scribbled note by Sir Robert mapping out his idea as to settling certain properties on his children ; also a long list of his election expenses in 1708, when, however, he was not the successful candidate. With these are papers relating to Ubbeston Hall from 1585 till 1710, which was, it seems, also known as Harefield House and Tile House. It may be further noted that one of the receipts in this collection dated 1751 was witnessed by "Jno. Van Kamp," who doubtless was a Dutchman. We do not know how he came to have anything to do with Dade or Kempes.

The following inscriptions on monuments to the Dades are existing in the Church of St. Matthew, Ipswich, with the arms of Dade impaling Kemp:

"IANAE, Filiae Natu Minimae / Dni Roberti Kemp De Ubbeston / In Comitatu Suffolciensi / Baronetti / Uxoris Johannis Dade, / De Gippovico In Medicinâ Doctoris. / Obiit Octavo Die Decembris. / Anno Dni 1724, et Aetatis 62."

Also under a lozenge with the Dade arms :

"Ianae, Filiae Natu maximae / Johannis Dade, Medicinae Dris / et Ianae, Filiae Roberti Kemp de Ubbeston in hoc comitatu. / Baronitti / Obiit Martii die 24 / Anno Dni. 1721. / Aetatis 23."

Sir Robert Kemp, the second Baronet, may be said to have been the first of this line to *establish* the spelling of his name without the final E ; in this he was merely following a custom of the age, and as we have said several times the only fixed exception to this change existed in Cornwall, the Kempe family, of which have studiously maintained the older spelling.

Sir Robert was buried at Gissing, his monument of white marble hangs on the North Wall of the Lady Chapel in Gissing Church, the inscription being as follows :

"Sir Robert Kemp of Gissing / in the County of Norff. Baronet / was born at Walsingham Abbey upon the 2nd of February / 1627 and died the 26 of September 1710, / in ye 83rd year of his age. His first lady was Mary the Daughter of Thomas Kerridge, by Susan his wife, she was born in London in February 1631, they were married July 15th 1650 and she died in June 1655. They had a son and two daughters born and Christened which died young. The second Lady of ye sd Sr. Robert Kemp was Mary the daughter of John Sone of Ubbeston in ye County of Suffolk, Gent, by Mary ye Daughter of William Dade and of ye said County, Esquire, she was born April ye 6th 1637, they were married November the 25th 1657, she died July 29th 1705 at Ubbeston, by whom he had 3 sons and 3 daughters. *Both these Ladyes were very prudent and pious—few exceeded ye former and scarce any the latter.*"

The curious unbiassed closing sentence of this monument must surely have been the outcome of very careful consideration on the part of the second Baronet, and with his portrait here reproduced,* will help us to form an opinion of his character.

His will was proved in the Suffolk Archdeaconry in 1710. The digest is given among Dade's collection above-mentioned.

The will, which is dated 3rd May, 1704, nominates Mary, the wife of the testator, as executrix. She, however, as we have seen, died before her husband. Sir Robert mentions Thomas and Peter Kemp, sons of his deseased brother, Matthew Kemp. This Matthew, as we shall presently note, had died in Virginia, where he and his relatives had done much to establish our British Colony. Robert, the eldest son, and Mary, the latter's daughter, are the recipients of legacies, as is also the testator's son, William Kemp. These two sons, with their sister, Jane Dade, are also the chief legatees under the will of RICHARD KEMPE of Ubbeston, their uncle, which was proved 21st July, 1714, in the same Court as the foregoing. He appears to have died without issue ; we do not know if he married, but possibly Jane Alexander,† whom he speaks of as his niece, and his kinsman, Thomas Alexander, were so related through his wife, as we have no further mention of them. (This will also is given in Add. MSS. 19, 138, in the British Museum).

* Portrait at commencement of chapter.

† The name Alexander was connected from this time with London Kemps who had come from the Kent. We do not think that the one family were connected with the other, it is however curious that a daughter of this third Baronet was buried at Ramsgate with which the Alexander Kemps were connected. *Vide Post* and the Kentish section.

of this Abbey at the same time were Galfrid Kempe, Hamo de Cumbe,
illiam o 'Willielmus de Coumbe and Johannes de Campo.)

daughte of Sir Thomas Aldon. (Perhaps living a widow in 1332.)

ghter of Sir Robert Lewknor.
th her husband at Wye.

, Archbishop of Canterbury, Cardinal,
Chancellor of England. 1380-1454.

Alice, dau. of Sir Ro
Lieutenant of the
London in 1424.

npe, of Fulham, Lord Bishop of London.
d at St. Paul's Cathedral, 1489.

Emelyn, dau. and co-
grand-niece of H
bishop of Canter
Souls' College, Ox

e, Vicar of Feltham, Middlesex, 1513-1533,
of Okeley Parva, Essex, in 1539.

Mary, dau. of Sir Ric
Knight. Afterwar
Sir William Haute

eginald
Capt.
stle of
f 1542.

Richard Kempe. (? of Boughton Aluph)

John Kempe.

Andrew Kempe. (? of London)

Edward Kempe. (? of Boughton Aluph)

George Kempe.

Ann Fogg=W

1st wife.
Catherine, dau. and co
Sir Thomas Chaney
Warden of the Cinqu
Captain of the Ca
Calais. Treasurer
King's Household.

ncis Neal
Naylor.

Mary Kempe.=Sir Nicholas Boughton.

Margaret Kempe.=George Fogge.

Anne Kempe (or Fogg)=... Cross.

Anne Kempe, mar in 1560, Sir Thomas Shirley.

u. of ...
of Ea
sister
Argal.

Moyle, 1553-4.

Moyle, 1555-85.

Moyle, living 1592.

William Kempe. (? of Dartford and Sheppey)

George Kempe, baptized at Wye, 1557.

Mary Kempe, of Chilham Castle.=Sir D
Ke
Ro

John Kempe, died without issue.

Anne Kempe, mar. Josias Clarke.

Dorothy Kempe, mar. Sir Wm. Denny.

Amy Kempe, mar. Maurice Tuke.

Among the same collection of papers are numerous Dade documents, including the marriage settlement of Jane Kemp with this Doctor of Physic. (It is, of course, mere coincidence that the arms of Dade as shown on the seal to this document closely resemble that of some Kemps, namely, *three sheaves* with a chevron between them). There is also among these manuscripts a scribbled note by Sir Robert mapping out his idea as to settling certain properties on his children; also a long list of his election expenses in 1708, when, however, he was not the successful candidate. With these are papers relating to Ubbeston Hall from 1585 till 1710, which was, it seems, also known as Harefield House and Tile House. It may be further noted that one of the receipts in this collection dated 1751 was witnessed by "Jno. Van Kamp," who doubtless was a Dutchman. We do not know how he came to have anything to do with Dade or Kempes.

The following inscriptions on monuments to the Dades are existing in the Church of St. Matthew, Ipswich, with the arms of Dade impaling Kemp:

"IANAE, Filiae Natu Minimae / Dni Roberti Kemp De Ubbeston / In Comitatu Suffolciensi / Baronetti / Uxoris Johannis Dade, / De Gippovico In Medicinâ Doctoris. / Obiit Octavo Die Decembris. / Anno Dni 1724, et Aetatis 62."

Also under a lozenge with the Dade arms:

"Ianae, Filiae Natu maximae / Johannis Dade, Medicinae Dris / et Ianae, Filiae Roberti Kemp de Ubbeston in hoc comitatu. / Baronitti / Obiit Martii die 24 / Anno Dni. 1721. / Aetatis 23."

Sir Robert Kemp, the second Baronet, may be said to have been the first of this line to *establish* the spelling of his name without the final E; in this he was merely following a custom of the age, and as we have said several times the only fixed exception to this change existed in Cornwall, the Kempe family, of which have studiously maintained the older spelling.

Sir Robert was buried at Gissing, his monument of white marble hangs on the North Wall of the Lady Chapel in Gissing Church, the inscription being as follows:

"Sir Robert Kemp of Gissing / in the County of Norff. Baronet / was born at Walsingham Abbey upon the 2nd of February / 1627 and died the 26 of September 1710, / in ye 83rd year of his age. His first lady was Mary the Daughter of Thomas Kerridge, by Susan his wife, she was born in London in February 1631, they were married July 15th 1650 and she died in June 1655. They had a son and two daughters born and Christened which died young. The second Lady of ye sd Sr. Robert Kemp was Mary the daughter of John Sone of Ubbeston in ye County of Suffolk, Gent, by Mary ye Daughter of William Dade and of ye said County, Esquire, she was born April ye 6th 1637, they were married November the 25th 1657, she died July 29th 1705 at Ubbeston, by whom he had 3 sons and 3 daughters. *Both these Ladyes were very prudent and pious—few exceeded ye former and scarce any the latter.*"

The curious unbiassed closing sentence of this monument must surely have been the outcome of very careful consideration on the part of the second Baronet, and with his portrait here reproduced,* will help us to form an opinion of his character.

His will was proved in the Suffolk Archdeaconry in 1710. The digest is given among Dade's collection above-mentioned.

The will, which is dated 3rd May, 1704, nominates Mary, the wife of the testator, as executrix. She, however, as we have seen, died before her husband. Sir Robert mentions Thomas and Peter Kemp, sons of his deseased brother, Matthew Kemp. This Matthew, as we shall presently note, had died in Virginia, where he and his relatives had done much to establish our British Colony. Robert, the eldest son, and Mary, the latter's daughter, are the recipients of legacies, as is also the testator's son, William Kemp. These two sons, with their sister, Jane Dade, are also the chief legatees under the will of RICHARD KEMPE of Ubbeston, their uncle, which was proved 21st July, 1714, in the same Court as the foregoing. He appears to have died without issue; we do not know if he married, but possibly Jane Alexander,† whom he speaks of as his niece, and his kinsman, Thomas Alexander, were so related through his wife, as we have no further mention of them. (This will also is given in Add. MSS. 19, 138, in the British Museum).

* Portrait at commencement of chapter.

† The name Alexander was connected from this time with London Kemps who had come from the Kent. We do not think that the one family were connected with the other, it is however curious that a daughter of this third Baronet was buried at Ramsgate with which the Alexander Kemps were connected. *Vide Post* and the Kentish section.

PEDIGREE OF KEMPE, OF WYE.

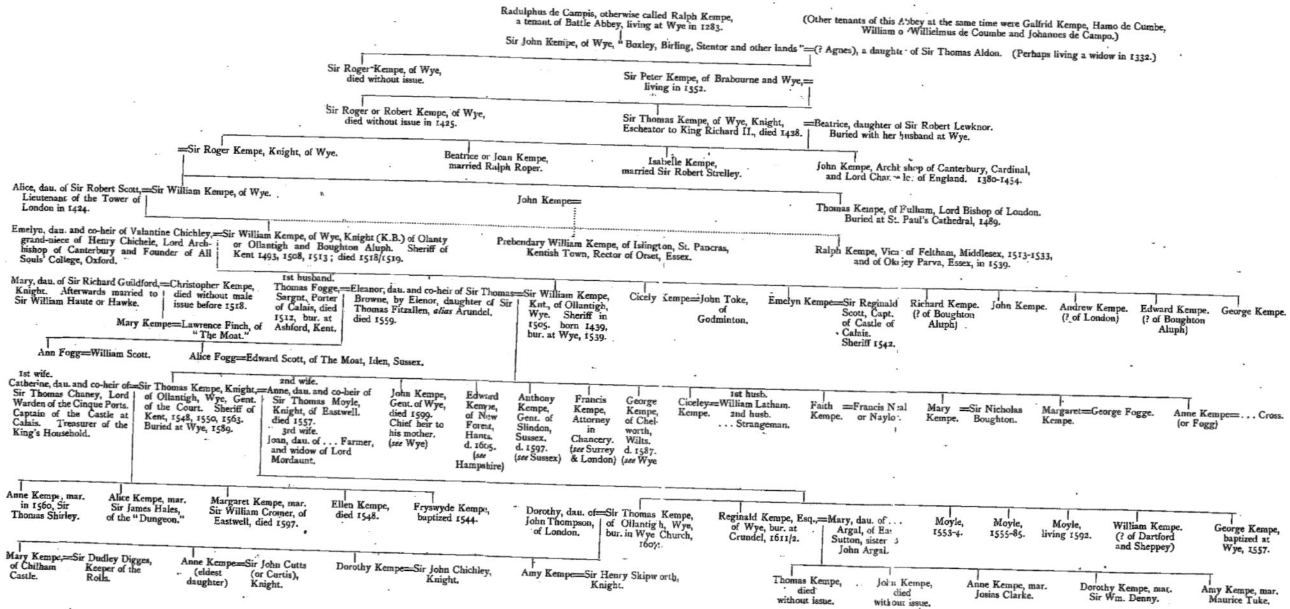
Radulphus de Campis, otherwise called Ralph Kempe, a tenant of Battle Abbey, living at Wye in 1283.
(Other tenants of this Abbey at the same time were Galfrid Kempe, Hamo de Cumbe, William or Willielmus de Coumbe and Johannes de Campo.)
Sir John Kempe, of Wye, "Boxley, Birling, Stentor and other lands"=(? Agnes), a daughter of Sir Thomas Aldon. (Perhaps living a widow in 1332.)
Sir Roger Kempe, of Wye, died without issue.
Sir Peter Kempe, of Brabourne and Wye,= living in 1352.
Sir Roger or Robert Kempe, of Wye, died without issue in 1425.
Sir Thomas Kempe, of Wye, Knight, Escheator to King Richard II., died 1428.
=Beatrice, daughter of Sir Robert Lewknor. Buried with her husband at Wye.
=Sir Roger Kempe, Knight, of Wye.
Beatrice or Joan Kempe, married Ralph Roper.
Isabelle Kempe, married Sir Robert Strelley.
John Kempe, Archbishop of Canterbury, Cardinal, and Lord Chancellor of England. 1380-1454.
Alice, dau. of Sir Robert Scott,=Sir William Kempe, of Wye. Lieutenant of the Tower of London in 1424.
John Kempe=
Thomas Kempe, of Fulham, Lord Bishop of London. Buried at St. Paul's Cathedral, 1489.
Emelyn, dau. and co-heir of Valantine Chichley,=Sir William Kempe, of Wye, Knight (K.B.) of Olanty grand-niece of Henry Chichele, Lord Archbishop of Canterbury and Founder of All Souls' College, Oxford.
or Ollantigh and Boughton Aluph. Sheriff of Kent 1493, 1508, 1513; died 1518/1519.
Prebendary William Kempe, of Islington, St. Pancras, Kentish Town, Rector of Orset, Essex.
Ralph Kempe, Vicar of Feltham, Middlesex, 1513-1533, and of Okesey Parva, Essex, in 1539.
Mary, dau. of Sir Richard Guildford,=Christopher Kempe, Knight. Afterwards married to Sir William Haute or Hawke.
died without male issue before 1518.
1st husband. Thomas Fogge, Sargnt. Porter of Calais, died 1512, bur. at Ashford, Kent.
=Eleanor, dau. and co-heir of Sir Thomas Browne, by Elenor, daughter of Sir Thomas Fitzallen, alias Arundel, died 1559.
=Sir William Kempe, Knt., of Ollantigh, Wye. Sheriff in 1505. born 1439, bur. at Wye, 1539.
Cicely Kempe=John Toke, of Godminton.
Emelyn Kempe=Sir Reginald Scott, Capt. of Castle of Calais. Sheriff 1542.
Richard Kempe. (? of Boughton Aluph)
John Kempe.
Andrew Kempe. (? of London)
Edward Kempe. (? of Boughton Aluph)
George Kempe.
Mary Kempe=Lawrence Finch, of "The Moat."
Ann Fogg=William Scott.
Alice Fogg=Edward Scott, of The Moat, Iden, Sussex.
1st wife. Catherine, dau. and co-heir of=Sir Thomas Kempe, Knight,=2nd wife. Anne, dau. and co-heir of Sir Thomas Chaney, Lord Warden of the Cinque Ports. Captain of the Castle at Calais. Treasurer of the King's Household.
of Ollantigh, Wye, Gent. of the Court. Sheriff of Kent, 1548, 1550, 1563. Buried at Wye, 1589.
Sir Thomas Moyle, Knight, of Eastwell. died 1557.
3rd wife. Joan, dau. of . . . Farmer, and widow of Lord Mordaunt.
John Kempe, Gent. of Wye, died 1599. Chief heir to his mother. (see Wye)
Edward Kempe, of New Forest, Hants. d. 1605. (see Hampshire)
Anthony Kempe, Gent. of Slindon, Sussex. d. 1597. (see Sussex)
Francis Kempe, Attorney in Chancery. (see Surrey & London)
George Kempe, of Chelworth, Wilts. d. 1587. (see Wye
Ciceley=William Latham. Kempe.
1st husb.
2nd husb. . . . Strangeman.
Faith =Francis Neal Kempe. or Naylor.
Mary =Sir Nicholas Kempe. Boughton.
Margaret=George Fogge. Kempe.
Anne Kempe=. . . Cross. (or Fogg)
Anne Kempe, mar. in 1560, Sir Thomas Shirley.
Alice Kempe, mar. Sir James Hales, of the "Dungeon."
Margaret Kempe, mar. Sir William Cromer, of Eastwell, died 1597.
Ellen Kempe, died 1548.
Fryswyde Kempe, baptized 1544.
Dorothy, dau. of=Sir Thomas Kempe, John Thompson, of London.
of Ollantigh, Wye, bur. in Wye Church, 1607.
Reginald Kempe, Esq.,=Mary, dau. of . . . of Wye, bur. at Crundel, 1611/2.
Argal, of East Sutton, sister of John Argal.
Moyle, 1553-4.
Moyle, 1555-85.
Moyle, living 1592.
William Kempe. (? of Dartford and Sheppey)
George Kempe, baptized at Wye, 1557.
Mary Kempe=Sir Dudley Digges, of Chilham Castle.
Keeper of the Rolls.
Anne Kempe=Sir John Cutts (eldest daughter)
(or Curtis), Knight.
Dorothy Kempe=Sir John Chichley, Knight.
Amy Kempe=Sir Henry Skipworth, Knight.
Thomas Kempe, died without issue.
John Kempe, died without issue.
Anne Kempe, mar. Josias Clarke.
Dorothy Kempe, mar. Sir Wm. Denny.
Amy Kempe, mar. Maurice Tuke.

CHAPTER XI.

THE THIRD BARONET.

WE must go back a little in order to review the chief events of the life of SIR ROBERT, the third Baronet (and eldest son of the last Baronet), who was some 43 years of age when his father died. He had graduated at Cambridge in 1683, and had married in rather a romantic way the daughter of the widow of Sir Robert Kempe, of Spains Hall, Essex, the latter being the same Sir Robert who had married as his first wife a sister of the first Baronet of Gissing. This widow of Sir Robert, of Essex, had remarried Captain Robert King, of Great Thurlow, in

Sir Robert Kemp, Third Baronet.
M.P. Dunwich M.P. Suffolk.

Essex, by whom she had only one child, Letitia King, who became the wife of the third Sir Robert Kemp, about 1693. We do not know the exact date of this marriage, which probably took place at Great Thurlow, but we find that their first child, named Letitia (Kemp), after the mother, was baptized at Ubbeston on 23rd April, 1694. This daughter became heiress to her mother, so far as the King estates were concerned, and to her grandmother, who was Elizabeth Steward, daughter of Thomas Steward, of Barton Mills, by Susan Wendy, sister of Sir Thomas Wendy, of Haslingfield, Cambridge. Thus Haslingfield and Wendy estates descended through the wives of two unrelated Sir Robert Kempes to a Letitia Kempe, and were passed by her marriage to Sir Edmund Bacon, of Garboldisham, the "Premier Baronet." This marriage took place at Ubbeston, on 27th November, 1712, but the bride's name is given in the parish register as "*Mary* Kemp, eldest daughter of Sir Robert Kemp, Bart." Sir Edmund Bacon was of the same family as those of the name who have repeatedly been mentioned as connected by marriage and in other ways with these Kempes from the time of Edward III.

Sir Robert Kemp lost his first wife within a few years of their marriage, for his first child by his second wife was baptized in 1697. The name of this second wife is given as Mary Elizabeth Brand Colt, but the children's mother appears merely as Elizabeth, the wife of Robert Kemp, *Esq*. The following children of these parents occur in the baptismal register of Hoxne Church:

Elizabeth, 26th September, 1697; Letitia, 27th October, 1698; Robert, 28th November, 1699; John, 27th December, 1700; Jane, 23rd January, 1701; Anne, 20th April, 1703, and Isaac, 27th September, 1704.

It would appear from these entries that Sir Robert lived at Hoxne (which is situated on the border of Suffolk, near Diss and the Gissing estates) from the time of his second marriage until the death of his mother, which event, doubtless, made it desirable that he should share Ubbeston Hall, and thus keep his aged father company. Thus we find that the Ubbeston Church Registers record the following baptisms, all of which, it will be noticed, are prior to his father's death. The parents in each case are Robert Kemp, *Esq*., and Elizabeth, his wife:

Thomas Kemp, 19th October, 1706; Edward, 5th November, 1707, and Benjamin, 4th January, 1708-9. Edward was buried there three days after his baptism, and Elizabeth, the second wife of Sir Robert, was buried there on 12th January, 1708-9—just after the birth of Benjamin.

It was within a year of this bereavement that the second Baronet died. After his accession to the family estates, Sir Robert, the third, married as his third wife, Martha, daughter of William Blackwell, of Mortlake, Surrey, Gent. And on her decease in 1727, he married as his fourth wife, Amy, daughter of Richard Phillips, of Edwardstone and widow of John Borroughs,* of Ipswich. This Borroughs had left an only daughter named Amy, who thus came under the care of Sir Robert as his third wife's step-daughter. Amy Borroughs became sole heir to her father, and under Sir Robert Kemp's influence married Nicholas Blois. She was buried in St. Nicholas's Chapel, Westminster Abbey, on April 9th, 1733, and is mentioned in Chester's "Register of Westminster Abbey," also in "Memorials of Westminster Abbey."

By his third wife, Sir Robert Kemp had a small family, who, like the issue of his preceding spouse, were baptized at Ubbestone. The registers give the following facts:

"Martha daughter of Sir Robert Kemp Bart. and Martha, baptized 7th September 1712, buried 8 September 1712."
"William Kemp son of Sir Robert Kemp Bart and Martha, baptized 26 February 1713/4."
"Martha Kemp daughter of Sir Robert Kemp Bart and Martha, baptized 4th May 1716."

Jane Kemp, the third daughter of Sir Robert, by his second wife, was married at this church 2nd March, 1730, to William Blois, of Yoxford, Esq. Thus this Baronet had two daughters and a stepdaughter married to members of the Blois family. It is no wonder, then, that Sir Robert and his executors and relatives had much to do with the Blois property. Unfortunately, Sir Charles Blois, the son of Sir Robert's eldest daughter, was declared to be insane, or at least too

* A John Borroughs, of St. Mary's, Whitechapel, London, Mariner, appeared to attest and prove the Will of Robert Kemp, of St. Christopher's (Middle Island) in 1732.

weak of intellect and physique to manage the estates which devolved upon him at a very early age. Much legal procedure was consequently necessary which must have been exceedingly trying to those responsible. We cannot go further into the matter here, but would refer those interested in the case to a mass of information in original documents to be seen in the British Museum (Add. MSS. 19, 138; 19, 186-7).

Martha Kempe, the Baronet's youngest child, married Darell Short,* of Wadhurst, Sussex, in September, 1738, her husband being connected with the Shorts, of Tenterden, in Kent, and others in Sussex:

Martha Short was one of the grantees of administration under the will of her half-sister, Elizabeth Kempe, who died at New Buckenham, a spinster, in 1763, and is mentioned in the wills of her brothers, Sir John and Sir Benjamin Kemp, the fifth and seventh Baronets, she being sole executrix to the latter in 1777, at which time she was living a widow, at Sevenoaks, Kent. She was buried at Ramsgate, in 1789, and in the old Parish Church (St. Lawrence), there is a white tablet to her memory, giving her relationship to the Kemps of Ubbeston, and as widow of Darell Short (junior), of Wadhurst, and stating her age to have been 77 at her death. Darell Short, of Wadhurst, her husband, died, according to a notice in the *Gentleman's Magazine*, in March, 1768.

Of the other children of the third Baronet, Isaac died young, while Robert, John and Benjamin succeeded in turn to the title, as will be further noted. William was a captain in the army, and appears to have left no issue. The third Sir Robert, after a very active public life, died in December, 1735, at the age of 68, when on his way from Ubbeston to take his seat in Parliament as the Tory Member for Suffolk. He seems to have been taken suddenly ill in his coach at Ufford (on the main road to Ipswich), and despite medical attention, succumbed before his relatives could reach him.†

He had, however, time to make a fresh will, for the one which was proved in the Prerogative Court of Canterbury in 1735 (104 Ducie) is dated the 7th December, 1734. The substance of it is given in the Additional MSS. at the British Museum (19, 138), and mentions the testator's wife, Amy, his brother William, his sons Robert, Isaac, Thomas, Benjamin, John, William, and his daughters Martha, Elizabeth, and "Blois," the last four being under the age of twenty-one.

Amy, the widow of the third Baronet, had inherited, under the will of her father, Richard Phillips, of Ipswich (dated 17th September, 1719), the reversion of property at Brockley, Suffolk. This property, however, did not pass to the Kemps as she released her interest, or devised her share to her brother Richard, by her will dated 11th October, 1745, and proved on the 18th February, 1746. She bequeathed to Christ's Hospital £240, which was placed out at interest and still benefits that Institution, to which his father was also a benefactor.

* We are indebted to George Dudley Short, Esq., of Brighton, for a number of notes on various Short families who have at different times intermarried with sundry Kemps. Martha Short's pedigree, and other particulars, may appear before long in a history of the Short families, for which our correspondent is collecting.

† The death of a well known man occurring in so tragic a way created considerable notice. See *Gentleman's Magazine* and the other papers and periodicals of the day.

CHAPTER XII.

THE FOURTH BARONET.

SIR ROBERT KEMP, the fourth Baronet, succeeded his father in 1734-5. He lived at Ubbestone for nearly eighteen years. He was M.P. for Orford. He was Lord of the Manor of Frenze as well as of the family Manors of Gissing and Flordon, and was also patron of the livings of Frenze, Gissing and Flordon. Judging from his portrait here reproduced (from a painting now at Mergate Hall) he was a man of intelligence and kind disposition. He seems, however, to have left very little record of his tenure of the estates, which he retained

Sir Robert Kemp, Fourth Baronet. M.P. for Orford.

intact but did not augment. He died unmarried in 1752, and was succeeded in title and estates by his next brother, John. He succeeded his father as M.P. for Orford in 1734.

SIR JOHN KEMPE, the fifth Baronet, married in 1742 Elizabeth, the daughter of Thomas Mann and widow of John Colt, Esq., of Tooting, Surrey, a lady of considerable fortune (vide *London*

Magazine, Dec., 1742). Her pedigree is not known to the compilers of this work, but it would appear likely that her husband belonged to the Colt family, who intermarried with the Kempes of Spains Hall. His marriage, occurring as it did before his accession to the title, led to Sir John making his wife's residence at Tooting his permanent home. He died there 25th October, 1761, and his will describes him as of Tooting, only mentioning Gissing as the place where he desired to be buried. He requests that his funeral be conducted in the same simple way in which his late brother, Sir Robert, was buried, namely, with a hearse and one coach only. He directed that all his personal estate was to be held in trust by his widow, Dame Elizabeth Kemp, and his friend, Eleaza Davy, of Ubbeston, Gent., who were to continue the annuities to his brother Benjamin under the will of his elder brother. Sir John's widow was provided with an annuity of £350 and a legacy of £500, as well as all the estates of her former husband, and other property which she inherited from her father. Further, she was to have Sir John's "chariot, chaise and horses," and all the stock of wine, beer, and certain other provisions at his house at Tooting. She was to enjoy the use of the family jewels during her life as well as the plate.

Among others who benefitted under this will we may mention the widow of the Reverend Thomas Kemp, of Flordon and Gissing, a brother of the testator, Martha, his sister, wife of Darell Short, his nephew, John Kemp, and Simon Adams, to all of whom annuities for life were bequeathed. Simon Adams was also to receive in all £3,500 ; he was at this time at school with the Rev. Cutting at Bungay, but how he was connected with the Baronet we are unable to explain, the large amount settled on him suggests that he was more than a mere acquaintance. This will was proved on 4th December, 1761, by Dame Elizabeth in the Prerogative Court of Canterbury (435 Cheslyn).

Dame Elizabeth Kemp survived her husband some seven years, her death being announced in the *Gentleman's Magazine* and other papers in 1768. Her will calls her Dame Elizabeth Kemp, of Tooting, Co. Surrey, widow of Sir John Kemp. She desired that she should be buried in a family vault at Tooting in which her grandmother and the latter's husband, Dr. Creighton, were buried, and directed that not more than £100 should be spent on her funeral. The will mentions many relatives, both her husbands and her own. Among the latter she especially dwells on her daughter, "Elizabeth Lady Trimlestown, wife of the Right Honourable Lord Trimlestown of the Kingdom of Ireland," to whom she leaves several miniature portraits set in diamonds and other valuable trinkets. These heirlooms have disappeared, the present Lord Trimlestown and the Hon. Mrs. Elliot declare that these miniatures and jewels never passed to their ancestors, but the treasures are certainly not among the Kemp heirlooms. The miniatures represented Mr. Brand, the Bishop of Ely, Dame Elizabeth Kemp's father and others. Several of the Barnwells are mentioned in the will, Mary Colt, the daughter of Lady Kemp, having married Bartholomew Barnwell in 1762. The will was proved in London 12th March, 1768, by William Mann Godshull, of Weston House, Surrey, and Eleaza Davy, of Ubbeston, the executors (P.C.C., 115 Secker).

The Rev. Thomas Kemp, the next younger brother of the fifth Baronet, had been presented by his father to the family livings of Gissing and Flordon, and married as his first wife Anne Mallum (or ? Marlow), by whom he had three children as follows : John, who became the sixth Baronet ; Robert, who died young, and Mary, who died single in 1784. This first wife having died before 27th May, 1753, the Rev. Thomas married Priscilla, daughter and co-heiress of Thomas Holden, Esq., of Tooting. Thomas, the father, died on 5th March, 1761, and thus just missed succession to the title, which consequently devolved upon his eldest son, Sir John Kemp. This Kemp was at Westminster School a minor when his uncle of the same name died. By the

Sir John Kemp, Fifth Baronet.

Sir Benjamin Kemp, Seventh Baronet.

latter's will £80 per annum was to be allowed for the maintenance of this nephew until he was seventeen years of age, and from that time until he became of age £200 a year was to be allowed. Unfortunately this sixth Baronet never saw his majority, having died unmaried at Duke Street, Westminster, on 16th January, 1771. He was buried in the Cloisters of Westminster Abbey, where a tablet to his memory may be seen on the east side against the last arch. We may here note that a celebrated John Kemp, Counsellor-at-Law and F.R.S., was buried here in 1738, also his wife and children, but we do not know with certainty that these were of the Baronet's family. The fact of Amy Blois being buried in the Abbey, together with the fact of his being resident in Westminster, may sufficiently account for his burial there instead of at Gissing with his predecessors. On his death his mother obtained letters of administration for his personal estate, the real estate with the title passing to Benjamin Kemp, his uncle.

Sir Benjamin Kemp, the seventh Baronet, was, we have seen, baptized at Ubbeston in 1708. He was, however, according to Burke, born in the parish of St. George, Hanover Square; London, in 1707. He entered Caius College, Cambridge, in 1731, and became M.A. in 1735; afterwards studying medicine and surgery. He practiced as a physician for many years at Coln Dean or Coln St. Denis in Gloucestershire, where he died unmarried in 1777. He was buried in the church of that parish. A monument of black and white marble bears his arms with the following inscription :

"Near this place is deposited, in Hope of Blessed Resurrection, the remains of Sir Benjamin Kempe Bart., who departed this life January 25 1777, aged 69 years."

His will was proved by his sister, Martha Short, widow, on 7th February, 1777 (P.C.C. 73 Collier). This will is probably the briefest will of any Kemp of this family ; he simply leaves the whole of his real and personal estate to Martha Short with the exception of one guinea for a mourning ring to Mary, daughter of his late brother Thomas, and £5 to the poor of the parish in which he dies. No mention of Gissing or other Kemp properties occurs. The witnesses to the will are, Jane Hughes, Giles Hancocke and Robert Berk, of whom we know nothing.

We may here conveniently note that his sister, Elizabeth, lived at New Buckenham, Norfolk, where she died unmarried in 1763. Her will was proved by Mary Blois on 28th March that year, a further grant on the death of the latter being made to Priscilla Merry (P.C.C., 135 Cæsar). This will is dated 1750, and mentions her brother, Thomas Kemp, then of Bracon Ash ; Judith, the wife of the Rev. William Leeth ; Sarah Young, of Bracon Ash, widow ; Ann Phillips and her brothers and sisters. Her kinsman, Richard Phillips, witnessed the document. Her brother and other relatives predeceased her.

Mary Kemp, the niece mentioned by Sir Benjamin, died at the "Gravel Pits," Kensington, but her residence had been Queen's Square, Westminster. It seems, from an obituary notice in the *Gentleman's Magazine*, that she had been an invalid from birth, enduring "misery" daily with the utmost patience and resignation for twenty-five years. Her character is said to have been exemplary, her disposition mild, and her piety and goodness of heart unbounded. Her Will was proved by Priscilla Merry, her mother, in 1784 (P.C.C., 395 Rockingham). She desired to be buried "in a private manner" at Gissing, and she left all her estate to the use of the Rev. Peter Pinnell, D.D., Prebendary of Rochester ; Thomas Birch, of Bond Street, Middlesex, banker, and Ingham Foster, of St. Clement's Lane, London, Gent., for the benefit of her mother, who also lived at Queen's Square.

On the decease of the seventh Baronet the title and chief estates passed to his first cousin, of whom we shall speak in the next chapter.

CHAPTER XIII.

THE EIGHTH, NINTH, TENTH AND ELEVENTH BARONETS.

WILLIAM KEMP, of Antingham, whose portrait as a child we reproduce, was second surviving son of the second Baronet by Mary Sone. He inherited the Antingham property from his father and there made his seat. He first married at Ubbestone Church, on 4th May, 1704, Jane Coleman, who it appears was related to Amy Phillips, wife of the third Baronet. She, however, died within a year and was buried at Gissing, where a mural inscription states that she died on 11th April, 1705, in her nineteenth year. By this wife,

Arms of William Kemp, of Antingham, in Mergate Hall.

therefore, William, of Antingham, had no family. His second wife was Elizabeth, daughter of Henry Shallcross or Shardelow. By this second wife William had three children, viz., William, who became the eighth Baronet; Robert, of whom we have no record; and Elizabeth, who married first John Cook, of Horsted, and afterwards James Gay, of North Walsham, as relict of whom she died in 1803, aged eighty-seven. In Antingham Church is a monument bearing the arms of Kemp

William Kemp, of Antingham, second son of Sir Robert Kemp, Second Baronet.

Elizabeth Kemp (sister of William Kemp, of Antingham)
the wife of Maurice Skelton and ancestor of Lord Nelson.

with a crescent for difference, and an inescutcheon of pretence or, charged with a chevron gules between three crosslets fitchée sable (*sic*). The inscription runs as follows:

"M. S. Gulielmi Kemp nuper de Antingham armigeri Qui obiit xij mo. die Maij Anno Domini MDCCXLIV. Aetatis suae LXIXmo. *Ac post mortem lucem in coelis sperat aeternum.*"

This allusion to the family motto is very noteworthy, and since it illustrates the possible meaning of the words *lucem spero* suggested in the introduction to Chapter I, namely, a desire for spiritual illumination and consequent felicity. No other similar example is known. It was doubtless for this William Kemp that the arms now in Mergate Hall were carved. It will be noticed that the crescent for difference is prominent in the illustration we give annexed. Possibly the book-plate with this difference, contained in the Kemp collection for the "History of Suffolk" (Harl. MSS. No. 901, Mus. Brit.), was also made for this Kemp. (His name appears on the Norfolk Polls of 1714 and 1734 as of Antingham.)

Sir William Kemp, the eighth Baronet, probably lived chiefly at Antingham, but latterly he resided at Worstead, where he died in October, 1799, aged eighty-four. He married Mary Ives whose father was seated at Coltshall. She died in 1762 leaving three sons, viz., William Robert Kemp, Thomas Benjamin Kemp and John Kemp.

The youngest of the three was twice married, his first wife was Mary, daughter of . . . Groat and widow of a Mr. Chandler. The name of his second wife does not appear. He left no issue by either.

William Robert Kemp, the eldest, became the ninth Baronet on the death of his father; he married Sarah, daughter of Thomas Adcock, of Carlton, by whom he had two sons, both of whom succeeded to the title. His death was due to a fall from a "Hobby" (the forerunner of the bicycle) being "killed instantly on the spot"—so the *Gentleman's Magazine* informs us. At the time of his death he is said to have been residing at Briston, in Norfolk, but we have no knowledge whether this was where the death occurred. The date of the fatal accident is set down as 6th October, 1804.

The next Baronet bore the same names and was the elder son of the last. This Sir William Robert Kemp was the tenth of his line and was born in 1791. He graduated M.A. at Corpus Christi College, Cambridge, in 1813, and afterwards took orders; we do not know what curacies he previously held, but we find that he was instituted as Rector of Gissing with Flordon, in 1816, he himself being the patron of both livings. He was thus lord of the manors, patron and spiritual overseer of these places, which complex position suggested the advisability of combining Manor House and Rectory. He therefore took the trouble to plan out for himself a building to comprise both, and in course of time built a fine mansion upon the garden and ground of the Rectory, and by turning a road and levelling some fences connected it with the ancient parts of the ancestral park.

He married Mary, daughter of Charles Saunders, Esq., of Camberwell, but had no children. His life was greatly occupied in expensive litigation, he having a keen sense of the rights and homages due to the family, which from the absence of his predecessors had become encroached upon, and taking, like so many of his predecessors, a practical interest in legal questions. He was a subscriber to a "General History of the County of Norfolk," by William Kemp, a copy of which may be seen in the Guildhall, London. This book is in two volumes, and the text is in places almost identical with Blomfield's "Norfolk." We cannot identify William Kemp, the author or editor, but he was presumably one of the family. Possibly the history was originally due to the collections made by William Kemp, of Antingham, and his ancestors, and the Robert Kempe, of Gissing, whose family and county manuscripts have found their way to the British Museum.

Sir William Robert Kemp, the tenth Baronet, died at Gissing Hall, on 29th May, 1874, in his eighty-third year.

Thus Sir Thomas Kemp, brother to the last and the eleventh successor to the Baronetcy, practically never enjoyed the estates, he was living a bachelor at Long Stratton, Norfolk, and died within a few months of his elder brother, in August, 1874, as the age of eighty.

Under the will of Sir William Robert Kemp, dated 1861, the family estates devolved, with the title, upon his cousin Kenneth Hagar Kemp, who for some years past had been treated by him as the heir and now became the twelfth Baronet.

Gissing Hall, rebuilt by the Rev. William Kemp, Tenth Baronet.

CHAPTER XIV.

THE TWELFTH BARONET'S FAMILY.

WE must now retrace our steps to Thomas Benjamin Kemp, second son of the eighth Baronet. This gentleman was of Swaffield, and married Sarah Cooke, by whom he had a son, Thomas Cooke Kemp, born in 1787, and the following daughters: Clarissa, who married Ebenezar Randall; Lucretia, who married Francis Woodrow; Melissa, who married Capt. Thomas Withers, R.N.; Sarah, who married Richard Fish; Elinora, who married Shephard Holmes, with others who died in infancy.

THOMAS BENJAMIN KEMP, the father, died 25th June, 1837, aged eighty-nine, and was buried at Antingham, in which church there is a mural inscription to his memory.

His son, Thomas Cooke Kemp, studied at Caius College, Cambridge, took his B.A. in 1811, and was presented by his kinsman, Bishop Tomline, to the Rectory of East Meon, Hampshire, in 1826. He married Jane, daughter of Robert Pretyman, Esq., of Eye, Suffolk, who bore him children, two sons named Nunn Robert Pretyman and Thomas Cooke. There were also *two other sons of these same names* who had died, and were buried at Dilham. The daughters were Martha Maria, who married James Barnard, of Bordean, on 28th October, 1830; Jane Sarah, who died aged four years, and Elinora Sarah Caroline and Lucretia Melissa, both of whom were unmarried, and Jane Louise who died, aged four years.

Thomas Cooke, the younger son, was married at St. Bride's, Fleet Street, London, on 17th June, 1841, to Mary Louisa, only surviving daughter of Anthony Canham, of Fordham, Cambs. He, however, left no surviving issue. The Rev. Nunn Robert Pretyman Kemp, the eldest surviving son of Thomas Cooke Kemp (senior), married Mary, daughter of the Rev. George Hagar, of Bourne, Cambridgeshire, grand-daughter of Admiral Hagar, and by her had five children, two of whom died young—the eldest, Edgar Kemp, was Captain in the 4th King's Own, and died in March, 1873, without issue, having married Ellen, daughter of Alfred Giles, Esq., M.P.; Kenneth Hagar Kemp and Caroline Russell Kemp. The latter married in 1875 the Rev. John Sharpe, D.D., Rector of Elmley Lovett, near Droitwich, sometime Fellow of Christ's College, Cambridge, and author of many Hebrew and theological works. Their son, Edgar Sharpe, was born in 1887.

SIR KENNETH HAGER KEMP, the twelfth Baronet, was born at Erpingham, Norfolk, on 21st April, 1853, and graduated at Jesus College, Cambridge, B.A. in 1875, being registered as a Student of the Inner Temple, on 22nd June the same year. He was called to the Bar on 26th January, 1880, and practised in the South Eastern Circuit.

In 1874, he inherited the family estates and Baronetcy from his cousin. He married Henrietta Mary Eva, daughter of Henry Hamilton, Esq., of Chilham, Kent, and late of Blackrock, Co. Leitrim, Ireland, in August, 1876, by whom he has had the following children, all now living. Robert Hamilton Kemp, only son and heir, born 11th September, 1877, who entered the Militia as Second Lieutenant of the 3rd Batt. Gordon Highlanders, and is now Lieutenant of the 3rd Batt. of the Norfolk Regiment. His coming of age was celebraced at Gissing, in 1898, by a feast in a building close to the site of the ancient hall, to the tenants of the estates. The presents sent on this occasion form an interesting cabinet at Mergate Hall. He is now serving with his regiment in South Africa.

The daughters of Sir Kenneth are Eva Constance, born 27th, August, 1878; Margaret Hagar, born 9th January, 1880; Violet Mary, born 14th February, 1881; and Ida Dorothy, born 16th August, 1882, and married at Flordon, in 1901, to Robert Gwilt, Esq., of Hartest, Suffolk.

[By a mere coincidence, Margaret Hagar Kemp was born at Chigwell, in Essex, where Alexander Davidson Kemp, a well-known London lawyer, had at this time a residence called "Ollanty." As a matter of fact, the ancestors of Alexander Kemp were long resident in Thanet, and no relationship between his family and the Baronet's exists (*Vide* Kempes of Thanet). It is well to note this, as the fact of a child of A. D. Kemp being born at Chigwell the same year (1880) might lead future generations to believe in some such near relationship.]

Sir Kenneth Kemp is a J.P. for Norwich, and until recently was a partner in the old Norwich Bank, styled Lacons, Youll and Kemp (now amalgamated with the Capital and Counties Bank). He has also taken an active part in the late South African War, having served as second in command of the 3rd Batt. Norfolk Regiment for upwards of a year.

During the first years of his tenure of the family estates he was much occupied with the setting straight of those legal difficulties and complications caused by the tenth Baronet. The Ecclesiastical Commissioners had to be settled with for the building of Gissing Hall on the Rectory grounds.

The whole of the estates have been greatly improved by the building of modern premises for the tenants and farmers, and a large amount has been expended in restoring Flordon Hall and Mergate Hall, but the most noteworthy items in the improvements are the fine roof and other restorations to Gissing Church, which is now one of the best furnished village churches with which we are acquainted in Norfolk. (This is, however, almost entirely due to his late brother-in-law, Dr. Sharpe, who was for some time rector.) The roof is of massive oak and enriched with

Mergate Hall (Bracon Ash) which passed to the Kemps in the fifteenth century by intermarriage with the heiress of John Appleyard. Queen Elizabeth dined here 16th August, 1578.

large well-carved angels and shields. The organ also is new and handsomely encased. According to the "Great Landowners of Great Britain," published by authority in 1876, Sir Kenneth held, in 1875, 2,133 acres in Norfolk, then valued at £3,163 per annum. To this he has added a strip of land running through the estates, which seems to have been sold by the first Baronet in his efforts to raise arms for the King. Sir Kenneth is a keen sportsman, and has twice contested North Norfolk in the Conservative interest—this being the division his ancestor, Sir Robert Kemp, represented in 1668.

We give illustrations of both Gissing Hall and Mergate Hall. The former, although having a splendid position and the advantage of modern construction, was not found so suitable a residence for the present Baronet as Mergate Hall, which lies some ten miles nearer to Norwich. Mergate Hall is not large nor imposing, but is a delightfully quaint country house. The oak panelling throughout the house date back to Elizabethan times, if not earlier, while the brick-work, although much reconstructed, must be much the same as when the hall passed to the Kempe in the fifteenth century. The Styles (whose family intermarried with the Kempes) had a lease of this house in the sixteenth century, and in the last century the Berneys, who own adjoining lands, held it on lease for sixty years. Entering the house one is struck with the oak-pannelled hall hung with family portraits from 1640, furnished with quaint oak furniture, and when, after viewing the oak mantelpieces in the panelled rooms, and the many curious and ancient memories of the family, including deeds from Henry I., we go outside to the bowling green at the back, we are conscious of having seen evidences of a family past and present which for nearly 600 years has given in each century an honoured name to the counties of Norfolk and Suffolk, which has not increased its wealth but retains the same lands, the same houses, the same names and the same position in Norfolk that it did more than five centuries ago.

CHAPTER XV.

COLONIAL AND OTHER BRANCHES.

THE compilers of the present work have addressed circulars to every Kemp in the directories of the United Kingdom, and as far as possible to those whose names appear in the directories of Colonial and English-speaking countries, with the request that the genealogical form supplied might be filled in, and inviting further information as to the origin and family history of the recipients. Although this world-wide request has produced a large return of matter, we have had no claim from any who can show *actual kinship* to the Baronets by direct *male* line. Notwithstanding this, many persons of the name of Kemp, both at home and abroad, have addressed letters claiming kinship, and very often asking financial assistance or help of some sort or another. The present Baronet has had many such letters, aud has frequently taken some trouble to give a polite reply, but in no case has a relationship been found to be more than "traditional" or imaginary; we beg that if any can show kinship, or believe that they come from the same (Kemp or Kempe) stock, they will be good enough to communicate with the compilers of this work, who will give the subject careful study in the light of numerous historical details relating to the family which they have not space to print in the present edition.

A prominent official of Norwich named Kemp, who is said to have displayed the Baronet's arms as his own, has written disclaiming relationship, and modestly saying that he was not of sufficient consequence to be even mentioned in this history.

An instance of a genuine claim occurred as far back as 1730, when one Dorothy Seaton, writing from Piankatank, Virginia, addressed the third Baronet in a piteous letter saying that she was a widow with several children, and in but reduced circumstances. She claimed to be the eldest and only surviving daughter of a Peter Kemp, son of Matthew Kemp, who was brother to the second Baronet. This letter is given in Add. MSS. 19, 185, now in the British Museum. On this subject much has appeared in the *Journal* of the Virginia Historical Society (to whose Secretary the compilers are indebted for many of the following details) with records of other Kemps too numerous to mention here.

Sir Robert Kemp, the second Baronet, in his will of 1704, mentions Peter and Matthew, sons of his *brother*, Matthew Kemp, deceased. According to the journal above mentioned a prominent Colonel Matthew Kemp died in 1683, but the *Journal* reasons that this Matthew was the son of an Edmund Kemp another brother of the Baronet. Even if this is so there is no doubt that Colonel Matthew and Dorothy Seaton were closely related to the Norfolk Kemps.

So early as 1622 there was a William Kempe settled in Virginia, who held considerable property and lived chiefly at Elizabeth City, of which he was a J.P. and Burgess in 1628 and 1630. He is recorded to have lodged a complaint against one, John Bush, in 1622, and to have had a son, Anthony Kempe, born in 1623. In 1624 he was living with his wife Margaret in Virginia. Possibly he paid a visit to England after 1630, for he, or one of his name, landed in the colony in 1635. There is no evidence that the J.P. of Elizabeth City was of the same stock as Richard Kempe, brother to the first Sir Robert Kemp, Baronet, of Gissing, who, doubtless, under this relative's influence obtained the appointment of Secretary to the State in 1634. The British State Papers and Virginia records contain numerous details of great interest concerning the acts of this first Secretary of Virginia, who served as Deputy Governor 1644 and 1645. Richard married Elizabeth Thomas, niece to Christopher Wormley, and had by her an only child, Elizabeth. In his will, which was proved in London on 6th December, 1656 (P.C.C., 455 Berkley), he bequeaths to his wife and child the whole of his estate in Virginia and all moneys due to him in England. During his daughter's minority his uncle, Ralf Wormeley, was desired to place out the portion due to her, and the testator desired that his property in the colony should be realised as soon as possible, and that both his wife and child should "depart the country." To his brother, Edward Kempe, he left £5, and to his nephew, Edmund Kempe, "one new servant." The will closes with a prayer for the prosperity of the colony and a request that Governor Sir William Berkeley would accept £10 and befriend his wife and child expediting their return to England.

Edmund Kemp, evidently the nephew mentioned in this will, acted as attorney for Sir Robert Kempe, of Spain's Hall, Essex, Knight, in Virginia in 1656. This Sir Robert Kempe, as we have already shown, was brother-in-law to Sir Robert Kemp, Baronet, of Gissing, thus it is natural that this Edmund Kemp, although of distinctly different family, should act for him. Edmund was a Justice of the Peace for Lancaster County (Virginia) from 1655 to 1657 and died in 1660, in which year the Lancaster County Court ordered that his estate should be appraised. His widow, Anne, married Sir Grey Skipworth, Baronet, of Lancaster County, who conveyed 900 acres in New Kent to his stepdaughter, Elizabeth Kemp, in 1661, Matthew Kemp being a witness to the deed. It was doubtless this Matthew who acted as attorney for Sir Grey Skipworth, Bart., "administrator of Edmund Kemp, Gent.," in 1662, and who, in, 1663 was granted administration of the estate of James Bonner as being next-of-kin, Elizabeth, the daughter of Edmund Kemp, having married one named Bonner.

A number of deeds ranging from 1653 to 1715 are cited by the *Journal* bearing out these and subsequent relationships. The will of Matthew Kemp of Middlesex County (Virginia), dated 4th May, 1715, was proved in that county on 2nd June, 1716. This will expresses the testator's wish to be buried in his orchard, and that his lands, negroes and other property should belong to his son Matthew, subject to a payment of £200 to the testator's daughter, Ann, when twenty-one years of age. Should this son die the estates were to pass to Ann, his sister, and in case of her death to revert to Sir Grey Skipworth. The will desires that Matthew, the son, should follow the advice of the testator's "father," Sir William Skipworth, and his friend, Major Edmund Berkley.

Matthew Kemp, Esq., was party to a deed dated 1687 with Adjutant-General Jennings, who had married Catherine Lunsford, daughter of Elizabeth, formerly wife of Secretary Richard Kempe, showing again that the third Matthew was evidently kinsman to the Secretary and hence to the Kemp Baronets, but it is not clear whether Colonel Matthew Kemp, who died in 1683, was the brother or nephew of the second Baronet of Gissing.

Peter Kemp was attorney to Mary, the wife of Thomas Kemp, of Kingstone parish, in Gloucester County (Virginia), in 1692, who calls him in her power of attorney "my loving friend." Thomas Kemp was a Justice of the Peace for this county in 1695, and with Peter patented land there in 1687. These two it would appear were respectively father and uncle of Dorothy Seaton, who, as we have said, wrote to the third Sir Robert Kemp, Bart., claiming kinship and practically asking for his financial assistance.

It is interesting to notice that when Colonel Matthew Kemp was denounced by the populace of Virginia as one of the officials said to be oppressors of the poor and a corruptor of the administration of the colony, he was in the same catagory as Sir Henry Chichley, Knight, who had married one of the daughters of the last Sir William Kempe, of Ollantigh, Wye, thus both Kempe families (Norfolk and Kent) were represented and denounced by "The Declaration of the People," which was signed by Nathaniel Bacon, Gent., a kinsman of the Kemps of Gissing. We need not venture a remark as to whether or no the charges against these "Oppressors" was just, but we can guess that personal interests and family fueds had somewhat to do with these affairs although concerning the whole State. It is further noteworthy that as the Essex Kempe family had twice intermarried with the Kempes of Gissing, Sir Robert Kempe, Knight, of Spain's Hall, was drawn to speculate in land in Virginia, his relative (by marriage only), Edmund Kemp, being his attorney concerning his colonial possessions in 1656. Again we have reason to believe that when the prospects of wealth induced many Puritans and others of Suffolk to emigrate to this colony, Kempes of that county were joined by Kempes of Middlesex, while Lord Berkeley, the governor, was certainly intimate with Cornish and other Kempes, thus it seems from the earliest formation of this colony, numerous distinct Kempe stocks were represented. Nor were these confined to those of British origin, for religious persecution again caused Dutch Kempes to make their home in this settlement. The wills and records of the colony have become very fragmentary, and it seems now impossible to trace every family to its origin. We may, however, record some later immigrations from which some of the present Kemps of Virginia may owe their lineage.

Among the Huguenots who settled in Virginia in 1742 and 1744 were Thomas Kemp, his wife Mary, and a daughter, Anne; while William, Peter, Daniel, Jack, Dick, Jenny and Kate appear with a Thomas Kemp as settling in Mannacan Town in Wiit, and are said also to have been Huguenots. Among still later emigrants to the colony we know of many Kemps, but space at our disposal forbids our bringing down the Kemp records to the present time.

An interesting collateral line involving the Kemps is that to which Lord Nelson belonged. Briefly, his descent from the Kempes of Gissing is as follows: The first Baronet in his will mentions his daughter, Elizabeth, who was then (1646-7) living as the wife of Maurice Shelton, Esq., of Barningham, Suffolk. Their daughter, Sarah Shelton, married Robert Suckling, of Wooton, who rebuilt the hall there and died in 1708. His arms were Per Pale Azure and Gules, three Bucks tripping or. Catherine Suckling, their daughter, was married at Beccles 11th May, 1749, and died in December, 1767 aged forty-two, having married Edmund Nelson, M.A., of Caius College, Cambridge, Rector of Burnham Thorp. He died in 1802 at Bath. These were the parents of Horatio Nelson, born 29th September, 1758, and who died in the service of his country at the Battle of Trafalgar. That the relationship was not lost sight of by the Kemps is shown by the tenth Baronet having offered to sell Ubbeston and Suffolk property as an estate suitable for the nation to purchase for Lord Nelson's family. Much concerning this proposal and its consideration by Parliament will be found in the "Historical Chronicle" of 1815, and in proceedings of Parliament. The estate offered by the Baronet comprised some 1,000 acres, and the price mentioned was £70,000. Earl Nelson, however, having expressed a preference for the Wiltshire estate, which was eventually purchased, the offer of Sir William Robert Kemp was not accepted.

CHAPTER XVI.

SOME MISCELLANEOUS KEMP(E)S.

WE have noticed more than once in previous chapters of this section, the coincidence of Sir Robert Kempe, a Knight of the Essex family, being seated in Norfolk at the time that Sir Robert Kempe, of Gissing, both a Knight and a Baronet, was living in the county. Sir Robert of the Essex stock lived at Heydon, where his father had made his home about 1599 on his marrying with Frances, daughter of John Mingaye, of Arminghall. As Sir Robert of Heydon eventually inherited Spain's Hall, we shall deal with the details concerning Heydon in the Essex section. We now pass on to a junior branch of his family, which appears to have been ignored by the county historians as well as the Heralds.

A reference to the Essex section will show the descent of George Kempe, of Cavendish, Suffolk, who had a son, George Kempe. This George probably lived at Cavendish before his father's death, for the latter died at the Rectory of Tottenham, which he had leased. Under his father's will he only received a legacy of £20, while his elder brother inherited Pentlow Hall and owned lands and "White House" in South Lynn, and the Manor of West Walton in Norfolk. The registers of Cavendish have not been searched, but it seems that George, the younger, had several of his children baptized at the adjoining Parish of Pentlow, where we find the following names duly recorded: Matthew, 25th March, 1611; Marie, 17th March, 1612; Ferdinando, 28th September, 1613; Anne, 27 December, 1614; Thomas, 18th June, 1617; Christopher, 30th March, 1619. The last two are entered as the children of Bridget; the others were probably by the first wife, Elizabeth Springham, but the mother's name is not given.

About 1620 George Kempe left Cavendish for Wooddalling, in Norfolk, where he died between 1644 and 1646, his will being proved in the latter year (Consistory Court of Norwich). The testator leaves sums of money to his sons Charles, George and Nathan Kempe, his daughter, Philippa, his wife, Bridget, and his grandchildren, John, George and Barbary Cooke. His sons,

John and Ferdinando Kempe, received all his property in Wooddalling (which estate we presume to have in some way descended to him from a John Kempe of Woodalling, whose will was proved in the Norwich Archdeaconry Court between 1545 and 1551).

John Kempe was a merchant, probably of Norwich; both he and Ferdinando appear to have died during the Commonwealth, which would account for their wills being missing from the local registers. The Wooddalling property evidently descended to Charles, the eldest son of John Kempe, who by will dated 1668 proved in 1671 (Nor. Arch.) left it to his son Charles. This will mentions also the testator's son Thomas, and daughters Bridget and Elizabeth; his nephews, Charles and John, sons of Mathew Kempe, with George Kempe, son of his brother, George Kempe. Thomas Newman, the Clerk of Heydon, was desired to assist the testator's son in administering the estate. Henry Waller, brother-in-law to the testator, is also mentioned.

No wife appears in the will, she having been buried in Wooddalling Church in 1646. The following inscription is copied from "Le Neve's Monumenta Angliæ":

Under this ancient gravestone is interred
The Body of Susan Kemp, hereby declared
To Charles Kempe, Gent., being wife
Both chaste and loving to him during life,
So constant also was as ever breathed,
Her soul in Heaven she thankfully bequeathed
To him who gave it for his service here
And now hath crowned it with his glory there.
Whose natural health of body did thus forsake her
Of much unnatural pain was made partaker,
Her soul God in mercy keep with heavenly love
Blessed with thankfulness he thereby did prove.
Glory, O God, to Thee, and unto Christ, Thy Son
And also to the Holy Ghost eternally be done
Her patience here on earth being firmly tryed
Upon the 11th of May then in peace she died.
A.D. 1646.

Charles Kempe (the grandson of John Kempe) of Wooddalling, made his will in 1703, it being proved in the Norwich Consistory Court by Martha, his relict, on 2nd February, 1714. She was to enjoy the local estates of her husband during her life, after which they were to revert to Charles, son of Charles Kempe, of Lyng, Norfolk. The testator leaves a legacy of £10 to his brother, Thomas Kempe, whose residence does not appear. Martha Kempe, the widow, died before 1717; her will proved that year (Norwich Arch., 119) mentions Frammingham Jay, Anne Draper, Thomas Neal, of Hackford and Charles Neal. The latter was to receive all the estate of the testatrix and to be executor. The couple, it would appear from the above wills, left no issue, and the Wooddaling property duly passed to Charles Kempe, of Lyng, for whose descent we must turn to Matthew Kempe, who was born at Pentlow in 1611, and who was a son of George Kempe, the founder of this branch of the Essex family in Norfolk.

In October, 1656, Susan Kempe was granted power to administer all the estate of her late husband, Matthew Kempe, of Lyng, Norfolk (P.C.C.), at which time, of course, her sons would still be minors. We do not know when she died, but we find that she had at least two sons, Charles and John, both of who were living in 1670. Charles, of Lyng, had, as we have seen, sons named Charles and John, who inherited the estate of their kinsman, Charles Kempe, of

Wooddalling. This youngest, Charles, removed from Lyng to Hunningham, where he died in 1721, his will being proved in the Archdeaconry Court of Norfolk that year. In it he mentions his lands at Lyng, leaving them to his wife Mary, with reversion on her death to his son, John Kempe, and his heirs, stipulating, however, that John should divide the rents among his brothers and sisters, whose names were Charles, Elizabeth, Susan, Thomas and William. What became of this family we have been unable to trace further, as the name of Kempe does not occur later in the calendars of the local Probate Courts either at Woodalling or Lyng.

An earlier mention of these places is found in the wills of a collateral line, the first of which was George, brother to Mathew Kempe, of Lyng, and the first Charles Kempe, of Wooddalling. This George Kempe was a mercer of Norwich, and lived in the parish of St. Simon and St. Jude in that city. By his first wife (whose name we have not traced), he had only daughters, named Bridget, Ann, and Mary. By his second wife, Margaret, he had sons named George and John, and daughters named Elizabeth and Margaret. His will is dated 1655, and was proved on the 8th August that year by his relict. All his personal estate was devised to his wife, while his sons were each to have £150 on coming of age, and each daughter by his second wife was to have £100 at twenty-one, the other daughters being left but £50 apiece.

The will of another George Kempe, of Norwich, was proved in the Peculiar of the Dean and Chapter of that city in 1712, which date would rather suggest that this was a grandson of the above mercer and not his son, but there is no intervening will of a George Kempe of the county. This will shows that the testator was of the same family, as he speaks of his kinsman, George Kempe, son of Charles Kempe, of Lyng, who is to inherit "Horningham" Grange after the death of his father. Charles Kempe, of Wooddalling, is also mentioned as a "cousin," a very indefinite term in documents of this and earlier periods; in this case the cousin is twice removed. Others mentioned are as follows: testator's sister, Durben, nieces Elmy, Framsham, Cady and Elizabeth Stephenson; cousin Robert Awborne, of King's Lynn, Martin Tolbot, of Burlingham and Elizabeth Tolbot, the latter's sister; also Ruth Davis, widow, Mrs. Vernon, Mrs. Sarah Vernon, Peele Maxey and Susan and Martha Kemp, these being the testator's sisters.

The George Kempe who was thus to receive Horningham Grange is, doubtless, the same as one of his name, son of Charles Kemp, of Horningham, who, under his father's will (1721), was merely bequeathed £5. There is a will indexed as of George Kemp, of Cawston, in 1728-9, which might prove to be his (Norwich Archdeaconry), and in 1747 another will of George Kempe was proved, this testator being a gentleman living at Brandeston, close to Cawston. There is, however, no mention therein of property at Lyng or Wooddalling, and no actual proof that he belongs to the foregoing Kemps of those places. His property extends to Surlingham, Yelverton, Holveston, Rockland, South Burlingham, Beighton and Upton, all in Norfolk. The whole of this he settled on his wife, Ann, for life, Surlingham and Yelverton land going after her death to the testator's brother, John Kemp, with the family plate; the rest of the land after the widow's death reverting to Robert Kemp, brother to the testator, in whose favour the devise to John was for some reason revoked. The following "sisters" are also left money, Elizabeth Church, Mary Whaites, Sarah Besfor, Martha Kemp and Susan Kemp. Robert Kemp, the brother, was the executor, and the witnesses were Mary Heath, Elizabeth Bradford and Jeremiah Berry. A codicil states that the testator was quite blind with the smallpox, and that consequently the will had been duly and distinctly read over to him. He desired to be buried at Surlingham.

Between 1746 and 1748 a will of George Kemp, of Surlingham, was proved in the Norfolk Archdeaconry Court: by this, presumably, the above properties passed to George Kemp of Brandeston. Robert Kemp, who next inherited the bulk of this property, perhaps made his residence at Stalham, for there is a will of Robert Kemp of that place entered in the Norwich Consistory Court in 1768. There is in the same court a will of John Kemp, of Catfield, which may be that of the John who inherited the residue of this estate.

In view of the fact that arms are justly due to any who can prove themselves representatives of this line, it will be interesting if further information concerning the descendants are sent to the compilers of this history.

We are unable to include the Kempes of Carlton Rode as an actual branch of the Kemps of Gissing, but although proof is wanting, the fact of their being established so close to Gissing from the sixteenth century makes it appear probable that both came from a common stock. There is, unfortunately, a break in the pedigree, due to the want of registration both in Probate Courts and Church Registers, that prevents the numerous descendants from the Carlton Rode family showing their right to the Kemp arms. Possibly in time further evidence will be forthcoming from deeds and local records which will make good the two missing links. The pedigree annexed is the outcome of much research, being derived from some twenty-five wills and numerous odd items from other sources. The wills are in every case to be found in the Norwich Probate Office; they contain, however, few items of interest other than the relationships shown. The family from the end of the sixteenth century, down to about 1740, styled themseves yeomen, and the senior branch by that time having acquired small estates deemed themselves entitled to be described as gentleman. The junior branches, however, have been content to continue as yeomen farmers, and many during the past century have left their agricultural pursuits to enter business in London and other commercial centres.

One of the last Kemp landowners of the family to hold property in and around Carlton Rode, was William Kemp, a solicitor's clerk in Norwich. His father, having suffered by the general agricultural depression, had heavily mortgaged his land, which consequently was relinquished by his son, who naturally had no desire to continue the unprofitable farming. This William Kemp eventually settled in London, and has a large family, who have spread out to such distant places as Manchester, Swansea, Leeds and Harrogate, while others have crossed the seas to California, Klondyke, and South Africa.

Another branch of the Carlton Rode Kemps is known as long associated with the "Society of Friends," and have by intermarriage with other Quaker families become nearly related to another Kemp Quaker family, of whom Caleb Rickman Kemp, Esq., J.P., of Lewes, is the present head, but whose family came originally from Kent.

Numerically the Kempes of Carlton Rode, Bunwell and Tibenham, were very important, but they are well pictured in "Grey's Elegy":

. . . "Their sober wishes never learned to stray;
Along the cool sequester'd vale of life
They kept the noiseless tenour of their way."

Now, however, having risen above the village life, many members of this old family are making good positions for themselves, and our colonies as well as our cities will benefit from their long dormant powers.

Another Kemp family long associated with Norfolk and Suffolk is represented by the lay Secretary of the S. P. G., William Francis Kemp, M.A., Camb., who acted as Secretary to the Ritualistic Commission of 1867, and who married, in 1860, Julia Lane Grace, third daughter of Sir Daniel Keyte Sandford, D.C.L., by whom he had a daughter, Geraldine Kemp, authoress of "A Modern Mirabah," "Ingram," and other novels, poems and songs which are making her name well known. "A Modern Mirabah" should find a place in the libraries of all fiction-loving

., NORFOLK.

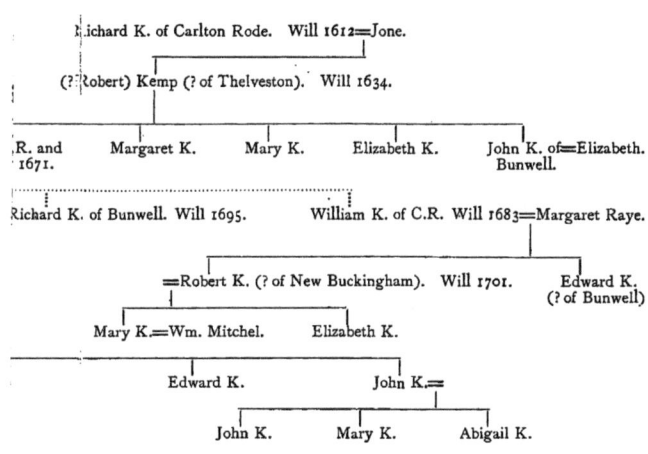

Richard K. of Carlton Rode. Will 1612=Jone.

(? Robert) Kemp (? of Thelveston). Will 1634.

,R. and 1671. | Margaret K. | Mary K. | Elizabeth K. | John K. of Bunwell.=Elizabeth.

Richard K. of Bunwell. Will 1695. | William K. of C.R. Will 1683=Margaret Raye.

=Robert K. (? of New Buckingham). Will 1701. | Edward K. (? of Bunwell)

Mary K.=Wm. Mitchel. | Elizabeth K.

Edward K. | John K.=

John K. | Mary K. | Abigail K.

Mary K. | George David K. of Heigham. Will 1854.

Hunt K. 1811. | Michael K. | John K. | David Thomas K. born 1814 in AUSTRALIA. | Frederick Charles K. 1817-65.

beth Hammond, born 1839, married 1865. | Alfred John K.=Maria Utting born 1851. | H. R. K. (Chemist) of Holloway.

a son (Chemist) of Holloway.

Leonard K. TH AFRICA. | Sidney Alfred K. of Leeds. | Gertie K. | Frank Edward K. of Harrogate.

Lewis Wilby K. | Hubert Alfred K. | Frederick K. | Florence Dorothy K.

residence at Stalham, for there is a will of Robert Kemp of that place entered in the Norwich Consistory Court in 1768. There is in the same court a will of John Kemp, of Catfield, which may be that of the John who inherited the residue of this estate.

In view of the fact that arms are justly due to any who can prove themselves representatives of this line, it will be interesting if further information concerning the descendants are sent to the compilers of this history.

We are unable to include the Kempes of Carlton Rode as an actual branch of the Kemps of Gissing, but although proof is wanting, the fact of their being established so close to Gissing from the sixteenth century makes it appear probable that both came from a common stock. There is, unfortunately, a break in the pedigree, due to the want of registration both in Probate Courts and Church Registers, that prevents the numerous descendants from the Carlton Rode family showing their right to the Kemp arms. Possibly in time further evidence will be forthcoming from deeds and local records which will make good the two missing links. The pedigree annexed is the outcome of much research, being derived from some twenty-five wills and numerous odd items from other sources. The wills are in every case to be found in the Norwich Probate Office; they contain, however, few items of interest other than the relationships shown. The family from the end of the sixteenth century, down to about 1740, styled themseves yeomen, and the senior branch by that time having acquired small estates deemed themselves entitled to be described as gentleman. The junior branches, however, have been content to continue as yeomen farmers, and many during the past century have left their agricultural pursuits to enter business in London and other commercial centres.

One of the last Kemp landowners of the family to hold property in and around Carlton Rode, was William Kemp, a solicitor's clerk in Norwich. His father, having suffered by the general agricultural depression, had heavily mortgaged his land, which consequently was relinquished by his son, who naturally had no desire to continue the unprofitable farming. This William Kemp eventually settled in London, and has a large family, who have spread out to such distant places as Manchester, Swansea, Leeds and Harrogate, while others have crossed the seas to California, Klondyke, and South Africa.

Another branch of the Carlton Rode Kemps is known as long associated with the "Society of Friends," and have by intermarriage with other Quaker families become nearly related to another Kemp Quaker family, of whom Caleb Rickman Kemp, Esq, J.P., of Lewes, is the present head, but whose family came originally from Kent.

Numerically the Kempes of Carlton Rode, Bunwell and Tibenham, were very important, but they are well pictured in "Grey's Elegy":

> . . . "Their sober wishes never learned to stray;
> Along the cool sequester'd vale of life
> They kept the noiseless tenour of their way."

Now, however, having risen above the village life, many members of this old family are making good positions for themselves, and our colonies as well as our cities will benefit from their long dormant powers.

Another Kemp family long associated with Norfolk and Suffolk is represented by the lay Secretary of the S. P. G., William Francis Kemp, M.A., Camb., who acted as Secretary to the Ritualistic Commission of 1867, and who married, in 1860, Julia Lane Grace, third daughter of Sir Daniel Keyte Sandford, D.C.L., by whom he had a daughter, Geraldine Kemp, authoress of "A Modern Mirabah," "Ingram," and other novels, poems and songs which are making her name well known. "A Modern Mirabah" should find a place in the libraries of all fiction-loving

PEDIGREE OF THE KEMPES OF CARLTON RODE, NORFOLK.

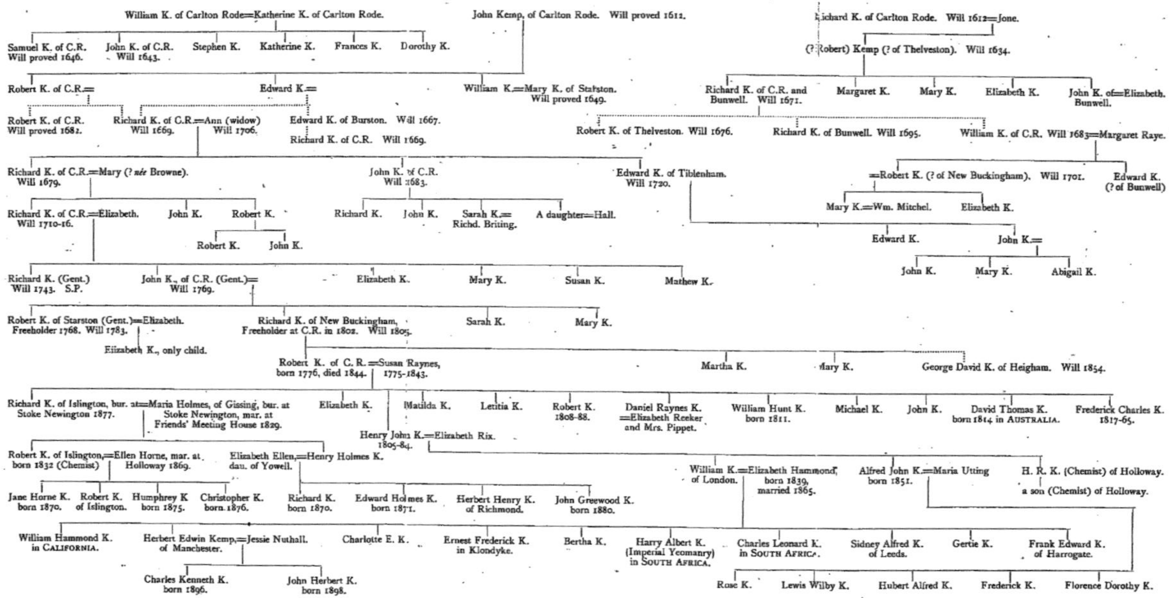

William K. of Carlton Rode=Katherine K. of Carlton Rode.
John Kemp, of Carlton Rode. Will proved 1611.
Richard K. of Carlton Rode. Will 1612=Jone.
Samuel K. of C.R. Will proved 1646.
John K. of C.R. Will 1643.
Stephen K.
Katherine K.
Frances K.
Dorothy K.
(? Robert) Kemp (? of Thelveston). Will 1634.
Robert K. of C.R.=
Edward K.=
William K.=Mary K. of Statston. Will proved 1649.
Richard K. of C.R. and Bunwell. Will 1671.
Margaret K.
Mary K.
Elizabeth K.
John K. of=Elizabeth. Bunwell.
Robert K. of C.R. Will proved 1681.
Richard K. of C.R.=Ann (widow) Will 1669. Will 1706.
Edward K. of Burston. Will 1667.
Richard K. of C.R. Will 1669.
Robert K. of Thelveston. Will 1676.
Richard K. of Bunwell. Will 1695.
William K. of C.R. Will 1683=Margaret Raye.
Richard K. of C.R.=Mary (? née Browne). Will 1679.
John K. of C.R. Will 1683.
Edward K. of Tiblenham. Will 1720.
=Robert K. (? of New Buckingham). Will 1701.
Edward K. (? of Bunwell)
Richard K. of C.R.=Elizabeth. Will 1710-16.
John K.
Robert K.
Richard K.
John K.
Sarah K.= Richd. Briting.
A daughter=Hall.
Mary K.=Wm. Mitchel.
Elizabeth K.
Robert K.
John K.
Edward K.
John K.=
Richard K. (Gent.) Will 1743. S.P.
John K., of C.R. (Gent.)= Will 1769.
Elizabeth K.
Mary K.
Susan K.
Mathew K.
John K.
Mary K.
Abigail K.
Robert K. of Starston (Gent.)=Elizabeth. Freeholder 1768. Will 1783.
Richard K. of New Buckingham, Freeholder at C.R. in 1802. Will 1805.
Sarah K.
Mary K.
Elizabeth K., only child.
Robert K. of C.R.=Susan Raynes, born 1776, died 1844. 1775-1843.
Martha K.
Mary K.
George David K. of Heigham. Will 1854.
Richard K. of Islington, bur. at=Maria Holmes, of Gissing, bur. at Stoke Newington 1877. Stoke Newington, mar. at Friends' Meeting House 1829.
Elizabeth K.
Matilda K.
Letitia K.
Robert K. 1808-88.
Daniel Raynes K. =Elizabeth Reeker and Mrs. Pippet.
William Hunt K. born 1811.
Michael K.
John K.
David Thomas K. born 1814 in AUSTRALIA.
Frederick Charles K. 1817-65.
Henry John K.=Elizabeth Rix. 1805-84.
Robert K. of Islington,=Ellen Horne, mar. at born 1832 (Chemist) Holloway 1869.
Elizabeth Ellen,=Henry Holmes K. dau. of Yowell.
William K.=Elizabeth Hammond, of London. born 1839, married 1865.
Alfred John K.=Maria Utting born 1851.
H. R. K. (Chemist) of Holloway.
a son (Chemist) of Holloway.
Jane Horne K. born 1870.
Robert K. of Islington.
Humphrey K born 1875.
Christopher K. born 1876.
Richard K. born 1870.
Edward Holmes K. born 1871.
Herbert Henry K. of Richmond.
John Greewood K. born 1880.
William Hammond K. in CALIFORNIA.
Herbert Edwin Kemp,=Jessie Nuthall. of Manchester.
Charlotte E. K.
Ernest Frederick K. in Klondyke.
Bertha K.
Harry Albert K. (Imperial Yeomanry) in SOUTH AFRICA.
Charles Leonard K. in SOUTH AFRICA.
Sidney Alfred K. of Leeds.
Gertie K.
Frank Edward K. of Harrogate.
Charles Kenneth K. born 1896.
John Herbert K. born 1898.
Rose K.
Lewis Wilby K.
Hubert Alfred K.
Frederick K.
Florence Dorothy K.

The Dawn of Love (p. 3)

Words by
Geraldine Kemp

Kempes, and the song, a portion of which we reproduce in fac-simile from her writing (and that of Mr. Percy Fletcher), is sure to be popular among those to whom the latest form of cultured love song appeals.* We regret that space at our disposal does not permit us to reproduce one of the "Kempe Traditions" which she specially set in verse for this work, it alludes to one of the Kemp crests, and is styled "The Legend of the Pelican feeding her young."

The Rev. Edward Curtis Kemp.

Miss Geraldine Kemp's grandfather was the Rev. Edward Curtis Kemp, M.A., for many years Chaplain to the *late* Duke of Cambridge, who presented him with a valuable gold snuff box, the illustration of which we here give. Edward Curtis Kemp was a writer of a very large number of tracts and small works of theological interest, the list of which is too long for us to give here, but that on "Nonconformity," published in 1837, may be mentioned as typical, while his rendering into Latin Dr. Watts' Divine Songs indicates his esteem for that worthy and a love of poetry which he has handed down. This Chaplain was a representative of two Kemp lines, who apparently derived their descent from the Kempes of Ipswich† in the fifteenth century. He was born at Melton, near Woodbridge, in 1795, and, after being Rector of Whissonsett, became the Incumbent of St. George's Chapel, Great Yarmouth, in 1865, where he remained until his death, which occurred in 1881.

† Copyright 1901, Boosey & Co. * *See* Section II., Chapter IV.

Snuff Box presented by the Duke of Cambridge to the Rev. Edward Curtis Kemp.

Section III.

The Kemp and Kempe families of Essex, Middlesex and Surrounding Counties.

The Kemp and Kempe Families of Essex, Middlesex and adjoining Counties.

CHAPTER I.

EARLY KEMPES OF ESSEX.

THE author of additions to Camden says that the Manor of Finchingfield, Essex, was given by William the Conqueror to Roger Bigod, who is recorded as holding it in Domesday, and that from him or his successors it passed to the "Compes," one John de Compes, holding this manor from Edward III. by the service of turning the spit at the coronation. This spelling of the name, even at so early a date, is uncommon, but there can be little doubt that Compes, Combes, and Kempe were at this time variants of one and the same name. As stated in the chapter on the origin of the name "comp," "komp" and "kamp" are early spellings of the word "camp." It is a curious fact that Sampford Magna, which adjoins Finchingfield, and which was partly owned by the Kempes after 1500, if not earlier, was held in the time of Edward II. by *Edward de Kemmesek*, who also possessed at his death Felstead and "Illebury" Manors in the same county, with other manors in Suffolk and Cambridgeshire. *Edmund de Kemesek* next held Sampford Magna, and within the same reign it passed to Petronilla, daughter and heiress of this Edmund. There is no conclusive evidence, however, to show that Kemesek became Kemp. Probably the occurrence of the two names at the same place is merely a coincidence.

If there may be doubt as to Compes being ancestors of the Kempes of Spains Hall, it is at least evident that as early as 1350 the Kempes were in the parish of Finchingfield, for in the Inquisitions and Assessments relating to Feudal Aids (preserved in the Public Record Office), for the period 1284-1431 we find that land there which formerly belonged to Thomas de Ruby was held by John Kempe and Agnes his wife between 1346 and 1350. From the same authority we find that in 1428 Richard Kempe, of Finchingfield, held land called "Snoterstones" in the parish, which formerly belonged to William Ambresburye. Between these dates we have further evidence in the Patent Rolls of 6 Richard II., from which we learn that John Kempe, of Finchingfield, had been charged with high treason (perhaps in connexion with the Wat Tyler insurrection), and his property at Newmarket, Cambridge, of the yearly value of 14*s*., had escheated to the Crown. The King, by patent dated 4th June, 1383, granted it to William Power, but this grantee surrendered it to John Kempe, of Finchingfield, to whom a pardon had been given.

In 1385 John Kempe, of Finchingfield, and Katherine, his wife, were concerned in the payment of a fine for land at Newmarket, Geoffrey Michael and William Hore being probably the purchasers. (Pedes Finium.) . These same Kempes held the Manor of Dullingham, Cambridge, or at least had some interest in it in 1382, *Alfredus de Veer*, Knight, being the other party to a fine then paid. Dullingham, it would appear, was for long connected with the Kempes, for a marriage license was issued in 1667 for Alice Kempe of that place to marry William Eade, of Cambridge,

Gent., her grandmother, Anne Harrington, being her guardian as her parents were dead. This license permitted the marriage to take place either at Dullingham, Worlington in Suffolk, Bury in Norfolk, or in the town of Warwick. The mention of the last place may point to the Kempes of that place being related to those of Finchingfield. (See Midland section.)

Another early Kempe, of Essex, of whom we have trustworthy record, was Richard Kempe, of "Little Horkesley," who appears on the Roll of the Hundred of Lexden in the time of Edward I. As Little Horkesley belonged in the eighteenth century to the Kempes, it is possible that the property had descended with that at Finchingfield. Morant's history states that John Kempe, who was living at Finchingfield in the time of the first King Edward, married Alice Gunter, and supports the statement by quoting a deed dated the twenty-fourth year of that reign, which grants a piece of arable land in Finchingfield, opposite Brent Hall, to Humphrey, and Agnes, his wife. In this document she styles herself "Uxor quondam Johannis Kempe." Nicholas Peche and others were witnesses to the deed. Where this deed was, or is, we are unable to say, but there is little doubt that the statement is correct. Morant next states that Nicholas Kempe, the son of this Alice, married Margaret, daughter of Richard de Hispania (*i.e.*, Spain), the possessor of Spain's Hall, which had descended to him from Hervey de Hispania, who built the original mansion about 1068. Whether Spain's Hall actually passed to the Kempes by this marriage we have no other authority than Morant for stating, but soon after this the family certainly made Spain's Hall their chief seat. Margaret Hispania was living in 1310, and her son, John Kempe, married a daughter of one surnamed Ramond from an estate which he owned at Finchingfield, he being the son of John de Lincoln. By this marriage the estate of Ramonds passed to the Kempes and remained with them for some three or four centuries, and the arms of the heiress were forthwith quartered by her husband. Her Christian name is not given by Morant nor in the Heraldic pedigree. The Inquisition and Assessment, however, point to her as *Agnes* Kempe, who was living between 1346 and 1350. A Nicholas Kempe held a part of West Winch, near King's Lynn, in 1346, and as the Essex Kempes continued to hold land in that district we suggest that Nicholas, of Finchingfield and West Winch, died about 1346, and thus John and Agnes were the head of the family at that time as the records imply.

Their son John married for his first wife a daughter of Armesbury. This wedding must have occurred before 1428, since the Armesbury property had passed to the Kempes, as we have seen, before that date; it is stated that Kempe and the daughter of Armesbury had a son living in 1371 named Richard, and this is quite reasonable. After his first wife's death John married Catherine, the same, doubtless, as mentioned in the deed on which a fine was paid in 1385. By her no issue is recorded. Richard is said to have married first a Katherine and secondly Margaret, daughter of Robert Jekell, a mercer of London. The name of Jekell has died out, and what little trace we have of the family was summarized in a short article in *Notes aud Queries* of 14th April, 1900. The property of Jekells and Justices passed with this Margaret Jekell to her husband in or about 1406. According to this date Richard must have been quite an old man at the time of his second marriage. We therefore incline to think that it was a son of the first Richard who married Margaret Jekell, and accordingly introduce his name as belonging to a distinct generation. They had a son, William, who is said to have married Alice, daughter and heiress of a gentleman named Mild or Miles, in whose right the Kempes quartered the arms of that family. What property she brought to William Kempe or her children we are unable to say; it was probably considerable, for her son, Robert Kempe, is the first recorded as buried in the Kempe Chapel at Finchingfield, of which he seems to have been the founder as well as of the Guild House, of which we shall presently speak. This Robert married first Ann Apulderfield,

e Combes, held land at Finchingfield by the=Alice Gunter, mentioned in a deed
rvice of turning the sp . at the Coronation, still existing, dated 1297.
living at time c Edward III.

Nicholas Combes or Kempe,=Margaret, d. of Richard de Hispania,
of Finchingfield. living 1310.

John Kempe=Agnes, d. of Raymond,
living 1346.

nchingfield, held prope y=Katherine, d. of Armesbury.
idgeshire 1383

f Finchingfield=Alice, d. of Miles or Mildes.

Finchingfield=Ann, d of Apulderfield, of Kent.

of John Maxey,
w of Yardley)

Seven sons and two daughters.

=George Kempe, of=Mary Corbet, 3rd wife.
Cavendish, d ed widow of
erfield= at Tottenham Woodhouse.
1606.

Margaret K.=Geo. Cavendish. 1st husb.
=Thos. Downes. 2nd husb.

Ann K.=Thos. Wright.

Pamen. Dorothy K.=R. Lee.

ard Colfer. Frances K.= . . . Doughty.

Mary K.=Nicholas Osbourne. 1st husb.
=John Kitchiner, of Norwich. 2nd husb.

pe.=Robert Green,
of Norwich.

George Kempe,=Elizabeth Spring.
of Norwich. 2nd wife.
Will pro. 1644. =Bridget.

Christopher Kempe,=Agnes, d. of Mathew
of Smithfield and Cockrode.
Finchingfield, Will proved
buried at F. 1630.

Thomas K. Christopher K. John K. George K. Charles K.
1617- of Norwich.
Will 1643. S.P.

f Richard Randall. Anne K.=. . . Gage. Elizabeth K.=J. Springham. Mary K.=Edward Chaplin.

ndrew Parne.

of Ralf Minors.

By third wife.

ebecca. Rebecca K.=Cooper. Elizabeth K.=Rogers.

Anne K.=Thomas Briscoe. 1st husb.
=J. Chaplin. 2nd husb.

Anne Kemp, Elizabeth Kemp. Catherine Kemp. Rebecca Kemp.
of London.
e,
don)

Gent., her grandmother, Anne Harrington, being her guardian as her parents were dead. This license permitted the marriage to take place either at Dullingham, Worlington in Suffolk, Bury in Norfolk, or in the town of Warwick. The mention of the last place may point to the Kempes of that place being related to those of Finchingfield. (See Midland section.)

Another early Kempe, of Essex, of whom we have trustworthy record, was Richard Kempe, of "Little Horkesley," who appears on the Roll of the Hundred of Lexden in the time of Edward I. As Little Horkesley belonged in the eighteenth century to the Kempes, it is possible that the property had descended with that at Finchingfield. Morant's history states that John Kempe, who was living at Finchingfield in the time of the first King Edward, married Alice Gunter, and supports the statement by quoting a deed dated the twenty-fourth year of that reign, which grants a piece of arable land in Finchingfield, opposite Brent Hall, to Humphrey, and Agnes, his wife. In this document she styles herself "Uxor quondam Johannis Kempe." Nicholas Peche and others were witnesses to the deed. Where this deed was, or is, we are unable to say, but there is little doubt that the statement is correct. Morant next states that Nicholas Kempe, the son of this Alice, married Margaret, daughter of Richard de Hispania (*i.e.*, Spain), the possessor of Spain's Hall, which had descended to him from Hervey de Hispania, who built the original mansion about 1068. Whether Spain's Hall actually passed to the Kempes by this marriage we have no other authority than Morant for stating, but soon after this the family certainly made Spain's Hall their chief seat. Margaret Hispania was living in 1310, and her son, John Kempe, married a daughter of one surnamed Ramond from an estate which he owned at Finchingfield, he being the son of John de Lincoln. By this marriage the estate of Ramonds passed to the Kempes and remained with them for some three or four centuries, and the arms of the heiress were forthwith quartered by her husband. Her Christian name is not given by Morant nor in the Heraldic pedigree. The Inquisition and Assessment, however, point to her as *Agnes* Kempe, who was living between 1346 and 1350. A Nicholas Kempe held a part of West Winch, near King's Lynn, in 1346, and as the Essex Kempes continued to hold land in that district we suggest that Nicholas, of Finchingfield and West Winch, died about 1346, and thus John and Agnes were the head of the family at that time as the records imply.

Their son John married for his first wife a daughter of Armesbury. This wedding must have occurred before 1428, since the Armesbury property had passed to the Kempes, as we have seen, before that date; it is stated that Kempe and the daughter of Armesbury had a son living in 1371 named Richard, and this is quite reasonable. After his first wife's death John married Catherine, the same, doubtless, as mentioned in the deed on which a fine was paid in 1385. By her no issue is recorded. Richard is said to have married first a Katherine and secondly Margaret, daughter of Robert Jekell, a mercer of London. The name of Jekell has died out, and what little trace we have of the family was summarized in a short article in *Notes aud Queries* of 14th April, 1900. The property of Jekells and Justices passed with this Margaret Jekell to her husband in or about 1406. According to this date Richard must have been quite an old man at the time of his second marriage. We therefore incline to think that it was a son of the first Richard who married Margaret Jekell, and accordingly introduce his name as belonging to a distinct generation. They had a son, William, who is said to have married Alice, daughter and heiress of a gentleman named Mild or Miles, in whose right the Kempes quartered the arms of that family. What property she brought to William Kempe or her children we are unable to say; it was probably considerable, for her son, Robert Kempe, is the first recorded as buried in the Kempe Chapel at Finchingfield, of which he seems to have been the founder as well as of the Guild House, of which we shall presently speak. This Robert married first Ann Apulderfield,

PEDIGREE OF THE KEMPES OF SPAIN'S HALL, ESSEX.

From "Visitations" made by the Heralds, with additions from original records.

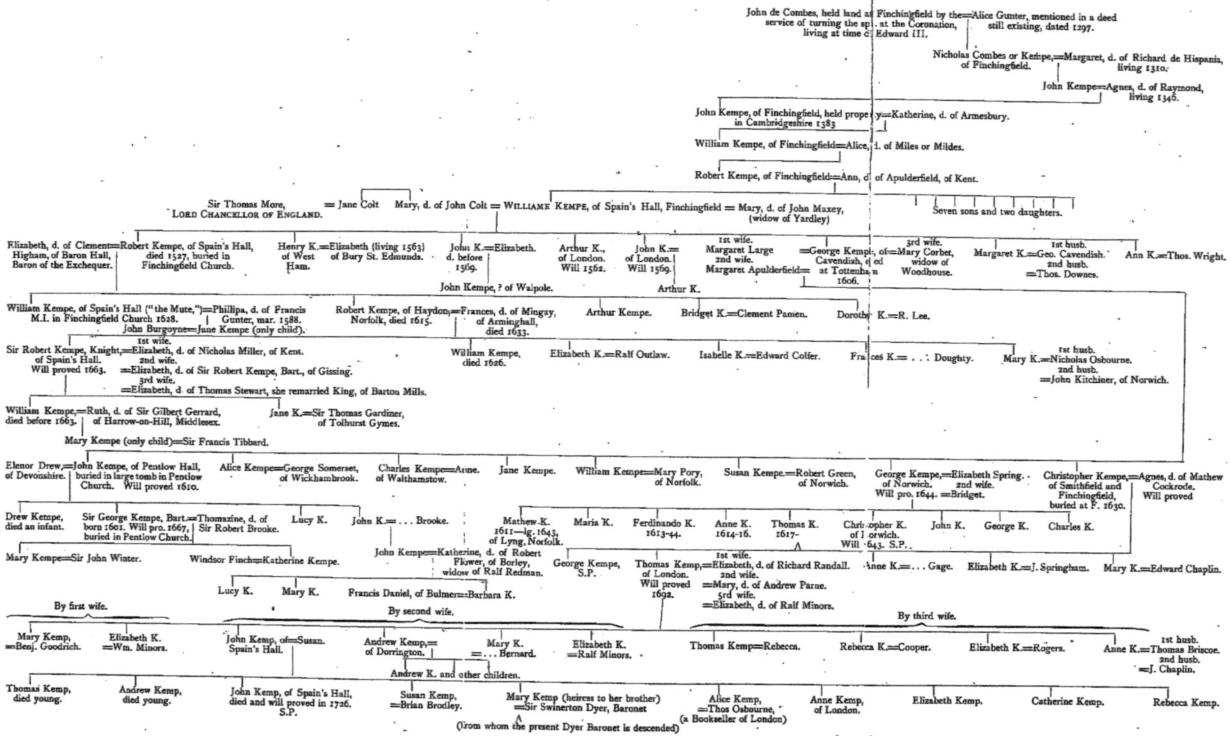

John de Combes, held land at Finchingfield by the service of turning the spit at the Coronation, living at time of Edward III.
=Alice Gunter, mentioned in a deed still existing, dated 1297.
Nicholas Combes or Kempe, of Finchingfield.
=Margaret, d. of Richard de Hispania, living 1310.
John Kempe=Agnes, d. of Raymond, living 1346.
John Kempe, of Finchingfield, held property in Cambridgeshire 1383
=Katherine, d. of Armesbury.
William Kempe, of Finchingfield=Alice, d. of Miles or Mildes.
Robert Kempe, of Finchingfield=Ann, d. of Apulderfield, of Kent.
Sir Thomas More, Lord Chancellor of England.
=Jane Colt
Mary, d. of John Colt = William Kempe, of Spain's Hall, Finchingfield = Mary, d. of John Maxey, (widow of Yardley)
Seven sons and two daughters.
Elizabeth, d. of Clement Higham, of Baron Hall, Baron of the Exchequer.
=Robert Kempe, of Spain's Hall, died 1527, buried in Finchingfield Church.
Henry K. of West Ham.
=Elizabeth (living 1563) of Bury St. Edmunds.
John K.=Elizabeth. d. before 1569.
Arthur K., of London. Will 1562.
John K.= of London. Will 1569.
1st wife. Margaret Large 2nd wife. Margaret Apulderfield=
=George Kempe, of Cavendish, died at Tottenham 1606.
3rd wife. =Mary Corbet, widow of Woodhouse.
1st husb. Margaret K.=Geo. Cavendish. 2nd husb. =Thos. Downes.
Ann K.=Thos. Wright.
John Kempe, ? of Walpole.
Arthur K.
William Kempe, of Spain's Hall ("the Mute,") M.I. in Finchingfield Church 1628.
=Phillipa, d. of Francis Gunter, mar. 1588.
John Burgoyne=Jane Kempe (only child).
Robert Kempe, of Haydon, Norfolk, died 1615.
=Frances, d. of Mingay, of Arminghall, died 1633.
Arthur Kempe.
Bridget K.=Clement Pamen.
Dorothy K.=R. Lee.
Sir Robert Kempe, Knight, of Spain's Hall. Will proved 1663.
1st wife. =Elizabeth, d. of Nicholas Miller, of Kent.
2nd wife. =Elizabeth, d. of Sir Robert Kempe, Bart., of Gissing.
3rd wife. =Elizabeth, d. of Thomas Stewart, she remarried King, of Barton Mills.
William Kempe, died 1626.
Elizabeth K.=Ralf Outlaw.
Isabelle K.=Edward Colfer.
Frances K.=. . . Doughty.
Mary K. 1st husb. =Nicholas Osbourne. 2nd husb. =John Kitchiner, of Norwich.
William Kempe, died before 1663.
=Ruth, d. of Sir Gilbert Gerrard, of Harrow-on-Hill, Middlesex.
Jane K.=Sir Thomas Gardiner, of Tolhurst Gymes.
Mary Kempe (only child)=Sir Francis Tibbard.
Elenor Drew, of Devonshire.
=John Kempe, of Pentlow Hall, buried in large tomb in Pentlow Church. Will proved 1610.
Alice Kempe=George Somerset, of Wickhambrook.
Charles Kempe=Anne. of Walthamstow.
Jane Kempe.
William Kempe=Mary Pory, of Norfolk.
Susan Kempe.=Robert Green, of Norwich.
George Kempe, of Norwich. Will pro. 1644.
=Elizabeth Spring. 2nd wife. =Bridget.
Christopher Kempe, of Smithfield and Finchingfield, buried at F. 1630.
=Agnes, d. of Mathew Cockrode. Will proved
Drew Kempe, died an infant.
Sir George Kempe, Bart. born 1601. Will pro. 1667, buried in Pentlow Church.
=Thomazine, d. of Sir Robert Brooke.
Lucy K.
John K.=. . . Brooke.
Mathew K. 1611—lg. 1643, of Lyng, Norfolk.
Maria K.
Ferdinando K. 1613-44.
Anne K. 1614-16.
Thomas K. 1617-
Christopher K. of Norwich. Will 1643. S.P.
John K.
George K.
Charles K.
Mary Kempe=Sir John Winter.
Windsor Finch=Katherine Kempe.
John Kempe=Katherine, d. of Robert Flower, of Borley, widow of Ralf Redman.
George Kempe, S.P.
Thomas Kemp, of London. Will proved 1692.
1st wife. =Elizabeth, d. of Richard Randall. 2nd wife. =Mary, d. of Andrew Parne. 3rd wife. =Elizabeth, d. of Ralf Minors.
Anne K.=. . . Gage.
Elizabeth K.=J. Springham.
Mary K.=Edward Chaplin.
Lucy K.
Mary K.
Francis Daniel, of Bulmer=Barbara K.
By first wife.
By second wife.
By third wife.
Mary Kemp, =Benj. Goodrich.
Elizabeth K. =Wm. Minors.
John Kemp, of Spain's Hall.
=Susan.
Andrew Kemp,= of Dorrington.
Mary K. =. . . Bernard.
Elizabeth K. =Ralf Minors.
Thomas Kemp=Rebecca.
Rebecca K.=Cooper.
Elizabeth K.=Rogers.
Anne K. 1st husb. =Thomas Briscoe. 2nd husb. =J. Chaplin.
Andrew K. and other children.
Thomas Kemp, died young.
Andrew Kemp, died young.
John Kemp, of Spain's Hall, died and will proved in 1726. S.P.
Susan Kemp, =Brian Brodley.
Mary Kemp (heiress to her brother) =Sir Swinerton Dyer, Baronet
(from whom the present Dyer Baronet is descended)
Alice Kemp, =Thos Osbourne, (a Bookseller of London)
Anne Kemp, of London.
Elizabeth Kemp.
Catherine Kemp.
Rebecca Kemp.

of Kent, and quartered her arms, which arms are also quartered by the Kempes of Kent by a distant descent through the Chiche family. Thus we might show a common ancestry to the Kent and the Essex Kempes, although so far as their Kempe ancestors are concerned they were in no way related. The connexion, however, was sufficiently close to bring members of the family together, while the heads of both families as men of social standing shared in raising arms for the safety of the Kingdom.

The children of Robert and his wife are said to have numbered ten—seven sons and three daughters—but their names are not known with the exception of the eldest, William Kempe, who inherited the property, including Spain's Hall, in 1524. According to this descent two generations

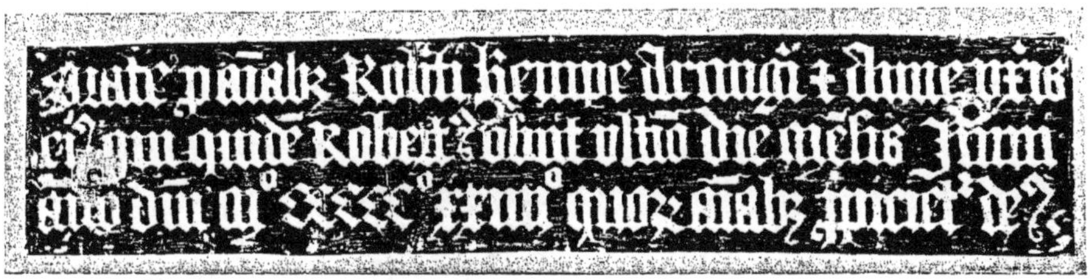

only held Spain's Hall during the whole century, 1400 to 1500, which is so unusual that we suspect another generation has been omitted. We are, however, unable to set this right, as no series of wills relating to Essex include wills of Kempes of that county until after the death of the Robert Kempe of whose memorial brass we here give an illustration (1527).

We may here briefly say that the chapel of the Kempes of Essex is still in existence, but is now the property of the Ruggles-Brise family, who purchased Spain's Hall so far back as 1729. Several inscriptions to the Brises now appear in the chapel, but the Kempe altar-tomb, and one to William Kempe still remain. The squires' pews have been turned to face the chancel, thus leaving much clear space which adds to the effect of the chapel from the nave. No stained glass is left in the church, which otherwise is full of interest to the antiquary. Adjoining the churchyard is the almshouse founded by the Kempes of Spain's Hall, which still fulfils its original purpose.

CHAPTER II.

SPAIN'S HALL.

WE now come to the period when records began to be carefully kept and preserved, so that we learn not only the descent of the heads of the family but also their brothers' and sisters' fortunes. The Finchingfield registers, we believe, are quite perfect, but we have been unable to obtain extracts from them. The earliest wills of Kempes of Essex are given here as a possible means of tracing earlier branches of the Spain's Hall family. It is, however, noticeable that in each instance given below the testators are "yeomen," whereas we should expect relatives of Finchingfield Kempes to style themselves "gentlemen." The following are wills and administrations proved or granted in the Archdeaconry Court of Essex.

John Kempe als. Campe, Dagenham,	1551.	Arthur Kempe (? Kemys),	1574.
Richard Kempe, Hutton,	1556.	John Kempe, Mucking,	1576.
Thomas Kempe, St. Osyth,	1560.	Edward Kempe, Canewdon.	1585.
John Kempe, Great Burstead,	1562.	John Kempe, Stanford-le-Hope.	1603.

During this period in the same court *Campes* appear at the following places: South Benfleet, 1493, Danbury, 1491, *Prittlewell*, 1504, and Nazing in 1539 and 1558. As to these *Campes* of Nazing, we should remark that the family were at Standon, in Hertfordshire, as early as 1463, and at Nazing before 1500, where we know that they remained for some 150 years or more. A branch of the family obtained arms, and members became citizens of London, but for the most part the *Campes* remained yeomen and continued in the county down to quite recent times. Camp, as an alias of Kemp, occurs at least down to the beginning of the last century, for even in 1797 we find an "Ann Kemp, otherwise Camp, formerly Ann Turner," proving the will of William Camp, her husband. At Prittlewell Kemp and Camp gravestones are placed close together as if to suggest that the Kemps of that place were related to the *Camps*. In this place, however, it is evident from the church registers that the names did not continue from 1504, for neither appear therein until about 1750 when both occur. In the Essex portion of the Archdeaconry of Middlesex no earlier instance of Kempe occurs than 1591, when Rose Kempe having renounced, her son, Thomas Kempe, of Braintree, obtained power to administer the estate of his late father, Thomas Kempe, of Castle Hedingham. Turning to the Prerogative Court of Canterbury (in which wills relating to more than one diocese had to be proved) we find the earliest will of a Kempe, of Essex, is indexed in 1562. This is the will of Arthur Kempe, Gent., of Lincoln's Inn and Finchingfield. His exact relationship is shown by a bequest of £10 towards the repair of *his brother* Robert Kempe's chapel and twenty shillings for books and ornaments in Finchingfield Church. He further mentions his sisters Downes, Cavendish and Wright; his brothers John, Henry and George; his nephew, Arthur, son of Robert Kempe; Alice and Jane, daughters of George, his brother; his nephew, William Kempe, and also Mary, Bridget, and Margaret Kempe, whose relationship is not stated. To the New Building of Lincoln's Inn he leaves £6 13*s*. 4*d*.; Arthur, son of Henry Kemp, receives £100. He leaves his law books and gown to Arthur, son of Robert.

Spain's Hall (front view), Finchingfield.
The chief seat of the Kempes of Essex, 1300-1720.

The residue of his estates goes to his brother George, who is appointed executor; Robert Kempe, Esq., and John Kempe, of London, draper, acting with him. The only real estate mentioned are leasehold lands in West Ham, in which place it will be seen Kempes of this and other families held property at various times if not continuously.

HENRY KEMPE, brother of the above testator, is, it appears, the same as one of his name whose will was proved in the same court in 1563 (P. C. C., 41 Chayre). He is described as "Gent.," of Bury St. Edmunds, and desired to be buried in the churchyard of "Swans" in that town. His estate he leaves to his wife, Elizabeth, subject to a small sum to St. Mary's for "tithes negligently forgotten." William Purdie is the appointed supervisor; the witnesses are named Wiffin, Nycholas and Stock.

JOHN KEMPE, the citizen and mercer mentioned above, was, he states, apprenticed to William Parker, to whom, by his will dated 8th September, 1569, he left £50. This John Kempe, the mercer, mentions his nephew, John Kempe, son of his late brother, John Kempe. It was by no means unusual during the reign of Elizabeth and earlier to baptize two brothers with the same name, and it makes the identification of the numerous John Kempes very difficult; in this case we cannot say what became of the nephew John, nor when or where his father died; his mother's Christian name was Elizabeth, and she was living in 1569. To the Universities of Cambridge and Oxford he left £200 each, and an annuity to Theodor Bacon, son of Thomas Bacon, and John Wynnesherst, that they might study at one of these universities. He mentions Robert, second son of his eldest brother Robert; John Kempe, eldest son of his brother George; and his own son, Arthur, who was at the time a minor. The only landed property named is a messuage in Bromley-at-Bow, relative to which we find fines recorded in 1566 and 1569. Andrew Young, Gent., with his wife, Margery, and John Barnby, Gent., were concerned in a moiety of this property. The messuage was bequeathed to Mary Aylyffe for her life and afterwards to the testator's son, Arthur, who is recorded to have paid a fine in 1585, when the other party to the transaction was Roger James. Others mentioned in this will are "Uncle" Thomas Colt and his daughter Joan; his sister, Anne Wright, deceased; his sister Margaret, wife of George Cavendish, and his friends Robert Crowley, Henry Middleton, Sir William Cordall, Knight, and Edward Lilsey. The will particularly states that the testator was born at Finchingfield, where one hundred sermons are directed to be preached, the clergy being paid for these out of the estate. At St. Antholm's (? London) also one hundred sermons

Spain's Hall (south side), Finchingfield.
The chief seat of the Kempes of Eesex, 1300-1727.

were paid for, and a third hundred were to be provided for at the discretion of Robert and George Kempe. One hundred pounds was bequeathed to St. George's, Southwark, with the object of starting young men in business, the money being lent to worthy individuals for that purpose free of interest. This sum is now the means of providing poor parishioners with bread.

The Register of St. Antholm, Budge Row, London, says that William Young, a servant to John Kempe, was buried there in 1563, and it also gives the baptisms of William and Francis, sons of Francis Kempe, in 1565-6, and the marriage of a Dorothy Kempe with John Token in 1569. We do not, however, know that these were connected with the Kempes of Finchingfield.

The will of an Arthur Kemp, Gent., of Suckles, Bradfield, was proved in 1595 (P. C. C., 63 Scott). It mentions his son, Henry Kempe, and leaves money to other children, who are not named. The widow, named Mary, was to hold the legacies until the children came of age. The witnesses to this will were Robert and William Jermyn, James Bacon, William Webb and Edmond Smythe. Persons of the name of Jermyn and Bacon were at this time closely related to the Kempes of Gissing, with which family it will be seen these Essex Kempes were intimate. It seems likely that this Arthur was the son of Robert Kempe, of Spain's Hall, and not son of John, the citizen and draper of London.

We do not know if the place here mentioned is identical with Bradfield, near Harwich, but it may be here noted that Aluric *Camp* held land at Bradfield so far back as the time of the Confessor ; it had, however, passed from the Camps in the Conqueror's reign.

It will be seen by the pedigree annexed that George Kempe mentioned above was founder of a branch which eventually inherited the chief estates. We shall deal with this line later, and therefore pass over the intervening wills to that of John Kempe, of London, Gent., which was proved in 1612 (P. C. C., Fenner 77). This is important, as showing a mistake which has been copied from the Heralds' Visitation into several county histories and other works. The testator more than once speaks of his son, Robert Kempe, of Heydon, in Norfolk, and of his son, William Kempe, of Spain's Hall. This, with other evidence, shews that again a generation has been omitted. William, Robert, Isabelle, Mary and Francis, all children of Robert Kempe, of Heydon, are mentioned, as also Anne, the daughter of Mr. Gawaynt Whittingham, of Tottenham, goddaughter of the testator. A piece of plate valued at £60 is devised to William Abbot, citizen and grocer of London, dwelling in London. This last was made overseer to the executor, Mr. Robert Kempe, of Heydon. William and Ambrose Abbott witnessed the will.

Concerning persons of the name of Abbott connected with various Kempe families we have several notes. The most distinguished was Archbishop Abbot, who crowned James I., and was co-founder of the Trinity Hospital, Guildford, with Sir Nicholas Kempe. Certainly Sir Nicholas did not belong to the Essex family, for his arms are displayed on his tomb as well as on seals ; yet in many points he seems more closely connected with friends of the Kempes of Spain's Hall than with either of those families whose arms he used. But, as we have said, Norfolk and Essex Kempes were repeatedly united by marriage, while the Kentish Kempes at this period are known to have bought property from both Essex and Norfolk Kempes, who also bought from the Kentish family, thus showing that the principal families of the name were intimate although of very distinct descent. A Richard Kempe, of Cornard, in Suffolk (close to the borders of Essex), mentions in his will, of 1584, his son-in-law, John Abbott : there may be thus an intermarriage with the Abbotts which occasioned or resulted from the intimacy of the two families. Richard Kempe, of Cornard, describes himself only as a "labourer," while the parents of Archbishop Abbot and his worthy brothers were very humble people of Guildford.

The Heydon Church Registers contain the following items, which confirm the statements in the will given above :

1599.	14th November.	Isabelle, daughter of Robert Kempe, Gent. (baptized)
1603.	8th September.	Frances, " " " " "
1604.	3rd February.	Mary, " " " " "
1609.	8th February.	William, son of " " " "
1612.		John Kempe, Gent. (buried)
1615.	28th July.	Robert Kempe, Gent. "
1626.	29th March.	William, son of Robert Kempe, Gent., and Frances his wife. (buried)
1633.	23rd December.	Mrs. Frances Kempe, Widow. (buried)
1664.	3rd June.	Mrs. Mary Kitchingman. (buried)

It will be seen by this that ROBERT KEMPE, of Heydon, only survived his father John some three years and was buried near him. His will was proved by Frances Kempe, his relict, in 1615, in the Norwich Consistory Court. To his wife he leaves his lands at Heydon and Sall for her life and then to his eldest son Robert Kempe, he paying to William Kempe, the younger son of the the testator, £20 a year out of it. He also leaves the profits arising out of his lands in Essex to his wife for the purpose of educating and bringing up his younger children. What these Essex lands were is not stated, but doubtless they were part of the patrimony of the Spain's Hall Kempes. To each of his daughters he left £200, to his son Robert half his household "stuff," to his sister Kempe he left a ring and to his brother William Kempe, of Spain's Hall, his hawks and five marks. The testator also mentions his father-in-law, John Mingay, of Arminghall, Esq., his mother-in-law Isabella Mingay, his brothers-in-law Henry Mingay and Clement Pamen, Gent., the last two being appointed overseers. A cousin William Peirce is mentioned also and Helen Pearce, Winifred Bell, Rebecca Barber and William Pearce were witnesses.

Frances, the wife of this testator, was, as will be seen, the daughter of John Mingay, of Norfolk, and it seems that she had, in addition to her husband's lands, other property at Heydon to which she became heir under the will of her father, proved in 1622. On this (by her will proved at Norwich 1633) she made a charge of £3 per annum to be distributed to the poor prisoners in Norwich Gaol and for preaching three sermons annually to them. This settlement however has now failed to have effect, for so long ago as 1808, on enquiry being made, only one instance of a donation being given from the fund could be cited. The Heralds who attended the funeral of John Mingaye made a certificate to the effect that Frances Kempe was his daughter and that she then had the following children : Robert and William, both living ; Elizabeth, wife of Ralf Outlaw or Utlaw, of Winningham, Norfolk, Gent. ; Isabelle, wife of Edward Colfer, of Wooddalling, Esq. ; Frances, wife of William Drury, of Hamworth, Norfolk, and Mary who was unmarried. Mary married soon afterwards however, for her monument in Heydon Church has the following inscription :

"Here lyeth the body of Mary one of the daughters of Robert Kempe Esq., sometime the wife of Nicholas Osbourne, Gent. and late wife of John Kitchiningman, Gent. who departed this life the 1st of June 1664."

Frances Kempe died in 1633 and was buried with her husband at Heydon, their monument there having this inscription :

"Here lyeth the body of Robert Kempe Esq., who descended of that Ancient Family of Spaynes Hall in Essex and departed this life in July 1615. Next unto him lyeth the body of his loving wife Mrs. Frances who died in December 1633."

Ralph Outlaw was of Little Winchingham (not "Winningham") and was party to a deed made between the two Sir Robert Kempes, dated 17th September, 7th of Charles I., relating to the marriage of Elizabeth Kempe, of the Norfolk family, with Robert Kempe, of Spain's Hall. It appears from this that certain lands at Old and New Buckenham were settled upon the bride or charged with an annuity in her favour. On this interesting document (which is noted in Howard's printed "Visitation of Suffolk") are seals as follows: A chevron engrailed between three estoiles. Crest, an arm, couped at the elbow, holding a chaplet, representing Robert Kempe, of Spain's Hall. Also, on a bend between two lions rampant, three dolphins embowed, for Osbourne,—doubtless the seal of Nicolas Osbourne, brother-in-law to Kempe, of Spain's Hall.

Before, however, this deed was made William Kempe, of Spain's Hall, brother to the above Robert, had died. He it was whose singular monument has given notoriety to a story which is still the chief tradition of Finchingfield. As told to-day in his native village it appears that this squire, returning from a banquet, used foul language to his wife, whose gentle nature was so hurt that her tears were with difficulty stopped. When the squire returned to his sober senses he vowed that for seven years he would speak no word to anyone. This vow he most rigorously kept, filling up his days with manual labour by way of further penance. His toil resulted in the formation of seven pools or fishponds, each one larger than the last, stretching away from the hall to the woods near the town. His self-inflicted punishment was just completed—they say that it was the very day that he could once more speak—when he died. The story, though told with variations, is founded on fact, for the tablet to the memory of himself and his wife, in the Kempe Chapel of Finchingfield Church, reads as follows:

"Here lyeth William Kempe Esquire, Pious, just, hospitable, Master of himself soe much, that what others scarce doe by force and penalties Hee did by a Voluntary constancy Hold his peace Seaven yeares. Who was interred June ye 10th 1628 aged 73.

"And Philip(pa) his wife, A woman of a chaste life and religion, discreet in both, who was outlived by her husband in ye course of her owne life five yeares, and interred August 21 1623, the parents of one onely Davghter and child Jane, married with a dubble portion of graces and fortune into the Ancient family of ye Burgoinies in Warwickshire.'

Philppa Kempe was the daughter and co-heir of Francis Gunter, of London and of Aldbury, Herts. Her marriage settlement is dated 10th October, 1588.

The husband of this child was John Burgoyne, of Sutton, in Bedfordshire, Esq., and it is believed that from this couple the present Vicar of Finchingfield is descended. John Burgoyne, of Sutton, was a grandson of Robert Burgoyne, of Wroxall, whose Inquisition was taken in 1613, which shows that the latter owned property in Staffordshire as well as in Warwickshire. It might hence be supposed the Kempes of those counties are an early branch of the Spain's Hall family, but it is more likely that John Burgoyne became acquainted with his wife through his mother's family—the Wendys, of Cambridge—one of whom married Thomas Steward, of Barton Mills, and had a daughter who eventually married Sir Robert Kempe, of Spain's Hall, thus twice linking the Wendy and Kempe families within some twenty years.

CHAPTER III.

SIR ROBERT KEMPE, KNIGHT.

ROBERT KEMPE, son of Robert Kempe, of Heydon, succeeded to the chief estates at Finchingfield on the death of his uncle William. This uncle had died intestate and powers of administration were granted (1629) to Robert on Jane Burgoyne (the only child) renouncing.

Robert Kempe had married, previous to this date, Elizabeth, daughter of Nicholas Miller, of

Kent, and had by her three or more children. She was buried at Wrotham Church, Kent, and the inscription on her tomb is given in Thorpe's "Registrum Roffense" as follows:

"Here lyeth the bodye of Elizabeth Kempe wife of Robert Kempe of Spains Hall in Finchingfield, in the County of Essex Esq, and daughter to Nicholas Miller Esquire who departed this life 28 June . . . 30 . . ."

We take the date to mean 1630, but believe that the inscription is not now existing. In the same church however are monuments to John Burgoyn and Margaret Burgoyn, probably relations of the John Burgoyne who married Jane Kempe, of Finchingfield.

Robert Kempe, as mentioned in the Norfolk section, was very intimate with Sir Robert Kempe, Knight, and afterwards Baronet of Gissing, and chose as his second wife Elizabeth Kempe, sister to this first Baronet. In the Dalry collection (Brit. Mus. Additional MSS. 19,138), deeds concerning this marriage are given dated 7th Charles I. and settling "all Finchingfield with patronage" on Sir Robert Kempe, of Gissing, the latter paying a peppercorn if demanded. This agreement was to be void if the marriage failed to be solemnized before 1st October, 1634. A second deed fixes the fine at £1,000 if the marriage does not take place, and a third settles £100 a year out of the mortgaged Finchingfield estates on Robert Kempe, of Spain's Hall. These deeds seem to point to extravagance on the part of the mortgagee and to a very determined wish to unite the two distinct Kempe families. There still exists in the great hall window of Spain's Hall a glass blazon of the arms of the Essex Kempes impaling those of the Kempes of Gissing, in evident allusion to this match.

This wife was living in 1645, for she is mentioned as "my sister Lady Kempe, of Spain's Hall, in Essex," by Arthur Kempe, of St. Michael's at Thorne, Norwich. This testator was brother to the first Kempe Baronet of Gissing, and was for a time Rector of Cricksea, in Essex. We do not know exactly when she died, but she left but one child, a daughter named Frances.

The third wife of Sir Robert, of Spain's Hall, was Elizabeth Steward, daughter of Thomas Steward or Stewart, of Barton Mills, Suffolk, Esq., the arms of whose family are as follows: Argent, a lion rampant gules, over all a bend ragulee or. It appears from the pedigree that this third wife was much younger than Sir Robert, however we are unable to give the date of her birth or marriage. As deeds of settlement were made between Thomas Steward and Robert Kempe in May, 1662, it is likely that this marriage occurred about that time; she had not borne a child before her husband's death, which occurred the following year, but provision was made by Sir Robert in case of a posthumous child. The will in which this occurs is dated at Finchingfield, 30th October, 1662, the testator styling himself Sir Robert Kempe, of Spain's Hall, Knight, and was proved by his widow on 20th November, 1663, in the Prerogative Court of Canterbury (140 Juxon).

The will is a very long one, characterized by many pious sentiments and contains numerous charitable bequests. Of these we shall speak presently under a notice of the Guild House. Of the family possessions he leaves the use of Spain's Hall for one year to his wife, and an annuity of £200, issuing out of the Manor of Spain's Hall The Manor of Jekells, then occupied by Robert Choate, with Bradfield Wood and Cheerewood, was charged with an annuity of £200 to the testator's daughter, Ruth Kempe, for her life and in full settlement of any dower. This Ruth was evidently the widow of William Kempe, son of the testator, for the next clause in the will provides for Mary Kempe, the testator's grandchild, the only child of this William and Ruth, his wife, who was the daughter of Sir Gilbert Gerrard, of Harrow-on-Hill. On this grandchild was settled a lease of two houses in Southampton Buildings, in the parish of St. Andrew, Holborn, and other reversions in case the testator had no son by his third wife. He also provides for his sisters described as follows: Elizabeth, wife of Ralph Outlaw, of Little Winchingham, Co. Norfolk; Isabell, wife of the late Edward Colfer, Esq., of Norwich: Frances Doughtie, of Hamur, in Norfolk, widow; and Mary, wife of John Kitchingman, of the City of Norwich, Gent. He also leaves legacies to his father-in-law, Thomas Stewart, Gent., and his sister, Sarah Stewart; also to his son-in-law, Sir Thomas Gardiner, Knight, and his brother-in-law, Edward Kempe, one of the Fellows of Queens' College, Cambridge. His nephew, Sir Robert Kempe, of Gissing, Baronet, and his "virtuous Lady," are to have mourning rings, also his nephew, Thomas Kempe, brother of the Baronet, and his niece Shelton. Several cousins are also mentioned, among them being Mary Chaplyn, William Leigh, Minister of Grotten (*hodie* Groton), in Suffolk, Clement and Henry Pamen. The will mentions many properties, freehold and leasehold, in Finchingfield, Sampford and Wimbush, the chief of which revert to the testator's kinsman, Thomas Kempe, citizen and draper of London, whose descent we shall presently show.

Elizabeth Kempe, the widow of Sir Robert Kempe, of Spain's Hall, married again within a few years of his death, her second husband being Robert King, of Great Thurlow, in Suffolk. By this husband she had an only daughter, Letitia, who eventually married Sir Robert Kempe, the third Baronet of Gissing, thus again linking the two Kempe families.

The fact of this Elizabeth having come from Barton Mills may explain the appearance of a Kempe family at that place, but we are unable to say for certain that the William Kempe, whose will was proved in 1674 (P. C. C., 16 Dycer) was of either family. He mentions his mother, Elizabeth, leaving her for life a messuage and land lying in Forncett and Tacolneston in Norfolk, which may have been settled on Elizabeth Kempe, the second wife of Sir Robert, of Spain's Hall, and sister to the Norfolk baronet. This William, of Barton Mills, otherwise called Barton Parva, speaks of his brother, Robert Kempe, his wife, Frances, and daughter Joice. After the death of this child all the testator's property was to revert to Robert and his heirs, failing which the reversion was to benefit Mr. Peter Watts, of Bungay, and his heirs. The mention of Bungay suggests that this William may have been related to a Robert Kempe of that place, whose will was proved in 1659 (P. C. C., 541 Pell), leaving his property to Margaret, his wife, and his children, Robert, Thomas, and Elizabeth Kempe. Robert, of Bungay, was an innkeeper, while William, of Barton Mills, was a vintner, trades which may well be connected, but which are somewhat unlikely occupations for such landed gentry as would be the sons of both Sir Roberts.

CHAPTER IV.

THE KEMPE ALMSHOUSES AND BENEFACTIONS.

IT is unknown when the guild or confraternity was founded at Finchingfield, but the names of the founders are given in Wright's "History of Essex" as Henry Onions, William Sergeant, Richard Walkfar, Richard Mortimer and a Kempe, whose Christian name is not shown. This religious association was formed for the purpose of finding a priest to sing masses, and was known as the Trinity Guild. It was at first endowed with lands in Finchingfield called "Onions" and "Mortimers," and had a "Yeld" Hall upon the hill.

This house, doubtless, was on the hill upon which the present Guild House stands, and on which the fine parish church is situated. It is possible that the chief timbers are part of the original "Yeld Hall," and that it dates from about 1450. We give an illustration of the present exterior and of the interior of the chief room, now used as a parish room. The floor, as will be seen, is curved excessively from the weight of the superstructure. In the building is a library containing a few old books. When these were seen the library was in disorder, and it is possible that among the old bundles of papers a careful searcher might find some of antiquarian interest. A weekly distribution of bread and other relief takes place still at the Guildhall, which, doubtless, includes the bequests of the Kempes. Those entitled to the alms produce a token of white metal in accordance with ancient custom. Adjoining the Guildhall are the almshouses, which if not founded by the Kempes were at least benefitted by them, and are now carefully tended by the family occupying Spain's Hall. At the extinction of the religious guild, the Guildhouse was evidently deemed the property of the Kempes, who seem to have kept it up for the benefit of the parish until Sir Robert Kempe definitely settled it upon the poor of Finchingfield as a perpetual almshouse. Adjoining this, as shown in our illustration, are other almshouses, founded about 1560 by Sergeant William Bendlowe, and frequently benefitted by the Kempes.

The Guildhall Almshouses at Finchingfield.

Interior of the Guildhall.

William Kempe, the silent, had settled, in 1623, an annual rent charged on the Spain's Hall estate, of £10, and Sir Robert, by his will of 1663, gave thirty-eight acres of land called Spains or Parkfield for the following purposes : For the "Minister" of Finchingfield to catechize in the church every month, on the first Friday at two o'clock, £6, and £3 to be expended by the church-wardens for bread, to be distributed to those who attend the catechizing, and if any abatement occur in the rent the minister's allowance is to be proportionately less, but the £3 is in any case to be distributed in bread or other alms. The will of this benefactor speaks of the almshouse as "my almhouses called the Guildhall, in Finchingfield," bequeathing to the inmates at his funeral a mourning gown. He further states that he made an engagement with his late "dear uncle, William Kempe," to found a Guildhouse for the poor and to settle upon it sufficient endowment. He also speaks of the Finchingfield Church as being the place where his "dear uncle William and many other of my ancestors have heretofore been buried, and where my wife, Dame Elizabeth Kempe, and three of my children lye already interred."

The chapel of the Kempes is now maintained by the Ruggles-Brise family as owners of Spain's Hall. It contains the mural monument of the celebrated mute William Kempe (1628), a brass, which we reproduce, of Robert Kempe (1527), and an altar tomb under which is the vault ot the Kempes. The chapel is at present very bare, devoid practically of seats, and is used as a vestibule by the Spain's Hall tenants. It contains an ancient chest, now the receptacle for the paraffin and cleaning rags for the lamps which light the church. No heraldic glass now remains to the Kempes or their relatives, but the chancel screen is the very same on which many generations of the family must have gazed, and the church is one of the finest and most interesting in the country.

CHAPTER V.

PENTLOW HALL.

WE have to return to George Kempe, son of William Kempe, of Spain's Hall, by Mary, daughter of John Colt. He was married three times, first to Margaret Large, by whom no issue is recorded ; secondly to Margaret Apulderfield, by whom he had a large family, and thirdly to Lady Mary Woodhouse, of whom we shall have more to say. The second wife was apparently an heiress, as the Heralds allowed her arms to be quartered by her descendants and they are emblazoned upon the tomb at Pentlow. These arms also appeared quartered by the Kempes of Kent and Sussex and point to the belief in the common descent of the families through the above marriage and the Chiches, which is interesting in view of the fact that the Kempe stocks were quite distinct. What lands she brought to George Kempe we cannot say for certain, but it seems likely that lands at Pentlow and Cavendish, formerly the property of the Feltons, had come to the Apulderfields before this heiress's union with the Kempes, for George Kempe was the first to hold Pentlow Hall, although his brother Arthur is the first to figure in the registers in the church adjoining the hall grounds.

The first entry is the baptism of Marie, the daughter of Arthur Kempe, Gent., on 10th August, 1589, after which no further record of Arthur occurs ; but John Kempe, Gent., has the following children baptized: Drew, 6th November, 1591; Margery, 6th August, 1599; Drewsella, 23rd December, 1601; George, 12th November, 1602; John, 13th May, 1604, and Tabitha, 8th August, 1606. George Kempe, a son of this John Kempe, Gent., was buried there 3rd May, 1594, and George Kempe, Esq., of Pentlow, grandfather of these children, was entombed in the Kempe Chapel, at Pentlow, on the last day of March, 1607, his will being proved in the Prerogative Court of Canterbury (35 Huddleston) on 14th April, 1607. It is dated at Tottenham, Middlesex, on 23rd March, 1605, and starts with a bequest of £25 13*s*. 0*d*. to the churchwardens of Pentlow and £3 6*s*. 8*d*. for the reparation of Pentlow Church. Of the first fund, which was to remain in stock for ever, eight poor folk dwelling in the parish were to share the interest. To his son Charles Kempe (who was of Walthamstow) he gave £200; to his son William Kempe £100 towards bringing up his children; to his son Christopher £20; to his daughter, the wife of Robert Green, Gent., £50, and to his granddaughter Theodora Green £200. To every child of his nephew, the late Arthur Kempe, £20, and to his nephew John Kempe £30. To John Kempe, his eldest son, he left the lease of the Rectory of Tottenham (which was held from the Dean and Chapter of St. Paul's), but the testator's widow was to have the occupation of it for twenty weeks next after her husband's death and option to take it on lease for six years at £20 a year. The testator left his eldest son sole executor, but begged him not to meddle with or enquire into any moneys which the widow claimed as her own by right of birth, by previous marriage or by settlement. George Kempe, another son, is mentioned, of whose descendants some account has been given in our Norfolk section under Wooddalling and Lyng.

Tomb of the Kempes in their Chapel at Pentlow, Essex.
Photographed by F. Stokoe, of Clare.

George Kempe, the testator, was a judge and a lawyer of some repute, a note book of cases in which he apparently took part was recently offered for sale by a Bristol bookseller, being marked Georgius Kempe. The *Gentleman's Magazine* of 1808 states that Lady Woodhouse was Mary, the daughter of John Corbet, of Sproughton, in Norfolk, Esq., and that she married first Sir Roger Woodhouse, and, as here recorded, afterwards George Kempe; of her identity there is no doubt, for John Corbet was a witness to this will and Mary Corbet witnessed a Kempe will in 1667, it is however confusing, as the above writer found, that at this period the Corbets were also closely related to some of the Gissing (Norfolk) Kempes. In the Middlesex County Records we find that on 2nd September, 1601, John Bryan, late of London, yeoman, broke burglariously into the dwelling-house of George Kempe, Esq. at Tottenham, and stole therefrom a pair of black silk garters, of the goods and chattels of Thomas Woodhouse, Esq., then a guest at the house. The culprit however obtained a pardon as he could read like a clerk.

JOHN KEMPE, Esq., the eldest son, inherited all his father's lands in Essex, and was evidently living at Pentlow Hall when his father died, as appears from the above register, and had married previous to 1591. His wife was Eleanor, daughter of . . . . Drew, of Devonshire, from which fact the first child received his Christian name. Drew Kempe however died young and consequently a daughter was baptised Drewsella. She bore fourteen children in all, but of these we only trace three who survived childhood, namely: George, who became a Baronet; John, who left a son of the same name, and a Lucy, who probably married a Mr. Taylor.

John Kempe, of Pentlow, was a student at Lincoln's Inn in 1580, and in the practice of the law acquired some wealth, for we find his possessions at death comprised Pentlow Hall and the Manors of West Walton and Whitehouse, in South Lynne, Norfolk, Wyleigh Hall and Park, Clapton Park, lands in Cavendish, and the advowson of the church at Pentlow; he was buried with his father and wife in the Kempe Chapel of Pentlow Church, and the fine tomb of which we give an illustration, still exists. The tomb was repaired about 1830 at the cost of the Rev. E. M. Mathew. The inscription on it is as follows:

George Kemp, whose life spake to his virtuous prayse,
Lies here entombed after his end of days.
Fame tells the world his life and death was such
On Truth's report can never prayse too much;
Religion, justice, mercy, bounty, peace,
With faithful plainesse was his fame's increase.
In King's Bench Courte full fifty years found just,
Who reads this truth but need commend him must.
From race of worship his life's beginninge spronge,
Of William Kempe, Esquire, the sixt, and youngest son
Whose Manor House, Spaines Hall in Essex knowne,
Tells from that roote this worthy branche was growne.
Seventy-six years he lived, and children eight,
Five sonnes, three daughters, on his age did wayte.
Monday, on March the three and twenteth day,
In peace Death's hand did take him hence away,
One thousand six hundred and six, of Christ the yeare,
His soule, as wearie of her mansion here
Made haste to heaven, with Christe for aye to dwell,
Happie are they that live and die so well.

Here lyeth John Kempe, that worthy esquire,
That never detracted the poor man's hire,
Of veritie and knowledge, a studious seeker,
Of word and promise a faithful keeper,
Chaste Elinor Drew of Devonshire,
Daughter of John Drew an Esquire
Was his virtuous wife, by mother honoured
To him children, seven and seven did she beare,
As by this monument to you doth appear;
He lived forty-eight yeare, too short a time,
And died the seventh of January,
One thousand, six hundred and nine.
Heaven hath his soule through Christian grace
Earth his bodye entombed in this place.

In the east window of the Kempe chapel there are fragments of heraldic glass, but being merely *painted* glass the colour has now almost disappeared. One can, however, distinctly trace the outline of the arms of the family there, a chevron engrailed between three estoiles, which arms are emblazoned on the tomb, with the seven other quarterings authorised impaling others.

The will of John Kempe, of Pentlow, Esq., was proved in the Prerogative Court of Canterbury (14 Wingfield). It is very long and gives much detail of his properties, which we cannot find space for here; it bequeathes to his wife, Elenor, his Manor of Pentlow for fifteen years and the use of lands there, and at Cavendish and Foxearth, she keeping such of the children who may be under age until their twenty-first birthday. The chief part of the estates passed ultimately to his son George.

The register shows that John Kempe, Esq., was buried on 8th January, 1609, and that a daughter of John Kempe, Esq., was baptized there on 1st August following named Magdalen. We do not know if this was a posthumous child or the daughter of John Kempe, the testator's son. She does not appear on the pedigree made at the Heralds' Visitation, and may, perhaps, have died young.

Pentlow Hall, a seat of the Kempes of Essex, 1500-1650.

The baptisms of children of George Kempe appear from 1611 to 1619, but the father of these settled at Wooddalling and Norwich, and has been already considered in the Norfolk section.

George Kempe, the son of John, was baptized as the son and heir on 12th November, 1602, and was therefore but a child at his father's death. He studied the law and became a prominent judge, residing chiefly in London. The Middlesex Session Rolls record that he and his grandmother, Lady Mary Woodhouse, otherwise Mrs. Mary Kempe, were recusants in 1641, he being then described as late of St. Giles-in-the-Fields, and she as late of St. Giles-in-the-Fields and of Saffron Hill, while in 1633 she appears to have been residing at St. Andrew's, Holborn. On 5th February, 1624, George Kempe, then of Pentlow, was created a Baronet by King James, and about this time married Thomazine, daughter of Sir Robert Brooke, who bore him two daughters, Mary, who married Sir John Winter, and Katherine, whose husband was Windsor Finch, Esq. Thomazine died in 1663 and Sir George in 1667, leaving no son to inherit the baronetcy.

The will of Dame Thomazine was nuncupative, and administration of her estate was granted to her daughter, Catherine Finch, on 20th July, 1663, Lady Mary Winter, the latter's sister, consenting. Thomazine died in the parish of St. Andrew's, Holborn, in which parish the family had a residence. (The will is to be found in the P. C. C., 91 Penn.) The will of Sir George Kempe styles him "Knight and Baron of Pentlow"; it is dated 20th March, 1663, and was proved by John Woolfe on 22nd January, 1666-7. At the date of making this will Thomazine was living, and provision was consequently made for her, while to his daughter Katherine (then single) he bequeathed his lands at Clacton, Essex, and the large diamond ring he was in the habit of wearing, and lands at Harking, Suffolk, the Manor of West Walton, Norfolk; lands at Walpole and Walsoken, in the latter county, were to be held in trust by his executors and the rents applied for the benefit of Mary Winter, his other daughter, and the testator's sister, Lucy Kempe, these estates reverting after their death to George Kempe, Gent., "nephew" (cousin) of the testator. Annuities were also provided for Elizabeth Jernegan, William Eldridge, Mrs. Taylor, "sister" of the testator, and his cousin, Mrs. Frances Quintain. It appears from this will that part of the Norfolk property mentioned had been devised to Katherine by the will of Sir Robert Brooke. Some at West Walton seem to have belonged to the Spain's Hall and Pentlow Kempes for generations.

By the last will the Pentlow estates were to pass to George, the son of Christopher Kempe, who was sometime a resident at West Smithfield and Clerkenwell, London. This Christopher was the fifth son of George Kempe, Esq., of Pentlow, and was buried there on 13th August, 1630. We have not found his will, and can but conjecture that administration was granted to his widow Agnes, who was daughter and heiress of Matthew Cockrode, whose arms were eventually quartered. Her children recorded were as follows: George, who inherited from Sir George Kempe, Bart.; Thomas, the latter's heir; Anne, who married . . . . Gage; Elizabeth, who married John Springham, of Edmonton, Middlesex, and Mary, who was the wife of Edward Chaplin. Agnes Kempe resided at Finchingfield, and was probably buried there, her will being dated in that parish on 4th February, 1652, and proved in London on June 17, 1656 (P. C. C., 220 Berleley). She leaves to her son, Thomas Kempe, citizen of London, £100, and a legacy to each of his children. To her daughters, Anne Gage and Mary Chaplin, and their children likewise legacies are left, while the poor of Finchingfield are also benefitted. It is possible that it was this Agnes Kempe, widow, who was described as *Anne* Kempe, widow, and was a recusant living at Saffron Walden with Lady May Woodhouse in 1633, at which time it may be noticed there was a William Kempe, Esq., recusant, living in Clerkenwell, London, where Christopher had been a few years previously. Of this William Kempe, however, we have no further knowledge by which to identify him. George Kempe, the eldest son of Christopher, died without issue, and his property thus passed to his younger brother Thomas, who married four times. His first wife was Elizabeth, daughter of Richard Randall, by whom he had two daughters, Mary, who married Benjamin Goodrich, and Elizabeth, who became William Minors's wife. The second wife was Mary, daughter of Andrew Parne, and she bore also two daughters (Elizabeth, who married Ralph Minors, and Mary, whose husband was a Bernard). She also had two sons, the younger being named Andrew, is said to have been seated at Dorrington, but we do not trace him at any place of that name; her eldest son was John, and he eventually inherited the Spain's Hall and other family estates. By his third wife, who was Elizabeth, daughter of another Ralph Minors, he had Thomas Kempe, who seems to have married a Rebecca Cooper; Elizabeth, who was married to a Rogers, and Anne, who was married first to Thomas Briscoe and secondly to Jernaghan Chaplin. The fourth wife of Thomas was Elizabeth Springham, by whom he left no issue. He died early in 1692, and his will was proved that year on the 8th February (P. C. C., 138 Fane) in London. This will, dated at Finchingfield the previous September 16th, mentions the following relatives: Elizabeth, his wife, his daughters, Mrs. Bernard, Mrs. Minors, Mrs. Cooper and Mrs. Rogers, his relative, Dame Elizabeth Kempe, widow of Sir Robert Kempe, Knight, and his grandsons, Andrew Kempe and John Kempe. Susan Kempe is mentioned, but her degree of relationship does not appear.

It is noticeable that the testator does not mention his sons, and the presumption is that the eldest, if not both, was dead. There is a will of a Thomas Kempe, clerk, of Foxearth, proved in 1718, though dated in 1692, and it is likely that, as the Kempes of Pentlow owned land at Foxearth, this Thomas was a near relative of the family, and thus was presented to the living through their influence. Curiously, this testator, like the last, speaks of his daughter Mary Barnard, he also leaves legacies to Elizabeth Holbrough, widow ; Francis, the wife of William Nicholls, and Thomas the son of Hannah Clopton. Bequests are also made to the poor of Foxearth and those of Preston St. Mary, in Suffolk, and the residue of his estate is left to his son Henry Kempe, who was appointed executor.

John Kempe, the eldest son of Thomas Kempe, of Finchingfield, married, but we have not traced the wife's name. They left a son named John, who inherited the Spain's Hall property, also two sons named Thomas and Andrew, who seem to have died young. Andrew was bequeathed both the water mill and windmill, under his grandfather's will, but we have no knowledge of his having been in actual possession of them. John Kempe, the heir, died unmarried in 1726, being the last male Kempe to possess the Spain's Hall property, which had been in the family some 400 years. His will was proved 2nd February, 1726, by his executrix and chief legatee, Mary Kempe, his eldest sister. He provides annuities for life to his sisters Anne Kempe, of London ; Alice, the wife of Thomas Osbourne, of London ; Elizabeth and Rebecca Kempe, of Finchingfield, and Spain's Hall, while the residuary estate is left to his sister Mary. With so large a fortune she quickly found a suitable husband in the person of Sir Swinnerton Dyer, Baronet, of Dunmow, ancestor of the present baronet of that name ; the property thus passed to the Dyers, who however soon parted with it. We have been unable to ascertain if any Kempe portraits or other relics of the family are still in the Dyer family.

CHAPTER VI.

THE LATER KEMPS OF ESSEX.

IN the reign of Elizabeth there was a suit in the Court of Chancery between Arthur Kempe and Anthony Golding, Esq., regarding the Manor of Waltons, in Purleigh, demised by the Earl of Oxford to George Golding, deceased, and by the latter assigned to Arthur Kempe. The identity of this Arthur is not absolutely determined, but he was in all probability one of the Arthur Kempes, of Finchingfield, mentioned in Chapter II., while from the time of these proceedings the Essex Kempes held at least an interest in this property. We however have not searched the local registers and must, for lack of evidence, leave a break in the records until 1688, when the will of Richard Kempe, of Purleigh, was proved in the Court of the Archdeaconry of Essex, by William Walker, Gent. (139 Parrett). The testator leaves all his household effects to his son Richard and daughter Frances Kempe. He leaves to his executor, the said William Walker, of Cold Norton Hall, in trust, his house called Purleigh Barnes and all the rest of his lands, the income to provide for the maintenance of the children until the age of twenty-one and then to become their absolute property. The will provides that in case both these children die before such age the estates are to pass to the children of *John Webb*, of *Southchurch*, in the same county, and in case of their death the property is to revert to the children of *Christopher Persons*, *of Southchurch.*

This is the first mention we have of a connexion of Kempes with Southchurch and, as will be presently seen, the Persons—otherwise Parsons—family were most important parishioners of this place, and were undoubtedly the relatives of the known ancestors of the present George Kemp, Esq., M.P. Before however we dwell further on this branch, who settled at Southchurch about 1700, we must digress to speak of a celebrated John Kempe who was connected both with the Earl of Oxford and one named Walker, and who seems to belong to this family.

It will be noticed from the foregoing chapters that the Kempes of Finchingfield showed evident sympathy with the Puritan preachers, at any rate from the close of the Commonwealth, although in his younger days Sir Robert Kempe, of Spain's Hall, had, with his friend Sir Robert Kempe, of Gissing, been a royalist and high-churchman ; this Puritan feeling evidently grew stronger in the succeeding generations, and both those of Southchurch, Prittlewell and the celebrated John Kempe's family were distinctly inclined to independency.

The father of the antiquary John Kempe was a merchant and a member of the Leathersellers' Company of London, and his mother was a Miss Hope Gilbert, who was married to John Kempe, the elder, by licence in 1665. In 1690 administration of her husband's estate was granted to her by the Prerogative Court of Canterbury, and her own will was proved in the same Court, by her daughters Hope and Mary Kempe, in January, 1714. This will is dated at Exeter on 27th April, 1710, and leaves the personalty to the daughters after a legacy to each of her sons John and William Kempe. The names of Elizabeth and Hannah Kempe and John Munsie (? Mounsey) appear as witnesses.

John Kempe, F.R.S., the elder son, had doubtless enjoyed the use of his father's residence in St. Martin's Fields from the time of his majority, and, having ample income and cultivated taste, devoted his time to gathering together a wonderful collection of ancient coins, curios and old works of art, of which he drew up a detailed explanatory catalogue. He became Fellow of the Royal Society in 1712. His tastes, if not his family connexion, led to intimacy with Lord Harley, son of the Earl of Oxford, to whom this unique collection was to be offered at the collector's decease for the sum of £2,000. Lord Harley however (the founder of the Harleian Library) declined the offer, and consequently the museum was parted with by auction in small lots for the total sum of £1,090 8*s*. 6*d*., and the account of the contents of the museum, written by himself, was edited by the noted Robert Ainsworth, and published by John's brother, William Kempe, in 1720, under the title of "*Monvmenta Vetustatis Kempiana*," being sold by J. Osborn, in Lombard Street, and other booksellers. One of the wills of the Spain's Hall Kempes mentions a relative named Osbourne as a bookseller. The fact that this John Kempe or his brother arranged with an Osborn to sell his book strengthens the supposition of the close connexion which then (1700-1720) existed between the Southchurch, Purleigh, St. Martin-in-Field, and the Finchingfield Kempes. Copies of the "Monvmenta" still exist in various libraries.

John Kempe, the antiquary, dated his will at St. Martin's-in-Fields, 26th March, 1716, and it was proved in the Prerogative Court of Canterbury by his brother William on 24th September, 1717 (171 Whitfield). The testator desired to be buried near his dear mother in Bunhill Fields, a burial place closely identified with dissent. To his sister, Hope Kempe, he left his Manor of Hockley Hall, lately surrendered by Ellena Swinsford ; to his sister, Mary Kempe, he left £200 South Sea Stock and money raised by the sale of his antiquities ; to his cousin, Elizabeth, daughter of his uncle James Kempe, South Sea Stock of the face value of £100 and debts due from William Paterson ; to his cousin, John Madden, a legacy; also rings or their value to his landlord *Walker*, William Tanner, goldsmith, in Cheapside, John Hannon, Dr. Crichlowe, Mr. Humphrey Wanley, Mr. Thomas Smith, of New Inn, and Samuel Noble, bookseller.

William Kempe, the brother, wrote as the will directed to Lord Harley, then Earl of Oxford, and his letters are to be seen in the British Museum ; a more recent note says that this William Kempe was an undertaker living or carrying on business at Surrey Street, Strand. We have no proof of this, and believe that having inherited the residence of his brother in St. Martin's-in-Fields he removed thither, for the goods, credits and effects of a William Kempe of that parish were granted to his widow, Martha Kempe, on 23rd April, 1746, by authority of the Prerogative Court of Canterbury.

Purleigh is but a short distance from Maldon, in Essex, and from the following details it will be seen that Thomas Kemp, of Abridge, otherwise Heybridge, now part of Maldon, was apparently akin to both Richard of Purleigh and the Kempes of Southchurch and neighbourhood. The will is dated 2nd June, 1720, and was proved by the executor, Henry Lewsley, *alias* Howsley, on 9th of the same month (P. C. C., 138 Shaller). To his son, Thomas Kemp, the testator left his farm and land at Little Wakering in the occupation of John Cattline, and an estate at Great Wakering to his daughters, Sarah and Mary Kemp, including his oyster-laying, stating that Arthur Kemp, his eldest son, had inherited an estate from his late mother and was therefore well provided for. Henry Hewsley, of Langford (near Malden), was instructed to sell a farm and land lying at South Shrewsbury,* Co. Essex, and to divide the sum so raised equally between the testator's four children. Edward Berry, of All Saints', Maldon, was also appointed executor and shared the responsibility with Howsley *als.* Lewsley.

Robert Johnson, William Remmington and Andrew Yardley witnessed this will. It will be noticed that a Johnson was made guardian of the infant son of Daniel Kempe of Barking, with whom it is likely that this testator was closely related.

Little and Great Wakering lie close to Southchurch on the east side of that parish, while Prittlewell adjoins Southchurch on the west. Within these four parishes from 1720 therefore it is certain that the Kempes held property, and within the next decade it is certain that they resided there, if, indeed, they did not do so much earlier. Christopher Parsons mentioned in the will of Richard Kempe, of Purleigh, as of Southchurch in 1688, was churchwarden, and is buried in a large altar tomb directly east of the chancel, while around him are the tombs of later generations of his family whose descendants still reside in the parish. The present vicar has been good enough to carefully search the parish registers and finds that the first mention of a Kemp occurs on 11th November, 1734, when Susannah, daughter of Thomas Kempe, by Susannah, his wife, was baptized. This couple also had the following children baptized there, Elizabeth Abigail, 1735, Johanna, 1736, Thomas, 1738, and John, 1739. These sons may both have died infants, for a Thomas Kemp was buried there in 1738 and a John in 1740. It is, however, possible that it was Thomas the father who was buried in 1738, and that the youngest son was posthumous, or baptized when older than usual.

The registers of Great and Little Wakering have been searched by ourselves, and the tombs at both examined, but no mention of a Kempe was found at either place ; however, it is evident that the Kempes had a residence here before that of Southchurch, for the estate of John Kemp of his Majesty's ship *Kent* in the King's service, formerly of Much Wakering, was granted in

* Thus in the Probate ; evidently a clerk's error for Shoebury.

1735 to Jane Kemp, widow, his relict. These were, we have little doubt, the ancestors of the subsequent Southchurch and Prittlewell Kemps, but as both died intestate it is extremely doubtful if proof will be forthcoming to actually establish this point.

The registers of Prittlewell have also been searched by ourselves, and are found to contain Kemp entries from 1754, in which year Henry Chacey, of Great Wakering married Hannah Kemp, spinster, of Prittlewell. It must be noticed that a Robert *Camp* married Mary Marsh at Prittlewell on 7th November, 1737, and although very late for such a change in the spelling it is not impossible that the numerous *Camps* whose graves mingle with the Kemps at Prittlewell are of the same family, although reverting to an old form of the name. The *Camp* entries continue to 1823 and perhaps later.

Close to the altar toub of the Marshalls, on the the south side of the church, is the earliest stone of the Kemps. It commemorates Martha Kemp, who died 6th September, 1742, aged twenty-five years, wife of John Kemp, who was buried in the same grave in 1757, aged forty-two. With them lie, as the stone informs us, eight of their grandchildren. In the last-named year we find an administration granted to Daniel Kemp, son of John Kemp, of Prittlewell.

Another stone in the churchyard records the name of John *D.* (? Durival) Kemp who died 18th June, 1810, aged seventy-two years. The second name of this individual is variously spelled Durival, Durivel, Durrival and Derwell. Why it was given is unknown, much research having failed to discover its existence as a surname in Essex or elsewhere. The most plausible suggestion made with regard to it is that it is a variant of Durrell used as a Christian name by the Shorts, of Kent, one of whom married Martha Kemp, of the Norfolk family. According to a tradition among the present representatives of the family their ancestors came from Norfolk. Elizabeth Rust, John Durival's grandmother, wrote the name in contracted form "Durr." which looks as if she regarded it as a well-known Christian name for which "Durr." was the recognized abbreviation. It is also possible that if Durrell or Durwell was derived from Kent it was through relations directly intimate with the Kemps of Prittlewell. That they *had* relatives in Kent of the name of Marshall is conclusively proved by names mentioned in the wills and polls of Kent for the period.

Among the administrations in the Prerogative Court of Canterbury is one granted in 1768-9 to John Durivel Kemp for administering the estate of his father John Kemp, late of Prittlewell, whose widow, Mary Kemp, died before she had taken out letters of administration. In the same year John Durival Kemp had to administer the estate of his brother Robert, who evidently died very shortly before his father, who should have performed this duty. Robert Kemp was a bachelor; we do not know of what he died, but three deaths in one househould so near together suggest some infectious disease as the cause.

A Bible in the possession of Clement Kemp, Esq., J.P., contains this inscription: "Elizabeth Rust's book, December 25th, 1775, which I promise to my grandson John Durr. Kemp when please God to call me." Evidently John Durival Kemp's mother was a Mary Rust. How he was related to John Kemp, who died in 1757, we do not know. He may have been nephew, but cannot have been grandson. John Kempe, of "His Majesties ship *Kent*," may very probably have been his grandfather. In 1759 administration of the goods of Mary Kemp, spinster, of Clerkenwell, was granted to Joseph Rust, he being nephew and next of kin. How they were related at all to J. D. Kemp we can only conjecture. "Nephew" may have been used to signify "cousin." John Durival Kemp's will shows that he was twice married, his first wife being named Martha and the second Mary. The latter died the 6th May, 1826, aged seventy-four. In the Prittlewell register a John Kemp is shown to have been united to Mary Beadle, a widow, on the 14th September, 1772. Whether the entry refers to John Durival is somewhat doubtful. Martha was the daughter of

Thomas Sumner, with whose son also, Thomas, her husband was for many years in partnership. She was buried at Prittlewell, as the will testifies. From 1784 to 1810 John Durival Kemp was rated as a householder at Southchurch, whither he probably removed on the death of Thomas Sumner, Sen.

John Durival Kemp is said to have been the father of eighteen children, but we do not know the names of all of them. A Thomas Sumner Kemp was baptized in May, 1772. He was unfortunately drowned on the 11th June, 1799, at the age of twenty-seven, as another stone placed "by a sincere friend," at Prittlewell, informs us. No other Kemp is recorded as having been baptized at Prittlewell till 1780, in which year their twin son and daughter, Henry Carr and Mira, were baptized on 15th October.

Alderman William Hunter, Lord Mayor of London.

We find however, in 1797, administration of the goods of William Marshall Kemp, of Southend, Master of the smack *Two Partners*, granted to John Durival Kemp. He cannot have been born later than 1776. John, who continued the principal family line, being married in 1793, and Robert Kemp, co-executor of John of their father's will, must have been among the elder members of the family, but the dates of their births are unknown. The following children were baptized at Southchurch: Elenor, 4th June, 1785; Frederick, 3rd June, 1786; Martha, 9th June, 1787; Charlotte, 11th October, 1788; Frederick Carr, in 1793. There were besides these, three daughters, Eliza, Louisa and Mary, whose ages are unknown. The rest of the children, of whom nothing whatever is known, probably died in infancy. Some account of John will be found in the next chapter. Robert emigrated to the United States where he continued the line, though little is known to the present writers of his descendants. Henry Carr Kemp died in 1837 without issue. His twin sister, Myra Sumner, married a Mr. Hardwick. She died 5th September, 1873, being the last survivor of the family of John Durival Kemp; her will was proved by George Tawke Kemp. Eliza became the wife of William Hunter, eldest son of William Hunter, of Bury St. Edmunds. He was an Alderman of London and held the office of Lord Mayor in 1852. Louisa married (first) a Mr. White and (secondly) a Mr. Mundy, a missionary in India, who published a brief memoir of her, largely made up of introspective excerpts from her diary. Mary married a Mr. Richardson. The late Rev. Henry Kemp Richardson, some time rector of Leire, was their son.

CHAPTER VII.

DESCENDANTS OF THE PRITTLEWELL KEMPS.

JOHN KEMP, son of John Durival Kemp, married Susan Stonnard, by whom he had seven sons and five daughters. He died at Thetford, 1844. She died at Cheltenham, 26th January, 1860, aged ninety years. With their family commences the connexion of the Kemps with LANCASHIRE, three of his sons having migrated from Essex to that county for different reasons. JOHN ABBOT KEMP, their eldest son, was born at Broomhills, Great Stambridge, 9th February, 1794. Why he received the name of Abbot (so spelled in his father's family Bible) is unknown. He married Elizabeth, daughter of John English Tabor, of Fenns, Bocking, 16th

John Abbot Kemp, ancestor of George Kempe, M.P.

Mrs. J. Abbot Kemp *née* Tabor.

August, 1821. He then lived at Stambridge, but soon afterwards removed to Prittlewell. He had three sons: Clement, born at Prittlewell, 15th January, 1824; Owen, born at Prittlewell, 19th March, 1826; and George Tabor, born in London, 3rd July, 1834, died 6th July, 1900. Two excellent likenesses of John Abbot Kemp and his wife, in their prime, are in the possession of the family, executed by a neighbour in London—Mr. Heffernan, an assistant in the studio of Sir Francis Chantrey. John Abbot Kemp retired to Southport for his health in 1860, and died there 20th May, 1869. He was for many years a deacon at Westminster Chapel. His widow died 31st July, 1875.

Mary Ann, the fourth child of John Kemp, was born 17th June, 1798. She became second wife to Mr. Henry Brown, of Thetford. She died at Sevenoaks, 5th March, 1875. Mr. Brown, by his first wife, became father of the late Edward Keer Brown, J.P., and the late William Brown, of Great Yarmouth. His second wife bore him a son, Henry, believed to have been lost at sea, and three daughters, Alice Louisa, Susan Stonnard and Ellen Kemp, all of whom died unmarried. Ellen Kemp, the last survivor, went out as a missionary to China, in connection with the Sheo-Yang Mission, after she was fifty years of age. She was killed by the overturning of a native cart in 1898. The fifth child was Susan, born 13th January, 1800, who married Robert Jacomb, afterwards Jacomb-Hood, of Bardon Park, Leicestershire. She died 8th June, 1873. Mr. Jacomb-Hood, who died in May, 1901, was a Director of the London, Brighton and South Coast Railway Company. He was an engineer by profession. Mr. Percy Jacomb-Hood, the well-known artist, is his son.

John and Susan Kemp's third son and seventh child was Frederick, born 12th March, 1803. When a young man he entered the employ of the late Sir P. Hesketh-Fleetwood, whose steward he was for many years. He had much to do with laying out the town of Fleetwood. His wife was Charlotte Titherington. He had two daughters of whom one married the late Major Poste, by whom she had a son, F. W. B. Poste (B.A., Camb., 1894). Frederick Kemp died 14th March, 1883 There is a stained window to his memory in the parish church of Bispham, where he lived. Emma Kemp, born 25th December, 1805, died unmarried at Cheltenhan, 15th December, 1862.

The twelfth and youngest child of John Kemp was George Tawke Kemp, late of Rochdale. He was in partnership in the silk trade at Spitalfields, and also at Middleton, Lancashire, with the late Thomas Stone, latterly a partner with Messrs. Peek, Frean and Company, biscuit manufacturers. Mr. G. T. Kemp also joined Mr. Frederick Kelsall, whose daughter he married, in the business of flannel manufacture. He died while on a visit to Egypt for his health March 20th, 1877, having been born on the 17th of the same month in 1810. He left a son, the present Major George Kemp, M.P. for the Heywood Division of Lancashire, and five daughters. He was distinguished for his liberality in religious and philanthropic causes. He was a liveryman of the Fishmongers' Company from 1837 and joined the Court of the Company in 1848. His widow still lives.

Two of George Tawke Kemp's daughters have entered the mission field. Miss Jessie Kemp first went out to India, but was obliged to return home on account of her health. She afterwards went to China under the auspices of the China Inland Mission. While engaged in this work she married Mr. T. W. Pigott. They and some other friends eventually formed themselves into an independent mission, the Sheo-Yang Mission. Mr. and Mrs. Pigott were murdered with their son, Wellesey, by the "Boxers" about 27th June, 1900. Mrs. Pigott's sister above referred to is Florence, now the wife of Dr. Edwards. They worked first with the China Inland Mission from which they seceded with Mr. Pigott. Miss Ellen Kemp Brown was another member of the Sheo-Yang Mission. Mr. George Kemp, M.P., was born in 1866. He was educated at Mill Hill, Shrewsbury and Trinity College, Cambridge, graduating B.A. with honours in the Classical Tripos in 1888. He distinguished himself as a cricketer, playing for Lancashire and for Cambridge University. He is a principal shareholder in the firm of Kelsall and Kemp, Ltd. He married the Lady Beatrice Mary, daughter of the Earl of Ellesmere.

Major George Kemp, M.P., served in South Africa with the Duke of Lancaster's Own Yeomanry for eighteen months; in his absence he was re-elected to represent his constituency. Since his return from the war Mr. Kemp has been gazetted as major. He has just accepted the command of a Yeomanry Regiment and is again going to South Africa for active service.

Turning to the family of John Abbot Kemp, Clement married Elizabeth Tabor, daughter of

John Tabor, of Bocking, by whom he had three sons. She died 8th November, 1895, aged seventy-four. He is a Liveryman of the Fishmongers' Company, having been admitted in 1847. He is also a J.P. for the Borough of Romsey where he resided from 1886-96. His business life was chiefly spent in Lancashire in the silk business of his uncle.

His sons, who were all born at Middleton, are John Tabor Kemp, M.A., Camb.; (B.A. Emman. Coll., 1884), born 5th October, 1860; Herbert Clement Tabor Kemp, now resident at Tarkastad, South Africa, proprietor of the *Tarka Herald*, born 26th September, 1862; and Cecil Tabor Kemp, pharmaceutical chemist in business at Hereford, born 16th April, 1868. Mr. H. C. T. Kemp married Edith Emily, daughter of Henry Hunt Wells of Rockwood, Coernay, Cape Colony, on 20th October, 1896.

Mr. Owen Kemp, younger surviving son of John Abbot Kemp, resides at Walthamstow; he passed many years of his life in Australia, where he married Miss Catherine Caroline Cater. George Tabor Kemp likewise emigrated to Australia, where he married late in life.

The arms of the Kemps of Prittlewell are said to be the same as those of the Kemps of Spain's Hall and Pentlow, the authority being, so far as we can ascertain, the semi-official acknowledgment of the claim of Alderman William Hunter, to impale such arms, in right of his wife (who, as stated above, was daughter of John Durival Kemp, of Prittlewell), contained in Burke's "Illustrations of Heraldry."

PIS held the same office 1231.
er," Robert Kempe and Matilda, at Uxbridge, 1331.
eld a messuage at Enfield, 1389. *Richard Kempe, at Harmondsworth*, 1407.

held lands in Tiburn Manor 1405 and Trinity, Aldgate, 1440-2. M.P. for . Will proved 1442.
roved at Lambeth 1458.

John Kempe, of Aldgate.

Robert Kempe, alias *Campe, living* 1442.

of London.=Agnes.

Robert Kempe, of Weston (Suffolk) and Gissing (Norfolk)=*Margaret or Elizabeth, d. of William Curzon, of Stutton.*
living 1473.

widow), 2-63.

George Kempe, of Hampstead, living 1523.

Ann Clifford,=*Robert Kempe, of Weston & Gissing, died* 1526.
of Kent.

Edmund Kempe, Citizen=*Bridget, d. of John Style.*
and Merchant of London. Will 1542.

Ralf Kempe, living 1473.

Finchley.=*Joan.*
1593)

Ann Allen,=*Bartholomew Kempe, of Gissing, died* 1554, *aged* 82.
of Bury St. Edmunds.

Margaret K. Benefactress. =*William Dane, Ald. of London.*

James Kempe=*Anne Powle, of Acton, living* 1566. (*mar.* 1544)

Powell Kempe.

Humphrey Kempe, (*claimed as ancestor by the Cornish Kempes*)

mythuin,=*Robert Kempe, of Gissing & Flordon, died* 1596, *aged* 80.
Buck-nshire.

Bartholomew Kempe, of London,=*Barbara Sharpe, bur. at Savoy Chapel* 1611.
M.P. for Eye 1586 & *Shaftesbury. held land at Hendon* 1565.

Edward Kempe, of London,=*Agnes Page, Will* 1594.
Citizen & Mercer

Robert K. Charles K. Edmund K. Margaret K.

ram.=*Richard Kempe, of Gissing, mar. at Hampstead* 1566.
ead.

Bridget Adlin.=*Bartholomew Kempe, of London and Croydon, living* 1626.

Nicholas Kempe, (*said to have died unmarried*)

Kempe, of Gissing, bapt. at Hampstead 1567.
= *d. of Arthur Harris, died* 1612.

Bartholomew Kempe, bur. at Croydon 1662.

Francis K. living 1626.

William K. *Robert K.*

Kempe, Baronet,=*Jane, d. of Sir Matthew Browne, of Betchworth.*
g, Flordon, &c.
ed 1647.

1st wife. *Cicely Kester*,=*Sir Nicholas Kempe, Knight*,=*Sarah James*
mar. 1577. *S.P.*
of Finchley and Islington. Will 1624. *J.P. for Middlesex. Steward of Fulham.*
2nd wife. *widow of Thos. Draper*

nchley.
1681.

ITTERHOUSE,=Mary, d. of George Nicholl, of Hendon, married 1682.
Hendon in
ed 1712.

Elizabeth Kempe.=Wm. Atley, of Shepherd's Bush.

Alice Kempe.=John Sutton, of Dollis, Hendon.

Anne K.

1st wife. Sarah . . =DANIEL KEMPE, of=Ellenor (? Arrowsmith) 2nd wife.
CLITTERHOUSE, Will proved 1749.

Susannah K.=Wm. Snoxall.

Joseph Kempe, bur. at Hendon 1693.

pe, of ower died nd St. p. 1797.

Daniel Kempe, d. an infant. 1719.

Sarah Kempe, =J. Pippin, mar. 1742.

Mary Kempe, =T. Dowdeswell, mar. 1745.

(both by licence at St. Paul's Cath.)

John Kempe, d. an infant.

Daniel Kempe, of=Dinah. Parson's Street, Hendon, d. 1763.

Edward Clarke.=Dinah Kempe. (only child)
mar. 1774/5.

3.

JOHN KEMPE, of CLITTERHOUSE and=Louisa, dau. of John Bishop, of=Dr. George Goodwin, of Queen Street, Westminster.
of Dover Street, Piccadilly, M.D., born 1740, bur. at Hendon. Will 1795.
Piccadilly & Hendon, by Mary Penny, of Wells, died 1838.

Susannah Kemp 1st husb. =Thomas Pitt. 2nd husb. =John Lodge.

Kemp, at 6.

Elizabeth Augusta Kemp, bap. 1775, of Hendon and Westminster, died .

Elenor Augusta Kemp, born 1780, of Hendon, died unmarried 1838.

The Rev. Samuel Charles Godwin, of Enhurst, Sussex, and of Charing Cross, died in Paris 1835.

sumed name n vault of

Frederick Brookes, born 1802, died 1824, bur. at Wells Cathedral.

Daniel Bowden Brookes, born 1807, died 1808.

hin, of The=Norah Goddard.
orn 1840.
4 *daughters.*

Charlotte H. 1842-73.

Louisa Clymer.=Thomas Hitchin, of=Eliza Golding.
London, born 1845.
widow of Alison.
1 *daughter.*

Louisa H. living at Margate.

a H.-K. ttie.")

Alice H.-K.

William Hitchin-Kemp, of Twickenham, born 1875.

Arthur Hitchin-Kemp, born 1877.

Nellie H.-K.

Hilda H.-K.

John Tabor, of Bocking, by whom he had three sons. She died 8th November, 1895, aged seventy-four. He is a Liveryman of the Fishmongers' Company, having been admitted in 1847. He is also a J.P. for the Borough of Romsey where he resided from 1886-96. His business life was chiefly spent in Lancashire in the silk business of his uncle.

His sons, who were all born at Middleton, are John Tabor Kemp, M.A., Camb.; (B.A. Emman. Coll., 1884), born 5th October, 1860; Herbert Clement Tabor Kemp, now resident at Tarkastad, South Africa, proprietor of the *Tarka Herald*, born 26th September, 1862; and Cecil Tabor Kemp, pharmaceutical chemist in business at Hereford, born 16th April, 1868. Mr. H. C. T. Kemp married Edith Emily, daughter of Henry Hunt Wells of Rockwood, Coernay, Cape Colony, on 20th October, 1896.

Mr. Owen Kemp, younger surviving son of John Abbot Kemp, resides at Walthamstow; he passed many years of his life in Australia, where he married Miss Catherine Caroline Cater. George Tabor Kemp likewise emigrated to Australia, where he married late in life.

The arms of the Kemps of Prittlewell are said to be the same as those of the Kemps of Spain's Hall and Pentlow, the authority being, so far as we can ascertain, the semi-official acknowledgment of the claim of Alderman William Hunter, to impale such arms, in right of his wife (who, as stated above, was daughter of John Durival Kemp, of Prittlewell), contained in Burke's "Illustrations of Heraldry."

KEMPS OF MIDDLESEX.

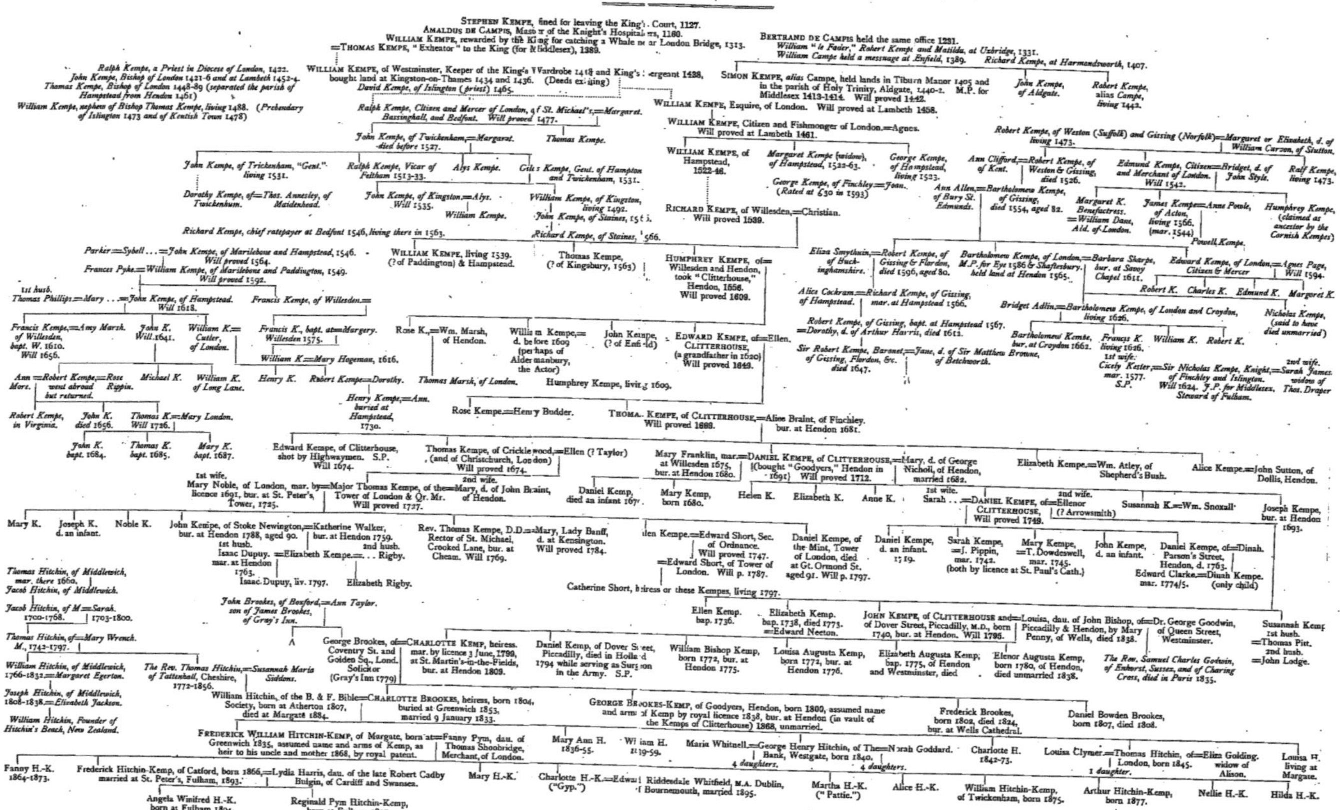

SECTION III. PART II.

CHAPTER I.

EARLY KEMPES AND CAMPES OF MIDDLESEX.

INCLUDING as it does the great metropolis, little doubt will be entertained that at one time or another every Kempe family in England must have been represented there. We cannot, of course, in this section deal with every individual Kemp, Kempe or Campe who has made London his home, or conducted his profession or trade there ; nor would this be necessary, for in many cases due mention of such residence has appeared in the section of this work in which his family are considered. Like other Counties, Middlesex was evidently the home of many individuals of the name (and its variants) from a very early period, and it is difficult to say whether the Stephen Kempe who was fined for leaving the Court of King Stephen in 1127 was then in London or at Winchester or other Royal City. As Prior of the Knights of Hospitalers, Amaldus de Campis and his successor Bertrand de Campis probably resided at St. John's, by Smithfield, close to which was the Hospital and Church of St. Bartholomew, of which one Rogerus de Kempele was Prior in 1359 ; both the Knights Hospitalers and Bartholomew Hospital had property in and around Paddington and both had interests at Hendon and Tiburn. (Concerning the exact *locale* of which there has recently been much debate in *Notes and Queries*.) The latter, being partially within the present district of Paddington, was held by the Knights of St. John of Jerusalem, whose badge, the Lamb and Flag, surmount still the church at Hendon, which in early times was attached to them. A portion of Tiburn was, as we remarked in the Norfolk section, leased at about 1490 to the Blaverhauset family who thenceforward had a residence at Hampstead within the ancient parish of Hendon, and intermarrying with the Kempes of Norfolk seem to account for some of that family being connected with this immediate district. Before, however, the Blaverhausetts obtained possession of these Middlesex lands, we know that a Thomas Kempe of the Kentish family was appointed an Escheator to the King for the County of Middlesex ; this was about 1389, at which time a William Campe held a messuage at Enfield, his inquisition being made in the 12th year of Richard II. In 1405 SIMON CAMPE held land then worth £10 in the manor of Tyburn, as is proved by the Middlesex Subsidy Roll of 6th Henry IV. SIMON CAMPE, who was presumably this same individual, was Member of Parliament for Middlesex in 1413 and the following year, and it is likely that he was also the same who possessed land in the adjoining County of Buckinghamshire in 1429, where his name appears as Simon *Kempe*. In 1440 we find the first Simon Kempe as a landholder in Kent, and in 1442 the will of Simon *Kempe alias Campe*, of Tiburn, Middlesex, was proved in the Prerogative Court of London. Stow, in his "Survey of London," before the Great Fire, says that ancient tombs of Simon and John Kempe were then existing in the Church of *Holy Trinity*, otherwise called Christchurch, *by Aldgate*, while the probate calendar describes Simon

Campe as of Holy Trinity *Priory*. There was another Priory of that name at Kilburn, close to Hampstead, Tiburn and Willesden, where from about this date the Kempes of Middlesex certainly established themselves.

Simon Campe's will is dated 25th August, 1442, and styles him "Esquire," a parishioner of St. Catherine's, near the Tower of London, and of *Holy Trinity, within Aldgate.* He desires to be buried at the "High Cross" at Aldgate, and bequeaths sums to Holy Trinity Priory, the Church of St. Catherine, the several houses of the Friars of London and to the house of the Carthusians, as well as the Hospital of Bedlam. He directs that his Chaplain shall be provided with "means according to the exigency of his need," with instructions to the said Chaplain, "Master William," to pray for the repose of the souls of the testator and his wife Margaret. John Burgh, the elder, John Burgh, the younger, and William Reynold were appointed the executors to see these charities and trusts duly carried out. To his brother Robert he left a sum of money, and to his brother John funds to enable him to pass through College. The lands mentioned by the testator were situated at "Tiburn, Lilleston, Westburn, Charing, Gye and elsewhere in Middlesex." These were left in trust for the benefit of his wife. No children are mentioned, but it is possible that the lands were entailed, in which case it would not be necessary to bequeath them to his son and heir.

Long, however, before this we trace Campes or Kempes to the district immediately around Willesden. In the Feet of Fines for Middlesex (printed by Hardy & Page) we have distinct evidence of individuals of these names holding land in the county, and although these records give but scattered information it wonld be reasonable to suppose that, from the earliest mention, 1331, the Kempes were men of some property around Uxbridge, which place stands on the border of this county and Buckinghamshire. Within the latter county some of the earliest known Kempes of Hendon certainly held property which may have been handed down to them. The Fine of 1331 records that William le Fader, Robert Kempe and Matilda, his wife, were concerned with a messuage in "Woxebridge," while in 1520 a Walter Champyon (another recognized variant of the name of Kempe), who was a Citizen and Draper of London, held premises at "Woxebridge" and "Hillyndon," now called Uxbridge and Hillingdon.

A few miles south of these places is Harmondsworth, whereat RICHARD KEMPE was a landholder in 1407, and is mentioned as such in a Fine made that year with Alan Wombe, clerk, William Ashe, Stephen Young and Matilda, the latter's wife. Within the Diocese of London there was a clerk named RALPH KEMPE, between 1422 and 1429, who seems to have gone to Harlow, Essex, as Vicar of that place; about this time, as we have noted in the Kentish section, a Ralph Kempe witnessed a deed of his relative Peter Kempe, of Brabourne, and it is very likely that, as this Ralph is not traced in Kent, he is identical with this clergyman. And it is further likely that from him the name of Ralph was handed down to several generations of Middlesex Kempes. On the other hand we know of a later Ralph Kempe, of Gissing, who also disappeared from his native place and may have come through the influence of the Blaverhausets to Middlesex as subsequent events seem to indicate. Before his time, however, we know of two WILLIAM KEMPES of considerable standing in the county, the first was an Esquire whose estate was administered, on his decease, by a John Cowper, of London (a point maker), by virtue of a commission, issued 13th July, 1458, under the seal of the Archbishop, as recorded at Lambeth Palace. The second WILLIAM KEMPE was a Citizen and Fishmonger of London, and his estate was granted on 3rd October, 1461, to Agnes Kempe, his widow, John Payne and William Harding. (Lambeth Wills and Administrations.) The fact of the grants of administration being obtained at Lambeth may indicate that the lands which these early Kempes of Middlesex held were part of the Episcopal estate of the Archbishop of Canterbury, and as JOHN KEMPE was the Archbishop and resident at Lambeth until within a few years of these grants it is extremely likely that he had admitted his own near kinsmen to the lands which he held in virtue of his position. He has been so constantly charged with nepotism that there can be little doubt that this was the actual case, and we suggest that it is probable one of these William Kempes was the father of the next Ralph Kempe known to Middlesex, and consequently founder of the Kempes of Marylebone and the earliest settlement of Kempes at Hampstead and Willesden.

In the 4th year of Edward IV. (1465) David Kemp was concerned with lands at Islington with Thomas Clifford and William Underhill. From this time the name of David was closely associated with clerical Kempes around Middlesex and away in Cornwall, the latter being possibly attributable to quite a different origin—the St. David of Wales and Cornwall.

In the extreme east borders of Middlesex undoubtedly the Essex Kempes held property from very early times, and before the middle of the sixteenth century they had tenements or interests in land at Hackney, and a little later at Tottenham, but of this see under the Kempes of Essex.

Turning to the earliest Calendars of the Commissary Court of London we find that the will of RADULPH CAMPE was proved in 1445; possibly this is a testament of that Ralph Kempe who we mentioned above as a cleric, which seems the more likely in that only three years before the wills of SIMON and MARGARET CAMP were recorded in the same Court (as well as being proved in the Prerogative Court of Canterbury), as of Tiburn, Holy Trinity Priory, and other lands in Middlesex. Simon was a name frequently occurring before 1440 among Kentish Kempes, after which it disappeared in that county and continued in Middlesex, thus giving some further evidence in favour of the Kempes of the latter being akin to the former.

Turning again to Commissary wills we find, in addition to the above Campes, the following Kempes in the Calendar, but unfortunately many of the original wills and the registers containing copies of them are now missing: Thomas Kempe, 1426; John Kempe, 1430; Stephen Kempe (see Kent), 1431; Richard Kempe, 1436; John Kempe, 1439; Richard Kempe, 1441; Robert Kempe, 1445; Thomas Kempe, 1464; Richard Kempe, 1462; Thomas Kempe (*circa*), 1466; Margaret Kempe, 1510, and Alice Kempe about the same time. In the Prerogative Court of Canterbury the first Kempe of Middlesex without the alias of Campe is one Ralph Kempe, whose will was proved in 1477, he being a merchant of St. Michael's, Bassinghall, London, and of Bedfont, in Middlesex; before however going into details of his family we may give a list of the earliest Kempes whose wills appear in the Calendars of the *Consistory* Court of London, which are as follows:—John Kempe, of Westminster, 1540-8; Thomas Kempe, between 1549 and 1559, and Ralph Kempe, between 1539 and 1559. The number of Campe and Kempe wills in the various Probate Courts under which the Middlesex lands were administered are sufficient to show that from very early times the name represented considerable people in the county, more particularly from the period at which John Kempe, Archbishop of Canterbury, and his nephew, Thomas, Bishop of London, held lands there. The latter, we know, instituted his relative William Kempe to the Prebends of Hoxton and Kentish Town (having their corps in this county), and presented him to the Rectory of Stepney so late as 1476. The Bishop was still living at the death of Ralph Kempe of London and Bedfont, and but for subsequent connexion of the Norfolk Kempes with the parish of St. Michael, Bassinghall, we should not doubt of this Ralph being distinctly near kin to the Bishop. Then, too, we have to notice that the later Kempes of this parish came through the influence of Sir James Yarford and the Greshams, and may have been but remotely, or totally, unconnected with this Ralph Kempe who was certainly buried there in 1477. The pedigrees of the families of Norfolk and Kentish Kempes, as duly noticed in their respective sections, still are unconnected so far as actual evidence can be found, but it seems possible that the connexion was far closer in the time of Archbishop Kempe than the pedigrees would lead one to suppose, for there was evidently friendly communication between the branches; and the fact of Archbishop Kempe benefitting places in Norfolk may indicate that in the Norfolk Kempes he acknowledged the senior branch of his family: be this as it may, we will treat of the two Kempe lines who resided in St. Michael's parish in the same chapter, as from each doubtless some modern Kempes of Middlesex descended.

CHAPTER II.

KEMPES OF ST. MICHAEL'S, BASSINGHALL, &c,

WE now come to the consideration of the earliest pedigree which we have been able to form from the available records of Middlesex.

RALPH KEMPE, of the Parish of St. Michael's, Bassinghall, in the City of London, was a merchant in the woollen trade, then, undoubtedly, the most profitable of English industries. From his will, which alludes to *garments of his own weaving*, it is evident that he manufactured the cloth as well as dealing with the raw material. From Kent, doubtless, he derived much of his wool, for then, as now, the county was particularly suitable for sheep farming, while the author of the "Scots of Scott's Hall" states his belief that a certain early Kempe, of Wye, described as a "scissor," was a merchant tailor akin to that celebrated Flemish weaver, John Kempe, who established the woollen cloth trade in England about 1331. We do not agree with this opinion as dates and records show that Kempes (or de Campis) were settled at Wye before the time of the weaver, nor do we think it likely that the name of the Kempes' seat at Wye, "Ollantigh," is derived from "Olla," meaning wool, and "tigh" a house, but it is at least interesting to notice how much the Kempes had to do with the woollen and weaving trade from the time of the Flemish settlement down to the last, and, indeed, the present century

Ralph Kempe probably inherited his lands at Bedfont from one of the Kempes or Campes whose wills we have mentioned in the foregoing chapter, and it is evident from his own will that he held lands also at Twykenham, Feltham, and Houndslow as well as his residence and place of business in Bassinghall Street.*

Ralph Kempe mentions in his will, dated 22nd October, 1477, Dame Katherine Burton, whose family had, about 1460, largely rebuilt the Church of St. Michael's, John Burton, a citizen and mercer of London, being then buried in the place of honour in the choir and his trade mark being carved on all the bosses of the roof in acknowledgment of his liberality. As usual at this period the testator (Ralph) left a considerable amount to religious institutions, hoping that the

* It may not be unworthy of notice here that nearly opposite the present Wool Exchange, in the next street (Coleman Street), was until the Fire of London an old wool shop known as "The Woolpack," on the site of which, subsequent to the fire, a new house was erected; this passed to the Kempes of Hendon, and the deed specifying that this property was on the site of the old "Woolpack" is still in possession of the head of the family (F. W. Hitchin-Kemp). This old building, although close to Bassinghall, stood within the parish of St. Stephen's, Coleman Street, of which the parishioners, as ordained by Bishop Thomas Kempe, elect their own Vicar.

various fraternities would "pray for the health of his soul." Among others he mentions as recipients of his charities Charterhouse, Austin Friars, Holy Trinity at Houndslow, and the Churches of Bedfont, Feltham, Twickenham and St. Michael's, directing that he should be buried in the Lady Chapel at the last named church. To his wife, according to the ancient custom of London, he left a third of his estate, and the remainder to his sons, John and Thomas Kempe, after legacies had been paid to his sister Ann, John and Florence Poynes, John Pothe or Potle, his cousin, Henry Bompstead, William Buxton, his cousin, Elizabeth Kempe, John Botiller and the Worshipful Sir Richard Pygot, Sergeant of Littleshull.

The lands at Twickenham and Bedfont remained with his issue for some generations, as we shall see, and it is worthy of note that within a couple of miles from Twickenham, at Kingston-on-Thames, a William Kempe, of Westminster, held lands so early as 1436, the original deed showing that he obtained it from a John atte Forde, being still preserved in the Record Office. "Atte Forde," at such a date would be likely to represent one named John *living at the ford of the Brent*," otherwise Brentford, which is a couple of miles north of Twickenham. Thus possibly William Kempe, of Westminster and Kingstone, was the William Kempe, Esquire, whose estate was administered in 1458, and he may have been father or kinsman of this Ralph Kempe, of London and Twickenham. Between the latter and Kingston lies Teddington, and there at a very early date it is claimed the ancestors of numerous Kempes long resident in the parish were settled ; if this is correct the ancestors must have been but humble folk, for we do not trace the name in the Subsidy Rolls, nor among the wills. From this stock the Kempes, who long held an inn on the river, descended, one of the family being now a well known optician in London. The tombs at Teddington bear witness to numerous Kemps who have been buried there in the last two centuries, and a long article saying that they were descendants of Danish "Kimpes" appeared in a local newspaper a few years ago.

In 1510, Margaret Kempe, of Isleworth (between Twickenham and Brentford), left or gave some cottages in that parish to the poor widows of the adjoining parish of Heston. Lysons says 1610, but this is clearly a mistake as seen from his remarks. These almshouses were doubtless founded under the will of Margaret Kempe, of Middlesex, which we have stated in the former chapter, was proved in or about 1510. Three years later we find that a Ralph Kempe was appointed to the Vicarage of Feltham, and surmise that this presentation was then in the hands of the Kempes, for this vicar was a grandson of Ralph Kempe, of St. Michael's. (Perhaps it was he who was, in 1539, presented to the living of Oakely Parva, Essex, and died there 4th March, 1540.)

In 1531 Ralph Kempe, clerk, John Kempe, gentleman, and Giles Kempe, gentleman, paid a fine concerning two messuages called "Richmonds" and "Hedgelands" and land in Twickenham, which further identifies this Vicar of Feltham with the others, while the same year another fine is recorded, the parties to the deed being John Kempe and Margaret, his wife, with Hugh Ellis, Henry Norres, Esq., Robert Norwych, Sergeant-at-Law, John Holden, clerk, Richard Heryng, clerk, and John Mores, concerning premises at Bedfont. Among the original deeds at the Record Office there is a grant by Ralph Kempe, Vicar of Feltham, *son and heir of John Kempe*, formerly of Twickenham, Esquire, to William Tyler, Knight, William *Cowper*, gentleman, John Holden, clerk, Thomas Stanard, Vicar of Twickenham, and John Crofton, Yeoman, "of a close in Twickenham called 'Andrew's merche.'" This is dated 10th January, 18 Henry VIII., *i.e.*, 1527. It will be remembered that one, John *Cowper*, of London, was administrator to William Kempe, Esquire, in 1458, thus again pointing to the kinship of this Twickenham Kempe family with him. A still later occurrence of the two names together is found in the Close Rolls of 15

Elizabeth (1573), John and William "Coper" being then concerned in transactions with a Thomas Kemp. Between Bedfont and Kingstone lies Hampton, it was there that Giles Kempe mentioned above resided in 1524, as shown by the existing Subsidy Roll, he, doubtless, deriving the property from the Twickenham Kempes. We find that a John Kempe left by will to his *father*, Giles Kempe, in 1537, a sum of money, to his Aunt Alice another sum, while his estate at Kingston-on-Thames was to be enjoyed by his wife of the same name. This will describes the testator as a taylor, and was proved in the Archdeaconry Court of Surrey. The aunt mentioned died the same year, her will being recorded in the same register and it describes her as also of Kingston-on-Thames; she, too, mentions Giles Kempe and friends named Frankys, Symonds, Warner, Sherwood, Hall, Buchard and Fox.

In the Subsidy Rolls of Middlesex, 1524 (which are the earliest that give the names of the ratepayers), we find that at that date the Kempes were well scattered about the county, and that they held some position as regards respective wealth. In addition to Giles living at Hampton there was a Richard "Campe" there who seems likely to be the Richard Kempe who died at Willesden in 1539 (of whom we shall speak in our next chapter), while at Hampstead at that date William Kempe heads the list, being rated at £15; and George Kempe and Margaret Kempe, widow, are each rated at £10 as residents of that hamlet. Parts of this Subsidy Roll are missing, but in 1549 there is further evidence confirming these settlements of Kempes and showing that John Kempe, rated at £20, was living in or near Kensington, William Kempe, rated at £11, was at Paddington, Richard Kempe, rated at £15, was at *Willesden* (second only to Sir Richard Read of that Parish), George Kempe was still rated at £10 at Hampstead, and James, living at Kentish town, was then assessed at £10 also.

Of the latter we get a glimpse from the will of Mychell Kempe, dated at Kentish Town in 1542 as a parishioner of St. Pancras. (Wherein the lands attached to the Prebend of the name lie and which had been enjoyed until about 1523 by William Kempe, the kinsman of Archbishop and Bishop Kempe.) The will is recorded in the Court of the Dean and Chapter of St. Paul's, and subject to a provision for the testator's wife Agnes and small legacies, leaves all the estate to James Kempe, *his brother*.

In 1564 Peter Kempe, gent., with Anthony Browne, Esquire; Sir Walter Mildmay, Knight; Sir Anthony Cooke, Knight, and Robert Wyngfeld were concerned with Sir William Cecil, Knight, in manors, lands, &c., in Lincoln, Northampton, Rutland, Hertford, and in the parishes of St. Clement Danes, St. Martin's, St. Margaret's, Westminster, Kentish Town and Enfield, in Middlesex. All these except Peter Kempe and Cecil appear as connected with the Kentish Kempes, and we think that this Peter Kempe must be the same as one of his name who was Steward to the first Lord Burleigh, but as to whose family connexions we are quite in the dark. No Peter occurs in the pedigrees of Kentish Kempes, but the name was in use soon after this date by the Slindon branch of that family, while it was also used by the Norfolk Kempes at a still later period.

We must refer once again in this chaper to a later Subsidy Roll, that of 1563, in which we again find that the Kempes retained their positions at Marylebone, Hampstead and Willesden with Hendon, while James Kempe appears at Acton and a Peter and William Kempe at St. Katherine's, near the Tower, and that at Bedfont Richard Kempe is a landholder. Presumably it was this last named Richard who with John Kempe, Gent., was fined with a Thomas Dove for premises in which they were jointly interested at Staines, which is near Bedfont. Richard was buried at St. Michael's Bassinghall, as appears from the register in 1576, while probably John was the same as he who died at Hampstead in 1574 (*vide* Chapter III.)

Here we leave for the present this earliest Middlesex Kempe family to notice EDMUND KEMPE, a citizen and merchant of London who flourished before 1542. This Edmund was undoubtedly son of Robert Kempe, of Gissing, and formerly of Weston, Suffolk, his mother being Elizabeth, daughter of William Curzon, of Sturton, in Suffolk. In his pedigree in the Harleian MSS. (1154) he is stated to be "heire elect" to Robert, of Gissing, and in his will (1542) he mentions many of his relations from Norfolk. There can therefore be not the least doubt as to his parentage, yet by a blunder of several genealogists he is repeatedly shown as eldest son of one of the Kempes of Ollantigh, Kent, and the wish being evidently father to the thought, he has been claimed as founder of the Kempe family of Cornwall. Without a knowledge of exact dates there might be some apparent ground for such a claim, as this Edmund had a son as mentioned in his will named HUMPHREY KEMPE, and that name was one of the early favourites among the Cornish family, but as will be seen in the notice of Kempes of Cornwall, the family was already established in that country when Edmund *was an infant*. Even admitting the claim that this Edmund was their progenitor their claim of direct descent from the Kentish Kempes must fail through this medium at least. Edmund Kempe was a prominent member of the Mercers' Company of London, who appointed him, in succession to Richard Gresham, Surveyor Accountant of St. Paul's School, which office he held from 1536 to 1537. In 1538 as a Mercer, rated at £40, he had to provide four suits of arms and armour for the protection of the City of London. He obtained lands at Acton and leave to erect a chapel there, in which perhaps he had intended to be buried, but finding that St. Michael's, Bassinghall, would afford him a more prominent burial place he was, at his request, buried beside Sir James Yardford, formerly Lord Mayor of London, connected with Emund Kempe through the latter marrying Bridget, daughter of Elizabeth Style, who married as her second husband the said Sir James Yardford or Yerford. In the register of St. Michael's it is recorded that Edmund Kempe was buried there on 2nd July, 1542, and that his wife, Bridget, was buried there on 7th April, 1540.

Edmund Kempe's will was proved in the Prerogative Court of Canterbury in 1542 (8 Spert), and is interesting as clearly stating many relationships and mentioning numerous influential London commercial friends, such for instance as his kinsmen Sir Richard Gresham, Knight, Sir John Gresham, Knight, and William Gresham, and his mother-in-law, Lady Yarford. We cannot give all the names and bequests, but it is sufficient to mention that he speaks of his relatives Nicholas Rokewood, Cisily Melton and Humphry Style to identify him with the Norfolk and *not* the Kentish line. To his chapel at Acton he bequeaths a vestment that lyeth there, and "a table with six leves of the Passion of Chryste that standeth on the Aulter there." To his son, James Kempe (see above) he leaves his house and lands at Acton, and the rest of his leases in Middlesex he bequeaths to Humphrey Kempe, his younger son, with an annuity of £10.

It is noticed above that at this time (1542) a JAMES KEMPE was living at Kentish Town with a brother named Mychell, possibly the latter had been so named from being born in the parish of St. Michael's; be this as it may the name was not (to our knowledge) handed down, and we find that James appears at Acton in the Subsidy Roll of 1563. In 1566 James Kempe, Gent., Anne, his wife, and their brother-in-law and sister, William and Margaret Dane, paid a fine for lands and premises in Acton, East Acton and Church Acton. This wife of James Kempe is shown on the pedigree above quoted as Anne, daughter of . . . Powell or Powle, "brother to him that was one of the six Clerks of Chancery," and we find from the marriage licenses that the marriage took place on 12th June 1544, two years after Edmund Kempe's death, the bride-groom being stated to be a "Gentleman of London." In 1556 James Kempe, Gentleman, John Garraway and Christopher Leyland were presented at the Court of the Countess of Bedford for keeping to pasture 100 acres of land in Acton, which land, according to agreement, should have been sown four times within the last . . . years.

No will of this James Kempe has been found, and the latest trace of him appears to be in 1566 when perhaps he parted with his Middlesex property to seek his fortune elsewhere. We have searched the early registers of Acton and St. Michaels, Bassinghall, but do not find that James was buried at either of these places. At the latter church his grandmother, the Lady Yarford was buried beside her second husband in 1548, and many of her family (the Styles) were with the Greshams buried there also. Her son, Sir Humphrey Style, Knight, of Beckenham, Kent, made his will in 1552, and mentions therein the children of his late "brother Kempe," leaving black gowns and memorial rings to James Kempe and his wife, "*Humphrey Kempe and his his wife*," Robert Rokewood and Bridget, his wife, and Ellis Wymarsh, all of whom belonged to the Norfolk Kempe family. This will affords us the only intimation that Humphrey Kempe was married, which event doubtless took place after that of James, and as no will of a Humphrey Kempe, of Middlesex, save that of Humphrey Kempe, of Hendon, has been traced one might be justified in believing that this younger son of Edmund Kempe, who inherited "other leases in Middlesex and an annuity of £10," was the founder of the Kempes of the parish of Hendon ; but with the pros and cons of this we will deal in our next chapter.

James and Humphrey Kempe had a sister named Margaret Kempe, who married Alderman William Dane, sometime Mayor of London. This Margaret Kempe was a lady of the Court of Elizabeth, and bequeathed to that Queen £200 for a necklace. Having no surviving issue and outliving her husband, she distributed her wealth to various City Companies. By her will, proved in 1579 (42 Bakon), she left £2,000 to the Ironmongers' Company, of which her late husband was a member. This handsome bequest was the cause of a portrait of this benefactress being erected in that Company's hall, which remains to this day. The portrait is not considered a good painting and is now the worse for age ; it represents Margaret kneeling at an oratory with a book of prayers in her hands, she is dressed in a scarlet robe, a black hood and ruff and many jewels. Out of the sum left to the Ironmongers £10 per annum was appointed for the Universities of Oxford and Cambridge, and several hospitals and prisons were benefitted, but the most singular of the bequests was the annual distribution of 1,200 faggots between the poor of the twenty-four wards of the City of London. Margaret Kempe was married to William Dane at St. Michael's, Bassinghall, on 22nd May, 1540, and desired to be buried at St. Mary Moyses in Friday Street, London, beside her husband. Her sister, Bridgett Kempe, married Robert Rokewood, of Stanningfield, Essex, and her other sister, Florence, was married to Robert Reice (Ap. Reis or Rice), who was of Preston, Suffolk. The last made his will in 1590.

According to the pedigree in the Harleian Collection above quoted James Kempe, the elder son of Edmund, had a son, Powle Kempe, who was "slayne in fight upon the bridge over the River Scaulde in the siege of Antwerpe" in 1585, without having left issue. This Pawle had two sisters, Dorothy, married to John Master, Parson, of Blechinglee, Surrey, and Elizabeth, who married John Shute (Sute or Chute), a captain in the Army, who was born at Willington in Somerset. The pedigree would have us believe that this was the only issue, but the registers of Acton show that James Kempe had a son baptized John there on 20th October, 1553, that Pawle Kempe was baptized there on 11th December, 1554, and that a second John Kempe ("son of James Kempe"), was baptized on 20th October, 1555. The registers further tell that a *Humphrey Kempe*, son of *John* Kempe, was baptized there on 28th July, 1548, but it seems probable that John in this case is a slip for James, while it is likely that the daughter, born between 1548 and 1553, was baptized in London. Neither of the John Kempes are traceable among the wills, nor can this Humphrey actually be shown to have reached manhood ; but the registers further record that in 1608 Margaret and Agnes Kempe were baptized at Acton, and that Henry Kempe (perhaps their father) was buried there on 17th May, 1616, and Anne Kempe was buried there in 1605, after which no Kempe occurs in the registers.

It is possible that these Kempes of Acton had representatives later at Hampstead and Willesden, which were but six miles or so distant, but the evidence to hand, after considerable research, seems to point to these latter being from the first Kempes of St. Michael's and of Bedfont.

It only remains to note in this chapter that in addition to the items above the following are recorded in the Registers of St. Michael, Bassinghall: 3rd November, 1541, Henry Kempe, the son of Stephen Kempe, baptized ; Elizabeth Kempe, baptized 23rd October, 1540 ; Margaret Kymp, widowe, buried 18th December, 1573 ; Rychard Kempe, son of Stephen Kempe, buried 1576 ; Matthew Kempe, son of Stephen Kempe, buried 1576, and Richard Kampey, buried 14th February, 1581.

CHAPTER III.

KEMPES OF PADDINGTON, WILLESDEN AND HENDON.

FROM the foregoing chapters it will be seen that CAMPES, otherwise KEMPES, held land belonging to Tyburn Manors as early as 1442, from which time probably the Kempes continued to reside on a portion of that manor lying in the hamlet of Marylebone, within the parish of Paddington. Jane Blavershauseth, widow, whose son married Margaret Kempe, of the Suffolk Kempe family, obtained a lease of lands at Tyburn before 1500, but if this led to Richard Kempe, of Gissing, making his home near by while studying the law, it may still not indicate that the Kempes of Marylebone, afterwards of Hampstead and Willesden, were his near kin.

It seems more likely that these were closely related to the earlier settlement of Kempes, first at Uxbridge and afterwards at Bedfont and Twickenham, mentioned in detail in the last chapter, although it is singular that the Styles who intermarried with Edmund Kempe, of the Suffolk family, also were of Uxbridge and Hampstead.

At Hampstead three Kempes were the chief landholders in 1524 (the earliest date at which the Subsidy Rolls of Middlesex record the ratepayers' names). In this Roll Marylebone does not appear and consequently we are unable to say whether Kempes were there then ; if not they were certainly at that place and Paddington in 1546 and 1563. We thus can trace William Kempe at Hampstead as the chief resident in 1523, and assume that George Kempe, the second largest taxpayer, was his younger brother or son, while Margaret Kempe, widow, was probably the mother of William Kempe, and may reasonably be the daughter-in-law of Ralph Kempe, of Bedfont and London. Margaret, the wife of his eldest son John, was living in 1531, but it is likely that he had another son of his own name who predeceased him.

In 1538 RICHARD KEMPE, of Wil(le)sden, made his will which was proved the following year in the Court of St. Paul's. The testator provides for the usual Masses for his soul and directs that he should be buried at Wil(le)sden. He provides an income for his wife Christian Kempe, and leaves his chief lands and leases to his eldest son William, who is rated as of Hendon in 1546 at £19. To his second son, Thomas Kempe, he leaves certain lands or equivalent value, as also to his *third* son HUMPHREY KEMPE. To his daughter Agnes Kempe he bequeaths such raiment as shall be necessary for her marriage; the residue of his estate he leaves to his wife Christian and appoints as executors of his will his wife and William Kempe, his eldest son, and as overseer, Robert Pumbe. The testator's curate, Thomas Hardy, and William Newland with others, were witnesses.

Of William, the eldest son, we have no will, but it was doubtless he who was rated at £19, and he is shown to have been living at Hendon in the Subsidy Roll of 1546. Widow Margaret Kempe. probably his relict, was living at Hendon in 1563, being then rated at £20, and it is likely that it was she who made her will in 1597, being then a grandmother. This will was not proved until 1607 (Commis. of London XX., 11) and shows that the testatrix had property at Newport Pagnell, Bucks, as well as at Hendon. The former proverty she leaves to her "son" (? son-in-law) William Franklin and his son, whose family long were people of importance in and around Willesden; their pedigrees and arms being duly recorded in the Heraldic Visitation. One William Franklyn lived to be 107 years of age and was buried at Willesden in 1628, this may reasonably have been the father of widow Kempe's son-in-law, and as will be seen by subsequent wills the Franklins and Kempes were long intimately associated. It may further be noted that the Franklyns of Norfolk had Middlesex property and may have been of the same stock as these of Middlesex and Buckinghamshire. As to the source of this Newport property held by Margaret Kempe we can only surmise that it may have been derived from the Annesleys of that town, for Henry Annesley married Dorothy, danghter of John Kempe of Twickenham, some time previous to 1570. Other landholders of Newport were the Mordaunts, one of whom married the last Kempe, Knight of Wye, and a Thomas Mansell, of Chicheley, who owned land at Newport as well as at Hulcote, Northampton, which may suggest that he was connected with the Kempes, of Northampton, of Norfolk origin.

Margaret Kempe mentions, in addition to the Franklyns, her son Robert Kempe and his daughters Elizabeth, Agnes and Dinah Kempe. This Robert does not appear in the local records, and we suggest that he was of Gilston, Herts. The testatrix further speaks of her servants Agnes Mery and Elizabeth White, also John Bethant and Thomas Hyngham, while *Edward Pecock* and Matthew Newman were witnesses.

(Edward Peacock was a landholder living at Finchley and was connected with the Kempes of Croydon (of Norfolk origin) through intermarriage with the Finches.)

Of THOMAS KEMPE, second son of Richard, of Willesden, we know little, but it is likely that he inherited property at Burnham (Bucks) and died 1544, for a will appears in the Prerogative Court of Canterbury in that year of a Thomas Kempe who bequeathed ground at Hedgley Hill, East Burnham Fields and "Sydnam" to Thomas God, and a carpet bearing *his coat of arms* to Thomas Kempe. with an annuity. The last-named Thomas died in 1560, and his will is also recorded (in the same Court) as of Burnham; he leaves to his wife, Margret Kemp, and Thomas, his eldest son, his lease of the Manor of "Sixeham." He speaks of his brother Anthony Smith and his son John, while *Humphrey Kempe* is a witness to the will. This Humphrey Kempe we presume to be the third son of Richard Kempe, of Willesden.

HUMPHREY KEMPE, we are informed by the Clerk of St. Bartholomew's Hospital, took a lease of the Manor of Clitterhouse (which lies within the parish of Hendon and adjoins the present district of Cricklewood) in 1556. Clitterhouse Manor was given to the above hospital by a Walter Green in 1441, and we think it likely that it was this same Walter Green who shared with Simon *Campe* the duty of representing Middlesex in Parliament in 1413. (See Chapter I.)

Humphrey Kempe in his will, proved in 1610 (Dean and Chapter of St. Paul's), distinctly states that he has purchased a lease of Clitterhouse wherein he then dwelt, and had settled the reversion of this property on his surviving son Edward Kempe. His other leases and a silver cup passed to Humphrey Kempe, eldest son of William Kempe deceased, who was the testator's eldest son. The testator also leaves legacies to his third son John and his daughter Rose, the wife of Thomas Marsh. He further mentions his maid Margaret "Bayle," William Huddle and Hugh Presswell, and makes John Hall, of London (notary), and William Franklin, of Hendon, his executors. We must not here follow each of the junior lines, nor the issue (if any) of Humphrey Kempe, the grandson, mentioned in the above will. Edward Kemp, the second but eldest surviving son, duly succeeded to Clitterhouse, for we find a singular mention of him in the Middlesex Session Rolls of the same year, it is as follows:

"7 February, 7 James I.

"True bill that at Hendon, in the night of the said day, George Newman alias Dorche, late of London, yeoman, Joan Elliott, late of London, yeoman, broke burglariously into the house of EDWARD KEMPE, and stole therefrom a woman's violet coloured gown worth forty shillings and many other articles of personal raiment, particularly mentioned and described in the bill of adictment, of the goods and chattels of the said Edward Kempe. George Newman alias Dorche, and Henry Courte were at large. Henry Elliott put himself not guilty, and was acquitted. Joan Elliott stood mute—Ideo h'et judicin pene fort et dure. (For that reason she was condemned to the punishment 'forte et dure.')" See "History of Hendon."

The punishment consisted of the culprit being laid naked on his back in a dark chamber, under as great a weight of iron as he could support, until he died from the pressure, his only sustenance being three morsels of the worst bread and draughts of putrid water on alternate days!

The Hendon Parish Registers are missing until 1656, it is thought they were taken away by the Vicar, Francis Wareham, who went to Little Hadham, Herts, about that date. Curiously a branch of the Norfolk Kempes had previously established themselves at that place and the author of the "History of Hendon" surmises that the Kempes of Hendon were descended from them, as (according to him) the two Kempe families bore the same arms. The author however states elsewhere that the Hendon Kempes used for their arms "Sable, three garbs or," while the arms of the Kempes of Little Hadham, in the Visitation of Middlesex, from which he presumably took their pedigree, clearly shows the others' arms as, Gules, three garbs or within a bordure engrailed on the last.

But to return to the missing registers,—we much regret their loss, for it is evident from the Subsidy Rolls that the Kempes were at Hendon from the institution of Parish Registers (1539), and as the Kempes do not appear in the registers of Hampstead until 1565, and in those of Willesden till 1572, the earlier baptisms, marriages and burials of the family were undoubtedly recorded at Hendon..

Margaret Kempe, widow above mentioned, expressed a desire in her will to be buried at Hendon, and Humphrey Kempe, of Clitterhouse, and his descendants also direct that they should be buried there, although in the wills down to 1649 they do not omit to mention the poor of Willesden and Hampstead as recipients of their charities; hence we may reason that from before 1556, when Humphrey took "Clitterhouse," the Kempes of this neighbourhood considered Hendon their chief residential parish. At the time Humphrey obtained his lease Sir William Herbert, Knight, ancestor of the Earls of Pembroke and Lords Powis, held the Manor of Hendon, it having been formerly the property of the Bishop of Westminster and granted to Sir William Herbert by

Edward VI. in 1550; this manor did not include that of Clitterhouse, but adjoined it, thus doubtless, although inferior in station, the Kempes of Clitterhouse must have been familiar with the Lords of the neighbouring manor. Lord Powis, son of the above Sir William Herbert, was buried at Hendon in 1655. When then we find that, in 1572, a Mr. John Kempe obtained a licence to marry "The Lady Herbert, commonly known as Grace Herbert," we must surmise that Grace Herbert was closely related to these Herberts of Hendon. However we have failed to identify either this Grace Herbert with any on the Herbert pedigree, and cannot certainly say which John Kempe it was who married her ladyship. It would be reasonable to think that if she had a daughter or grand-daughters her Christian name would be passed to them, hence we seek for Grace Kempes. We find that John Kempe, a noted preacher and "the Parson of Freshwater," in the Isle of Wight, speaks of his daughter Grace in his will dated 1587, and as he also mentions a son John, it is likely that Grace was his daughter-in-law and identical with Grace Herbert; when too we find that Caleb Kemp, of Totteridge, in his will of 1638, identifies himself as grandson of this Parson John Kempe, we may further reason that John Kempe's family, although holding property in Surrey, were akin to those of Hendon.

CALEB KEMPE speaks of his "mother, Mistress Phœbe Cooke," who was by birth a Lister, of Yorkshire, and was married first to the Rev. Caleb Kempe, son of Parson John Kempe and Rector of Bradford, in Yorkshire, and second to one named Cooke. Caleb, the younger, married Rose, daughter of John Rippin, of Totteridge, both these being alive in 1638, as well as Caleb's brother John Kempe and his "cousins" Moses and Mary Jenkins. As to these "cousins" it is at least singular that Edward Kempe, of Clitterhouse, speaks in his will (dated 1647) of Richard Jennings* and Parnell his wife, thus making it doubtful whether in this case Jenkins and Jennings represented the same family. Caleb Kempe's brother John probably succeeded his father as Vicar of Bradford, for one of his name held that living.

EDWARD KEMPE, of Clitterhouse, must have died in 1648 or 1649, his will having been dated in the former and proved in the latter year. It is recorded in the Prerogative Court of Canterbury (184 Fairfax) and provides an annuity for his wife Ellin and bequeaths to her the use of his furniture and household effects. To his son Thomas he leaves his lease of Clitterhouse and his other lands, and legacies to the four children of this son at their respective ages of sixteen. To his daughter Rose, the wife of Henry Budder, and to his sister Rose Marsh he leaves sums of money, and makes his "loving friend" William Franklyn, the elder, of *Brent Street*, Hendon, his overseer, and his son Thomas, executor.

This is the first mention of "Brent Street," the property in which soon passed to the Kempes and is still retained by the head of the family, but from the title deeds of this estate it is clear that "Goodyers," in Brent Street, with the fields (just converted to Hendon recreation grounds) were long before this occupied by one Margaret Kempe who married in 1624 a John East, at St. Mary, Aldermanbury—John East being the son of John East, of Goodyers, who was living there in the 43rd year of Elizabeth. Their posterity sold it to Daniel Kempe, of Clitterhouse, in 1691, from whom it has descended to the present generation.

We may here digress a moment to speak of a Kempe, of St. Mary, Aldermanbury, with whom Margaret Kempe was doubtless connected. This parish is in the heart of the City of London, and was in the reign of Elizabeth the parish most frequented by the Shakesperian actors, indeed it is in this parish churchyard that a monument has recently been erected to commemorate them; when

* It will be found in the Kentish section that an Ann Kempe had just prior to this married a *Jerins*, ot Norfolk, while some named JENNINGS were related to the Kempes of Antingham through the latter's intermarriage with Calthorps. The spelling, even at this date, being far from uniform we cannot determine how each of these were related to one another.

therefore we find (from the Feet of Fines) that a William Kempe held a house in this parish in 1584, we have reason to believe that the actor of that name was resident here until that year, he then selling his house and removing with his brother actors to Southwark, where we find, from the "Sacramental Token Book" of St. Saviour's, that he resided in 1600 and 1602, Peter Hemings and Robert Nashe appearing on the same list. Some of the name of Hemming were certainly related to Kempes at this time, for the estate of Joanna Kempe, of St. Peter, in Chepe, was granted to Rose Hemming by the Archdeaconry Court of London in 1564, Rose being her next of kin, probably her daughter. While those of the name of Hall were as certainly connected with Shakespeare himself, as well as the Kempes of Acton and Hendon; thus it seems likely that William Kempe, the comedian, actor, author and celebrated dancer, was of the family of Hendon Kempes, and we may thus recount in this section what is known or surmised of his work.

The Camden Society reprinted and published, in 1840, his book entitled, "Kemp's Nine Daies Wonder," and added to it very ample introduction and notes, while *Notes and Queries*, the *Gentleman's Magazine* and the "Biographical Dictionaries" have frequently added or questioned Malone's account of him. It is generally stated that he died between 1603 and 1607, aged about fifty-four. It is said that the cause of his death was a wound received from a rapier accidently inflicted while acting at the Globe Theatre, but others believe that he died abroad while on a theatrical tour. In support of the first theory an item in the Burial Register of St. Saviour's, Southwark, has been put forward as evidence; it reads:

"1603, November 2nd William Kempe, a man," (buried)

If this indeed was the celebrated actor, it is strange that his profession should not have been mentioned in place of merely "a man," but the date and the fact of his having been a communicant at St. Saviour's, favours the belief of this being the actor. And he may be that William to whom Humphrey Kempe, of Hendon, alludes in his will, dated 1609, as "my late son William Kempe." If this last conjecture is accepted it will be further evident that the actor had a son William living in 1609, as well as other children. Perhaps it was this William, the younger, who was married at St. Bartholomew's-the-Less to Annis *Howard* on 10th February, 1605-6. (One John Howard is mentioned in the will of Sir Nicholas Kempe, of Finchley and London, in 1624.) The actor attracted much attention in 1599 by dancing from London to Norwich, and to repudiate exaggerated accounts of this exploit he published, in 1600, his book "Kempe's Nine Daies Wonder." Many other Jigs and plays, as well as educational books, have been attributed to him, but in the "Nine Days Wonder" he declares that this is his *first* publication, hence it is very doubtful if many books bearing his name were actually his production. It is however likely that he had some hand in the writing of several plays popular at the Court of Elizabeth, at which he was a welcome guest. From the fact that many Norfolk Kempes were at the Court of this Queen and that he selected Norwich (near which the head of the family was seated) as the goal of this Morris Dance, it has been reasonably stated that the actor was some connexion of the Kempes of Norfolk; certainly the welcome accorded to him by the officials of Norwich on that occasion was due chiefly to his name as Shakespeare's comedian, but it is likely also that he was known as a member of the local family of Kempes.

He dedicated his "Nine Daies Wonder" to "Mistris Anne Fitton, Mayde of Honour to . . . Queen Elizabeth," who was undoubtedly acquainted with Margaret Dane, a Lady of Queen Bess's train and a grand-daughter of Robert Kempe, of Gissing; thus, if not related to those of Gissing, he was at least known to some of them. Roger Weld was the Mayor of Norwich when the Civic

Officials went out in State from that City to meet "Will. Kempe," the actor, being presented with the following lines :

"W With hart, and hand, among the rest,
E Especially you welcome are :
L Long looked for as welcome guest,
C Come now at last you be from farre.
O Of most within the Citty, sure,
M Many good wishes you haue had ;
E Each one did pray you might endure,
W With courage good the match you made.
I Intend they did with gladsome hearts,
L Like your well willers, you to meete :
K Know you also they'l doe their parts,
E Eyther in field or house to greete
M More you than any with you came,
P Procur'd thereto with tromp and fame.
your well-willer,
T. G."

(T. G. was Thomas Gilbert, who had been selected by the citizens to express their welcome ; possibly the Mayor, Roger Weld, was related to a "Mrs. Weld" mentioned in the will of Caleb Kempe, of Totteridge.)

In "Hazlitt's Handbook to his Bibliographical Collections" the following are attributed to William Kempe : "A Dutiful Invective," 1587 ; "Education of Children in Learning," 1588 ; "A Translation of Peter Rannee's Arithmatic," 1592 ; "New Jigge between a soldier, a miser and Sam, the Clown," 1595 ; "New Jigge of the Kitchin-stuffe-woman," 1595 ; "New Jigge of the Broomeman," 1594-5, and the above "Nine Daies Wonder" in 1600. Of the second and third of these we believe William Kempe, of Plymouth, a schoolmaster, to be the author (see Cornish section) between whom and the actor there appears to be no connexion.

CHAPTER IV.

KEMPES OF HENDON, HAMPSTEAD AND FINCHLEY.

WE shall continue the line of the Kempes of Clitterhouse, but for chronological reasons we must go back to the earliest mentions of Kempes in the registers and wills of Willesden and Hampstead.

The very first mention of a Kempe in the Hampstead parish books is in 1566 when appears the marriage of Richard Kempe (of Ipswich and Gissing), with Alice Cockerham, whose father, Phillip Cockerham, was a resident of this parish ; in the following year (1567) their eldest son, and ancestor to the Kempe Baronets, was baptized there.

Four years earlier than this baptism, however, it appears from the Subsidy Roll that a John Kempe was resident at Hampstead ; he certainly was there until 1574, in which year he made his will, which was witnessed by the above Phillip Cockerham and by Joyce "Cockram" From this one might infer very close relationship between Richard Kempe, of Gissing, and John Kempe, of Hampstead, but from our investigations it seems that at least two generations before the ancestors of John Kempe were at Marlibone and Hampstead.

In the Subsidy Roll of 1546 John Kempe, of "Marybone," was rated at £18, and the same individual appears also in the Subsidy of 1563 at the same place. He died the following year, and his will was proved in the Commissary Court of London in 1564. By it he bequeathed to his wife, Sybbell, his household goods and a sum of money, and to his son, William Kempe, he bequeathed his land so soon as he attained twenty-one years. William Bowington and Robert Westerfield were appointed executors, and the testator desired to be buried at "Maribone" by his seat in the church. He provided funds for the mending of the highways between *Kilbourne* Bridge and *Paddington*, and for alms to the poor of the latter place as well as other legacies. The witnesses were James Powel, Harry Wrench, Nicholas Brayfford, Moyses Tisdalle, John Crosse, John Prue and Edward Ellet.) The will is chiefly important as mentioning ground at "Wilsden Grene," "where Bankes dwelleth"—which Sybbell was to enjoy for life, thence reverting to the testator's son or his issue—thus showing the connexion between the Kempes of Marylebone and Paddington with those of Willesden.

In 1574, as we have said, John Kempe, of Hampstead, made his will, which is recorded in the same court as the above. This testator desired to be buried at Hampstead, and left his domiciliary house to his wife Joane, with the land adjoining, for her life, after which it was to devolve upon John Bradley, his daughter's son, or in the event of her issue failing to WILLIAM KEMPE, of MARYBONE, whose relationship to the testator is not stated. This John Kempe provided for the mending of the ways between Dolefield Grene and Figg Lane, from which fact it seems evident that his property at Hendon was reached by this lane and may have been "Dolles," which has since belonged to the Hendon family.

William Kempe, of "Marylebone," evidently he who is referred to in both the foregoing, dated his will 27th April, 1592, and it was duly proved by his mother (who had remarried to one named Parker) on 12th June following in the Commissary Court. He bequeathed his property at Hampstead to his wife Frances, and all the rest of his lands and tenements to his son John Kempe, his residuary estate being equally divided between his son, William Kempe, and his daughters, subject only to legacies to his cousin, Susan Kerrott, his servant, John Tailor, and to John Thorne and Walter Clarke, Sibell Mathen and Joan Ware. The testator left his lands at "WILSDEN" to his father-in-law, Henry Pyke and Anthonie Nicoll, in trust for his younger children, William and the daughters being still minors. This will draws together the lands at Marylebone, Hampstead and Willesden, and makes it apparent that the Kempes of these parishes were of the same stock as those of Hendon.

The Hampstead line continued down to the end of the seventeenth century as will be seen by the pedigree, but we need not support every step in this with quotations from the numerous wills and extracts from the registers (which we have duly and carefuly searched), for the family after entering the City life of London appear to have been influenced by the success of their remote kinsmen in Virginia, and selling their property here emigrated. It is doubtful if any Kempes from this line (Hampstead) are now living, but we shall be glad to furnish further information as to the records of Hampstead Kempes to any who can lay claim to lineal descent.

As we have mentioned in the first chapter, the earliest Subsidy Roll to show the names of ratepayers at Hampstead is that of 1523, on which William Kempe heads the list, George Kempe being second, and Margaret Kempe, widow, the third in ratable value in this parish. George Kempe appears there in both the Subsidies of 1546 and 1549, after which probably he moved to Finchley, but three miles distant, for we find tnat George Kempe and his wife Joan were concerned with Thomas Dobbys and Isabelle Harryett, widow, in paying a fine in 1553 for premises in "Fincheley." Perhaps it was this same George who was of Edmonton and Northawe in 1593, but as "Widow Kempe" was buried at Finchley in 1569, it is likely that George, of Northawe, was son to this couple. We have searched the Registers of Finchley but do not find any further Kempe item, although we know that NICHOLAS KEMPE (afterwards Knighted) was living at this place in 1606 as evidenced by his deed, now in our hands, to which his signature and seal are attached. The seal is quite perfect and shows his arms as ***three sheaves within a bordure engrailed***, similar in detail to one used on the deeds of the Kempes of Norfolk at this date. Singularly, although Sir Nicholas Kempe was a very prominent judge and active in many capacities around London, his parentage is not known, the only clue to his connexions with Kempes being his location at Finchley, and the mention in his will (P.C.C., 74 Bryde) of a Ralph Kempe, of Winchcombe. Those who have a general knowledge of Kempe pedigrees would be disposed to connect him with Cornwall, for the name of Nicholas was long in use among that family, but the record of wills at Ipswich show that many Nicholas Kempes were resident in Suffolk before 1650, and were doubtless of the same family as the Gissing Baronets who came from that county. When we turn to the name of Ralph we find it first at Kent as the claimed founder of the Kempes of Wye, second at Norfolk, about 1480, and third in Middlesex as mentioned in the first chapter. Winchcombe Registers have been examined by the present incumbent, but although we have some details of the Kempes of that place, including three named Ralph, no Nicholas appears, and it is open to conjecture as to whether those Kempes went from Middlesex or whether Sir Nicholas came from that place. We are inclined to think that the former is most likely, as it is on record that Ralph at least was married at St. Bartholomew's-the-Great (London) before he settled at Winchcombe, while many of the Middlesex Kempes, including those of Hendon, were connected with both the St. Bartholomew's, of West Smithfield, as well as the hospital of that name.

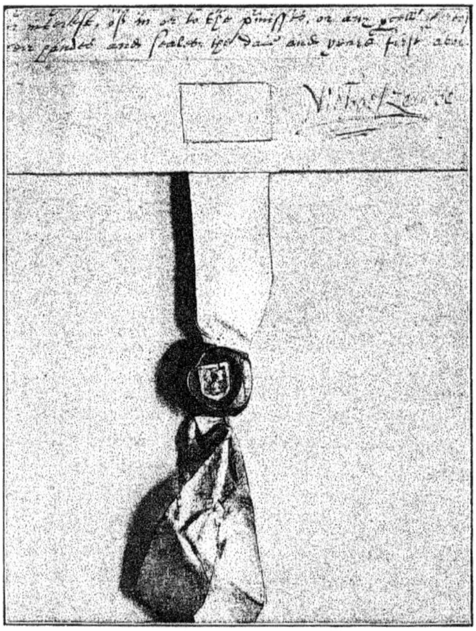

Signature and Seal of Sir Nicholas Kempe, Knight, 1606.

There is, however, another connexion of Sir Nicholas Kempe which may help to determine his exact relationship with other Kempes. He is recorded to have been Steward of St. Albans, and patron of Gilston, Herts. At the former there was an earlier Kempe in the same office, while soon after the death of Sir Nicholas there was a wealthy Joseph Kempe, a schoolmaster, who bequeathed his house called "Beggin" for an almshouse for the poor of Hitchin, for which purpose it still serves. His will mentions several persons connected with the Kempes of

Winchcombe. At Gilstone, according to the registers, in 1647, "Robert Kempe ye clerke aged neere a hundred years was buried Octob. 3." This may give rise to the question was this the "son Robert" mentioned by Widow Margaret Kempe, of Hendon, in her will of 1597-1607?

Later on Sir Nicholas was made Steward of the Episcopal Manors of Fulham, which office he held for a considerable time, during which Francis-Kempe, a descendant of Norfolk Kempes, settled at Fulham. (See Chapter VIII.)

Nicholas was knighted by James I. at Theobald's Park on 3rd October, 1617, and was a Justice of the Peace for Middlesex from that time until his death, which occurred in his seventy-fourth year—1624. He had married first Cisily Kester at St. Dunston's-in-the-West, on 24th January, 1577, but she left apparently no surviving issue and died in June, 1617, being buried in Islington Church near the vault of the East family. His second wife was Sarah, daughter of Roger James, of Holland (Essex), and widow of Thomas Draper, of Lincoln's Inn. She had by her first husband several children, but none by Sir Nicholas Kempe, who consequently left much of his property to the before-mentioned Ralph Kempe, of Winchcombe, while to the University of Oxford he bequeathed £2,000. To his almshouses at Guildford he left £500, and plate to the value of £500 to the co-founder, George Abbott, Archbishop of Canterbury; to the repair of St. Paul's Cathedral, £200, and for the repair of the highway between Islington and Stroud Green he also provided, as well as for charity to the poor of Islington and St. Sepulchres. To his wife he gave his coaches and horses, all his property at Islington and Stroud Green and his household effects, and he gave to his "antient" servant, Anthony Rigby, his windmill at St. Margaret's Hill, Southwark, and his houses in the Parish of St. Andrew's, Holborn. It is in reference to the purchase of this same windmill that the deed of 1606 mentioned above was executed, thus identifying *Sir* Nicholas with Finchley.

Sir Nicholas Kempe, Knight, 1554-1624.
Specially drawn for this History by Miss Lucy Kemp-Welch, after the original painting at Trinity Almshouses, Guildford.

Sir Nicholas was chiefly identified as the co-founder with Archbishop Abbot of the Trinity Almhouses at Guildford, at which his portrait and that of Abbott still hang. This hospital is of much better proportions than the average almshouses of the period, and the chief rooms are so well preserved and the carving so handsome that every Kempe tourist to Guildford should seek admission; we must not, however, devote space to describe in detail this still effective foundation. We reproduce the portrait of Sir Nicholas, which Miss Lucy Kemp-Welch has specially drawn for this purpose from our photograph of the original painting, which, unfortunately, has been damaged by unskilful varnishing.

CHAPTER V.

KEMPES OF CLITTERHOUSE, HENDON.

IN Chapter III. we showed as far as possible how the Kempes settled at Clitterhouse in 1556, and brought down the record of that family to 1649, when Edward Kempe left a wife named Ellen and a son called Thomas, who had at that time four children living. His sister, Rose Marsh, widow of William Marsh, an official of the Lord Mayor's Court, was also living, and seems to have left a daughter-in-law of her name, for it can hardly be she who made her will in 1711, mentioning her son, Thomas Marsh, her grandchildren, John Nicholl, John Sutton and Ann Rippin, yet these names are clearly relatives of the Kempes.

THOMAS KEMPE, the son of Edward, was a "Head-borough" for Hendon (North) in 1633, and doubtless held office later, but the records are missing from 1647 until 1679 when his son Thomas held that position. Thomas, the elder, lived still at Clitterhouse, and it seems he had secured the adjoining land and house known as Cricklewood. He died in 1667, his will being dated in April and proved in December that year (P.C.C., 170 Carr). By it he settled Clitterhouse upon his son Edward, with all the stores and cattle there, while he left Cricklewood to his second son Thomas. To his third son, Daniel Kempe, he left land in "Wilsden" called "ffeasant field" and a house and land called Burrows Close in Hendon. He also left legacies to his daughters, Elizabeth and Alice Kempe, and the residuary estate to his wife Alice. This wife was sister to John and George Brent, but her father's name does not appear in the will; she lived until 1681 at Finchley, where she dated her will 9th April, 1679. This will is full of details conclusively showing the various relationships set forth on the pedigree we submit, mentioning her grandchildren William, Elizabeth and Jane Atley, and John and Christopher, sons of her daughter Alice, who had married John Sutton. She speaks of her sons Thomas and Daniel, but Thomas as well as Edward predeceased her. John Sutton was appointed executor, and George Brent and Daniel Kempe overseers. Like the majority of women's wills this enumerates minutely pieces of jewellery and other personal effects bestowed upon various friends and relatives, but it does not omit the poor of Hendon, and desires that Mr. Staysmore should preach her funeral sermon.

It is probable that EDWARD KEMPE was appointed one of the "Constables" for Hendon in 1674, and that it was in virtue of his office that he took a prominent part in the exciting chase after a "notorious gang of highwaymen," whose career made a lasting impression on the community. Two or more books published at the time commemorate this event, one being called "Jackson's Recantation: or the Life and Death of the Notorious Highwayman," and the other "The Confession of Four Highwaymen," from which it appears that having been a terror on the main roads round London for some years the gang had grown so bold that they often appeared in broad daylight in the smaller towns; it was so on the 18th March, 1674, they having robbed the Windsor Coach on Hounslow Heath only two days previously, they yet had the audacity to stop two coaches in Bedford Lane, near Staines, about noon; expecting to be quicky followed they made off over the fields to Acton, thence to Harrow-on-Hill, where news of their approach had caused some forty or fifty people to assemble armed with guns. Thus they turned, rode to Paddington, thence through Kilburn to Hendon, being followed all the way by such as could keep pace with them. At Hendon their progress was checked by EDWARD KEMPE and others, and being brought to bay they emptied their pistols at the little band, a shot lodging in the breast of Edward. During the pause caused by this the brigands got away, but were stopped finally at Hampstead, where after due trial Francis Jackson was hanged in chains on the Heath for the murder of Edward Kempe and one Henry Miller. His gibbet is said to form the mantel shelf at "Jack Straw's Castle."

Edward Kempe evidently had time to make a fresh will, but he died within a few days of his wound; for the Register at Hendon records that he was buried there on the 26th March, 1674. His will was proved in the Commissary Court on the 17th April following by his brother, Thomas Kempe, to whom he bequeathed Clitterhouse and other lands subject to the payment of £500 to his younger brother Daniel; and £100 to Elizabeth Atley's four children, and £100 to his sister, Alice Sutton, and the residue of his effects to his mother and brother, Thomas Kempe, jointly. The will mentions also his cousin, Henry Budder, his relatives Andrew and George Brent and Daniel Brown. It is evident that Edward left no issue nor widow, and that his brother duly inherited the property.

This brother, THOMAS KEMPE, however, died the same year, his will being registered in the same book as Edward's. It is dated at Hendon, 29th November, 1674, and was proved by his widow, Ellin Kempe, on the following 18th of December. To his brother, Daniel Kempe, he bequeathed Clitterhouse, mentioning that the sum of £500 bequeathed by Edward was still due to this younger brother, to his sisters, Atley and Sutton, the legacies were also due, and subject to the payment of these his residuary estate including Cricklewood was left to his wife and son.

It is clear that in 1674 Thomas, the son, was still a minor, as his mother was to hold his portion of the estate in trust; when he was born is not certain, but his father as a second son seems to have settled in business in Newgate Street, London. Possibly his wife was by birth Taylor, for a marriage licence was issued by the Court of Faculties on 20th September, 1669, for Thomas Kempe and Ellenor Taylor. If this was the Hendon couple the son Thomas could only be a child of five or so when his father died, unless by a previous wife, but he married by licence Mary Noble in May, 1691, by which time he was most likely just twenty-one. In April the following year his first child, Mary, was baptized at Christ Church, Newgate, and an infant son, Joseph, was buried there in 1693. After this date, and before 1697, Thomas Kempe became an officer stationed at the Tower of London, where his family remained just 100 years. His eldest surviving son John was baptised at St. Peter ad Vincula, in the Tower in 1697, and the other children, viz., Thomas, Daniel, Ellen, Elizabeth, Noble and Mary were all born or baptized in the precincts, while Mary, his first wife, was buried at St. Peter's on 2nd April, 1727.

It is evident from his will that Major Thomas Kempe, of the Tower, married a second wife named Mary, who was daughter of John Braint (or Brent), of Hendon, doubtless related to the other Brents mentioned in the previous wills; by this wife, however, he left no issue. Noble Kempe was buried at Hampstead on 8th January, 1701, but the other children all attained a good age, as we shall record. Thomas Kempe was Quartermaster at the Tower from 1699, and lent considerable sums to officers. We find him as Major of the Tower Hamlets Militia in 1712 and as Quartermaster at the Tower in the Army List of 1722, and in the Treasury Papers of 1725 and 1726 several references are made to the petition of Quartermaster Thomas Kemp of the Tower, who appeals for the annexation of the estate of Brigadier Munden, to whom he had lent £1,700. Brigadier Richard Munden was the officer selected to receive the surrender of the "Six Rebel Lords," and was an important witness at the State trial of them in 1716, for which services he was probably appointed Out-Ranger of Windsor Forest, holding which office he died on 19th September, 1725, in debt to Thomas Kempe. The Lords of the Treasury granted his estate to

Thomas Kempe until the debt was satisfied, and it seems that Thomas Kempe, was selected to succeed Munden in the office of Out-Ranger, but he died suddenly in the following year at the Tower, and consequently John Short, from the Tower, was appointed to Windsor. The will of Major Thomas Kemp merely describes him as Thomas Kemp, of the Tower of London, Gent.; it is dated 5th September, 1716, and was proved (P.C.C., 16 Brook) by his wife Mary on 20th January, 1727. The testator mentions each of his six surviving children, leaving his Cricklewood property to John, the eldest son, with land also at Willesden, all of which was let and occupied by tenants of the Kempes. To the other children sums of money were left, the residue of the estate being settled upon his widow for life and reverting to Thomas, the second son. No will of the widow was necessary, nor has one been found; she was buried in St. Peter's ad Vincula on the 12th of March, 1763.

John Kempe, the eldest son, had married a wife named Katherine, whose arms as impaled on his tomb at Hendon, claim her as a Walker, of London, but she seems to have been either a daughter or widow of Jones, of Walthamstow. She was buried in a railed vault at Hendon in October, 1759, and the inscription states that she was a "devoted parent," but how many children she had, or where they were baptized, has not been traced. We only know of one daughter, Elizabeth, who married first Isaac Dupuy, by whom she had a boy named Isaac, and secondly to one named Rigby, by whom she had a daughter named Elizabeth. Both she and her two children were living in 1797. Her father, JOHN KEMPE, died at Stoke Newington in 1788 aged ninety-one, and was buried with his wife at Hendon, but we have failed to trace either his will or letters administrating his estate. The arms on his tomb are well carved and are interesting from the fact that no bordure surrounds the three sheaves representing the Kempes and that this impales a fess between three crescents, the tinctures in neither case being indicated. As head of the senior branch of the Hendon Kemps he must have held plate older than that which has been handed down by the collateral line, and as it is likely that portraits and documents have descended to the Rigbys or Dupuys which would add to our knowledge of this family, we shall be glad to receive any notes or enlightenment as to present representatives of these families.

Thomas Kemp, the next younger brother of this John, went to Oxford, being entered at St. John's College as "Thomas Kemp, of the Tower of London, Gent.," and graduating there B.A. on 20th May, 1723, and as M.A. in April, 1727. He was made Doctor of Divinity in 1736, and was presented by his College to the Rectory of Cheam, Surrey, where he remained until 1747 when he exchanged this living for that of St. Michael's, Crooked Lane, London, where he remained until his death. He was, however, buried at his request in Cheam Church, where a stone remains in the old (disused) chancel to his memory. He had officiated at Hendon on the occasion of his niece's wedding with Isaac Dupuy, which was solemnised by licence on 24th October, 1763 (Dupuy being a widower of St. Martin's-in-Fields), aud it is noteworthy that Dr. Earle,* at this time Vicar of Hendon, was formerly Rector of St. Michael's, Crooked Lane.

The REV. DR. KEMP married Mary Lady Banff, daughter of Captain Ogilvie and widow of the Earl of Banff (who was drowned while bathing); she left no children. Dr. Kempe's will is dated at Cheam 3rd July, 1745, but he did not die until 1769, in which year it was proved by his widow (Commissary of London). The will mentions specially his sermons and MSS., which he desired to be disposed of by his wife "according to instructions he had given her." He left the arrears of his pay as Chaplain of Plymouth, and all rents, debts, his plate and all personal estate to his widow. She died in 1784, and her will was proved that year (P.C.C., 6 Rockingham) by Edward Short, son of Edward Short, of the Tower of London, by Ellen, daughter of Major Thomas

* Other Earles were long closely connected with the Kempes of South Malling, while a third family spelling their name *Erle* succeeded to Ollanty, so long the seat of the Kentish Kempes.

Kempe. The testatrix had omitted to get witnesses to her signature to two codicils, consequently before proving the will Daniel Kempe, brother to her late husband, and Catherine Short, the latter's great niece, had to testify that the codicils were in the handwriting of the testatrix. This helps to show the undoubted identity of all the parties. "Mary Kempe, *alias* Mary Lady Banff," it appears, died at Camberwell, but since her husband's decease she had been living at Kensington. She left legacies to her nephews, Archibald and Alexander Ogilvie, and her niece Mary Ann Ogilvie, but her "fortune" she left to Catherine Short, who afterwards became heiress to her great uncle Daniel. Lady Banff mentions also Captain "ffoulis," Sarah Thompson and Miss Anna Ismay, but except for certain bank annuities the will does not tell in what her "fortune" was invested.

In the *Gentleman's Magazine* of 1732 it is announced that in March "Edward Short, Esq., Secretary of the Office of Ordnance, married the daughter of the late Major Kempe." This Edward Short made his will in 1747, and it was proved the same year by *Ellen* Short his widow.

The will describes the testator as a "gentleman of the Tower of London," it leaves the interest in Bank Annuities to his sister, Martha Gibson, for life, and afterwards the principal was to revert to John Lansdell, Chrysostom Lansdell and Daniel Kempe. It mentions his freehold estates in Windsor Forest, which were to be held in trust for his son, Edward Short, and it bequeathed to the testator's "sisters," Elizabeth and Mary *Kempe*, one third of his freehold estate in Fleet Street for their lives with reversion for his said son. The residuary estate was bequeathed between the latter and the testator's widow, who with her brother, Daniel Kempe, were the executors. It seems likely that the Windsor property had come from that John Short of Windsor Castle mentioned above and whose will was proved in 1731.

Ellen Short, the widow, lived at the Tower of London until 1786, when administration of her estate was granted to her son, Edward Short, Esq. (jun.) The latter dated his will at the Tower the 19th April, 1785; it is very brief, leaving all his estate to his daughter, Catherine Short, subject only to the payment of 300 guineas to his servant, Hannah Mann. On the 11th January, 1787, Daniel Kempe, of the Tower, Esq., and John Sudlow, of Monument Yard, London, Gent., deposed that this will was in the handwriting of the executor, no witnesses' names having been attached, and on the following day the will was duly proved by Catherine Short, the testator's daughter.

Daniel Kempe, the third son of Major Thomas, made a report to the Treasury in 1737 on the utensils in use at the mint, which was then located at the Tower of London, at this time he was one of the Moneyers. He became Provost of the Company of Moneyers within a few years, and retained this office until he retired shortly before his death, which occurred in 1797. His will was proved that year by his grandniece, Catherine Short, to whom he left the bulk of his property, those receiving legacies under his will being as follows: Elizabeth Rigby, his great-nephew, Isaac Dupuy, his cousins Ellen, Elizabeth, and Ann Flower, and his friends Joseph Sage and William Atkinson. He left £50 to his coachman, £30 to his footman, and £70 to his maid servant, also £100 to the Alicium, or Orphan House for girls, and £100 to St. Luke's Hospital in Old Street. His consideration for others is shown by a sentence at the close of his will, which says that he desires to be buried at Walthamstow or Wanstead, "the funeral to be private," and the mourners each to have a "heavy ring," but they ***need not attend the funeral!*** His reason for wishing to be buried at Walthamstow was that his grandmother was connected with the Jones's of that place.

Daniel Kempe died at Great Ormond Street, Bloomsbury, situated close to the Foundling Hospital, and we therefore may presume that it was one of his family who as a "Mr. Kempe" collected funds and published a report thereon for a branch of this establishment, which it was proposed to establish at Shrewsbury about the year 1765. Singularly in the catacombs under the Foundling Hospital lie buried two other Kempes, namely, Joseph Kemp, who died, aged seventy-three on January 3rd, 1819, and Mrs. Elizabeth Kemp, his widow, who was buried there in August 1842, aged ninety-one. They lived in Great Ormond Street, and the latter resided at Hampstead after her husband's death. Their wills are duly recorded in the Prerogative Court of Canterbury in the above years; we do not know how these were connected (if at all) with Daniel Kempe of the Mint, the relatives mentioned by them are as follows: The Rev. Joseph Wright, Edmund Nelson Wright, Elizabeth Wright, Benjamin and Sarah Thorpe, Mrs. Letitia Marchant, Mrs. Sarah Stone, Samuel Barker and Thomas Davis. Joseph Kempe bequeathed to the British Museum a medal, which was presented by the Empress Catherine of Russia to the testator's friend Paton.

The present Secretary of the Mint has taken some trouble to search the records, and tells us that in virtue of his office Daniel Kemp removed all his papers when he retired, but that several letters and entries are in evidence relating to John, Nicholas and Alfred John Kempe, of the Cornish Kempe family, who were successively engaged in the Mint in minor capacities. Of these we shall give due notice under Cornwall, it is however necessary here to mention the fact of a second distinct Kempe family being associated with the Mint.

In further reference to Daniel Kemp's will, we may say that just behind St. Luke's Hospital, in Old Street, was that fashionable resort of the eighteenth century founded by William Kempe, a wealthy jeweller of London, and known as the "Peerless Pool." The site of this was formerly known as the Perilous pond, from the fact that on several occasions when people resorted to skate there, some were drowned by the breaking of the ice. William Kempe constructed from it two large swimming baths, and built dressing rooms, promenades refreshment rooms and a commodious residence for himself in the grounds, of which a picture appeared in Hone's "Every Day Book" (1838), with much interesting information concerning the charges made to bathers and anglers, for whom a fish pond was also provided. The will of this William Kempe was proved in 1755 (P.C.C. 399 Glazier); it bequeathed the "Peerless Pool," consisting of three tenements, gardens, pleasure baths, cold bath, several buildings and a large fish pond, held of *St. Bartholomew's Hospital*, to his son Philemon and Nathaniel Kempe, and his son in-law Mr. George Roadley, in trust that they paid certain sums to the testator's wife Sarah and to his younger children, namely: William, Charles, Samuel and Jane Kempe, and Sarah the wife of the said George Roadley. From the fact that this property belonged to St. Bartholomew's Hospital, and that a Roadley had married a grandchild of Thomas Kempe, of Clitterhouse, Hendon, it seems likely that William Kempe belonged to that family, but we have no definite proof of this, nor can we say for certain what became of the children mentioned in this will.

Catherine Short, as we have seen, inherited not only the estate of Daniel Kempe, but that of her great-uncle and great-aunt the Rev. Thomas Kempe, D.D., and Mary Lady Banff; it is important therefore that we should know what became of her fortune. We have made, and are still making, search for her will, and can only suggest that it was she who married a Mr. Perry in 1827, at St. George's, Hanover Square, of which parish her relative John Kemp, of Dover Street, was a parishioner.

CHAPTER VI.

KEMPES OF CLITTERHOUSE, HENDON—*continued.*

DANIEL KEMPE (the third son of Thomas Kempe, of Clitterhouse) inherited, from his two elder brothers, Clitterhouse and other Hendon property in 1674; he married at Willesden on 7th October, 1675, Mary Franklin, by whom he had a son Daniel in 1678, but who died the following year, also Mary Kempe, born 1680, who survived. Mary, the first wife, was buried at Hendon in February, 1681, and Daniel married in 1682, Mary, daughter of George Nichol, of Hendon. Some amusing love-letters of this Mary Nichol are still preserved by her descendants and show that Daniel Kempe and Randell Nichol, her cousin, had been rival suitors for her hand before Daniel's first marriage. We may give a specimen of her style, which is as follows:

"11th Oct., 1679.

"COUSIN RANDOLL.

"I do thankfully acknowledge all your loving kindness which I have received from you. But as for me to study a requitall is more than I can attain to.

"Cousin as to your love for me I am satisfied in it though you are pleased to call my love imperfect. But I think if my love with yours were weighed in the Balances I should not be found much wanting, I am confident I could equall yours were it not for its consequence; therefore knowing the cause pardon me if you find not that here which you do expect.

"Cousin I shall not make an apology for these weak lines knowing that your love will cover it with a favourable construction; at this time I shall say no more, only this, to desire you to unbind yourself of cupid's bonds lest you are intangled by them, so I Rest and Remain,

"Your friend for ever,

From Dallis (Hendon). "(Signed) M. M. MARY NICHOLL.

"Farewell till your time be expired."

By this wife Daniel Kempe had the following children: Helen, Elizabeth (who died an infant), a second Elizabeth baptized in 1686, Ann, Sarah, Susannah, Joseph and Daniel. Daniel, the elder, was buried at Hendon in 1712, his will being proved that year in the Commissary Court of London. He bequeathed to his eldest daughter Mary, by his first wife, £250; to his daughter Elizabeth, land called "Dollis" (which probably is meant by Dallis in the above letter and since called Dollis Farm) also Thorn Field, all in Hendon; to his daughter Helen, land at Cricklewood and £250; to Susan, the wife of William Snoxall, also a portion of his property jointly with her sister Ann. This last bequest was for their lives only, and consisted of the house and grounds called "Goodyers," fields called the "Upper and Lower Mead," and two fields in Braint Street called "Stubble" and "Little Goodyers." GOODYERS, as has been stated, had belonged to relatives of the Kempes for a hundred years before this, but Daniel Kempe purchased it in 1691, from which time to the present it has remained with his descendants. His will further mentions his late sister Alice Sutton and her son John Sutton, to whom he bequeaths a legacy. The testator leaves all the rest of his estate, including Clitterhouse, to his son Daniel (who at this time had not attained twenty-one years), begging him to listen to the advice of his relatives.

From the time when Daniel Kempe inherited Clitterhouse the *junior* branch of this family remained at Hendon, while, as we have seen in the last chapter, the senior branch lived in London, terminating with Catharine Short, who practically inherited their lands and fortunes. The earliest silver now held by the representative of the Clitterhouse Kempes dates from this Daniel Kempe, and includes a large silver pot with cover, weighing some 16 oz., on the handle of which D.K. has been stamped (not engraved). On the face of the pot is engraved a coat of arms,—*three sheaves within a border engrailed*, the tincture of the field is not indicated, but the charges and border are indicated as gold; this shield is of course the coat used by the Kempe Baronets, the Kentish Kempes and Sir Nicholas Kempe, Knight of Finchley (1606), but we fear that Daniel Kempe could not have shown by what right of descent he used these arms. From this time however it is evident that the motto "Honestas et Veritas" was adopted by this family, indicating at least that they did not blindly and ignorantly copy those used by the Baronet.

DANIEL KEMPE, the surviving son of the last, lived also at Clitterhouse, his first wife was named Sarah, but her surname does not appear; it is just possible that she was an Arrowsmith, for a shield of the Kemp arms, impaling argent, two arrows in saltire between four (? bulls) heads caboshed, was emblazoned about the time of this marriage, and is still preserved in the family. These arms do not appear correct but closely resemble those of Arrowsmith. By this wife he had two sons named Daniel, the first however died an infant in 1719, the second, born in 1728, lived at Parsons Street, Hendon, during his father's life. The other children of this marriage were as follows: Mary Kempe, baptized 1723, who married Thomas Dowdeswell, and Sarah Kempe, born 1724, who married John Rippin, and John Kemp, baptized 1725, buried the following year. Daniel Kempe's second wife was named Elenor, she died in April 1791, aged ninety, having given birth to the following children: Ellen Kempe, baptized 1736; Elizabeth Kempe, baptized 1738, who married Edward Neeton and died at Harrow-on-Hill in 1773, and Susan Kempe, who married first in 1773, Thomas Pitt, and secondly John Lodge, of Mill Hill; she also had a son named William Kempe, born 1743, but he died in 1746 just prior to his father; her surviving son was John Kempe, of whom we shall speak later.

Silver Pot, dated 1710, which belonged to the Kemp(e)s of Clitterhouse.

The will of Daniel Kempe (the second of his name at Clitterhouse) was proved in 1747, with codicils made in May and April of that year. He provided an annuity for his wife, and settled upon his daughters—namely, the wife of John Rippin and the wife of Thomas Dowdeswell—for their joint lives, "Goodyers" and the Brent Street Estate, and certain rentals on his daughters Elizabeth and Susanah Kempe. He mentions as part of his lands in Hendon, the following: "Rowlands," "Southfields," "De La Heys," "Dole Street," "Thornfields," "Drivers," and his lease of Clitterhouse which he left to John Kempe, his son, and his heirs, or in default to his son William and his issue. As we have said, William died an infant and consequently the whole of the estate remained with John.

Daniel Kempe (the third of his name) died in 1763, intestate, and his wife Elizabeth was granted administration of his estate. During his tenure of a portion of his father's estate (which he probably received by deed of gift) a return was made of landholders on the Manor of Hendon:

at this time (1756) we find that Daniel Kempe held 150 acres in Hall Lane besides some fields near the church and his residence in Parson's Street.

In a map of this period "Kemp's Wood" is shown (in a map of 1610 it is indicated but not named), this however has now been cleared; it was situated a short distance north-west of Clitterhouse, to which it belonged.

JOHN KEMP, under his father's will, inherited Clitterhouse and the other family property mentioned above; eventually, on the decease of the widow of his half-brother Daniel Kemp, he also received the house in Parson Street and the leases of Hall Lane, subject to provision for Dinah Kempe (daughter of the said Daniel) who married Edward Clarke. This Dinah, by her marriage settlement, had an interest in Goodyers but released this to John Kemp in 1774. Edward Clarke was a merchant of Bishopsgate Street, London, and was connected with the Clarkes of Marston Magna, Somerset (which may account for the subsequent intermarriage of the Kempes with West of England families), he had a son of his own name and a grandson who was living in London in 1813. John Kemp, as a second son, was intended to follow the profession of a physician, and studied at St. Bartholcmew's Hospital, at which he obtained a certificate in 1762 (which is still held by the family); it is interesting to notice that this certificate was issued to a tenant of the hospital, whose family had continuously been tenants of the hospital for over two hundred years. During his elder brother's life he practised as an apothecary, and resided at Dover Street, Piccadilly; he married Louisa, daughter of John Bishop, of Piccadilly, at St. George's, Hanover Square, on 8th October, 1769. The mother of Louisa Bishop was Mary Penny, of Wells, who was niece to a Phillis Hodges of that place and of Westminster, who lived to be a great age and died about 1773. John and Louisa had the following children: Daniel Kempe, born 1771; William Bishop Kemp and Louisa Augusta Kemp (twins), born 1772; Elizabeth Augusta Kemp, born 1775, and Charlotte Kemp, born 1776. Of these, William Bishop died in 1775 and was buried at Hendon under a tomb on which the family crest is well carved; Louisa Augusta, his twin sister, being buried in the same grave the following year.

DANIEL KEMP, the only surviving son, studied at St. George's Hospital and there obtained a certificate as a qualified surgeon in 1792. He practised for a short time as an apothecary in Dover Street, Piccadilly, but was soon appointed as a surgeon in the army; in that capacity he served in Holland and there died, while on active service, on the 29th December, 1794. He had not been married.

The news of his death proved the death-blow to his father, who died on 28th October following, and was buried in a vault which he had had prepared at Hendon. The vault is dated 1791 and bears the Kemp crest and inscriptions to three generations. His will is dated in 1792 and consequently mentions this son Daniel as his heir, but by a codicil dated 24th November, 1795, he left his estate in trust to provide an income for Louisa his wife and for his daughters Elenor Augusta Kemp and Charlotte Kemp with ultimate remainder to them and their lawful issue. The lands mentioned in this will include Goodyers, Brent Street and Dole Street; other property he mentions is a "two-handled silver chased cup marked," also a "curious Egyptian stone snuff box gilt with gold," which he bequeathed to his daughter Charlotte, but these are not now among the family plate. He also mentions a silver tankard "*with the family arms*" which he intended should descend to his son, and a silver pint mug marked "F.L.K.," which he left to his daughter Elenor. We are curious to know who the initials F.L.K. represented? The large silver cup, as we have said, dates from the time of Queen Anne and belonged to the first Daniel Kempe, of Hendon.

LOUISA KEMP, the widow of John, benefitted under the will of her father John Bishop, who amongst other properties in and around London had curiously a house in "Bishop's Court," Old

Bailey; this court however was so named through being once possessed by the Bishops of London and not because of its association with a family named Bishop. Another of his properties worthy of mention consisted of a row of houses in Kensington High Street, which had belonged to the Munden family, one of whom was the Brigadier Richard Munden mentioned in the previous chapter; this property was however derived by purchase and not, as might be supposed, through Munden's estate being mortgaged to Major Thomas Kempe. Louisa Kemp had a brother named Matthew Bishop who was an officer in Colonel Parker's Regiment stationed in the Isle of Guernsey; his residence was at Diddington, Oxford, where he died in 1763, in that year he made his will bequeathing his estate to his father John Bishop, then dwelling in Piccadilly. John Bishop, the father, had also a house at Hendon, at the corner of Butcher's Lane, which was until recently standing, being last known as "Fosters"; his will is however dated from his last town residence, Queen Street, Golden Square, on the 25th October, 1802.

Louisa Kemp, widow, remarried; her second husband being Doctor George Goodwin, of Great Queen Street, Lincoln's Inn Fields, her will is dated from Queen Street, Golden Square, and bequeathed to her daughter Elenor Augusta Kemp, spinster (then residing with her), her freehold land at Brent Street and "Goodyers," and to her grandchildren, George and Charlotte Brookes, the only surviving issue of her daughter Charlotte, her land at Dole Street and various London property. She mentioned her son-in-law, Mr. George Brookes, of Spur Street, Leicester Square, and Mr. and Mrs. Henry Brookes, of Chamberlayn Street, in the City of Wells. She also left a legacy to her son (by her second husband) "Charles Goodwin, clerk, late of Enhurst, Sussex, but then residing at Charing Cross"; also legacies to Mrs. Mary Ann Goodwin, wife of Dr. Goodwin, and to Edward Turner, of Hart Street, Covent Garden, the curate of Orange Street Chapel.

The Rev. Dr. Samuel Charles Goodwin, mentioned above, died in Paris in 1835, and we do not know of any representatives of the Goodwin family now living, but it is possible that certain portraits of the Kempes were retained by Louisa Kempe's second husband, as such are not now in the hands of the descendants by her first marriage.

CHAPTER VII.

HITCHIN-KEMPS.

CHARLOTTE, the only daughter of John and Louisa Kemp to have issue, married George Brookes, a solicitor of Coventry Street and Beake Street, London, at the Church of St. Martin's-in-Fields by licence on 3rd June, 1799. George Brookes appears in the Register of Gray's Inn as the son of John Brookes, Esquire, of "Boxford," Sussex, and St. Andrews, Holborn, and his father appears to have been the son of James Brookes of the latter parish, where he was married to Ann Taylor of Bath in June, 1732 (James Brookes died 28th August, 1784.) George Brookes was a liberal supporter of the Volunteer Movement, and among the family plate is an interesting silver teapot which was presented to him by the Hendon Corps of the "S.M.L.B." for his services as secretary and solicitor to that Volunteer Brigade; the inscription, which is very laudatory is dated 1802. By the co-heiress of the Kemps of Clitterhouse George Brookes (senior) had the following children: George, born 29th October, 1800; Frederick, born 2nd December, 1802; Charlotte, born 29th December, 1804, and Daniel Bowden, born 22nd November, 1807. The last named died 22nd August, 1808. Frederick was placed at school with Mr. Lotherington, of Hammersmith, whence he addressed many interesting letters to his relatives which are extant. On reaching manhood he fell into a decline and died while on a visit to his uncle, Henry Brookes, Chancellor to the Bishop of Bath and Wells. He was buried in 1824 at Wells Cathedral beside several of his Brookes relations, and a little book on his life was written and published by his brother George that year, a copy of which may be seen at the British Museum.

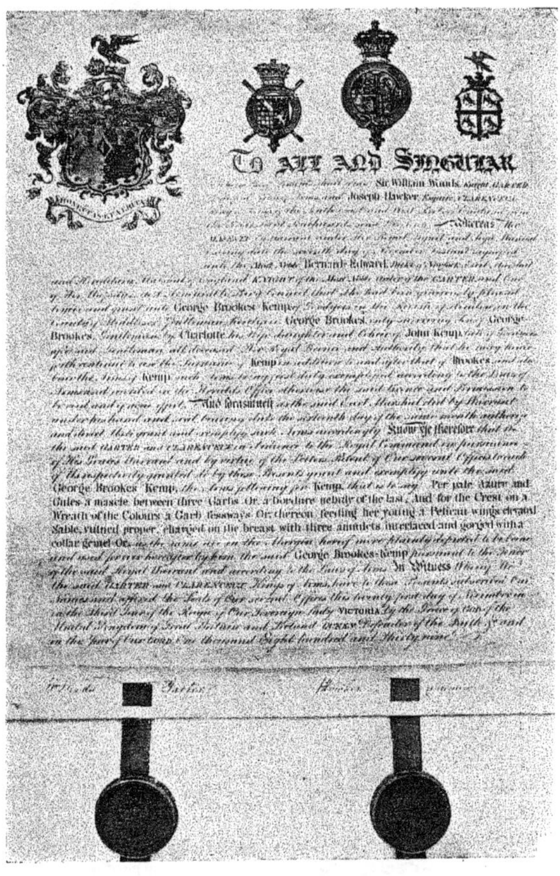
To All and Singular

Royal Patent granting Arms of Kemp to George Brookes.

George Brookes (the younger) became heir to his mother, and thus on the death of his maiden aunt, Ellinor Augusta Kemp (the other co-heiress of the Kemps of Clitterhouse), assumed by Royal licence the name and arms of Kemp in 1838. He had studied the law with a view of following his father's profession, but took little active interest in the business, which consequently devolved upon a Mr. Pike (whose descendants still carry on the practice of solicitors at Old Burlington Street, and have continued to act for the Hendon Kemp property). George Brookes-Kemp did not marry, living a batchelor life chiefly at London hotels, but took

The Hitchin-Kemp's "Home." (Front view.)

The Hitchin-Kemp's "Home." (Side iew.)

much interest in Hendon local politics and carefully arranged and preserved the papers and relics of the Kemps which devolved upon him. His will, proved in 1868, bequeathed the Kemp, Brookes and Bishop Estates to his nephew, Frederick William Hitchin, on condition that the heir took the name and arms of Kemp, and directed that the family plate should descend with "Goodyers." He was buried in the "Vault of the Kemps of Clitterhouse," on the north of Hendon Church, in 1868. The estates duly passed to his nephew, Frederick William Hitchin, who was the son of William Hitchin (Accountant and Assistant Secretary of the British and Foreign Bible Society) by Charlotte Brookes, the co-heiress of John and Louisa Kemp.

We may here give a few notes as to the Hitchin (formerly written Hitchen and Hytchen) family on whom the Kemp estates of Middlesex devolved. The above William Hitchin—from his great interest in the propagation of the Scriptures—was pleased to dwell upon the fact that Tyndall, the translator of the Bible, was known both at college and during his persecuted life as "William Hychins, otherwise Hitchins," this name appearing in his works. We cannot say for certain that the Hitchins of Cheshire came from his stock (who were natives of Somersetshire) but the Hitchins first appeared at Middlewich, Cheshire, during the Commonwealth, and it is not improbable that their settlement there was due to the influence of Cromwell. The name occurs in the Middlewich Registers frequently from 1662, but it is evident that the family were staunch supporters of the Puritan doctrines, and it is known that the Independent Chapel at Middlewich was founded by them. The present chapel was erected over their graves, and the tombstones, commemorating several generations of them, are now grouped together within a special enclosure in the old Dissenting burial ground. At Newton, in the Parish of Middlewich, still stands the house—a stiff, double-fronted Georgian edifice—in which the Hitchins lived for a century, it was there that the Rev. Thomas Hitchin, second son of Thomas Hitchin, by Mary Wrench, his wife, was born in 1772. This Rev. Thomas Hitchin founded several chapels in the Midland Counties, and was one of the earliest supporters of the Provincial Bible Societies. Late in life he came to London and formed the congregation, which afterwards worshipped at Dr. Allan's Chapel. When over seventy years of age he frequenty preached at the Independent Chapel, Greenwich, where his son William was a deacon, and where his grandchildren were members of the congregation. It was at this chapel that his daughter-in-law Charlotte, the Kemp heiress, was buried in January, 1853. The Rev. Thomas Hitchin was buried at Nunhead Cemetery in 1856 in the family grave of his son.

The first Hitchin-Kemp—Frederick William.

The Rev. Thomas Hitchin married at St. Margaret's, Westminster, on 24th May, 1791, Maria Siddons, who was related to the great actress of her name. She studied under Dr. Jenner, and is believed to have been the first lady to vaccinate her own children. By her he had several children, his eldest son, William, having been born at Atherstone, Warwickshire, on 9th April, 1807. It was this son who married Charlotte Brookes and thus became father of Frederick

William Hitchin, the heir to the Hendon Kemp property. Another William Hitchin, son of Joseph Hitchin, of Middlewich (nephew of the Rev. Thomas Hitchin), was the founder of "Hitchin's Beach," New Zealand, where he is still living.

The above-mentioned Frederick William Hitchin on the death of his maternal uncle, George Brookes-Kemp, in 1868, assumed the name and arms of Kemp by Royal licence. He was born at Tibberton Square, Islington, on 18th January, 1835, he commenced his business life in the Bible House, but soon entered the Bank of William Deacons and Co., London; while there, however, his health failed, and it was thought desirable that he should be placed at Margate; thus he entered Cobb and Co.'s Bank there in 1855 (afterwards amalgamated with Lloyd's), in which he remained for over forty-five years, retiring in 1900. He married on 19th June, 1863, Fanny Pym, daughter of Thomas Shoobridge, of London, her mother being related to the Hampdens and Pyms of Devonshire, in which county she spent much of her childhood. Mrs. Hitchin-Kemp is an Associate of St. John's Ambulance Association, and is well known for her original modes of impressing a moral by means of a working model accompanied with a story. Her models, although intended originally for the amusement and benefit of her own family, have been the means of earning funds annually for the Church Missionary Society, and these with their stories have been a great feature at local, and even distant, bazaars for some twenty-five years. Over twenty of her Christmas stories have been printed, and many copies have been sold in aid of various charities. She has presented her husband with ten children, the eldest died aged nine in 1873, but the others are all living — three sons and six daughters. Charlotte

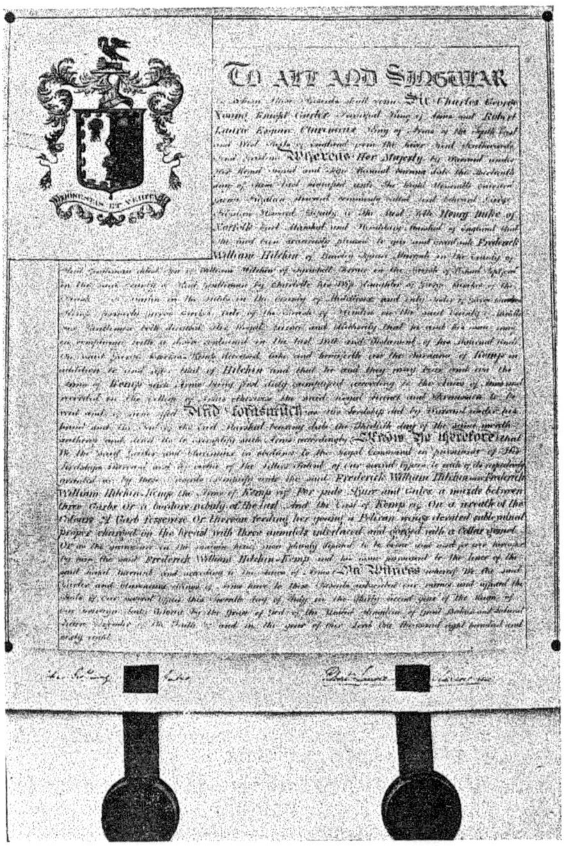
To All and Singular

Royal Patent granting Arms of Kemp to F. W. Hitchin-Kemp.

Hitchin-Kemp, the third daughter, married in 1895 Edward Riddlesdale Whitfield, M.A., of Dublin, now residing at Bournemouth ; Alice, the fifth daughter, is devoting her life to nursing the sick poor of the East End of London, the other daughters are unmarried. Frederick Hitchin-Kemp, the eldest son, was for many years engaged in shipping and army agency work in London, and is the compiler of the present history. He married in 1893 Lydia Harris, sixth daughter of the late Robert Cadby Bulgin (formerly a shipowner of Swansea and Cardiff), by whom he has had two children —Angela Winifred and Reginald Pym. William Hitchin-Kemp, the second son, was articled to a firm of sanitary specialists, and later to C. H. Cooper, M.I.C.E., Engineer to the Wimbledon Local Board, and on the completion of his articles was appointed junior assistant to their engineer. He has since held similar appointments at Willesden and Twickenham. (It is worthy of notice that thus a member of the Hendon Kemp family has been officially connected with these two places in the twentieth century in both of which his ancestors were interested four hundred years previously.) Arthur Hitchin-Kemp, the third son, was articled to Blandford and Lawrence, Incorporated Accountants of London, and having passed all the examinations of the Society of Accountants and Auditors (Incorporated), is now an Associate of that body.

The head of the Hitchin-Kemp Cot.
(An heirloom to which each generation is asked to add carving)

We give illustrations of the house built by the first Hitchin-Kemp in 1870-2, after the designs of Alfred Mercer-Drew. Also of a cot in which the younger members of the family have successively slept, the carving on which is representative of the various families of their name and kindred.

CHAPTER VIII.

KEMPS OF FULHAM, CHELSEA, AND OTHERS.

ROBERT KEMP, of Gissing, by Ann, daughter of Clifford of Kent, had a son, Bartholomew, who succeeded to the Norfolk Estates in 1527. The latter had a large family, among whom was FRANCIS KEMPE, who settled at Little Hadham (Herts). Francis married Armynell, daughter of John Brooke, of London, by whom he had three sons, Francis, William, and Thomas. William, the second son, entered the Merchant Taylor's School in 1574, but is recorded in the school register to have "died young." Francis, the eldest son, was an Attorney of Common Pleas, having a residence for a while in Fleet Street, he married first Barbara, daughter of Leonard Cocks, of London, by whom he had the following children: Leonard, baptized 1593, became an M.A.; Bartholomew, baptized 1595, also an M.A. and Rector of Graylingham, Lincolnshire; Henry, who was of the Inner Temple; Frances, baptized 1596, married Ralph Pemberton, of St. Albans, in 1616; Elizabeth Catherine (who married Humphrey Shalcrosse, of London), and Susan.

The first two children of Francis (the younger) were baptized at St. Dunstan's-in-the-West, Fleet Street, but the other children probably were baptized at Fulham, for we find that on the earliest rate book existing for that parish, viz., 1615, "Francis Kempe, Gent.," was rated, and continued to be a ratepayer until 1635, when the word "gone" appears against his name; his daughter, however, Elizabeth Shalcrosse, lived subsequently in the parish, but was buried at Digswell, Herts, in 1667, aged seventy-two. A monument in the church there states that she was the mother of thirteen sons and two daughters! The arms of Shalcrosse impaling Kempe appear on the monument.

The Court Rolls of Fulham were kept for some years prior to 1624 by Sir Nicholas Kempe, Knight, as Steward of the Manor, his arms were the same as those of Francis Kempe, but how these two were related we have not discovered, and we are inclined to think that the connection (if any) must have been quite remote; it is, however, singular that during the tenure of his office Sir Nicholas should have enrolled this Francis as a tenant.

The Court Rolls in 1626 record that Francis Kempe was appointed one of the trustees for the "Poor's Land" at Parr Bridge, and that in 1631 the same Francis was a "defaulter" and consequently was fined 12d. In 1615 Francis Kempe, of Fulham, Esq., became tenant of five acres called "Hale," abutting on Danes Lane (now Lily Road), but he resided in Bear Street (now Fulham High Street), retaining his London residence.

His third son, Henry, had two sons, Edward, born 1642, and William, born 1650; also a daughter, Ann, who married Anthony Southby. So far the pedigree of this family is recorded in the "Visitation of London," made by the Heralds in 1633, and as from this date Kempes appear in the adjoining hamlet of Parsons Green and the neighbouring Parish of Chelsea, it appears likely that William Kempe, who was living at Chelsea in 1680, was the William mentioned above. William Kempe, of Chelsea, had a house at Parsons Green, overlooking Eelbrooke, which he settled upon his son John in 1680, the father being recorded in the Manor Rolls as a brewer; he appears in 1686 as a *malster*, of Chelsea, with his wife, Dorothy, to have surrendered the same house at Parsons Green to William Kempe, his youngest son, and Elizabeth, his (the latter's) wife. The brewer was evidently a troublesome tenant, for he is charged at the Court Leat, and Court Baron for "suffering his swine to go at large in the streets," for which he was fined two-and-six, while on another occasion he was fined thirty-shillings for permitting overcrowding in two of his houses. William Kempe, the son, also described as a brewer, of Chelsea, had a marriage licence in 1686, his bride being Elizabeth Lumas, he being then twenty-five years of age and she twenty-three. (In the following year a Daniel Kemp, also a maltster of Chelsea, and aged twenty-four, had a licence to marry Catherine Fraser, of Westminster. This couple removed at once to Barking, and Daniel died there in 1691, his will being proved that year in the Archdeaconry Court of Essex. He bequeathed his property to his son William, or in the event of his death during infancy to Francis and Samuel, brothers of the testator, and his wife equally.

He mentions that £200 was due to him under a prenuptial settlement from his "father Kemp and father Fraser."*)

Both William and John Kemp, of Chelsea, as tradesmen of means and repute, were licensed to issue tokens, of which we have obtained specimens, they are respectively marked as follows :

"William Kempe of Parsons Green" (in four lines), and on the other side "Neare Fulham. His Halfe Penny (in four lines) ½d."

"John Kemp in Putney," The Cordwainers Arms, on the reverse "Batersey 1663 His Half Penny."

"John Kemp in," the Corwainers Arms, on the reverse "Putney or Batersey I. B. K. 1663 ½d."

From these it will be seen that the Kempes of Chelsea crossed the river and established their business on the other side, and it seems that William Kemp was in 1678 Churchwarden of

COPIES OF TOKENS ISSUED BY KEMPS

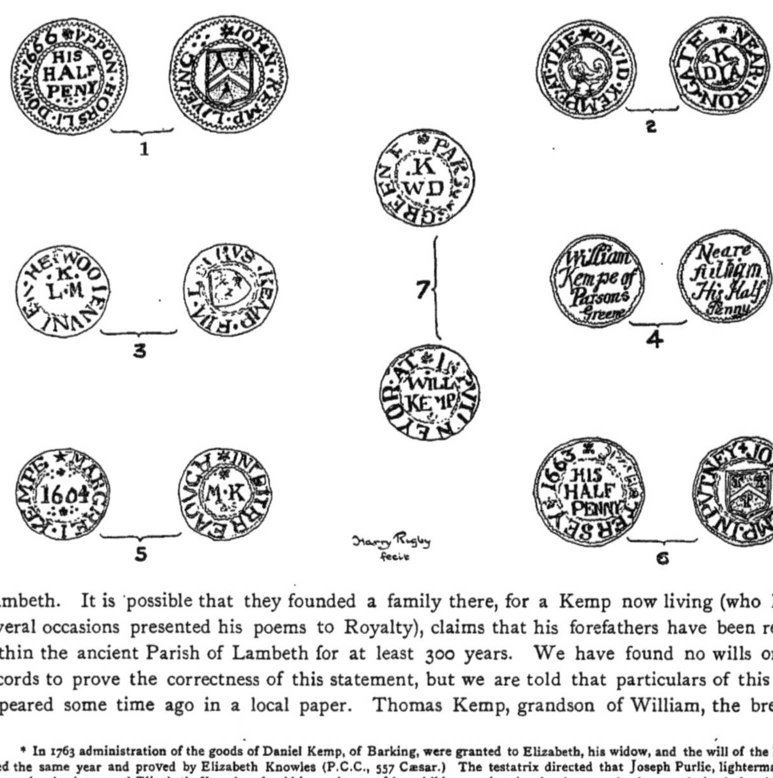

Lambeth. It is possible that they founded a family there, for a Kemp now living (who has on several occasions presented his poems to Royalty), claims that his forefathers have been resident within the ancient Parish of Lambeth for at least 300 years. We have found no wills or other records to prove the correctness of this statement, but we are told that particulars of this family appeared some time ago in a local paper. Thomas Kemp, grandson of William, the brewer of

* In 1763 administration of the goods of Daniel Kemp, of Barking, were granted to Elizabeth, his widow, and the will of the latter was dated the same year and proved by Elizabeth Knowles (P.C.C., 557 Cæsar.) The testatrix directed that Joseph Purlic, lighterman, should carry on her business, and Elizabeth Knowles should have charge of her children and maintain them on the income derived thereby. It is a singular thing that Daniel Kemp, of the Hendon family, died in 1763, we, however, believe this Daniel Kemp to be connected with the Kemps ot Lamarsh, Essex, several of whom were named Daniel.

Chelsea, seems to have died in 1726, for a will of Thomas Kemp, of Putney, dated 1725, was proved that year. He left his estate, which included houses and gardens in Putney and Wandsworth, to his wife, Francis Lucy, with the remainder to their children, John, Lucy and Elizabeth. He mentions his "sister Arnold," his brother-in-law, John Fletcher, and others. Francis Lucy, the widow, died the following year, and Catherine and Thomas Cotton were appointed curators of the children, who seem to have disappeared from the neighbourhood.

A John Kemp, connected with Lambeth, was a barrister, residing at St. Martin's-in-Fields, he was buried in the North Cloister of Westminster Abbey, 20th October, 1738, and his wife, Elizabeth, the daughter of John Staunton, Esq., of Longbridge (Warwick), was buried there 6th May, 1739; they left two children, namely, Boyle Staunton Kemp and Henrietta Kemp, who were placed under the guardianship of John, Earl of Orrery. The will of this Elizabeth Kemp is dated from St. Margaret's, Westminster, March 21, 1739, and was proved by the Earl the following year (P.C.C., 106 Henchman). Boyle Staunton Kemp was specially bequeathed his father's gold watch, snuff box, rings, and portrait, the residue of the estate being equally divided between the two children. Boyle Staunton, described as "late of St. Mary, Lambeth," died in August, 1786, his estate being granted that year to his widow, Mary.

The next Kemp of whom we hear connected with Lambeth is the Rev. Primate Kemp, who died 1789, his estate being administered by his widow, Keturah Kemp, who was buried there, a tomb to her memory recently existed in Lambeth Cemetery. The Rev. Primate Kemp was Rector of Shenley, Bucks.

At Chelsea there still exists "Kemp's Row"; this had, we believe, no connexion with the Kemps mentioned above, but was built about 1800 by one of the Kemps of Somersetshire, who was well known as the builder of churches in and around Bristol. (It has been thought that Nicholas Kempe, a porter of the Royal Mint who resided at Chelsea, was responsible for this Row, but this is a mistake.)

We may note here that the Church of St. Anne's, Soho, was built about 1678 on *Kemp's Field*, which was formerly within the Parish of St. Martin's-in-Fields; and that "Kempes Court," near Oxford Street and Broad Street, still exist; we cannot say for certain how these names originated, but close to the latter was a brewery, the proprietors of which were for several generations of a Kemp family, then living at Bloomsbury.

Leaving the western districts of London we must notice a family of Kempes, who for 200 years held a little property between Shoreditch and Bishopsgate. Several old maps of this district show "Kempe's Garden" at the corner of Cock Lane, near Shoreditch Church. The first mention of the parish as connected with Kempes occurs in 1665, when Judith Snow, of St. Leonard's, Shoreditch, widow, twenty-two, was licensed to marry Ralph Kemp, a widower, twenty-six, of St. James's, Clerkenwell; her estate—which, doubtless, included this Shoreditch land—was granted to her husband in 1681, she having died intestate. (*See* Ralph Kemp of Winchcomb.) We must not give in detail the generations of this family, some members of which were wealthy distillers and victuallers, while others were goldsmith's and watchmakers. One of their relatives was a soldier serving in the West Indies, connected with whom was Nathan Crossley, who lies buried in a church at Shoreditch. Thomas Kemp seems to have been the last to reside on the Cock Lane property, he was living there in 1807. Close by was Spittalfields, where at this date more than one Kemp carried on business; a little later a Kemp from Prittlewell wasengaged in the Spittalfields silk trade, but these last two Kemps were unconnected with the old local family.

In conclusion of these notes on the various groups of Kemp(e)s settled in Middlesex, we may mention three parishes, with which numerous Kempe families were at one time or another connected. The first is St. Dunstan's, Stepney, which before the seventeenth century was a residential suburb; the second was St. James's, Clerkenwell, which enjoyed for a time a good reputation as a residential quarter; the third is St. Dunstan's-in-the-West, Fleet Street, which was much patronised by most of the Kempes connected with the law and some others.

CHAPTER IX.

KEMPES OF HERTS, BERKS, BUCKS AND SURREY.

HERTFORDSHIRE.

THE number of Kempes we have found settled in Middlesex from early times would lead one to expect that many from this source might be found in the neighbouring counties of Herts, Berks, Bucks and Surrey, but a careful search in the various Probate Courts to which these were subject shows but few Kempes, mostly widely separated as to time and residence —the chief settlers of standing coming from a distance, viz., Kent and Norfolk.

Taking first our gleanings of Kempes in Hertfordshire, we find in the Archdeaconry Court of St. Albans one, John, in the callendar for the period extending from 1471 to 1536, his abode is not given. From about 1554 a Nicholas Kempe, Esq., was Steward of St. Albans, he being succeeded in this office by SIR NICHOLAS KEMP (Knight), who was also patron of Gilston. At the latter place Robert Kempe, "nigh a hundred years old," was buried in 1647. It was also in the latter parish that Sir John Gore lived, who married one of the Kentish Kempes. David Kempe was Archdeacon of St. Albans from 1560 till 1580, being also Vicar of Rickmansworth and Prebend of Harleston (which points to his being connected with the Kempes of Twickenham), he seems to have been also at Croydon, and is probably the testator of a will proved at Gloucestor 1581, which states that the David of that city was a priest living in the close of the Cathedral.

We have mentioned that a Francis Kempe from Gissing resided at Little Hadham about 1570, but he seems to have returned to his native county, and it was probably his younger son, Thomas, who was described in a London Poll as a "stranger" in Farringdon Ward in 1595, and belonging to the County "of Hertford, Gent." In 1593 George Kempe, of Northawe, was assessed at £30 for the defence of the Kingdom; he, we believe, was formerly a resident of Hampstead, and is perhaps the same as a Jesuit of his name who was with others charged with conspiracy in connexion with a London plot in 1626; this would account for no will being traced, as his property would probably be confiscated. In 1566 Stephen Kempe, son of William Kempe, of Broxbourne, was apprenticed to William Cooke, a citizen and stationer of London.

JOSEPH KEMPE, of Hitchin, Gent., married Anne Luke, and by his will, dated and proved in 1654 (P.C.C., 231 Alchin), he bequeathed to the town his "mansion house" called "Beggin" for the benefit of the poor of the parish, endowing it with lands and appointing as the first trustees of this charity the following: Ralph Skinner, of Hitchin, Gent., Robert Draper, Francis

Audley, James Turner, Jeremy Carter and Nathaniel Hobbs. The two first of these were certainly connected with Sir Nicholas and the Kempes of Winchcombe, while the will shows that the testator had "hereditaments" in the Parish of Godmanchester, where his "kinsman, John Sell," lived. He mentions Susan Tapenden, widow, his sister, Helen Kempe, and his "half sister, Mary, wife of . . . Farmer." Several other names appear, but we have failed to trace his exact connection with the Norfolk or Kentish Kempes, whose arms, impaling those of his wife, appeared over his tomb. This almshouse is still a benefit to the poor, a good account of it with illustrations has recently appeared.

In 1696 the will of an Edward Kemp, of Chipping, Barnet, victualler, was proved, he left sons named Edward and John, and daughters named Hannah, Elizabeth, Sarah, Susannah; his wife, Hannah, being executrix and residuary legatee. The next will of a Kemp in this county was proved in 1744, this being the testament of John Kempe, of Sawbridgeworth. The Probate Register for this period, however, does not exist, so we have no details. About this date a William Kempe was appointed Attorney-General of New York, we do not know that he was connected with this county, but on his decease his office was given to John Tabor Kemp, who we may presume was either his son or at least a relative. This John Tabor Kemp was Attorney-General of New York for many years, and on his return to England resided at St. Margaret's Herts, from which his will is dated in 1792 (P.C.C., 471 Fountain) stating his late official position, and that he had formerly resided at Marylebone and Jermyn Street, Westminster. To his son, Edward, then a minor, he bequeathed the ultimate residue of his estate, providing an annuity for his wife, Grace, and portions for his daughters, Maria, Elizabeth, Anne and Henrietta. The will directs his executors to endeavour to trace and recover some stocks (valued at £2,125), which had been settled on his wife after the death of her mother, Abigail Cox. Edward Kemp, the son, became a clergyman, and was the founder of a "Kempe Fund," now benefiting the Bristol Blind Asylum. He lived at Bath and aftewards at Bristol.

BERKSHIRE.

Berkshire had a family of Yeoman Kempes at least as early as the end of the fifteenth century; how they were connected with other families of the name we are unable to say; the earliest will we have traced as representing them was proved in the Archdeaconry of Berks in 1531. The testator was of Westbrook, in the Parish of Boxmoor, and mentions his wife, Margaret, and his son, William. The will of the latter, dated 1542, and proved in the same Court, speaks of his mother, Margaret, as still living, his wife Alys, and his daughters, Joan and Alys; he left his property at Boxworth to his son Robert. (Richard and John Kempe were witnesses.) The will of John Kempe, of Westbrooke, was proved in 1557, and describes the testator as a "husbandman," he bequeathed to his children, John and Ann, at the respective ages of twenty-one, his farming stock; his wife, Margaret Kempe, inheriting his residuary estate. Another will of a Kempe of Boxworth (or an Administration of his estate), was registered in 1558, after which the family seem to have removed to Welford and Kentbury. William Kempe's estate at Welford was administered in 1621; and that of Simon Kempe, of Kentbury, in 1630. The will of a Thomas Kempe, of Welford, was proved in 1672, and one of "Fetiplace Kemp*ber*," of Kentbury, in 1697. Richard Kemp, of Kentbury, must have died about 1719, for inventory of his personal effects with a bond for their administration are entered in the Archdeaconry Book of that year. Thomas Kemp, of Boxford, a Yeoman, dated his will 1728, but it was not proved until 1741 (Cons. Sarum); it mentions his wife, Joan Kemp, his daughter, Frances Castle, and his grandchildren, Mary Castle, Mary Sarah and Elizabeth Wells. An administration of the goods and effects of Simon Kemp, of Welford, was granted in 1749; this is the last Kemp will recorded in the Archdeaconry, and we have no evidence of the name occuring at Welford later. Not far, distant, however, is Enbourn, where Kemps, doubtless related to the above, lived from at least the middle of the sixteenth century until about 1700 or later, their wills having been proved in 1591, 1632, 1641, 1670, and 1690. Beside the above there were a few scattered Kemps at Reading, Farringdon, Newbury, Shrivenham, Hungerford and Abingdon.

BUCKINGHAMSHIRE.

From at least the thirteenth century Kemps have been found in Buckinghamshire, but it is singular that many of these early Kemps appeared to have resided in the county merely on account of their ecclesiastical appointments. Alan Kempe was concerned at "Little Willeston" between the years 1250 and 1272 with William De Bellocampo, who was one of the Earls of Warwick; a second instance of a Bellocampo and a Kempe occurs in Buckinghamshire at an early date, and, as we have had occasion to remark earlier, there appears just reason for supposing that some Kempes derived their name from that illustrious family. In 1311 Alan Kempe was made Rector of Great Loughton. In 1381 William Kempe and others were appointed by the King to arrest certain men charged with felony at Stoke, by Stony-Stratford, and charged to bring them to Windsor Gaol. In 1404 a grant was made of lands in the Parish of Chalfont-St-Giles, Bucks, to Henry Kempe; and in 1407 John Kempe, afterwards the Archbishop, was presented to the Rectory of Slapton.

In 1533 Queen Mary presented William Kempe to the Rectory of Cotteslow, and soon after this date David Kempe, the Archdeacon of St. Albans, held the Vicarage of Rickmansworth, close to the Middlesex border of this county.

We have mentioned under Hendon Kempes two Kempes of Burnham (in Cotteslow Hundred) who died respectively in 1544 and 1560, these evidently used a coat of arms, but their connexion is a little uncertain, and we do not find any trace of Kempes in this locality after the latter date.

About 1600 Robert Kempe, son of Edward Kempe, of the New Forest, and grandson of one of the Kempes of Ollantigh, settled at Chipping Wickham (or Wycombe), having married Dorothy Elliott, of Hampshire; he made his will in 1621 (P.C.C., 15 Savile), bequeathing an annuity of £100 to his wife, as well as a legacy of £200. He mentions also his daughters, Elizabeth and Dorothy, and his sons, Francis and Thomas. The will also mentions his brothers, Francis and Thomas; the last named had settled in Hampshire, while Francis subsequently removed from Basingstoke to Wycombe, where he died in 1649. His will was proved that year and describes him as "of Cliffords Inn, London, Gent.," and expresses his wish to be buried in the Church of St. Dunstan's-in-the-West. He left his house known by the sign of "George and the Three Cups," situated at Chipping "Wicombe," to his daughter Susannah for life, with reversion to the issue of Henry Kemp (the testator's son), or in default of such issue to his daughters, Ann and Susan. To his daughter, Elizabeth Catherine, he left £500; to his daughter Frances £400; to his son Leonard £500; to his son Bartholomew £400; and to his wife £500 and an annuity of £140. The will also mentions his "brother," Humphrey Clarke, of London, dyer. A blunder appears to have been made by the Heralds, as the issue mentioned in this will is attached to a pedigree of a branch of the *Norfolk* Kempes, whereas this man clearly belonged to the Kentish stock. The error seems to have arisen from the coincidence that a Francis Kempe from each family was a parishioner of St. Dunstan's-in-the-West (See *anti* Fulham Kempes). In 1651 administration of another Francis Kempe, Gent., of Wycombe, was granted to Anne

Kempe his relict, but it is not clear whether this was a son of Robert or Francis Kempe, as both had sons of the name. That this grant does not refer to the Francis who made the above is clear, for the former mentioned his wife, Helen, who was daughter of Gawton, of Southwark. "Francis Kempe, second son of Francis Kempe, Gent., of Wycomb," was born 1st November, 1644, and entered at the Merchant Taylor's School in 1657, this evidently was the grandson of Robert Kempe of Wycombe,

The principal monument in the Church of Chipping Wycombe is within the Communion rails, the inscription on a brass plate being as follows:

"Here lyeth the body of Robert Kempe, who departed this life the 20th November, A.D. 1621. / Wife, children, wealth, this world, and life forsaken. / In silent dust I sleep; whence once awaken, / My Saviour's might a glorious change will give, / So losing all I gayne, and dying live, / My fame I trust the world with, for 'tis true, / Posterity gives every man his due."

His daughter, Dorothy, married by licence, dated 29th November, 1632, John Gore, of Bassetsbury, a widower, then aged thirty-four, she being described as the "daughter of Robert Kempe, *late* of Wycombe, Esquire," and her age being stated to be twenty-four. Sir John Gore, Knight, was afterwards seated at Gilston, Herts, where Sir Nicholas Kempe, Knight, had previously been patron of the Church. The second daughter of Robert Kempe married William Adams, of London, citizen and draper; their son, Robert Adams, was knighted, and seems to have been married to another Elizabeth Kempe at West Quantoxhead, Somerset, on 23rd February, 1654, by John Tuberville, Esq., J.P., being the official appointed to celebrate marriages under the order of the Cromwellian Parliament. This Elizabeth Kempe was the daughter of John Kempe, of West Quantoxhead, who made his will in 1662 (and which is recorded at Wells), mentioning his grandchild, Robert Adams, son of Robert Adams of the same place. This testator also speaks of his daughter, Elizabeth Adams, Mary Bartlett, and his grandchildren, John and Alexander Kempe, of Coombe Florey, to whom was due legacies under the will of an Andrew Kemp.

The will of Anne Kempe, of Wycombe (widow of Francis, who died 1651), was proved in 1665 (P.C.C., 73 Hyde). It left to her son, Francis Kempe, certain bonds for £250 given by James Bigg, of "Chipping Wicomb," and legacies to her daughters, Dorothy and Ann, and to her son-in-law Marshall Bridges and his wife, Mary. The testatrix also states that her son, William Kempe, of London, Merchant Taylor, was indebted to her, upon bond, for some £800, which she desired should be paid to her two unmarried daughters. From the parish register of St. Dionis Barkchurch, London, we find that Marshall Bridges of that parish, linendraper, married Mary Kempe, of St. Michael's, Cornhill, on 28th April, 1659. In Wells Cathedral is a flagstone surmounted by their arms (argent, on a cross sable a leopard's face Or) of "Kempe Bridges, son of Marshall Bridges, Chancellor and Canon Residentiary of that Cathedral, by Frances Kempe, of Wycombe, Bucks." He was born in 1665, became a Fellow of All Soul's (by right of descent from the Founder's kin), and married Frances, daughter of Robert Creighton, only surviving son of Robert Creighton, Bishop of Bath and Wells. The stone also commemorates a second Kemp Bridges of Wells, who married Eleanor Dawson, and dying in 1792 left a son, Kemp Bridges, born 1749. The *Gentleman's Magazine* of the period stated that Kemp Bridges, formerly of Bedford Street, Covent Garden, died at his apartments in Manchester in January, 1792 in his seventy-seventh year, and that he was the youngest son of the Rev. Marshall Bridges, the Chancellor of Wells. The latter is mentioned in the will of Anne Kempe, relict of Robert Kempe, of Shenstone, Co. Hereford, as then (1677) of Tiberton Court, which was long the residence of the Bridges. Robert Kempe, of Shenstone, was son of Edward Kempe, and nephew to Robert Kempe, of Wycombe. William Kempe, the eldest son of Francis and Anne Kempe, of Wycombe, was living in 1665, as mentioned above, he then being a merchant of London. We have not traced his will, but that of a Mary Kemp, widow, of "Chipping Wycomb," dated in 1719 and proved the following year (Arch. Bucks) may be his wife's. It directs that she shall be buried in the middle of the chancel of the church at Chipping Wycomb, and bequeaths legacies to her grandchildren, William and Ann Taylor, and to Kemp Parker, son of her daughter Mary, wife of William Parker; others mentioned are Ann, wife of John Cock, of Wycomb, Ralph Whitnell (Tanner), and Ambrose Eldridge, Gent. From the fact that no sons are named we may surmise that this widow was the last of the Kempes of Wycombe, we having no evidence to the contrary. At Iver (Bucks) Philip Kemp died between 1736 and 1742, his will being proved in the later year (P.C.C., 191 Trenley). It bequeaths his property, as to one-fourth, to his nephew, William Kemp; as to another fourth part to Ann Mitchell, and the remaining two-fourths to his kinsman, Philip, the son of his nephew, William Kemp. Elizabeth and Thomas Martin were witnesses. We may remark that the family of Franklins who were akin to Hendon Kempes were connected with Iver, but we cannot say this testator was related to the Wicombe Kempes or those of Middlesex.

As to other Kempes of Buckinghamshire we can only allow space to give a mention of wills and administrations recorded, although we have many details concerning them. In the Archdeaconry Court of Bucks the following, in addition to those above mentioned, occur: Margery Kemp, of Great Missenden, 1680; William Kemp of same, 1680; another William Kemp of same in 1688; John Kemp, 1692; William Kemp, of Langley, 1693; William Kemp, of Akeley, 1694; Thomas Kemp of same, 1767. Three named Thomas Kemps respectively in 1760, 1776 and 1818 of Swanbourne. William Kemp, of Great Missenden, 1808, and William Kemp, of Great Horwood, 1826. In the Prerogative Court of London (except those mentioned above) we find only one administration of a Kemp of this county, *viz.*: The goods of Mathew Kemp(ff?) were granted to Susannah, his mother, in 1699, he having died a bachelor intestate. He is stated to have lived formerly in the parish of St. Andrews, Holborn.

The Rev. Alfred Arrow Kempe, Rector of Wexham, belongs to the third branch of the Cornish Kempe family. In the official return of the "Greater Landowners" in 1874, he is shown to have then held some twenty acres of land at Wexham.

The name is now represented in the County at Aylesbury and Great Horwood—William Kemp being a leaseholder at the former place and a Mrs. M. A. Kemp residing at the latter.

CHAPTER X.

SURREY KEMPES.

AMONG the earliest known Kempes of Surrey we have notes of the following individuals, but so little can be ascertained concerning them that we fear they were not a thriving family in this county. Ailwin Kempe held a small quantity of land in the Hundred of Blackheath (near Guildford) in 1205, and in 1272 Martin Kempe, of Guildford, had some interest in lands in Hampshire, which then were settled upon Netley Abbey; a copy of the deed with his signature is in the possession of James Kemp-Welch, Esq. Perhaps this Martin Kempe was identical with a Martin de Campo, who at this period held land in Norfolk. In 1235 one, Gilbert Kemp, resided at Chertsey, and in 1285 Hamo de Campo was residing at Rotherhithe.

At Kingston-on-Thames, certainly, a Kempe of standing held property, for a deed exists at the Record Office showing that William Kempe, of Westminster, bought of John atte Forde, of Yvere, lands at Kingston in 1436. This William Kempe, of Westminster, was, we suggest, related to the Archbishop, for while the latter was rising to fame William Kempe was appointed Keeper of the King's Wardrobe at Westminster, and subsequently he was known as the "King's Sergeant." Perhaps William Kempe, who paid the account of the fête called "Kynggam," celebrated in the twenty-first year of Henry VII. (1505), was a grandson or great-grandson of this individual. In 1535 a John Kempe, of Kingston-on-Thames, made his will, he being a tailor. He, too, we think, may be a connexion of both William of Westminster and the Kempes of Twickenham. The will of Alys Kempe, of Kingston, was proved in 1537, after which the Kempes seem to disappear from this spot, although it has been stated in the local papers that the Kempes of Teddington (adjoining) have continued from before the sixteenth century down to the present time. How true this is we have no means of proving, as both Subsidy Rolls and Probate Records give no evidence of their early establishment there, however from at least the early part of the nineteenth century Kempes were certainly numerous at Teddington, and one family resided there until the last decade. One representative of this family is an optician of London, Henry Cornelius Kemp, of Thavies Inn, and another is Henry Herbert Kemp, of West Kensington.

In the fifteenth century we find that Kempes of Kent were intimate with the Brownes of Betchworth, and in the following century an alliance united these two families. It is just possible that this marriage was the reason for Kempes establishing themselves in and around Betchworth a little later, but before we trace their advent we find that a branch of the Norfolk Kempes settled at Croydon, they being also subsequently connected, though but distantly, with the Brownes of Betchworth.

The founders of the Surrey branch of the Norfolk Kempes were Bartholomew Kempe and Barbara Sharpe, who were married at St. Martin's-in-the-Fields on 14th September, 1562. In 1565 this Bartholomew paid a fine for lands in which he held an interest at Hendon. We do not know when he died, but in the will of his widow she states that he was buried in the Savoy Chapel, and she desired that her body should rest beside his there. Her will (P.C.C., 41 Wood) was proved in 1611 and mentions her grandchild and son, both named Bartholomew Kempe, also Thomas Cotton, of Bartholomew's-the-Less, and her steward, Walter ffinch. Among the silver enumerated were spoons "*with falcons on their tops*," evidently in allusion to the Kempe crest. Also a "bell silver salt" with a cover and *her husband's coat of arms* engraved thereon. The will of Walter Finch, of Croydon, was proved in 1626 (P.C.C., 125 Hele), and mentions as chief legatees Bartholomew, William and Francis, the three sons of Bartholomew Kempe, "*late* of Croydon, Gentleman."

Turning to the early records of the Surrey Archdeaconry Court we find that the will of a John Kempe, of Godstone, was proved in 1530, that another probate of a John Kemp of that place is registered in 1549, that of a Joan Kemp, of Godstone, appears in 1550, and a mention of property at Godstone occurs in the will of a celebrated John Kempe, "Parson of Freshwater," dated 1579. John, of Freshwater, seems to have been connected in some way with the Kempes of Middlesex, but possibly only through his grandson's intermarriage with a Rippin, of Totteridge. The land mentioned was bequeathed by Parson Kemp to his sons, Tobias, Caleb and John, and the eldest surviving heir.

Ewell, Dorking, Banstead, Moulsey and Cobham have also had families of Kempes, but these appear to have been but birds of passage, and little worthy of note attaches to them. Guildford and Southwark in the eighteenth century had also many Kempes; one, William Kemp, of Guildford, a brewer, is said to be the ancestor of a Sussex Kemp family, if so he was also of Wapping and came from Kent (*vide* Sussex).

Returning to the Kempes of Croydon we may say that their pedigree—going back to the early ancestors of the Norfolk Kempe Baronets—is included in the printed "Visitation of Surrey." As, however, it gives but two generations actually resident in this county, and the last named thereon returned to Norfolk, we have not thought it worth printing here. Several entries concerning these Kempes are contained in the local Church Registers, and have also been printed in the County Histories. On this pedigree appears the name of a Nicholas Kempe, who is marked as having died a bachelor. Apart from that statement it is evident from the dates inferred that it was *not* this Nicholas Kempe who was co-founder with Archbishop Abbott of the Trinity Hospital, Guildford.

en, of Tregothnan (by Eliz. d. of Nicholas Lower, Harl. MSS. 1164, 70)

. of (? Tremayne) widow of Tozar.

d. of Robt. Smith, of Tregoneck, married at Blisland, 20 Sept. 1540.
rl. MSS. 1079, 196) Will proved 1586.

29 Sept. 1572. | Elizabeth Kempe. | Christopher Kempe.

Honour K. bap. 1573. | Jane K. bap. 1575. | John K. bap. 1578. | Robt. K. *vide* Chart, bap. 1579. | Digory K. bap. 1582. | Humphrey K. bap. 1586. | William K. bap. 1589.

of St. Ewe. | . . . d. of . . . Maunder, of Probus. = Nicholas Kempe, of Crugsillick, in Veryan.

m Kempe, 1681. | Richard Kempe, l. 1681. | d. . . of . . Foot, of Trecossick, in Veryan. = Nicholas Kempe, s. and heir. | Re Thomas Kempe, died at sea, s. of John, of Gerrans, at Col. 1682, aged 16. Beneficed in Somerset 1692/1708. Will 1689/96.

child.

John Kempe, s. & h. = Grace, d. of Sir Nich. Trevanion, Knt., Gov. of Pendennis. | Henry Kempe, ob. S.P. = Mary, d. of Sir. N. T. | Nicholas Kempe, of Plymouth, *vide* Chart II.

= Ann Kempe, sole heir of her brother. | James Kempe, d. unmarried. | Hannah Kempe, d. unmarried.

Ursula Kempe, = David Hewis, of Truro. | John Kempe, s. and h. of Crugsillick, ob. 22 Aug. 1814. S.P. = Letitia Maria, d. of John Coryton, of Crocaden. | Anne, d. of J. Coryton, of Crocaden. = Arthur Kempe, 3rd son. Admiral, born 1740, of Palone, Cornwall, d. æt 80.

M. A. Kempe, d. unmarried. | Sophia Kempe, d. unmarried. | Harriett Kempe, = Admiral Sir John Devonshire.

Eliz. Mary,‡ b. 16 Feb. 1786. = Wm. Courtenay, of Walreddon Devon, 4 June, 1807. | Anne Coryton Kempe, = §Mathew Garland Gregor, of Gerrans, 4 Aug. 1803.

Coryton Sylvanus Sampson Kempe, 61st Regiment. d. S.P. | Wm. Hussey Blomfield Kempe, = laie of Custom House, drowned in "Princess Alice." | Maria Kempe, Wriford, ob. S.P.

empe, use, m. = Maria, only d. of W. J. Harper, of Shoreham. | Wm. Sandford B. K. | Edw. Ar. K. | Gilbert Bunington K. | Arthur Kempe, of Exeter, M.D., M.R.C.P. =

as K. | Wm. Coryton K. | Arthur Marshall K. | Earnest Harper K. | Agnes May K. | Gladys Noel K.

CORNWALL, No. I.

(NOTE.—Sir John MacLean states that the ancestors of this Richard (or William) were long seated at Trevelver, Cornwall, whence they removed to Lavethan in 1475. Consequently this cannot be a great-grandson of any Kempe Knight, of Ollantigh.)

Richard Kempe, of Lavethan, Cornwall (called by some genealogists William Kempe, and claimed to be a grandson of Edward Kempe, Citizen and Merchant of London, and great-grandson of Sir William Kempe, Knight, of Ollantigh, Kent.=Grace, d. of John Boscowen, of Tregothnan (by Eliz. d. of Nicholas Lower, Harl. MSS. 1164, 70)

1st wife.
Alice, d. of Thomas St. Aubyn, of Clowance.=John Kempe, Lavethan.=Juliana, d. of (? Tremayne) widow of Tozar.

William Kempe, of Lavethnan.=Margaret, d. of Robt. Smith, of Tregoneck, married at Blisland, 20 Sept. 1540. (Harl. MSS. 1079, 196) Will proved 1586.

Catherine, d. of Lawrence Courtney, of Ethney, in St. Winnow, living 1542.=Thomas Kempe, of Lavethnan, (not mentioned by Margaret K. widow in 1586) | John Kempe.=Winifred, d. of Philip Penkivell, mar. 29 Sept. 1572. | Elizabeth Kempe. | Christopher Kempe.

2nd son. Richard Kempe, bap. at B. 28 Apr. 1566. | Humphrey Kempe, son and heir.=Jane, d. of Thos. Peyton, of Edmundsbury, Customer of Plymouth by Cicily Bouchier. | Dorothy Kempe, bap. at B. 11 Apr. 1568.=John Truebody, of Castle, in Laulivery. | Honour Kempe, bap. at B. 11 Nov. 1563. | Jane Kempe, bap. 30 Aug. 1572. | Nicholas Kempe, of Rosteage, which he purchased of Reg. Mohun 1619, in par. of St. Gerrans, Cornwall. 1647. ? Ad. to Joan K. widow.=Juliana, d. and heir of ... Budge, of Darley, Linkenhorn. | Honour K. bap. 1573. | Jane K. bap. 1575. | John K. bap. 1578. | Robt. K. *vide* Chart, bap. 1579. | Digory K. bap. 1582. | Humphrey K. bap. 1586. | William K. bap. 1589.

Humphrey Kempe, a sailor, bur. at B. 1682. S.P. Will 1686, P.C.C. 61, Pile | Cecilia Kempe, bap. 13 Mar. 1603, bur. at B. 3 Apr. 1642. | J... Kempe, a dau. | William Kempe, s. and heir, ob. 1629 I.P.M.=Florence. | ...gan Kempe, 3 May, 1602, ... Mar. 1603. | Grace Kempe, bap. 13 Nov. 1608. | Ann, d. of Wm. Williams, of Treworagy, in Probus.=John Kempe, s. and heir, of Roseague, St. Gerrans.=2nd wife. ... widow of ... Hix, of St. Ewe. 3rd wife. =... d. of ... Leonard. | ... d. of ... Maunder, of Probus.=Nicholas Kempe, of Crugsillick, in Veryan.

Phillipa, d. of ...=William Kempe, sold Lavet... bap. 23 Ap... | ...4 and settled at Veryan;

Richard Kempe, of Tragony, b. 1683, d. at Bath 1736. Will proved.=Anne, d. of James Day, of Little Colan. Ad. 1738. | P... | ...mpe=Katherine Penwarne. No. 1717 Penryn Reg. | Mary, eldest d. of Arthur Spry, of Place, by Mary, d. of Richd. Gayer.=Nicholas Kempe, of Rosteague, St. Gerrans. l. 1681. | Henry Kempe, of Middle Temple. Will 1680, b. 1654. at Ex. Col. Ox. 1672=Ann, d. of Francis Bonny, Goldsmith, mar. by l. 27 Feb. 1677-8. | William Kempe, l. 1681. | Richard Kempe, l. 1681. | d... of .. Foot, of Trecossick, in Veryan.=Nicholas Kempe, s. and heir. | Re Thomas Kempe, died at sea, s. of John, of Gerrans, at Col. 1682, aged 16. Beneficed in Somerset 1692/1708. Will 1689/96.

James Kempe, Sheriff 1711-12. | Phillip Kempe. | Francis K. ob. an infant 1680, only child.

James Kempe, s. & h. l. 1736, d. unmarried, Will dated 1738, proved at Bodmin. | William Kempe, d. unmarried, l. 1736. | Elizabeth Kempe, co-h. to her bro., l. 1736. =Joseph Taunton, 1738, ob. 1793. | Ann Kempe, l. 1736. =John Thompson, of Penryn. | Ursula Ke... l. 173... =Samuel ... wi... of Penryn. | Francis Kempe, l. 1736. | Arthur Kempe, of R., s. & h.=Honour, d. of Chris. Huddey, of Trethevan. | Lucy Kempe, Edward John. | Thomazine Kempe. | John Kempe, s. & h.=Grace, d. of Sir Nich. Trevanion, Knt., Gov. of Pendennis. | Henry Kempe, ob. S.P.=Mary, d. of Sir. N. T. | Nicholas Kempe, of Plymouth, *vide* Chart II.

Dorothy, d. of James Borlase, of Treludry=NICHOLAS KEMPE, of Rosteague, s. & heir, b. 1699, SHERIFF OF CORNWALL 1761. | Amy, d. of Sir Nic. Trev... and widow of Capt. ... on | 3rd son. Arthur Kempe, Governor of St. Mawes Castle. 1726, xxi. 27 (Honor K,=Wm. Wills) | 2nd son. Charles Kempe, of Creigsillick, in right of his wife.=Ann Kempe, sole heir of her brother. | James Kempe, d. unmarried. | Hannah Kempe, d. unmarried.

Jane Geak, h. of Bonithons, mar. lic. Court of Exeter, 16 June, 1833.=Samuel Kempe, of Carlclew, born 1728. | Dorothy Kempe,=Rev. Bennet, of Mary Tavy, Devon. | Mary Ke... born 17.. | Ursula Kempe, died unmarried. | Catherine, d. of ... Hockin, of St. Judy.=2nd son. Charles Kempe, Rector of St. Mabyn. | 4th son. James Kempe, of Truro, Surgeon.=Mary, d. of Christopher Warnell, of Truro, | Ursula Kempe,=David Hewis, of Truro. | John Kempe, s. and h. of Crugsillick, ob. 22 Aug. 1814. S.P.=Letitia Maria, d. of John Coryton, of Crocaden. | Anne, d. of J. Coryton, of Crocaden.=3rd son. Arthur Kempe, Admiral, born 1740, of Palone, Cornwall, d. æt 80.

Samuel Kempe, d. on a voyage of discovery with Capt. Cook, 1747. | Capt. Nicholas Kempe, R.N., ob. 1829, æt 72, buried at Bridgend, (unmarried) 25/4/1829. | Arthur Kempe, died young, unmarried. | John Kempe, Merchant, of New York, d. S.P.=Eliz. Dunbar. | ...IAM KEMPE, ... on & Glamorgan.=Sarah, d. of Rev. John Lyne. A *see* Chart III. | Jane Kempe, Larbeck. | Honour Kempe, =John Stevens, Esq., of Surrey. | Rev. John Kempe, Vicar of Fowery, ob. 1862.=Frances, d. of Rev. Cory, of Costelort, died at Fowery, 22 May, 1848, æt 70 M.I. | M. A. Kempe, d. unmarried. | Sophia Kempe, d. unmarried. | Harriett Kempe,=Admiral Sir John Devonshire.

Charles Travenion Kempe, s. & h. Vic. of Breage, Rec. of St. Mich. Carhayes, ob. 1851, æt 74.=Eliz. d. and co-heir of Rev. Edward Marshall, Vic. of Breage. | Col. Jo... Arthur Kempe, of E... India Co. ob. 18... ...Oct. 1830.=Eliz. d. of John Penhallow, Peter Crugnurrion, in Philleigh. | ... d. of Jenkin, of Truro.=William Peter Kempe, J.P. § of Malabar and Leman Ho, Truro, b. 1786. Capt. E. I. Co., d. 1866, H.E.I.C.S.= Eliz. Mary,† b. 16 Feb. 1786. =Wm. Courtenay, of Walreddon Devon, 4 June, 1807. | Anne Coryton Kempe,=§Mathew Garland Gregor, of Gerrans, 4 Aug. 1803.

Augustas, d. of Capt. W. P. Daykin, of Hartley Ho, co. Devon, d. 1862. S.P.=Rev. Edward Marshall Kempe, Vicar of Linkinhorne. | Wm. Coryton K... | ...nny Helen Dumpster Douglas, d. of Gilbert Burrington, of Chudleigh, Devon. | John Kempe, Fel. of Exeter Col. Oxford, bapt. 13 July. 1827. | Coryton Sylvanus Sampson Kempe, 61st Regiment. d. S.P. | Wm. Hussey Blomfield Kempe, late of Custom House, drowned in "Princess Alice."= | Maria Kempe, Wriford, ob. S.P.

Charles K. b. 1799. d. unmar. | John Kempe, Com. R.N. b. 1804.=Susan, d. of John Rundle, of Alan Prym, Col. of Customs at Fowey. | Frances K. b. 1806. | George Henry Kempe, Rector of Bicton, b. 1809.=Sophia, d. of Rev. ... Hole, Rec. of Wooli... worthy, co. Devo... | ...aria Letitia K. d. unmarried. | Rev. James Cory Kempe, born 1810, mar. 1843, Rec. of Huish & Merton, co. Devon.=Laura, survg. d. of Rear-Admiral Pulling. | Arthur Kempe, of Exeter, Surg. born 1802, d. unmarried. | Chas. Marshall Kempe, of Chantry House, New Shoreham.=Maria, only d. of W. J. Harper, of Shoreham. | Wm. Sandford B. K. | Edw. Ar. K. | Gilbert Bunington K. | Arthur Kempe, of Exeter, M.D., M.R.C.P. =

Charles Patrick K. of London, Surgeon. =Eleanor M. Taylor. | Maria Letitia K. born 1833. =Stephen Roberts, of Crego, in Ruan, Lanihorne. | Catharine Eliz. K. b. 1836, m. 1863, =John Wm. Harvey, Com. R.N. | Louisa K. born 19 May, 1846, died 10 Jan. 1855. | Rev. George Henry K. Vicar of Croydon, born 4 July, 1844. | John Arthur K., F.R.C.S. of Birmingham, born 26 Oct. 1851. | Frances Cath. Mary K.

John Henry Kempe, born 1844. | James Arthur K. born 1848. | Emily Mary K. | Henrietta Frances K. | Fanny K. | Mary K. | Edith K. | Alice Maria K. | Laura K. | Chas. William K. died infants. | Chas. Gilbert B. K. M.D., M.R.C.S., B.S., Surgeon Salisbury Hospital, | Edith Douglas K. | Wm. Coryton K. | Arthur Marshall K. | Earnest Harper K. | Agnes May K. | Gladys Noel K.

Section IV.

The Kemp and Kempe families of Cornwall, Sussex and the South of England.

THE

Kempes of Cornwall, Sussex and the South of England.

CHAPTER I.

TRADITIONS AND EARLY KEMPES AND KYMPES.

IT may be well to state the *traditions* of the Cornish family before entering upon the *facts*, as while the latter do not entirely support the former, the result of our researches proves that these Kempes have been longer established in their native country than their pedigree and traditions claim. Briefly, we may say that the several pedigrees which have been lent to us by recognised chiefs of the various branches show that their first claimed Kempe ancestor of Cornwall was a grandson of one Edward Kempe, a citizen and merchant of London, the latter, being stated by Burke and others, to be third son of Thomas Kempe, Knight, of Ollantigh, while Burke says that Richard Kempe was living at Lavethan in 1500. The second tradition rests largely on this first one, as members of the family have explained that the Kempes of Cornwall used the three sheaves on a red ground as their arms, *without* the engrailed border used by the Kentish Kempes, as the border was used to indicate that the first known user of it (Archbishop Kempe) was a younger son, whereas they claim that the elder branch, which they represent, did not use the border until many years after the Archbishop had died, the subsequent use of his addition to the shield being the outcome of a natural pride, and the desire to identify themselves more plainly with him and his nephew, who it is known also used the border.

The traditional absence of the "bordure engrailed" is borne out by many deeds relating to Cornwall, which bear as the seal of Cornish Kempes three garbs without any bordure, and by these arms being emblazoned on the chief family tomb of the Kempes of Lavethan, in Blisland Church, dated 1624.

We have pointed out, both in the Kentish and Norfolk sections, that Edmund Kempe, the well known citizen and merchant of London, was not of the Ollantigh family, but claimed himself to be "heire elect" to Robert Kempe, of Gissing and Weston, and using the latter's arms (with the bordure) and quarterings—which are quite different from the quarterings used by Kentish Kempes. He is further stated in the "Visitation of Middlesex" to have been a native of Suffolk, and his will, still extant, proved in 1542 (P.C.C., 8 Spert) fully confirms his relationship to the Norfolk and Suffolk families, and shows that his two sons, James and Humphrey, were not at that date even married, hence neither could have been, as the Cornish Kempes would have us believe, founder of the Cornish family. Again, as both must have used the bordure engrailed, they are not likely to have handed down the coat without it. It is useless therefore for the Kempes of Cornwall to try to attach themselves to the Kentish Kempes *through Edmund Kempe or his sons*, but this does not necessarily prove that they did not spring from the same stock as those of Ollantigh. Although no coat without the bordure engrailed is recorded to have been used by the earliest Kempes of Wye, the explanation of the border being used to indicate a junior line is feasible if it were claimed to have been so used before the fifteenth century. By the usage, however, of the sixteenth century the younger branch would be indicated by cadency or "house-marks," which were, and are still, *exact* in their significance. In order therefore to explain the use of the recognised coat of the Cornish Kempes we must suppose that their branch was severed from the Kentish or Suffolk family not later than about 1400, and to presume that before that date their family had been using arms. No record of the Heralds attributes arms to Campes, Kempes, or Kympes so early as this, and strange to say the arms so long proved to have been used by Cornish Kempes have *never* yet been authorized by the Heralds' College, although Burke gives their pedigree and remarks on their arms in his History of the Commoners. Sir John MacLean, who gave some account of the Kempes of Blisland in his history of that parish and Trigg Minor, wrote to James Fletcher Kempe, of Liverpool (who claimed to be the head of the family), that it was very desirable that the pedigree he held should be recorded officially. Seemingly the expense which this would entail has hitherto barred its accomplishment. We know of some 200 representatives living, and suggest that one of them should take the initiative and get the others to subscribe to a general fund to effect this undertaking, so that the pedigree, if not the right to ancient arms, may be *authenticated*..

We will now notice as briefly as possible the earliest recorded existence of the name of Kempe in Cornwall, Devonshire, Somerset and districts, taking into account possible variants of the name. Cornwall being in touch with Ireland some Kempes of the latter country are likely to have been akin to the Cornish Kempes.

The very earliest mention of a Kempe in the Calendars of the Prerogative Court of Canterbury (the jurisdiction of which covered the whole of the south of England) is in 1418, when John Kempe, a "clerk" (*i.e.*, priest), of Budleigh, Devon, is recorded to have left a will. It is dated 1416, is written in Latin, and describes the testator as of "Budlegh," in the Diocese of Exeter, but gives no clue as to his family connexions. In the same Probate Court, in 1425, the will of Nicholas Kempe, of Mark, Somerset, was proved; this also is in Latin, and except for wills relating to Kempes of Middlesex, is the second earliest now recorded south of Ipswich, thus giving some ground for the claim that as regards property and social standing the Kempes of south-west England took the lead. Curiously this testator also was a priest, being chaplain of Mark; it is possible that he was from Kent, and owed his presentation to the influence of Archbishop Kempe, who by this time was in power. This seems the more probable, as the name of Nicholas Kempe is recorded on the Kentish Subsidy Rolls in 1418 and subsequently disappears. The testator leaves legacies to his brother John Kemp, Robert, the son of his "cousin," John Thomas, John Pogge, William Baggerly, Lord Sutton (*sic*) of Bristol, and several others, and the will was proved by John Lynde, of Lyndefield, apparently on behalf of the executors, John Thomas and the testator's brother, John Kemp, who were residuary legatees.

It is worth mention, that throughout this will the final e is omitted, and, indeed, although for the past two centuries the Cornish Kempes have most carefully maintained the use of the fifth letter, the early wills and other local records show that KEMPE was not the most common spelling adopted by their ancestors, Kympe being certainly more used down to say 1600. Indeed, Kympe, or Kimpe, is found as a frequent variant throughout the south-west of England as the following facts testify. At Wells, Somerset, are copies of the following wills: John Kympe, Portishead, 1597; Alice Kemp, Portishead, 1615; John Kempe, Portishead, 1615, and Robert Kempe, Backwell, 1623. These documents, which have been searched, clearly show that these spellings represented the same family, the first also being spelled Kimpe. These Kempe and Kympes appear from the wills to be closely related to those in Gloucestershire, from the borders of which they were but a few miles distant. At Gloucester we find that while testators spell their names Kempe in 1558 and 1560, Kympe, Kimpe and Keempe occur in 1558, 1566, 1592 and 1619. Some of these testators indicate that they are foreign weavers, but Robert Kempe, of Winchcombe (1560), we have reason to believe, had a right to arms (Gules three garbs or within a bordure engrailed of the last) being near kin to Sir Nicholas Kempe, of Middlesex. The Calendars of Wills at Bodmin have not been searched by the present compilers, as Sir John MacLean having evidently examined these when writing his Cornish parochial histories, the chief representatives now living have thought our making the search quite unnecessary. The Wills of Devonshire, recorded at Exeter, do not include any Kympes, but are noticeable as spelling the name with only two exceptions without the final e, there being ten ***Kemps*** between 1592 and 1742, the exceptions being Toby Kemp*e*, of Stoke Damerel, 1644, and John Kemp*e*, of Mawnan, 1720. The last, certainly, was of Cornish descent, but those of Stoke Damerel had been settled there for many generations and were akin to those of Rame, one of whom is called so late as 1613 "Robert Campion, Rector of Rame."

The historical family of Kempe, of Liskeard, is certainly descended from John ***Kympe***, who is recorded in the Manorial Rolls of that place in 1502. Nor was this spelling merely a fault of the scribe, for in 1540 William "Kympe" paid XII pence at the Homage to the Lord the King, from whom he held some land at Liskeard. In the following year with his co-tenants, John Harell and John Kyng, he paid another XII pence, the name again being spelled "Kympe." In 1618 Thomas Kympe was rated for an acre of timber of forty years growth, and a tenement in Bodnell South; the first occurrence of the spelling Kempe being towards the close of Queen Elizabeth's reign, when "H. Kempe," otherwise called Humphrey Kemp, appears as a suitor for lands held of the Queen at Blisland.

The Manor of Liskeard was the subject of an inquiry in 1624, when it was found to be a portion of the Duchy of Cornwall, and the evidences then collected are preserved at the British Museum (Ad. MSS. 24, 748 and 24, 750); they show that Blisland in the fourteenth century was the property of Bello Campo, Earls of Warwick, with whom (as we have before stated) we have reason to suspect many "Kempes" were akin, if not actually descendants of that noble family.

It would, at least, be reasonable to suppose that descendants of a previous proprietor would hold an interest in part of his estate, hence we suggest that this is quite as likely an origin of the Cornish Kempes as the traditional one. Touching on this interchange of Kempe and Campo we may refer to the Kentish Section, Chapter II., where the coincidence of an Arnulphus Kempe and Campo Arnulphi are mentioned as existing contemporaneously. Some of the earliest Kympes, of Cornwall, do not appear to have been large landholders, but the earliest marriages on the pedigree certainly point to the Kempes of Lavethan being persons of some social standing, while Sir John MacLean tells us that before 1475 they were "seated" at Trevelvar, moving their principal residence to Lavethan in Blisland in that year! This authority further states that in the reign of Edward I. John Kempe, junior, sued John Hyke ("Bocher") in a plea of trespass at Trevelver. Accepting this statement—the original authority of which we are not told—it rather favours our belief that the Bello Campo family may have been progenitors of these Cornish Kempes. In 1572 John Kempe, second son of Thomas Kympe or Kempe, of Lavethan, was seated at Trevelver, showing that for 100 years at least those of Lavethan held their property at Trevelver.

John Kemp held lands at Miniver valued at 53*s.* 3*d.* per annum in 1521-3, and these descended to Margaret Kemp, who was assessed there in 1571. In the former year an Arthurus

Kemys was a tenant at St. Miniver, which suggests another origin, for Camois, otherwise Kemys, was a family of great power in South Wales, and certainly had some representatives in Cornwall; yet we know of instances in which Kemys and Kempes were interchanged, and we think that this Arthur Kemyes was most likely a Kympe, otherwise Kempe. At Tintagel in 1546 there was at least one "K*i*mpe"; and a Walter K*y*mpe, of Swilly, living in 1563, son of Argent was the founder of a family of Kempes who were long resident in and around Plymouth. In the chapter on the origin of the name, it is shown that Kemp and Kemys probably have the same meaning, the latter being a translation of the former. All the landholders in Cornwall mentioned in "Domesday" have Saxon names. It is therefore in entire accord with reason to suppose Kemys to be the Cornish equivalent of Kemp.

Concerned with this Walter Kympe were several persons named Rede, his wife being Rose Rede, on whom lands in Plymouth and Stoke Damerel were settled. The name of Rede is mentioned in the will of Thomas Kempe, Bishop of London, the individual being "a boy of my (*i.e.*, the Bishop's) chapel"; possibly the Redes of Devon and Cornwall were earlier related to the Kentish Kempes, but of this we have no actual evidence. Seemingly the Stoke Damerel Kempes were people of some property, and it is possible that the arms ascribed in British Armourals to Kempes of Devon, viz., Gules a bend vair between three escallops argent, pertained to them.

Before closing this chapter we may note a connexion of distant Kempes with the south-west of England. The Kempes of Norfolk claim descent from one, "daughter of Barnstaple," which name is suggested to be associated at a remote date with this part. The members of the same family early in the sixteenth century intermarried with *Masters*, of Somerset, and *Cockerhams*, of Devon. The Essex Kempes had at the end of the sixteenth century relatives in this part in consequence of intermarriage with an "Elenor Drew, of Devonshire," and the Kentish Kempes were represented in Cornwall about 1600, as Elizabeth, daughter of Sir Thomas Shirley, by a daughter of Sir Thomas Kempe, of Ollantigh, married Edward Onslow, of St. Tudy.

CHAPTER II.

LAVETHAN AND BRANCHES.

SIR JOHN MACLEAN in his "History of Blisland" tells us, that the Manor of Barlandew, in the Parish of Blisland, was so called from "lande"—God's inclosure—and "bar"—over—thus signifying the summit above God's enclosure. This derivation well accords with the site on which the Kempes built their house "Le bidhen," (corrupted to Lavethan, originally meaning simply "the meadow,") which is beautifully placed about half a mile from the church. It was hither that they removed from Trevelver in 1475. For the next 200 years they were among the chief landowners in Blisland, being Lords of the Manor of Barlandew, which in 1654 consisted of the following: Twelve messuages, six cottages, two water corn mills, two tucking mills, sixteen gardens, sixteen orchards, 400 acres of land, fifty acres of wood, fifty acres of moor, 300 acres of furze and heath and 18*s*. rent in Barlandew, Lavethan, Hevycroft, *Kemyes*.

house, Atwell Brownwelly, Nailboro, Whitstile (otherwise Puddietown), Scribbell Stokesley, and appurtenances in St. Blisland and St. Breward, all of which were then sold by William Kempe, Esquire, to Christopher Walker.

The pedigree of the family as given in the above "History of Blisland" commences with a William Kempe, of Lavethan, who is said to have married Grace, daughter of John Boscawen, of Tregothnan, by Elizabeth, daughter of Nicholas Lower. This marriage is supported by a reference to Harleian MSS. 1164, fo. 70, and except for the fact that this Kempe is called Richard by Sir Edmund Burke, we have no reason to question its correctness. Whether Richard or William does not matter, but it must be admitted that the ancestors of this man were Kempes *long settled at Blisland and that he was not* (as erroneously claimed by modern genealogists of the family) grandson of Edmund Kempe, of London. Alfred John Kempe, himself a descendant of these Lavethan Kempes, is mainly responsible for this mistake. Being an antiquary of considerable repute the present compilers regret the necessity of contradicting him, but in face of considerable evidence it is important that members of the family should correct their pedigrees in this particular.

The second generation shown on the Blisland pedigree is a John Kempe, of Lavethan, who is stated to have married, first, Alice, daughter of Thomas St. Aubin, of Clowance, by whom he had a son, William Kempe, his successor. John married for his second wife (so the pedigree asserts) Juliana, the widow of Toser, but by her no issue is recorded, although it is likely that she was the mother of several children. We are disposed to think that this widow was the daughter of Tremayne, for Margaret Kempe, widow of William Kempe (the next generation), who is said to have been a daughter of Robert Smith, of Tregoneck, had as witnesses to her will dated 1586 Richard, John and Jane Tremayne, and mentions her brother, Robert Smith, her sons, John and Christopher Kempe, her daughter Elizabeth, and Winifred, wife of her son, John Kempe. Although dated at Clerkenwell, London, her will clearly identifies her with Cornwall apart from these names, as she speaks of her personal property at Trevelver, and leaves 40*s*. to the poor of St. Miniver. This will (P.C.C., 43 Windsor) is further of considerable importance as showing another slight error in the pedigree, for Winifred, wife of John Kempe, is undoubtedly the same as Winifred Penkiville, daughter of Philip Penkiville, of Ross Crowe, who married John, second son of Thomas Kempe, of Lavethan, seated at Trevelver. Presumably Trevelver reverted to him on his mother's death under a provision of his father's will.

John Kempe and Winifred Penkiville were the ancestors of all the branches known to be represented at the present time, who on the strength of the pedigree claim Royal descent from Catherine Courtney, who is stated to have married the son of this Margaret and William Kempe of Lavethan. The name of the son is given as Thomas Kempe, who was buried at Blisland on 23rd March, 1571. If this is correct it follows that John Kempe was not of the Courtney blood, being merely brother-in-law to Catherine Courtney, hence his descendants have no right to the Royal lineage which the pedigree claims through this intermarriage. The Courtney-Kempe alliance, however, undoubtedly left issue, which for a time remained at Blisland, but at length seem to have become involved in costly litigation which so impoverished them that the head of the family had to part with the Lavethan property as above stated in 1654. He then settled at Veryan, where his second son, Philip, was married in 1690, his wife being Katherine Penwarne. RICHARD KEMPE, the elder brother of the last named Philip, having settled at Tregony and married Ann, daughter of James Day, of Little Colan, by whom he had two sons, who died unmarried, and two daughters, the eldest of whom, Elizabeth, marrying Joseph Taunton, and Ursula Kempe, the younger, marrying Samuel Hawis, of Penryn. Elizabeth became heir to her brothers and thus conveyed the estates to her husband in 1738. This seems to have been the last of the senior Kempe line; meanwhile the second branch, starting with John and Winifred Kempe, had been gaining in property and in position, and established themselves at Rosteage as we shall presently see.

We must, however, first note a few facts concerning the decadence of the Kempes of Lavethan, and the records of them at Blisland Church.

We greatly regret that our efforts to obtain an illustration of their important tomb have failed, but we still hope to secure a drawing or photograph from which copies could be made for the numerous Kempes who now represent the family. Sculptured in low relief on an altar tomb are three figures, on the dexter side male and on the sinister female. The first two males appear as civilians, and are marked respectively H. K. and W. K. The third is girt with a sword and is marked H. K. The three females are respectively marked I. K., G. K., and C. K. Behind the first is a skull, and above is an escutcheon of arms—Gules, three garbs or., impaling Or. a cross engrailed sable, representing the Kempe intermarriage with Peyton. The inscription on the tomb is as follows:

"Here lyeth the bodye of Humphrey, sonne and Heyre to Thomas Kempe of Lavethan, Esquire, who departed this life the tenth daye of November Anno Domini 1624 and married Jane, the daughter of Thomas Peytonne, Esqvire, Customer of Plymouth and Cornwall. No sweeter comfort dothe betide mankinde Then to depart this life with a quiet minde, Firme confidence, pure conscience unmolested By Gviltiness of sinne or vice detested; Such hap I hope, such Grace had I the rather Because I dyde a husband and a father. Dyde, no vent hence, for they that leave posterite Live in their offspringes, dye not properly."

The figure of the son girt with a sword represents, undoubtedly, Humphrey Kempe, whose will was proved in 1630 (P.C., 61 Pile). It commences with: "*I Humphrey Kempe intending God Willing some long Voyage wherefore have thought it expedient to leave for lynds* (*? lines*) *to be executed by my mother Mrs. Jane Kempe and Cecilie my sister*," and proceeds to bequeath £50 in the hands of his brother to the sister Cecilie, and £20 to his sister Grace, £2 each to his brother's "four children," and the residue of his effects to his mother, with whom, he adds, he was then living. He was probably a sailor. His mother was the daughter of Thomas Peyton, the latter being son of Christopher Peyton, of Bury St. Edmunds. Frances, sister to Thomas Peyton, married John Hart, of Highgate, Middlesex, and left a son, Sir Eustace Harte, whose half brother, Henry Harte, is frequently mentioned as a relative connected with the sale of Lavethan.

It seems that in February, 1599, two years before the sale of the Manor of Blisland to the Stanhopes, the Queen granted to Humphrey Kempe and Jane, his wife, with John their son, a farmhouse, seven acres and outmoors at a rental of 30*s.* per annum. In 1602 the outmoors were released by the Kempes to the Stanhopes, and by deed dated 11th December the same year the Stanhopes sold to William Kempe, son and heir apparent of Humphrey, the reversionary interests of the above farmer's house and other buildings and orchards. There was about this time litigation as to the ownership of a mill and other property which had been held by the Kempes, but it seems that their title was not good, and they consequently had to relinquish it. Presumably as a result of this loss they had to mortgage other property, and being still in difficulties Humphrey and Jane, and William, their son, sold their interest at Lavethan to Sir Eustace and Henry Harte by deed, dated 6th November, 1624.

(Sir Eustace Harte, Knight, of Highgate, was buried at St. Paul's Wharf, London, in which parish Kempes appeared about the time of this breaking up of the Lavethan estate. One, William Kempe, of St. Peter's, Paul's Wharf, a clothworker, had married Elizabeth Gardiner, widow, there in 1579-80, and at that church in 1608 Elizabeth Kempe, late of Kingston, married John Bodleigh. We, however, cannot say for certain if these belonged to the Cornish family which Eustace Harte befriended.)

In the church at Blisland there are, or were recently, two more epitaphs to the local Kempes. They are given in the "History of Blisland" as follows:

"Here lyeth the Body of John Kempe, who lived in Alternum and was born in Tresineck, being aged 75 years, Anno Domini 1728. Heares peace and rest within my Grave / Which in my life / Could never have."

"Here lyeth Mary the wife of John Kempe who was born in Stoke Klemsland, whose name of Smeath, being aged 84 years. / The heart knoweth his own bitterness and a stranger does not inter meddle with his joy, For in the presents of God is fulness of Joy, / At his right hand are pleasures for ever more."

A note states that according to the register Mary Kempe was buried on 28th October, but the year is not stated. We can only wonder what was the cause of this couple's unhappiness. Kempes are shown to have been frequently, if not constantly, at Alternon between 1605 until the above date, the will of a miller of this place named John Kempe was proved at Bodmin in April, 1667, and an Edward Kempe, also a miller there in 1679.

The Registers of Blisland contain numerous Kempe items from their commencement down to 1742, when Edward Kempe, aged about twenty-three, was buried there; but it seems impossible to include all the items in one pedigree, and there is little doubt that strangers of the name frequently came to the parish from other Kempe centres. Anyway, the Kempes of Blisland lost their prestige before 1750.

CHAPTER III.

LISKEARD AND ST. GERMANS.

WE mentioned in Chapter I. that so early as 1502 John Kympe held land at Liskeard, and that in 1540 William Kympe had succeeded him; the next note we have is the Subsidy Roll of 1544 for the hundred of Trigg, when John Kympe is rated at £20 and William Kympe at £15. In 1554 Jacob, otherwise James Kemp, was Member of Parliament for Liskeard, while John "Keym" was M.P. for Helston. In 1577 John Kemp with others was indicted as a Papist, for aiding and abetting of the Bull, and was adjudged upon the Statute of Premunire "to lose lands and goods and to undergo pepetual imprisonment at the Queen Majesty's pleasure." We cannot say with certainty that this Kemp was of Liskeard, but the bill of indictment describes the offenders as "Papists of Cornwall," thus it seems likely that the testator, whose will was proved in 1593 as William Kempe, of "Lyskeard," Cornwall, may have been his son, for the will directs his friends, John Notle and John Kempe, "in special confidence to labour and endeavour to recover "his" interest and right in several tinworks in Lankhooles and Hondrethin," and to apply the profits, when obtained, for the benefit of James Blaye's children, John Bloye and Jone Bloye, Jane Notley, John Ingowe; Elizabeth Jago, Robert Fudge, William Marshe and John Vosper are also mentioned, but no Kempe relationships are stated.

We hear nothing more of the tinworks, so fear that they were *not* recovered. The next will of a Kemp at Liskeard is that of Peter Kemp, dated 1622 and proved the following year (P.C.C., 16 Swan). To Thomas Kemp of the same parish, yeoman, £20 was bequeathed, and bequests to his sister Alice Edle and brother Edward. Humphrey Virler is designated the testator's "cousin," and Patience Bishopp, Mrs. Faith, Jane Penrose, Mr. Pennant and others are mentioned. A charity of some unknown date was founded at Liskeard by a John Kempe, and in 1588 William Kempe was a subsidy payer there and termed a "superior burgess." Peter Kempe was Town-Sergeant of Liskeard for some years prior to 1662, about which time Richard Kempe, of Liskeard, was licensed to issue farthing tokens, of which specimens still exist though rare. His token was marked on one side "Richard Kemp, 60," with three fleur de lis, and on the other "In Lisscard, 1/4." It is likely that the fleur de lis were in allusion to his arms, for a recognized Kempe coat was "ermine, on a saltire engrailed five fleur de lis, Or," while in Ireland Kempes had a similar shield, namely, "Or, on a saltire gules five fleur de lis of the first, the crest pertaining to which was an Antilope passant, Or, collared azure. This, or another similar one, is also said to have been used by some Kemp family of Scotland.

The first Kemp(e) will recorded at Exeter is that of Henry Kemp, of St. Erney, which place is close to St. Germans and between Liskeard and Rame. It is likely that this Henry was from the latter family, as one, Henry Kempe, of Crede, is mentioned in 1573 as party to a Rame deed. We have not, however, seen the will and must leave this in doubt.

We will briefly give the evidence concerning the Kempes of Rame and Plymouth, many of which details are found in "Miscellanea Genealogica," under a notice of the Furneaux family, one, Emma Kempe, having married John Furneaux on 25th February, 1652, at Stoke Damerell, as recorded in that parish register. Possible Furneaux was a variant of "Fyneaux," if so perhaps John Fyneaux mentioned as concerned with lands of the Kentish Kempes about 1520 was related to this John Furneaux. Rose Rede, daughter and heir of Thomas Gaynor, and widow of Stephen Rede, held lands in Plymouth and Stoke Damerell for her own use in 1533, the reversion being entailed first to Robert Rede and his issue, which failing, the remainder was for Richard Rede, and if his issue failed the remainder was settled upon Argent Kempe and his right heirs, or the last failing then to the right heirs of the donor. The lands concerned were then valued at 34*s.* 4*d.* In 1563 lands at Wortha, in Mary Tavy, were granted by Simon Rowe and Rose his wife to Walter Kympe and Anne, his wife. In 1566 the latter couple, with Symon Rawe and Rose, his wife, were jointly interested in a freehold lease and tenement and close at Plymouth, which they seem to have made over to Phillippa Dingle. In 1571 John Rede released his right to lands in Stoke Damerell and Plymouth and Compton to the right heir of Rose Rede, widow, namely, Mr. Walter Kempe, of Stoke Damerell. In 1573 lands in Marwell were held by Henry Kempe, of Crede, Elizabeth, his wife, John, their son and heir apparent, who together settled the property on Richard and Robert Kempe, sons of the above named John, who, however, is called "son of Walter." That same year Robert Kympe had a grant of annuity from John Ernestsettle, of St. Budeaux, Robert apparently having married Emma, daughter of this grantor, the annuity being charged on land in Plymouth. In 1606 Sir John Hele and Mary, his wife, made over a lease of three parts of Swilly for life to Mr. Tobias Kempe and Joan Dawe, and in 1611 Robert Kempe settled by deed on his son, Tobias Kempe, his lands in Plymouth, Stoke Damerel, and at Mary Tavy. This Tobias was aged thirty years at his father's death, and married Joan, daughter of . . . Dawe, of Maker. She was living a widow in 1647, as she then assigned her interest in the above three parts of Swilly to her daughter Emma, this being confirmed on the daughter's marriage to John Furneaux in 1652, and a further gift made of lands in Stoke Damerel and Plymouth as well as at Heavitree. In 1689 the will of John Furneaux was proved and settled upon his issue these lands. Meanwhile, however, other interests in Swilly, Stoke Damerel and Plymouth were retained by the Kempes; Pascho Kempe, of Swilly, brother to Emma Furneaux, holding at least one eighth of Swilly in 1647. This moiety he bequeathed to his sister, whose husband purchased another moiety from Abraham Rowe, and the balance of the interests from Sir E. Hungerford. How Sir E. Hungerford obtained his moieties we cannot say, but we must remark that a Richard Hungerford in his will of 1510 mentions his "cousins," Margaret Kempe and Robert Blaverhauset, both of whom were connected closely with the Kempes of Gissing as well as with the County of Warwick.

An early Kempe of note evidently connected with Rame, was William Kempe, Master of the Grammar School at Plymouth, erroneously supposed by some to be identical with the actor. William Kempe, the schoolmaster, made his will in 1601, and it was proved the same year, whereas the actor was living in 1603, and possibly later. The will mentions his father, Walter Kempe, his brother Robert, and his sisters, Thomasine and Jon*as*, leaving to the latter his smallest volume of the English Bible. He further mentions his brother-in-law, John Honkin, his cousin, Pascowe Kempe, of Rame, and his wife Joan, while he gives the names of his children as William, Judith, Elizabeth, Joan and Wilmot; besides these he speaks of his property at Ware, and leaves alms to the poor of Plymouth, Stoke Damerel, Stonehouse, and St. Budork. It was, undoubtedly, this William Kempe who wrote "A Dutiful Invective" in 1587, and in the following year another book "Education of Children in Learning." He also translated Peter Ramus' Arithmetic in 1592. The name Pascowe is derived through a marriage between Thomasine Kempe and John Pascowe, and the widow of the latter we find married Francis Croker, Gent., at St. Stephen's Church.

In the Church of Rame is a floor slab commemorating the following: Paschoe Kempe, of Rame, who died 18th July, 1628; Aquila Blake, son of John B. of this parish, died 1631, also Joan, wife of Pascho. Evidently other names were inscribed, but these now are obliterated. The will of this Pascowe Kempe was proved in 1628 (P.C.C., 112 Barrington). It described the testator as of Rame, and bequeaths charity to the poor of that parish and of Stoke Damerel, St. Johns and St. Anthony. The will mentions the testator's cousin, Nicholas Kempe, and his brother, Thomas Kempe, John and Edward, sons of the latter, and numerous other relatives. His sister Wilmot is doubtless the Wilmot mentioned in the former will. It also mentions Tobias Kempe, of whom we have already spoken.

The will of another Pascho Kempe, a resident of Stoke Damerel, was proved in 1649 (P.C.C., 39 Fairfax). It speaks of lands and tenements in Plymouth and Stoke Damerel, Nether Swilley, and "Cumpton" (? Cullompton), also Wortha Mills, which he had inherited, he states, from his father, Tobias. The bulk of these he left to his sister "Emb" Kempe. Among other friends he mentions Honor Dingle, daughter of John Dingle, of Lavaniche, and John Webb, a brazier, of Plymouth.

The will of a third Pascho Kempe was proved in 1651 (P.C.C., 244 Grey). It commences "Be it remembered that Pascho Kempe, late of Stoke Damerel," and goes on to bequeath his estate in trust to his wife for life, with a remainder to his daughter Joan. This Joan married Blake, who became administrator, Elizabeth Kempe, the widow, having died without proving the will.

We hear no more of the Kempes of Stoke Damerel until 1769, when Anthony Kemp, a mariner of His Majesty's ships *Norfolk* and *York*, but late of Stoke Damerel, a bachelor, left a little property, which was administered by his sister, Ann Martin, a widow.

We know of a few later Kemps of Plymouth, but it does not follow that these belong to the old family. One instance is the Rev. Thomas Kemp, D.D., of the Hendon family, who was for a time Chaplain of Plymouth, as he states in his will proved 1769. Between Liskeard and Rame is the parish of Saltash, where Edward Kempe died between 1634 (when his will was made) and 1637 (when it was proved) (P.C.C., 149 Goare). This testator mentions John Horrenden, Thomas Bignell, Robert Walker and others, but he mentions no Kempe relatives with the exception of his only daughter, Elizabeth, who had married John Horrenden, father of the above legatee. This testator is described as a merchant, and was evidently in the weaving trade, for he leaves to Thomas Bignall one pair of his looms, "if he be so minded as to follow the trade of weaving." We do not know at what this testator's estate was valued, but we presume that he was wealthy, for he instructed his executors to bury him in the middle of a chancel of the parish of St. Stephen's, to the poor of which parish he left 40*s*. "to keep them at work, but not otherwise."

CHAPTER IV.

PENRYN, FALMOUTH AND GERRANS.

We cannot attempt to dwell on each intermarriage shown in the accompanying pedigrees, but it will be seen that Nicholas Kempe, son of John Kempe, by Winifred Penkivell, purchased Rosteage, in the Parish of Gerrans, from Reginald Mohun in 1619, from which time the senior branch of John Kempe's issue made this their seat. We have not found the will of John Kempe, of Levethan, nor that of Nicholas, of Rosteage, the first Kempe will connected with this place being that of Jone Kempe, proved in 1653. She is described as a widow, of Rosteage, in the parish of Gerrans. She mentions John Kempe, her eldest son, Wilmutt Kempe, and her daughters-in-law, Mary Kempe and Grace Kempe, and her grandchildren, John, Thomasine and Anne Kempe, also her daughters, Phillippa Fudge, Ann Hawke, Susan Hobbs and Rebecca Webber, from which it appears that despite the pedigree she was closely connected with the Kempes of Stoke Damerel and Plymouth. The only estate mentioned is "Pentawadden," in the parish of Gerrans, with deeds appertaining thereto dated 1640, and deeds giving title to an estate called "Cellerin Petegrew" in the same parish dated 1632, which she left to her son James, while the residue of her personal estate was to be divided between her four sons, Anthony, Nicholas, Richard and this James. The younger sons do not appear on the pedigree, but undoubtedly left issue, which, however, we cannot attempt to follow. Her son John was in the parish of Gerrans in 1672, and her grandson Nicholas was there in 1698, and later in Penryn.

Arthur Kempe, of Rosteage, son of the last named, was customer at Falmouth, and in 1711 and 1712 was sheriff for the county, John Worth, of Penryn, evidently his kinsman, being the other sheriff in those years. He married Honor, daughter of Christopher Huddy, by whom he had Nicholas, his son and heir, and Arthur Kempe, who became Governor of St. Mawes Castle, and a son Charles, of Crugsillick. Nicholas, the eldest son, was sheriff for Cornwall in 1761, and the banner which he used during his shrievalty is still preserved, being now in possession of James Fletcher Kempe, Esq., of Liverpool, who is declared to be heir-at-law to the late head of this family. The illustration of this banner, which we reproduce, is from a photograph taken personally. It is worthy of notice that although the family has been accustomed to use as their motto an appropriate text of scripture in Latin, the sheriff gave its English equivalent: "They that sow in tears shall reap in joy," for the benefit of his pious supporters. The will of this sheriff styling himself Nicholas Kempe, of Rosteage, Esquire, was proved in 1768 (P.C.C., 206 Secker). After pious phrases—not common at this period—he bequeathed to his brother Charles, of Carsillich, and his sister Ursula in trust all his lands, tenements and personal estate, instructing them to pay all the debts of his late father, Arthur Kempe, and afterwards to raise £900 for the benefit of his three daughters, Mary, Dorothy and Ursula, and the remainder of his estate was left in trust for his son, Samuel Kempe, and his heirs. This will is dated 7th September, 1754, and the original probate is in the hands of the above-mentioned James Fletcher Kempe. Attached to the will are copies of accounts kept by the executors showing how the estate was administered.

Banner of Nicholas Kempe.

Samuel Kempe, the eldest son, was born in 1728, and was therefore not a minor at his father's death, and the estates were evidently put in the hands of the testator's brother and sister in order to realise sufficient to pay mortgages on the estates, the testator feeling that his son was not a suitable person to be entrusted with this responsibility. Indeed, there can be no doubt that the honour of serving as sheriff had lead the two last generations into great expense, and that Samuel Kempe was not inclined to economise. When at length, after satisfaction of the debts of his forefathers, Rosteage came into his hands, he found he was unable to keep up such an establishment as it necessitated, and either by deed—of which there is no evidence—or by mortgage, or other arrangement, Rosteage passed into the hands of the Harris family. It has long been a bone of contention that the Harris's had no real title to the estate, but we fear now that too many years have elapsed to permit of the Kempes making good their title. Nicholas Kempe, the eldest son, was a commander in the Royal Navy, and died in 1829, aged seventy-two, and his brother, John Kempe (who purposely dropped the final "e" from his name), became a merchant in New York, where he died in 1824. William Kempe, the third son, was living in 1824, and was the only one of these sons whose issue survived. He had sisters named Jane and Honor. These five children give rise to a serious question in law. The first and second having died without issue, the issue of the third son would naturally be heirs-at-law to the Rosteage property, if recovered, while the personal estate, if entailed, should have passed to William Kempe's eldest son. It is important therefore that exact evidence, with proofs of the decease ***without issue*** should be put in, in case of Nicholas, John, and other heirs-at-law. Thanks to the trouble which James Fletcher Kempe has taken to gather together official copies of probates and certificates, he has established his title to the personal effects of his grandfather, William Kempe, who resided for a time at Tyne Villa, Devon, and afterwards on the continent, where he died. It is noteworthy that some Kempes of New York and Bermuda, who have for some generations been most careful to preserve the final "e" to their name, were told by their father that the reason for doing this was because they were the head of a family who had considerable property in Cornwall.

The tradition spontaneously sent to us by the head of this Bermuda family, who had no exact knowledge of the Kempe family of Cornwall, is to the following effect: "My father, William Kempe, was a native of Cornwall, England, and born in 1804. Left his home when quite a boy and joined H.M. Navy. Served for some time under Admiral Lord Dundonald (or Cockerhan) in American waters. Returned to England and entered the coastguard service. Married Miss Mary Elizabeth Bullen, of Hampshire, by whom he had three sons, Richard, William and James. Later joined the convict service and came to Bermuda, bringing his family with him. Shortly after coming out his wife died (about 1849). Some years later he retired from service on a pension, and remained here till his death, which occurred 23rd January, 1865. The three sons are still living, and have issue" . . . "I remember when very young my father taking me to his mother's home (his father being then dead), and his two sisters were then living. I also remember being told by my father that ***his brothers were lost at sea***, and that he was the *youngest child*, but *only* surviving son."

This statement, if compared with the pedigree, will be found to coincide with the facts as given by James Fletcher Kempe, the heir-at-law, with but a slight difference as to the date of birth of William Kempe, father of Richard Kempe, the writer of the above letter. It may be nothing more than a mere chance, and the two families may not be connected, but as we have not received or found proofs of the death of the elder brothers of James Fletcher Kempe's father, it is still open for us to suggest that one of these brothers was the founder of the Bermuda Kempe family. If this founder proves to be an elder brother, his issue would be *morally* entitled to any relics of the Cornish family which might be considered heirlooms. It is not for us, however, to enter upon the legal aspect of this strange coincidence, but it is our duty to state that James Fletcher Kempe, on his return from New Zealand, made application to the Court of Chancery, who granted to him as apparent heir the personal effects of his grandfather, which included the family banner above mentioned, a signet ring which had long been in the family, and numerous family documents.

The will of John Kemp, late merchant of New York (mentioned above), was dated in London on the 19th March, 1818, and written in the form of a letter, states, that he was then leaving for New York, and thus appointed as attorneys and executors his brother, Nicholas Kempe, and his sisters, Mrs. Janes Larbeck and Mrs. Honor Stevens. The will leaves his property in New York to Eliza Kemp, his wife, for life, with residue (subject to a few legacies), to his brothers and sisters. This was proved in Liverpool on 9th July, 1824, the said brothers and sisters, with a brother William, having given evidence to support the validity of this will. By an arrangement made between these parties it was agreed that the estate should be invested in the British funds, and the interest from £1,500 each was to be respectively paid to the four parties. The estate is said to have proved of considerably less value than was expected, owing to the small value of American stocks, which had to be realised.

The will of Jane Larbeck was dated at Chepstow, 5th March, 1840. She mentions her grandsons, William Kempe Larbeck and John Kempe Larbeck, also her nephew, WILLIAM KEMPE, junior, and her nephew, Nicholas John Kempe; also James Fletcher Kempe, William Kempe, Sarah Kempe, and Mary Ann Kempe, sons of her nephew, Nicholas John Kempe. Administration of this will was granted to her *brother* William, 18th December, 1843.

The will of Honor Stevens, widow, was dated from Roath Castle, Glamorganshire, 21st February, 1841. She states that she was lately residing at Farnham Surrey, and she wished to be buried beside her late husband, John Stevens, at Lewisham. She left legacies to her *nephew*, William Kempe, junior, and her nephew, Nicholas John Kempe, and stock (of the face value of £1,000) to her *brother*, William Kempe, of Roath Castle.

William Kempe, of Roath Castle, Glamorganshire (formerly of Liverpool), sold his residence about 1830 to Lord Bute's agent, and then purchased Teign Villa, which he sold after the death of his wife, and in 1851 he left England for France, where he is said to have died in 1858, aged eighty-nine. This William was the fourth son of Samuel Kemp, and born at Rosteage in 1770, where he lived for ten years. At the age of fifteen he went to Lisbon, and is said to have made a fortune there. Coming home in 1805 he went into partnership and lost the greater portion of it. This William Kempe probably married in 1805, and we suggest that William Kempe (afterwards of Bermuda) was born in 1806, and therefore was the *elder brother* of Nicholas John Kempe, father of the present legal head of the family.

Among the documents descended to James Fletcher Kempe is an interesting map and architectural drawing of Roath Castle and its estate. The castle was an embattled edifice with a wide front built in five sections, and stood in a park of about fifty acres in all, with Ty-yn-y-coed farm, it included 143 acres adjoining the property of the Marquis of Bute and the Cardiff Corporation.

A biography of Nicholas Kempe, R.N., who died at Bridgend, South Wales, aged seventy-two in 1829, appeared in the *Gentleman's Magazine* in July that year. It is very interesting, the more so that it was written by his learned kinsman, Alfred John Kempe, the antiquary. In addition to the fact that this Captain Nicholas went on a voyage of discovery with Captain Cook, it states that during the revolutionary war with the United States he was much on the American station, and was for three years in East India, *and latterly in the West Indies.* The circumstance of his having been in the West Indies, coupled with the fact of his brother being a merchant in New York, appears a very good reason why a nephew of his should settle at Bermuda. Richard Kempe and William Kempe, now of Bermuda, and their brother James Kempe of New York, are sons of the William Kempe, "a native of Cornwall" mentioned above as settling in the West Indies in 1848. They have each several children living.

CHAPTER V.

THE SECOND BRANCH.

We have said that Nicholas Kempe, of Rosteage, mentioned in his will Charles Kempe, his second brother, seated at Crugsilich. This Charles married his kinswoman, Ann Kempe, heir to her brother James, who died unmarried, which James was a son of John Kempe, eldest son of Nicholas Kempe, of Crugsilich and Veryan, the last named being second son of the first Nicholas Kempe, of Rosteage. Thus two branches were represented by the issue of Charles Kempe, of Crugsilich, and Ann. Their eldest son, James, was a surgeon at Truro. His children, however, were all daughters, and their line passes from our notice. Charles, the second son, was Rector of St. Mabyn, and the founder of a family which we shall notice presently. Arthur Kempe, the third son, was an Admiral, and is at present represented by Edward Marshall Kempe, of New Shoreham. Charles Kempe, of St. Mabyn, left a son John, who was Vicar of Fowey, and died in 1862, leaving the following family: John, commander in the R.N.; George Henry, Rector of Bicton; James Cory, Rector of Huish and Merton, Devon, and Arthur Kempe, of Exeter, surgeon. John Kempe, R.N., left two daughters and a son, Charles Patrick Kempe, a physician, who practised in Bayswater, and died aged sixty-six on the 12th May, 1900. His will was proved that year in the principal registry, and his son, also a doctor, now represents the second line of this ancient family.

George Henry, the Rector of Bicton, left two sons, both unmarried as yet, viz., George Henry, now a vicar of one of the Croydon churches, and John Arthur, a medical practitioner, living at Birmingham. The elder has inherited the principal estates at Veryan, which have been in the family for some 200 years. Dr. John Arthur Kempe has been good enough to send us a copy of his book-plate, which, however, he states, perhaps jocularly, to be "the only genuine one," and claiming that his brother, George Henry, is the senior representative of the Kempes of Veryan. As, however, their father was born in 1809, and Charles Patrick Kempe's father was born in 1804, it will be seen that the Rev. George Henry is a junior representative to Charles Patrick's eldest son. Dr. Charles Patrick Kempe, as head of the Veryan family, inherited the books collected by successive generations, and cut from one of these a book-plate, which is at least 150 years old, and which is now in our possession, while that sent in by John Arthur Kempe is a fine modern example.

Book-plate used by Nicholas Kempe.

The issue of James Cory Kempe were John Henry and James Arthur, with several daughters, who are also represented.

Arthur Kempe, of Exeter, Surgeon, born in 1812, met with his death in the great disaster, the wreck of the *Princess Alice*. At the time Arthur Kempe, his eldest son, was a student at college, and not yet prepared as a qualified surgeon. This fact, and his lack of knowledge of the family estates, we understand resulted in considerable loss to the family, but he has now one of the best practices in the West of England, and still holds a considerable portion of his father's estate. He has to regret the loss of an ancestral ring which it was his father's habit to wear. This was a Cornish diamond of considerable size, very heavily mounted, and we understand bore his arms. It dropped from the finger of his father when on a visit to Cornwall and has never been found. He owns a pedigree showing the descent of his family, not merely from the Kempes of Levethan, but from the Kings of England and numerous old Cornish families, with the arms of those which his family represent.

Arthur Kempe, the Admiral, had the following sons as well as daughters. The eldest, Charles Trevanion, was Vicar of Breage; the second was John Arthur, Colonel in the East India Company, and the third, William Peter, a Captain in the same Company. The eldest left a son, Edward Marshall Kempe, Vicar of Linkinhorne.

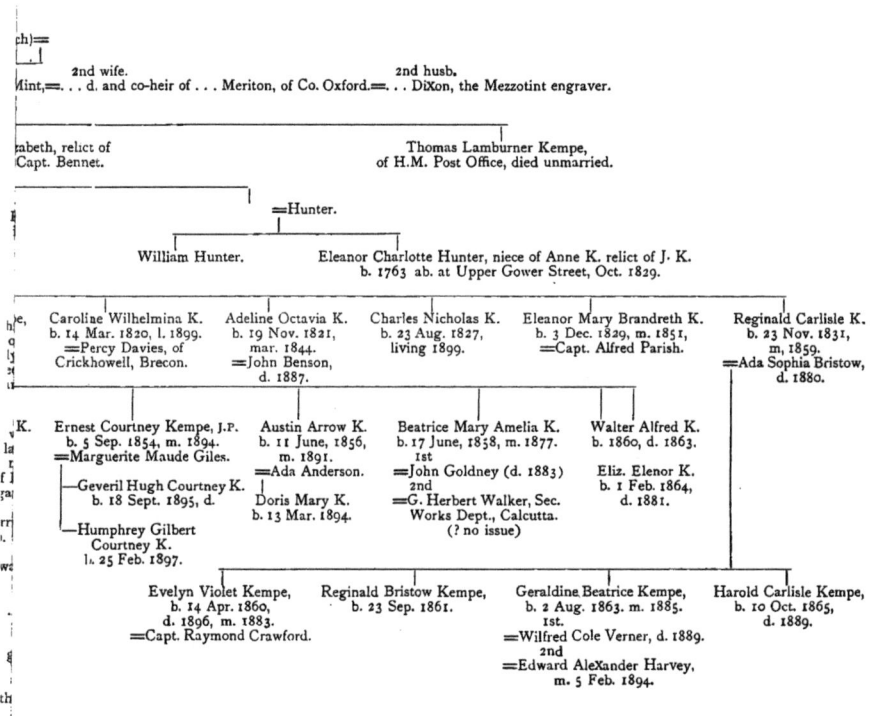

ch)=

2nd wife. 2nd husb.

Mint,=. . . d. and co-heir of . . . Meriton, of Co. Oxford.=. . . Dixon, the Mezzotint engraver.

zabeth, relict of
Capt. Bennet.

Thomas Lamburner Kempe,
of H.M. Post Office, died unmarried.

=Hunter.

William Hunter.

Eleanor Charlotte Hunter, niece of Anne K. relict of J. K.
b. 1763 ab. at Upper Gower Street, Oct. 1829.

Caroline Wilhelmina K.
b. 14 Mar. 1820, l. 1899.
=Percy Davies, of
Crickhowell, Brecon.

Adeline Octavia K.
b. 19 Nov. 1821,
mar. 1844.
=John Benson,
d. 1887.

Charles Nicholas K.
b. 23 Aug. 1827,
living 1899.

Eleanor Mary Brandreth K.
b. 3 Dec. 1829, m. 1851,
=Capt. Alfred Parish.

Reginald Carlisle K.
b. 23 Nov. 1831,
m, 1859.
=Ada Sophia Bristow,
d. 1880.

K.

Ernest Courtney Kempe, J.P.
b. 5 Sep. 1854, m. 1894.
=Marguerite Maude Giles.

—Geveril Hugh Courtney K.
b. 18 Sept. 1895, d.

—Humphrey Gilbert
Courtney K.
b. 25 Feb. 1897.

Austin Arrow K.
b. 11 June, 1856,
m. 1891.
=Ada Anderson.

Doris Mary K.
b. 13 Mar. 1894.

Beatrice Mary Amelia K.
b. 17 June, 1858, m. 1877.
1st
=John Goldney (d. 1883)
2nd
=G. Herbert Walker, Sec.
Works Dept., Calcutta.
(? no issue)

Walter Alfred K.
b. 1860, d. 1863.

Eliz. Elenor K.
b. 1 Feb. 1864,
d. 1881.

Evelyn Violet Kempe,
b. 14 Apr. 1860,
d. 1896, m. 1883.
=Capt. Raymond Crawford.

Reginald Bristow Kempe,
b. 23 Sep. 1861.

Geraldine Beatrice Kempe,
b. 2 Aug. 1863. m. 1885.
1st.
=Wilfred Cole Verner, d. 1889.
2nd
=Edward Alexander Harvey,
m. 5 Feb. 1894.

Harold Carlisle Kempe,
b. 10 Oct. 1865,
d. 1889.

th

CORNWALL, No. III.

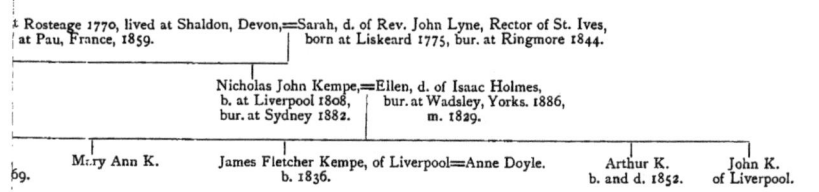

t Rosteage 1770, lived at Shaldon, Devon,=Sarah, d. of Rev. John Lyne, Rector of St. Ives,
at Pau, France, 1859. born at Liskeard 1775, bur. at Ringmore 1844.

Nicholas John Kempe,=Ellen, d. of Isaac Holmes,
b. at Liverpool 1808, bur. at Wadsley, Yorks. 1886,
bur. at Sydney 1882. m. 1829.

69.

Mary Ann K.

James Fletcher Kempe, of Liverpool=Anne Doyle.
b. 1836.

Arthur K.
b. and d. 1852.

John K.
of Liverpool.

issue of Charles Kempe, of Crugsilich, and Ann. Their eldest son, James, was a surgeon at Truro. His children, however, were all daughters, and their line passes from our notice. Charles, the second son, was Rector of St. Mabyn, and the founder of a family which we shall notice presently. Arthur Kempe, the third son, was an Admiral, and is at present represented by Edward Marshall Kempe, of New Shoreham. Charles Kempe, of St. Mabyn, left a son John, who was Vicar of Fowey, and died in 1862, leaving the following family: John, commander in the R.N.; George Henry, Rector of Bicton; James Cory, Rector of Huish and Merton, Devon, and Arthur Kempe, of Exeter, surgeon. John Kempe, R.N., left two daughters and a son, Charles Patrick Kempe, a physician, who practised in Bayswater, and died aged sixty-six on the 12th May, 1900. His will was proved that year in the principal registry, and his son, also a doctor, now represents the second line of this ancient family.

George Henry, the Rector of Bicton, left two sons, both unmarried as yet, viz, George Henry, now a vicar of one of the Croydon churches, and John Arthur, a medical practitioner, living at Birmingham. The elder has inherited the principal estates at Veryan, which have been in the family for some 200 years. Dr. John Arthur Kempe has been good enough to send us a copy of his book-plate, which, however, he states, perhaps jocularly, to be "the only genuine one," and claiming that his brother, George Henry, is the senior representative of the Kempes of Veryan. As, however, their father was born in 1809, and Charles Patrick Kempe's father was born in 1804, it will be seen that the Rev. George Henry is a junior representative to Charles Patrick's eldest son. Dr. Charles Patrick Kempe, as head of the Veryan family, inherited the books collected by successive generations, and cut from one of these a book-plate, which is at least 150 years old, and which is now in our possession, while that sent in by John Arthur Kempe is a fine modern example.

Book-plate used by Nicholas Kempe.

The issue of James Cory Kempe were John Henry and James Arthur, with several daughters, who are also represented.

Arthur Kempe, of Exeter, Surgeon, born in 1812, met with his death in the great disaster, the wreck of the *Princess Alice*. At the time Arthur Kempe, his eldest son, was a student at college, and not yet prepared as a qualified surgeon. This fact, and his lack of knowledge of the family estates, we understand resulted in considerable loss to the family, but he has now one of the best practices in the West of England, and still holds a considerable portion of his father's estate. He has to regret the loss of an ancestral ring which it was his father's habit to wear. This was a Cornish diamond of considerable size, very heavily mounted, and we understand bore his arms. It dropped from the finger of his father when on a visit to Cornwall and has never been found. He owns a pedigree showing the descent of his family, not merely from the Kempes of Levethan, but from the Kings of England and numerous old Cornish families, with the arms of those which his family represent.

Arthur Kempe, the Admiral, had the following sons as well as daughters. The eldest, Charles Trevanion, was Vicar of Breage; the second was John Arthur, Colonel in the East India Company, and the third, William Peter, a Captain in the same Company. The eldest left a son, Edward Marshall Kempe, Vicar of Linkinhorne.

CORNWALL, No. II.

Nicholas Kempe, of Plymouth, (3rd son of Nicholas K. of Crugsillich)=

1st wife. Elizabeth, d. of James Humphreys, of Deptford, Ad. 1762.=Nicholas Kempe, of "The Villa," Chelsea, Bullion Porter of H.M. Mint, b. 1688, d. 1744 (and of Deptford in 1762)=2nd wife. . . . d. and co-heir of . . . Meriton, of Co. Oxford.=2nd husb. . . . Dixon, the Mezzotint engraver.

John Kempe, son and heir, Bullion Porter at H.M. Mint, b. 1748, d. 1823, *vide* Biography, *Gents. Mag.* 1823, *pp.* 569 and 603.=Anne, d. of James Arrow, of Westminster, Esq., b. 1745/6, d. 17 Mar 1835, æt 90.

Capt. James Kempe, R.N., *vide* Memoir, *Gents. Mag.* July, 1829.=Elizabeth, relict of Capt. Bennet.

Thomas Lamburner Kempe, of H.M. Post Office, died unmarried.

Children of John Kempe and Anne Arrow:

- Jemima Kempe, died an infant.
- Edward Gibbon Kempe, died an infant.
- Alfred John Kempe, F.S.A., b. 14 June, 1784, d. 1846, bur. at Fulham.=Mary, d. of J. Prior, a Capt. in the Army, related to Prior, the Poet, b. 9 Dec. 1791, d. 1864.
- 1st Chas. Stothard, F.S.A., d. 1821. (Artist)=Anne Eliza Kempe. d. 1883. (Authoress)=2nd Rev Edward Atkins Bray.

Daughter of Capt. James Kempe and Elizabeth: =Hunter.

- William Hunter.
- Eleanor Charlotte Hunter, niece of Anne K. relict of J. K. b. 1763 ab. at Upper Gower Street, Oct. 1829.

Children of Alfred John Kempe and Mary Prior:

- Rev. John Edward Kempe, Rector of St. James, Piccadilly, Chaplain to the Queen and Author, b. 9 Mar. 1810, liv. 1899.=Harriet Wood, mar. 1843. d. 1872.
- Mary Anne Kempe, b. 22 Dec. 1811, living 1899.
- Selina Augusta Woodcock, mar. 1846, d. 1884.=Rev. Alfred Arrow Kempe, b. 12 Apr 1813, liv. 1899, Rec. of Wexham, Bucks.
- Ann Eliza Kempe, b. 22 Jan. 1815, mar. 1846. =Rev. Arthur Mozley, d. 1892.
- Jemima France Martha K. b. 22 Dec. 1816, d. 1888, mar. 1841. =Albin Martin.
- Augusta Kempe, b. 1818, d. 1827.
- Caroline Wilhelmina K. b. 14 Mar. 1820, l. 1899. =Percy Davies, of Crickhowell, Brecon.
- Adeline Octavia K. b. 19 Nov. 1821, mar. 1844. =John Benson, d. 1887.
- Charles Nicholas K. b. 23 Aug. 1827, living 1899.
- Eleanor Mary Brandreth K. b. 3 Dec. 1829, m. 1851, =Capt. Alfred Parish.
- Reginald Carlisle K. b. 23 Nov. 1831, m. 1859. =Ada Sophia Bristow, d. 1880.

Children of Rev. John Edward Kempe and Harriet Wood:

- Rev. Edward Wood Kempe, Chaplain to the Queen, b. 9 Jul. 1844, m 3 Sep. 1879, Vic. of Forty Hill, Enfield. =Margaret Miller Challis.
  - Harriett Mary K. b. 19 Aug. 1870.
  - Edward Challis K. b. 11 Feb. 1881.
  - Wm. Alfred K. b. 21 Aug. 1882.
  - Margaret Caroline K. b. 18 Mar. 1884.
  - Katherine Eleanor K. b. 30 June, 1886.
- John Arrow Kempe, Dep. Chairman of H.M. Customs, b. 5 Jan. 1846, m. 1872. =Mary Jane Edwards.
  - Dorothy K. b. 31 Aug. 1873.
  - Edward K. b. 15 Nov. 1874.
  - Harriet Elizabeth K. b. 24 June, 1876.
  - Mary Cicely K. b. 14 July, 1878.
  - Ronald Northcote K. b. 11 Mar. 1881.
  - John Erskine K. b. 12 Mar. 1888.
  - Harry Francis Christopher K. b. 13 Oct. 1889.
- Caroline Mary K. b. 22 Sep. 1847, mar. 1872. =Rev. Erskine Wm. Knollys, Vic. of Folkestone.
- Alfred Bray Kempe, F.R.S. Chancellor of St. Albans, Newcastle and Southwell, b. 6 Jul. 1849, m. 1887. 1st =Mary Bowman, she d. 4 June, 1893. 2nd =Ida Meadows White, m. 1897 (no issue)
- Henry Robx. Kempe, b. 1 Mar. 1851, mar. 1880. =Helen Catherine Byng,
  - Mabel Harriet Ellen K. b. 6 Dec. 1881.

Children of Rev. Alfred Arrow Kempe and Selina Augusta Woodcock:

- Grace Augusta K. b. 7 Feb. 1849.
- Gerald Steuart Kempe, b. 6 July, 1850, m. 1883. =Mary Ann Russell.
  - Selinor Eleanor K. b. 15 Dec. 1883.
  - Ernest Ravenscroft K. b. 12 Apr. 1885.
  - Edward Hull K. b. 23 Nov. 1887.
  - Gerald Austin K. b. 17 Dec. 1889, d. 1897.
  - Constance Isabelle K. b. 14 Oct. 1891.
- Arthur Granville K. b. 17 Sep. 1852, d. 1897.
- Ernest Courtney Kempe, J.P. b. 5 Sep. 1854, m. 1894. =Marguerite Maude Giles.
  - Geveril Hugh Courtney K. b. 18 Sept. 1895, d.
  - Humphrey Gilbert Courtney K. b. 25 Feb. 1897.
- Austin Arrow K. b. 11 June, 1856, m. 1891. =Ada Anderson.
  - Doris Mary K. b. 13 Mar. 1894.
- Beatrice Mary Amelia K. b. 17 June, 1858, m. 1877. 1st =John Goldney (d. 1883) 2nd =G. Herbert Walker, Sec. Works Dept., Calcutta. (? no issue)
- Walter Alfred K. b. 1860, d. 1863.
- Eliz. Elenor K. b. 1 Feb. 1864, d. 1881.

Children of Reginald Carlisle K. and Ada Sophia Bristow:

- Evelyn Violet Kempe, b. 14 Apr. 1860, d. 1896, m. 1883. =Capt. Raymond Crawford.
- Reginald Bristow Kempe, b. 23 Sep. 1861.
- Geraldine Beatrice Kempe, b. 2 Aug. 1863. m. 1885. 1st. =Wilfred Cole Verner, d. 1889. 2nd =Edward Alexander Harvey, m. 5 Feb. 1894.
- Harold Carlisle Kempe, b. 10 Oct. 1865, d. 1889.

CORNWALL, No. III.

William Kempe, born at Rosteage 1770, lived at Shaldon, Devon, died at Pau, France, 1859.=Sarah, d. of Rev. John Lyne, Rector of St. Ives, born at Liskeard 1775, bur. at Ringmore 1844.

vide A Chart I.

- William Kempe, of Liverpool, living 1843 (? of Bermuda) born at Lisbon 1806.
- Nicholas John Kempe, b. at Liverpool 1808, bur. at Sydney 1882.=Ellen, d. of Isaac Holmes, bur. at Wadsley, Yorks. 1886, m. 1829.
  - Sarah K.
  - William K. b. 1832, d. 1869.
  - Mary Ann K.
  - James Fletcher Kempe, of Liverpool, b. 1836.=Anne Doyle.
  - Arthur K. b. and d. 1852.
  - John K. of Liverpool.

The second had a son, John, who was a Fellow of Exeter College, Oxford, and the third left two sons, of which Coryton Silvanus Sampson Kempe was of the 63rd Regiment, while his brother, William Hussey Blomfield Kempe, was one of the chief officials of Her Majesty's Customs.

Space at our disposal prevents us commenting upon many members of the family who have distinguished themselves, but the ancestral wills show that the second branch of the Cornish family, namely, that of St. Veryan, have continued for over 200 years to maintain their position as worthy members of this ancient family.

CHAPTER VI.

THE THIRD BRANCH.

NICHOLAS KEMPE, of Plymouth, third son of Nicholas Kempe, of Crugsilich, might be termed a junior line of the second branch, but the descendants have carved out for themselves such a distinct course of life that we prefer to treat them in a separate chapter. Nicholas, of Plymouth, was an officer of that port, connected chiefly with the collection of duties. It was probably due to this Government appointment that his son secured the honourable position of bullion porter in the Royal Mint. It is very singular that at this time a Daniel Kempe, of the Hendon family, was Provost of the Company of Moniers, and was therefore the officer under whom Nicholas, the bullion porter, served. Between these families, if any connexion existed at all, the distance must have been very great, for both families can count their ancestors back to 1500 for certain, while in both cases also it is evident that their ancestors were respectively settled in their native places for some generations earlier. It is still more remarkable that, side by side with the Kempes of Hendon, three successive generations of the Cornish Kempes held offices in the Tower of London. The Master of the Mint has been good enough to make an exhaustive search among the records, and has sent in about twenty references to the Cornish family. We cannot give space to reproduce these interesting items in full; but, briefly, they include the following:

14th May, 1756. Appointment by the Treasury of Nicholas Kempe to be porter of His Majesty's Mint, within the Tower of London.

10th July, 1759. Nicholas Kempe, as porter, being entitled to a salary of £45, and standing indebted to a William Mills, of Mark Lane, merchant, as surviving executor of the last will of James Hatch, of London, for £200, he assigned the said salary of £45 a year "for so long a term as the said Nicholas Kempe shall live."

28th January, 1763. Nicholas Kempe's renewed appointment as porter of the Mint.

27th July, 1774. Probate of the will of Nicholas Kempe, Esq., late of Chelsea, appointing his wife, Mrs. Ann Kempe, sole executrix.

29th June, 1774. Petition of Nicholas Kempe to the Treasury reminding them that he had served in capacity of porter "for eighteen years with a character unimpeached," and begging that as severe indisposition renders him unfit to attend to the office himself, that their Lordships will permit him to resign in favour of his son John Kempe, who has officiated for him for the last two years! (We may remark on this item the cool way in which the porter introduced his son and thus freed himself from handing over his pay, which, as above recorded, was mortgaged to satisfy a debt, so long as he held the appointment, for naturally the pay of another could not be claimed by his creditors.)

12th August, 1774. Appointment of John Kempe as porter of the Mint.

21st June, 1820. John Kempe is relieved from part of his duties, instead of which other responsibilities are imposed.

12th February, 1822. Mr. John Kempe having become, from age and infirmities, incapable of giving requisite attendance to his office, which consists in his attendance on the Receipts and Deliveries of the Bullion weighed into the Mint, in the arrangement and assortment of the several Ingots in the Strong Hold, his superannuation is applied for. Certificate and length of service of Mr. Kempe is enclosed, giving the former as 65 and the latter as 50 years. His allowance for the remainder of his life is fixed at £105 per annum.

4th June, 1822. The allowance reduced to £90 per annum.

10th August, 1822. A request from John Kemp for increase in the allowance.

30th July, 1823. The probate of the will of the late John Kempe was exhibited this day at the Mint Office; Ann Kempe, widow of the deceased, and Alfred John Kempe were noted as the executors.

6th December, 1811. Appointment of Mr. Mushet in place of the late Mr John Kempe.

4th October, 1815. Acknowledgment and receipt of a petition of H. A. Kempe for a position on the staff of the Mint.

Mr. A. J. Kempe being unfitted by ill-health to execute the duties of his position as third clerk at the Mint, is forced to retire, and begs that as some recompense for the loss of his position he may receive a computed sum in lieu of annuity.

21st October, 1815. Petition of Mr. Kempe again praying for financial assistance or a minor appointment.

5th November, 1815. Their Lordships reply that the shortness of his period of service prevents them granting him an allowance.

On the 9th July, 1829, A. J. Kempe, addressing from Rodney Buildings, Kent Road, tenders his prices for supply of coals to the Mint, and a reply from the Clerk of the papers regretting that he cannot accept the same.

We must now return to Nicholas Kempe, the first porter who held office. He married, first, Elizabeth, daughter of James Humphreys, of Deptford, by whom he had three sons; John, the eldest, as we have seen, succeeded his father at the Mint; James, the second son, was a Captain in the Royal Navy and married Elizabeth, relict of Captain Bennett, by whom he had children, one of whom married a Mr. Hunter. Except for the latter's issue, Captain James Kempe left no surviving children. He died in 1829, and a memoir written by his nephew, Alfred John Kempe, appeared that year in the *Gentleman's Magazine*. Thomas Lamburner Kempe was the third son of Nicholas Kempe, and held a position in His Majesty's Post Office, dying unmarried. Nicholas Kempe lost his first wife in 1762, and administration of her estate was granted to him that year; his second wife was the beautiful co-heiress of the Merton family of Oxfordshire, a lady whose portrait is frequently to be seen in collections of engravings. To her Nicholas was most deeply attached, and left the whole of his property unreservedly to her. On his death she married Dixon, the celebrated Mezzotint engraver, and consequently conveyed the Cornish relics and estate to this husband. The children consequently were shorn of their just expectations. The villa at Chelsea, where Nicholas Kempe dwelt, was a rendezvous for all the men of letters and art of this period, and among his treasures he had the veritable piano used by Haydn in his early compositions.

John Kempe, the eldest son, as we have stated, was for some fifty years at the Mint. He married Ann, daughter of James Arrow, of Westminster, but whose family was of Irish extraction; her father was architect to the king, and remembered playing as a child with the little prince, afterwards George III., and jumping him up and down the staircase at Hampton Court in a basket. Mr. Arrow had a large house in Tothill Fields, afterwards used as a barrack. By this wife John had the following children: Jemima, Edward Gibbon, Alfred John and Ann Eliza. The first two died in infancy, the last inherited her grandfather's love of art, and in conjunction with her brother published sketches and descriptive matter of an antiquarian nature. It was owing to this that she became acquainted with, and eventually married, Charles Stothard, F.S.A., the compiler of that great standard work, "Monumental Effigies." The death of this husband was very tragic. While the guest of a friend he had obtained permission to make detailed drawings of an altar piece, and had arranged for his friend to call at the church at a certain time to drive him back to dinner. When the friend entered he was horrified to find the poor artist lying dead at the foot of a ladder, having evidently dropped insensible from a blow which he received in too quickly ascending the ladder from some protruding masonry. Ann Eliza, his widow, afterwards married the Rev. E. A. Bray, M.A., Vicar of Tavistock, who had exchanged the Bar for the more congenial duties of a Clergyman. This husband was well known to the literary world as the adapter of the orthodox sermons of our old divines to a more modern and popular style. After her second marriage, as Ann Elizabeth Bray, she wrote numerous books, which are not yet forgotten.

ALFRED JOHN KEMPE, the only son of John, as we have seen, was the third generation to hold office at the Mint. He was educated first by Monsieur Lepere, who had been curé of Fecamp, in Normandy, and afterwards by Monsieur Rivoult, who kept a school at Walworth. These instructors led him to a taste for French literature, and being a great lover of theatrical performances he translated and adapted some of the Comedies of Moliere. At an early age he evinced a great talent in the exercise of his pencil, both in sketching from nature and in humorous delineations of character. With these qualifications, it is regretted that Alfred John Kempe was not brought up to some profession in which he would have undoubtedly been led to eminence. In early life his only occupation was that of an officer in the Tower Hamlets Militia, in which he held commission for five years. He next, as we have seen, spent some time at the Mint, but was unfitted for clerical work such as this involved. His taste for antiquities having been cherished during some excursions which he took with Charles Stothard, he was led to write occasional articles on the subject for the *Gentleman's Magazine*, and was engaged by that publication to review books. Gradually he became known as an authority in antiquarian matters, and was elected a Fellow of the Society of Antiquaries. He visited many places in England, and carried out considerable excavations in Roman encampments and ancient sites, publishing the result of such labours in such books as "Tavistock and its Abbey" and the antiquities of "St. Martin le Grand." One of his most interesting papers was a report of curiosities found on the site of St. Michael's, Crooked Lane, which had been pulled down for the construction of the present London Bridge. It was at this church that John Kempe, the Archbishop, was a Rector, and from the pulpit of which that great man became known as a powerful preacher. It was also at this church that a Thomas Kempe, of Hendon, was for many years the Minister.

Alfred John Kempe, Antiquary.

Alfred John Kempe married Mary, daughter of J. Prior, a Captain in the Army, in 1808, and had by her eleven children, ten of whom lived to advanced ages, and the majority have left such large families that there are at the present time nearly 150 descendants of this marriage. Alfred died in 1846, and was buried in Fulham Churchyard with his sister Ann Eliza. The simple but handsome monument over them gives merely their age with the legend "brother and sister." His wife died in 1864. The eldest son, John Edward Kempe, born in 1810, is still living, and is well known from his religious works and sermons. He was for many years the Rector of St. James', Piccadilly, and was Chaplain in Ordinary to her late Majesty Queen Victoria; his son, Edward Wood Kempe, Vicar of Forty Hill, Enfield, enjoyed the same honour. Both are now Chaplains to the King. John Edward married, in 1843, Miss Harriet Wood, who died in 1872. Their second son, John Arrow Kempe, born in 1846, is Deputy Chairman of His Majesty's Customs. Alfred Bray Kempe, the third son of John Edward, was born in 1849, and is Chancellor of the Dioceses of St. Alban's, Newcastle and Southwell, and is the author of "How to Draw a Straight Line; a Lecture on Linkages." He was called to the Bar in 1873 and joined the western circuit, was elected a Fellow of the Royal Society in 1881, and in 1898 became its Treasurer and Vice-President. Perhaps the most noteworthy event in his life was his service as Secretary to the Royal Commission on the Ecclesiastical Courts at the historical trial of the Bishop of Lincoln for Ritualistic practices in 1889-90, he being junior counsel This memorable trial was depicted by Mr. and Mrs. Floris, representing the Bishops and officials on that occasion. A copy of this now hangs in Lambeth Palace Library, where Mr. Alfred Bray Kempe will be found amongst the group. He was married at St. James', Piccadilly, in May 1877, to Mary, second daughter of Sir William Bowman, Bart., on whose official pedigree at the Heralds' College this marriage is duly recorded. She however died in 1893, and in 1897 he married Miss Alice Ida Meadows White, daughter of the Rev. Preb. Bonell White, by whom he had a son born in 1900.

Alfred Arrow Kempe, second son of Alfred John Kempe, was born at Windmill Row, Camberwell, in 1813, and was educated at St. Paul's School, where, like his elder brother and Alfred Bray Kempe, he greatly distinguished himself. Thence he went to Magdalene College, Cambridge, and has for many years been Rector of Wexham, Bucks. His sons are Gerald Stuart, Arthur Granville, Ernest Courtenay, Austin Arrow and Walter Alfred. Gerald Stuart Kempe has settled in Australia, his present residence being Carandale, Mintaro. We give in our page of Colonial portraits a reproduction of photographs of himself and his son Reginald Lewis, who will doubtless spread the family name in that colony.

Charles Nicholas Kempe, the third son of Alfred John, was born in 1827, his birth being mentioned in an interesting letter written by his father from Rodney Buildings, New Kent Road, dated September 22nd, 1827. (The letter is addressed to his friend J. B. Nicholls, the compiler of "Londinium Redivivum," introducing a Mr. James John Harris, who the writer says was an able Professor of Music, formerly tutor to their family, who wished to present a copy of his selection of "Songs and Hymn Tunes" to Mr. Nicholls in the hope of getting this mentioned in Nicholl's magazine). The letter says, "My sister and I are much indebted to you for your notice of the monumental effigies" . . . . "I also truly thank you for the record of my late dear child which you inserted in your obituary. I am happy to say that my anxiety on Mrs. Kempe's account has been dissipated by the birth of a son on the 23rd of last month, and that both mother and infant are tolerably well." Charles N. Kempe, the child thus mentioned, entered the Civil Service and for a long period was private secretary to four successive parliamentary secretaries at the Admiralty, namely, Mr. Bernal Osborn, Admiral Lord Clarence Paget, Lord Northbrook and Lord Henry Gordon Lennox, and at the time of his retirement was head of the Secret and Military Branch. He is unmarried, and lives at 128, Piccadilly. He is a member of the Junior Athenæum Club, and although seventy-four years of age may be said to be in robust health and travels much.

Reginald Carlisle Kempe, the youngest son of Alfred John, was born in 1831, and married Ada Sophia Bristowe. He is patron of Hawkwell in Essex, but in consequence of his having joined the Roman Catholic Communion forfeits his prerogative to the University of Cambridge. He is still living at Brighton, and has two sons, Reginald Bristowe Kempe and Harold Carlisle Kempe.

Charles Nicholas Kempe, finding it impossible to remember all the names of his numerous relatives, took the trouble some years ago to formulate "a family list," giving the dates of birth, marriage and death of every descendant of his father, of whom over 140 are now living.

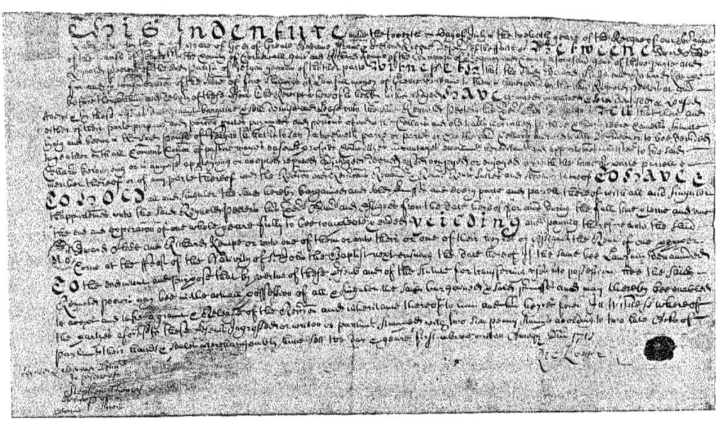

SECTION IV. PART II.

CHAPTER I.

EARLY AND SLINDON KEMPES.

IN our Kentish section we noted the apparent identity of the Kempe family with that represented by tenants of Battle Abbey entered on the Rolls as "de Campis." The earliest date at which a *Kempe* is recorded in Sussex is in the time of Edward I., when an Adam Kempe held land in Sullington, which is but six or seven miles south of Slindon. In the same reign or the following one, Galfrid Kempe held messuage and twelve acres from Battle Abbey, but these apparently were in Surrey; he may, however, also have held land at "Apeldraham." In 1403 Thomas Kempe, of Nuthurst, held lands there, and received a grant of others at Horsham from John Colme of that place, the deed being preserved at the Record Office. In 1436 John Kempe represented the Borough of Shoreham in Parliament, he, probably, being of the Kentish family. In 1452 at the rebellion led by Jack Cade (and aimed directly at the power of Archbishop Kempe and his party), one John Kempe, a *labourer* of Mundefield, with Richard Roper, Richard Elliot and others, were followers of Cade from this county. Thus it will be seen that at this early date there were Kempes in the lower classes as well as those in influential position. We know that one of the Kempes, of Ollantigh, was connected by marriage with this county; it may be in consequence that a very important branch of the Wye family established themselves at Slindon. This seat, however, was obtained by a grant from the Queen, and not through any connexion with that Adam Kempe who held land close by. The wills relating to the county are preserved partly at Lewes and partly at Chichester, those at the former court being apparently the more important. They commence in 1541, and in 1547 the first will of a Kempe appears. This is the will of John Kempe, of Preston, close to Brighton; and it has been claimed that he was the ancestor of the Kempes who founded Kempe Town in the last century. From Preston the Kempes appeared at Battle and Whatlington, then at Aldbourne, and afterwards at Brighton, Salehurst and South Malling. These, however, although admittedly connected with the Kempes, of Kempe Town, were a yeoman family until the seventeenth century, and no connexion between them and the wealthy Kempes of Slindon is traceable, nor probable.

The Chichester wills commence in 1511. No Kempe appears before 1545, but the names Cames, Comes, and Combes occurring early may be variants. We will first speak of the Kempes of Slindon. It was in the first year of Queen Mary that Geoffrey Poole, keeper of the manor and park at Slindon, granted the entire estate under the Queen's sanction to Anthony Kempe, of the Kentish stock, who was at this time in the Royal household. We find among the State papers a letter of his, dated at the Royal Palace of Greenwich the 25th February, 1556, and addressed to the Earl of Devonshire. The writer makes excuses for not communicating earlier owing to "being so engaged in posting between Greenwich and Brussels." He remarks, "the King has not yet returned to England, and whose absence makes the Queen melancholy." Another letter of Anthony Kempe's, also preserved in the State papers, is dated June 14th, 1556, at Brussels. He says, "I am sorry to hear that the plague has visited your house. The Queen is in good health. . . . Some of the traitors in the late conspiracy have been executed. . . . The King is still detained in Brussels." These letters are sufficient to show how closely connected the Kempes were with the affairs of State and the Royal Household. Anthony Kempe's mother was present at the baptism of Queen Elizabeth in 1533, and Anthony himself was present at most of the Court ceremonies of his time. He lived to be very old; indeed, his age was a source of considerable trouble to his relatives, as he accused his faithful medical attendant of hurrying his end. In the papers and manuscripts collected during the reign of Queen Elizabeth by the great Lord Burleigh are letters from Sir Thomas Shirley (who married Ann Kempe, daughter of Thomas Kempe, of Ollantigh) addressed to Sir Robert Cecil, and saying that Anthony Kempe is greatly abused by one, Walmesley, and "is very aged and even worn to the last." We have seen from the will of his mother (Kentish section) that Anthony Kempe was a staunch supporter of the Roman Catholic cause, and that it was under Queen Mary that he received his grant of considerable estates in and around Slindon and other places. At the accession of Queen Elizabeth, although known as a Romish recusant, he escaped attainder (doubtless owing to the great friendship which existed between that Queen and many of the other Kempes), and he maintained the Roman ritual at Slindon House, where a chapel and secret priest chamber were only recently dismantled. Throughout many generations, indeed, until the final heiress caused the estates to pass into other hands, the rites of the Roman Church were kept up at Slindon without interruption.

Anthony Kempe married, first, Ann, daughter and co-heir of John, Lord Conyers, by whom he had two children, Henry and Mary. This wife was buried at the Savoy chapel beside her mother-in-law. Anthony's second wife was Margaret, daughter of Sir Edward Gage, of Firle, Knight, by whom he had Garret, George, Anthony and Elizabeth. He died on the 29th October, 1597, and was buried with his first wife, his will being proved in the following year (P.C.C., 61 Kidd). The will bequeaths 1,000 marks to his daughter, Elizabeth, three score acres of woodland and twenty-eight of meadow in Plumstead to his son George, or in default to his son Anthony, to the latter his manor at Wallmore, Gloucestershire, to his daughter Mary, wife of Humphrey Wallrond, 1,000 marks, and the residue, subject to legacies to the testator's "cousin," Edward Gage, of Bentley, Sir Thomas Sholling and others, was bequeathed to Garret Kempe, his eldest surviving son. By codicils his jewels were equally divided between his daughters, and his mansion house at Blackfriars, London, was bequeathed to his nephew, Sir Thomas Shirley.

Henry Kempe, the eldest son of Anthony, was born in 1574, and at the age of fifteen was entered at Gloucester Hall, Oxford, where he duly matriculated. He died without issue in 1592, in which year a Post Mortem Inquisition is entered. Garret Kempe, the second, but eldest surviving son consequently—as we have seen from his father's will—inherited Slindon House and the numerous other manors which had been held by his father. We gain some idea as to the extent of his property by a casual mention in the proceedings of Chancery during Queen Elizabeth's reign, he suing his factor for failing to duly account for money collected in Yorkshire, Surrey, Gloucester, Wilts and Sussex. Garret was entered at Gray's Inn in 1618, probably living for a time in the parish of St. James', Clerkenwell. He was knighted by James I. in 1626, and married Elizabeth, daughter of John Carrell, of Warham, Sussex, by whom he had issue, which we shall presently follow. His brother George, as we have seen from the above will, inherited lands at Plumstead, Kent, which had belonged to the Moyles and the Kempes of Ollantigh. He, however, does not appear to have resided there, and is probably the George Kempe, a Jesuit, who was taken with other conspirators at a house of their society in London about the year 1626, of which some account occurs in the "History of St. James', Clerkenwell," and in the State papers. This may have occasioned the confiscation of his property and thus explain the absence of a will or other trace of him. However, as his father had property in Gloucestershire, this George may be the ancestor of the Kempes of Shepton Mallet, with whom the name of George was the constant favourite.

Anthony Kempe, the younger brother of this George, inherited Walmore, Westbury, but died at Ham, Wilts, in 1648, and in 1649 his will was proved (P.C.C., 184 Fairfax). An infant of his, named Anthony, was buried at St. Dunstan's-in-the-West in 1584, and he had two daughters, namely, Jean (who married Thomas Osborne) and Elizabeth ; also a son, Robert, who inherited the bulk of his father's property and made his will in 1656 at Ham ; he, probably, was the ancestor of the Kempes of Trowbridge, of whom we shall presently give some record. Returning to Garret Kempe, Knight, of Slindon, he had the following children : Philip, who was at Gray's Inn in 1619 and married Frances, daughter of Sir John Webb, of Oldstock, Wilts, by whom he had Garret, who died an infant, and Catherine, who married Thomas Eyre, of Hassop, Derby ; she was living in 1634. The Eyre family were connected with the Rogers, of Surrey, and both these families with Christchurch, and we are inclined to believe that it is due to this connexion that the ancestors of the Kemp-Welch family became identified with that town, at which another member of the Kentish stock lived about this time, namely, John Kempe, a leading Roundhead and member of the Parliamentary Committee in the time of Cromwell. Thomas Kempe, the second son of Sir Garret, was of Ypres, in Flanders. He married Mary, daughter of Sir Anthony Briggs, of Essex, by whom he had but one child, Mary, who married George Heneage, of Hainton, Lincoln. Garrett Kempe, the third son, eventually succeeded to Slindon, and married a daughter of Beale, by whom he had issue as will appear. The daughters of Sir Garret were as follows : Mary, who married Francis Croote, of Essex ; Jane, who married Patrick Plunket, of Ireland ; Elizabeth, who married Thomas Arundell, of Dorset, Margaret and Bridget.

Garret Kempe, of Slindon, by the daughter of Beale, left two sons. William, the youngest, had a son named Garret, who was buried at Clerkenwell in 1629. Anthony, the eldest son, succeeded to the Slindon estates in 1666 and married Mary, daughter of Sir Thomas Gage, Bart., of Firle—this is the second occasion of an intermarriage between the Kempes of Slindon and this family of Gage. More remarkable is the fact that Sir Garret and the Gages united in a sale of property at Shelwood and other places in Surrey and Sussex to Sir George Kempe, of Pentlow, Bart., who was of entirely different stock and diverse arms. Deeds relating to these transactions are preserved at the British Museum (Add. Charters 18,906 and 18,944), to which several interesting seals are attached, Sir Garret apparently using as his badge a spread eagle or similar heraldic bird ; replicas of this seal occur on the original wills of several Kempes connected with Worcester, Gloucester and other parts of England, the testators of which have not positively been traced as connexions of the Kentish stock. We may here remark that another deed in the same collection (19,016) is an indenture signed by Anthony Kempe, of Slindon, relating to Goodwood Park and other property, he having bought the now renowned racecourse with its appurtenances from John Carrell for the sum of £3,500. It is hardly necessary to say that Slindon House has frequently entertained Royalty even in recent times. The last named Anthony Kempe, who died in 1715, had the following family : Anthony, his heir ; John, who died unmarried ; Thomas, who left no issue ; Philip, who died at Ghent in 1728, and the administration of whose estate was granted to his eldest brother that year, and Mary Kempe, who married Sir Henry Tichborne, Bart., of Hampshire. Sir Henry was buried at Tichborne on 20th July, 1742, and his will was proved in the following year.

Anthony Kempe, the eldest son and heir, again followed tradition, marrying Anne Brown, daughter of Henry, fifth Viscount Montagu, two of whose family had intermarried with Kempes, the first to a Kentish Kempe, Knight, and the second to a Norfolk Kempe, Baronet. By this wife he had two children. On her death he married Jane, daughter of the Hon. Charles Stourton, third son of William Stourton, niece to Lord Stourton. This marriage took place in July, 1734, and notice of it appears in the *Gentleman's Magazine*. Anthony died in 1753, aged eighty-five, administration of his estate being granted in 1754 to the Hon. Barbara Radcliffe, wife of the Hon. James Bartholomew Radcliffe, commonly called Lord Kynnaird, she being daughter of the deceased, and the Hon. Jane Kempe, widow and relict, having first renounced. Administration of the estate of Jane Kempe, the widow, formerly of Slindon, but who died in the city of Liege, Germany, was granted to John Maire, Esq., the attorney of the Right Hon. William Lord Stourton, her brother, on the 9th April, 1770. In addition to Barbara, who, as stated, married Lord Kynnaird (afterwards Earl of Newburgh), Anthony had a daughter Anne, who died aged forty-three in 1765 unmarried. Barbara was married in 1749, and is the ancestress of the present Earl of Newburgh and Lord Kynnaird, who are now chiefly known by their Italian titles.

She inherited Slindon and all the Kempe estates, which passed to her husband, and thence descended. Slindon House, of which we give an illustration, is still standing, and bears ample evidence of the Kempes, their arms and quarterings being repeatedly carved and emblazoned within the hall. It is said that the present building was rebuilt by Sir Garret Kempe about 1600, but traces of the earlier mansion are evident.

Slindon House.

CHAPTER II.

SOUTH MALLING AND DESCENDANTS.

A MASS of tradition and possibly superstition surrounds the origin of those Kempes identified with Kemp Town and Lewes. Their pedigree seems to have first seen print about 1828 in Berry's "Sussex Genealogies," and then in Burke's "Commoners," in both cases it commences with a George Kempe, of Lewes, who married Grace, daughter of Thomas Stonestreet. This couple are represented as living about 1750. Burke in his usual questionable introduction states that "one branch of the Kempes, of Ollantigh, is represented by the present Thomas Read Kemp, Esq., of Kemp Town, near Brighton." Charles Eamer Kempe, Esq., M.A., who now represents this family, and who has collected Kemp(e) items enthusiastically for a number of years, has repeatedly been approached by the editors of genealogical works with a view to his publishing that line of ancestors by which he claims connexion with the Ollantigh Kempes, but his reply is to the effect that he questions the trustworthiness of the works soliciting these details. His brother, Captain William Kemp, of Arundel, in answer to our inquiries states that so far as his knowlege goes the pedigree of his family goes back some 200 years in a rather disjointed manner. A third relative of Thomas Read Kemp, who has also collected a great many genealogical notes of the Kempes of Sussex, confirms the latter statement, and although both have a vague idea that their ancestors were for a long time connected with South Malling, we believe that the following details will afford them fresh information and a better knowledge of the subject. We, however, cannot profess that the line is without flaws, nor do we believe that it will give them indisputable right to the ancient arms of the Kempes of Ollantigh.

Roger Kempe possessed tenements at Hamsey in 1590; he seems to have died intestate. In 1601 Thomas Kempe was connected with Albourne and Preston. His will names Edward and William, sons of his brother John, with Edward, Alice and Agnes, children of his uncle Robert, who may be the same individual as Roger Kempe above. In 1615 we have the will of William Kempe, of Albourne, who desires to be buried at Preston, the poor of which parish he remembered. His wife, Alice, and children, William, Edward, Richard and Mary survived him. This last William Kempe may be identical with the first William Kempe, of whom we have record in connexion with South Malling, who was rated at Hamsey for 30*s*. 8*d*., and whose will was proved in 1656 (P.C.C., 459 Berkley). This will states that he was a yeoman, and that he had a son William and a daughter Grace, his wife is not mentioned. It is evident that he had a little property, for he left a tenement and land, valued at £10 per annum, to his daughter Grace, and the residue to his son William. This son, William, was also of South Malling, a yeoman, but in 1662 obtained a *grant* of arms under the hand of Edward Bysshe, Clarenceaux, which was as follows: Gules, a fess, ermine, between three garbs Or, within a bordure of the second. And for his crest, on a helmet and wreath of his colours, a falcon volant, ermine, standing on a garb Or, mantled Gules, doubled argent. This coat and crest, which are reproduced in colour in "Miscellanea Genealogica," are similar to those used for a time by Richard Kempe, of Wash-brooke, Suffolk, who was the ancestor of the Kempe Baronets, but it does not follow that the Kempes of South Malling were in any way connected with the Norfolk Kempes. William Kempe, mentioned in the last will as then aged seventeen, was placed at Christchurch, Oxford, and became a student of the Inner Temple in 1674, whither we shall follow him. He had, however, a relative, namely, Edward Kempe, of Albourne, a yeoman, whose will appears in 1667. This mentions a wife, Anne, and sons named Edward and William, the last named being appointed executor, while the testator's "kinsman," William Earle of Bartons, was appointed overseer. The two families were from this time for at least 100 years closely connected. In the following year a deed was made between Edward Kempe, of Albourne, styling himself Gent., and John Whitpaine, of Hurstperpoint, relating to some lands at Cowfold. We may presume, therefore, that the will proved in 1668 (P.C.C., 56 Coke) of William Kempe, of Hurstperpoint, was that of his son and executor. It leaves all his farm, lands and tenements in Preston, then in the occupation of Samuel Friend, to his loving friend Elizabeth Luxford, one of the daughters of Thomas Luxford, of Randalls, Gent. The testator does not describe himself as either a yeoman or gent., but as a "singleman," so we suggest that Elizabeth was his intended wife. William Kempe, son of William Kempe, Gent., in his will of 1689 styles himself "esquire," and he seems to have considerably added to the importance of his family and to his estate; he certainly had the honour of representing South Malling in Parliament. He desired to be buried in the chancel of South Malling Church with a marble slab over him. This request was complied with, the inscription was until recently to be seen there. The following inscriptions with others are now in the churchyard at South Malling on one very large altar tomb: "Mary Kempe, wife of William Kempe, the elder, now living, she was buried September 3rd, 1664"; and "Here lies the body of Mary Kempe and John Kempe, dafter (*sic*) and sown of William Kempe and of Mary, his wife, she was buryed Desembar 24th, 1657. He was buryed April 15th, 1662." The above will mentions lands and tenements, barns and malthouse at Albourne, and lands called Sparhaws, in the parish of Hamsey, also lands at South Malling, Rugnor and Hartfield, which he leaves to his loving kinsman, Edward Burtonshaw, woollen draper; no children or other relatives appear in the will, and we may presume that he left no surviving issue. It was consequently from the second son of Edward Kempe, of Albourne, that the subsequent line of Kempes of South Malling was continued. We do not know for certain that this was so, but in 1720 William Kempe, of South Malling, "Esquire," made his will. With many pious phrases he desired his body should be buried in the church at South Malling, and he left to his wife, Timothy, all his capital messuage, &c., called The Deanery or College, with appurtenances, wherein he then dwelt, with the advowson of the church, and also lands called Beaches, Bruxells, and Blackfield, lying in Hartfield, and lands called Islewoods and other lands in the parish of St. Johns, under the Castle of Lewes. The will is a very long one, and is particularly interesting because it gives us a glimpse of a family trouble. William, by his wife Timothy, had but one child, Mary, who married against the will of her parents Richard Russell, of Lewes, M.D. The man was an accomplished physician, and was the author of several medical books, and his family were certainly equal, if not superior, in station to the Kempes of South Malling. The objection therefore to him appears to have been that William and his wife held religious tenets entirely opposed to this worthy doctor. In any case, the above will states that the daughter having caused her parents great pain and impaired the health of her mother, notwithstanding the many and frequent admonitions and persuasions used by her father, should forfeit the fortune which would otherwise be hers, and that it should consequently be held in trust for her eldest son, and that he only should inherit the South Malling estates on condition that he absolutely and for ever renounced his paternal name of Russell and assumed the name of Kemp (with authority to use the Kemp arms) without the addition or alias of Russell. Timothy Kemp, of South Malling, made her will in 1728. It is very brief, and leaves to her daughter, Mary Russell, all her real and personal estate whatsoever. Probate was granted to her daughter in 1760, before which time her husband had died.

Richard and Mary Russell had several children, and the eldest son, named William, complied with the requirements of his grandfather's will, renounced the name of Russell, and was granted by due authority the name of Kemp, with the use of the following arms : Gules, three garbs or, within a bordure of the last charged with eight pellets gules. These arms it is necessary to notice were entirely new, and although similiar, except for an addition to the border to the arms used by the old family of Kempes in Kent, do not imply at all that the heralds believed him entitled by descent to claim kinship to these worthies. Further, had his ancestors been direct descendants of that William Kempe, of South Malling, who obtained arms mentioned above, he would probably have been granted the use of that coat instead of the new one. It will be seen that if William Russell, who assumed the name of Kempe, left issue, that his descendants cannot claim direct descent by *male* line from even the Kempes of South Malling.

(It is necessary to make this remark, because the papers of the day frequently speak of Mr. Charles Eamer Kempe as a direct descendant of the great Archbishop of his name, when mentioning that some window of his design and manufacture has been erected in a church or public building. Of course the Archbishop was not permitted to marry, and we are sufficiently satisfied that he left no issue.)

William Russell, *alias* Kempe, who did succeed to the Kempe property at South Malling and Lewes, was a Serjeant-at-Law, and is credited with having a considerable knowledge of the history of his family's estate. In the local histories they have generally omitted to mention that his father's name was Russell, and merely say that the property was inherited from his grandfather, William Kemp, who is said to have obtained this property from Richard Evelyn in 1639—100 years before the said William Kemp was alive! There are many letters from Mr. Sarjeant Kemp in the British Museum relative to the local Parliamentary elections, and mention is made of him in the *Gentleman's Magazine*. He died on the 19th June, 1797, aged seventy-six, and his will was proved the following year (P.C.C., 39 Walpole). He is therein described as William Kemp, of South Malling, Serjeant-at-Law, and the will is dated 27th October, 1794. He leaves to his daughter, Timothea Kempe, the watch of her late mother, a five guinea Queen Anne piece and a medal of Queen Anne, as well as her mother's clothes. To his daughter, Wilhelmina Sophia, as well as the above daughter, he left some money, and divided his goods, Government funds, and the Deanery of South Malling, between Richard Russell Kempe, his son, and the second daughter. He also mentioned his nephews, John Ley Martyn, Esq., of Southampton Row, London, and the Rev. Arthur Fredel, Rector of Newhaven, Essex. There is a clause in his will which must be recorded. It is to the effect that he had intended to marry his deceased wife's sister, but that ill health had prevented this marriage being carried out. He, however, provided for an expected child. (The will was proved by Lestock Wilson, Esq., Abraham Driver, a land surveyor in Kent, and the Rev. Arthur Fredel, clerk.)

We now come to George Kemp, of Lewes, the first individual mentioned in the pedigree in Berry's "Sussex Genealogies," and so repeated by Sir Edmund Burke. This George Kemp married Grace, daughter of Thomas Stonestreet, by whom he had the following children : Thomas Kemp, Nathaniel Kemp, of Rottingdean, Grace, who married John Pain, of Patcham Place, and Elizabeth, besides the following children who died young: Nathaniel, George, Grace and Anne. The eldest son married Anne Read, of Brookland, heiress of Henry Reid, by whom he had several children; he was M.P. for Lewes, which borough was afterwards represented in Parliament by his son, Thomas Read Kemp, who had the honour of receiving in this capacity the King and Queen on their visit to Lewes in 1830. An account of this visit was published that year, and fully sets out the speech he made on that occasion at the banquet, and his many acts of gallantry in escorting Queen Adelaide to the gates of the Friars, and thence to Lewes Castle, and finally to the Infant's School, where Her Majesty made many inquiries concerning the mode of teaching the art of needlework as performed by the girls. Throughout these proceedings the name of Mr. Kemp occurs as the leading spirit, and from this time until the death of the King he was permitted frequent access to the Royal residences. A picture commemorating the visit, and including portraits of the King and Queen with Thomas Read Kemp, was for a time hung in the Town Hall, and is now the property of the Earl of Chichester. We reproduce a portrait of this distinguished M.P., and regret that space at our disposal prevents us giving further details of his many public and philanthropic acts. It was he who laid out and founded Kemp Town, near Brighton; it was he who bought Hurstmonceaux Castle, which had belonged for a time to the Kempes of Slindon, and it was he who ran through three fortunes and finally died—it is believed by his own hand—in Paris. His death was announced as "sudden," but no details were published. He was for a time a lay preacher, and started a chapel on original lines, which has given rise to the rumour that he founded a sect, his doctrines, however, seem to have died with him, and their very nature is now a matter of doubt. The property on which Kemp Town was built came to him through a family named Friend, a member of which has been mentioned above as a tenant of William Kempe, of South Malling. A part of this property, indeed, was mentioned in a will before cited as "Beeches," and the title deeds relating thereto, with various legal opinions thereon, are now preserved in the British Museum. It is presumably from these documents that the printed pedigree was derived. Thomas Read Kemp was married at Beddington, Surrey, 12th July, 1806, to Miss Baring, daughter of Sir Francis Baring, Bart., of Stratton Park, Hants, and on the 27th May, 1807, his first child, a daughter, was born at Hill Street, Berkeley Square. On the 21st August, 1810, his son and heir was born at the house of Sir Francis Baring, at Lee (Kent), and on the 3rd May, 1811, the death of his father was announced at the age of sixty-five, the papers of the day calling attention to the fact that he represented the Borough of Lewes in six Parliaments. In January, 1812, the birth of another son was announced, Thomas Read Kemp, then being described as of Lewes, M.P., while on the former occasion he was mentioned as of Hurstmonceaux. In 1825 the building of Kemp Town was described in the papers as proceeding

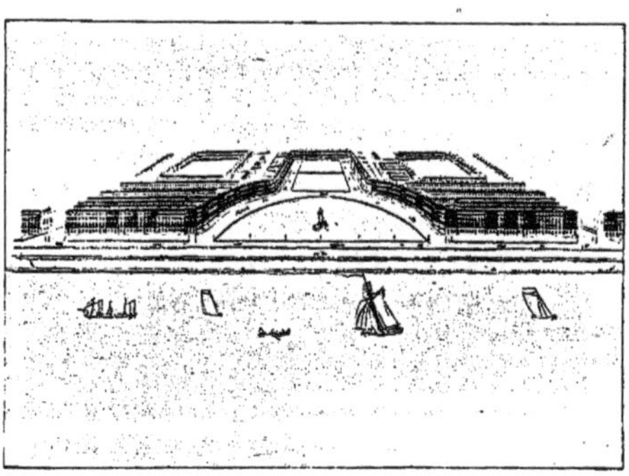

Original scheme for the building of Kemp-Town.

rapidly, and in the same year the death of Frances, wife of T. R. Kemp, M.P. for ***Arundel***, was announced in the ***Gentleman's Magazine***. In 1827 Thomas Read Kemp was interested in the building of Belgrave Square, at one of the corners of which he had a residence.

Nathaniel Kemp, brother to Thomas Kemp, M.P., for Lewes, lived at Preston House, Preston, near Brighton, and at Rottingdean, and married a daughter of John Eamer, Esq., Sheriff of London, by whom he had two surviving sons, the eldest is Charles Eamer Kempe, M.A., the well-known manufacturer of stained glass, and who owns some 300 acres in Sussex, the younger son being Captain William Kemp, now of Arundel. The last named has been good enough to send us a seal which is used by himself. It is a fine example of a modern imitation of the Tudor period, and shows his authorised arms impaling those of Marsh in right of his wife; the arms selected, however, for his wife are not authorised by the Herald's College, and much doubt exists as to whether his wife's family can claim *any* arms; her father, however, was an admiral of distinction. We may mention that Anne Frances, youngest daughter of the late Thomas Read Kemp, Esq., married Thomas Jesson, Esq., eldest son of Thomas Jesson, Esq., of Beech House, Hants, on the 6th October, 1846, at Stotfold, Bedfordshire, a descendant of which marriage has lent us his MSS. collections concerning the Kemps of Kemp Town, to which we owe many of the foregoing details, and the portrait of Thos. Read Kemp. At the crossways in Kingston, juxta Lewes, is a spot known as "Nan Kemp's Grave," which is said to be the burial place of a murderess (S.A.C., xxix. 165).

CHAPTER III.

THE QUAKER FAMILY.

LIKE the family so long settled at Slindon the ancestors of Caleb Rickman Kemp, J.P., of Lewes, came from Kent, but it is not certain how they were connected with the Kemps of Wye, whose arms they claim. According to one "family tree" in possession of a member of this family their first known ancestor was a WILLIAM KEMP, of Guildford, a brewer, living about 1750, while another pedigree states that this same William was of Wapping. Both versions are likely to be true, for in a will of Sarah Kemp, spinster, of the parish of St. John's, Wapping, the testatrix speaks of her "uncle, William Kemp," and relatives living both in Kent, Surrey and Sussex. William Kemp, of ***Brewhouse Lane***, aged sixty-six, was buried at St. John's, Wapping, on 28th November, 1756, and administration of his estate was granted that year to his widow, Susannah Kemp, who is recorded to have been buried at the same church, aged sixty-eight, in March, 1757. This couple is shown to be the same as a couple who were married at Beakesbourne by license in 1714 by the Kentish Freeholders' List of 1734, when William Kemp, of ***Wapping***, held land at Wickham Breux, of which place his wife, formerly Susannah Shooler, was a native. They had two children baptized at Beakesbourne, namely, Mary, in 1715, and Edward, in 1717; after this they certainly removed from that parish and probably were at

Guildford for the next ten years, thence removing to Wapping where the brewer was established in 1734. In 1748 William Kemp, of St. John's, Wapping, was married to Sarah Bing, of Wickham, Kent, at St. George's, Canterbury, and we have little doubt that this was the son of the elder brewer, but we cannot identify him as having left issue at Wapping. In April, 1751, Edward Kemp, of St. John's, Wapping, was married by license at St. Paul's Cathedral to Elizabeth Dare. This Edward was probably the son of the brewer baptized at Beaksbourne, the will of his wife appears to be that proved in London 21st January, 1795, mentioning her nephew, Charles Dare, the elder, of Dowgate, and her sister, Sarah Goodyer, of Cobham, Surrey, to the latter of whom she bequeathed certain house property in Shoreditch, John Crabtree, of Newington Butts, Surrey, and James Goodyer were the executors. She does not mention any children of her own, and we believe, as shown by the pedigrees sent in, that the only son of the Wapping brewer to leave issue was JOHN KEMP, who lived at Grange Walk, Bermondsey, and was a coalfactor. The name of John Kemp's first wife is not recorded, but she left daughters whose descendants were named Lane and Viner. His second wife was Elizabeth, daughter of Robert Horne, of Arundel (by Mary, daughter of John Grover, of Brighthelmstone), to whom he was married at the Arundel Friends Meeting House on 6th July, 1764. He died on 10th August, 1785, his age being stated to be fifty-five years. If this is correct it would appear that he was born much later than those of the brewer's family mentioned above ; indeed, it would seem just possible that he was a grandson of William Kemp, of Beakesbourne. His wife lived to her eighty-fifth year, being buried at the Friend's Burial Ground at Long Lane, Southwark, in July, 1817. She was the mother of the following family : Robert, who died aged six months ; Mary, who died aged sixteen months ; John Kemp, of whom we shall speak directly ; Elizabeth, born in 1771, marrying Thomas Edmunds, of High Wycombe, in 1792, and dying in 1836, leaving a great many female descendants ; Marv Horne Kemp, died aged five months, and Thomas Kemp, who was born 27th November, 1778. This son married Maria Todd, by whom he had at least three children, named Robert, Thomas and Maria ; he lived in London, but his children went abroad, and except that one was in the army nothing is known as to them or their issue. Sarah, the youngest daughter of John Kemp, of Bermondsey, was born in 1775 and was married at the Southwark Friend's Meeting House on 23rd March, 1813, to George Neave, of Poole, a merchant. (It is noteworthy that at the time of her marriage the ancestors of the Kemp-Welches were important townsmen of Poole, and their religious views were almost as strict as those of the Quakers ; it is, however, believed that the Kemps of Poole were descendants of the Hampshire branch of the Ollantigh family, and were but remotely, if at all, connected with these Bermondsey and Sussex Quakers.)

We now come to JOHN KEMP, the eldest surviving son of the coalfactor. He was born at Bermondsey on 29th March, 1769, and was married at the Friend's Meeting House at St. Peter's Court on 21st April, 1791, to Benjamina, daughter of Joseph Rickman, a merchant of Stockwell. He carried on his father's business at Bermondsey for a time, but being more disposed for study than for a business career he went to Brighton as a schoolmaster, and was there buried at the Quaker's burial ground in April, 1827, his wife having predeceased him and having been buried at Long Lane, Southwark, in 1799, aged only twenty-eight. She left the following family : Grover Kemp, with whom we shall deal below ; Rickman John Kemp, born in 1798, who lived at Chelsea, but died at Poole on 26th July, 1824 ; Benjamina Kemp, born at Bermondsey Square in 1794 and married Richard Penny, of Poole, a merchant. He died in 1835, aged forty-two, and she was buried in the Friend's Burial Ground at Poole in 1867 leaving eleven children, four of whom married and left descendants, Anne Rickman Kemp, the youngest daughter of John and Benjamina, was born in 1796, and met her death by playing with fire on 28th February, 1799.

GROVER KEMP, the eldest son of John and Benjamina, was born at Bermondsey on 10th November, 1792, and was educated at a large school at Earl's Colne in Essex (conducted by John Kirkham), and afterwards at Hitchin and Epping. On his mother's death his father went abroad, consequently Grover with his sister Benjamina was placed under the guardianship of his grandfather, Joseph Rickman, of Staines, and their aunt, Mary Rickman, to whose influence is attributed that earnestness in religious and philanthropic matters which both children evinced as they grew older. At the age of only fourteen Grover was apprenticed to Mr. John Glaisyer, a chemist at Brighton, with whom he subsequently became a partner, keeping active in this business until within six years of his decease. Feeling a keen interest in study as a means of benefitting others, and regretting that his education should have ceased at so early an age, Grover studied both ancient and modern languages in all his available time during his apprenticeship, and while still a youth wrote many essays showing depth of thought and care for the spiritual and temporal improvement of the community. In 1816 he was married at the Chichester Friend's Meeting House to Susannah, daughter of Robert Horne, of Arundel (by Elizabeth, daughter of Caleb Rickman, of Shipley, Sussex), by whom he had but one son, namely, Caleb Rickman Kemp, who is the last male descendant of this family. Grover Kemp began to speak at meetings in his nineteenth year, and when twenty-six spoke as a minister and was recorded as such by the Lewes and Chichester Monthly Meeting in 1823. Actively associating himself with the Friends he restarted many disused Meeting Houses, not merely in Sussex, but eventually in the West of England and the Midlands. He especially devoted himself to reaching the artizans of Wapping and Ratcliffe, and those at the potteries and pitmen in some colliery districts. In 1832 he visited the South of France, in 1839 the Friends in Dublin, and in 1843 those meeting at Manchester, Liverpool and Birmingham. In 1855 he went on a similar mission to the Isle of Man, and the following year to the Scilly Islands. He next went to the Channel Islands where he held many meetings, and in 1857 and 1858 he went with his youngest son to the West Indian Islands with a view of freeing the black population. In this humane work he was greatly aided by missionaries already settled there who lent their places of worship that he might state to large congregations his views and scheme. In this same work, one James Kemp, of Hoxton, had already taken a considerable part. Between these two anti-slavery Kemps, however, no connexion is known (*vide* Middlesex). So late as 1862 Grover Kemp was authorized by the Friends to hold special services in the Eastern Counties, thus in the course of a long ministry he probably visited more meetings throughout England than any other of the society had previously done; indeed, it is very doubtful if any other member of the Quaker body has since equalled his work or visited more places in the execution of ministerial duties. He was also one of the first and most active supporters of a saving's bank in Brighton. After publishing many tracts (copies of which may still be obtained) he died 21st December, 1869. He was buried at the Friend's Burial Ground at Black Rock, Brighton, and a memoir of his life appeared in the "Annual Monitor" of 1871. His portrait is still among the most valued in the society's gallery at Bishopsgate Street, London. His wife died on 27th March, 1882, and was buried beside her husband. Her name also occurs at the time of her death in the "Annual Monitor," which also included notices of other members of this family, namely, Benjamina Kemp, afterwards Penny, in 1868, Mary Rickman, afterwards Binns, in 1852, and numerous other Kemps, who, however, were chiefly connected with that Quaker family of Kemps which we have noticed in our Norfolk section.

CALEB RICKMAN KEMP was born at Brighton on 18th June, 1836, and married Jane Morland, of Croydon. Like his ancestors he has taken a very active part in the work of the Society of Friends, and was one of the representatives selected to congratulate King Edward the VII. on his accession, before whom he appeared at St. James' Palace in February, 1901. He was President of the Society of Friends in 1900, and has for years taken a great interest in the work of the British and Foreign Bible Society, of which he is Vice-Chairman. He is a Justice of the Peace for Lewes, represents the Lewes Castle Division on the (East) Sussex County Council, is an Alderman of Lewes, and has held many other municipal positions. Alderman Kemp has had no children, and devotes his life to philanthropy in its varied forms.

We may here mention that the County Hospital at Brighton stands on an elevated site which was given for the purpose by Thomas Read Kemp, M.P., mentioned in our last chapter, he gave in all some £5,000 towards the erection and maintenance of this institution, at which Charles Gilbert Barington Kempe, M.B., B.S., M.R.C.S., Eng., has for some time been assistant house surgeon. A Mrs. Kemp is the treasurer of the Girls' Training Home, Delap Hall, Lewes, thus at the present time we have four or five distinct Kempe and Kemp families represented in the County of Sussex. Charles G. B. Kempe and Charles Marshall Kempe, the Medical Officer for Health at Shoreham, being of Cornish origin, while the others claim origin from Kentish and possible Norfolk stock.

CHAPTER IV.

HAMPSHIRE AND ISLE OF WIGHT.

SO early as 1272 there is no doubt that bearers of the name of Kempe were resident in Hampshire, and a deed of that date still exists mentioning Martin Kempe as a tenant of some lands which were then settled upon the Abbey of St. Edward at Netley. In the following century a ring bearing the name of Kempe was presumably lost in the county, for a note of such being found and ascribed to that period occurs in the archæological journals of a few years back. This ring appears from its description to have belonged to a foreigner of the name, and from this we might infer that some of the numerous early Kempes in this county were of direct foreign origin. Both to the east and west, namely, in Sussex and Dorset, we find that John Kempe was a name of considerable repute in the fourteenth and early fifteenth centuries, for one of this name represented Lyme Regis in Parliament from 1337 to 1340 and again in 1354, while another of the same name was M.P. for the Borough of Shoreham from 1436 to 1440. In the year 1584 Bartholomew Kempe—who, we believe, was of the Norfolk family—represented Shaftesbury, and in the time of Charles I. and during the Commonwealth John Kemp, of Heywood, sat for Christchurch. This last alone seems to be traceable as a descendant of the Kentish family, although in the sixteenth century several Kempes who *may* have come from Ollantigh were ratepayers in Hants; the Manor of Bishopstoke belonging to a Francis Kempe who held it direct from Queen Elizabeth. In 1582 Robert Kempe held a house in Northbrook Street, Basingstoke, and about the same time he, or another of the same name, held a house in Church Street, Basingstoke. It is worthy of note that within the hundred of Basingstoke so early as 1334 there was a piece of land known as "Kempeshete" or "Kempeshote," and this retained its name at least down to the time of Elizabeth; we might from this fact reason that the Kempes from 1344 held this site, but the absence of records to prove this rather suggests that the Kempes who held property from the Queen were related closely to the Kempes of Gissing or Wye, both being represented at the Royal Court at this time.

We must now turn to the known branch of the Kentish family, who for a comparative brief period exercised considerable power in Hampshire.

The founder of this branch was EDWARD KEMPE, sixth son of Sir William Kempe, Knight, of Ollantigh, by Ellenor, daughter and co-heiress of Sir Thomas Browne. This Edward settled at "Conns," in the New Forest, and married Elizabeth, daughter of . . . Wilmot, of Oxford and Gloucestershire. This wife was related to John Wilmot, of Marilebone, and Rose Wilmot, who married Robert Bromfield, connected with whom were some of the Kempes of Hampstead. Edward, of the New Forest, died in 1605, and is commemorated by the following inscription which appears on a brass in Beaulieu Church:

> "Here lyeth the body of Edward Kempe
> Gent: the sixt sonne of Sir William
> Kempe, Knight, who hath left Eli
> Zabeth his wife with Thomas, Edward
> Frauncis and Robert their sonnes. He
> Died the VIIth of March ano dni. 1605."

We have failed to trace any will or administration mentioning this couple, but we find that Thomas, the eldest son, was born in 1557. He appears to have been at Oxford in 1581, and on the death of his father inherited the patrimony and lived thenceforward at Beaulieu, where he died in 1622, having married Mary, daughter of Sir William Oglander, Knight, by whom he had three sons, Francis, Robert and John and two daughters, Elizabeth, who married John Ford, and Frances, who married Henry Bromfield, J.P., of Dorset. The will of THOMAS KEMPE, of "Gins," in Beaulieu (pronounced and sometimes written Bewley), was proved in 1623 (P.C.C., 52 Swan); the opening is indicative of the Roman faith, and he bequeathed sums of money to the poor of Bewley and several servants. He mentions also the following relatives: his brother Francis, the widows of his late brothers Robert and Edward, Sir John Oglander, Knight, Arthur Bromfield, Esquire, his "kinsman," Robert Dillingham, Esquire, his brother-in-law George Oglander, Gent., his wife Mary, and his children, John, Robert, Francis, Elizabeth, Frances and Amy. He mentions several items of his real estate at Beaulieu, Boulnor and elsewhere, the bulk of which with his stock and cattle was left to his wife for life and, subject to her interest, to John, his eldest son, to whom he specially bequeathed his father's "sealed ring." (Impressions from this ring are extant at the British Museum and doubtless elsewhere, but we fear the ring itself has passed away.)

JOHN KEMPE, the eldest son, duly inherited the estate, and it was he who represented Christchurch and Lymington in Parliament, and conveyed to the imprisoned King Charles at Carisbrooke Castle the demands of the Parliamentary Party. He was Mayor of Christchurch in the following years, 1625, 1633, 1640, and several letters of his are still preserved in the Corporation chest of Christchurch. He lived chiefly at Bucker's Hard, near Beaulieu, but was buried at Boldre Church, where a bust with the following inscription still exists there.

> D. M. S.
> Iohannes Kempe, armiger, pietate in Deum,
> patriam, parentes et cognatos nulli secundus;
> modestia, humanitate, et vitae integritate
> omnibus bonis notus; e civibus supremi senatus

Anglicani non postremus ; exactis 41 vitae annis
mortales exuvias hic deposuit resumpturus
immortales in resurrectione.
Non diu fuit, sed diu vixit.
Obiit die quinto Octobris anno Dni 1652.
Hoc monumentum Henricus Bromfield, armiger,
sororis suae maritus, in perpetuum amoris
testimonium, moestus posuit
Qui clarus fuit, qui charus amicis,
qui patriae fidus, cui decus omne fuit,
occidit ante diem, fatis ablatus iniquis,
et rediit in cineres (proh dolor) ipse suos,
Quod mortale fuit tumulo requiescit in isto ;
sed nescit leges mens, libitina, tuas ;
nanque expers lethi mortales despicit omnes,
et tenet aetheria pegmata coeli post.

The church register records that John Kempe, Esquire, was buried 7th October, 1652. His will dated at Haywood, in the parish of "Bolder, in the New Forest," on 23rd October, 1647, was proved in London on the 28th October, 1652. The will opens with a request that the testator should "be buried according to the rancke, qualitie and degree it hath pleased the Lord to place me in," but this clause was struck out before signing. It bequeaths to his mother, Mary Bromfield, £500, £300 to his "sister," Frances Bromfield, and subject to other legacies it leaves the residuary estate in trust for William Bromfield, during whose minority his father, Henry Bromfield, is appointed executor. The testator mentions his lands in "Bewley," Christchurch, Boldre, Whippingham and at Shalfleete, the two last being in the Isle of Wight. Among the legatees are the following: Elizabeth, daughter of John Ford (Gent.), the testator's "brother," Amy, wife of John Button, Margaret Tollesbury, John Baywood, Robert Dillingham, Esq., William Oglander, Esq., the servants on the estates and the local clergy. From this will it appears evident that this John Kempe left neither widow nor children, and that his possessions passed to the Bromfields, his mother, as indicated by the will, having married Henry Bromfield, of Southampton. Thus it seems that William Bromfield, the principal legatee, was half brother to John Kempe, M.P. We find that "John Kempe, son of Thomas Kempe, of Bewley, Co. Southampton, Esquire," was entered at Gray's Inn on 2nd May, 1631, there can be no doubt about this entry referring to the above M.P. for Christchurch, but it is evident that there was a second John Kempe, of Christchurch, who died there just two years later, his will being proved in the same Court as the foregoing (P.C.C., 187 Wotton) in 1658. It is dated 3rd October, 1657, and describes the testator ss "John Kemp*t*, of Weeke, within the parish of Christchurch, *Gent.*" It mentions the testator's son-in-law, Henry Hopkins, his daughter Mary Hilles, and his two daughters-in-law, Dorothy and Alice Warwicke, and a grandchild Thomas Hills. The chief legatee of this will is Tobias Kemp*t*, who also was sole executor. From the mention of married children and of the grandchild, we infer that this John Kempt was older than the M.P. Possibly he was the son of Parson John Kempe, of Freshwater, Isle of Wight, who had sons named John, Tobias and Caleb.* We may therefore now turn to the notes gleaned of Kempes settled in that

* We say *possibly*, for whereas Kempts requently become Kemps the converse is rare, the rule being that the more difficult form to pronounce or write yields to the easier form. John Kempt may have been a migrant from Scotland.

Isle, the earliest of whom, so far as our information goes, is the said Parson, who is said to have been beneficed at one time at Clanfield, Hants. The state papers contain many references to him, and John Fox, in his "Acts and Monuments," states that he was persecuted in Queen Mary's time. This JOHN KEMPE is believed to be one of those of his name included in the Alumni Oxonienses, he being either at All Souls in 1541 or 1546. In either case the fact of his being at that college points to his being a recognised relative of the Kentish Kempes, who as descendants of the Founder's Kin (Archbishop Chichele) were entitled to privileges as noticed in our Kentish section ; he, however, seems to have come from Godstone (Surrey), where the records show that a line of Kempes had long been settled. The State Papers of 1587 announce his death, Sir George Carey writing from Carisbrooke Castle to Sir Francis Walsingham says, "The Parsonage of Freshwater is vacant by the death of Parson Kempe . . . the place is fit for Mr. Browne, Mr. Eades or some good preacher. (The suggestion as to Mr. Browne also points to the likelihood of this John being near kin to the Kempes of Ollanty, as Elleanor Browne, daughter of Sir Matthew Browne, of Betchworth Castle, Surrey, was grandmother to Thomas Kempe, of Beaulieu.) The will of the Parson was proved in 1586-7, being dated at Freshwater in July, 1579. It bequeaths sums to the poor of that place and to the poor of Gatcomb. Piteous mention is made of the testator's persecutions in former times, and he explains his actions which have given rise to questions as to his orthodoxy. He bequeathed his great Bible to his wife, Anne, with three other books, and his small Bible to Thomas Banks. He leaves family silver to each of his five children, John, Tobias, Caleb, Hannah and Grace, and left his real estate at Godstone (Surrey) to Tobias, his son, and his heirs, or in the event of Tobias dying without issue then to the issue of the said John and Caleb Kemp. A list of debtors and creditors of the testator was affixed to the will, mentioning Story, Smith, of Havant, Earle, of Havant, and the testator's brothers Richard and Edward.

TOBIAS KEMPE, presumably the same mentioned in this will, became steward to the Oglanders, and is buried under an alter tomb which still exists in the chancel of Brading Church. We have not traced his will, and, as the records of such at Winchester seem to be very imperfect, we have little doubt that his is among the documents which have disappeared. We have no trace of his marriage, but as Kempes were from that time (1620) settled in the parish, it seems likely that the numerous Kempes of Brading were his descendants or kinsmen. One of the modern representatives of this family was the late Dixon Kemp, whose father (Edward) and grandfather (John) were both baptized at Brading, where their ancestors are commemorated for generations back by tombstones and numerous entries in the registers. Dixon Kemp was born at Ryde in 1839, and from boyhood was an enthusiastic boat builder. His knowlege of naval architecture grew rapidly, and as a practical yachtsman he gained early fame. One of his books on boat-building has been translated into German by the order of the Emperor, and is now the recognised text book in the German Naval Schools. He was a member of many of the chief yachting clubs, yachting editor of *The Field*, and contributed articles on aquatic sports to the daily and other papers for a long series of years. His last work was a huge volume (now sold at £4 4*s*.) on Naval Architecture, an authority which will always be a book of reference. He died after a short illness at his residence at Kensington in 1899 leaving (by his wife, Georgina M. B. Gordon) two children, Gordon Kemp, born in 1870, and Dorothy Morison Kemp, born ten years later.

We may mention that Dixon Kemp had two great uncles who started branches away from their native town (George, the eldest brother of his grandfather, remaining at Brading). Charles Kemp was a silversmith in Fore Street, London, and James was a carriage builder who long flourished at Lime Kiln Lane, Bristol. Descendants of the last still live at Bristol, but we have

Miss Lucy Kemp-Welch,

Margaret Kempe, wife of William Dane,
some time Lord Mayor of London.

5,

Sarah . . .= d. 1813.

Mary K. 1768 1816.

Thomas Kemp, b. 1758, d. 1763.

Martin Kemp, added name of Welch in 1795 by Royal Licence, b. 1772, d. 1837. =Elizabeth Watts, b. 1780, m. 1801, d. 1867.

George K =Elizabeth

Issue in Ame

rray K. Augustus K. Anna Maria K. Julia K.

A *see below.*

James Kemp-Welch, =Mary Ann Hill, b. 1806, d. 1887. m. 1830, d. 1856.

Emily Olive 1832-65

W. Janet Maria K.-W. b. 1836.

Harriet Sophia K.-W. b. 1838, m. 1860. =Wm. Pratten.

a Oakes, m. 1867.

Kemp-Welch, ist.

Elizabeth K.

live Brown, m. 1879.

a daughter.

Frank K.-W. b. 1853.

Thomas K.-W. b. 1842.

Emma K.-W. =Alex. Paris. b. 1846, m. 1877.

K.-W. 1830.

Thomas K.-W. b. 1819, d. 1842.

Harriet Sophia K.-W.=Wm. Pratten, m. 1860. of Bristol.

Phoebe K.-W

Catherine K.- m. 1863.

ce Leckie.

Harry K.-W. =Mary Bevington. b. 1847, m. 1874.

John K.-W. =Julia A. Grindall. b. 1658, m. 1884.

Beryl K.-W.

Erratum: John Kemp-V

THE KEMP-WELCH FAMILY.

Martin Kemp, of Poole, Dorset, born 1723,=Mary, dau. of Robert Welch, of Lymington, born 1735, died 1772. Will proved mar. 1755, died 1805, buried at Christchurch.

Sarah . . =George Kemp, =Elizabeth Pearce, widow, d. 1813. b. 1756, d. 1845. m. 1815, d. 1856. — Mary K. 1760-64. — John Kemp, =Elizabeth Wools, b. 1762, d. 1833. m. 1783, d. 1851. — Martin K. 1764-9. — James Kemp, =Elizabeth Jordon, b. 1770, d. 1856. m. 1808, d. 1853. — Mary K. 1768-1816. — Thomas Kemp, b. 1758, d. 1763. — Martin Kemp, added name of Welch in 1795 by Royal Licence, b. 1772, d. 1837.=Elizabeth Watts, b. 1780, m. 1801, d. 1867.

George Kemp, =Elizabeth Miller. Issue in America. — Elizabeth.=Henry K.=Jane Crew, m. 1810, d. 1872. — Mary K. =Richd. Hamer. — Sarah K. — Elizabeth K. d. 1862. — Edward K. d. 1817. — Mary Anne K. d. 1877. — John K. d. 1873. — Sophia K. d. 1872. — James K. — Frederick K. — Charles Murray K. — Augustus K. — Anna Maria K. — Julia K.

Emily K. — Jane K. — Sarah K. — Ellen K. — Thomas K. — Francis K.

Comley Olive,=George Kemp-Welch, b. 1797, d. 1876 b. 1802, d. 183-. — Martin Kemp-Welch,=Sophia Forrest, b. 1804, d. 1884. m. 1827, d. 1844. — James Kemp-Welch,—Mary Ann Hill, b. 1806, d. 1887. m. 1830, d. 1856. — A see below.

Emily Olive K.-W. 1832-65. — Elizabeth Amelia K.-W. 1833-37. — Martin K.-W. b. 1837, d. 1844. — Caroline K.-W. b. 1839. — George Martin K.-W.=Lucy Pemberton, b. 1844, d. 1883. m. 1878, d. 1881. — John Bunn K.-W. b. 1829. — Martin Forest K.-W. b. 1831, d. 1858. — Edward Buckland K.-W. b. 1834. — Janet Maria K.-W. b. 1836. — Harriet Sophia K.-W. b. 1838, m. 1860. =Wm. Pratten.

George Willoughby Kemp-Welch, born 1879. — Ridson D. Cope K.-W.

=Elizabeth Oakes, m. 1867.

Lucy Elizabeth Kemp-Welch, Artist, of Kingsley, Bushey. — Edith Mary Kemp-Welch, Artist.

Elizabeth K.-W.=Joseph Walton. — Jesse Hall K.-W. b. 1832, d. 1854. — Mary Ann K.-W. b. 1835, d. 1853. — Catherine K.-W.=W. Watmough. b. 1838, m. 1867, d. 1853. — Agnes K.-W. =Chas. Coate. b. 1839, m. 1864, d. 1873. — James Kemp-Welch, of=Olive Brown, Weybridge, b. 1850. m. 1879. — Frank K.-W. b. 1853. — Thomas K.-W. b. 1842. — Emma K.-W. =Alex. Paris. b. 1846, m. 1877.

Maurice Kemp-Welch, b. 1880. — a daughter.

A

Edward Ashburnham K.-W.=Martha Whitchurch, b. 1818, d. 1869. m. 1836, d. 1814. — John K.-W. =Maria Ransford Cooper. b. 1810, d. 1885. b. 1816, d. 1885. — Elizabeth K.-W. b. 1815, d. 1830. — Thomas K.-W. b. 1819, d. 1842. — Harriet Sophia K.-W.=Wm. Pratten, m. 1860. of Bristol.

Phoebe K.-W. — Emily Martha K.-W. — Mary Grace K.-W.=Hy. M. Aldridge. — Samuel Edward K.-W. b. 1847, d. 1888. S.P.

Catherine K.-W.=L. White. m. 1863. — John K.-W. b. 1840, d. 1853. — Stanley Kemp-Welch,=Wilhelmina Larit, b. 1843. m. 1868. — August K.-W.=H. Bush. b. 1843, m. 1873. — Charles Durant K.-W. b. 1845. m. 1st 1870 Jessie Ann Lambert. m. 2nd 1876 Emma L. Truefitt. — William K.-W. =Alice Leckie. b. 1847, m. 1877. — Harry K.-W. =Mary Bevington. b. 1847, m. 1874. — John K.-W. =Julia A. Grindall. b. 1658, m. 1884.

John Kemp-Welch. b. 1869. — Stanley Kemp-Welch. — Beryl K.-W.

Erratum: John Kemp-Welch, "b. 1658" should read "b. 1858."

no actual knowledge of the present representatives of the second London branch of this Brading Kemp family.

Returning to the issue of the old Parson Kemp we may note that Caleb, as stated in our Middlesex section, was Vicar of Bradford, Yorkshire, and left issue. We surmise that the other son John was he who married Alice, daughter of John Talk, of Havant (as stated by Berry's "Hampshire Pedigrees"), and that it was he who died at Christchurch in 1656, he apparently being M.P. for that place in 1653 and 1655. The present representative of Sir William Oglander still resides on the family estates within the parish of Brading, and on referring to the MSS. of Sir William and his descendants he finds many mentions of the Kempes, who seem to have been tenants of his family for the last 300 years. The Vicar of Brading has been good enough to sketch the tomb of Tobias Kemp, and gives the inscription thereon as follows: "Mr. Tobye Kempe, Ob. 1637, clarke to Sir John Oglander, Knight, of Nunwell."

Another and later connexion of Kempes with Hampshire is shown to have occurred by the will of Anne Kempe, relict of Henry Kempe, of the Inner Temple, proved in 1685 (P.C.C., 46 Cann), for this testatrix bequeathed to her daughter Susannah all her real estate in the parish of Milford, near Lymington, Co. Southampton, with other lands at Whitton, in the parish of Twickenham, Middlesex, and at Studley Marsh and Padbrooke, in the parish of Lydiard Tregoze, Wilts. This testatrix was the daughter of William Yorks, of Basset's Down, Lydiard Tregoze, and her husband, according to an accepted pedigree in the "Visitation of Middlesex" made in 1663, was son of Francis Kemp, a descendant of Bartholomew Kemp, of Gissing. Thus this Henry was of an entirely different stock from those Kempes of Christchurch and Beaulieu. Henry died only a few months previous to his wife and was buried in the Temple Church. His will proved and registered in the same year and book as his wife's, bequeathed his real estate to his son Edward, who was the executor appointed. Edward Kemp was at Christchurch College, Oxford, in 1661, and at the Inner Temple in 1669, after which we have no definite trace of him. Possibly he may be the ancestor of the Dorset Kemps, of whom we shall speak in our next chapter.

CHAPTER V.

THE KEMPS OF DORSET.

WE have already alluded to the very early Kempes who represented Lyme in Parliament from 1337 to 1340, and again in 1354, and of a Bartholomew of the Norfolk family who represented Shaftesbury in 1584. But so far as we can trace the Kempes of Poole were not connected directly with either of these. Their ancestors, the Welches, had long been settled at Beaulieu, Lymington and Christchurch, but it is not known yet how Martin Kemp, of Poole, the first known ancestor of the Kemp-Welches was connected with those recorded in our last chapter. One of the family and a friend, who is an expert archæologist, have searched the local registers and several in the Isle of Wight, but have not found the baptism of this Martin nor any other Kemp so named. We suggest that it is probable that the name of Martin as a christian name was derived from the surname, as we know of several instances previous to his date of birth (*circa* 1722) of Martins marrying Kemps. These are, however, in each case at a distance from Poole, the nearest being "Luce Martin als Kempe, of Nettlecombe, Co. Somerset," a widow, who made her will in 1660 and died in 1663, leaving her daughter, "Ursula Martin als Kemp," executrix and principal legatee. She mentions also her son Baldwin, her daughter Dorothy, and her grandchildren, Joane and William Clerke. Susannah Kemp, of Richmond, in her will dated 1684 (P.C.C., 32 Lloyd), desired to be buried near her father and mother in the Church of St. Dunstan-in-the-West, London, with eight or ten escutcheons of arms over her. She left numerous legacies, but we need only mention here that she included the names of Elizabeth, wife of Humphrey Clerke; her niece, Rodya Martin, wife of John Martin, of Old Change, London; her nephew, Sir Francis Pemberton, Knight, and her niece, Anne Southby. These names identify the testatrix as a member of the Buckingham branch of the New Forest Kemps, and thus near kin to John Kempe the M.P. for Christchurch. It would seem highly probable therefore that Martin Kemp, of Poole, derived his name from these Martins, and that he was akin to the Kemps of High Wycombe, Bucks, and their Hampshire cousins. Against this theory, however, we must range the following evidence, which is local but very scattered. Edward Kempe, of Poole, married Edith Hawkins in August, 1665; Edith Kemp, a widow, was buried there in 1715; Edward Kemp, baptized at Poole in 1666 (evidently the eldest son of this couple), married Joan Guy there in 1690, and a son Edward was baptized there in that or the following year. In 1709 Edward Kemp, a maltster, of Poole, married Jane Crocker, a widow, and in 1722 Benjamin, the son of Edward and Rachell Kemp, was baptized there. Beside these we have the following apparently collateral line. Benjamin, the son of the first named Edward, was baptized there in 1668. Administration of his estate was granted to Edith Seagar in 1707, and Nicholas, the son of Nicholas and Mary Kemp, was baptized there in 1716.

The Kemp-Welch family held property in the Isle of Wight, but there are no wills at Winchester recording such property; indeed, it is astonishing that all the Kempes of Brading should have passed away without having recorded one will or administration. Calbourne is one of the places in the Isle of Wight which comes under notice, and the registers have been searched. They, however, included but two rather late Kemp items, William, buried 1781, and John, buried 1782. These were, it is thought, the sons of Thomas Kemp, of Brexford, who, with Ellen Grey, were administrators of the estate of Elizabeth Kemp, their mother, formerly of Newton, who died about 1740, she being the widow of Richard Kemp, of Calbourne, whose will was proved in London 1732. Arreton Registers also include a few Kempes between 1694 and 1704, and those of Newport contain Kemp entries between 1680 to 1813. In the last case at least more than one family of the name is represented, for Lucretia, daughter of John Purcell Kemp, who was baptized there in 1741, was certainly of a Yorkshire family, her baptism being performed here owing only to her father being temporarily stationed with his regiment in the Isle of Wight. The aunts of this John Purcell Kemp were employed in the British and German Royal Courts as governesses or some such capacities, and they are frequently mentioned in the state papers and treasury papers of the period. It is not impossible that they were related to the Kemps of Poole, but we do not think this at all probable.

We must in any case leave the matter in doubt as to the parentage of the first MARTIN KEMP, of Poole, his baptism, as we have said, has not been traced, and except that he is said to have been nearly fifty years of age when he died we have no clue as to the date of his birth. We know that he married at Poole on 16th April, 1755, Mary, the daughter of Robert Welch, of Lymington. Both were buried at the Congregational Chapel at Poole, he in 1772 and she in 1805. His will was proved in London within two months of his death (P.C.C., 297 Taverner). Therein he is described as a merchant, of Poole, and he bequeathed to his wife his household goods absolutely, and the leasehold estates in the Isle of Wight (which he held from Sir John Barrington) to her for life, after which this and his residuary estate was to be divided among his children, George, John, Mary and James, all of whom were minors. Martin Kemp is not mentioned in the will; indeed, being posthumous double probate was obtained that he might obtain in due time his share of the property, consisting largely of the merchant business, which, in accordance with directions in the will, was carried on by John Green, of Poole, and John Holding, of the City of London, banker, until the eldest child, George, could manage it. The business proved well founded, and under its new management prospered exceedingly.

We need not give here details of all the baptisms, marriages and births recorded in the registers of Poole Church and the Congregational Chapel there; it will suffice to say that nearly all the descendants of this Kemp and Welch alliance were stout supporters of Congregational Churches, most, indeed, being identified with that of Poole, while those who migrated to Bristol, London and elsewhere have mostly identified themselves actively with the churches of the same body.

George Kemp, of Poole, the eldest son, married twice, first to Sarah . . . and secondly to Elizabeth Pearce, by whom he had two sons and two daughters. His eldest son George married Elizabeth Miller, and several of his descendants are now in America. George Kemp, the elder, died in 1845 aged eighty-nine, and his son George died at Michigan, United States, in 1865, aged seventy-five. Henry, the second son, also married twice and had two sons, Thomas and Francis, and three daughters. He died in 1872 aged eighty-three. Mary, one of the daughters of George Kemp, the elder, married Richard Hamer in 1821, her sister Sarah dying unmarried.

The second branch of the senior George Kemp's family is represented by Francis H. N. C. Kemp, of Brecknock Road, London, who is a son of Francis John, the second son of Henry Kemp, the second son of George Kemp, the elder.

Returning to the second Martin Kemp, of Poole, we noted that he was born shortly after his father's death in 1772; he married Elizabeth Watts in 1830, she being related to Isaac Watts "the Divine," so well known from his hymns. It was this Martin Kemp who by Royal Patent added the name of Welch to his paternal surname. The *London Gazette* of May 16th, 1795, contains the following, dated from Whitehall:

> "The King has been pleased to grant unto Martin Kemp of Tower Hill, London, son of Martin Kemp of Poole, Dorset, His Royal Licence and Authority that he and his issue may take the surname of Welch in addition to that of Kemp in compliance with the wish of hi smaternal Uncle George Welch Esquire, of the City of London, Banker."

All the descendants have duly used the compound name, but we are not sure that every person at present styling themselves by that name is an actual descendant of the second Martin Kemp, to whose *issue* the use of that name was limited. Strange to say, although some £500 was paid for this licence, no arms were accredited to the Kemp-Welches, and there is a doubt as to the correct bearings for Welch as well as in right of the Kemp descent. Candlesticks, formerly the property of the above mentioned banker, George Welch, bear as a crest a goat's head caboshed with an amulet for difference, and the arms of Welch as quartered with the arms of the Kempes of Kent are engraved on the signet ring of one of the family.

Section V.

The Kemp and Kempe

FAMILIES OF

The Midlands, Western Counties

AND

North of England.

The Kempes of the Midlands, Western Counties and North of England.

CHAPTER I.

EARLY ONES.

IN 1352 an enquiry was made as to the extent of the Borough of Stratford-on-Avon, the report of which records that "Robert de Kemesei" held a piece of land there at a rental of twelve pence, and two other pieces at two shillings per annum. At the same period "Petras de Kemes" held land at about the same value. It might not unreasonably be supposed that these individuals were forerunners of the name and a family of Kemp. As a matter of fact, however, the addition to the christian names simply identifies them with the parish of Kempsey in the adjoining county of Worcester. In the case of Robert this explanation admits of no doubt; Peter may have belonged to one of the places called Kemeys. But though we may not claim those persons as representatives of the Kemp families, the place name Kempsey, meaning Kemp's Island, attests the existence of the name Kemp at a far earlier period in this part of the county. Kempsey is situated on the Severn about two miles South of Worcester. It contains a residence known as Beauchamp Court, from which it is presumable that the Earls of Warwick, whose surname as has already been stated more than once was de Bello Campo, held property here. As the chief or sole landowners their name, as often happens in the case of place names, was used to distinguish the locality. These facts lend additional support to the views that the Kemp and Beauchamp (or Bello Campo) families are derived from the common stock, though we are unable to state the actual line of descent. The name of Bello Campo appears on the Battle Abbey Roll, which however contains no Kemp. As some of the Kemps, Edward Kemp, Sheriff of Belton, for example, used the royal supporters with their arms in the belief that their ancestors came over with the Conqueror, we are again forced to turn to the line of the house of Warwick in justification of the tradition. The earliest mention of the actual surname of Kemp(e) in the county of Warwick is in 1384 when Henry Inge was charged before the king's clerk with having caused the death of Richard Kempe, of Austeley, *hodie* Austray, on the Leicestershire border of the county.

Arms used by Edward Kemp, Sheriff of Rutland.

Another tradition still rife among the Leicestershire Kempes is that their stock was akin to JOHN KEMPE the noted Flemish weaver, who under the special protection of Edward III. founded his craft at Kendal in 1331. Much fiction has doubtless gathered round this man, but the royal patents and other original records give us authority for saying that long before 1331 the Kempes were manufacturers of woollen stuffs at Ghent, where a street was devoted to their weaving shops and was called "Kempe's Street." We must not be too ready to believe that this weaver of Flanders was necessarily of Flemish *origin*, for thirty or forty years before his settlement in England, Guy and Robert *Kempi* or Campe were important British officers engaged round Hull to arrest the unauthorized exportation of wool. And still earlier a merchant of Florence named Cempe was engaged in the woollen trade with England, his name being spelled in various forms recognizable as variants of Kemp. (This merchant was a member of the "Falcon" Guild of Merchants, it is therefore singular that a Falcon was one of the earliest Kemp crests.)

In 1327, Philippa, daughter of the Earl of Hainault, was wife of Edward III., at whose court it was the fashion to wear Flemish cloth, but this was a source of trouble to that king, who was anxious that his people should be able to produce as good a material as any imported. The Green Cloth of Kendal had already become known through the civilized world, but the withdrawal of court patronage had led to the manufacture falling into disrepute. Hence when the Count of Hainauit, in 1330, found the Kempe weavers of Ghent getting so powerful that he feared further increase of their influence (and even charged them with treason and conspiracies) they were glad to accept the invitation of Edward III. to come to this country "with all implements of their craft, their looms and their dyes." A thrilling story of their landing, apparently founded upon the result of considerable research, was printed in the *Kendal Mercury* of December, 1865. It tells of the natural misgiving of the native weavers of Kendal at the inroad, under the king's protection, of these hated foreign rivals. But the local weavers were soon converted into willing friends when they found John Kempe to be a generous hearted man, ready to teach all his modes of manufacture to the British subject. He is said to have had no son, but brought with him two nephews named Kempe and a daughter who was of phenomenal beauty and the embodiment of kindness. This lovely daughter is not a creation of modern fiction, for she is recorded to have married John, Baron de Roos, of Kendal Castle, who took the Kempe weavers under his personal care. It is strange if this *is* merely tradition, that the Roos or Rous family and the Kempes of Suffolk were so intimately connected during the next century, John Kempe, of Woodbridge, being buried beside many of the Rous family, who founded the church at that place.

Few references to the name of Kemp(e) have been found at Kendal, but it appears that in 1544 one of the Kempe weavers was factor or park keeper to Walter Strickland, Esquire, of Sizergh Castle, which lies close to Kendal. This Nicholas, with others of the Kempes as subjects of this "Lord" of Sizergh, fought with the other Kendal men (who were renowned for their skill at archery) against the Scots at Flodden Field, as evidenced by a letter narrating the fight written at the time by the Earl of Surrey. Nicholas was not a common name among the Kempes, but from this time the Cornish and other families frequently selected it for their children, possibly on account of the repute in which this man of their name was held. We have not traced the will of this individual, but it is likely that it may yet come to light in one of the Northern Courts. Although Kempes remained at Kendal and carried on their weaving until the introduction of machinery, they do not appear to have acquired any landed property there until the end of the eighteenth century. Under the successive lords of Kendal and Sizergh Castles they were doubtless tenants, for from time to time the name appears until, on the last great guild procession of the Kendal weavers in 1761, one reputed descendant of the first John Kempe's nephew took the principal part in the proceedings. This may have been the forefather of a John Kemp, who as a landowner under Sizergh and in the township of Helsington, received a grant as his share of an enclosure which was allotted to the freeholders, dated at Heversham Church, 14th June, 1815. We have received an authentic copy of this interesting award from John Kempe, A.M.I.C.E., lately Surveyor of Kingston, Middlesex, who was born at Natland, close to Sizergh Castle, and is a descendant of this freeholder of Kendal, and in all probability a representative of the same stock as the weaver.

One of the last Kempes of Kendal.

We are greatly indebted to an enthusiastic antiquary, Mr. Thomas Jennings, of Kendal, for a quantity of newspaper cuttings for years back, for many extracts from Kendal, Natland and other local registers, and much miscellaneous information besides. Mrs. Langley, of Bolton-le-Sands, has very kindly presented us with photographs of one of the old Kempes of Westmoreland, from whom she is descended, as well as an illustration of a jug made by a Westmoreland Kempe for his relative, whose name appears thereon. The jug bears date 1802 and has descended with other Kempe relics to Mrs. Langley. To John Kemp, Esq., now settled in Australia, we are indebted for the loan of the *Kendal Mercury* for Decembers in 1865, 1866 and 1867 containing the historical tales* bearing on the Kempes of Kendal, Sizergh and Natland.

From Kendal the Kempes had frequently to cross the country to the port of Hull, and we know that under the laws made for the woollen trade they would visit, from time to time, the centres appointed as woollen markets. We cannot *prove* that in this way they spread from Kendal, but apart from tradition, which says that the Kempe weavers of Spott (N.B.) were a direct branch, it is reasonable to presume that at least some of the many early Kempe weavers of the West of England and around the greater towns were descendants. It is very noteworthy that the Kempes of Lancashire, Cheshire and Leicestershire have continued to be closely connected with the woollen and other weaving trades from the earliest available records until the present time. *This section of the Kempe History worthily represents the industrial enterprise of England.*

* The papers are now out of print, and there being no copyright we would suggest to those Kempes who are interested in collecting matters pertaining to their name that these stories should be printed by subscription.

We must conclude this chapter with a mention of a few of the instances of early Kempes in the Midlands, Lancashire and Cheshire.

One Kempe was a tenant at Liverpool in 1324, Simon Kempe was a Member for Parliament for the Borough of Appleby in 1329, 1330, 1335 and 1337. Anthony Kempe, Gent. (Kentish family), represented the County of Westmoreland in Parliament in 1557-8. William Kemp was a Sheriff of the City of Chester in 1404, and in the Chester Recognizance Rolls of 1517 Arnold Kemp is recorded to have held land at Norley, Cheshire (under Sir Thomas Gerrard, Knight) at a rental of three pence per acre. In the records of the Duchy of Lancaster the name of Kempe appears, one Randall Kempe being interested in a wood and lands at Newton Heath (1582), while "Kemp's Hill," otherwise called "Kympton Hill," near Belgrave Bridge, Leicester, was a matter of litigation in the same Ducal-Lordship, between Stephen Harvey and others. In 1603 Hugh Kempe, Ralph Jackson and others were parties to a suit concerning lands at Nuthurst, Oldham and Chadderton, and in the will of James Chetham, of Nuthurst, dated 1613, Hugh Kempe and Isabelle Jackson and Katherine Jackson are mentioned, and Nicholas Kempe is a witness thereto. Of these we believe Nicholas, Hugh and Arnold to be strangers recently become temporarily interested in the counties,* but the others are likely to be some of the connexions of the celebrated weaver, unless Simon Kempe is found to be, as seems probable, a kinsman of the powerful Earls of Warwick who would be likely to influence his return to Parliament.

Although the wills recorded at Chester are preserved from 1545, no Kempe or Campe appears in the list until 1615. In the neighbouring county of Staffordshire we find one John Kempe paying a subsidy in 1535 as a Burgess of Stafford, and in Lichfield Probate Court we find several early Kempe wills, namely, in 1533, George Kempe, of Sudbury; 1539 Reginald Kempe, of Leek, and in 1541 Richard Kempe, of Abbott's Bromley. This latter place was the nest from which a very important British family of Kempes came, most of whom have been engaged in commerce and industry. Generation after generation they have increased both in numbers and in wealth. To them we must devote the next chapter.

CHAPTER II.

ABBOTT'S BROMLEY AND ISSUE.

WE had fully intended to give abstracts from the long series of wills which confirm the pedigree we present, but the cost of printing the latter runs into such a large proportion of the amount subscribed by members of this family, that we have regretfully to restrict ourselves to the limited space left at our disposal, and can only briefly mention the wills in order, with some few details of property and other items.

In addition to the wills, which have been personally examined, we are indebted to the present Rector of Abbott's Bromley for about 100 extracts concerning Kempes from the parish register.

* The name Arnold will be recollected in connexion with the Kempes of Kent and Cornwall.

(As this required great labour and patience on his part, and has been *entirely gratuitous*, we trust that some of the descendants of this old family will at least benefit the church, if not offer some personal recognition to the rector.) The parish is a picturesque one and well worth a visit, but we fear that no trace of a Kempe monument is now to be found.

The first of this series of Kempe wills show that *previous* to 1541 ancestors had been buried at the church, for the testator begged that his body should be laid "beside his fathers in Bromley Churchyard." This testator left his land and tenements to his son John, provided he paid an annuity to his wife Alys. He also mentions his son, Thomas Kempe, who was to enjoy the deceased's "tack," otherwise called "intack," which, we believe, was an enclosure from the Common-fields of the town and held by copyhold. Alys was to have the use of a certain house in Bromley until the youngest child was of age and the residue of his personal estate. An inventory attached to this will shows that Richard Kempe, of Abbott's Bromley, was a yeoman possessing a fair farm. The estate was appraised by William Harvey and others (which William Harvey may have been connected with Stephen Harvey mentioned in our last chapter). Passing by the many Kempe wills proved between this and 1590 we come to that of Thomas Kempe, of Abbott's Bromley. There is, however, no copy of the will itself, although the probate is duly recorded, with a grant of administration to Jone, his widow, and an inventory made of his estate by Nicholas Harvey, Nicholas Browne, Thomas Wakelyn and Nicholas Joneson. The latter shows that the farming stock had increased, and that in addition to "peuters" he had "silver salts" and silver candlesticks and "fine linen sheets," which were by no means common. The most interesting items, however, are the "loomes" and tools connected with the home manufacture of woollen and linen goods. Edward Kempe was a witness to this inventory, to which is attached a business-like account of moneys lent, due, or owing, which probably represents his rent roll. George Kempe is a debtor to the deceased for 8*s.*, which would be sufficient rent for a house and garden suitable for his station as a yeoman. It is perhaps this same George Kempe whose inventory was made at Abbott's Bromley 1st April, 1615; this again is drawn up by a Harvey, with the assistance of William Wall and Michael Donne. Again looms and woollen cloth are among the chief items, and the value of the personal effects has risen from £38 to £79, in addition to which some £5 are owing from John Jackson and others. (Jackson may also be one of those connected with Nicholas and Hugh Kempe mentioned as suitors interested in Nuthurst, while another debtor is James Atkins, of Rugeley, and a third "goodwife" Hemming.)

The will of EDWARD KEMPE of the same place was made and proved in 1618, and records the same request that his body should be buried "where my father, mother and other friends were buried"; he mentions his lands not only at Abbott's Bromley, but others which he held of the Manors of Cannock and Rugeley; also his daughters Joan, Elizabeth and Marie, and his brother Thomas Kempe, William Vanes, and his cousins Hand and niece Bridget Kempe. His niece, Dennis Cartwright, and others are left legacies; and a bequest left to his "Uncle Robert" Kempe. No inventory is attached, but the total value of the estate indicates that he was not at this time the head of the family. Robert Kempe, probably the "uncle," was apparently a "scrivener," or *writer* at Warwick, and in that city his "father" (? father-in-law or godfather) was buried at St. Nicholas Church. His own father and mother Kempe were then living, for he left to them the house which he had in Bromley for their lives, and 20*s.* per annum out of a house at Warwick. The testator mentions his brother, Richard Kempe, his brothers-in-law William Stratford and William Cartwright, his cousin Robert Morrell; and he leaves to his wife, Catherine, his tenement in Warwick, "near the Pillory," two tenements in West Street and one in Smith Street, also his residence in the Market Place, Warwick. This will was proved in 1624 (P.C.C., 37 Bride) and no inventory is attached. As to the "father Wakefield," we may note that in the will of John Kempe, of the Savoy, London, proved in 1588 (P.C.C., 24 Rutland) the testator mentions his "son-in-law, William Wakefield," and his wife, to whom he was married in 1581 at St. Michaels, Cornhill, as Sybble Lambe, died in 1590. Administration of her estate as "Sibelle Kempe *als* Lambe *als* Cook *als* Wakefield, late of the parish of the Savoy, Middlesex, widow, was granted to her son, Nicholas Wakefield. From this we may deduce that this John Kempe, of Savoy, who was a Merchant Taylor of London, was at least connected with those of Abbott's Bromley, although we must bear in mind that the Kempes of Kent had Royal apartments at the Savoy so late as 1560. Sybelle may have been connected with the Phoebe Cooke who married Caleb Kempe, Vicar of Bradford, Yorks, in that case numerous Kempes of Yorkshire would be connected with those of Staffordshire, while a connexion between these and the Kempes of Hendon through the Cooke family would be traced.

In 1627 Thomas Kempe, a dyer, of the Borough of Warwick, died, and his will was proved (P.C.C., 12 Barrington). It leaves charities to the poor of St. Nicholas, Warwick, Kingstone, in the same county, and to Bromley Paget's, otherwise called Abbott's Bromley. It mentions his father and mother, Robert and Elizabeth Kempe, and his "cousin," son of his brother Robert Kempe, also the Cartwright family, William Stratford and the latter's daughter Elizabeth Morrell. He appointed his brothers William Kempe, "Master of Arts," and Richard Kempe executors. By a codicil he left his workshop and all the tools, utensils and coppers used in dying cloth for the purpose of carrying on his business, in favour of his wife Dennis, and he left a further legacy to his kinsman Thomas Kempe, of Vanbrooke, in the parish of Abbott's Bromley. In 1652 we come to a very important will, that of HENRY KEMPE, who states that he was of Loughborough, but formerly of Houghton-on-Hill, Leicestershire, but on proving the will it was necessary for William Kempe, of *Abbott's Bromley* to attest the will, he *being testator's eldest brother*. From this will we consequently trace a long line of mercantile Kempes who spread over Leicestershire, Nottingham, Northampton, Lincoln, and have now many representatives in London as well as throughout our colonies. This junior line, however, we must leave to the next chapter.

The will of Margaret Kempe, of Abbott's Bromley, dated 5th January, 1681, recorded at Lichfield the following May, directed that she should be buried at Bromley. She left bequests to her sons Edward, Richard and Robert Kempe, the two former to be executors and Sarah, the daughter of the son Robert, and the testatrix's daughter Elizabeth, wife of Robert Lawrence, are also mentioned. On the 8th December, 1682, the will of EDWARD KEMP, of Abbott's Bromley, made on 14th June previous, was proved at Lichfield by Richard Kempe and Thomas Andrews, both of Bromley. This will left all his estate in trust to his wife to maintain their children until their respective ages of twenty-one, Richard Kempe, the eldest son, inheriting the lands which the testator held of Walter Bagott at twenty-one and the residuary estate, eventually, after portions were paid to the other children on their attaining that age. WILLIAM KEMPE of the same place, elder brother to the above mentioned Henry of Loughborough, made his will in May, 1684, and it was proved the following year. The testator was "sick and weak" at the time of signing this document, and directed that when his debts had been paid the residue of his estate was to be held in trust by his wife Hannah for the benefit of their sons Thomas and Edward equally, and "to their heirs for ever." Thomas Adderley, of Drayton, yeoman, and William Bradshaw, of Dunstall, were the executors, and *George Wright* one of the witnesses. The seal bears the initials G. W., which doubtless refer to this witness, possibly the notary who made the will. It occurs again on the will of RICHARD KEMPE, proved in 1699. This testator had £130 due to him from tenants and others, and his executors having renounced, Thomas Barker and Walter Toone proved the will.

William Kempe, of Stafford.
Will 1559.

Robert Kempe,

Kempe.=. . . Painter.

ohn Kempe. bap. 1566.

George Kempe, of Abbott's Bromley,=Marie Cartwright (Weaver?) Inventory 1615. b. A.B. 1564, bur. A.B. 30 Apr. 1615.

Marie Cartwright mar. A.B. 1593, bur. A.B. 1618.

Margaret Kempe, bap. A.B. 1569.

Francis Kempe. bap. A.B. 1561. bur. 1571.

Robert Kempe, bap. and bur. 1594, other infants bur. 1596-1609.

Joy... n.

Elizabeth Kempe, bap. A.B. 1613.

Bridget Kempe, b. 10 Dec. 1615, m. 1 Nov. 1638. =Wm. Baggerley.

Edward Kempe, bap. A.B. 31 Oct. 1619, bur. (? 1702)

Robert Kempe, bap. 24 Feb. 1624, ? of Belton, bur. 27 Feb. 1684.

Thomas Kempe, bap. 10 May, 1629.

Ann...

...rge Kempe, bap. 1640, 1670 ? 1681) Will 1670, Siston, ...andman)

Robert Kempe,=Margaret . . . of Warwick, Weaver. Will 1686

Margaret . . . Will 1712.

Susannah K. (? Sarah).

Elizabeth K.

Richard Kempe,=Jane Walklake, of A.B., yeoman, Will 1699, bur. A.B. 1699. Bromley, Hurst & Ashbrook.

Jane Walklake, mar. A.B. 1668, bur. A.B. 1704.

Marian Kempe, b. A.B. 1642, m. 1676. =John Grane.

Edith Kempe, m. A.B. 1701, =Richard Smith.

...(widow) Bourne ...mar. A.B. ...July, 1709.

Edith K. living 1699. =Thos Smith, (of Elford)

Anne K. b. A.B. 1668.

Mary K. b. A.B. 1672, bur. A.B. 1687.

Jane Kempe, b. A.B. 1673, m. A.B. 1705. =John Kilby, of Lichfield.

Richard Kempe, b. A.B. 1677.

Elizabeth K. b. A.B. 1679.

Wil... B...

Edith=Jno. Bourne.

Robert Kemp Bourne.

Aaron Bourne.

Sarah Bourne.

Richard Kempe, s. of Richard, bur. A.B. 1710.

Wi...

...Kemp, of =Joan. . . . ...on Linford, ...bandman, ...ll 1718.

William Kemp,=Hannah Sharpe m. A.B. 1671. (younger son)

Hannah Sharpe Dorothy

John Kemp.

Rose Kemp, m. 1659. =Henry Collins.

Alice K. =(? John) Hill.

Th...

...nckley, ...1.

Hannah K. bap. & bur. A.B. 1676.

Henry Kemp, bap. & bur. A.B. 1672.

Hester Kemp, bur. A.B. 1682.

Edward Kemp, bap. A.B. 6 Oct. 1681.

=Sarah, widow of William Ward.

Ja... b. E...

Sa... b. E...

Elizabeth Ward, (? Ann or Eliza Ann)=William Kemp, of Hinckley and Belton, mar. B. 11 July, 1701. lands at Allexton, died before 1751.

Sarah K.=Dewall

one child.

V... b. E...

...of East Norton, Grazier, ...1703. Will 1749.

Elizabeth K. bap. B. 27/4/1704. Eliz. K. b. B. 11 Sep. 1715.

William Kemp, of Belton, Co. Rutland,= bap. B. 28 May, 1705. Ad. 1788.

H... b. E...

Elizabeth Kempe, only child, bap. Belton, 21 Feb. 1737, died a spinster 7 May, 1793. M.I. Belton. Will 1793.

Su... b. E...

Mary Kemp, Geo. Godfrey.

Thomas Kemp, died unmarried, bur. B. 7/2/1823, aged 79.

Ellenor.=Francis Kemp, b. 1747, bur. B. 6/3/1826.

Eleanor Kemp, bur. B. 18/6/1833. æt 84.

John Kemp, of=Ann. Belton, Butcher, bur. B. 20/8/1826. aged 73.

Ann. bur. B. 14/5/1805 æt 48.

...ter ...n.

Sarah K., bap. B. 7/11/1788, bur. B. 9/12/1788.

Susannah K. B. 6/5/1790

John K., bap. 29/1796, bur. B. 15/7/1796

...ancis Kemp, of London, 1783 ...

Godfrey Kemp, b. 1785, d. 1850,=Isabelle Malim, d. of Geo. M.,

John Kemp,

...her, b. ... 1805.

Sheriff of Rutland, of Belton 1835.

of Higham Ferrers (by Sarah Jennup, of Spalding)

bap. 10 Jun. 1787. *see below.*

Isabelle Charlotte Kemp, bap. B. 1 Aug. 1849.

The Rev. Godfrey George Kemp, M.A.,—Harriet Ann Malim, b. at Belton 26 Aug. 1845, bap. 2 Oct. 1845, of Rawreth, Essex.

Harriet Ann Malim, born Grantham.

Willia... b.

Edith Hilda K.

Irene K.

Minda Mary K.

Cyril Godfrey K.

Ernest W. G. Kemp.

d. 1895. ...ton,

Helen Kemp.

Sophia Kemp, m. 1849, =J. T. Springthorpe, Sheriff of Rutland, mar. Uppingham, 16 Aug. 1849.

Chas. Kemp, b. & d. 1825.

Charles Godfrey Kemp. b. 1831, d. 1863 (at Leicester) educated at Uppingham School.

...K.

Emily K.=G. M. Frean. b. 1856.

John Kemp.=Eleanor. b. 1787.

...nry.

Margaret.

..., of ...m,

James Kemp, b. 1825, d. 1825,

Josiah Kemp, b. 1826. =Jane Kirby

Maria Kemp, b. 1818.

Helen Kemp, b. 1819.

Fanny Kemp, b. 1828, d. 1828.

...y K. 1884.

Ellenor Mary K.

Francis William K. =Alice Rose Lester.

Jane Maria K.

Josiah K. =Ruth Mary Ward.

Sarah Ann K.

no inventory is attached. As to the "father Wakefield," we may note that in the will of John Kempe, of the Savoy, London, proved in 1588 (P.C.C., 24 Rutland) the testator mentions his "son-in-law, William Wakefield," and his wife, to whom he was married in 1581 at St. Michaels, Cornhill, as Sybble Lambe, died in 1590. Administration of her estate as "Sibelle Kempe *als* Lambe *als* Cook *als* Wakefield, late of the parish of the Savoy, Middlesex, widow, was granted to her son, Nicholas Wakefield. From this we may deduce that this John Kempe, of Savoy, who was a Merchant Taylor of London, was at least connected with those of Abbott's Bromley, although we must bear in mind that the Kempes of Kent had Royal apartments at the Savoy so late as 1560. Sybelle may have been connected with the Phoebe Cooke who married Caleb Kempe, Vicar of Bradford, Yorks, in that case numerous Kempes of Yorkshire would be connected with those of Staffordshire, while a connexion between these and the Kempes of Hendon through the Cooke family would be traced.

In 1627 Thomas Kempe, a dyer, of the Borough of Warwick, died, and his will was proved (P.C.C., 12 Barrington). It leaves charities to the poor of St. Nicholas, Warwick, Kingstone, in the same county, and to Bromley Paget's, otherwise called Abbott's Bromley. It mentions his father and mother, Robert and Elizabeth Kempe, and his "cousin," son of his brother Robert Kempe, also the Cartwright family, William Stratford and the latter's daughter Elizabeth Morrell. He appointed his brothers William Kempe, "Master of Arts," and Richard Kempe executors. By a codicil he left his workshop and all the tools, utensils and coppers used in dying cloth for the purpose of carrying on his business, in favour of his wife Dennis, and he left a further legacy to his kinsman Thomas Kempe, of Vanbrooke, in the parish of Abbott's Bromley. In 1652 we come to a very important will, that of HENRY KEMPE, who states that he was of Loughborough, but formerly of Houghton-on-Hill, Leicestershire, but on proving the will it was necessary for William Kempe, of *Abbott's Bromley* to attest the will, he *being testator's eldest brother*. From this will we consequently trace a long line of mercantile Kempes who spread over Leicestershire, Nottingham, Northampton, Lincoln, and have now many representatives in London as well as throughout our colonies. This junior line, however, we must leave to the next chapter.

The will of Margaret Kempe, of Abbott's Bromley, dated 5th January, 1681, recorded at Lichfield the following May, directed that she should be buried at Bromley. She left bequests to her sons Edward, Richard and Robert Kempe, the two former to be executors and Sarah, the daughter of the son Robert, and the testatrix's daughter Elizabeth, wife of Robert Lawrence, are also mentioned. On the 8th December, 1682, the will of EDWARD KEMP, of Abbott's Bromley, made on 14th June previous, was proved at Lichfield by Richard Kempe and Thomas Andrews, both of Bromley. This will left all his estate in trust to his wife to maintain their children until their respective ages of twenty-one, Richard Kempe, the eldest son, inheriting the lands which the testator held of Walter Bagott at twenty-one and the residuary estate, eventually, after portions were paid to the other children on their attaining that age. WILLIAM KEMPE of the same place, elder brother to the above mentioned Henry of Loughborough, made his will in May, 1684, and it was proved the following year. The testator was "sick and weak" at the time of signing this document, and directed that when his debts had been paid the residue of his estate was to be held in trust by his wife Hannah for the benefit of their sons Thomas and Edward equally, and "to their heirs for ever." Thomas Adderley, of Drayton, yeoman, and William Bradshaw, of Dunstall, were the executors, and *George Wright* one of the witnesses. The seal bears the initials G. W., which doubtless refer to this witness, possibly the notary who made the will. It occurs again on the will of RICHARD KEMPE, proved in 1699. This testator had £130 due to him from tenants and others, and his executors having renounced, Thomas Barker and Walter Toone proved the will.

PEDIG K OF MIDI

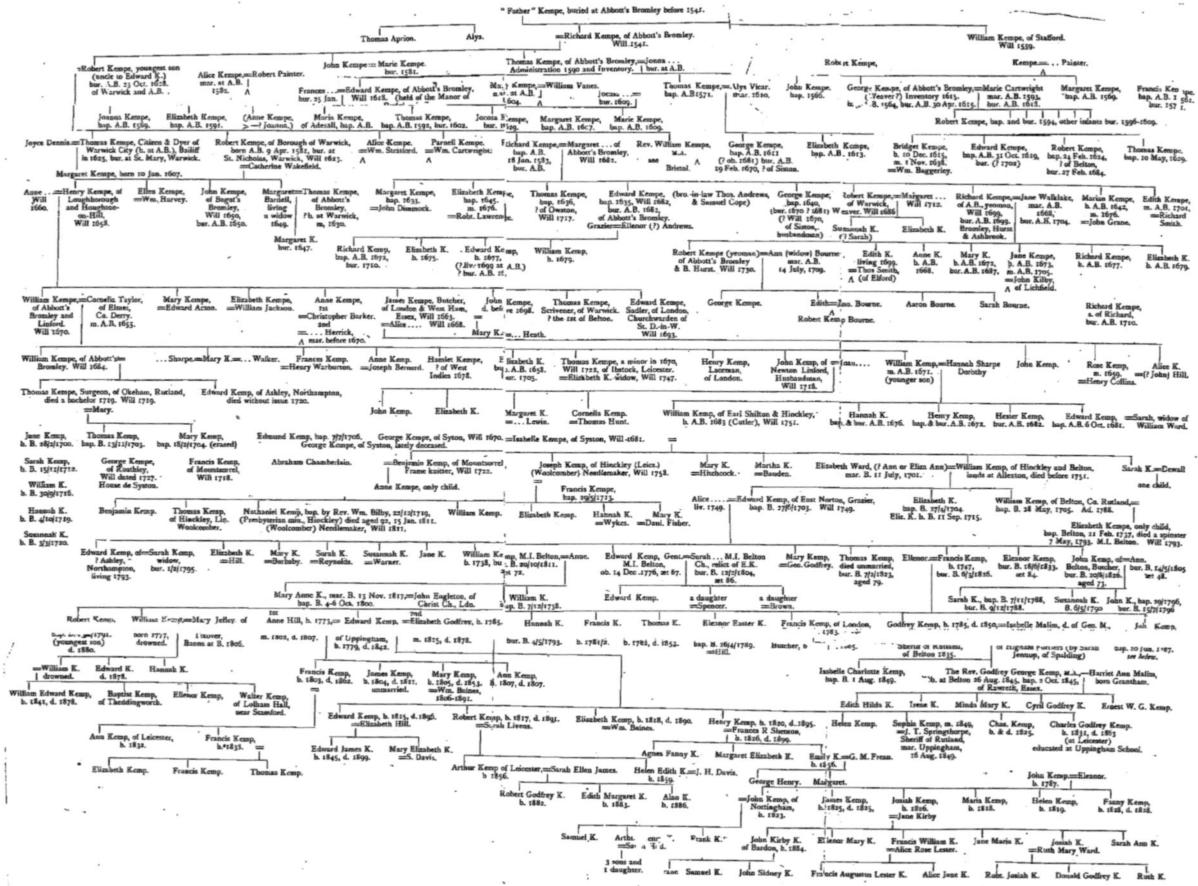

TSHIRE.

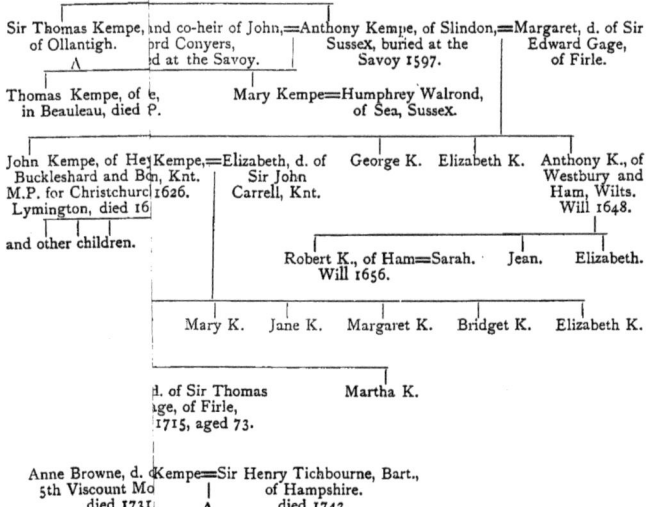

Sir Thomas Kempe, of Ollantigh. — ...nd co-heir of John, ...rd Conyers, ...d at the Savoy. = Anthony Kempe, of Slindon, Sussex, buried at the Savoy 1597. = Margaret, d. of Sir Edward Gage, of Firle.

Thomas Kempe, of ...e, in Beauleau, died ...P.

Mary Kempe = Humphrey Walrond, of Sea, Sussex.

John Kempe, of He... Buckleshard and B... M.P. for Christchurc... Lymington, died 16...

and other children.

...Kempe, ...n, Knt. ...1626. = Elizabeth, d. of Sir John Carrell, Knt.

George K.

Elizabeth K.

Anthony K., of Westbury and Ham, Wilts. Will 1648.

Robert K., of Ham = Sarah. Will 1656.

Jean.

Elizabeth.

Mary K. Jane K. Margaret K. Bridget K. Elizabeth K.

...d. of Sir Thomas ...ge, of Firle, ...1715, aged 73.

Martha K.

Anne Browne, d. o... 5th Viscount Mo... died 1731...

...Kempe = Sir Henry Tichbourne, Bart., of Hampshire. died 1742.

PEDIGREE OF THE KEMPES OF SLINDON, NEW FOREST, AND WILTSHIRE.

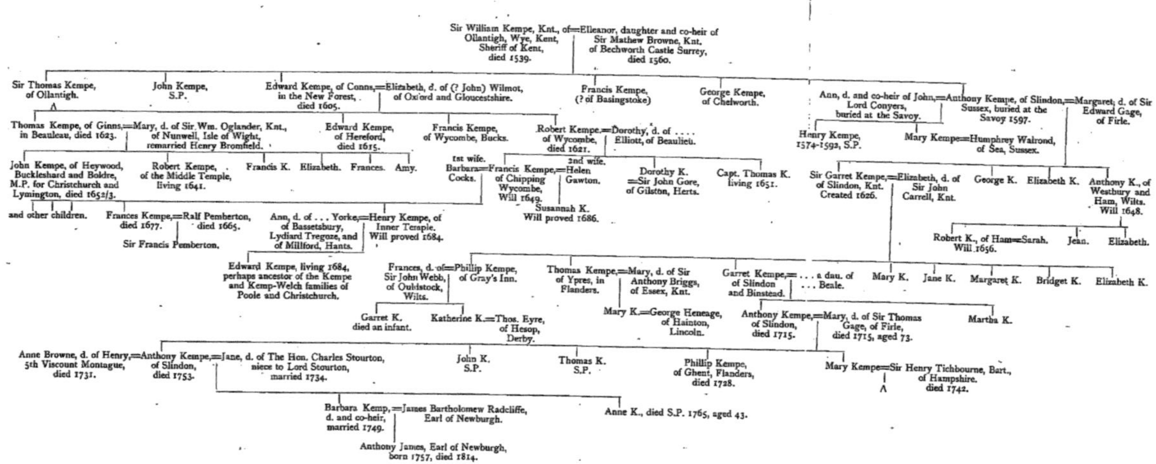

In 1686 Robert Kempe, of Warwick, a weaver by trade, left by his will a house, in which his cousin John "Savadge" then lived. Margaret, his wife, was empowered to sell this provided she settled certain sums upon her daughters Susannah and Elizabeth when they were twenty-two years of age. No sons are mentioned, and the testator's cousin, Mr. John Wilson and Richard Hands (his kinsman) were appointed executors. This will bears a seal marked "T.K." which, doubtless, belonged to Thomas Kempe, of Warwick, and which appears on later wills. The inventory attached to this shows that Robert Kempe, the weaver, had some books of value, and that his stock in trade included three looms, one "weeping" (*sic*) bar and frame, a twisting mill, and other weaving plant, these items being modestly valued at £10.

The will of Margaret Kempe, of Warwick, widow of the above Robert Kempe, the dyer, was proved at Worcester on 31st May, 1722; it mentions the same properties he left her which devolved next upon her daughters Elizabeth and Sarah. The executors were James Fish, of St. Mary's, Warwick, and Samuel Farr, of Stratford-on-Avon.

This apparently ended the line of Kempes at Warwick, but in a previous generation it seems that a branch of the family had been established at or near Rowington, from which descends Thomas Kemp, Esq., J.P., who now resides at Warwick, and who has published several most interesting books on the ancient history of that borough.

There are about this period several wills relating to Abbott's Bromley, the testators of which had become merchants in London. We shall not introduce them here, but pass to that of Richard Kemp, of Abbott's Bromley, dated and proved in 1699. He was residing at Bromley Hurst, and left his residence, a cottage, Ashbrooke Field and other real estate to his wife during her widowhood, subject to the payment of certain sums to their children Robert, Jane, Edith and Elizabeth Kempe, who were to share the eventual residue equally. The personalty was valued at £335 19*s*. 6*d*. In 1730 the will of Robert Kempe, of Bromley Hurst, was proved, it made "Edith, wife of his son-in-law," chief heir, mentioning for small bequests Hannah Willington, of Castle Hays, in the parish of Titbury, Staffs., his sister, Edith Smith, his godson Robert Kempe Bourne, his son-in-law Aaron Bourne, Jonathan Kilby, of the City of Litchfield, and Thomas Smith, of Elford.

The long line of Kempes at Abbott's Bromley ended with Robert Kempe, his burial there in 1730 being the last entry of a Kemp found. This family, however, as we have said, is by no means extinct, for in London several branches are represented, while as we shall see in our next chapter, as numerous an offspring is found in Rutland as that reviewed at Abbott's Bromley.

CHAPTER III.

LEICESTERSHIRE AND RUTLAND.

THE records of the borough of Leicestershire have just been published covering the period between 1300 and 1500, but the name of Kemp does not appear therein. Two mentions of "Campes" living about the middle of the fifteenth century in Leicester occur, and knowing how frequently this spelling changed to Kempe during the next century we conclude that at least some of the Kempes of Leicestershire came from that *Campe* stock. The wills now preserved at Leicester commence in 1495, but no Campe or Kempe has been found before 1538, when the will of "Sir" John Kempe, Vicar of Hungerton, was proved. We have remarked upon the coincidence that the Kempe family very frequently sprang up around a place in which the clerical members of the family were beneficed, and as we find numerous Kempes settled in Leicestershire from this time, we are inclined to believe that the first family came as the result of John Kempe being appointed the vicar at Hungerton. We must not, however, allow space for details concerning the family who made Hungerton their residence for some 100 years, but having well studied the evidence of many wills relating to them, we have come to the conclusion that the Vicar Kempe belonged to the Norfolk family of his name. His will is very interesting, for he left a sum of money to every person, "man, woman or child" in his parish, and he bequeathed his own cloak to a poor blind woman who was one of his parishioners..

He speaks of "Ludwick Kempe," his brother, and of his nephews William and John, of South Croxton. Ludwick is but another form of the name Lewis, and as a Lewis Kempe, of Gissing—who had remainder entailed in the Norfolk property—disappeared from that county about this time; we suggest that it was he who founded the long line of Kempes of Croxton.

We do not know of any will which could be his, but in 1563 the will of John Kempe, of South Croxton, was proved. This clearly shows that the testator was the nephew of the above vicar, and it mentions John Ward, a name distinctly associated with the Kempes of Gissing.

In 1576 John Kempe, of Hungerton, mentions in his will "Lodwick," the son of his brother, and numerous other relatives, and leaves charities to the poor of Croxton, Hungerton, and Beeby. In 1615 the will of Bryan Kempe, of Hungerton, was proved, and mention his children, Francis, Alice and William, Thomas and John, also his brother Henry, the sons (who were minors at that date) have been traced to other localities.

From this family a branch was founded at Harby before 1580, for in that year the will of Matthew Kempe, of Harby, was proved, it mentions his brothers, "Ludwick" and Thomas, his *son* "Ludwick," and other relatives. The will of Ludwick Kempe of the same place was proved in 1620, and mentions his son and grandson both named Matthew Kempe. We cannot give details of each generation, but it is clear that the Kemps remained at Harby until the last century. In 1798 James Kempe, of Harby, left by his will his residence, situated in that parish, and Stathern to his wife *Olivia* for her life, and the reversion of this, with other lands, to his son James, or in case of the latter's death then to his second son William, and remainder to Thomas his youngest son. He also mentioned his daughters, Elizabeth, the wife of William Dalby, *Olivia* Mary, and Sarah Kempe. In the official return of the Land Holders of Great Britain in 1874 it is recorded that George Kempe was a freeholder then at Harby. In response to our circulars three independent descendants of this family have sent in details of their forefathers which connect them with Harby and Woolsthorpe, the senior representative of this old family appears to be Henry Kempe, now Postmaster of Bradford, his father, Eustace Compton Kempe, was born at Woolsthorpe in 1801 and was buried there in 1868, his grandfather, William Kempe, was born at Harby in 1774 and was buried at Woolsthorpe in 1823, and his great-grandfather was William Kempe mentioned in the above will. Another branch of this family is represented by William Kempe, of Grantham; Compton Kempe, of Doncaster, and John James Kemp, of Maidstone. Miss *Olivia* Kemp, of South Kensington, is one of the many who owe their christian name to the Harby family.

Returning to the early Kemp(e) wills proved at Leicester we find, in addition to those already mentioned, several testators of the name at Kirby Frisby, Saltby and Saxby, some of which, if not all, appear to be connected with the Kempes of Croxton and Hungerton. The facts derived from these wills, however, are insufficient to form a pedigree without abstracts from the parish registers, and we have had to leave this matter undone, both the funds for the research and the space at our disposal, preventing our including the detailed history of these families.

We now turn to the *immigration* of Kempes to this county and Rutland, which, as noticed in our last chapter, occurred about the middle of the seventeenth century. HENRY KEMPE, who was third son of William Kempe, of Abbott's Bromley, left his native place to seek his living "in pastures new"; why he selected Loughborough is not evident, but shortly before his death he moved to Houghton-on-Hill, where he died in 1657. His will proved by Anne Kempe, his widow, in 1658 (P.C.C., 671 Wotton), mentions his sons in order of age, namely, William, James, John, Thomas, Edward and George, and his duughters Mary, the wife of Edward Arton; Elizabeth, wife of William Jackson, and Anne, wife of Christopher Barker (she remarried Herrick), and he leaves legacies to his grandchildren, who, however, he does not mention by name. To prove the will the testator's *son* William Kempe, of Abbott's Bromley, swore to the following effect: That on or about the 1st March, 1657, the testator "doubting whether he might survive his wife," directed the deponent to add a codicil providing for an income for his wife, this being done the deponent asked the deceased if he would name an executor, but the testator then delayed saying he would consider the matter, finally requesting that the codicil should be expunged, which the deponent according did.

The widow Ann made her will in November, 1659, and it was proved at Leicester on 24th December, 1660, it mentions the above sons and daughters, also James, the son of her son George, and Henry, Mary, Francis, Ann and Elizabeth, the children of her son William. (The seal attached to this bears the initials "A. H." which, doubtless, were those of her daughter Ann Herrick.) WILLIAM KEMPE, the eldest son, married Cornelia Taylor, of Elmes, Derby, in 1655, and as we have seen was at Abbott's Bromley until after his father's death; he then moved to Linford, Leicestershire, where he made his will in 1670 (P.C.C., 136 Penn). His will mentions his children as follows: William, John, Henry, Hamlet, Mary, Frances and Ann; and his properties in the Borough of Leicester, in Abbott's and Bagot's Bromley, and at Newtown-Linford; also his wife Cornelia, his sisters Ann Herrick, Elizabeth Barker and cousins Jackson. The will was proved by WILLIAM KEMPE the eldest son. The will of this son was, as we have said in the last chapter, proved in 1685 and mentions his sons Edward and Thomas. The last named was a surgeon practising at Oakham, he died a bachelor in 1719, and his will was proved in 1721 (P.C.C., 149 Buckingham); it mentions his tenements and hereditaments in Abbott's and Bagot's Bromley and at Barrow, which he bequeathed to his brother Edward subject to his paying £40 to his "brother" Samuel Green. The household effects were left to the surgeon's servant, Mary Faulkner. His brother Edward died without having administered the estate, and administration was consequently granted to Margaret Walker, widow, their aunt and next-of-kin.

The *senior* line from Henry Kempe, of Loughborough, thus became extinct, but by John Kempe, son of William Kempe, of Linford, the family was continued in Leicestershire, his will (which was proved at Leicester in 1719) describes him as of Newtown-Linford, and mentions his son John and his daughters Elizabeth Kempe, Margaret Lewin and Cornelia, the wife of Thomas Hunt; and it appointed his wife Joan and his brother Thomas Kempe, of Ibstock, executors, and his "brother," William Hunt, of Bramstone, supervisor. With regard to these witnesses William Kilsby and Joan Greening, we may notice that John Kilby married Jane Kempe, and that Mary Greening married a John Kempe, ancestor of Thomas Kempe, Esq., J.P., the historian of Warwick. THOMAS KEMPE, of Ibstock, died in 1722, his will being proved at Leicester, and that of his wife Elizabeth, of Ibstock, at the same Probate Court in 1747.

William Kempe, the youngest brother of this last couple, had several children. Joseph Kempe of Hinckley, a needle-maker, made his will in 1758, in which year it was proved by his sons Thomas Kempe, of Hinckley (wool-comber), and Nathaniel Kempe (needle-maker), of the same place; there were also sons named Benjamin and William, and daughters, Elizabeth Kempe, Hannah, who had married in 1755 James Wikes, and Mary, the wife of Daniel Fisher. William was indebted to his father and was consequently not to participate in the distribution of this estate; he, however, had doubtless invested his loan in a profitable manner, and seems to have lived as a squire at Belton.

The last named William Kempe was of Hinckley, and formerly of Earlshilton, a cutler, and by his will dated and proved in 1751 (P.C.C., 147 Busby) he bequeathed to the five children of his late *son* William, and the one child of his daughter Sarah Dewell, all his estate equally divided at the respective ages of twenty-one, until which age the testator's brother, Joseph Kempe, was to control the property in their interest.

The *Gentleman's Magazine* of 1787 announced the death of "William Kempe, Esq., of Belton, Rutland," who died on 29th November. Administration of his estate was granted to Elizabeth Kempe, spinster, his *only* child, on 26th April, 1788. The will of the latter was proved in 1793 (P.C.C., 322 Dodwell) by William Kempe, power being reserved for Frances and George Godfrey. The will is a very long one, providing for numerous eventualities, and we need but say that an estate which she held at Allexton was settled upon William Ward, of *East Norton*, son of William and Sarah Ward, of Belton, and that property at Ashley, Northampton, was settled on Edward Kempe, son of Elizabeth and Edward Kempe of that place, while her residence at Belton, "formerly the estate of Francis Ward, deceased," then in the occupation of William *Godfrey*, was settled upon George Godfrey in trust for the benefit of the testatrix's cousins, William Kempe, John Kempe and Francis Kempe, all of Belton. Legacies were bequeathed to William Hodges, the elder, of Leicester, several other Hodges, Mary, the wife of John Nield, and her servants.

The will of Edward Kempe, of East Norton (uncle to Elizabeth Kempe, of Belton), was proved in 1749. We believe that his wife was the daughter of William Ward, and that the Wards and Kempes were thus relations by half-blood, while George Godfrey was also a relative, having married Mary, daughter of the above Edward Kempe. Edward Kempe, the younger, of Ashley, and afterwards of East Norton, had five sons: William, who was Sheriff for the County of Rutland in 1801, John, who was of Belton, Francis, Edward and Thomas. The eldest son, William Kemp, died in 1811, and by his wife Ann left an only child, Mary Ann Kemp, who died in 1870; she married in 1817 John Eagleton, of Christ Church, London. There is a monumental inscription to her father and mother in Belton Church, the latter died in 1836. The issue of Edward Kempe, the younger, was a son, Edward, and two daughters, who respectively married a Spencer and a Brown; the issue of Edward, the son who was born in 1738, is not further known, but monuments to Edward and his wife are also to be found in Belton Church. Thomas, the third son died unmarried, and was buried at Belton in 1823, John Kempe, the youngest son, was also at Belton, and married Ann, who died in 1805 aged forty-eight; they had a son John, and a daughter Sarah, both of whom died infants, also a second daughter Sarah who died unmarried.

Francis Kemp, the fourth son, consequently seems the only one of these five sons whose issue survives to the present day, he married Elenor . .. by whom he had the following children: William, Edward, Thomas, Francis, Godfrey, John and Robert, Eleanor Ester and Hannah. Francis, the father of this family, was buried at Belton in 1826. His eldest son, William, married Mary Jelly, of Tixover, in 1806, and had by her three children, William,

Edward and Hannah ; both William Kempes, father and son, were drowned. The younger left the following children : William Edward, born 1841, died 1878 ; BAPTIST Kemp (who settled at Theddingworth) ; Eleanor Kemp and Walter Kemp, who lives at Lolham Hall, near Stamford. Edward Kemp, the second son of Francis and Eleanor, was born in 1779 and died in 1842, having married first (in 1802) Ann Hill, by whom he had Francis Kemp, James Kemp, Mary, who married William Baines, and Ann ; and secondly to Elizabeth Godfrey, by whom he had Edward, Robert, Elizabeth (who became the second wife of William Baines), Henry, Sophia (who married J. T. Springthorpe, Sheriff of Rutland) and Charles Godfrey Kemp.

The will of Edward Kemp, who died in 1842, is dated at Uppingham, 30th May, 1839 ; it bequeaths legacies to his son Francis and his daughter Mary. And he appoints as his trustees and executors his brother, Godfrey Kemp, his wife, Elizabeth Kemp, William Baines and William Toller, who were directed to carry on his business and to apply the profits for the education, support and maintenance of his children during their minority, during which time his wife was to have the use of his residence, and after the youngest child had attained the age of twenty-one the whole of the profits of the business were for the sole use of his wife, subject, however, to £100 per annum (from the testator's decease) being invested in Government Stocks, which was for the purpose of raising a fund out of which the trustees were empowered to advance the sum of £400 to either of his children at twenty-one; or in the case of the daughters marrying earlier their portions might be paid according to the discretion of the trustees. Francis Kemp, the eldest son, died in 1862 leaving two children, Ann, born 1832, who lives at Leicester, and Francis Kemp, who was born in 1838. The latter has three children living, Elizabeth, Francis and Thomas. James Kemp, the second son of Edward, of Uppingham, was born in 1804 and died in 1821 ; Mary, the eldest daughter, married William Baines, and left three daughters and a son, Frederick James, who was born in 1836, the latter being married and having two daughters. Edward Kemp, the third son of Edward, of Uppingham, born 1815, married his cousin, Elizabeth Hill ; he died at Leicester in 1896 leaving a son, Edward James Kemp, who for some years was a member of the Leicester Board of Guardians and a Town Councillor ; he died without issue in 1899, and a daughter, Mary Elizabeth, who married Samuel Davis, of Leicester. Robert Kemp, the fourth son of Edward, of Uppingham, born in 1817, died in 1891, having married Sarah Livens, who is still living at Leicester, and left two children, one son and one daughter. The son, ARTHUR KEMP, was born 1856, and married in 1880 Sarah Ellen James, of Towcester,

Arthur Kempe, Esq., of Leicester.

and has three children living, namely, Robert Godfrey Kemp, Edith Margaret Kemp and Alan Kemp. The daughter, Helen Edith (born 1859) married John Henry Davis, who is manager of the Leicester Permanent Building Society. They have no family.

Henry Kemp, the fifth son of Edward, of Uppingham, born 1820, died in 1895, he married Frances Richards Shenton, by whom he had three daughters, two of whom died unmarried, and the youngest, Emily Sophia (born 1856) is married to George M. Frean, and has two children. Charles Godfrey Kemp, the youngest son, born 1831, was placed at Uppingham School and practised as a dentist in Leicester, but died in 1863 without issue. Thomas Kemp, the brother of Edward Kemp, of Uppingham (born in 1782) died in 1853, and we have not traced any descendants; his brother, Francis Kemp, settled in London, where he died in 1865, we have no information as to his marriage, but are inclined to think that one Godfrey George Kemp, now living in Australia, is one of his family. *Godfrey* Kemp, who was executor to Edward, of Uppingham, was born in 1785, became Sheriff of Rutland; he died at Belton in 1850, having married Isabelle, daughter of George Malim, of Higham Ferrars (by a daughter of Sarah Jenneys, of Spalding), by whom he left only one son, the Rev. GODFREY GEORGE KEMP. The Rev. Godfrey George Kemp was a Fellow of Pembroke College, Cambridge, from 1870-3, having graduated as 10th wrangler in 1869 and was Curate of St. Botolph, Cambridge, from which he was transferred in the latter year to the Rectory of Rawreth, Essex. The church at Rawreth (to which his college presented him) was in a serious state of dilapidation and the parish poor; it therefore required persistent and unflagging interest to raise the necessary sum for the present church. Not only has he accomplished the rebuilding, but he has obtained a good organ in place of the barrel instrument which he found in the parish, and he has embellished the church with oaken screen, choir stalls, and all the legal ornaments. Two windows in the choir were erected (at his own cost) in memory of two of his children, who lie buried in that churchyard. He married Harriet Ann Malim, by whom he has the following children living: Irene, Minola Mary, and Ernest Wentworth Guy Kemp.

Rev. Godfrey George Kemp.

Before leaving these Leicestershire Kemps we must notice briefly some of their members who came to London. So early as 1588 there is reason to believe that a John Kemp, merchant tailor and citizen of London was from Abbott's Bromley. THOMAS KEMP, a clergyman, was a curate at St. Dunstan's-in-the-West, and we believe him to be the same as the one of his name who was beneficed in Warwickshire. In the *Alumni Oxonienses* it is noted that Thomas Kemp, of Warwick, a clergyman's son, matriculated at University College in 1581, aged twenty-four. We next find that Edward Kemp, son of Henry Kemp, of Loughborough, and his brother James, settled in London about the time of their father's death (1658). James died in 1663, and by his will (P.C.C., 65 Juxon) he bequeathed lands which he bought at Westham to his wife Alice for her life, with remainder to his son John, or if the latter died without issue then this property was to be shared equally by the testator's daughters Rose (who had married in 1659 Henry Collins) and Alice (who had married in 1662 John Hill). James left a donation to the poor of St. Sepulchre's, Newgate, in which parish he probably lived; he left his friends John Hill (the elder), John Benton and Richard Low, rings, begging them to be overseers. His wife Alice dated her will at Hamerton, Middlesex (Com. London, 1668), and mentions her son, John Kemp, and her daughter, Rose Collins, to which children she left considerable silver plate, as well as the estate mentioned by her husband; she also mentioned her "kinsman" John Bent (a mercer), and her brother-in-law, Mr. Edward Kemp (a saddler).

EDWARD KEMP, the last named, belonged to the Saddlers' Company, and was a citizen of London of considerable wealth and influence. He was for many years a churchwarden of St. Dunstan's-in-the-West, in which capacity he was instrumental in collecting funds for a new organ, which still exists. He and his nephew, Henry Kemp (a "laceman") both resided in the Ward of Farringdon, and both were impanelled and returned as jurors, serving as such at the State trials of Lord Russell in 1689 and of Rouse in 1690. The will of Edward Kemp (P.C.C., Coker, 1693) desires that he should be buried *in* the church of St. Dunstan-in-the-West, near his late wife, and that about 100 persons should be invited to his funeral, each of whom was to be presented with a ring, and that £100, or "thereabouts," should be expended on his obsequies. To his cousin, Henry Kemp, he left £220, provided that he first managed to clear himself of debts by composition or otherwise, so that "he may go quietly and without fear of arrests or troubles, and betake himself to some employ or business." Legacies are also left to his cousins, Mary (the wife of Thomas Sharpe), Frances, (the wife of Henry Warburton), Ann (wife of Joseph Bernard), Ann Muston, Mary Heath, Rose Collins, Elizabeth Wingfield, Elizabeth (late wife of William Jackson), Anne Bonyman, daughter of his late sister Ann Herrick, and William and John Kemp the two youngest sons of his late brother William Kemp. Among other items of charity he bequeathed £20 to Bridewell Hospital, of which he was governor, £5 to the Saddlers' Company, £5 to the poor of St. Dunstans and £5 to the poor of Hungerton, where (he states) he was born. We cannot give the names of all the influential friends mentioned in his will; suffice to say that among them were Sir Peter Rich, Sir Thomas Kelsey, the Rev. Doctor Sherlock, Doctor Henry Dove, Mr. Thomas Fiser and George Ashby, Esq., of Queenby Hall. (This hall is an old moated building long held by the Ashby family.)

We do not know what became of the nephew Henry Kemp mentioned above, but possibly he was the father of the following James Kemp, of Benson, Oxford and Isaac Kemp of St. Sepulchre; if not it would at least appear that he was connected with them. Isaac Kemp, of Upton, in Essex, by his will dated 1767 (P.C.C., 425 Alexander) left to his son, Anthony Facer Kemp but £50, for the reason that he had a few days previously paid him his "fortune"; he left to his second son, Samuel Scattergood Kemp, £400, and to his daughter, Martha Seccombe, £200, with the residue of his estate to his wife Martha. Martha Kemp, widow, of Well Street, Cripplegate, by her will dated 1785 (P.C.C., 83 Holman) left legacies to the same three children, and her will was witnessed by Edward Bernard, Joseph Lamb and William Jackson, of Mark Lane. Anthony Facer Kemp was appointed on the committee of the Livery of London appointed in December, 1781, to effect a "better popular representation in Parliament." At Long Ditton, Surrey, there was a tomb on which the following was inscribed: "Underneath lieth the body of Mrs. Susannah Kemp, wife of Mr. *A. F.* Kemp, of the City of London, merchant. She died August 31st, 1792, aged fifty-five." We are unable to say for certain that this refers to Anthony Facer Kemp, but it seems likely that he was a merchant of London.

Another branch of the Leicestershire Kemps who were much connected with London, lived sometimes at Nottingham, but more often in Moorfields. John Kemp, of Middle Moorfields, was a bankrupt in 1765, and it is probable that he was the father of Samuel, Richard, Mary, Joseph, Ruth and William. The last named was of Coventry Court, St. Martin's-in-the-Fields, and his administration, which appears in 1772, was granted to his daughter Mary. Samuel was a framework knitter, of Nottingham, and his will was proved in 1776 (P.C.C., 376 Tyndall); it mentions his mother Ann Kemp, his sisters Ruth Kemp and Mary Williams, his brother-in-law Thomas James and his brothers Richard and William. This Samuel, we believe, married Ruth, and had a daughter Martha baptized at St. James', Clerkenwell, in 1701. RICHARD KEMP, of Whitecross Alley, Moorfields, was also engaged in the knitting and weaving industry, and in 1762 obtained a Royal Patent in conjunction with Henry Fisher, of New Bond Street, hosier, to make "silk pieces in gold and silver figured," in a stocking frame; this was to hold good for fourteen years. He died in Moorfields, September, 1787, his death being announced in *The Gentleman's Magazine*. His will proved that year (P.C.C., 417 Major) mentions his sons, Richard, Thomas, Samuel, John, and William, also James Dewey, of Artillery Lane, and George Wolfe, of Wellclose Square and William Marriott, of Hoxton Square, the last two being executors. He mentions his property at Poplar consisting of twelve houses and gardens, and also states that under the will of the late Mr. Horne he held a freehold estate in Kent in trust with one John Duplex; as to this last property we have no definite information, and the Hornes were connected with so many different Kemps that we have been unable to identify this testator. Catherine, the widow of this Richard Kemp, was buried beside him in the Old City Road in 1803, aged seventy-nine, Richard Kemp, the eldest son, was a partner in the firm of Baxter, Kemp and Noble, of St. Mary's-at-Hill, and was one of the trustees of Wesley's Chapel, Old City Road, where he was buried in 1798, his will being proved that year (P.C C., 660 Walpole), he describes himself as of Camberwell, and states that his business was that of a wine merchant. He left legacies to his partners in business, Richard Noble and Timothy Baxter, and appointed Peter French and Henry Goldfinch, of Lombard Street, his executors. To his wife Harriet Elizabeth he left an annuity of £200 for life, also an annuity to his brother Thomas Kemp, of Hoxton, with reversion to Sophronica Kemp, the latter's daughter. He also mentions his brothers, William, Thomas, Samuel and John, and his sister Ann Church. John Kemp, brother of the last, appears in the "Directory of London" in 1760 as "at Mr. Hydes, Mark Lane," and later we find that he was declared a bankrupt; this was in 1803, and he was described then as a "wine merchant, of Mark Lane." Probably it was his wife, Elizabeth Ann, who was buried in "the grave of Richard Kemp, of Moorfields," in 1820 with her son also, who died in 1818, aged nineteen. Thomas was of Hoxton, and was buried with above in 1836, aged seventy, and his wife Elizabeth was also buried there in 1844, aged seventy-six, leaving "a numerous family." William Kemp, the other brother, was of Whitechapel, a tobacconist, he died aged thirty-nine in 1800, having married Ann. His will was proved the same year.

We must draw attention to the coincidence that at Hoxton also another Kemp family were living at this time, who likewise were buried in the Old City Road. "Mr. JAMES KEMP, late an inhabitant of Hoxton, a deacon of the Independent Church in that place for more than twenty-two years in his seventy-fourth year." This James Kemp is said, in a biography of his life, to have been "a native of Scotland." He married Mary Sperry, with whom he was the actual founder of the first Sunday School, although Rakes has always had the credit for so doing. James Kemp on coming to London about the year 1772 came under the influence of a celebrated preacher, the Rev. Edward Hitchin, of the chapel in White Row, Spitalfields; under this ministry he and his wife gathered together the first school of young people known as the Hoxton Academy, and for some forty-five years Mrs. Kemp laboured there; she died on the 9th September, 1837, and was buried at Bunhill Fields, where her eldest son, "Mr. John Kemp, of Old London Street," had been buried in 1830, aged fifty-three. With them also lie the bodies of the latter's grandson, Alfred Pratt White, Mrs. Tabitha Kemp and Mr. Samuel Kemp.

Connected with one of these Hoxton families we may note that at Poplar Church there is a stone to Richard Kemp, Vestry Clerk there for many years, who was buried in 1831, aged fifty-two, and that at St. George's-in-the-East there is a stone to Elizabeth Kempe, who died in 1843, aged seventy-four. Near these parishes there was a family of Kempes who owned a printing business early in the last (nineteenth) century, one of these married a daughter of Henry Stone, and left a son Richard, who emigrated to New South Wales, and a son Samuel Kemp, who was a linguist, and also settled abroad.

We have mentioned that a widow of Edward Kemp, of East Norton, married William Ward of that place, these being important ancestors of the chief living representatives of the Abbott's Bromley family, thus a mention of the will of a Sarah Ward of London will not be out of place here. The probate has been lent to us by a descendant of the Kempe-Ward alliance, now secretary at "Shakespeare's Birthplace." It was proved in 1819 (P.C.C., 193 Ellenbro') and a fresh administration was granted in 1830. The testatrix says she was a "spinster formerly living at King Street, Moorfields," but in 1816 living at Old Street Road, Middlesex. She bequeathed to James Kemp, the elder, of Hoxton Town, James Kemp, his son, of the Bank of England, and John Prior Ward, of Godliman Street, London, all her estates at Budbrook and Pillerton in Warwickshire in trust for the benefit of any persons who could "prove consanguinity or degree of kindred not beyond that of third cousin" on her *father's* side. Advertisements were to be inserted in three newspapers in London and one in Warwickshire or Northampton, four or more times in order to trace any who had claim to such property; and should no claim arise she bequeathed her estate, subject to several large legacies, to the above trustees absolutely. The special bequests included £1,000 to Robert Wheeler, of Stratford-on-Avon, £1,000 to Mr. Miles Birkett, of Bunhill Row, stockbroker, and the interest from £1,000 stock to James Kemp, the elder, for life, reverting to his wife and thence to their son, Mr. Samuel Kemp absolutely. It appears probable that these James Kemps were those connected with the Sunday School at Hoxton, notwithstanding the fact that the founder of that institution was said to have been a "native of Scotland," and a will of Samuel Kemp, which is in the P.C.C. Calendar of 1833 and 1838 is likely to be that of Samuel who inherited under Miss Sarah Ward's bequest.

James Kemp, Deacon of the Independent Church.

CHAPTER IV.

KEMPES OF THE WEST OF ENGLAND.

THE West of England has never been thickly scattered with families of Kemp(e)s like the Eastern Counties, but from early times the name is traceable. Even before the noted Flemish weaver made his home at Kendal, "John Kemp" was a name of importance in the County of Westmoreland. Apparently from Westmoreland the Kempes spread to Cheshire and gradually southward, but several settlements of West of England families of the name are of southern origin. The chief of these as measured by social rank was founded by an Edward Kempe, who was the son of Edward Kempe, of the New Forest, and grandson of Sir William, Kempe, Knight, of Ollanty, Kent. This Edward appears to have settled in the County of Hereford owing to a grant of land which he obtained from his uncle, Robert Benett, at the time Bishop of Hereford. The lands included Middleton-on-the-Hill, Chenson and Waterson, and a lease of the parsonage and glebe of Almeley, all of which are mentioned in the will of Edward Kempe which was proved at London in 1615 (P.C.C., 82 Rudd). The will mentions also his uncle and aunt Benett, and bequeaths the property to his son Robert, subject to the life interest of the testator's wife Elizabeth. The mention also of his "friend, Sir Robert Oxenbridge, Knight," and many relatives distinctly shows the exact connexion of the testator to those of Hampshire and Kent. Further interesting evidence is furnished by several deeds now preserved at the British Museum relating to these lands and others and bearing the signature and seal of Edward Kempe and his relatives.

Elizabeth, his widow, resided at Middleton on his decease, and her will is dated there. It was proved in 1631 (P.C.C., 135 St. John) and bequeaths the lease which she held from the Bishop of Hereford of the rectory and tithes of Middleton to her daughter, Margaret Bourne, and the lease of the rectory and tithes of Docklow to her daughter, Anne Jeffries. To her son Robert she left her household furniture, and legacies to Edward Smith, her "nephew and grandchild," The will states that to secure the wardship of her son from the Court of Wards she had paid a considerable sum, part of which she had borrowed from her son-in-law, William Jeffries, whom she begged to act as the said son's guardian.

At the time the will was proved it is probable that Robert had attained manhood, for in 1629 we find that he petitioned the king for pardon, he having been accused of crime by "a woman of mean condition" named Mary Elizabeth Cook. We have not traced his will, but that of his wife Anne, styling herself "relict of Robert Kemp, of Shenstone," dated 1677, was proved that year at Hereford. It mentions her son Robert Kemp and her daughters, Ann Kemp, Rachael Kemp and Elizabeth Freeby, also her grandson Thomas Kemp and her granddaughters Elizabeth, Ann and Rachael Freeby.

The daughter Rachael mentioned above made her will at Wormbridge, and it was proved at Hereford in 1681. It mentions her brothers Robert and Roger Kemp and her cousin Dorothy Gurnons, also her sister Ann and the children of her brother Robert, whom she said were to be paid legacies by her kinsman Marshall Bridges. From this we get a glimpse of the fourth generation of Herefordshire Kempes, but their movements thenceforward are shrouded in mystery. It would at least appear evident that they no longer retained considerable property in the county, and it is probable that they left Herefordshire, one branch going south to Redwick, in the parish of Henbury, near Bristol, and another settling in the north of Shropshire. If this surmise is correct it is still necessary to retrace our steps and mention earlier Kempes of that adjoining county.

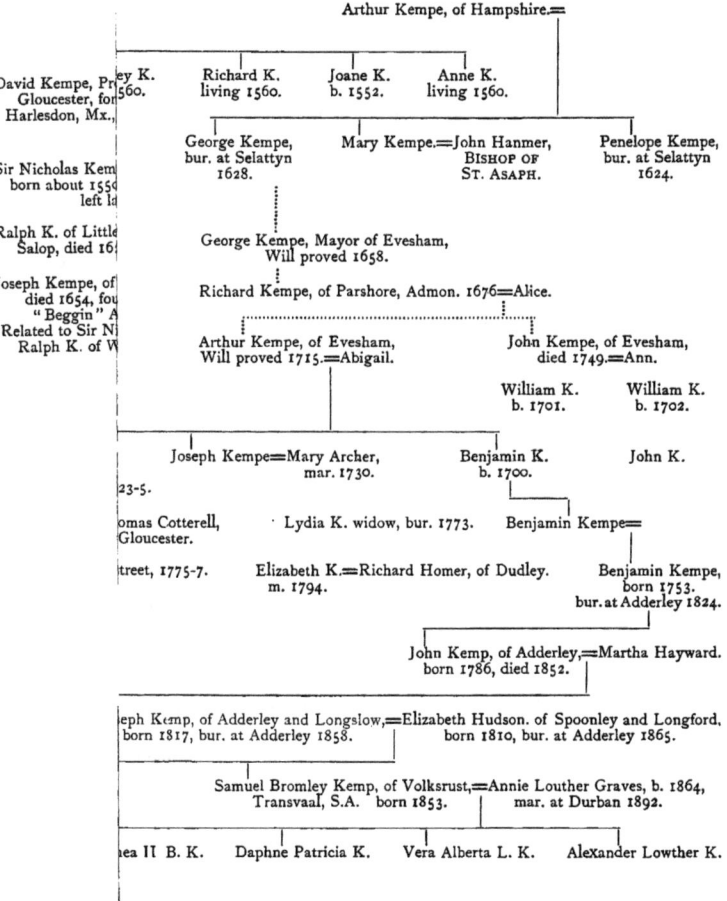

Arthur Kempe, of Hampshire.=

David Kempe, Pr
Gloucester, fo
Harlesdon, Mx.,

ey K.
560.

Richard K.
living 1560.

Joane K.
b. 1552.

Anne K.
living 1560.

George Kempe,
bur. at Selattyn
1628.

Mary Kempe.=John Hanmer,
BISHOP OF
ST. ASAPH.

Penelope Kempe,
bur. at Selattyn
1624.

Sir Nicholas Kem
born about 155
left l

Ralph K. of Littl
Salop, died 16

George Kempe, Mayor of Evesham,
Will proved 1658.

Joseph Kempe, of
died 1654, fo
"Beggin" A
Related to Sir N
Ralph K. of W

Richard Kempe, of Parshore, Admon. 1676=Alice.

Arthur Kempe, of Evesham,
Will proved 1715.=Abigail.

John Kempe, of Evesham,
died 1749.=Ann.

William K.
b. 1701.

William K.
b. 1702.

Joseph Kempe=Mary Archer,
mar. 1730.

Benjamin K.
b. 1700.

John K.

23-5.

omas Cotterell,
Gloucester.

· Lydia K. widow, bur. 1773.

Benjamin Kempe=

treet, 1775-7.

Elizabeth K.=Richard Homer, of Dudley.
m. 1794.

Benjamin Kempe,
born 1753.
bur. at Adderley 1824.

John Kemp, of Adderley,=Martha Hayward.
born 1786, died 1852.

eph Kemp, of Adderley and Longslow,=Elizabeth Hudson. of Spoonley and Longford,
born 1817, bur. at Adderley 1858.
born 1810, bur. at Adderley 1865.

Samuel Bromley Kemp, of Volksrust,=Annie Louther Graves, b. 1864,
Transvaal, S.A. born 1853.
mar. at Durban 1892.

ea H B. K.

Daphne Patricia K.

Vera Alberta L. K.

Alexander Lowther K.

CHAPTER IV.

KEMPES OF THE WEST OF ENGLAND.

THE West of England has never been thickly scattered with families of Kemp(e)s like the Eastern Counties, but from early times the name is traceable. Even before the noted Flemish weaver made his home at Kendal, "John Kemp" was a name of importance in the County of Westmoreland. Apparently from Westmoreland the Kempes spread to Cheshire and gradually southward, but several settlements of West of England families of the name are of southern origin. The chief of these as measured by social rank was founded by an Edward Kempe, who was the son of Edward Kempe, of the New Forest, and grandson of Sir William, Kempe, Knight, of Ollanty, Kent. This Edward appears to have settled in the County of Hereford owing to a grant of land which he obtained from his uncle, Robert Benett, at the time Bishop of Hereford. The lands included Middleton-on-the-Hill, Chenson and Waterson; and a lease of the parsonage and glebe of Almeley, all of which are mentioned in the will of Edward Kempe which was proved at London in 1615 (P.C.C., 82 Rudd). The will mentions also his uncle and aunt Benett, and bequeaths the property to his son Robert, subject to the life interest of the testator's wife Elizabeth. The mention also of his "friend, Sir Robert Oxenbridge, Knight," and many relatives distinctly shows the exact connexion of the testator to those of Hampshire and Kent. Further interesting evidence is furnished by several deeds now preserved at the British Museum relating to these lands and others and bearing the signature and seal of Edward Kempe and his relatives.

Elizabeth, his widow, resided at Middleton on his decease, and her will is dated there. It was proved in 1631 (P.C.C., 135 St. John) and bequeaths the lease which she held from the Bishop of Hereford of the rectory and tithes of Middleton to her daughter, Margaret Bourne, and the lease of the rectory and tithes of Docklow to her daughter, Anne Jeffries. To her son Robert she left her household furniture, and legacies to Edward Smith, her "nephew and grandchild," The will states that to secure the wardship of her son from the Court of Wards she had paid a considerable sum, part of which she had borrowed from her son-in-law, William Jeffries, whom she begged to act as the said son's guardian.

At the time the will was proved it is probable that Robert had attained manhood, for in 1629 we find that he petitioned the king for pardon, he having been accused of crime by "a woman of mean condition" named Mary Elizabeth Cook. We have not traced his will, but that of his wife Anne, styling herself "relict of Robert Kemp, of Shenstone," dated 1677, was proved that year at Hereford. It mentions her son Robert Kemp and her daughters, Ann Kemp, Rachael Kemp and Elizabeth Freeby, also her grandson Thomas Kemp and her granddaughters Elizabeth, Ann and Rachael Freeby.

The daughter Rachael mentioned above made her will at Wormbridge, and it was proved at Hereford in 1681. It mentions her brothers Robert and Roger Kemp and her cousin Dorothy Gurnons, also her sister Ann and the children of her brother Robert, whom she said were to be paid legacies by her kinsman Marshall Bridges. From this we get a glimpse of the fourth generation of Herefordshire Kempes, but their movements thenceforward are shrouded in mystery. It would at least appear evident that they no longer retained considerable property in the county, and it is probable that they left Herefordshire, one branch going south to Redwick, in the parish of Henbury, near Bristol, and another settling in the north of Shropshire. If this surmise is correct it is still necessary to retrace our steps and mention earlier Kempes of that adjoining county.

KEMPES OF THE WEST OF ENGLAND.

(Grandmother) Smith.=

Robert Kempe, of Winchcombe,=Margaret, d. of John Dyson.
living there 1540, will proved 1560.

Arthur Kempe, of Hampshire.=

David Kempe, Prebendary of=Catherine.
Gloucester, formerly of
Harlesdon, Mx., died 1582.
a daughter.

John K. b. 1542. | Henry K. b. 1544. | Edward K. b. 1550. | Giles K. living 1560. | Roger K. living 1560. | Reginald K. living 1560. | Humphrey K. living 1560. | Richard K. living 1560. | Joane K. b. 1552. | Anne K. living 1560.

John K. of Muckleton, held lands in Cheshire. | Ralph Kempe, of Gloucester, Will proved 1562. | Thomas K. of Upton Magna, Administration 1590. | Robert K. living 1590.

George Kempe, bur. at Selattyn 1628. | Mary Kempe=John Hanmer, Bishop of St. Asaph. | Penelope Kempe, bur. at Selattyn 1624.

Sir Nicholas Kempe, of London, J.P., born about 1550, died Sept. 1624, left lands to ——> Ralph Kempe, of Winchcombe,=Ellen Jusnell, mar. at St. Bartholomew's,
(heir to Sir Nicholas K. and to John K. above.) West Smithfield, London, by license, 16 August, 1574.

Henry Kempe.

Ralph K. of Little Ash,=Katherine.
Salop, died 1624.

George Kempe, Mayor of Evesham,
Will proved 1658.

Joseph Kempe, of Hitchin, Herts.
died 1654, founder of the
"Beggin" Almshouse.
Related to Sir Nicholas K. and
Ralph K. of Winchcombe.

Ralph Kempe, of Winchcombe,=Grace Grinnell, mar. by licence 1610.
and of St. Margaret's, West- Will proved 1656.
minster, Mx. Will proved 1645.

Richard Kempe, of Parshore, Admon. 1676=Alice.

Thomas Kempe,=Deborah. d. before 1656. | Ralph Kempe. | a dau.=Leonard Adams. | a dau.=John Levenworth. | a dau.=Peter Holland.

Arthur Kempe, of Evesham, Will proved 1715.=Abigail. | John Kempe, of Evesham, died 1749.=Ann.

Ralph Kempe, b. 1655, at College 1672. | Ralph Adams, living 1656. | Ralph Levenworth. | Elizabeth Holland.

William K. b. 1701. | William K. b. 1702.

Thomas Kempe, of Winchcombe, Will proved 1665. | Ann K. | Ralph K. (?=Judith Snow, of London, 1665)

Arthur K. bur. 1727. | Sarah.=Thomas K.=Hannah. | Joseph Kempe=Mary Archer, mar. 1730. | Benjamin K. b. 1700. | John K.

Henry Kempe, 1723-5.

Margaret, living 1674.=William Kempe, of Acton Raynold, in the parish
of Shawbury, and taxed for 2 hearths at
Gt. Withyford, 1674. Will 1674.

Thomas K. bap. 1721. | Charles Kempe, of=Elizabeth, d. of Thomas Cotterell, Evesham, Will 1787. of Campden, Gloucester. | Lydia K. widow, bur. 1773. - Benjamin Kempe=

Robert Kempe, of Albrighton-by-Shrewsbury. | Henry Kempe.=Martha.

Charles Kempe, of London & Chelmsford. | Francis Stonestreet, 1775-7. | Elizabeth K.=Richard Homer, of Dudley. m. 1794. | Benjamin Kempe, born 1753, bur. at Adderley 1824.

Henry K. b. 1674. | Richard K. b. 1683, Churchwarden=Joan. at Albrighton, 1726-36. | Elizabeth K. | Thomas K. b. 1688.

John K. of Warfield=Elizabeth Roberts, of Madelay, mar. 1706. | Mary K. | Elizabeth K.

John Kemp, of Adderley,=Martha Hayward.
born 1786, died 1852.

Joseph Kemp, of Adderley and Longslow,=Elizabeth Hudson, of Spoonley and Longford,
born 1817, bur. at Adderley 1858. born 1810, bur. at Adderley 1865.

Joseph Hayward Kemp, of Walton,=Mary Bennion,
Wellington, Salop, born 1851. b. 1853.

Samuel Bromley Kemp, of Volksrust,=Annie Louther Graves, b. 1864,
Transvaal, S.A. born 1853. mar. at Durban 1892.

Thomas George Juckes, eldest=Ada Kemp. m. 1902. | Mabel Kemp. | Evelyn Kemp.
son of Thos. J., of Tern.

Damaris Dorothea H B. K. | Daphne Patricia K. | Vera Alberta L. K. | Alexander Lowther K.

Among the old MSS. of the Shrewsbury Corporation is an undated deed recording the sale and quit claim by "Vincint, son of Reginald Kemp," to Robert, the son of Roger de Cornlegh, of a rent of elevenpence which William le Knave used to pay to the said Vincint. The deed would appear to be earlier than the sixteenth century, otherwise these names certainly point to a connexion with the Kentish family, Reginald and Vincent being two of the last male line resident at Wye, Reginald, however, died in 1610. Among the same collection of deeds and municipal papers is a letter dated 31st October, 1593 addressed from "My house at Coton in Wemes parish" to the bailiffs of the Earl of Essex, by William Harrison, expressing readiness to cease sueing Robert Kemp for a debt, "being bidden by Crist to forgive those that trespass." The letter mentions a Mr. John Newport, of Wellington, deceased, to whom the writer owed some rent. Perhaps the Robert Kemp mentioned belonged to the district of Wellington, for the present head of a local family of Kempes has property there, although the little evidence that we have been able to gather points to the extreme north of the county as being for generations the home of his ancestors. This brings us to another episcopal connexion of the Kempes.

John Hanmer, who had formerly been Prebend of Worcester, was Bishop of St. Asaph from 1624 to 1628, and married Mary, daughter of Arthur Kempe, Gent., of the County of Hampshire. Doubtless like Bishop Benett, Hanmer admitted some of his Kempe relatives to leasehold property which he obtained in virtue of his bishopric. At Selattyn, on the north-western border of Shropshire (which came under the Archdeaconal Court of Asaph), lived George and Penelope Kempe. Penelope was buried there on 9th December, 1624, the parish register describing her as "Penelope Kempe, spinster, sister-in-law to the Lord Bishop Hanmer." George Kempe, said to have been her brother, was buried there on 18th December, 1628, and is described as a "Gentleman" in the register. We have not identified his will, nor that of Arthur Kemp, of Hampshire, and are not able to say for certain that these were a branch of the Kentish stock, but it seems probable that Benett and Hanmer were friends and perhaps connected by marriage. There is, however, some evidence which may lead us to connect these Kempes of the north of Shropshire with a family settled for several generations at Winchcombe.

In 1624 Ralph Kemp, of Ash Parva, or Little Ash, Shropshire, who was by trade a *weaver*, bequeathed legacies to the children of his brother, John Kempe, of Mucklestone, and to his god-child, Ann Hitchin. He appointed his wife, Katherine, executrix and residuary legatee, and Ralph and Richard Jackson, of Little Ash, "his loving neighbours," overseers to the will.

There can be no doubt that this Ralph Kempe was related to Sir Nicholas Kempe, Knight and J.P. of London, who mentioned in his will (proved 1624) "Ralph Kempe, of Winchcombe," and we have evidence that in 1603 one, Ralph Jackson, probably the above, with Hugh Kempe and others were suitors in the Queen's Court (Pleadings Ducatus Lancastriæ) concerning boundaries of property at Chaderton, Nuthurst and Oldham. As mentioned earlier the will of James Chetham, of Nuthurst, dated 1613, mentions Hugh Kempe, Nicholas Kemp and Isabel and Katherine Jackson, thus linking Sir Nicholas with Jackson, and the latter with Ralph Kempe, of Little Ash.

The mention of Winchcombe gives rise to the question, at what date were the Kempes established there? The answer comes from the registers of the parish church, which have kindly been searched for us by the Rev. John Taylor. The parish books were in accordance with the law commenced in 1539, but in common with the majority throughout the Kingdom it is clear that at first the registration was very irregular. The first entry of a Kempe occurs on 7th October, 1541, when William, son of Robert, was baptized; then follow other children who were baptized as here given: John, 1542, Henry, 1544, Edward, 1550, and Joan, 1552. In addition to these children we find from the will of Robert Kemp, of Winchcombe, which was proved at Gloucester in 1560, that he had sons named Gyles, Roger or Robert, Reginald, Humphrey, Richard and a daughter Anne. This will mentions "a velvet nightcap," "a best doublet," "satin shoes," and other clothes of fine material, indicating that the man was a gentleman, or at least a well-to-do yeoman. He speaks also of his silver cups and other plate silver spoons, which had been left by his *father-in-law*, John Dyson, to his sons, and he left a considerable sum to his wife Margaret, and to his children. Mention is made of a bequest left to John, the testator's son, by his "grandmother Smythe." The will is witnessed by "Raffe Kempe" and others.

Ralph Kempe, of the City of Gloucester, in his will proved there in 1562, directed that he should be buried in the Church of Graceland in that city, and bequeathed his lands at Cheltenham to his son, Thomas Kempe, subject to the payment of legacies to his sisters Agnes, Sibel and Mary, and he mentions a bowl, made of silver gilt, and other plate. This last testator was probably the son of the former, and his will helps us further to identify him, as at Graceland (*i.e.*, land belonging to the Church of Our Lady of Grace), at Gloucester died the Rev. David Kempe, who was for a time Prebendary of that Cathedral.

This same David Kempe was formerly Prebendary of Harlesden, and subsequently the Prebend of Willesden in St. Paul's Cathedral, London, and he was also vicar of Rickmansworth, Middlesex, and Archdeacon of St. Alban's, with the latter of which at least Sir Nicholas Kempe was identified; thus we reason again that between the Kempes of Winchcombe and Shropshire there was a close connexion at this time. The will of David Kempe, dated in 1581 from the Close of Gloucester Cathedral, was proved in 1582, and mentions his wife Catherine and his daughter and her children. The executor, Thomas Kempe, was bequeathed a "shamise purse, wt. the silver locke," the relationship between David and Thomas Kempe is not stated. In 1596 the will of John Kempe, of the parish of "Our Blessed Lady of Grace," Gloucester, an apothecarye, was proved, leaving all his lands and tenements in the City and County of Gloucester to John Kempe, his son, one hundred marks each to his son Edward Kempe when twenty-one years of age, and to his daughter Susan. The residue of his estate being left to his wife Elizabeth, who was sole executor. Walter "Brommedge" and Richard Ward, *Gent.*, were the overseers.

Returning to the relatives of these at Winchcombe we find that Ralph Kempe, described as of the parish of St. Margaret's Westminster, was granted a license to marry Grace Grinnell on 22nd June, 1610. Very shortly after this date he was at Winchcombe, where he made his will in 1644. It was proved at Gloucester the following year, and bequeaths to his wife *Grace* certain lands lying at Winchcombe called "Hitchingsfields" for her life with reversion to her son, Thomas Kempe, while to his son Ralph and his heirs for ever he leaves his "inheritance." The testator leaves legacies to his sons-in-law, Leonard Addams, John Leavenworth and Peter Holland, and his brother Henry and kinsman William Greening are also mentioned.

It was no doubt this Ralph Kempe, of Winchcombe, who was intended to benefit by the will of Sir Nicholas Kempe. The will of Grace Kemp, Ralph's wife, was proved in 1656 (P.C.C., 404 Berkley), and directed that her body should be buried *in* the church of Winchcombe. She mentions her son "Raphe" Kempe and her sons-in-law as mentioned above, also her son-in-law Edmund Mutson and her brother-in-law Henry Kempe. We may remark that "Raufe Skinner" was a trustee under the will of Joseph Kempe, of Hitchin, in 1654, and we have no doubt that the said Joseph was related to the Winchcombe Kempes, his arms as displayed over his tomb were *Gules 3 garbs within a bordure engrailed, Or*, as used by Sir Nicholas. "Ralph Kempe, son of Ralphe Kempe, of Winchcombe," matriculated at New Inn Hall, Oxford, in 1672, aged seventeen. He must have been the grandson of Grace Kempe. The estate of Ralph Kempe, late of the ship

Fauconberge, bachelor, was granted to his brother, Ephraim Kempe, in 1696; we cannot say, however, if this is the same individual. One, Ralph Kempe, of St. James's Clerkenwell, married before 1675, for in that year he was granted administration of the estate of Susanah, his wife. Several Ralph Kempes of a latter period are known to us, but here we need only say that the Kemp line at Winchcombe must have ceased before the beginning of the eighteenth century, and that the last will relating to this place was that of Thomas Kempe, proved in 1665. The testator mentions his "mother-in-law Deborah Kempe," and his "half-brother Ralph Kempe," and his "half-sister Ann Kemp," from which we conclude that "mother-in-law" in this case means *step*-mother. The will also mentions Ralph Addams, the elder, and Elizabeth Breaks, widow, and is witnessed by Edward Slaughter and others. (A seal attached bears the impression of a crest, a griffin's head, the facsimile of which occurs on a later will and also on some Middlesex Kempe deeds.)

From Winchcombe to Evesham and South Littleton is a distance of some eight miles. It would appear likely that as Kempes were at both these places at this time (1590-1665) these were connected with the above, but an interesting will of a foreign Kempe proved in 1566 shows that those at Beckford and Harvington, close by, were kinsmen of his and but recently settled in this kingdom. This testator was named James Kempe, and the will shows that he was a weaver of some wealth living at Beckford. He leaves many specific legacies to relatives named Kempe and sums of money for his poor kinsmen in his "native country." Which country this was is not indicated, but is likely that he was one of the Hugenots who took refuge in this country about 1544. We may however remark that although some of our subscribers have claimed descent from such, the name of Kempe does not occur either in any known list of Hugenots settled in England nor in the registers of the Hugenot church, which is still maintained at Canterbury. James Kempe speaks of his looms and other stock-in-trade, and an inventory of his goods includes cattle, sheep and some silver plate. He particularly mentions as kinsmen Henry Kempe, of Siston, Thomas Kempe, of Harvington, and a Randall Kempe. The clergy and poor of Ashton and Dumbleton were also bequeathed money. Some of these immigrants doubtless returned to their native land, but the parish registers of Harvington show that others of the Kempes remained in that parish. In 1595 Magdalen Kempe was there married to Robert Harward, and from that time Kempe became a constantly-used christian name among the local Harwards and kindred families. Administration of the estate of John Kempe, of Harvington, was granted to his daughter, Judith Jarratt, in 1615. In 1618 Kempe, the son of William Abell, was baptized at Harvington, Kempe Harwarde and Samuel Demetrius (of Priors Salford) being witnesses. In 1644 an inventory was made of the goods of John Kempe, of Harvington (a blacksmith), and administration was granted to Elizabeth Kempe, of the Boro' of Evesham, spinster, and to George Kempe of the same place, Elizabeth being the deceased's daughter and George Kempe probably his brother. The inventory was signed by Kempe Harvard and George Kempe, who stated that John Kempe, of Harvington, had died *about fourteen years before*, since which his wife had held his property, which consisted of a house "built of (? on) the lord's waste," a little furniture, and his tools as a blacksmith. This inventory shows at least that the widow had lived on her capital and thus reduced the estate, for in his lifetime John Kempe had been the chief resident at Harvington, as appears from the Subsidy Roll of 1601, his name then headed the list of parishioners, he being rated at £5. At Evesham at that time Richard Harvard was rated at £4, and we can surmise that it was due to the influence of that family that George Kempe settled there. At South Littleton at the same rating Agnes Bussell, widow, was registered, and we think this worthy a mention, as Kempe as a christian name was adopted by subsequent Bussells. In the Abell family it continued until the eighteenth century, one Kemp Abell, of Bidford, with

Thomas Osborne, of Broom, being at Stratford-on-Avon Petty Sessions in 1736. Connected also with the foreign Kempe of Beckford we have no doubt was Henry Kempe, a husbandman, of *Siddenton*, whose will was proved at Gloucester in 1559; this testator mentioned his sons Thomas, Robert, Richard, James, John, Harry and Roger and a daughter Joan, leaving his property to his wife Joan for her life with reverson to the sons. He left various amounts for charity at Stratford-on-Avon, being included under the bequests to poor. We cannot attempt to follow the issue of this Henry of Siddenton, but must return to those of Evesham, which place for some two centuries was the home of a small family of Kempes.

George Kempe, who as stated above, was the appraiser of the small estate of John Kempe, of Harvington, was thrice elected Mayor of Evesham in the years 1634, 1643 and 1654. His will, dated 1650, was proved in 1658 (P.C.C., 20 Wooton), and describes him as a "Gent.," of Shinehill, in South Littleton. His estate at Evesham and Shinehill he bequeathed to John Nicklis, and to William Nicklis he left a piece of land, while to Samuel and Jonathan Nicklis, both of London, he left some property at Shinehill, and his house and demesne lands to his daughter Elizabeth Kempe, the wife of Thomas Bushell (otherwise written Bussell). The most notable bequest, however, was twenty bibles, which were directed to be given to the poor people of Littleton and Bengeworth at the discretion of his executors, and sums of money to Mr. Henry Ballard, Mr. Hopkins, Mr. Dolphin, of Honnybourne, and Mr. Matthews, "ministers of the gospel," for that they had "suffered for righteousness sake." George Hopkins was Vicar of All Saints', Evesham, and Thomas Matthews gave a piece of ground at Evesham—the profits from which were to be applied "to apprentice poor children to some honest trade." The local Probate Register Records are not perfect, and doubtless some wills of the Kempes have been unregistered; thus the next of which we have a knowledge is of one Arthur Kemp, of Evesham, dated and proved in 1715. The testator is described as a "fellmonger," and bequeathed to his wife Abigail his house and lands in the parish of All Saints', Evesham, for her life, and afterwards this property was to pass to their son Arthur, besides whom they had children named Thomas, Joseph, Benjamin, Joan, Mary and Abagail. Mary married William Green, of Weston-sub-Edge, Joan died single in 1749, John, another son, had been buried in infancy, Joseph died about 1785, Benjamin married Lydia, who was buried a widow at Evesham in 1773. Thomas married first a Sarah, by whom he had a son Thomas, and secondly a Hannah, by whom he had a son Henry baptized 1723 and buried 1725. Thomas, the younger, married Sarah Russell in 1776, and Arthur, the eldest son was buried at All Saints' on 20th December, 1727. The registers show also that John and Ann Kemp had two sons named William who were baptized in 1701 and 1702; that Margaret Kempe married Edward Cole in August, 1719, and that Israel* Kemp married John (*sic*) Crump in 1739; Joseph Kempe, by a wife named Catherine (who died in 1728), had children baptized named Joseph and Martha in 1723 and 1727, Joseph, the elder, marrying as his second wife Mary Archer in 1730. These, doubtless, are only a few of the Kempes who during the seventeenth and eighteenth century must have been constantly represented at Evesham, but we have no exact information as to the parentage of the next testator whose will relates to this place. Before, however, passing on we must note that on the last quoted will there is still a seal bearing an evident allusion to a crest of several Kempe families. It is a bird with wings raised, standing on an *upright* sheaf, at the foot of which are a serpent and lion, while a motto has evidently been broken from the top of the seal the word "OVR" being alone readable. Many Kempes in Australia have sent us impressions of seals bearing the bird on an *upright* sheaf, and

* Perhaps Israel is a mistake for Isabel, or John a mistake for Joan.

even modern heraldic artists when purporting to give the arms of the Kemp Baronets have *erroneously* drawn the sheaf thus instead of "fesswise" (*i.e.*, horizontally). In this case, however, it is clear that the testator used the seal as a badge, which would be sufficient to distinguish him as a Kempe without encroaching on the rights of a family to which perhaps he did not belong.

The will of CHARLES KEMP, of Evesham, was proved in 1787, his death being announced in the *Gentleman's Magazine* as occuring on 14th September and the register stating that he was buried at All Saints' on the 16th of that month, 1787. He is styled "Gent." in his will, and states that he had inherited under the will of his father-in-law, Thomas Cotterell, of Campden, Gentleman, a freehold estate at that place, and that he also had property in Drury Lane, Great Queen Street and Hampstead, all in Middlesex, which, subject to his widow's life interest, he left to his son Charles, who was bound to allow to his sisters sufficient annuities for their maintenance. The will mentions Mr. Owen, bookseller at Temple Bar, London, Mr. John Brown, stockbroker, and Mr. John King, of Chancery Lane. These last names and the Middlesex property casts a doubt upon his connexion with the early Kempes of Evesham, but although the Kempes of Hendon also had property at Hampstead, Drury Lane and Great Queen Street, we are not able to state that he belonged to that family. We find that a Charles Kemp, Esquire, of Evesham, subscribed for a copy of "The History and Antiquities of Evesham" in 1768, and that a Charles Kemp, possibly his son, was an officer on the *Chaser*, and made his will in 1788; in this, the testator names his "good friends" Frederick and Hannah Westerlins, of the parish of St. George's-in-the-East, Middlesex, as residuary legatees, but his estates are not enumerated. Another CHARLES KEMP, formerly of the East Indian Maritime Service, was buried in Brixton Church in 1840, aged forty-six years, and a will, which doubtless is his, was proved in London that year. Perhaps this also was a relation of the Evesham Kempes, of whom we find no later trace locally. The last entry of a Kemp in the Evesham registers is the marriage of Elizabeth Kemp in 1794 to Richard Homer, of Dudley. One other entry, but earlier, is however curious, that of the baptism in 1775 of Frances Stonestreet, daughter of Charles Kemp; she was buried in 1777. It is a singular coincidence that Grace, daughter of Thomas Stonestreet, of Lewes, married George Kemp, grandfather of Thomas Read Kemp, the prospector of Kemp Town, with whose family the name of Russell mentioned above as intermarried with Kemps of Evesham, was also linked. (*Vide* Sussex.)

CHAPTER V.

GLOUCESTER AND BRANCHES.

WE have had occasion in the foregoing chapters to mention several early Kempes of Gloucester, and must here note others whose wills we have seen at the Gloucester Probate Registry, namely, JOAN KEMPE, of Maisemore, 1599; William Kempe, of Maisemore, 1566; William Kempe, of Churcham, 1591; Anne Kympe, of Churcham, 1672; Joanna Kemp, of Bulley, 1619, and Thomas Kemp, of Bulley, 1660. These places are near Gloucester, and from the wills we judge that the testators were connected with David Kempe,

Prebendary of Gloucester Cathedral, mentioned earlier. It is important to add that the William of Maisemore desired to be buried near his father and mother at Maisemore; thus this settlement was evidently at least one generation earlier in this parish. William was forty-four years old when he died, and he left a son Richard and daughters Elizabeth, Agnes and Margaret; he also had a stepbrother of his name, the brother was the testator of the will of 1591, and left a son Richard, whose widow's will appears in 1619, the son of the latter probably was the husband of Ann Kemp, of Churcham proved in 1670, the last leaving a son, Richard Kempe, whose children named "Londerence," Richard, Joseph, Margaret, Marcy and Mary were then living. This last will bears a seal bearing the impression of a bird with wings raised, evidently another allusion to the crest or badge of the chief Kemp families.

The mention of Master Skidmore in the will of 1591 calls for the note that a family of this name was connected about this time with Middlesex Kempes, with whom we have previously surmised this west country family to be akin.

The Kempes of Almondsbury, in the south of Gloucester, who for over 100 years were small landowners there, seem to have originated from Abbot's Bromley; one, WILLIAM KEMPE, who was born at that Staffordshire nest in 1587, being a clergyman much persecuted during the Commonwealth. This William was educated at Magdalen Hall, Oxford, and became Greek lecturer there; he was presented to the Rectory of Easton Grey, from which he was transferred to Puddimore-Milton, Wilts. It was during his pastorate there that he, with his eleven children, was driven from his house into the streets and all his property plundered by the Parliamentary soldiers. One account states that his children when turned out "were naked to their shift and shoses." Thus turned from his rectory he had to get a living by practising as a doctor at Hawkshead and Tachbrook. After the Restoration he petitioned the King for his late rectory and was given a prebendal stall in Bristol Cathedral, which, however, he did not long enjoy, his death occurring in 1663. He had been present the previous year at the reception of the King and Queen at Bristol when the mayor entertained the royal party at the "Great House" at Bridge End. Administration of his estate was granted in 1663-4. He left several sons, one of whom was the writer of a remarkable book on the cure of the Plague, which was well received in London during the pestilence. A copy of this is at the British Museum, it is entitled, "A Brief Treatise of the Nature, Causes, Signes, Preservation from, and Cure of, the Pestilence," collected by W. Kemp, "Mr. of Arts," and printed and sold by D. Kemp at his shop at the Salutation, near Hatton Garden in Holborn, 1665. We were very amused with a perusal of this, it contains a wonderful mixture of science, superstition and logical sermonizings; we gather from internal evidence that the author or editor was born at Bristol about the beginning of the seventeenth century. The other sons of the Prebendary William Kempe were scattered, some seeking their fortunes in "foreign countries." Of this family the eldest, named William, seems to have settled at Almondsbury, from which time the family had representatives there; William seems to have been a chaplain in the "Fleet"—not in the navy, but in that horrible prison so called for debtors in London. Doubtless he had become involved in some financial difficulty, and was detained there until his death, which occurred in 1687, his brother, Thomas Kempe, being authorised to administer his estate at Almondsbury and elsewhere. He had apparently married Jocosa Hodges, for her estate was granted to him in 1679. It does not appear that this unfortunate clergyman left children, and the following are surmised to be the issue of his brother Thomas. At Almondsbury lie buried Thomas Kemp, who died in 1729, aged thirty-eight, Thomas Kemp, whose wife Hester was buried there in 1763, aged thirty-three, and Thomas Kempe, who lived for a time previous to 1776 at Westbury-on-Trim.

Connected undoubtedly with these were two Kempes named Lazarus. The elder made his will in 1664 at Wotton-under-Edge, leaving to his eldest son William all his land at Almondsbury "which William Kemp, clerk, deceased," purchased of Nicholas Parnell, excepting a lease which the testator left to his son Lazarus. Both these sons were minors in 1663, their mother, Mary Kemp, being appointed their guardian. Silver goblets and other plate, as well as further lands are mentioned, and the deceased's brother William Kemp, clerk, of the City of London, with Mr. Cresswell Wheatley, "preacher of God's word at *Todmarton*, Oxford, were appointed overseers to the widow, who was executrix. The second Lazarus "Kempp" was licensed to issue tokens, and a specimen of his coin is extant, one side being marked "Lazarus Kemp in" with a fleece D.S.S., and the other side bearing "Wotton Undridge, 1667," with the words "His Half-penny ½" across the centre. The fact of the fleece being used as his sign may indicate that he was engaged in the cloth manufacture, which has for centuries been largely carried on in the neighbourhood of Wotton, but of this we have no actual proof, no will or administration of his being traced.

The mention of Oxfordshire in the last will, and the discontinuance of Kempes at Wotton-under-Edge, may point to a migration thither, and we thus may mention here one James Kempe, who was entered on the books of Oxford University as a coach proprietor. His will is dated at Benson, and describes him as an innholder; he, however, bequeathed his share in the Cirencester Stage Coach with his horses and harness to his grandchildren equally. He mentions in his will his sons Edward and James, his daughter-in-law Susannah Kemp, widow, his daughter Elizabeth, wife of John Stevens, and his daughter Jane, leaving to the last named his house called the "Red Lion," in Benson, with coach house, stables and barn. This will was dated 1776 and proved the following year (P.C.C., 319 Collier).

We must now note a Somerset family, of whom we have but little detail; we have already said that a very early line in this county was settled at and around Portishead. These spelled their name chiefly as "K*y*mpe," but that slight difference was also made by several other West of England Kempes occasionally, and is not distinctive though most common in Cornwall. In the sixteenth century relatives of both the Kent and Norfolk Kempe families were settled in this country, and again there seems to have been a fresh colony connected with Ashbrittle, Brunton Regis and Tolland who held a little property during the first half of the seventeenth century, and several wills at Wells relate to Kempes of Cloford. We cannot give details of these but pass to Shepton Mallet, where for some generations a yeoman Kemp family lived. George Kempe of this place in his will of 1687-8 mentioned three sons, George, Thomas and William, also a nephew William Kemp and a sister Elizabeth Stout. His wife's name was Mary, and to her he bequeathed his house at "Bradford's Lye"; the inventory made of his estate amounts to £203. The will of his son, George Kempe (who was a minor at his father's death), was proved in 1751 (P.C.C., 260 Busley), and it leaves an estate at North Bradley, Wilts, called "Hawkins," to his daughter Mary Rose, with the "broad loom therin standing." To his daughter Ann Fox and her son Stephen other lands, and to his daughter, Phoebe White, he left "White House" at Great Gadston and lands at Shepton, with reversion to her son George White. To his grandson George Kempe he bequeathed "a great bedstead that was his *great-grandfather's*" and his tools, also a garden at Southwick and certain "water rights." Charles Hawkins was a witness to this will, and we may conjecture that the lands called "Hawkins" had some connexion with this witness's family. We may also say that Mary Hawkins was a witness to the will of Robert Kempe, of Ham, Wilts, in 1657, thus it seems likely that these Kemps of Shepton were from the same stock as those of Ham, namely, from the old Kentish one; this is the more probable when we recall that those of Ham were content to style themselves "yeomen," and had ceased to use the arms which were their birthright. GEORGE KEMPE, the grandson mentioned above, or another of his name and line, made his will in 1781, this being duly proved at Wells in 1785. He mentions first his cousin, Robert White, of Wanstrow (where his grandfather had lived), and left the bulk of his estate to his daughter Catherine, the wife of James Doddrell, to whose children £100 was bequeathed. We conclude that he left no other issue, and the Kempes who later had a quarry near Frome were probably a collateral line. Of their family we know little, except that each generation had a John Kemp, the last being a builder, known chiefly for his intrepidity in climbing steeples. After building many churches in and around Bristol he built Kemp's Row," Chelsea, which still bears that name. The line ended in a daughter, who married a Mr. Bussell, from whom is descended the Rev. Walter Kemp Bussell, of Spanish Town, Jamaica, who was born at Bristol in 1852; he lived for a time at Saltash, Cornwall, leaving there for Jamaica in 1883. He married Edith Wilson, of Scottish family, the following year, and had a son in 1885, who, however, died an infant. Two daughters are still living with their parents at Spanish Town after a prolonged residence in England.

We may here note that two other Kempes, of Jamaica, have replied to our circulars, namely, Thomas Kemp, J.P., of Constant Spring, who is of Scottish birth, and James Wheeler Kemp, who was born at Peshawar, N.W.P., India, in 1851, his father being James George Kemp, a descendant of the Kempes of Thanet, his grandfather, Ebenezer Chapman Kemp, having gone to India in the employ of the Royal Navy, while several of the Thanet relatives were engaged in the merchant service with India.

The foregoing family of Wilts were closely connected with Wiltshire, and we must again revert to that county, where at Trowbridge Johns were heads of the Kemp branch for several generations. Indeed, we believe that these were a branch of those near Frome, but the date of foundation is uncertain. John, the first of whom we have a certain knowledge, was born there in 1783, and his son John also was born there in 1811, the third John in 1843, and John Henry, the fourth generation, in 1881. In 1874 when a return of the "Greater Land Holders of England" was made by authority, two John Kemps, of Trowbridge, had freehold in the county. These are distinguished as "senior" and "junior," and the value of their freehold was then estimated at nearly £700 per annum. The present John Kemp, of Trowbridge, is senior partner in the firm of Kemp and Hewitt, cloth manufacturers; another John Kemp, of Wilts, is a farmer at Lower Studley, but we have no particulars of his family connections. Miss Emily Kemp, of Wotton-under-Edge, is a representative of the Trowbridge family. Mr. Clement Kemp and his family, one of whom is Mr. John Tabor Kemp, part author of the present work, resided at Wotton-under-Edge for several years. Details of his relationship are given under the Essex section.

CHAPTER VI.

KEMPS OF THE NORTH OF ENGLAND—YORKSHIRE.

WE have in previous chapters mentioned various early Kempes who are known to have existed in Northumberland and Yorkshire from the time of Edward II. Some of these must certainly have been possessed of lands, but so little trace of them exists that we cannot speak of these northern Kempes as *families*. The long period during which Archbishop Kempe and his nephew held office in the province of York would lead one to expect that some of their kinsmen would have settled in the district over which these worthies exercised so much control in the fifteenth century. We have, however, but the barest evidence of such being the fact. Their kinsman, Anthony Kemp, of Slindon, a century later had property in both Northumberland and Yorkshire, but it is quite probable that this was acquired by his own personal power at Court and not in any way as the outcome of the Archbishop's nepotism.

In 1567 an Inquisition Post Mortem of one, Anne Kempe, of Yorkshire, is recorded, but what her estate comprised we have not ascertained. The next individual of the name of some position in the county appears to be the Rev. Caleb Kempe, Vicar of Bradford, who, undoubtedly, was the son of the noted preacher, Parson John Kempe, of Freshwater. To him was granted administration of his widowed mother's estate in 1599, she being then resident at Bradford with this son. Caleb married in 1602 Phoebe, daughter of Thomas Lister, whose family were gentry of Yorkshire, and by her had a son Caleb, who married Rose Rippin, of Totteridge, Middlesex. On the Rev. Caleb Kempe's decease, which occurred before 1638, his widow, Phoebe, married one named Cooke, for she is styled "my mother, Mistress Phoebe Cooke," in her son's will, which was proved in London in 1639 (P.C.C., 22 Harvey). Possibly it was another son of the Rev. Caleb who founded the family at Hedon in Yorkshire, and that it was his descendant who afterwards became another Vicar of Bradford.

Of the family who resided at Haddon or Hedon we have but a glimpse; the registers of Oxford University record that Guy, the son of Thomas Kemp, "*Pleb.*," of Hedon, matriculated in 1695, aged seventeen. The wills preserved at York are by no means perfect, but from the calendars of the Richmond Deaneries it is evident that there was a fair number of Kempes in Yorkshire and Lancashire from the sixteenth century. It is, however, unlikely that any of these retained their property for many generations, or became possessed of much land or influence until the eighteenth century, when one family of Kempes, who intermarried with the Wyvell family, enjoyed much Royal patronage. Edward Wyvell, Henry Kemp and Francis Twisden were witnesses to the will of Sir William Playter in 1668, but apparently it was later than this that "Major Kemp," whose christian name appears to have been Robert, married Priscilla, daughter of Sir William Wyvell, fourth Baronet, of Constable Barton (by Anne, daughter of James Brooke). Major Robert Kemp with Margaret Collingwood and others petitioned the Lords of the Treasury in 1715 for certain arrears of pay which were due to officers, widows and children connected with the Hon. Col. Fox's late Regiment of Foot, of which Colonel Collingwood was formerly commandant. There was a Major Thomas Kemp at this time stationed at the Tower of London, and as both are frequently mentioned in the Treasury and State Papers of this period, often without their christian names, it is somewhat difficult to identify them. Major Kemp, of the Tower, died in 1727, and apparently Major Robert Kemp died two years later, but we have not traced his will and do not know where he was buried. He left five daughters and two or more sons.

Henrietta Maria, the eldest daughter, outlived the others, dying at Beverley in 1787 unmarried. Frances, the second daughter, was governess to the Hesse Royal family, and died at Hesse Castle, Germany, in 1758, her will being that year proved in London (P.C.C., 221 Hutton). It is very interesting but too long to give here; we must be content to mention one or two of her bequests. To His Serene Highness Prince Charles of Hesse she left any two of the drawings in frames done by Her Royal Highness the Princess of Hesse, and two others by the same Royal artist to Prince Frederick of Hesse, and others to Prince William of Hesse, together with "a small picture of King James I. in water colours done by Her Royal Highness, and a portrait of Her Royal Highness by her own hand. The testatrix gave a large silver tea kettle to her sister Priscilla Wastale with a portrait of her late sister Anne Kempe. To her sister Henrietta Kemp she left a silver writing stand, silver forks, spoons, pepper box, salts and other articles, an ivory tea box and £200. To her niece, Mrs. Lucretia Kempe, she left "a silver bowl for washing hands in," a looking glass in a silver frame and a gold repeating watch, as well as other jewels and diamonds. To her brother, John Purcell Kempe, she left all her books and a watch, and with many keepsakes to friends she left the ultimate residue of her estate in trust for her two nieces, Lucretia Kemp, daughter of this said brother, and Mary, daughter of her sister Mrs. Elizabeth Mill.

"Sister Anne" mentioned above had died a spinster at St. James', Westminster, before 1756, and her will proved that year (P.C.C., 201 Glazier) bequeathed her father and mother's portraits to her brother, William Kemp, and a seal *bearing her arms* to her niece, Lucretia Kempe. Other legatees being Mrs. Margaret Purcell, Mrs. Ann Mein, Miss Elizabeth Wyvell, Miss Jenny Margaret Twisden, Mrs. Honor Pratt and the testatrix's sister Priscilla Wastell, Elizabeth Mills, Henrietta Maria Kempe, Frances Kempe and Mary Eyre. The brother, William Kempe, died in 1768 at sea when returning from Calcutta. His estate was granted to his sister Henrietta Maria that year, the grant of administration styling the deceased as William Kempe, *Esquire*, late of Calcutta, in the Kingdom of Bengal, a batchelor, the administratrix being his sister and next-of-kin. It would appear from this grant that John Purcell Kempe had died before this date, but we have little trace of him except that he attained the rank of major in the army, and that his daughter Lucretia was baptized in March, 1741, at Newport, in the Isle of Wight, where he was then stationed. She, as mentioned in the foregoing wills, was living in 1756 a spinster, and is again mentioned in the will of her aunt Henrietta Maria. This testatrix made her will at Beverley, Yorks, in 1785, and it was proved by her said niece, Lucretia Kempe, in 1787 at London (P.C.C., 133 Major). The testatrix mentioned the following: Mrs. Mary Appleton, of Beverley; her niece, Mary Ayres, of Stratford; her niece, Lucretia Kempe, of Pontefract; Dinah and Lucretia Hodgeson, Dinah Hodges (*sic*) and the Rev. Mr. Wyvill, of Burton Hall. This will has several codicils attached varying small specific bequests to her servants and companion, but the residuary estate was from the date of the will left to Lucretia Kempe, the executrix. It is evident that this lady died unmarried, for on 2nd August, 1824, a fresh grant of administration of this property was made to Lucretia Hodgeson, widow, and administratrix of the goods of Lucretia Kempe. The last will states that the Rev. Mr. Wyvell, of Burton Hall, paid into Drummond and Co.'s bank regularly an annuity of thirty pounds for the benefit of the testatrix, and it also mentions a nephew named Stephen Stephen (*sic*) Kempe as living in 1785, to whom she left certain bank annuities. Possibly this nephew was named Stephen *Smith* Kempe, for there is a will of one so styled recorded in the Principal Probate Court in 1838, he, however, being resident in Surrey. We know of no present representatives of this interesting family, and shall be glad to be enlightened as to the connexion which entitled these ladies to arms which they evidently used.

The only armorial bearing recorded as pertaining to Kempes of the North of England is, so far as we are aware, the shield as used by Achbishop Kempe, which is given also as the right of "Kempe of Alnwick." Anthony Kempe, of Slindon, Sussex, who held property in the north, was also authorised to use the same, but we cannot give any date or details of the family at Alnwick who are said to have used such. We think that these Kempes must have existed before the fifteenth century. There is, however, living a clergyman named John Kemp who was connected with Alnwick, and to whom perhaps the arms were attributable.

In the Treasury Papers of 1731 to 1733 are several mentions of Mrs. Kempe and Mrs. Purcell as then being engaged in the royal household at St. James's Palace, and apartments, both at that palace and at Hampton Court, were luxuriously furnished at the expense of the Treasury for Mrs. Kempe's use. This was presumably for *Anne* Kemp (spinsters then being styled Mrs.), but her christian name does not appear, nor is the capacity in which this Mrs. Kemp served the Princess Mary exactly stated. In 1734 she was in attendance on the Princess on her wedding eve, from which time perhaps Anne Kempe enjoyed a sinecure position at the palaces until her death.

A Captain Kemp, of H.M. 36th Regiment, married Mary, daughter of the Rev. G. T. Clare, Rector of Bainton, Yorks, at Ottery St. Mary on 14th January, 1847. We have, however, no knowledge of this Captain Kemp's family connexions. A Joseph Kemp was quartermaster in the same regiment in 1810. The name is prominent in the official return of the Greater Land-owners of England made in 1874, the following then being freeholders in Yorkshire: The Rev. H. W. Kemp, of Hull, G. G. Kemp, of Hornsea, —. Kemp, of Elvington, Edward Kemp, of East Layton, R. Kemp, of Wakefield, and a William Kemp at Leeds, Maltby, Swinton Bridge and Tickhill. Of these the most worthy of note is the first. He, however, was not an actual native of Yorkshire, having been born at St. Peter's, Thanet, on 23rd June, 1820. He was educated at Beverley Grammar School, proceeding thence to Christ's College, Cambridge, of which he was a scholar. He graduated in 1843 as nineteenth wrangler, also was ordained the same year. He became curate of St. John's, Hull, in 1846, and vicar in the following year. There he had one of the largest congregations in the North of England. In 1868 he became Master of the Charter House, Hull, and held this position until his death. In 1886 the prebendal stall of Riccal in York Cathedral was conferred on him. He was also President of the Hull Literary and Philosophical Society, and he was the author of popular sermons published in 1854 and other works, and died at Charterhouse on 7th March, 1888. His portrait appeared in the *Church Portrait Journal* of 1881 (II., 21-4) with his biography. He married at Rugby in 1847 Ann Maria, widow of the late Joseph Simons, Esq., M.D., of that place.

The above G. G. Kemp, of Hornsea, represented a family long settled in that parish. Simon Kemp of that place, who was born in 1810, and lived subsequently at Market Rasen and Bradford, was buried at Hull in 1856 leaving a son Robert Thomas Kemp, who was born at Hornsea in 1837, and now carrying on business at Aldermanbury, London. The Wakefield Kemps are now represented by the Rev. James Vickerman Kemp, of Escombe Vicarage, Bishop Auckland, whose eldest son has now settled at Byers Green, Durham. The father of this clergyman, named James Kemp, was buried at Chicago in 1861, but left no male issue to represent him *there.*

The well known tenor Edward Kemp, Vicar Choral of Lichfield Cathedral, is the son of Edward Kemp, of Gawthorpe, Mr. Taylor Kemp, of Batley, being a representative of the same family. Many members of this family are known as vocalists and have appropriately been named after Handel, Haydn and other celebrated composers. Numerous Kemp families of Yorkshire originated from Leicestershire, one of whom is Postmaster of Bradford, while others, particularly in the south of the county, come from an old Lincolnshire stock.

KEMPS OF LINCOLN.

It is most noteworthy that in the years 1555, 1556 and 1557 three Kempes represented places in the North of England in Parliament, these being Anthony Kemp, "armiger," for Westmoreland County, Robert Kempe, "gent.," for Boroughbridge, Yorks, and Francis Kempe, "armiger," for Lincoln City. These dates being within the reign of Queen Mary, in whose confidential service was Anthony Kempe, of Slindon, suggests that all three of these were of the then influential Kentish Kempe family and closely related; there is, however, no conclusive evidence of this, although all three names (and the fact of their being styled armiger) agree with names shown on the Kentish pedigree as living at this period. Neither retained his seat in the first Parliament of Elizabeth.

One of the most important Kempes found connected with Lincolnshire and the adjoining counties was Peter Kempe, "Gent.," who for some years was steward to the first Lord Burleigh, and was largely responsible for laying out the Burleigh Park and other possessions of the Cecil family. It seems impossible to trace his exact relationship to others of his name, but his connexion with Anthony Browne, Esquire, and John Conyers points to his being probably a close relative of the William Kempe, Knight, of Ollantigh (Kent) who married Elinor, daughter of Sir Matthew Browne, whose son, Anthony Kempe, of Slindon, married a daughter of Conyers. We find that with Sir William Cecil, Sir Walter Mildmay, Sir Anthony Cooke and the above Browne and Conyers he paid fines on the settlement of properties in the Counties of Lincoln, Rutland, Northampton, Hertford, and in the London parishes of St. Clement's Danes, St. Martin's and those of St. Pancras, St. Margaret's, Westminster, Kentish Town, Enfield and St. Gregory's in the year 1564. Before this, namely in 1561, Peter Kempe is mentioned in the state papers as being then laying out Burleigh Park and building there; in the following year Peter petitioned Sir William Cecil to make him bailiff of Stamford, and this request seems to have been granted forthwith, for numerous letters addressed from Stamford by the petitioner to Cecil exist, covering the years 1564 to the date of his death. His last letter, which is in possession of the Marquis of Salisbury, who permitted us to copy many of this steward's letters now at Hatfield, is dated 17th September, 1575, and gives a quaint but pathetic picture of his endeavours to carry on the building work at Burleigh with the population in the neighbouring villages decreasing rapidly from the plague. He says "that the people are dying at the rate of fifteen a day!" We regret that space does not permit of our giving the text of this series of letters, nor reproducing some of his architectural drawings and plans. One of the latter is a sketch of a simple, but original plan, for laying on a water supply in the house by water pipes, which were at the period almost, if not entirely, confined to the outer walls. The drawing looks like a present day shower bath.

The plague was evidently the cause of the steward's death, which must have occurred very soon after the date of this letter. His will was proved in London the following year (P.C.C., Doughtry 1).

A Kempe family, ascribed by the Heralds to *Norfolk* origin, settled in Lincolnshire in the seventeenth century, evidence points to these also being of the *Kentish* stock, but we have sufficiently mentioned that matter in the Middlesex section (Sub Fulham).

The oldest Kempe family in this county claims to have held land as tenants of Fulney Abbey, which was desolved more than 350 years ago. They appeared at Thimbleby first in the eighteenth century, then residing at Hallgarth Manor House, and owned the manor attached thereto for about 150 years. The parish register of Thimbleby records as the earliest item pertaining to this family that Henry Kemp and Eleanor Panto were married there in 1723, they having a numerous family including Michael, Thomas and Robert baptized between 1723 and 1740. Thomas was married in 1768 and his brother Robert in 1766. Robert and Thomas were the favourite Christian names in this family, which is now represented by the Rev. Edwin Richard Kemp, Chaplain and Warden of St. Annes Bede Houses, Lincoln, and many other Kemps at Grimsby, Horncastle and other places within the county. The above name of Michael recalls the titles of two books written by the late Mrs. Woodroofe more than fifty years ago, namely, "The History of Michael Kemp, the Happy Farmer's Lad" and "Michael Kemp, the Married Man," which is a sequel to the former. We do not know whether the hero was so named in real life, but as the Michael Kemps of Lincoln, as well as their namesakes at Alphamstone, in Essex, *were* farmers, it is perhaps possible that the books actually relate to one of these.

Jewels and Rings, heirlooms of the Kemp Baronets.

The Calendars of Wills proved at Lincoln, and the marriage licences of the diocese, have been searched for us, and should information therefrom be of special interest to subscribers of this work we shall be pleased to communicate any item; space, however, prevents our noticing each group of yeomen Kemps scattered about the county from the sixteenth century. Boston was evidently the centre from which many Kemps spread. One, John Kemp of that place, having licence to marry Mary Ingram of "Huttoft" in 1622. John Kemp, of Horsleydowne, in the parish of Southwark, who was a citizen and joiner of London, was probably a son of this couple, for in his will proved in the Archdeaconry Court of Surrey, 1672, he mentions his brother Thomas Kemp, of Boston, in Lincolnshire. This John Kemp, the younger, has left us a very interesting momento in the shape of a tradesman's token which he issued under licence in 1666, it bears his name, and the arms of the Joiners' Company, of which he was a member. (See illustration of tokens in Middlesex section.) He left a son Edward Kemp, who inherited houses on the south side of the old spinning-ground at Southwark, and others which the testator had built in Free School Street in the same parish. There is in the same Probate Court the will of an earlier John Kemp, of Southwark, proved in 1634, but there is no means of identifying this as that of the elder John of Boston, or in any way connected with the joiner.

At Crowland, Lincolnshire, there were Kemps for some generations, and it is likely that the Boston Kempes came from this place. Between these lies Fossdyke, at which Jervis Kemp was a freeholder for many years, he being succeeded by Charles Kemp, who frequently styled himself Christopher; his son was baptized Shadrack, but prefers to be known as Sidney Kemp, and is a master mariner, who sails chiefly from Liverpool.

LIVING REPRESENTATIVES.

Sir Kenneth Kemp, Bart.

George Kemp, M.P.

Geo. W. Kemp India.

Ernest Courtenay Kemp, Warrina, S. Australia.

Edward Kemp, Vicar Choral of Lichfield Cathedral.

G. S. Kemp, Chief Assistant to Signor Marconi,
Inventor of Wireless Telegraphy.

George Meikle Kemp, Architect..

Section VI.

THE KEMP AND KEMPE FAMILIES OF SCOTLAND, IRELAND THE BRITISH EMPIRE & UNITED STATES.

The Kempes of Scotland, Ireland, the British Empire and the United States.

CHAPTER I.

GENERAL REVIEW—SOUTHERN

IT will be convenient to begin the Scottish section of the work by setting down the principal facts which have been ascertained as to the early occurrence and distribution of the name Kemp, which is various in the northern Kingdom. Of alternative forms of the name, the most frequent in the older records is KEMPT. Indeed, it is doubtful whether in some districts of Scotland, particularly in Aberdeenshire, it is not more common than Kemp, although very rarely met with in England. The two spellings often occur with reference to a single individual. Other variations of the name will be noted, as occasions for mentioning them arise. When in the following account the name Kemp is spoken of as being very frequent in certain parts, the reader should bear in mind that the comparison refers to its general prevalence in Scotland alone, in which country the name is not nearly so common anywhere as in England in many parts. The number of Scottish Kemps who have attained some degrees of distinction make the name appear a more common one than it actually is in the country of their birth. As readers acquainted with Scottish history would expect to be the case, the name Kemp is found frequently in the border country of Berwick and the Lothians, being the region in which the Saxon element in the population assumes its highest proportion. The name is less frequent in the central Highlands, while further north it is almost entirely confined to certain centres, which it is noteworthy are all situated on or near to the East Coast. The name is very rare in the "Southern Uplands," as Sir Archibald Geikes designates the elevated region between the Lowlands and Solway Firth, while in the central and northern Highlands it is scarcely known.

In the south, Haddington has been an important centre of the Kemps for several centuries at least. In 1565 we find one, John Kempt, concerned in lands belonging to the constabulary of Haddington and the Sheriffdom of Edinburgh. A notarial instrument dated 6th October in that year, relates that "'an honourable man, John Knight,' acknowledged receiving from 'an honourable man, Patrick Hepburn, of Wanchtown,' the sum of 1,200 merles Scots, for the redemption and release of an acccount rent of 108 merles Scots, which the said John had yearly from the said Patrick's lands and barning of Luffness, situated as above stated which had been alienated and inpignorated by the said Patrick to the said John, his heirs and assignees, under reversion of 1,200 merles." Patrick having paid back the sum for which he pledged that part of his estate, John gives an instrument renouncing all rights over it.

The pages of history have preserved the memory of another Kemp living at Haddington a little before this time, a person, probably, of less account in the social scale than the "honourable man" mentioned above, but one who through circumstances of the time was brought into intimate contact with royalty itself. The infant destined to become known as Mary Queen of Scots was born in Edinburgh Castle on 7th December, 1542. A nurse was required for the mother and child. This important office was conferred on Janet Sinclair, wife of one John Kemp, of Haddington, who had already proved herself to be a good nurse by attending on the deceased Prince James, the Queen of Scots' eldest brother. As a reward for her services, which were much esteemed by the Queen mother, some Crown grants were made to her husband.

In 1688, in the baptismal register of Haddington, we find the baptism of John Kemp, son of John Kemp and Agnes Sanderson. In the following year a Robert Kemp, possibly John's brother, and Marion Wail had a son, Alexander, baptized, who probably died in infancy, for in 1693 the same couple had another son called Alexander. From this time upwards the name of Kemp occurs frequently in the registers of Haddington. (*Vide* Chapter V.)

The Haddington Kemps are now represented by Thomas Kemp, of Dalkeith, who is well known as a Journalist. He is a member of the Institute of Journalists, included in the International Press Bureau of Correspondence, and is connected with the Press Association. He owns a printing business at Dalkeith and is an active member of the Local Scientific Association, he is also interested in paper mills and other commercial concerns. He was born in 1869. Other representatives of this group of Haddington Kemps are George Kemp, of Brockley, Kent, and his younger brothers, Joseph Pattinson Kemp (Chairman of the London Lothian's Association), Richard Watt Kemp, now serving with the Imperial Yeomanry in South Africa, and Thomas William Kemp, Chamberlain of the Burgh of Haddington and of the 7th Bat. Royal Scotts.

Thomas Kemp, of Dalkeith.

One of the chief objects of interest in Edinburgh is associated with the name of Kemp, to wit, the Scott Monument, designed by George Meikle Kemp. He was not himself born in the city, but was the offspring of one of the Kemp families scattered about the south of Scotland. Edinburgh, however, claims as her genuine sons the professors of chemistry in her University, Kenneth Treasurer Kemp and Alexander Kemp.

Another native of Edinburgh was David Kemp, who carried on a business as a chemist at Portobello, he had four daughters, two married, and their families reside in Scotland and CANADA. He had the honour of being appointed an Examiner to the Pharmaceutical Society of Great Britain.

Sir James Kempt, G.C.B., Governor-General of Canada, 1828-30, and who distinguished himself on many occasions in the Peninsula War, sprang from one of the Kemp families in the neighbourhood of Edinburgh, though himself born near Southampton.

Lasswade is a parish a few miles south of Edinburgh, which seems to have contained two or more families of Kemps among its population in the eighteenth century. Robert Kemp, coal-hewer, of Lasswade, married Lilias Dun in 1761 or 1762.

The earliest known occurrence of the name of Kemp in Scotland is in the burgh of Linlithgow. A charter or deed is extant by William Blackbourne, burgess of Inverkeithing, in favour of John Brady, burgess of Stirling, of an annual rent of thirteen shillings and fourpence, usual Scot money, from a tenement of William Kemp, burgess of Linlithgow, situate at Linlithgow. The deed is witnessed among others by David Kemp, burgess of Linlithgow, and bears date 13th August, 1422.

Another charter connected with Linlithgow and dated 5th August, 1447, is attested by a William Kemp. Linlithgow Palace being at that period a royal residence of great importance, it is likely that the Kemps in the royal household of the sovereigns were connected with these Linlithgow burgesses.

King James V. had a personal attendant named Henry Kemp*t*, and described as of Thomastown, who had lands at Beridale and Auldwick in Caithness-shire conferred on him. It was probably a son of this Henry Kemp or Kempt (or a brother named Alexander Kemp, styled Sir Alexander Kemp) who James V. married to the heiress of Dury, near Cupa, and which Kemp had to adopt the surname of Dury.

Henry seems to have been highly esteemed by his royal master, for in 1526 we find him granted lands at Gargettown, with lands at several other places. In 1529 the king granted him the ward relief and marriage of the heir of the lands and pertinents belonging to Andrew Oliphant, of Beridale, Caithness, deceased. In 1540 a grant was made to Henry Kempt of the dires of the lands since the decease of the same Andrew. This grant was confirmed two years later. In 1545 Queen Mary granted the lands given in 1526 to another party, the document stating that they had been resigned by Henry Kemp*t*, of Thomastown. This Kemp also received the Ward of Proncy in the Sheriffdom of Inverness, formerly belonging to the Earl of Sutherland.

Before leaving the region south of the Forth we may briefly notice a few miscellaneous records of Kemps resident there to the close of the eighteenth century.

At Elphinstone, in the parish of Tranent, Haddingtonshire, James Kemp, described as "servant to Mr. Nicholas," married Agnes Thompson in 1779 (or perhaps earlier), who bore him at least nine children.

At Garvald in the same country an individual described as John Kemp, in Baro', was husband of Isobelle Lillico in 1745. The baptism of two children are recorded, among the witnesses being Henry Kemp and William Kemp.

At Larkhall, Lanarkshire, we find a James Kemp, weaver, in 1790. Another weaver, named Alexander Kemp, lived in Newbigging, in Midlothian, at the same time. George Meikle Kemp was born in the village of Monsford, in the extreme south of Midlothian. His father was a shepherd, but he had uncles who were respectively a lawyer and a doctor.

A family of Kemps was long connected with Spott, a village near Dunbar. They were most of them weavers, and believed themselves descendants of John Kemp, the weaver, who came from Flanders in 1331 and settled at Kendal. Mr. David Skinner Kemp is a representative of this family, and it was he who established the firm of Kemp and Co., chemists, at Bombay.

At Dunny, in the County of Stirling, we find a family of Kempts living in 1675, in which year a father and son, both named James Kemp, of that place, witnessed an instrument of sasine.

The southern section will fitly conclude with a reference to the town of Stirling itself. The register contains the name of Jone (*sic*) Kemp, described as ZWNGER (*i.e.* younger), as witnessing baptisms in 1589 and 1591.

CHAPTER II.

GENERAL REVIEW—NORTHERN.

PASSING to region north of the Forth we find Kemp families resident for several centuries in certain localities, notably at St. Andrews, Aberdeen and Dingwall. They seem never to have penetrated far into the Highlands. The facts concerning their distribution point unanimously to the Kemps as belonging to the Saxon element in the population of Scotland. In the south they are chiefly found in Berwickshire and the Lothians, where the Saxons displaced the ancient Celtic population. In the uplands and the western counties the name is more rare. (There, though Anglicized, the population is essentially Celtic. In the north the Saxons settled in greater or less numbers at various places on the east coast, they never ousted the ancient inhabitants.)

James Kemp, innkeeper, of Doune, in the south of Perthshire, gave evidence in connexion with the rebellion of 1745. At Perth we find in the register under date 16th November, 1561, the marriage between George Conqueror and Nanse Kempt. It may be added that the Conquerors were an important family at Perth, some of whom occupied public stations. We therefore conclude, in default of evidence to the contrary, that that Kempt family were likewise of good standing.

In St. Andrew's the Kemps are an old established stock. In 1569 an Andrew Kempt was among the prebendaries and choristers of the Collegiate Church of Salvator. He was Master of the Song School there. A copy of the Te Deum harmonised by him dated 1575 is among the MSS. at the Bristish Museum. The Register of Kirk Sessions from 1570 had many references to a certain Andro (*sic*) Kempt, who appears to have been minister of the church. He had evidently committed some offence against two members of the church, viz., David Sympson and his mother, for which he is required to crave pardon on his knees after sermon on a certain Friday. In November, 1573, he is referred to as dead. His widow, Isobel Adesonn, described as "relict of urquhill Andro Kempt," being in grevious sickness, a collection was made for her which the assembly direct to be paid to her at the rate of eightpence a day as long as it lasts. In 1587 we find "the minister, elders and deacons" of the congregation arranging to apprentice "Patrick (*sic*) Kempt, lawful son to urquhill Andron (*sic*) Kempt, minister," for five years to David Husband, a tailor in St. Andrews, at a premium of twenty-four merks, which sum appears from late entries to have been paid by instalments. We shall hear of Patrick Kempt again.

Aberdeen has been for several centuries the home of Kemps and Kempts, many of whom occupied honourable positions in connection with the city or the university.

The "Register of Burgesses of Guild and Trade of the Burgh of Aberdeen" contains many entries relating to the name of Kemp. The earliest is under date 23rd September, 1464, and refers to James Kemp, goldsmith, for seven years in the service of T. Leman, goldsmith. In the sixteenth and early part of the seventeenth centuries the Kempts evidently held a prominent position in the trading community of the burgh. Several were bakers, one was a "flesher," another a sea captain, and another, Patrick Kempt, a tailor. This last is almost certainly the individual who figures in the records of St. Andrews. He appears to have settled in Aberdeen in 1616. In 1625 we find him receiving as apprentice a youth named Johne Taileour. In 1603 Alexander Kempt was granted by Act of Council the entry of a burgess in recognition of "his avancemtis that year in the tounis advis." In 1617 his youngest son Alexander, described as "pupil," was admitted *ex gratia*. Another Alexander Kempt, son and heir of John Kempt, was granted entry *ex gratia* in January, 1579-80.

An Instrument of Sasine of 1504 mentions one, Martin Kemp, as owning some land in Green Street. In the Chartulary of St Nicholas' Church we find another mention of the same land in 1587 as formerly belonging to Martin Kemp, but now James Collisonn's. The rent was received by the chaplains of the church. Another entry speaks of land belonging to Johne Kemppt baxter (*i.e.*, baker). He is probably identical with the John Kempt mentioned above who is described as a baker. Among the witnesses to a deed dated 9th January, 1602, connected with the family of Skene, of Skene, burgess of Aberdeen, most likely the same individual referred to in the other entries.

On 30th November, 1641, one James Smith, described as a "wobster," with Alexander Kempt, "wicht," were convicted of burglary at the house of Alexander Sangster, a "wobster," "vnder clovd and silence of the night, and braking up the dore of the said Alexanderis hous with ane foir hamer, and entering the samen with draven suordis in thair handis." For this they were sentenced to be banished the town.

Various Kempts are recorded among the students of King's College and Marichal College, but they are perhaps more appropriately mentioned in connexion with their birth place or lives if sufficiently noted.

From the town of Aberdeen as a centre Kemps probably emigrated to other places in the regions around. The Records of Aborfar in that country mentions "Mr. Thomas Kemp, servitor to Mr. James Farguharson, W.S." The fact of his being dignified with the title "Mr." indicates that he was a confidential clerk preparing, if not actually prepared, to practice the law on his own account. John Kemp, the mathematician and professor in Columbia College, was a native of Auchlossen, Aberdeenshire. James Kemp, second Bishop of MARYLAND, was born at Keith Hall in the same country.

The last centre of the Kemp families which we have to mention is Dingwall. In 1516 King James V. is recorded to have presented Sir Thomas Kemp to the chaplaincy of St. Lawrence in the Castle of Dingwall when it should be vacated by the resignation of Sir John Auchtlek. In 1526 Patrick Kempt is mentioned as possessing land at the Gray Stane, Dingwall. He appears to have been the father of Sir Thomas Kemp. An interesting tombstone to Patrick and Thomas still exists in Dingwall Churchyard, and measures about 6 feet by 4 feet; it is much worn through long exposure to the weather and having been walked upon. The illustration is from a photograph of a rubbing somewhat restored, which has been kindly prepared expressly for this work by Dr. Joass. He has devoted much time and thought in endeavouring to correctly decipher the Latin inscriptions. The legend round the margins he translates thus:—"Here lie . . . and Patrick Kemp, wife and son of William Kemp, founder of the Chapel of St. Clement, A.D. 1529." The inscription in the lower right compartment reads: "Sir Thomas Kemp caused me to be made A.D. 1531." In the "Origines Parochiales Scotiæ," vol. ii., part 2, p. 484, it is stated that "in 1516 King James V. presented Sir Thomas Kemp, Chaplain, to the Chaplaincy of St. Lawrence, in the Castle of Dingwell, when it should be vacant."

It may be noted in passing that the Christian name Patrick occurs early in two or three of the East Lothian families; thus in Humbie in 1654 the marriage of Patrick Kemp and Janet Young is recorded; and again in Bolton, Richard Kemp and Janet White had a son Patrick born 1695.

Among the burgesses of Dingwall in 1563 appears a Donald Kemp. Ninety years later another Donald Kemp described as "in Usie," was called as a witness before the Presbytery of

The Dingwall Kemp Stone; from a drawing by the Rev. J. M. Joass, LL.D., Golspie.

Dingwall. The records of the presbytery a few years later, viz., in 1666, mention Donald Kempe, "indweller in Dingwell," as a suppliant for divorce against his wife. In 1655 we find Agnes Kempt in Gairloch protesting before the Presbytery that her marriage was forced against her will. James Kempt, a burgess within the burgh of Dingwell, appears as a witness before the Presbytery in 1653. No doubt members of the family left Dingwall to settle in the neighbourhood as the husband of Agnes Kempt probably did. Among the Graduates of Aberdeen University, Hugo Kemp, Rossensis (*i.e.*, a native of Ross-shire), is recorded as receiving the degree of Master of Arts on 29th March, 1733.

Bishop Forbes's journal for 1770 mentions Ciscelie Kemp, of Ord, as a communicant at Ord Meeting House, and Gillie Kemp, of Ord, as a candidate for confirmation. Several variants of the name remain to be noted. In 1598 John Kempie, maltman, appears as a burgess of Perth. Among those who have complied with our request for information as to their own ancestry is Mr. Peter Kemp, of *Currency Creek, South Australia*, but a native of Comrie, Perthshire; he states that his great-grandfather and father were known respectively as James and Peter Kemp, of Kempy; the former was born at Carrevechten, near Creief. This fact is of great interest in connexion with the origin of the name. "Kempy" is defined in the "Historical English Dictionary" as "a kemp or champion, one given to fighting; a rough or uncouth fellow." The illustrative quotations range from 1525 upwards. A very similar variant is Kemptie. John Kemptie is described as "writer in Aberdown." The name of William Kemp*yen* appears in the records of the "Edinburgh Commissariat" under the year 1569. "Sir William Kemp*ton*, chaplain and notary public," witnessed a lease in connexion with the names of Kirkliston, Linlithgowshire, in the year 1546.

CHAPTER III.

GENERAL REVIEW—BIOGRAPHIES.

THE REV. DAVID KEMP. THE REV. JOHN KEMP, D.D.

THE Rev. David Kemp, sometimes minister of the parish of Gask, studied at St. Leonard's College, taking the degree of A.M. in due course at the University of St. Andrew's, 11th April, 1738. He was examined and found qualified for the school of Auchtergaven, Perthshire, but does not appear to have retained the appointment long, vacating it for the mastership of King James VI.'s Hospital at Perth. In 1761 he was licensed by the Presbytery, and in December, 1765, was presented by George III. to the parish of Gask, being ordained 3rd April in the following year. In 1795 he removed to Edinburgh, where he died 22nd February, 1798, at the residence of his son. He wrote "Account of the Parish of Gask," published in Sinclair's "Statistical Account of Scotland."

The Rev. David Kemp married in 1743 Jane Stewart, who died 7th March, 1784. By her he had a son, the subject of the following memoir.

John Kemp, son of David Kemp and Jane Stewart, was born in 1745. Like his father he studied at the University of St. Andrews. Having been licensed by the Presbytry he was presented by the Earl of Kinnoul to Trinity Gask, and ordained 4th April, 1770. In 1776 he was translated to New Greyfriars Church, Edinburgh. In 1779 he accepted the Collegiate or Second Charge of the Tolbooth Church in the same city. Ten years later he was appointed secretary of the society in Scotland for Propagating Christian Knowledge. It is in connexion with this Society that he is chiefly remembered. For many years he travelled through the Highlands visiting and reporting on the Society's schools and missions. In 1793 he received the degree of D.D. from Harward University.

The following stories are related of Dr. Kemp. On approaching the Tolbooth Church one Sabbath he noticed a small knot of people listening to the singing of a blackbird in a cage which was hanging outside one of the small shops with which the church was surrounded. He was so incensed that he carried the bird in its cage off to the Tolbooth Prison.

Rev. Dr. John Kemp, Edinburgh.

An anecdote which reveals him in a pleasanter light is the way in which he captivated the attention of the boys of the Heriot Hospital School when preaching on Jacob blessing the sons of Joseph. The point of this story appears to be that in those days for a preacher to really engage the sympathies of a youthful audience was so unusual an occurrence that the fact that anyone could do so was regarded with some astonishment.

Dr. Kemp was thrice married. His first wife was Beatrice, daughter of Andrew Simpson, merchant, of Edinburgh, whom he married 2nd October, 1780. By her he had a son, David, who married the eldest daughter of Sir James Calquhoun, of Lass, Bart., and a daughter named Agnes Beatrice Kemp died 12th March, 1796. On 2nd June, 1797, Dr. Kemp married Mary Anne, youngest daughter of the Earl of Northesk, who died 10th August, 1798. His third wife, whom he married 26th August, 1779, was the seventh daughter of the Earl of Hopetoun. She died 17th September, 1801, aged thirty-three. Both the latter seem to have been childless.

The following is a list of Dr. John Kemp's publications:—(1) A sermon entitled "The Gospel adapted to the State and Circumstances of Man." This has as an appendix "facts serving to illustrate the character of Thomas, Earl of Kinnoull." Edin.: 8vo, 1788.

(2) "Account of the Society in Scotland for Propagating Christian Knowledge." Edin.: 8vo, 1796.

(3) "The Character of the Apostle Paul in some of its features delineated." Edin.: 8vo, 1802.

Dr. Kemp's death occurred on the 18th April, 1805.

SIR JAMES KEMPT, G.C.B.

We have not space in the present volume to give more than the briefest sketch of the long and varied career of this eminent man.

Sir James Kempt, G.C.B.

James Kempt was the son of Gavin Kempt, merchant, of Edinburgh, and his wife Sarah, daughter of Alexander Walker, brewer, of Edinburgh. He appears to have been born at Botley Hill, near Southampton, where his father had a residence. The year of his birth was 1764. He was gazetted ensign in the 101st Foot in *India* 31st March, 1783. This regiment of which he was then lieutenant, was disbanded in the spring of 1785, and Kempt spent some years in retirement on half pay. During this period he is said to have been in Cox and Co.'s Bank, London. In 1794 he returned to active service as captain of the 103rd Foot, which regiment he had assisted in raising in Ireland. Passing over several minor appointments, we find him in 1799 acting as aide-de-camp to Sir Ralph Abercromby, at that time Commander-in-Chief in Scotland. He soon afterwards went with him to Holland where he was present with Sir Ralph in many engagements. In 1801 he accompanied Sir Ralph to Egypt as aide-de-camp and military secretary. Sir Ralph was mortally wounded at the battle or Alexandria on the 21st March of that year. He was succeeded by General John Hely Hutchunson, under whom Kempt continued his former duties. His services in the expedition were recognised by the conferment ot the Turkish Gold Medal. In 1806 Kempt went with the expedition to Sicily, where the light brigade under his command distinguished itself at the battle of Maida, 2nd July. From 1807 to 1811 Kempt was in North America in the capacity of Quartermaster-General. At the close of the latter year he was appointed to the staff of the Peninsular army with local rank of Major-General. Wellington had formed a high opinion of Kempt's capacity in military affairs from reports of his previous career which events amply justified. He distinguished himself in the storming of Fort Picurnia. Under a horrible fire from the enemy Kempt coolly and skilfully directed the attack. A few days later while heading an assault on the Castle of Badajoz Kempt was struck down and severely wounded. On his return to the Peninsular after his recovery he was present in various engagements, including the battle of Vittoria, Nivelle, Nive, Orthez and Toulouse. At Nivelle he was again wounded severely, but remained in the field directing operations. In 1814 he again went to Canada in command of a brigade sent to reinforce the army there. He did not remain long away. He took part in the battles of Quatre Bras and Waterloo. In the latter he took the place of Sir Thomas Picton, who, while leading a charge, was instantaneously killed by a musket shot.

Kempt was made K.C.B. in January, 1815, and in June of the same year was advanced to the honour of G.C.B. In 1816 the title of G.C.H. was conferred upon him. He was also the recipient of various foreign decorations. For Maida, Vittoria, Nivelle, Nive, Orthez and Waterloo he held medals.

For some years Kempt was Governor of Nova Scotia. In 1828 he accepted the office of Governor-General of Canada. The Duke of Wellington was then Prime Minister, being succeeded by Earl Grey on 22nd November, 1830. Two days later Kempt gave up his duties as Governor-General. His action under difficult circumstances was approved by the Duke of Wellington. On 8th December, 1830, he was nominated a Privy Councillor.

Kempt was Master-General of Ordnance from 1834 to 1838. He was gazetted Lieutenant-General in 1825 and General in 1841. He died in London on 20th December, 1854, at the age of ninety.

Arms were granted to him, and he used as his motto the suitable word "promptus."

GEORGE MEIKLE KEMP.

Although General Sir James Kempt rose to such distinction, the average Scot associates the name of George Meikle with the name and forgets the hero of Badajoz. To the Edinburgh man particularly, the artist and architect is the greatest Kemp, Kempe or Kempt that ever lived. He competed with all the best designers of the day for the honour of designing the memorial to Sir Walter Scott, and although he was then looked upon as little more than a working carpenter, his plans and drawings were accepted and he secured the honour, as well as the money, which was by no means unacceptable to the struggling young man. His life is fully set forth by his relative Thomas Bonnar, F.S.A., in a well printed and beautifully illustrated biography, published by Blackwood and Sons in 1892, and we do not attempt to record here the surroundings of his boyhood and his setting forth to see the great buildings of Europe with but his skill to support him. His father was a poet who never committed his thought to paper; his mother was gifted and accomplished, and it was doubtless due to her influence that the lad broke away from the pastoral life so dear to his father and made great use of his opportunities. Leaving his home near Moorfoot he first became an apprentice to an upholsterer in Edinburgh and spent all his spare time studying and drawing, he noted down every peculiarity of architecture that struck him and grasped the various styles and periods, thus after a prolonged wandering he returned to Edinburgh qualified by study to equal any architect there. He was naturally extremely sensative and fearful lest a want of education should be apparent in him when in conversation with others; this characteristic stood greatly in his way, and it was by the sheer excellence of his work that he came into notice. His death was one which was extremely pathetic. While the masterful monument was nearing completion he was suddenly cut off from his family. The exact details can never be known, but it seems evident that he lost his way home one evening when a heavy mist was falling, and some days later his body was found in the river. His eldest son, a youth of much promise, had the pleasure of placing the topmost stone to the great memorial, which is a lasting momento, not only of the greatest Scottish novelist, but to the honour of George Meikle Kemp. He was born in 1795 and drowned on 6th March, 1844.

One of his uncles was a Provost and another a doctor. The only son to reach maturity now lives in Edinburgh, and sad to relate, although a clever artist, he is forced to remain inactive having lost the use of his hands by severe illness. The last surviving daughter died only this year (1902).

Masonic Chair
made by George Meikle Kemp.

KENNETH TREASURER KEMP.

The Kemp families of the South of Scotland have produced several chemists of distinction. First in order of time stand the brothers Kenneth Treasurer and Alexander Kemp, both of whom held the post of lecturer on chemistry at Edinburgh University. Their father, Alexander, along with another son, were in business as clothiers and hatters in College Street, Edinburgh, and resided in the same street, the one side of which is occupied by the University buildings. The youthful Kemps were thus reared in an atmosphere of learning, which no doubt essentially influenced them to adopt professional careers. Their mother was a daughter of Kenneth Treasurer, a merchant in Edinburgh.

Kenneth Treasurer Kemp was born in Edinburgh on the 17th April, 1805. He early displayed an interest in the science of chemistry. His first appointment was that of lecturer on practical chemistry in Surgeon's Square. He proceeded thence to a similar position at the University, which he held until his early death. He seems to have possessed great experimental skill. Among other subjects he investigated the laws of combustion and the liquefaction of gases. He was the first chemist in this country who succeeded in solidifying carbonic acid gas, which he appears to have hoped for for equal success in relation to every other gas. He told his students that they might one day see him carrying a stick of solid hydrogen! When the recently formed British Association met at Edinburgh in 1834 he read a paper on the "Liquefaction of Gases," only the bare mention of it occurs in the proceedings of the Association for that year. K. T. Kemp also devoted attention to electricity and magnetism. He introduced amalgamated zinc plates for galvanic batteries; he was the discoverer of various chemical compounds.

Kenneth Treasurer Kemp died 28th November, 1842, at the age of thirty-six, the cause of his death being an aneurysm. He was buried in Greyfriars Churchyard, Edinburgh, where a tablet was placed to his memory. He was succeeded in the lectureship at the University by his brother Alexander.

Alexander Kemp was born 10th January, 1822, and died 30th April, 1854. He was author of various scientific papers as well as inventor or improver of many pieces of experimental apparatus. He was a member of the Royal Society of Edinburgh; he was buried in Greyfriar's Churchyard as a tablet there records.

DAVID KEMP, Chemist.

The subject of this notice was a native of Edinburgh. After serving an apprenticeship with the famous pharmaceutical chemists, Messrs. Duncan, Flockart and Co., he commenced business at Portobello, and resided there all his life. He was much more than a dispenser of drugs; his extended knowledge of their properties and of the science of chemistry gained for him the honourable position of an examiner to the Pharmaceutical Society of Great Britain. Although he never thrust himself into prominence his worth did not pass unnoticed. He was appointed a magistrate and also elected as a member of the schoolboard for Portobello; he was an enthusiastic admirer of Scottish poetry, and was particularly fond of Jacobite songs. In celebration of the centenary of Burns in 1859 banquets were held all over the country, and at the one in Portobello Mr. Kemp acted as croupier and gave the toast, "the Poetry of Scotland." Late in life, having retired from active business, he accepted the honorary office of co-pastor of Bristo Palace Baptist Church, Edinburgh, along with the Rev. William Grant. He was a clear, argumentative and evangelical preacher; very calm and incisive, and he rarely used notes. As an illustration of great coolness it may be related that on one occasion he had not proceeded far with his sermon when he announced to his astonished and large congregation that he had completely lost the thread of the discourse, and "would they sing a song whilst he tried to collect his thoughts." He afterwards rose and delivered an unusually eloquent address. He died on the 15th July, 1888. His services as a pastor were cordially appreciated, many beyond his own family lamenting his decease. His age was seventy-two. Mr. Kemp had four daughters, the two eldest were married and had families, Borthwicks and Edwards, the latter are in Canada.

BISHOP JAMES KEMP.

James Kemp, the second Bishop of Maryland, was born at Keith-Hall, a parish of Aberdeenshire, being the son of Donald and Isabel Kemp. He was educated at Aberdeen Grammar School and Marischal College, where he graduated in 1786. After studying for another year he emigrated in the spring of 1787 to Maryland in the United States, where he remained till his death. Having forsaken Presbyterianism, in which he had been brought up, he decided to take orders in the American Episcopal Church. He was ordained deacon and priest on 26th and 27th December, 1789, by Bishop Claggett, of Maryland. In August, 1790, he was appointed Rector of Great Chopbank parish in the same diocese and state, where he remained more than twenty years. He was afterwards for a short time Associate Rector of St. Paul's, Baltimore. The advanced age of Bishop Claggett, who still presided over the diocese, compelled him to obtain the help of a younger man. Kemp was chosen for the post of suffragan bishop, being consecrated on 1st September, 1814. Bishop Claggett assigned him the eastern portion of his diocese, which has since been entirely severed, and now forms the Bishopric of Easton. In 1816 Bishop Claggett died, Kemp being appointed to succeed him, and for about eleven years he continued to preside over the whole diocese of Maryland. In 1827 he went to assist in the consecration of Bishop Ondderdonk, of *Pennsylvania*. On the return journey he met with a coach accident in consequence of which he died on 28th October in that year at the age of 63.

Kemp received the degree of D.D. from Columbia College, New York, 1802. He was the author of the following works: "Tract on Conversion," 1807; "Letters in Vindication of Episcopacy," 1808; "Sermon on Deathbed Repentance," 1815; "Sermon on the Death of Bishop Claggett," 1816.

Portraits of Bishop Kemp are said to give impression of a stony Scottish face, not lacking kindly humour. Bishop Claggett greatly valued his aid both before and after his consecration. He is said to be the only bishop suffragan ever appointed in the American church.

PROFESSOR JOHN KEMP.

John Kemp, who became famous as professor of mathematics and other subjects in Columbia College, is generally stated to have been born at Auchlossen, Aberdeenshire. He is, however, thus described in the records of Marischal College "Joannes Kempt, f. Joannes in Coull." It is quite possible that his parents may have removed from Auchlossen and settled in the neighbouriug parish of Coull. He was born on 10th April, 1763; he graduated as M.A. at Marischal College in 1781; his display of intellectual ability as a young man is evidenced by his election as a Fellow of the Royal Society of Edinburgh in 1783. In 1787 he received the degree of LL.D. from King's College, Aberdeen. He emigrated to AMERICA 1783, settling first in Virginia. Two years later he went to New York, where, after acting for a short time as a teacher, he was appointed Professor of Mathematics in Columbia College in 1786.

In 1795 he was transferred to the chair of geography, history and chronology. He was a friend of De Witt Chiston, Mayor of New York, and was frequently asked to advise in reference to municipal affairs; he died at New York 15th November, 1812. At what time in his life he changed his name from Kemp*t* does not appear. His portrait in oils hangs in the library of Columbia College, the compilers of this work are securing a copy, but regret that this is not to hand in time to appear here.

THE REV. HUGH KEMP.

The Rev. Hugh Kemp was minister of the Church of Scotland, of whom some slight memoirs have been handed down, though he does not appear to have been a man of any special eminence. At the end of the seventeenth century he was minister of Forgan in Fifeshire. He was appointed clerk to the Presbytry of St. Andrew's in 1693. In 1701 he was admitted minister of the church of Dunfermline. This church was occupied jointly by the Episcopalians and the Church of Scotland, the Episcopal minister officiating at one service and the Presbyterian at the other. Hugh Kemp does not seem to have liked the arrangement, his ministry not being submitted to by some of the townspeople. He was therefore glad to accept a call to Carnbee in the same county in 1704. He died in 1718 leaving an only child James by his wife, Margaret Gowlay, widow of Thomas Shens, of Lathallan.

CHAPTER IV.

TRADITION.

THE name of Kemp is not unknown in Scottish tradition. Among the ballads current among the peasantry in the early decades of the nineteenth century, and which were collected and published by William Motherwell in his "Minstrelsy: Ancient and Modern" (1827), are some verses entitled "Kemp Owyne," which we here quote:

Her mother died when she was young,
Which gave her cause to make great maun;
Her father married the worst woman
That ever lived in Christendom.

She served her with foot and hand
In everything that she could dee,
Till once in an unlucky time
She threw her in ower Craigy's Sea.

Says, "Lie you there, dove Isabel,
"Till all my sorrows lie with thee,
"Till KEMP Owyne come ower the sea
"And borrow you with kisses three;
"Let all the warld do what they will
"Oh! borrow'd you shall never be."

Her breath grew strong, her hair grew lang,
And twisted thrice about the tree;
And all the people far and near
Thought that a savage beast was she.
Their news did come to KEMP Owyne,
Where he lived far beyond the sea.

He hastened him to Craigy's Sea,
And on the savage beast look'd he;
Her breath was strong, her hair was lang,
And twisted was about the tree;
And with a swing she came about,
"Come to Craigy's Sea and kiss with me."

"Here is a royal belt," she cried,
"That I have found in the green sea,
"And while your body it is on
"Drawn shall your blood ne'er be;
"But if you touch me tail or fin,
"I vow my belt your death shall be."

He stepped in, gave her a kiss,
The royal belt he brought him wi',
Her breath was strong, her hair was lang,
And twisted twice about the tree;
And with a swing she came about,
"Come to Craigy's Sea and kiss with me."

"Here is a royal ring," she said,
"That I have found in the green sea,
"While your finger it is on
"Drawn shall your blood ne'er be;
"But if you touch me tail or fin,
"I swear my ring your death shall be."

He stepped in, gave her a kiss,
The royal ring he brought him wi';
Her breath was strong, her hair was lang,
And twisted once about the tree;
And with a swing she came about,
"Come to Craigy's Sea and kiss with me."

"Here is a royal brand," she said,
"That I have found in the green sea,
"And while your body it is on
"Drawn shall your blood ne'er be;
"But if you touch me tail or fin,
"I'll swear my brand your death shall be."

He stepped in, gave her a kiss,
The royal brand he brought him wi',
Her breath was sweet, her hair was short,
And twisted nane about the tree;
And smilingly she came about,
As fair a woman as fair could be.

Several other versions of the ballad exist which we have not space to quote at length, though some of the chief points of difference may be noted. Some of these versions are considerably longer, having twenty verses or more instead of eleven. Of the additional verses some are addressed to the supposed listener to the recitation:

Come hither, come hither, you cannot choose
And lay your head low on my knee,
The heaviest weird I will you read
That ever was red to gay ladye.

Other verses relate additional incidents or emphasize the terribleness of the lady's case.

The hero is called KEMPION instead of KEMP OWYNE, and he is said to be the King's son.* The place where the lady is confined is Estmere Crays. Instead of the hero having to be called from beyond the seas

Now word has gane to KEMPION.
That siccan a beast was in his land.

Kempion determines to inspect the strange creature of which he has heard so much :

" Now by my sooth," said KEMPION,
" This fiery beast I'll go and see."
" Now by my sooth," said Segramon,
" My al brother, I'll gang wi' thee."

Then bigged hae they a bonny boat,
And they hae set her to the sea,
But a mile before they reached the shore
Around them she gar'd the red fire flee.

Oh, Segramon, keep the boat afloat,
And let her na the land o'er near ;
For this wicked blast will sure gae mad
And set fire to all the land and mair.

Syne has he bent an arblast bow,†
And aimed an arrow at her head,
And swore if she didna quit the land
Wi' that same shaft to shoot her dead.

" O out of my stythe ‡ I winna rise,
(And it is not for the awe of thee)
Till KEMPION, the kingis son,
Cum to the crag and thrice kiss me."

Kempion leans over the crag three times and kisses the beast.

He's louted him o'er the lofty crag,
And he has given her kisses three,
Awa she gaed and again she cam,
The loveliest ladye e'er could be.

Here the following stanza is found in some versions, but not all :

Nae cluding had this ladye fair,
To keep her bodye frae the cold ;
But KEMPION took his mantle off,
And around his oin true love did fold.

The following are the concluding stanzas of one version. Others have variants on them :

" O was it warwolf in the wood ?
Or was it mermaid in the seas ?
Or was it man or vile woman,
My ain true love that mishaped thee ? "
" It was-na warwolf in the wood,
Nor was it mermaid in the sea,
But was my wicked stepmother,
And wae and weary may she be."
" O a heavier weird shall light her on
Than ever fell on vile woman,
Her hair shall grow rough, and her teeth shall grow lang,
And on her four feet shall she gang."
" None shall take pity her upon,
In wormeswood she aye shall won ;
And relieved shall she never be,
Till St. Mungo come over the sea.
And sighing said the weary wight,
" I doubt that day I'll shall never see ! "

Several places in different parts of Scotland are named after Kemps who are not known in tradition, but who may nevertheless have been real persons. Near Dollar, in Clackmannanshire, is an ancient castle named Castle Campbell and Castle of Gloom. It overlooks a glen at the bottom of which is a stream. From the castle a narrow passage concealed under the foliage of the slope goes down to the burn. Owing to the depth of the cleft between the rocks and the thickness of the overhanging vegitation the passage is almost completely dark. It originally had steps, but these have long since been concealed by fallen earth. The passage is called KEMP'S SCORE, and is said to have been made by one William Kemp, a noted robber. The object of the work

* The Kemp who married the heiress of Dury was the natural son of King James V. by a Kempe.

† The reference to the cross-bows under the word arblast is of great importance as an indication of the date of the ballad. This word passed out of popular use prior to 1500. Although occasionally met with in literature to the present time, it became essentially an archaic term by the end of the fifteenth century, and is very unlikely to have been inserted in a nautical version of a folk-tale after that period.

‡ Stythe appears to be an antiquated word. In the third line there is an interesting lective " the king's own son." There can be no manner of doubt but that "Kingis son" was the original reading, Kingis or Kinges being the middle English possessive form When it ceased to be intelligible owing to the changes in the language, the reading King's son was substituted as the nearest metrical equivalent. This again is proof of the antiquity of the ballad.

was evidently to enable the residents at the castle to obtain water from the stream below. Kemp is said to have beeen a man of gigantic stature and immense strength with a resolute and fearless disposition. One day he entered the royal palace at Dunfermline and carried off the King's dinner. A young nobleman, in disgrace for improper behaviour to the King's daughter, having heard of the occurrence pursued Kemp, and succeeded in cutting off his head, which he brought back to the palace. The King was so delighted at being rid of such a dangerous outlaw that he pardoned the young man and received him into favour. The date of the occurrence, and even the name of the King, do not appear to have been handed down! Kemp's body is said to have been thrown into a deep pool in the River Devon known as "Willie's Pool."

The Pass and Kemp's Score.

KEMP'S HOLD, or the Soldiers' Fastness, is a spot in the parish of Caputh, Perthshire, near the top of the Craig of Stenton, a detached conical hill situated about a mile west of Caputh Church. It has evidently been fortified at some time or other. Kemp in the name Kemp's Hold may signify a soldier, not an individual called Kemp.

On the summit of Turin Hill, in the parish of Rescobie, Forfarshire, is another fortified stronghold known as KEMP CASTLE or Camp Castle. The place is difficult of access from any side; in front it has an impregnable rock resembling Salisbury Crags.

While speaking of fortified places concerning Kemp as an element of their names, we may mention an antiquity known as KEMPE STONES, near Dundonald, County Down, as well as KEMPSTONE, a hill in Fetteress parish, Kincardshire. KEMPOCK POINT is a headland of Renfrewshire on the west side of Gourock Bay. KEMPE is a quandam moated mound in Renfrew parish, Renfrewshire. There is also KEMPLAW, a place with vitrified fort, in Dundonald parish, Ayrshire, and at one time there were lands called KEMP'S FIELDS, in the County of Haddington, evidently from some Kemp owning or leasing them.

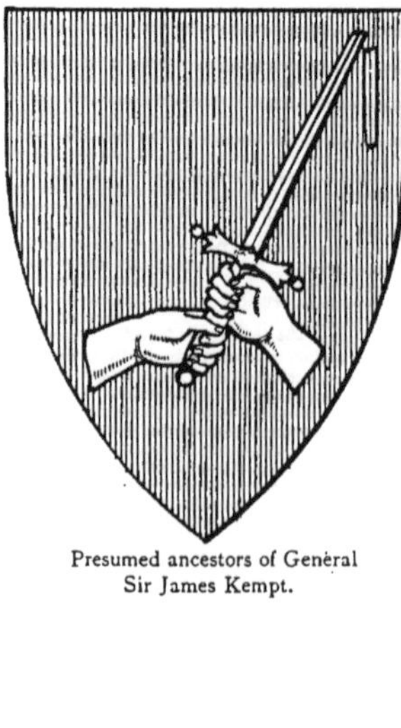

Presumed ancestors of General Sir James Kempt.

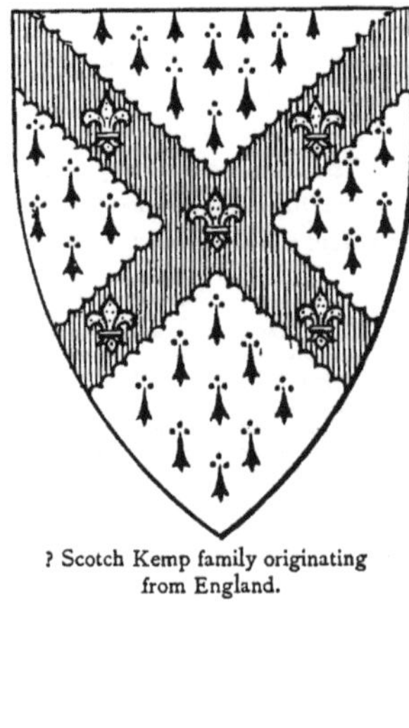

? Scotch Kemp family originating from England.

CHAPTER V.

THE KEMPS IN THE LOTHIANS.

MID, East and West Lothians, or the counties respectively of Edinburghshire, Haddingtonshire and Linlithgowshire, were for several centuries the homes of numerous groups of Kemps, but there is no evidence that they were all of one common, and that a Scottish stock. That there existed a distinctive Scottish family appears probable, but there were undoubtedly Kemps of English origin who settled on the borders, and who may have come with the English armies. Tradition has it that some who had sought an asylum from the fierce religious persecution following on the Reformation were of Flemish origin, and had settled in various localities on the eastern coasts of England and Scotland. The oldest of these groups, of which we have authentic records, were those in and around the ancient and royal burgh of Haddington, which date from the fourteenth century. A little further to the east other large groups were located in Spott, Dunbar and neighbouring parishes. The Mid Lothian groups probably sprang from some of the Haddington families, which for several generations centred in Pencaitland, Temple and adjoining parishes. In West Lothian the groups were not so numerous, but there were burgesses of the name in Linlithgow in the beginning of the fifteenth century, who appear to have been related to those of Edinburgh and Haddington, many of whom had official positions in the royal households during the reigns of James V., Queen Mary and James VI.

Sir Alexander Kemp, a favourite of King James V., married the heiress of Thomas Dury, of that Ilk, a ward of the King's. Henry Kemp, in that and following reigns, received grants of lands in various counties in Scotland. The wife of John Kemp, of Haddington, was the nurse of Prince James (who died), and of his sister the Princess Mary, who subsequently became the Queen of Scots Many other Kemps are recorded as owning property in the three royal burghs referred to, but the parish registers are not sufficiently perfect to enable us to show the exact line of descent to the present generation.

About the middle of last century the families, numerous though they had been, entirely disappeared from many of the parishes. This was certainly not that they had become extinct, but as they were nearly all of the landless class, mostly tradesmen, weavers and labourers, they migrated to the towns north and south ; and very many emigrated to the COLONIES and are now scattered over the world—quite a Scottish characteristic.

Of one of the older Mid and East Lothian families Daniel William Kemp, J.P., is the present Scottish representative. An early projenitor, of whom there is authentic record, settled in Humbie in the beginning of the seventeenth century, and had a son Alexander born in 1670 ; he married Janet Gaat and resided in Temple, where his large family of four sons and six daughters were born ; several died young. His son, Alexander, married Agnes Wadie in Temple in 1731, and there reared a family of five sons and one daughter. John, the youngest, married Mary Brown in 1771 and resided in Edinburgh, Rosewell and Pentland, at which places their children were born, six sons and three daughters. The eldest son, David, married (1) Janet Mossman, no issue ; (2) Agnes Kilpatrick, widow of — Gairns, and had one son, John, who emigrated to Melbourne, AUSTRALIA. The second son, Alexander, settled in Westport, Co. Mayo, IRELAND, and his descendants all emigrated to the UNITED STATES. Three sons are believed to have died young. John, the fifth son, born in 1789, married Janet Davidson, daughter of Daniel Davidson, of Larkhall, Lanarkshire, had four sons and three daughters, two of whom died young.

DANIEL KEMP, the eldest son, born 1810, married (Janet or) Jessie Steele, daughter of John Steele, a burgess of Edinburgh. Her mother, Christian Donaldson, claimed to be a direct descendant of Alexander Selkirk (or Selcraig), the father of Alexander Selkirk, the prototype of De Foe's "Robinson Crusoe." Of his family hereafter.

David Kemp, the second son, born 1816, married Mary Gibson, of Edinburgh, had four daughters; his career has already been sketched, page 12.

William Kemp, third son, born 1820, married Johanna Stewart, of Edinburgh; had six sons and two daughters. The family emigrated to the UNITED STATES. His second eldest son, Robert Stewart Kemp, at present resides in Brooklyn, NEW YORK CITY.

Mary married Stephen Cooper, of Edinburgh; the family emigrated to AUSTRALIA.

Ninian Kemp, of Galashiels, representing the Cloth and Dyeing Industries of Scotland.

Catherine, married Peter Craigie Roughead, of Edinburgh, had one son, Thomas, and six daughters.

Reverting to the above Daniel Kemp, shortly after his marriage in Edinburgh and the birth of two daughters (both of whom died), he migrated to Chester, where his daughter Margaret Ecking was born (called after an old Chester lady, Miss Ecking). The family removed to Wrexham, Denbighshire, where three sons and one daughter were born, John Davies Kemp (died young), Daniel William Kemp, David Robert Kemp, Janet Kemp. In 1856 the family returned to Edinburgh.

Margaret Ecking Kemp married in 1875 Andrew Ferguson Bowie (his second wife), and had one son and two daughters.

Janet married John Murray Duncan, barrister, London, and had several sons.

Daniel Kemp commenced life as a confectioner, but eventually became connected with the management of the poor while in Wrexham, and this led to the appointment of Governor of the City of Edinburgh Poorhouse, which important position he held till his death in 1887. Like his younger brother David he took a deep interest in the Baptist denomination, and was for many years a pastor (unpaid) of the Bristo Place Baptist Chapel, Edinburgh. On his retirement from the pastorate the Church presented him with a handsome cabinet containing the "Encyclopedia Britannica," a marble clock, &c., with suitable inscriptions. He was spared to celebrate his golden wedding, when he and Mrs. Kemp entertained a large party of relatives and friends, five of whom had been at their wedding fifty years previously. The aged couple received several valuable mementoes of the interesting event.

DANIEL WILLIAM KEMP, the second son of Daniel Kemp as stated above, was born in Wrexham in 1844, and was educated at the Grammar School of that town and subsequently at Newington Academy, Edinburgh, his parents having again come to reside in the city. At the early age of fourteen he gave indications of the bent of his mind by writing an essay on Hydrogen, which was published with illustrations in the school annual in Edinburgh. That early impulse after science became intensified, and thus it is that to-day he is such an ardent student. He is a life Fellow of the Royal Scottish Society of Arts, and has been awarded several medals by this Society for papers on original subjects. In 1870 he suggested the formation of the Edinburgh Association of Science and Art, and on that association attaining its majority in 1891 he was presented with a Diploma of Distinction as its founder. In the early days of volunteering he threw himself into the movement, and was largely instrumental in raising the 5th Highland Company of the Queen's Own Rifle Volunteer Brigade—which at that period donned the kilt—and was its first Ensign. Visiting the far north he formed a strong attachment to the romantic county of the 93rd and Reay Fencibles. He made himself intimately acquainted with the history, topography and antiquities of Sutherland. He has published a number of works bearing on that county. These include an edition, with notes and illustrations, of "Bishop Pococke's Tours in Sutherland" in 1760, published for the first time from the original MSS. in the British Museum (1888); "Notes on Iron Smelting in Sutherland" (1887); "The Democracy of Sutherland" (1890); "An Eccentric Sutherland Dominie" (1892); and "Selections from the Sutherlandshire Magazine of 1826" (1898); "The Taylor Family of Ross, Cromarty, Sutherland and Caithness" (1895), &c. On the formation of the Scottish History Society in 1887 he was requested to undertake the editing of its first volume—a complete edition of "Pococke's Tours in Scotland, 1747-1760." This Society's publications now number forty volumes, which are highly valued by Scottish historical students.

Daniel William Kemp, J.P.

He possesses probably the largest and most complete collection of Sutherland books extant. He is a Justice of the Peace of Sutherland. The Royal Burgh of Dornoch bestowed on him the privilege of its "freedom" in April, 1890, and he has represented this burgh for many years at the Convention of Royal Burghs. With the political life of Leith he has long been associated, and for twelve years he has occupied the position of President of the Leith Liberal Club. In commercial and mercantile affairs he is a member of both the Edinburgh and Leith Chamber of Commerce. In religious matters his sympathies, like his father's and uncle's, are with the Baptists. In 1867 he joined the old established firm of R. Anderson and Co., metal merchants and paint manufacturers, Leith, where he still resides. In 1869 he married Helen Primrose Bell, fifth daughter of Peter Bell, of Edinburgh, and has one son, Charles Norman Kemp, born 1883, who is at present a student at the University of Edinburgh.

DAVID ROBERT KEMP, youngest son of Daniel Kemp, was, as before stated, born in Wrexham in 1846; he was educated chiefly in Edinburgh on the return of his parents to their native city. On leaving school he entered the service of the Union Bank of Scotland and rose to the position of secretary in Edinburgh. The *Banker's Magazine* for April, 1894, vol. lvii., pp. 573-6, contains a sketch and portrait of him, the occasion being his leaving Edinburgh to enter on new duties as manager of Dalgety and Co., Limited, London, which he still occupies. He is a Justice of the Peace of Edinburgh, and was connected with many commercial and financial concerns in that city. He has visited Australia on three occasions, travelling outwards by India and homewards by United States; he has travelled extensively on the continent. In 1868 he married Margaret Anne, fourth daughter of Peter Bell, of Edinburgh—thus the two brother's wives are sisters. He has one son, Edwyn Arthur, and one daughter.

David Robert Kemp.

EDWYN ARTHUR KEMP, born 1869, was for several years with the Union Bank of Scotland in Edinburgh, but is now in London. He early joined the Volunteers and devoted all his leisure to acquiring an extensive knowledge of the military profession; he attended camps and cavalry barracks and became an expert horseman. In 1887 he obtained a commission in the 5th V. B. the Royal Scots, and rose to the rank of captain; for five years he was A.D.C. to Brigadier-General the Right Honourable Lord Kingsbury, C.B., commanding the North V. I. Brigade, and in that capacity was at camps and reviews at Aldershot. On his father's removal to London he also removed thither to the London office of the Union Bank of Scotland. Subsequently he went into commercial life, and is at present secretary of an Australian Trading Company in London. His sister, Ethel Margaret Kemp, born in Edinburgh, 1873, who married in London John Morison Inches, brewer, Edinburgh, on 29th June, 1898; has a daughter, Ethel Vera Morison Inches.

The artist to whom the Kemp history is indebted for heraldic illustrations, Mr. ALEXANDER KEMP, of Edinburgh, comes of a family long settled at Spott, at which place several monuments and records of members of his family still exist. His first ancestor, so far as the artist knows, was a George Kemp, who appears to have been near kin to one of the East Lothian groups. He was born about 1740, and resided latterly in Whittingham parish, but during his long life of *nineiy-six* years lived in various places in the South of Scotland. He married Margaret Carter, from Earlston, who is said to have been the daughter of a Highlander of the Pretender's army, who settled either in the Lothians or on the borderland. Margaret died at the advanced age of *ninety-four*. (It may be noted that a William Carter married a Catherine Kemp and lived for a time in Hilldown, Spott, about 1736, from which place Earlston is not greatly distant.) George Kemp, of Spott, had a daughter Elsbeth, who was baptized in 1775 and died in 1856 unmarried, and a son Alexander, who was born in 1782. This son resided chiefly in Stentor parish, where he was the precentor of the church ; he married Jean Goodall (born 1784) in 1809, and by her had six children, two of whom died in infancy. Alexander died in 1864 leaving the following children : George, born 1810, who died in 1893 ; Marian, born in Cockburnspath parish in 1811 ; Margaret, born in Stentor parish in 1814, and Ann, born in Whittingham parish in 1817, who is still living. The last named married a merchant named William Knox, of Chirnside, whose business she continues to conduct ; she is a member of the Berwickshire Liberal Association, in which she still takes a deep and active interest. The eldest son, George Kemp, in his early life travelled throughout Scotland in the interests of his business, even including England and Ireland in his rounds. Eventually he settled down in Edinburgh where he married in 1844 Marion Hall (born in Dirleton 1821, died 1891). Their son, Alexander Kemp, the artist, was born in 1845 at Edinburgh where he now resides. He married in 1881 Margaret Watt, of Edinburgh, and has a daughter named Maggie Livingstone Kemp. Mrs. Kemp died in 1882, and Alexander married as his second wife Helen Morrison, also of Edinburgh, in 1893, but by her there has been no issue. (We may suggest to subscribers to the Kempe and Kemp history, that those who desire designs for book plates or similar drawings cannot do better than commission this artist to undertake their work. Apart from his long study of heraldry and his skill at designing, he has a special interest in all that in any way pertains to Kemp(e)s, and from our own experience we can say that he takes infinite care to carry out the wishes of his clients with due attention to heraldic laws.)

Edwyn Kemp.

Francis Kemp, the Deputy Chairman of Williams, Deacons, the Manchester and Salford

Bank, was born at Edinburgh on 13th August, 1831, and entered business as a clerk in the Friendly Insurance Office there in 1844; subsequently he was on the clerical staff of the British Insurance Office, Edinburgh, and in 1852 he was appointed cashier in the Lancashire Insurance Office; In 1856 he was made resident secretary in that company's London office, and from this position he resigned in 1861 to enter the Manchester and Salford Bank at Manchester; in the same year he became secretary and subsequently sub-manager, then manager and general manager of that bank, with which Williams, Deacon and Co. was amalgamated. He is a member of the Manchester Reform Club, and of the National Liberal Club (London), and resides at Parkside, Altrincham, Cheshire. (Of his family we have no details.)

David Campbell Kemp, shipowner, of Belfast, is one of a family of six, his father, David Kemp, having been a merchant of Glasgow. This Mr. David Kemp was first cousin to the two eminent chemists Kenneth and Alexander Kemp mentioned in foregoing chapters. C. Kemp now carries on the business founded by his father David at Glasgow; John L. Kemp, another son of the Glasgow merchant, was until recently a brewer at Northgate, Chester. He died during the progress of this work leaving a widow. David Kemp, of Glasgow, was the son of Hugh Kemp, by Ann Campbell, which Hugh was the son of one Henry Kemp, by a Margaret Cameron, and was closely related to Gavin Kemp and the worthy General, James Kempt, of whom we give a portrait. This family claim arms, but except for the *direct* descendants of Sir James Kempt, the right of Kemps now living, to Scottish arms, is at least " not proven."

Arms of General Sir James Kempt.

Arms of Kemp of Haddington and Edinburgh.

KEMPS OF ALBANY AND NEW YORK.

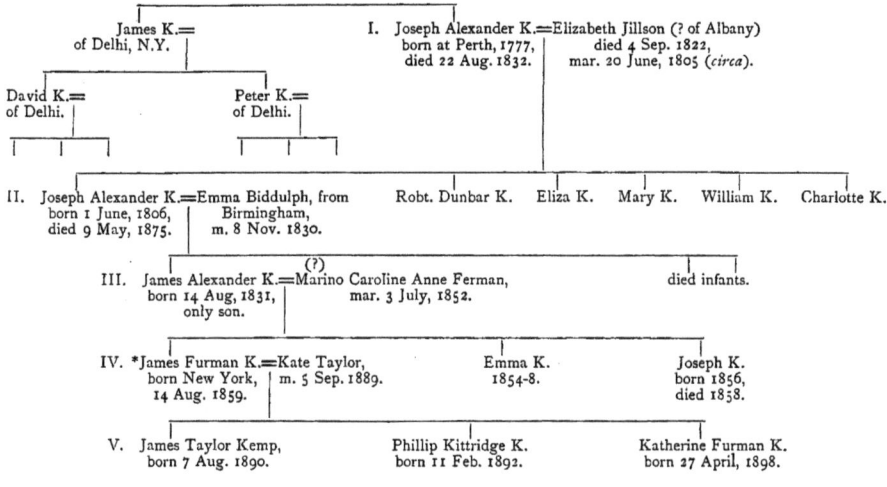

James K.= of Delhi, N.Y.

I. Joseph Alexander K.=Elizabeth Jillson (? of Albany) born at Perth, 1777, died 22 Aug. 1832. — died 4 Sep. 1822, mar. 20 June, 1805 (*circa*).

David K.= of Delhi.

Peter K.= of Delhi.

II. Joseph Alexander K.=Emma Biddulph, from Birmingham, m. 8 Nov. 1830. — born 1 June, 1806, died 9 May, 1875.

Robt. Dunbar K. | Eliza K. | Mary K. | William K. | Charlotte K.

III. James Alexander K.=(?) Marino Caroline Anne Ferman, mar. 3 July, 1852. — born 14 Aug, 1831, only son.

died infants.

IV. *James Furman K.=Kate Taylor, m. 5 Sep. 1889. — born New York, 14 Aug. 1859.

Emma K. 1854-8.

Joseph K. born 1856, died 1858.

V. James Taylor Kemp, born 7 Aug. 1890.

Phillip Kittridge K. born 11 Feb. 1892.

Katherine Furman K. born 27 April, 1898.

CHAPTER VI.

IRISH KEMPES

SO early as 1293 we have a trace of the name of Kemp in Ireland, one Robert Kemp being a witness to a deed of Christianna de Glascote, of Dublin, on 26th May that year. In 1338 Henry Kemp was a witness to a similar document of Elyas Heyford and Walter le Marshal, of Dublin; it was probably the same Henry Kemp who in 1345 witnessed a deed in the same city, the parties to which were William de la Felde and Robert Fled. In November, 1383, William Kemp and Nicholas Walse (chaplain) were acting as attorneys in Ireland for William Ponufrayt. These items are furnished by the Deputy Keeper of Public Records in Ireland in his Appendix to his Twenty-six Report, which covers the period from 1270, and it is noteworthy that there are no cases of Kemps witnessing or being party to deeds between 1383 and 1471, from which we may reason that the Kemps were either few in number and of little property, or that they entirely disappeared during the greater part of this hiatus. There is another fact derived

* James Furman Kemp is Professor of Geology in Columbia University.

from these records which is contrary to the general rule in England, namely, that the above earliest examples of the name all appear without the final E, and that even later the name in Ireland is usually spelled "Kemp." In 1471 the will of John Kempe was proved in Dublin, but the details of this testament are not available. Again from this date we find no mention of the name until the time of Cromwell, when both tradition and fact agree in stating that certain Kemp soldiers, both from England and Scotland, founded families in Ireland.

In 1641 Henry Kemp and John Mathews petitioned the Committee of Irish Affairs, and about the same time Hannah Kemp had a license to marry John Wright. In 1665 Thomas Kempe, of St. Patrick Street, Dublin, an inn-keeper, made his will and died, and Elizabeth Kemp, a widow, left a will which was proved at Dublin in 1730. In 1738 Robert Kemp of the same place left property by will which was duly proved, and another Robert Kemp, who is described as a mariner, of Dublin, left a will in 1757. Three years later Elizabeth Kemp was licensed to marry Joseph Malone, and a license was issued in 1776 for the marriage of Robert Kemp to Margaret Hennesy, and two years later Mary Kemp and John Naylor were married at Dublin. During this period Scottish Kemps frequently immigrated and settled in the North of Ireland, one family having a little property at and around Cavan. Like so many of the Irish families these Kempes found farming unremunerative and land almost valueless, and it was in consequence of real poverty that the first of this family migrated to New York in search of work. This young man's father had died at Cavan in 1829 leaving a large family unprovided for. Edward Kemp found hope in New York, and soon returned to Cavan to convey his mother and her children to America. There he was able to make steady headway, and eventually he felt some strong desire to look again on his native soil. Despite his mother's objection to the effect that he would find nothing of family interest at Cavan Edward went his way, and on arrival in his native place he was surrounded with Kemps who were awe-struck with his liberality and apparent wealth. After benefitting these poor cottagers he returned to New York regretting that he had been to Ireland, and when in course of a month or two a large colony of Kemps turned up in New York claiming his aid as a wealthy kinsman he was the more regretful; however, we understand that he did assist them, and gave them a chance of making a fortune for themselves. Edward Kemp, of New York, is now seventy-two years of age, an immense man, but as active as many men half his age. He still conducts a merchant's business, resides in Fifth Avenue, New York, and when frequently visiting England he makes the Hotel Metropole his headquarters. He married Mary Augusta — in New York, but has had no children, and, we believe, he has but one relative, a niece, who is now living in England.

The Kempes of the South of Ireland have been long settled at and around Cork, the directories of a hundred years ago give many persons of the name, these being engaged in various trades more or less connected with shipping. John Lovekin Kemp was born there about 1800, and married a Miss Annie Leighton, by whom he had a son, John Kemp, born at Cork in 1832, who married Emily Bird, of Woodchester. They have had no children, the next of kin to John Kemp, of Cork (now living at Cleveden, Somerset) being three sisters, who are still living in their birth-place.

Another Kemp family of Cork is now represented by the Rev. Richard Lavers Kemp, of St. Paul's Vicarage, Blackpool, Lancashire, whose father, Joshua Joseph Kemp, was born in Cork in 1839, the latter's father being a William Kemp, of Cork. The Rev. R. L. Kemp married at Newcastle-on-Tyne Miss Emily Maud Woodhouse (formerley of Farnley, Leeds), by whom he has three children, Mona, Norman and Bryan Charles Lavers Kemp, the eldest son being now seven years of age.

CHAPTER VII.

SUNDRY KEMPES OF THE EMPIRE—INDIA.

AS might be expected Kempes and Kemps of India are chiefly connected from the first with the Army and the Government. Before the disestablishment of the East India Company many Kemps were frequently in India as merchants and seamen, but these left no family so far as we can gather until a century ago, when a representative of a Kentish Kemp family, formerly a sailor, settled at Calcutta.

Of his ancestors we have a mass of interesting details from the wills proved at Canterbury. It seems highly probable that the tradition current in the family which claims connexion with the Kemps of Wye is correct, for certainly that illustrious family had property in the fifteenth century in Thanet, since which time the Kempes were settled around St. Lawrence and participated in the important continental shipping business for many generations. A branch of these Thanet Kemps settled as merchants and glass makers in London, and it was due to their looking-glasses being so esteemed by Indian natives that led to the establishment of the sailor Kemp at Calcutta. His success led to a cousin going out, but the second Kemp left a young wife at home, and being a devoted husband and father he returned after a voyage or two, and his descendants have made England their home, although several members of the family have held important positions in India. For instance, ALEXANDER DAVIDSON KEMP (who was the third or fourth of that double Christian name) was for many years a prominent administrator of the law in India, and on return to England he continued to practice as a solicitor. He had residences at Kensington, Bath and Chigwell, in Essex, and married Ann, the only daughter of Major Webster, of Lansdown, by whom he had three sons, namely, ALEXANDER DAVIDSON KEMP, the REV. WILLIAM EDELMAN KEMP, of Chiswick, and F. F. KEMP, of Kensington. A. D. Kemp, the father, was born at Calcutta in 1827 and died at Chalcomb, Bath, in 1901; his eldest son married Harriet Edith Frary, of Norwich, in 1895, and has two sons and a daughter. It is interesting to mention that the gallant General French, who has taken so prominent a part in the South African campaign, is a second cousin to Alexander D. Kemp, both being descended from Colonel Thomas Webster, of the Indian Army, by Selina French. We have before us over 100 letters written by members of Alexander Kemp's family from India and Africa one hundred years ago, one dated at Cape Town 6th March, 1803, has the following interesting clause:—

> "I have without the smallest recommendation got forward and have done so well as could have been expected, and, indeed, I'm not a litfle disappointed at the simplicity of our Government in giving up the key to India, which I doubt not they will be sorry for hereafter. . . . We are now under the Dutch flag, and CAPE TOWN—which was a few weeks past flourishing, fine place—is now as desolate as a village. So great is the change as almost impossible to conceive. I think with good reason the inhabitants are very sorry for the change."

The writer of this letter found business did not flourish at the Cape under the new government, and soon after this letter went to India whence he wrote more hopefully of his business prospects.

Another family, who were for some long period connected with India, was that of the Kemps of Kemp Town. Owen Lomer, Esq., of the 21st Bengal Infantry, having married Elizabeth, youngest sister of Colonel Kemp, of the Polygon, Brighton, on 8th September, 1828. Colonel George Rees Kemp was living at the Polygon in 1827, in which year the birth of a daughter was announced; in that notice the Colonel is described as "Commandant of the 15th Foot, B. N. I." He died at Spring Lodge, East Hoathly, Sussex, aged eighty-one, on 16th September, 1861, being then Colonel of the 22nd Regiment, B. N. I.

General George Rees Kemp had a brother, William Kemp, who was of the Seventh Light Cavalry, and subsequently in the Public Works Department, Trichinopoly. His son, William Kemp, who died at Trichinopoly, had eight sons, out of which family but two survive, namely, Alexander Kemp, who now resides at Chudderghat, Hyderbad (aged eighty), and ALARIC GARNETT KEMP, now of Naini Tal., N.W.P. The last named was born at Trichinopoly in 1835 and married in 1858 Miss Georgiana Macqueen, by whom he has one daughter, Nina Rose Georgiana.

Another Indian branch of the Sussex Kemp's was founded about 1840 by a Thomas Kemp; he, however, was not related to the last named, being connected with the Quaker family of Brighton, who, as we have said, are traceable to Kent. He went to India as a soldier and was lost sight of by his English relatives, and his descendants are not in a position to absolutely prove their identity, although it was desirable some time since for them to put forward their claim to certain estates—freehold in Sussex and Kent. Connected with this branch there are now living two widows, both being known as MRS. JOHN MAINWARING KEMP. The REV. JOHN KEMP, of Haughley, Suffolk, belongs to this family, being son of Major John Kemp, of ' t K.B. Guards, late of Loose Court, Maidstone. JOHN WILLFRED KEMP, now of the North W . Province Police Force, Allahabad, is the son of the Rev. John Kemp, and was born at Sar .k (Borneo), on 9th June, 1871. He went to India in 1888, and is now one of the special (secret, police. G. C. Kemp, late of the R.E., Forozpur, also belongs to this group.

Another British Kemp family in India was established by E. C. Kemp, Esq., late of Calcutta, whose widow died in 1850 leaving a daughter, who married the Rev. S. J. Lyon, M.A. (for some time Incumbent of Moorfields, Sheffield), in 1845. James Lyon Kemp, son of Henry Kemp, Esq., formerly of the East India Company's service, was drowned at Bunbury, Western Australia, in 1847 by the upsetting of a boat. His age was twenty-two.

The Cornish Kempe family were also represented in India, Peter Kempe, being a Captain in the H.E.I.C.S. His daughter, Ann Eliza Kempe, married in 1846 at Whitechurch, Devon, Benjamin Sampson, Esq., of Tullimaer.

The Norfolk Kemps are represented in India by G. W KEMP, Esq., late of the Alliance Bank of Simla. (His ancestors lived for generations beside the Kemp Baronets, but the actual connection between the two families has not been proved.)

The Scottish Kemp's were represented in India 100 years ago, and have continued to send out fresh branches, two of the most prominent being DAVID SKINNER KEMP, who established Kemp and Co., Limited, chemists, at Bombay, and his brother, JAMES KEMP, who was formerly editor of the *China Mail*, and eventually editor and proprietor of the *India Mail*, wrote considerably on Oriental life, including "Voices from the Verandah." D. S. Kemp has a son, David Claude Kemp, who is now a lieutenant in the Indian Medical Service, and another son, NORMAN WRIGHT KEMP, a barrister-at-law, Bombay. A character sketch and portrait of Mr. DAVID SKINNER KEMP appeared in the *British and Colonial Druggist* of 5th February, 1887. A niece of his, Miss Nora Kemp, is a doctor (M.B. and C.M.) at the "Retreat," York.

AUSTRALASIA.

We attempted to get access to the list of passengers carried to Australia in the early days of colonisation, but this proved impossible, and our information as to any early settlement of Kemp families there is very meagre. It would seem probable that many of those of the name at Melbourne and Adelaide are the third or fourth generation of their respected families in the

Antipodes. Those of more certain origin are as follows: Stewart Kempe, of Carandale, Mintaro, South Australia, whose pedigree is given in our Cornish (South of England) section.

PETER KEMP, of Currency Creek, who is of a Perthshire family (*vide* Scottish section, Chapter II.), and Walter Kemp of the Titles Office, Melbourne, whose family were from Middlesex, England. The last named uses as his crest a vulture on a wheatsheaf fesswise with wings endorsed, similar to that used by the Hitchin-Kemps and Kemps of Norfolk, but avoiding the mottoes of these families he uses "Sit Copia Campis,"—a neat allusion to the early spelling of the name of Kemp, which from this root is fittingly signified by the three golden sheaves on a blood red field. These sheaves, and a similar bird on a sheaf (upright), are claimed as the arms of Dr. WILLIAM GEORGE KEMP, M.D., late of Australia and Wellington (N.Z.), who has two old seals cut with these heraldic devices. The last named is of the Indian branch of the Sussex and Kent family mentioned above, and is now resident in England.

Samuel Bromley Kemp, Volksrust South Africa.

New Zealand had a very prominent Kemp, whose figure was borne on a flag as a tribal ensign. He wrote a Maori grammar and dictionary which have proved valuable books.

Many Kemps from the Lowlands of Scotland, the Midlands, the South of England and Cornwall have been mentioned in other sections of this work as having settled in Australasia and need not be reviewed here.

SOUTH AFRICA.

During the present war (which is just concluded by the declaration of Peace as this section of the History goes to the press), Kemps have been prominent on both sides. GENERAL KEMP was second in command of Delarey's force, and Lord Milner has had on his staff Herbert Henry Kemp, who is the son of William Kemp, of Norton Fitzwaren, Taunton, Somerset. He was born at Minehead, Somerset, in 1877, but belongs by descent to a Devonshire branch of the Kempes.

GEORGE KEMP, M.P. for South Lancashire, has been twice to South Africa. On his first expedition he served for over a year, and was under fire on several occasions; he arrived out in command of Lancashire Yeomanry shortly before the close of the campaign.

COLONEL SIR KENNETH H. KEMP, BART., was second in command of a Norfolkshire battalion, and his son "ROBIN" KEMP has also been out on active service, while numerous Kempes from London, Leicestershire and Kent have gone as Yeomanry troopers, and WILLIAM ROUS KEMP is serving in the Army Medical Corp at one or more of the field hospitals. As it is probable that he may become a Colonist, we may here record that his father, George Lucas Kemp, was a native of Norwich and son of William Rous Kemp, of Stourton, Warwickshire by Jane Meadows, of Idbury Hall.

Samuel Bromley Kemp, of Volksrust, who has suffered in business from the prolonged war, is a native of Shropshire, and some account of his family will be found in our West of England section.

Many other Colonists of the name of Kemp have already been mentioned under previous headings.

CANADA.

We issued circulars to a large number of Kemps whose names appear in Canadian Directories, but the return of details on the forms supplied has been very small. A. E. Kemp, of the "Kemp Manufacturing Co.," Toronto, appears to be one of the most prominent of his name in the Dominion. Of his family connexions, however, we have no evidence. Another correspondent states that he (D. K. Goodfellow, of Beauharnois, Quebec) is descended from the Kempe family of Ontario, which family he gives us to understand settled at Ontario at the close of the Revolutionary War, members serving the Crown in 1812-4 and during the Upper Canadian Rebellion of 1837. Mr. Alfred Edward Kemp, of Melita, Manitoba, is a native of Tunbridge Wells, Kent (England), being the son of John Kemp. a farmer, of Adisham. The latter married twice, first to a Miss Pack and secondly to Miss Harriet Potter. His brother George was a soldier and served in India. Two Kemps of Canada owe their origin to Scottish parents, one of these has taken considerable trouble to compile a list of Kemps now living in Canada, which, however, we do not find space to include here.

WEST INDIES.

Major Robert Kemp died at St. Christopher's, Middle Island, in 1732, and his will was proved in England in that year by Peter Lamotte, attorney to Nathan Crossley the executor. A mural tablet to Nathan Crossley appears in the Church of St. Leonard's, Shoreditch, and wills of Kemps connected with the parish suggest that he was related to the Kemps of Shoreditch. The will is very interesting as mentioning "trooping accoutrament," saddles, pistols, carbine, "Buccaneer Gunns," silver-hilted sword and *negroes*, which formed part of this major's estate. His property was left in trust for the deceased's wife, Martha Kemp, during her life, and the reversion was to be divided between the testator's brother and sister, Nathan Crossley, senior, and Jane Crossley. Apparently Robert Kemp left no issue.

We have already mentioned (*vide* Cornwall chapter) the Kempes of Bermuda who came from Cornwall. Besides these there are two other Kemp families in the West Indies. James Wheeler Kemp, of Jamaica, was born at Peshawar, N.W.P., in 1851, his father being James George Kemp and his mother Harriet Wheeler (of Simla), and his grandfather Ebenezer Chapman Kemp, who commanded vessels to and from India, was a brother to the Alexander Davidson Kemp, who as we have stated above was of East Kent origin and connected with a London firm of glass silverers. He was born about 1770, and for a while was in the Royal Navy.

The Rev. W. Kemp Bussel, of Kingstone, Jamaica, is the representative of an old family of Kemps long settled in Somersetshire, and yet another James Kemp, of the West Indies, hails direct from Scotland.

UNITED STATES.

Although the States now form no part of the British Empire we have had frequent occasion to mention various Kemps who have held important posts in the States. Two were State Attorneys of Philadelphia and Province of New York during the eighteenth century, and at the present time the Professor of Geology in the Columbia University, New York, is a Scottish Kemp. We have numerous short pedigrees of Kemps, of New York and the States, and shall be glad to correspond with representatives of the name in the U.S.A, but we cannot include here more than the passing mention of the fact that a very large proportion of the Kemps in New York are not of British descent, the name being widely spread on the European Continent as well as throughout the late Transvaal Republic.

NEWFOUNDLAND.

As mentioned in the South of England section, a family connected with the Kemp-Welches settled in Newfoundland, and this George Kemp died there, aged eighty-nine, in 1845, leaving a large family. In his obituary notice in the *Gentleman's Magazine* he is stated to have been one of the principal Newfoundland merchants.

LEEWARD ISLANDS.

Captain Kempt was agent for provisions of war at the Leeward Islands in 1804 and agent of transports at Barbadoes in 1805, in which year he was promoted to Post-Captain and placed in command of the *Egyptienne* prison-ship. In 1813 he was made agent for transports on the lakes of North America.

SUGGESTED SUPPLEMENT TO

THE HISTORY OF THE KEMP FAMILIES.

In view of the number of genealogical forms which are still coming in pertaining to living representatives of the various Kempe, Kempt and Kemp families, the compiler of this history believes that it will be found desirable to publish a supplimentary book giving the recent generations of many descendants from the old British families. He will be glad to receive any additions and corrections to be included in this supplement, and suggestions as to better arrangement of facts. Meanwhile he is at work on a similar

HISTORY OF THE VARIOUS FAMILIES

NAMED

BROOKE, BROOK, BROOKES AND BROOKS,

and will be indebted to any readers who will make the prospective work known to those interested; and he takes this opportunity of thanking the large number of genealogists and others who have assisted in the "History of the Kemp(e)s."

Fred. Hitchin-Kemp.

6, Beechfield Road, Catford,
London, S.E.

CORRIGENDA.

SECTION I.

Page 20, line 16: *For* "High Ferrars" *read* "Higham Ferrers."
" 30, " 8: *For* "Middlesex" *read* "Hertfordshire."
" 38, " 26: *For* "Chetham" *read* "Chatham."
" 42, " 8: *For* "Southwich" *read* "Southwick."
" 47, " 15: *For* "Loue" *read* "Loué."
" 55, " 5: *For* "insticiam" *read* "iusticiam."

SECTION II.

Page 33, line 7: *For* "Smallbridge" *read* "Smallborough."
" 44, " 14 from bottom: *For* "Laybourne" *read* "Layham."
" 47, " 4 " : *For* "Essex" *read* "Suffolk."

SECTION III.

Page 2, line 2: *For* "Bury" *read* "Burgh."

SECTION IV.

Page 18, line 22: *For* "Preb. Bonell White" *read* "the late Judge Meadows White."
" 21, " 5 from bottom: *For* "Warham" *read* "Warnham."
" 26, " 15 " : *For* "Essex" *read* "Sussex."

SECTION VI.

Page 1, line 3: *For* "which is various" *read* "with its variations."
" " 7 from bottom: *For* "Knight" *read* "Kempt."
" " 6 " : *For* "Wanchtown" *read* "Wauchtoun."
" " 6 " : *For* "merles" *read* "merks."
" " 5 " : *For* "account" *read* "annual."
" " 4 " : *For* "barning" *read* "barony."
" 2, " 12: *For* "Wail" *read* "Wait."
" 3, " 11: *For* "who" *read* "whom." *For* "Cupa" *read* "Cupar."
" " 14: *For* "Gargettown" *read* "Gargestoun."
" " 17: *For* "dires" *read* "dues."
" " 11 from bottom: *For* "Monsford" *read* "Moorfoot."
" " 9 " : *For* "They were most of them weavers" *read* "Some of them were weavers."
" " 5 " : *For* "Dunny" *read* "Denny."

CORRIGENDA.

Page 4, line 7: *After* "north" *add* "though."
" " 12 and 14: *For* "Kempt" *read* "Kemps."
" " 18 from bottom: *For* "Adesonn" *read* "Adesoun."
" " 17 " : *For* "urquhill" *read* "umquhill" (and in line 14).
" " 14 " : *For* "Patrick" *read* "Patrik."
" 5, " 6: *For* "Collisonn" *read* "Collisoun."
" " 10: *After* "Skene of Skene" *add* "is Johne Kempt."
" " 13: *For* "wicht" *read* "wricht."
" " 21: *For* "Aborfar" *read* "Aboyne."
" 7, " 10: *For* "Gillie" *read* "Gillies."
" " 15: *For* "of Kempy" *read* "or Kempy. *For* "Creief *read* "Crieff."
" " 21: *For* "Kempton" *read* "Kempyon. *For* "names" *read* "mains."
" 8, " 9: *For* "Harward" *read* "Harvard:"
" 9, " 2 from bottom: *For* "Hutchunson *read* "Hutchinson."
" 10, " 4 " : *For* "upholsterer" *read* "carpenter."
" 11, " 11: *For* "river." *read* "canal."
" " 11 from bottom: *For* "which" *read* "while."
" 12, " 15: *For* "Palace" *read* "Place."
" " 11 from bottom: *For* "Chopbank" *read* "Choptank."
" 13, " 5: *For* "stony" *read* "strong."
" " 19: *For* "Chiston" *read* "Clinton."
" " 2 from bottom: *For* "Gowlay" *read* "Gourlay."
" 15, " 1: *Delete* footnote, the ballad being of much earlier date than the incident referred to.
" " 2: *For* "Crays" *read* "Crags."
" verse 1, line 4: *For* "al" *read* "ain."
" " 7, " 4: *For* "oin" *read* "ain.
" last verse, line 4: *Delete* "shall."
" line 8 from bottom: *For* "not" *read* "only."
" Note ‡, line 1: *For* "lective" *read* "lection."
" " " 3: *For* "King's son" *read* "King's own son."
" 19, line 2 from bottom: *Delete* "where he still resides."
" 21, " 8: *For* "Elsbeth" *read* "Elspeth."
" " 11: *For* "Stentor" *read* "Stenton" (and in line 20).

INDEX OF PERSONS.

Numerals in brackets thus (2) after a name denote different individuals bearing the same name. For examples, *see* "Adams" and "Andrews."

Index of Persons.

C

D

Index of Persons.

Index of Persons.

Index of Persons.

Y

INDEX OF PLACES.

Roman numerals denote the sections of the work, while the pages of each section are indicated by Arabic figures.

References in heavy type contain the principal information relating to the places concerned.

The letter *f* immediately after a page number indicates that a further reference is contained in the following page. Where *ff* is added the references extend through three or more successive pages.

The letter *n* or *and n* attached to a page number directs attention to a footnote.

Where the name of a place is followed by an entry in square brackets, the former represents the usual modern spelling, while the bracketed form is that used in the text in one or more places. Some of forms in brackets are genuine antique spellings, while others are mere writer's or printer's errors which escaped notice till too late for correction.

Index of Places.

C

D

Index of Places.

Index of Places.

Index of Places.

LIST OF SUBSCRIBERS.

Kemp, Sir Kenneth Hagar, Bart.,
Mergate Hall, Braconash, near Norwich, and Gissing Hall, Norfolk.

Kemp, George, M.P.,
71, Portland Place, W., and Beechwood, Rochdale.

Kemp, Mrs. John Mainwaring,
Claughton, Beulah Hill, Norwood.

Kemp, the Rev. Godfrey Geo., M.A.,
Rawreth Rectory, Battlesbridge, Essex.

Kemp, the Rev. John, M.A.,
Haughley Vicarage, Suffolk.

Kemp, Wm. Geo., M.D.,
(late of Wellington, N.Z.), Tarana, Avenue Road, St. Peter's Park, St. Albans.

Kemp, Alexander,
227, Dalkeith Road, Edinburgh.

Kemp, John T., M.A.,
Devon Villa, 4, Cotham Grove, Bristol.

Kemp, Clement, J.P.,
Devon Villa, 4, Cotham Grove, Bristol.

Kemp, Arthur Henry,
144, Stockport Road, Manchester.

Kemp, John,
The Laurels, Trowbridge.

Kemp, Professor James F.,
Columbia University, New York City.

Kemp, John,
Fairholme, Park Road, Blackpool.

Kemp, Richard,
Hamilton, Bermuda.

Kemp, Henry Charles Edward, B.A.,
Suffield Park School, Cromer.

Kemp, Edward,
135, Water Street, New York, U.S.A.

Kemp, John Frederick,
1, Theobald Road, Cardiff.

Kemp, F. W.,
Chasewood, 100, Melton Road, Leicester.

Kemp, Edward,
(Vicar Choral), 19, Sturgeon's Hill, Lichfie

Kemp, Geo. Watts Hill,
Southampton, East Bermuda.

Kemp, D. S.,
52, Coverdale Road, Uxbridge Road, W.

Kemp, Sydney Faithful,
33, Elmfield Mansions, Upper Tooting, S

Kemp, Compton,
61, Broxholme Avenue, Doncaster.

Kemp, R.,
Cobden Villa, 4, Shaftesbury Street, Nottingham.

Kemp, Miss Olivia M.,
33, Trevor Square, Brompton, S.W.

Kemp, John Oddie,
3, Waveney Terrace, Bungay, Suffolk.

Kemp, Alfred,
Fairmeadside, Loughton.

Kemp, Arthur,
Littlecote, Stoneygate Avenue, Leicester.

Kemp, Wm. H.
27, Sidney Road, Richmond.

Kemp, Captain W., J.P.
Lyminster House, Arundel.

Kemp, Caleb Rickman, J.P.
Bedford Lodge, Lewes.

Kemp, James,
70, Waterloo Rd., Freemantle, Southampton.

Kemp, Wilkinson,
2, Richmond Terrace, Manchester.

Kemp, William,
Victoria Terrace, 240, Dewsbury Rd., Leeds.

Kemp, Daniel W., J.P.,
Ivy Lodge, Trinity, Edinburgh, and Temple, N.B.

Kemp, F. E.
Supt. Bengal Police, Faridpur, Bengal, India.

Kemp, Mrs. David C.,
Clanbrassil, Cultra, Belfast.

Kemp, Miss Janet,
11, Hailes Street, Edinburgh.

Kemp, the Rev. Robert, M.A.,
The Manse, Blairgowrie, Scotland.

Kemp, the Rev. Arnold Low, M.A.,
255, Rosemount Place, Aberdeen.

Kemp, Herbert Henry,
Office of His Excellency the High Commissioner for South Africa, Johannesburg,

Kemp, the Rev. W.,
Clergy House, Stockport.

Kemp, Albert Edward,
Melita, Man, Canada.

Kemp, J. Hayward,
Walton, Wellington, Salop.

Kemp, Wm. D.,
Academy Street, Inverness.

Kemp, the Rev. Robt. Sangster, M.A., B.
Manse of Deer, Mintlaw, Aberdeenshire.

Kemp, Thos., M.J.I.,
Ellonville, Dalkeith, N.B.

Kemp, Miss,
12, St. Fillans Terrace, Morningside, Ed burgh (deceased).

Kemp, Samuel Bromley,
Volksrust, South Africa.

Kemp, Amos, M.J.I.
2, Gloucester Street, Warwick Square, S.

Kemp, Syd. S.,
137, High Park St., Princes Park, Liverp

Kemp, C. T.,
7, Eign Street, Hereford.

Kemp, H.
43, Curzon Road, Bradford, Yorks.

Kemp, Geo. Lucas,
Umballa, Punjab, India.

Kemp-Bussell, W.,
Clifton Villa, Spanish Town, Jamaica.

Kemp-Paris, Charles,
Becton House, New Milton, Hants,

Kemp, Robert,
Halstead, Essex.

Kemp, H. C.,
(Life Fellow I. Inst.), 7-8, Thavies Inn,

Kemp, Jesse,
Albion Villa, 338, Liverpool Rd., Highb

Kemp, Thomas, J.P.,
Constant Spring, Kingston, Jamaica.

Kemp, Peter,
Glen Royston, Currency Creek, South Australia.

Kemp, F. W. J.,
The Treasury, Whitehall.

Kemp, Wm. Rous, B.A., Camb., F.S.A.,
172, Blomfield Terrace, Paddington.

Kemp, A. N. B.,
Stoke-under-Ham.

Kemp, James Wheeler,
Pennants, Charleton, Jamaica.

Kemp, Miss Agnes,
54, Frederick Street, Edinburgh.

Kemp, John, A.M.I.C.E.,
Leitrim Lodge, Hampton-on-Thames.

Kemp, Herbert E.,
37, Arcade Chambers, Manchester.

Kemp, H.,
Lulworth, Rodney Road, New Malden, Surrey.

Kemp, F.,
Linthwaite, Windermere.

Kemp, the Rev. W. Edelman,
Ridgmount Gardens, W.C.

Kemp, John H.,
Denial Bay, South Australia.

Kemp, Miss,
Bispham Lodge, Poulton-le-Fylde.

Kemp, Mrs. E. L.,
Beechwood, Rochdale, Lancs.

Kemp, Geo. Stephen,
"Ferndale," Upper Cedar Road, Bevois Mount, Southampton.

Kemp, Thomas,
10, Jury Street, Warwick.

Kemp, David Robert,
109, Eaton Place, London, S.W.

Kemp, Edwyn, A.,
61, Belsize Park Gardens, N.W.

Kempe, Arthur Wightman, M.B., M.R. -M.R.C.P.,
Exeter.

Kempe, the Rev. Preb. John Edward,
14, Montague place, W.

Kempe, Charles N.,
126, Piccadilly, W.

Kempe, Alfred Bray, F.R.S., K.C.,
10, Rochdale Square, W

Kempe, James,
2485, Broadway, New York City, U.S.A

Kempe James Fletcher,
41, Lawton Road, Waterloo, Liverpool.

Kempe, A. A.,
61, Gordon Road, Ealing.

Kempe, Ernest Courtney, J.P.
Warrina, South Australia.

Kempe, G. S.,
Carandale, Mintaro, South Australia.

Kempe, Chas. G.B., M.R.C.S., L.S.A.,
17, Endless Street, Salisbury.

Kempe, John Arrow, C.B.,
14, Montague Place, W.

Kempe, C. M., M.R.C.S.,
Chantry House, Shoreham, Sussex.

Kempe, H. R.,
Brockham, Betchworth, Surrey.

Kempe, R. B.,
Junior Athenæum Club, W.

Kempt, Irvine,
Forest Hill, Kelvinside, Glasgow.

Kemp-Welch, Henry,
Parkstone, Weybridge.

Kemp-Welch, Miss Lucy,
Kingsley, Bushey, Herts.

Kemp-Welch, John,
Sopley, Christchurch.

Kemp-Welch, James,
Parkstone, Weybridge.

Ashton-Gwatkin, the Rev. W. H. Trelawney, M.A.,
The Vicarage, Margate.

Bulgin, Mrs. Robert C.,
Willesden.

Bullen, the Rev. R. Ashington,
Pyrford Vicarage, Woking, Surrey.

Davies, Mrs. Percy,
Crichowell, Breconshire.

Fletcher, Percy E.,
25, Union Road, Clapham, S.W.

Hazlewood, the Rev. F. G., LL.D., D.C.L.,
Chislet Vicarage, near Canterbury.

Hayman, Howard,
157, White Ladies Road, Bristol.

Hitchin-Kemp, F. W.,
Addington House, Margate.

Hitchman, John,
51, Cherry Street, Birmingham.

Hovenden, Robert, F.S.A.,
Heathcote, Park Hill Road, Croydon.

Jacomb-Hood, S.,
3, Aubrey Road, Campden Hill, W.

Jesson, Thomas,
6, Duke's Avenue, Chiswick.

Johnston, Geo. P.,
33, George Street, Edinburgh.

Langley, Mrs. J.,
Croftlands, Bolton-le-Sands, Carnforth, La

Machell, Mrs. Isabella,
Aynsome, Cartmel, near Ulverstone.

Mercer, W. John,
12, Marine Terrace, Margate.

Price, Arthur,
26, Old Burlington Street, W.

Stewart, Mrs. E.,
Glendevon, Sutton, Surrey.

Tuer, Mrs. A. W.,
18, Campden Hill Square, W.

Waters, Mrs.,
Millo, Gorleston, Great Yarmouth.

Williamson, Mrs. Isabel A.,
The Warrens, Camelford.

Williamson, Mrs. R. H.,
The Warrens, Camelford, Cornwall.

Wolterbeek, Mrs. Louisa (née Jacon Hood),
Zeestraat, 71A, The Hague, Holland.

Lightning Source UK Ltd.
Milton Keynes UK
UKHW021602030519
342068UK00006B/903/P

9 781332 131518